About Island Press

Island Press is the only nonprofit organization in the United States whose principal purpose is the publication of books on environmental issues and natural resource management. We provide solutions-oriented information to professionals, public officials, business and community leaders, and concerned citizens who are shaping responses to environmental problems.

In 2005, Island Press celebrates its twenty-first anniversary as the leading provider of timely and practical books that take a multidisciplinary approach to critical environmental concerns. Our growing list of titles reflects our commitment to bringing the best of an expanding body of literature to the environmental community throughout North America and the world.

Support for Island Press is provided by The Nathan Cummings Foundation, Geraldine R. Dodge Foundation, Doris Duke Charitable Foundation, Educational Foundation of America, The Charles Engelhard Foundation, The Ford Foundation, The George Gund Foundation, The Vira I. Heinz Endowment, The William and Flora Hewlett Foundation, Henry Luce Foundation, The John D. and Catherine T. MacArthur Foundation, The Andrew W. Mellon Foundation, The Moriah Fund, The Curtis and Edith Munson Foundation, National Fish and Wildlife Foundation, The New-Land Foundation, Oak Foundation, The Overbrook Foundation, The David and Lucile Packard Foundation, The Pew Charitable Trusts, The Rockefeller Foundation, The Winslow Foundation, and other generous donors.

The opinions expressed in this book are those of the author(s) and do not necessarily reflect the views of these foundations.

About The Nature Conservancy

The Nature Conservancy is a leading, international nonprofit organization that preserves plants, animals, and natural communities representing the diversity of life on Earth by protecting the lands and waters they need to survive. The Conservancy is known for it's non-confrontational approach, bringing science to the table, and working in collaboration with diverse partners, corporations, indigenous people and traditional communities all over the world. The Conservancy works in all 50 United States and 27 countries and, together with its more than one million members and numerous supporters, has been responsible for protecting more than 117 million acres of land. The Conservancy's efforts to protect freshwater biodiversity have grown significantly during the past decade and follow the Conservancy's success in working across traditional geographic, political, and intellectual lines since ecological systems rarely coincide with human-drawn boundaries. Please visit nature.org for more information about The Nature Conservancy and nature.org/initiatives/freshwater/ or www.freshwaters.org for more information about The Nature Conservancy's efforts related to freshwater biodiversity conservation.

A PRACTITIONER'S GUIDE TO
Freshwater Biodiversity Conservation

A PRACTITIONER'S GUIDE TO
Freshwater Biodiversity Conservation

EDITED BY
Nicole Silk and Kristine Ciruna

WITH CONTRIBUTIONS BY
David Allan, Ronald Bjorkland, David Braun, Mark Bryer, Rebecca Cifaldi,
Jonathan Higgins, Mary Khoury, and Catherine Pringle

The Nature Conservancy

ISLANDPRESS

Washington • Covelo • London

First edition © 2004 The Nature Conservancy
Reprint edition published by Island Press © 2005 The Nature Conservancy

ISLAND PRESS is a trademark of The Center for Resource Economics.

Citation: Silk, Nicole, and Kristine Ciruna, eds. 2005. A Practitioner's Guide to Freshwater Biodiversity Conservation. Washington, DC: Island Press.

Library of Congress Cataloging-in-Publication data.

A practitioner's guide to freshwater biodiversity conservation / edited by Nicole Silk and Kristine Ciruna with contributions by David Allan ... [et al.].— 1st ed.
    p. cm.
  Originally published: Boulder, Colo. : Nature Conservancy, c2004.
  Includes bibliographical references and index.
  ISBN 1-59726-043-6 (cloth : alk. paper) — ISBN 1-59726-044-4 (pbk. : alk. paper)
 1. Freshwater biological diversity conservation. I. Silk, Nicole. II. Ciruna, Kristine. III. Title.

QH96.8.B53P73 2005
333.95'2816—dc22

                         2005018129

British Cataloguing-in-Publication data available.

Photo credits for chapter opening pages: Chapter 1–Harold E. Malde, Chapter 2–Harold E. Malde, Chapter 3–Jerry and Marcy Monkman, Chapter 4–Harold E. Malde, Chapter 5–David Harp. Photo credits for photographic tabs: Chapter 1–Jim Stimson, Chapter 2–Milton Rand, Chapter 3–James C. Godwin, Chapter 4–Harold E. Malde, Chapter 5–Adriel Heisey

Printed on recycled, acid-free paper

Manufactured in the United States of America

10 9 8 7 6 5 4 3 2 1

Contents

Preface and Acknowledgments:

The Development of
A Practitioner's Guide to Freshwater Biodiversity Conservation

A Practitioner's Guide to Freshwater Biodiversity Conservation was developed to help conservation practitioners become better able to meet the challenges of freshwater biodiversity conservation. It should also help practitioners identify conservation actions that will make the greatest contribution towards stemming freshwater biodiversity decline and establish a process for refining and improving upon these actions over time. Conservation practitioners are defined here as anyone pursuing conservation goals or objectives at a particular place—professional staff of conservation organizations and government agencies, water resource managers, policy level decision-makers, etc.

This guide presents information about the global challenge of freshwater biodiversity conservation, explores how ecosystems are structured and function to support this biodiversity, and explains approaches for identifying the most important biodiversity to protect across large geographic areas as well as at specific locations. These preliminary chapters provide important contextual information followed by a detailed review of the four primary causes of freshwater biodiversity decline (water use and management, invasive alien species, land use and management, and overharvesting and fisheries management) and a wide range of promising strategies at various institutional and geographic scales for abating these threats and conserving freshwater biodiversity. The final chapter of this guide describes design considerations and methods for measuring freshwater conservation success within an adaptive management framework.

The collective wisdom gained through The Nature Conservancy's Freshwater Initiative contributed a great deal to the structure and content of this guide. The Freshwater Initiative was launched by The Nature Conservancy in 1998 to build organizational capacity in freshwater biodiversity conservation. Originally designed as a five year program with a lofty goal of raising $10 million, the Initiative included three components: identifying areas of freshwater biodiversity importance for future conservation action and developing tools and methods to help others identify freshwater priorities; developing breakthrough strategies to common causes of freshwater biodiversity decline as well as methods for more effective applied freshwater biodiversity conservation; and creating a Freshwater Learning Center to build a community of freshwater conservation practitioners, offer opportunities for collaboration and skill-building, and develop products (articles, guidance documents, videos, web sites, etc.) for sharing knowledge and lessons learned across a variety of audiences. Although only 15 people, as a result of the focused creativity harnessed through this team, between 1998 and 2003 the Initiative had access not only to available literature and experts, but also to conservation planners and practitioners from around the globe. Working with these conservation planners and practitioners, and through a series of direct and virtual interactions, the Initiative effectively became a learning laboratory to test ideas, approaches, tools, strategies, and methods. Towards the end of the Freshwater Initiative, staff also developed a course on freshwater biodiversity conservation and disseminated regionally customized versions of this course to hundreds of practitioners within and outside of the United States. This guide is, in essence, the companion text for that course, complete with some of the best information from around the world. It delivers what Freshwater Initiative staff believed to be of most use to others engaged in freshwater biodiversity conservation.

Although the Freshwater Initiative officially disbanded in 2003, work on this guide continued through The Nature Conservancy's Sustainable Waters Program. Contributors to this guide include Nature Conservancy staff, staff from Nature Conservancy of Canada, staff and graduate students affiliated with the University of Georgia's Institute of Ecology and the University of Michigan's School of Natural Resources. These contributors represent a wide range of disciplines (ecology, hydrology, economics, law, etc.) and professional backgrounds (field-based conservation practitioners, university professors, professional experts, etc.), which mirror the complexity and multi-disciplinary nature of the challenge of freshwater biodiversity conservation. Contributors central to the content of individual chapters and sub-chapters include: Chapter 1: Nicole Silk; Chapter 2: Kristine Ciruna and David Braun; Chapter 3: Mark Bryer, David Braun, Mary Khoury, and Jonathan Higgins; Chapter 4: Introduction: Nicole Silk, Kristine Ciruna and David Braun; Chapter 4: sub-chapter on Water Use and Management: Ronald Bjorkland and Catherine Pringle; Chapter 4: subchap-ter on Land Use and Management: Rebecca Esselman and David Allan; Chapter 4: subchapter on Invasive Alien Species: Kristine Ciruna; Chapter 4: subchapter on Overharvesting and Fisheries Management: Ronald Bjorkland and Catherine Pringle; Chapter 5: David Braun; Appendix A: Kristine Ciruna and Allison Aldous; and Appendix B: David Braun. In addition to the contributors listed above, this guide was also peer reviewed at various stages by over 40 practitioners working on freshwater conservation challenges at individual projects, building capacity to engage in this type of work, or contributing to the efforts of others. Special thanks are also extended to Nicole Rousmaniere for the graphic design of, assembly of images included within, and "friendliness" of the final lengthy product, and to Kristine Ciruna for editing contributions and project management assistance. Development of this guide was partially supported by the U.S. Environmental Protection Agency, Office of Water, through Grant X–82773901 and its ammendments.

We hope this guide helps you in your efforts.

—NICOLE SILK

Chapter 1

The Global Challenge of Freshwater Biodiversity Conservation

Nicole Silk

OVERVIEW AND LEARNING OBJECTIVES

This chapter briefly examines the need for and importance of freshwater biodiversity conservation. The chapter begins with an overview of the value of global freshwater resource, examines current trends in the decline of freshwater biodiversity, and considers prospects for improvement from a global perspective.

THE FRESHWATER CRISIS: WHY SHOULD WE CARE?

The Global Importance of Freshwater and Its Biodiversity

The most critical component for human survival is access to a sufficient supply of freshwater. However, the supply of freshwater is surprisingly low globally. Approximately 70% of Earth's surface is covered by water, yet only 2.5% of Earth's water is freshwater (McAllister *et al.* 1997). Most of the freshwater is locked in polar ice caps, stored in underground aquifers (many with recharge cycles measured in millennia), or part of soil moisture and permafrost. Only 0.01% of Earth's water is available as freshwater in rivers and lakes (McAllister *et al.* 1997). This one-hundredth of a percent of Earth's water that occupies only 0.8% of the Earth's surface (McAllister *et al.* 1997) provides us with a vast array of environmental services:

- Waste disposal;
- Energy to fuel our electricity needs;
- Transportation corridors to carry raw products and finished goods to customers;
- Drinking water to quench our thirst;
- Irrigation for agriculture and aquaculture;
- Water to make manufactured products;
- Places to recreate; and
- Aesthetic, spiritual, and religious values.

Freshwater ecosystems also support an exceptional concentration of biodiversity. Species richness is greater relative to habitat extent in freshwater ecosystems than in either marine or terrestrial ecosystems. Freshwater ecosystems contain approximately 12% of all species, with almost 25% of all vertebrate species concentrated within these habitats (Stiassny 1996). The richness of freshwater species includes a wide variety of plants, fishes, mussels, crustaceans, snails, reptiles, amphibians, insects, microorganisms, birds, and mammals that live beneath the water or spend much of their time in or on the water. Many of these species depend upon the physical, chemical, and hydrologic processes and biological interactions found within freshwater ecosystems to trigger their various life cycle stages.

As with terrestrial species richness, freshwater species richness increases strongly toward the equator —there are many more freshwater species in the tropics than in temperate regions. Preliminary estimates suggest that the world's tropics may be home to a disproportionately large share of the world's freshwater-species richness. Central Africa, Southeast Asia, and northern South America have high numbers of fish species, including many endemic species that occur only in limited areas (Revenga *et al.* 2000). However, certain freshwater groups, such as freshwater crayfishes, are much less diverse in the tropics than temperate regions. Indeed, some temperate regions are exceptionally high in aquatic biodiversity. The United States, for example, ranks first in the world in the diversity of freshwater mussels, snails, and salamanders as well as three groups of freshwater insects: caddisflies, mayflies, and stone-flies. U.S. waters contain approximately 30% of the world's freshwater mussel species.

Despite what is known, much of the diversity of life that thrives in the world's freshwaters remains largely unknown, unstudied, and unquantified due to the challenges of sampling, the focus on objectives other than biodiversity conservation, and limited resources for inventory.

What is clear is that freshwater biodiversity is a story not only of species, but of communities and ecosystems. The history of geologic and climatic change and species evolution in every area of the globe has produced dynamic assemblages of species that interact with each other and with physical environments in unique ways:

- Pacific salmon return to the headwaters of the Columbia River Basin to spawn and die, completing their lifecycles. Through this journey they also bring vast quantities of nutrients from the ocean as their spent bodies decay, enriching freshwater and terrestrial life in these systems.
- The floodwaters of the Amazon River enable huge numbers of fish access to bottom-lands necessary for feeding and reproduction. These floodwaters also push vast quantities of organic matter from these bottomlands back into the river, where it becomes food for other organisms and those that feed on them.
- The native freshwater mussels of North America need species-specific host fish to reproduce. These

Illustration courtesy of Toronto and Region Conservation Authority.

mussels release thousands of microscopic larvae called glochidia, some of which find their way to the gills of host fish. The unsuspecting host fish then carries these glochidia to new habitats. Eventually, the glochidia drop from the host fish, settle into their new homes, and grow into adult mussels.

Such tales of complex interactions emerge wherever freshwater ecosystems are studied.

All terrestrial organisms (plants, animals, etc.) also need freshwater for their survival. River, lake, and wetland ecosystems support almost all terrestrial animal species, since these species depend on freshwater ecosystems for water, food, and various aspects of their life cycles. Finally, all freshwater that runs into our rivers, lakes, and wetlands also eventually ends up in the ocean. There, the endless cycle of life and death in the freshwater world provides a steady stream of incoming food, sediments, and nutrients to nearshore marine ecosystems. The diversity of life in the world's freshwaters, estuaries, and the sea are thus closely linked as well. Given the range of life dependent upon freshwater ecosystems, it is clear that we can easily lose tremendous biodiversity by the deterioration of just a few freshwater ecosystems.

The Crisis

The decline of freshwater biodiversity has reached alarming rates. The extinction rate of freshwater bio-diversity is predicted to be five times faster than all other groups of species (Ricciardi and Rasmussen 1999). Researchers have estimated that during recent decades between 20% and 35% of the world's freshwater fish species have become endangered, threatened, or extinct (Ricciardi and Rasmussen 1999, Revenga *et al.* 2000, Gleick *et al.* 2002). As well, 20% of threatened insects have freshwater larval stages, 57% of freshwater dolphins are vulnerable or endangered and 70% of freshwater otters are vulnerable or endangered (McAllister *et al.* 1997). Declines in freshwater biodiversity are found in every country, but perhaps are most disturbing in areas with the greatest known current native species richness. In addition to species loss, entire freshwater ecosystems are also in decline. For example, since 1970, the health of the world's freshwater ecosystems has declined by 50% (Loh 2000). Eighty-five percent of freshwater ecosystems in Latin America and the Caribbean are in critically endangered or vulnerable condition (Olson *et al.* 1998). Rates of decline in Africa and Asia are similarly precipitous. Actual rates of freshwater biodiversity loss may even be much higher then these estimates since only partial data exists for most species and even less exists for entire freshwater communities and ecosystems. One projection suggests that unless dramatic steps are taken today, 20% of the world's freshwater fish may become extinct in the next 25–50 years (Moyle and Leidy 1992).

The reasons for this deterioration are easily under-

TABLE 1.1. Freshwater Ecosystem Services

	Streams & Rivers	Laks & Ponds	Wetlands
Electricity	✓	✓	
Drinking Water	✓	✓	
Waste Removal	✓	✓	✓
Crop Irrigation & Landscaping	✓	✓	✓
Transportation	✓	✓	
Manufacturing	✓	✓	
Fish	✓	✓	✓
Flood Control	✓	✓	✓
Recreation	✓	✓	✓
Religion & Sense of Place	✓	✓	✓

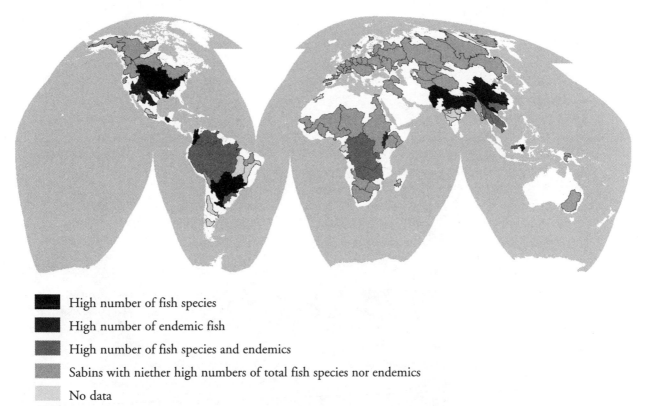

High number of fish species

High number of endemic fish

High number of fish species and endemics

Sabins with niether high numbers of total fish species nor endemics

No data

FIGURE 1-1. Freshwater Fish Species Richness and Endemism

Source: Revenga, C., S. Murray, J. Abramovitz, and A. Hammond. 1998. Watersheds of the World: Ecological Value and Vulnerability. Washington, DC: World Resources Institute. Reproduced with permission of the World Resources Institute.

stood: the world's growing human population uses freshwater for the vast range of services shown in Table 1-1. In doing so, freshwater ecosystems are disrupted, starved, contaminated, and sometimes completely eliminated. For example, the world's rivers are now obstructed by more than 45,000 large dams, including 19,000 in China and 5,500 in the U.S. (World Commission on Dams 2000). More than 85% of the world's large dams have been built during the last 35 years (Postel 1995). Half of the world's wetlands have been eliminated—to make way for other land uses such as forestry, agriculture, and new homes—or modified to serve water needs by groundwater extraction as well as through the placement of dams and diversions (Revenga *et al.* 2000).

Collectively, these changes continue to have devastating impacts on native freshwater species that evolved in close interaction with each other and the distinct patterns of chemistry, sediments, hydrology, temperature, and other physical regimes within these freshwater ecosystems. Indeed, as described above,

many species require certain combinations of these patterns to trigger critical aspects of their lifecycles. For some species, when these conditions are eliminated, they can no longer reproduce. Further complicating this picture is the loss of native species due to the effects of invasive alien species introductions and poor fisheries management.

The deterioration of freshwater ecosystems results in a loss of freshwater species, communities, and ecosystems. It also results in a loss of all other animals dependent on freshwater, and degrades the ability of these systems to provide the services for humans previously mentioned. Many rivers can no longer provide flood control for downstream communities, since they have been channelized or engineered to stay within their banks and their watersheds have been altered through land clearing, the draining of wetlands, and the expansion of impervious surfaces (e.g., through paving). When the flood comes, it is often larger and more destructive than would have occurred naturally as it moves into the river more quickly, has no place to

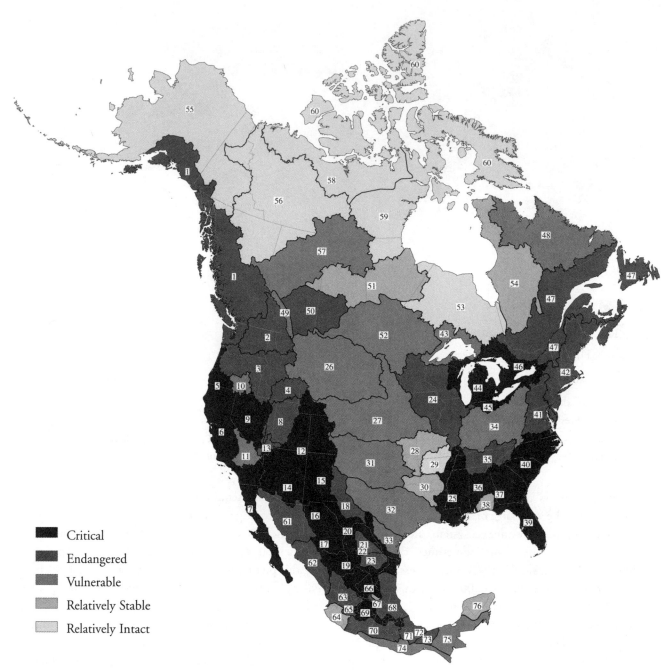

FIGURE 1-2. Freshwater Ecoregions of North America

Source: Abell, R., D.M. Olson, E. Dinerstein, P. Hurley, J.T. Diggs, W. Eichbaum, S. Walters, W. Wettengel, T. Allnutt, C. Louks, and P. Hedao. 2000. Freshwater Ecoregions of North America: A Conservation Assessment. Island Press, Washington, DC.

meander or spread, and moves faster to downstream locations. In many areas of the world, water extracted from rivers, lakes, and groundwater is no longer safe for drinking without additional and often costly treatments. Rates of infection from diseases carried by water are on the rise (Gleick *et al.* 2002). Many commercial as well as recreational fishing catches in fresh-

water and marine ecosystems have declined or have been eliminated.

This crisis may become more devastating in the near future given the increasing human demands for water. Annual water consumption has increased worldwide in the last 50 years. In Western Europe between 1950 and 1990, per capita water consump-

Pacific Bioregion

Coastal Complex
1. North Pacific Coastal
2. Columbia Glaciated
3. Columbia Unglaciated
4. Upper Snake
5. Pacific Mid-Coastal
6. Pacific Central Valley
7. South Pacific Coastal

Great Basin Complex
8. Bonneville
9. Lahontan
10. Oregon Lakes
11. Death Valley

Colorado Complex
12. Colorado
13. Vages-Virgin
14. Gila

Arctic-Atlantic Bioregion

Rio-Grande Complex
15. Upper Rio Grande (Rio Bravo)
16. Guzmán

17. Rio Conchas
18. Pecos
19. Mapimí
20. Lower Rio Grande (Rio Bravo)
21. Rio Slado
22. Cuatro Ciénegas
23. Rio San Juan

Mississippi Complex
24. Mississippi
25. Mississippi Embayment
26. Upper Missouri
27. Middle Missouri
28. Central Prairie
29. Ozark Highlands
30. Ouachita Highlands
31. Southern Plains
32. East Texas Gulf
33. West Texas Gulf
34. Teays-Old Ohio
35. Tennessee-Cumberland
36. Mobile Bay
37. Apalachicola
38. Florida Gulf

Atlanitc Complex
39. Florida
40. South Atlantic
41. Chespeake Bay
42. North Atlantic

St. Lawrence Complex
43. Superior
44. Michigan-Huron
45. Erie
46. Ontario
47. Lower St. Lawrence
48. North Atlanitc-Ungava

Hudson Complex
49. Canadian Rockies
50. Upper Saskatchewan
51. Lower Saskatchewan
52. English-Winnipeg Lakes
53. South Hudson
54. East Hudson

Arctic Complex
55. Yukon
56. Lower Mackenzie
57. Upper Mackenzie

58. North Arctic
59. East Arctic
60. Arctic Islands

Pacific Bioregion
61. Sonoran
62. Sinaloan Coastal
63. Santiago
64. Manantlan-Ameca
65. Chapala
66. Llanos El Salado
67. Rio Verde Headwaters
68. Tamaulipas-Veracruz
69. Lerma
70. Balsas
71. Catemaco
72. Catemaco
73. Coatzacoalcos
74. Tehuantepec
75. Grijalva-Usumacinta
76. Yucatán

FIGURE 1-2. *Continued*

tion grew from 100 to 560 cubic kilometers a year. In Asia, consumption has increased from 600 to 5,000 cubic kilometers between 1900 and the mid-1980s. Globally, freshwater withdrawals have almost doubled since 1960 (Loh 2000). Estimates suggest that freshwater use is growing at 2.5 times the rate of human population growth. In fact, some scenarios suggest that water withdrawals will increase 50% in developing countries and 18% in developed countries during the next 25 years, placing even greater pressures on

freshwater ecosystems and potentially leading to severe water shortages across two-thirds of the total world human population by the year 2025 (Szollosi-Nagy *et al.* 1998). And as populations and economies grow, they will place ever increasing demands on freshwater ecosystems for hydropower, transportation, and the disposal of wastes. To all this is added the uncertainty associated with the potential effects of global climate change.

OUR CHALLENGE

Clearly, we must act now if this precious freshwater heritage is to remain. We must alter our practices so that these ecosystems continue to support both freshwater biodiversity and human life. Our survival and obligation of stewardship demands that we help these

freshwater ecosystems to remain healthy, properly functioning, and capable of supporting viable populations of native plants and animals. The following chapters of this guide will help conservation practitioners meet this challenge.

Threats to freshwater biodiversity include invasive alien species such as zebra mussels, attached to a native pink heelsplitter mussel, (above, photograph by K.S. Cummings, Illinois Natural History Survey), hydrologic alteration by dams and other diversions (upper right, photograph courtesy U.S. Army Corps of Engineers), and overexploitation of water resources for agriculture and other activities (lower right, photograph by Jeff Vanuga/USDA NRCS).

REFERENCES

Gleick, P.H., M. Cohen (contributor) and A.S. Mann (contributor). 2002. The World's Water 2002–2003. The Biennial Report on Freshwater Resources. Island Press, Washington, DC.

Loh, J. (ed). 2000. Living Planet Report 2000. UNEP-WCMC, WWF-World Wide Fund for Nature, Gland, Switzerland.

McAllister, D.E., A.L. Hamilton and B. Harvey. 1997. Global freshwater biodiversity: Striving for the integrity of freshwater ecosystems. Sea Wind 11(3): 1–140.

Moyle, P.E. and R.A. Leidy. 1992. Loss of biodiversity in aquatic ecosystems: Evidence from fish faunas. In: P.L. Fiedler and S.K. Jain (Eds.). Conservation Biology: The theory and practice of nature conservation, preservation and management. Chapman and Hall, New York.

Olson, D., E. Dinerstein, P. Canevari, I. Davidson, G. Castro, V. Morisset, R. Abell, and E. Toledo (eds.). 1998. Fresh-water biodiversity of Latin America and the Caribbean: A conservation assessment. Biodiversity Support Program. Washington, DC.

Postel, S.L. 1995. Where have all the rivers gone? World Watch 8: 9–19.

Revenga, C., J. Brunner, N. Henninger, K. Kassem, and R. Payne. 2000. Pilot Analysis of Global Ecosystems: Freshwater Systems. World Resources Institute. Washington, DC. 65 p.

Ricciardi, A., and J.B. Rasumussen. 1999. Extinction rates of North American freshwater fauna. Conservation Biology 13(5): 1220–1222.

Stiassny, M.L. 1996. An overview of freshwater biodiversity: With some lessons learned from African fishes. Fisheries 21(9): 7–13.

Szollosi-Nagy, A., P. Najlis, and G. Bjorklund. 1998. Assessing the world's freshwater resources. UNESCO. Nature & Resources 34(1).

World Commission on Dams. 2000. Dams and Development: A new framework for decision-making. The Report of the World Commission on Dams.

Chapter 2

Freshwater Fundamentals: Watersheds, Freshwater Ecosystems and Freshwater Biodiversity

Kristine Ciruna and David Braun

OVERVIEW AND LEARNING OBJECTIVES

This chapter explains the form and function of freshwater ecosystems and their associated watersheds. This chapter explores climate and the associated hydrologic cycle, geology, and watershed vegetation, all essential ingredients in shaping the location and characteristics of freshwater ecosystems across the landscape. The chapter also describes the major types of discussion of the adaptation of species to freshwater ecosystems and the abundance and distribution of freshwater biodiversi-

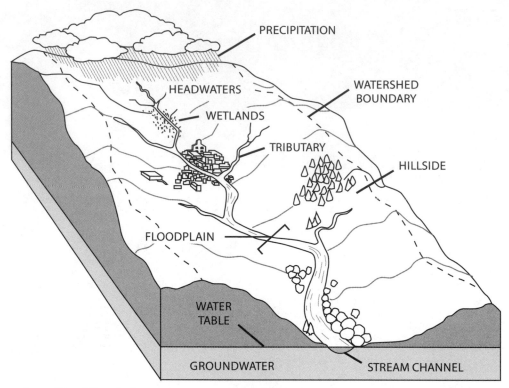

FIGURE 2-1. Large River Watershed

Source: Adapted from USEPA, Office of Water. 1997. Volunteer Stream Monitoring: A Methods Manual.

WATERSHED FORM AND FUNCTION

ty globally. Figure 2-9 at the end of this chapter explains the context of this information in relation to the entire guide.

What is a Watershed?

A watershed is an area of land that collects water arriving as rain and snow and then drains that water to a common outlet at some point along a body of freshwater (Dunne and Leopold 1978). All freshwater ecosystems—lakes, rivers, wetlands—have an associated watershed. Watersheds vary tremendously in size. The watershed at the headwaters of a river may be just one or two hectares (2–5 acres), whereas the watershed of the river that this small stream flows into may contain thousands of hectares of land.

Figure 2-1 represents a watershed for a large river

system. The watershed boundary or divide consists of a line of highest land elevation extending around the entire watershed area. Water falling on one side of this divide will eventually flow out of the watershed outlet while water falling on the other side of the divide will drain into another watershed. The diagram in Figure 2-1 also shows that this large river system includes smaller streams or tributaries, headwaters, and wetlands. Each of these parts of the larger system has its own watershed that is a sub-watershed of the larger system. Larger watersheds are commonly made up of smaller sub-watersheds as illustrated in Figure 2-2. The tree-like branching of streams in a watershed is the drainage network of the watershed.

The variables that influence the size of a watershed include geology, climate, and land cover. These variables also determine the speed and direction of water flow within a watershed and the wash of sediments, nutrients, dissolved minerals, and a wide range of

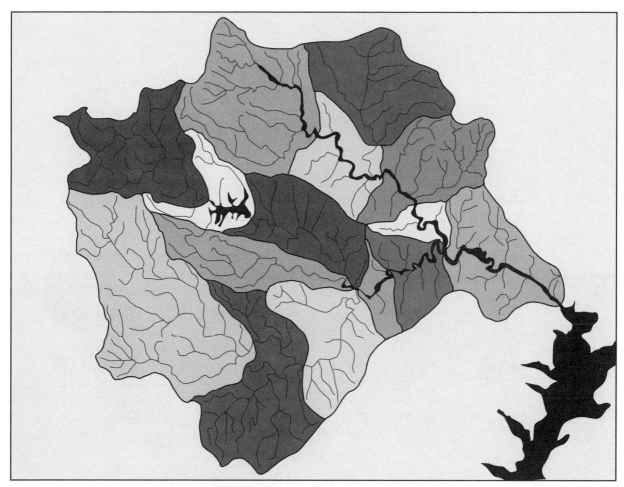

FIGURE 2-2. Sub-watersheds Within a Larger Watershed

plant matter with this water and influencing the water chemistry of freshwater ecosystems within watersheds in the absence of human intervention and alteration. Understanding global processes underlying these variables is essential to understanding watershed form and function.

Global Processes that Shape Watershed Form and Function

Geology and climate are large-scale processes that shape the Earth's physical features. Finer scale environmental processes and factors shape biological organization across the landscape, from the distribution of genes to ecosystems. These finer scale environmental processes and factors—such as vegetative cover, a river's flow

regime, or a wetland's nitrogen cycle—also depend on geology and climate within a localized setting.

CLIMATE

Climate refers to an aggregate of both average and extreme conditions of solar radiation, temperature, humidity, precipitation, winds, and cloud cover measured over an extended period of time. The climate of a watershed heavily influences its vegetation communities, streamflow magnitude and timing, water temperature, and many other characteristics of key ecological factors for freshwater ecosystems.

Climate not only shapes the average weather for a watershed, but also the extremes of weather that can occur from one year to the next, or from one decade or even century to the next. Extreme events, such as

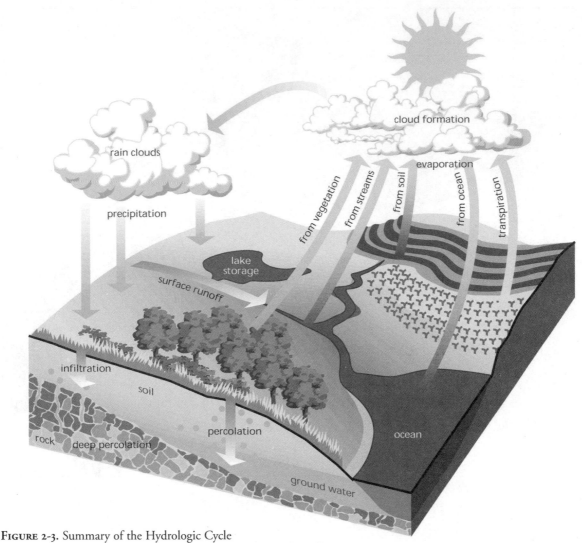

Figure 2-3. Summary of the Hydrologic Cycle

Source: The Federal Interagency Stream Restoration Working Group. 1998. Stream Corridor Restoration: Principles, Processes, and Practices

floods, droughts, destructive downpours, and ice build-up, may not happen every year or decade, but they do occur. Such disturbances are natural phenomena which influence a watershed. The species present in any freshwater ecosystem will have evolved ways to cope with (or even take advantage of) these kinds of disturbances or else they would not exist in the watershed climate-driven disturbances act like giant biological filters, temporarily or even permanently driving out species that cannot tolerate or protect themselves from extreme conditions, clearing out established vegetation and animal colonies, reshaping the physical habitat, and opening up new opportunities for colonization. These dynamics are natural features of freshwater ecosystems.

Hydrologic Cycle

The hydrologic cycle—the continuous cycling of freshwater from the atmosphere to the earth to the oceans and back again—is intimately tied to climate and forms the backbone of all freshwater ecosystems. The details of the hydrologic cycle—the pattern of precipitation, evaporation, runoff, groundwater recharge and return flow, and concentration of the water in lakes, rivers, and wetlands—will differ from

The flows of the San Pedro River in Arizona are dependent upon groundwater. Photo by Harold E. Malde

one watershed to another because of differences in watershed climate, geology, and vegetation.

As depicted by the hydrologic cycle (see Figure 2-3), when water falls to Earth's surface as precipitation, it can do one of many things. The water may simply evaporate again. It may fall directly onto a body of freshwater and from there either evaporate or flow downward through a river system back to the ocean. It may fall as snow or freeze upon hitting the ground, and remain in this condition until weather conditions allow it to melt. After hitting the ground, or after melting, it may flow over the land surface as runoff, eventually becoming part of a lake, river, or wetland. Lakes, rivers, and wetlands are actually ecological terms for the different forms of surface water within a watershed. Precipitation may also soak into the ground (either immediately or after melting), where it adds to soil moisture. Once it soaks into the ground or flows into a water body, the water may also be extracted and used by plants before returning to the atmosphere as water vapor through plant transpiration.

Precipitation Patterns

Precipitation in a watershed directly influences the patterns of variation in streamflow and the water levels in lakes and wetlands. Precipitation affects the topography of a watershed by continually eroding and depositing materials as it moves across the land surface. Precipitation also strongly influences the chemistry of the water flowing through a watershed. While in the atmosphere, water droplets absorb gases, including airborne pollutants, and dust particles. Droplets swept up off the ocean surface by the wind carry dissolved ocean salts with them. As a result, the water that returns to Earth as precipitation contains not just water, but a dilution of acids, gases, and salts. Once on the ground additional minerals, gases, and organic matter from soils and underlying geologic materials in the watershed combine with these other substances to supply essential chemicals (e.g., carbon, silicon, nitrogen, and phosphorous) to freshwater ecosystems. These chemicals dissolved in the water link the hydrologic cycle to

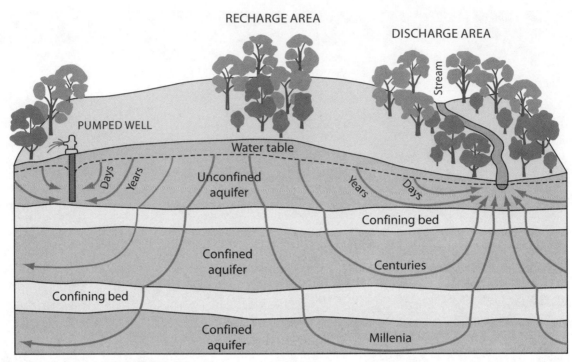

FIGURE 2-4. Confined and Unconfined Aquifers

Source: T.C. Winter, J.W. Harvey, O.L. Franke, W.M. Alley. 1998. Ground Water and Surface Water: A Single Resource. USGS Circular 1139. Denver: USGS.

other nutrient cycles and contribute to the distribution and abundance of all living things.

Groundwater

Water that soaks into the ground usually continues to percolate further downward, adding to or recharging the water stored in the geologic materials of the watershed as groundwater. Groundwater is water that fills the spaces between soil particles and the fractures in rock formations below the ground. Approximately 22% of all freshwater on the planet occurs as groundwater compared to 0.01% in lakes and rivers (McAllister *et al.* 1997).

Many types of soils and rock formations hold groundwater and therefore are effective aquifers. An aquifer is a soil or rock formation that both holds a substantial amount of groundwater and is permeable enough for water to be extracted. For example, basalt is a dominant type of surficial aquifer in the northwestern U.S. and many other parts of the world. It is composed of many tiny, interconnected fractures that

can hold large volumes of water. Unconsolidated materials such as sand and gravel, semi-consolidated sand, sandstone, and carbonate rock can also be effective aquifers. Other rocks or soil formations that are extremely dense, contain few fractures, or have extremely small pore spaces, such as granite and clay, are generally not very permeable and therefore do not make effective aquifers. These latter types of materials can act as barriers to groundwater movement, preventing surface water from percolating far into the ground or preventing groundwater from seeping back to the ground surface. An impermeable geologic layer that prevents deep groundwater from mixing with groundwater in some higher layer or from seeping back to the ground surface is called a confining layer. The groundwater confined in this manner is generally under pressure.

Groundwater flows from points of recharge (water infiltrating the ground) to points of discharge to surface water ecosystems and generally flows downward with gravity. However, groundwater trapped beneath a confining layer can develop a great deal of pressure.

When this pressurized water meets a fracture in the confining layer, it will force its way upward, sometimes emerging at the ground surface as a spring or geyser. Groundwater also flows more quickly through some geologic formations than through others, depending on the permeability of the formations. As a result, the route that groundwater travels underground—called its flow path—is often complex. Groundwater flow paths differ greatly in length, depth, and travel time, from one aquifer and watershed to another. In fact, groundwater systems are structurally complex. Aquifers exist at many different levels below Earth's surface, depending on the different layers of geologic materials. Many aquifers and several confining layers are often stacked up layer upon layer, each with its own geological characteristics (Figure 2-4). Similarly, an unconfined aquifer is one that is not capped by a confining layer. Generally, the aquifer nearest the ground surface, also referred to as a surficial aquifer, is an unconfined aquifer; the top of groundwater in such an unconfined aquifer is called the water table. Surficial aquifers which interact directly with river, lakes, and wetlands can have a huge influence on these freshwater ecosystems through their influence on patterns of water flow, temperature, and chemistry within freshwater ecosystems.

Confined aquifers that occur only deep in the ground are regional aquifers. Water movement into these deep aquifers and then back to the surface can take thousands or even millions of years. Intermediate level aquifers are generally closer to the surface than regional aquifers and generally have a water residence time of hundreds of years. Water in surficial aquifers may have a residence time of days to years. All aquifers interact not only with surface water but with each other; except where confining layers prevent it, aquifers constantly exchange their water supply with each other. Patterns within both deeper and more surficial aquifers are often unrelated to watershed boundaries. Eventually (sometimes in a few days, sometimes only over millions of years), all this groundwater will seep back out to the Earth's surface and combine with other waters. Some seeps out beneath the ocean along the coast and the rest discharges into rivers, lakes, and wetlands contributing to their water levels and flow patterns.

GEOLOGY

The geology of a landscape influences its freshwater characteristics in seven crucial ways. First, geologic history determines the location of the landscape's watersheds and the freshwater ecosystems within them. Specifically, uplifting, faulting, warping, and erosion of the Earth's crust determines watershed boundaries and the avenues down which a river will run; depressions on the surface of Earth's crust provide the location for the formation of a lake and so forth.

Second, geology determines the detailed spatial patterns of flow of water across and below the land's surface within each watershed (Figure 2-5). The permeability of soil and underlying rock formations dictates whether water hitting the land as rain or snow will soak into the ground to become groundwater or remain on the surface as runoff. As noted earlier, groundwater typically does not remain locked underground, but eventually seeps back out to the land surface along geologic fractures or at low points across a watershed, where it helps form and sustain rivers, lakes, and wetlands. Rivers and streams in watersheds composed of mainly permeable soil and rock formations tend to have fairly constant minimum amount of flow throughout the year driven by groundwater contributions—called baseflow. These rivers rarely ever run dry because a significant fraction of the precipitation within such watersheds infiltrates the ground and sustains the groundwater system. The resulting slow seepage of groundwater back to the land surface provides a stable source of flow year-round. However, even streams with strong base flows have water levels that fluctuate, due to the effects of snow melt and rainfall. At the opposite extreme, rivers that have watersheds composed of impervious soils and underlying rock formations (or parking lots!) tend to be very flashy or prone to fast runoff and may become dry during prolonged periods of little or no precipitation.

Third, the geology of a landscape determines not only whether water infiltrates to become groundwater, but where that recharge can take place, how the water moves beneath the ground, and where the groundwater can return to the land surface. As noted above, different soils and rock formations at and beneath the land surface differ in their permeability and hence in

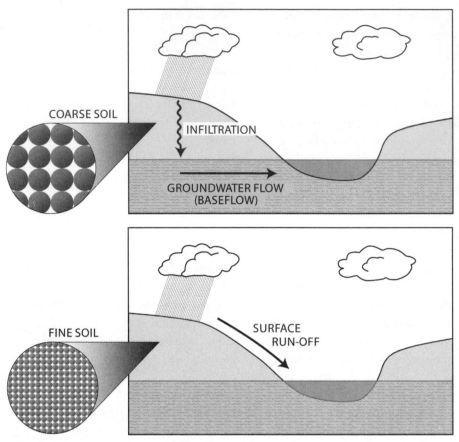

FIGURE 2-5. Influence of Basin Surficial Geology on Water Flow

their ability to recharge, store, and transmit ground-water. The distribution of geologic formations also determines where and how easily groundwater may re-emerge at the land surface as seeps or springs. As a result, neither the recharge nor the reemergence (discharge) of groundwater takes place evenly across any watershed.

Fourth, geology also strongly influences the water chemistry of freshwater ecosystems. As water moves through a watershed, both across the land surface and through the groundwater system, it dissolves some of the minerals and organic matter in its path, as noted above. These dissolved materials react with each other, with plant and animal life in the water, with, gases dissolved from the air, and with other ingredients brought along from the atmosphere to create a unique pattern of water chemistry in every watershed. Water that enters a surface water body from the groundwater system typically contains higher concentrations of dissolved minerals than does runoff water because of the

longer time it spends in contact with the watershed's geologic materials. Water temperature, one aspect of water chemistry, is also affected by geology. Groundwater generally is cooler than surface water in a watershed during warm seasons and may in fact be warmer than surface water fed streams during cold seasons as it stays nearly the same temperature year-round. In volcanic regions groundwater may become quite hot. By determining how and where groundwater discharges into surface waters, the geology of the watershed influences where and to what extent these releases may modify surface water temperature.

Fifth, the geology of a watershed determines the types, sizes, and shapes of the mineral materials that create the physical habitat substrate of every freshwater body—the shores and bottoms of lakes, the banks and beds of streams and rivers, and the sub-soils of wetlands. Most important among these materials are the sediments that get washed into rivers and lakes and carried along by currents in these waters. Water

Topographic features of a large river watershed include headwaters, streams of varying sizes and gradients, as well as lakes and wetlands. Photographs by National Park Service (top left), Harold E. Malde (top right, middle left, bottom left, bottom right), Brian Richter/TNC (middle right).

can exert a lot of force on these materials, loosening and carrying them off when flowing fast, for example, during a severe storm, and dropping them again when the flow abates. This almost constant reworking of the landscape and the substrate of the water bodies is a distinctive characteristic of all freshwater ecosystems, and the way these processes shape the physical habitat

of these ecosystems depends strongly on the geologic materials available.

Sixth, the geology of a watershed determines where natural breaks may occur within the drainage system, creating natural barriers to the movement of freshwater species. Such breaks may consist of waterfalls or severe rapids or may consist of zones of porous geologic

Beaver dam. Photograph by Charlie Ott.

materials that allow the water to sink in rapidly to recharge the groundwater system and potentially cause the stream to sink out of sight altogether.

Finally, geology determines the amount and distribution of relief, or variation in elevation, present across a watershed. Relief shapes several features of freshwater ecosystems. For example, the overall slope of the watershed determines how rapidly water runs off into its water bodies, and the gradient of a river determines how fast the river will flow and the size of a river's bottom substrate material. The shape and gradient of a river valley also determine how readily the river may flood the land when the water runs high. Lakes and most wetlands will form in areas of flat topography where water can pool. Changes in topography, such as a break in slope along a hillside, may determine where a wetland will form. Lastly, topography is critically important to the connectivity of freshwater features. Changes in topography, such as the creation of levees along a river's course, will dramatically alter the river's connection with its floodplain, specifically the transfer of water, nutrients, sediments, and species between the river and its floodplain.

WATERSHED VEGETATION

Except in the most harsh mountain and desert climates, watersheds are covered with vegetation that evolved over time through a unique combination of geologic, and climatic factors. The vegetation across a watershed shapes freshwater ecosystems in four ways as described below and illustrated in part by Figure 2-6.

First, the vegetation of a watershed exerts a strong influence on water chemistry. Plant matter becomes incorporated into the soil as it decays. As it decays, it releases a wide range of organic compounds that percolate further into the soil and are also washed out of the soil by precipitation and flooding. These dissolved organic materials vary in their chemistry, depending on the kinds of plants and soils present across the landscape; all are rich in carbon, but some may be rich in nitrogen, some highly acidic, and some even toxic to aquatic life. Once they wash into a freshwater ecosystem, they help shape the chemistry of the water and also provide an important source of nutrients for microorganisms, helping drive the food chain of the ecosystem. Vegetation may also provide shade, modifying water temperature within an ecosystem.

Second, the vegetation of a watershed, particularly the vegetation living near freshwater bodies, provides a steady source of plant litter—leaves, twigs, fruits, and

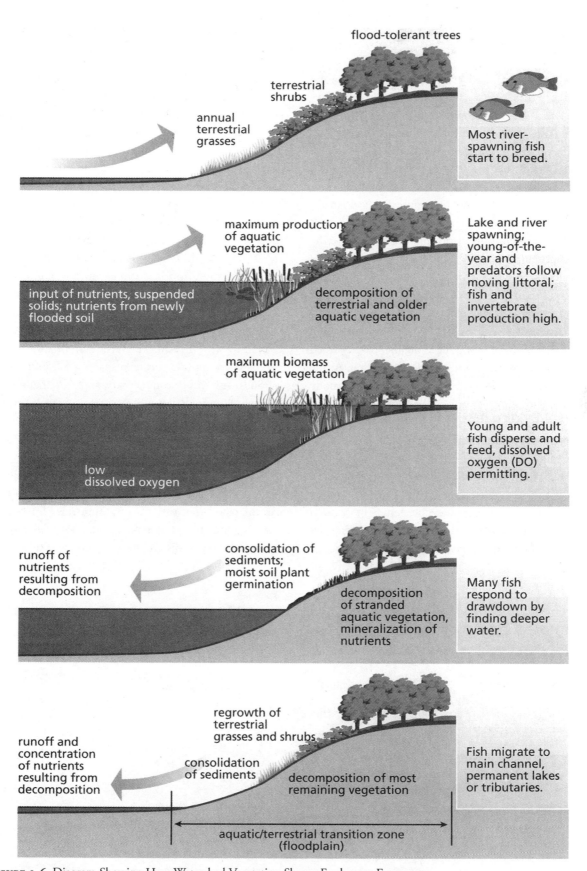

FIGURE 2-6. Diagram Showing How Watershed Vegetation Shapes Freshwater Ecosystems

Source: Peter B. Bayley. 1995. "Understanding Large River-Floodplain Ecosystems." BioScience, vol. 45, March 1995, p. 154. Copyright, American Institute of Biological Sciences.

even whole bushes and trees—that may fall or be washed into these freshwater bodies. This detritus plays two crucial roles in freshwater ecosystems: as food for freshwater life and as solid material that adds complexity to the physical habitat. Seeds and fruits that fall into the water rapidly become food for fishes and waterfowl; and any plant material that falls into the water also rapidly becomes food for microbes, insect larvae, snails, and other aquatic invertebrates. In some freshwater ecosystems, these inputs of organic matter may be the most important source of carbon in the entire ecosystem, and carbon is a crucial building block for the entire food chain. As part of the physical habitat, plant detritus can serve as raw material for nests and the protective casings of some insect larvae. Larger material may become wedged along the shoreline, bank, or bed of a freshwater body, creating shade and shelter. At the largest scale, the trees and tree limbs or large woody debris that falls into a stream can create large eddies and pools, shelter and basking surfaces for many fish and reptiles, perching surfaces for waterfowl, and even temporary dams. Beavers in the Northern Hemisphere deliberately carry woody debris into streams in order to build their dams and lodges, exerting a strong influence on the shape of the freshwater ecosystem. The removal of beavers from much of their range by trapping has resulted in dramatic changes in watershed dynamics.

Third, the vegetation of a watershed strongly influences the way that water behaves on the land surface after it falls as precipitation or is released by the melting of snow or ice. The more dense the vegetation and plant litter covering a watershed, the more it slows down and holds back runoff and delays the time it takes for a drop of water to wash into a freshwater body after hitting the ground. This effect of vegetation on storm runoff detention plays a crucial role in shaping the hydrology and chemistry of freshwater ecosystems. By slowing runoff, it spreads out the time it takes for the precipitation from a storm event to reach its destination in a stream, river, lake, or wetland. This moderates the potential for flooding and also gives the water more time to soak into the soil itself, as well as to react chemically with the soil. The vegetation of a watershed also plays an important role in shaping soil permeability. Soils with lots of root activity, and soils that attract burrowing animals because of their covering vegetation, are naturally more permeable than other soils.

Finally, vegetation plays a key role in each watershed's micro-climate. Plants pull water from the soil through their roots and transpire it from their leaves. Plants in fog-prone regions have evolved ways to collect the cloud moisture directly onto their leaves and needles, directing the moisture to then fall to the ground to help moisten the soil and be available to

Cloud forest, Tariquia Flora and Fauna Reserve, Bolivia. Photograph by Ivan Arnold.

plant roots. The more heavily vegetated a watershed, therefore, the more water gets taken out of the soil, and sometimes out of the air itself, and released back to the atmosphere without ever reaching a freshwater body. The amount of and type of vegetation in a watershed, consequently, has a large effect on the humidity of the air over a watershed, which itself exerts a strong influence on the kinds of plant and animal life that can live in that environment. In extreme cases, such as in the cloud forests of Central and South America and in the forests of giant redwoods of the North American Pacific Coast, watershed vegetation creates the very micro-climate on which the forest ecosystem depends, which in turn shapes the hydrology of the watersheds' rivers, lakes, and wetlands as well.

The preceding text of this chapter discussed the formation and function of watersheds and the importance of climate and the associated hydrologic cycle, geology, and watershed vegetation in shaping the loca-

FRESHWATER ECOSYSTEMS AND THEIR VARIABILITY

tion and characteristics of freshwater ecosystems on the landscape. The following section provides an overview of the major types of freshwater ecosystems and the key ecological factors that determine their ability to remain healthy and able to support resident biodiversity.

A freshwater ecosystem consists of a group of strongly interacting freshwater and riparian/near-shore species and communities linked by shared physical habitat, environmental regimes, energy exchanges, and nutrient dynamics. Freshwater ecosystems vary in their spatial extent, can have indistinct boundaries, and can be hierarchically nested within one another depending on spatial scale. Conserving freshwater biodiversity is best accomplished not by conserving habitat for a few species and communities alone, but by conserving entire freshwater ecosystems.

Types of Freshwater Ecosystems

The features that perhaps most distinguish freshwater ecosystems from terrestrial ecosystems are their variability in form and their dynamic nature. Freshwater ecosystems are extremely dynamic in that they often change where they exist (e.g., a migrating river channel) and when they exist (e.g., seasonal ponds) in a time frame that we can experience. Freshwater ecosystems are nearly always found connected to and dependant upon one another, and as such they form drainage networks that constitute even larger ecological systems. Freshwater ecosystems exist in many different forms, depending upon their underlying climate, geology, veg-

etation, and other features of the watersheds in which they occur. Many classifications exist to describe in great detail freshwater and freshwater-related ecosystems (i.e., Cowardin *et al.* 1979, Maxwell *et al.* 1995, and Higgins *et al.* 2003). In very general terms, however, freshwater ecosystems fall into three major groups:

- Standing-water ecosystems (e.g., lakes and ponds);
- Flowing-water ecosystems (e.g., rivers and streams); and
- Freshwater-dependent ecosystems that interface with terrestrial ecosystems (e.g., wetlands and riparian areas).

Cave systems often have both standing and flowing water and unique aquatic biota that have evolved in them. The resulting underground freshwater ecosystems present a unique set of challenges to conservation, which this guide cannot address due to its highly specialized demands. Estuaries, formed where rivers and streams discharge to the sea, constitute another type of freshwater-influenced ecosystem with complex conservation challenges beyond the scope of this guide.

LAKES AND PONDS

Lakes and ponds are inland depressions containing standing water derived from glaciers, river drainage, surface water runoff or groundwater seepage. They vary in size from less than a hectare to large bodies of open water covering thousands of square kilometers such as the Great Lakes bordering the U.S. and Canada. Lakes in temperate climates display seasonal

Link Lake, Deschutes National Forest, Oregon, Photograph by Charlie Ott.

characteristics. The difference between a lake and a pond is in the depth and not the size. In a pond, sunlight reaches all the way to the bottom, whereas in a lake the light does not reach the bottom. It is possible, therefore, for a pond to be larger in surface area than a lake. The lack of light at the bottom of lakes means that plants do not grow there. This in turn affects the distribution of plant-eating organisms and also carnivores. Given the greater complexity of lakes, the remainder of this section focuses on lakes.

Three distinct layers of water temperature develop in lakes during summer months. The top layer (the epilimnion) is the warmest, followed by the middle layer (the metalimnion), with the bottom layer (hypolimnion) being the coldest. Since sunlight is the strongest in the top layer, the majority of a lake's biomass (phytoplankton) occurs within the top layer of the lake during the summer. During spring and fall, cooler air temperatures cause the top layer of water to cool, resulting in greater mixing of the lake waters. As a result, the water temperature is more uniform throughout lakes due to increased water flow (mixing), allowing for fish and other wildlife to occur in all areas. In areas with cold winters, lakes can form distinct temperature layers, providing protection for organisms needing to stay within warmer waters: water that cools to 4°C or below is lighter than warmer water and therefore floats to the surface carrying ice or forms a cold top layer and organisms can stay well below this surface water where the environment is warmer. In tropical climates, of course, the temperature patterns in lakes tend to behave as if it were summer year-round.

Although called standing water bodies, the water in lakes and ponds does not stand still. The water arrives as precipitation, direct runoff, and inflow from streams and areas of groundwater discharge and leaves as evaporation, outflow to streams, and groundwater recharge. The flushing rate of water through a lake is greatest in lakes connected to river ecosystems where river inflows and outflows create a constant flow pattern. Wind and changes in water temperatures cause further mixing. In larger lakes, all of these same factors apply, but temperature differences with depth can also create distinct temperature zones and deeply circulating currents, prevailing winds can create steady currents, particularly along the shoreline, and the pull of the moon's gravity can actually create modest lake tides. The patterns of water flow in ponds and lakes play a crucial role in shaping the availability and spatial distribution of habitat over time.

RIVERS AND STREAMS

True flowing-water ecosystems—rivers and streams—

are distinguished by water moving along distinct channels within a watershed, creating rich but often challenging habitat for a unique spectrum of organisms. Factors such as the amount and depth of water flowing, the source of the water, how the flow naturally changes over time, and the location of the ecosystem within a watershed all combine to further determine the type of the river ecosystem and the organisms living in it. Nearly all stream and river ecosystems are directly connected to other streams and rivers (and ponds, lakes, and wetlands as well), and eventually to estuarine and marine ecosystems. This connectivity serves a critical role in shaping the movement of energy, material, and biota throughout the entire system. Riparian ecosystems—the ecosystems of streamside lands, especially those subject to flooding—serve as transition zones between streams, rivers and the terrestrial world, providing key habitat (e.g., floodplains as fish nurseries), material inputs (e.g., woody debris for structure and nutrients), and other ecological services (e.g., temperature control from shading) to these ecosystems. Rivers and streams are so closely linked to their adjacent floodplain riparian corridors, it often makes sense to treat the river and floodplain as a single ecosystem. This is particularly true in large river valleys where seasonal flooding covers vast areas of the adjacent lowlands for months at a time, such as along portions of the Amazon River and Rio Paraguay.

Streams and rivers vary dramatically in their size, from the smallest headwaters high in a mountain range to the largest rivers such as the Amazon, Mississippi, Congo, Danube, Mekong, or Nile. The terms *stream* and *river* are general terms for relatively small and large flowing waters and have no precise definition. Flowing waters form drainage networks across a watershed. The small streams high in a watershed join to form larger streams, that join to form rivers, which eventually drain out to the sea.

Important changes occur in the physical, chemical, and biological aspects of flowing waters in any watershed, as one moves downward from small headwater stream to larger rivers. Other factors that influence stream and river ecosystems and their biota include variation in hydrologic regime, geomorphology, stream temperature, chemistry, and biogeographic history.

WETLANDS

Wetlands are an ecotone or transitional zone between terrestrial and freshwater ecosystems. They support both freshwater and terrestrial species. Wetlands are areas where water covers and permeates the soil or is present either at or near the surface of the soil all year or for varying periods of time during the year, including during the growing season. The prolonged presence of water creates conditions that favor the growth of specially adapted plants and animals and promote the development of characteristic wetland soils. Wetlands occur on every continent except Antarctica. Fifty-six percent of the world's wetlands are in tropical and subtropical regions. The remaining are primarily boreal peatland in arctic and subarctic regions. Wetlands also perform many important services within a watershed:

- They have often been described as the kidneys of the landscape, because they filter out nutrients, pollutants, and sediments from the water that passes through them;
- They serve as water storage sites moderating floods in the wet season and releasing water in times of drought;
- They provide critical breeding and migratory stopover habitat for numerous species including ducks, wading birds, and shore birds and also provide critical habitat for many globally declining reptile and amphibian species, which are rapidly declining world-wide;

TABLE 2-1. Distribution of Freshwater Ecosystems by Continent

	Africa	Europe	Asia	Australia	North America	South America
Large Lakes	30,000	2,027	27,782	154	25,623	913
Rivers	195	80	565	25	250	1,000
Wetlands	341,000	'Eurasia' 925,000		4,000	180,000	1,232,000

Data refer to volume in km³, except for wetlands which refer to area in km². All estimates are approximations and vary according to the methods used to derive them. (*modified from Korzun et al. 1978*)

Satellite image of the Nile River, one of the world's largest rivers, flowing into the Mediterranean Sea. Image by Jeff Schmaltz, MODIS Rapid Response Team, NASA/GSFC.

- They host a suite of rare and endemic plants and significantly high species richness.

A summary of the extent of these major freshwater ecosystem types for every continent is found in Table 2-1.

The Importance of Natural Variability in Freshwater Ecosystems

Freshwater ecosystems are not static. Life is constantly in motion, reproducing, growing and dying, and evolving through natural selection. This grand drama plays out on a stage of environmental variation, in which the details of climate and geology change daily, seasonally, yearly, and over longer periods of decades, centuries, and millennia. Wet seasons vary with dry ones, wet years vary with droughts, watersheds slowly erode, lakes fill up with sediment, and rivers meander. Sometimes

these details change only slightly or gradually; sometimes they change catastrophically as a result of floods, disease epidemics, earthquakes, or volcanic events.

Species could not persist in a specific ecosystem if they are intolerant of the range of variation in environmental and biological conditions that the system naturally faces and creates. Indeed, all species have evolved adaptations to the environmental and biological conditions they face, including the natural variation in these conditions. The biological diversity found in any ecosystem therefore exists not despite, but because of, this natural variation. Changes to the natural variation in these patterns alter interactions among species and interactions of species with their physical environment and environmental processes. These changes, in turn, make it difficult (or impossible) for some species to persist in the system, or make it possible for invasive alien species to establish and

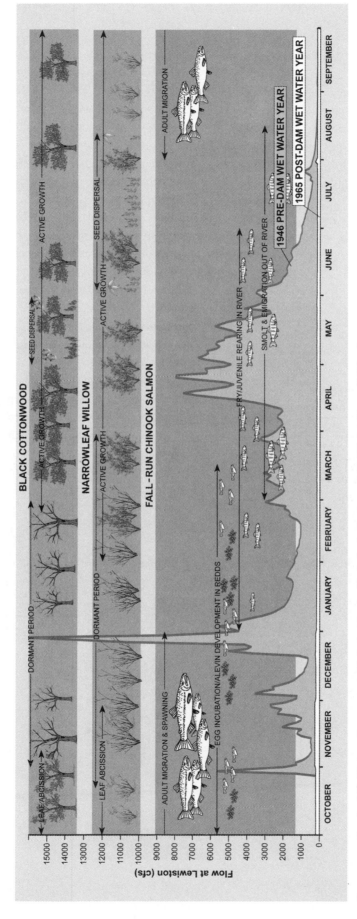

FIGURE 2-7. Species Life History Responses to Variation in the Hydrologic Regime of the Trinity River, California

Source: Courtesy of McBain and Trush, Inc., Arcata, California.

thrive, and thereby potentially altering the ecosystem's biodiversity (Figure 2-7).

Every freshwater ecosystem (lakes, rivers, wetlands) experiences a specific combination of geologic and climatologic processes, terrestrial ecological processes, and biological history. These influences create a unique pattern of key ecological factors for each freshwater ecosystem (Figure 2-8).

1) Hydrologic Regime: The pattern of variation in the amount and movement of water in the system over time.
2) Water Chemistry Regime: The pattern of variation in water chemistry over time, including temperature and the composition of dissolved and suspended materials.
3) Physical Habitat Conditions: The physical habitat conditions created by the underlying geology, vegetation, and other materials that form the solid substrates of the ecosystem.
4) Connectivity: The arrangement or pattern of different water bodies across the landscape, and the physical connections among them, and the extent to which this arrangement allows or impedes the movement of life forms (animals, larvae, seeds, and fruit, etc.) among them.

5) Biological Composition and Interactions: The biological structure, composition, interactions, and critical biological processes that characterize the ecosystem, including trophic dynamics (how energy is captured and moved through the ecosystem).

These five categories of key ecological factors not only define the essential character of every freshwater ecosystem, but also determine how the ecosystem will respond to disturbance—whether from extreme weather, geologic shifts, or human intervention. Conserving freshwater ecosystems therefore involves conserving all five of these categories of key ecological factors in as natural a state as possible. More precisely, in order to conserve freshwater biodiversity, we need to characterize a freshwater ecosystem's key ecological factors and make sure they are functioning within their natural ranges of variation.

Appendix A - Ecological Characteristics of Freshwater Ecosystem Types provides an in-depth overview of each of the major freshwater ecosystem types (lakes, rivers, and wetlands). Specifically, Appendix A explains what they are, how they are formed, and provides a detailed description of the fundamental structure, composition

Hydrologic Regime
(surface flow, groundwater, surface inundation, and soil moisture regimes)

Physical Habitat Conditions

(woody debris, riparian canopy, geomorphology, sediment/soil regime)

Biological Composition & Interactions

(energy regime, feeding, 1• & 2• production, target structure & composition, competition & predation, reproduction, disease & parasitism, mutualism)

Connectivity
(up-down gradient continuity, water-wetland-land connectivity)

Water Chemistry Regime

(salinity, alkalinity, hardness, temperature, dissolved minerals, dissolved gases, turbidity, pH, ORP, radioactivity, organic compounds)

Photo by Will Van Oberbeek.

FIGURE 2-8. The Five Types of Key Ecological Factors for Freshwater Ecosystems

FRESHWATER BIODIVERSITY

and function of these freshwater ecosystem types with respect to their key ecological factors. Appendix A provides the foundation for understanding the major components of each freshwater ecosystem type that must be conserved in order to ensure the conservation of freshwater biodiversity.

The key ecological factors for freshwater ecosystems, formed from unique combinations of geology, climate and zoogeographic history, create the settings in which individual freshwater species have evolved over millennia. Estimates suggest that over 45,000 described species rely on freshwater habitats. With the inclusion of undescribed species, this number could increase to include over one million species (SSC/IUCN Freshwater Biodiversity Assessment Programme, 1998). Although the number of freshwater species overall (species richness) is low compared to marine and terrestrial groups, freshwater species richness is high relative to the amount of area on Earth in which these species occur. For example, among all known fish species, approximately 40% (ca. 10,000) are freshwater forms and 60% marine, despite the fact there is over 10,000 times as much seawater as there is freshwater habitat. This high diversity of freshwater fish relative to habitat is undoubtedly promoted by the extent to which freshwater ecosystems are geographically isolated from each other.

Distribution Patterns of Freshwater Biodiversity

Biodiversity in freshwater ecosystems is distributed in a fundamentally different pattern than that of marine or terrestrial systems. Species adjust their ranges to some degree as climate or ecological conditions change. However, freshwater habitats are relatively discontinuous, and many freshwater species do not disperse easily across the land barriers (watershed boundaries) that separate river drainages into discrete units. Therefore, the spatial extent of strictly freshwater species tends to correspond to presently or formerly continuous river basins or lakes. Watershed boundaries and, for most freshwater species, the intolerable conditions of the ocean into which most rivers flow

are the principal barriers to the dispersal of freshwater species between systems. Species can extend or become restricted in their ranges within a river basin relatively easily, but usually can do so between river basins only as a result of geologic changes that affect the locations of watershed boundaries. For example, large-scale glaciation brought formerly neighboring river basins into contact with each other along the margins of the ice. This glaciation also created debris dams that separated formerly connected basins from each other. One river can also capture another by eroding into a neighboring valley, and large-scale geologic movements can allow species formerly restricted to one system to move into another. Species can also extend their range accidentally, for example, through the accidental transport of eggs by waterbirds, or by flooding, and in even some documented accounts by tornadoes or water spouts! This combination of factors limiting species distributions has three important consequences regarding the distribution pattern of freshwater species:

- Freshwater species cannot readily migrate outside their drainage basins to avoid catastrophic climatic and ecological events;
- The ranges of some freshwater species, communities, and types of ecosystems can be highly localized; even small lake or stream systems can harbor unique, locally evolved forms of life; and
- Freshwater species diversity among neighboring watersheds in a single region may be high, even if the number of species in any single watershed is low due to local endemism and variation within this region.

Freshwater lakes are classic examples of habitat islands (freshwater islands surrounded by a terrestrial sea). Like islands, the larger, older lakes tend to have high levels of endemism. For example, the rift lakes of Africa harbor hundreds of species, and over 90% of these species are found nowhere else in the world.

In many cases, a species range within a freshwater ecosystem will also be restricted by particular habitat requirements, such as the need to seek out or avoid locations with particular patterns of water turbulence

Global processes, including geology and climate, interact to produce...

The Watershed Context of Freshwater Ecosystems

- Location
- Waterhed vegetation cover
- Watershed elevation, gradient, and drainage patterns

which establishes the natural patterns of variation in...

The Five Key Ecological Factors of Freshwater Ecosystems

- Hydrology
- Physical habitat structure
- Water chemistry
- Connectivity
- Biological composition and interactions

which in turn can be altered by...

Human Activities

- Land use and management
- Water use and management
- Invasive alien species
- Overharvesting and fisheries management

because of the adverse effects these activities can have on...

Geophysical Conditions	Aquatic Biological Conditions
• Watershed vegetation cover	• Taxonomic and genetic composition
• Soil erosion rates	• Individual health
• Surface and groundwater hydrology	• Biological processes
• Soil and water chemistry	• Ecological processes
• Channel/shoreline morphology	• Evolutionary processes

which must be prevented or abated by...

Conservation Strategies

- Restoration and land/water protection
- Specific land use policies and practices
- Specific sustainable water management policies and practices
- Invasive alien species management policies and practices
- Fisheries management and harvesting policies and practices
- Etc.

and we improve our success through...

Monitoring and Adaptive Management

CHAPTER 2

CHAPTER 4

CH 5

FIGURE 2-9.

Freshwater species with special adaptations: the American dipper, Cinclus mexicanus, (above left, photograph © 1999 Dan Kirchner) has specialized wings to dip under the water to catch fish; freshwater mussels like Lampsilis reeveiana (below left, photograph © Chris Barnhart) have lure-like extensions designed to attact fish to serve as hosts for the mussels' glochidia; and the spider Argyroneta aquatica (above right, photograph © Gerard Visser) is able to live almost entirely under water by relying on air stored in bubbles carried from the surface.

or speed, shelter, substrate, etc. These habitat preferences usually differ between different stages in a species' life cycle. For example, some freshwater fish require different conditions and different sites for egg deposition and development, for early growth of fry, and for feeding and breeding of adults.

Many cave or subterranean freshwater species (e.g., of fish, amphibians, and crustaceans) have very restricted ranges, in some cases consisting of a single cave or aquifer, and very limited opportunities for dispersal, depending on the surrounding geology and the consequent morphology of the freshwater ecosystem within which they live.

Insects with an aquatic larval phase but a winged adult phase are often restricted to particular river basins; even if the adults disperse widely, they may not find suitable habitat elsewhere. In general, however, such insect species are less restricted in their ability to move between watersheds than are other freshwater species. A relatively large number of species,

particularly crustaceans, have evolved the ability to occupy temporary pools by producing or undergoing a desiccation-resistant life stage. In this form, such species can undergo long-range passive dispersal between drainage basins; some of these species are therefore widely distributed.

Vascular aquatic plants evolved from terrestrial ancestors. Most inland water plant species are relatively widespread, ranging over more than one continental land mass. Many are cosmopolitan, occurring around the world and on remote islands. Of the widespread forms, some are predominantly northern temperate species extending into the tropics; some are mainly tropical. Tropical regions of Asia, Africa, and South America appear to be most rich in species restricted to a single continent, or to a single country or smaller area (WCMC 2000).

Adaptation and Abundance of Freshwater Biodiversity

Organisms that typify freshwater ecosystems have adapted to live in different freshwater habitats through morphologic and behavioral adaptations. The following are some examples of these unique adaptations:

- Freshwater fish species, like their marine counterparts, have developed gills that extract oxygen from the water. They also have specialized kidneys to excrete excess water from their bodies while conserving the salts necessary for their physiological processes. Small invertebrates with gills, such as insect larvae and worms, often have to wave their gills to create a current of water from which to extract oxygen.
- Freshwater species that live underwater have also adapted morphologically by evolving hydrodynamic body shapes that enable them to move easily through the water without expending a lot of energy. Bottom dwelling river species have evolved specialized appendages that allow them to attach themselves to the river's substrate, to avoid being swept downstream. Many fish and freshwater plant species utilize water flow to help with the dispersal of eggs, juveniles, and seeds.
- Submerged freshwater plants have also adapted morphologically. Instead of tough outer surfaces to prevent water loss or thick stems to support themselves underwater, many have evolved root systems to hold themselves in place where currents might otherwise dislodge them. Many have evolved ways to use the flow of water for seed dispersal.
- Freshwater animals that live in turbid water, such as in muddy rivers, have adapted ways to navigate, locate food, and avoid predators by feeling the water and substrate and by sensing chemical scents and electromagnetic fields that surround other animals. Some even communicate with each other through chemical and electromagnetic means. ·
- On the margin between land and freshwater live specialists that depend on both terrestrial and freshwater ecosystems for their survival. Amphibians breed in water but live on land. Frogs and toads lay long strings of eggs in the water, which develop into aquatic tadpoles, then into air-breathing adults. Some reptiles, on the other hand, live in the water but lay their eggs on dry land. Examples of these reptiles include water snakes, Monitor lizards, freshwater turtles, and crocodiles.

There are 19 major taxonomic groups of organisms that live in freshwater ecosystems. They are sum-

TABLE 2-2. The Major Groups of Freshwater Organisms (World Conservation Monitoring Centre 2000).

	General Features	Significance in Freshwaters
Viruses	Microscopic; can reproduce only within the cells of other organisms, but can disperse and persist without host.	Cause disease in many aquatic organisms, and associated with waterborne disease in humans (e.g., hepatitis).
Bacteria	Microscopic; can be numerically very abundant, e.g., 1,000,000 per cm^3, but less so than in soils. Recycle organic and inorganic substances. Most derive energy from inorganic chemical sources or from organic materials.	Responsible for decay of dead material. Present on all submerged detritus where a food source for aquatic invertebrates exists. Many cause disease in aquatic organisms and humans.
Fungi	Microscopic. Recycle organic substances; responsible for decay of dead material; tend to follow bacteria in decomposition processes. Able to break down cellulose plant cell walls and chitinous insect exoskeletons.	Present on all submerged detritus where a food source for aquatic invertebrates exists. Some cause disease in aquatic organisms and humans.

	General Features	Significance in Freshwaters
Algae	Microscopic and macroscopic; include variety of unicellular and colonial photosynthetic organisms. All lack leaves and vascular tissues of higher plants. Green Algae (Chlorophyta) and Red Algae (Rhodophyta) include freshwater species; Stoneworts (Charophyta) mostly freshwater.	Responsible for most primary production (growth in biomass) in most aquatic ecosystems. Free-floating phytoplankton main producers in lakes and slow reaches of rivers; attached forms important in shallow parts of lakes and streams.
Plants	Photosynthetic organisms; mostly higher plants that possess leaves and vascular tissues. Mosses, quillworts, ferns important in some habitats. Some free-floating surface species (e.g., Water Fern Salvinia, Duckweed Lemna); most are rooted forms restricted to water margins.	Provide a substrate for other organisms and food for many. Trees are ecologically important in providing shade and organic debris (leaves, fruit), structural elements (fallen trunks and branches) that enhance vertebrate diversity, in promoting bank stabilization, and in restricting or modulating flood waters.
Invertebrates: protozoans	Microscopic mobile single-celled organisms. Tend to be widely distributed through passive dispersal of resting stages. Attached and free-living forms; many are filter-feeders.	Found in virtually all freshwater habitats. Most abundant in waters rich in organic matter, bacteria or algae. Feed on detritus, or consume other microscopic organisms; many are parasitic on algae, invertebrates or vertebrates.
Invertebrates: rotifers	Near-microscopic organisms; widely distributed; mostly attached filter-feeders, some predatory forms.	Important in plankton communities in lakes and may dominate animal plankton in rivers.
Invertebrates: myxozoans	Microscopic organisms with complex life cycles, some with macroscopic cysts. Formerly classified with protozoa but are metazoa.	Important parasites in or on fishes.
Invertebrates: flatworms	A large group of worm- or ribbon-like flatworms, includes free-living benthic (Turbellaria), and parasitic forms (Trematoda, Cestoda).	Turbellaria include mobile bottom-living predatory flatworms. The Trematodes include various flukes, such as the tropical schistosome that causes bilharzia; Cestodes are tapeworms: both these groups are important parasites of fish and other vertebrates, including humans. Mollusks often intermediate hosts.
Invertebrates: nematodes	Generally microscopic or near-microscopic roundworms.	May be parasitic, herbivorous, or predatory. Typically inhabit bottom sediments. Some parasitic forms can reach considerable size. Poorly known; may be more diverse than recognized.
Invertebrates: annelid worms	Two main groups in freshwaters; oligochaetes and leeches.	Oligochaetes are bottom-living worms that graze on sediments; leeches are mainly parasitic on vertebrate animals, some are predatory.
Invertebrates: mollusks	Two main groups in freshwaters; Bivalvia (mussels, etc.) and Gastropoda (snails, etc). Very rich in species; tend to form local endemic species.	Snails are mobile grazers or predators; bivalves are attached bottom-living filter-feeders. Both groups have speciated profusely in certain freshwater systems. The larvae of many bivalves are parasitic on fishes. Because of the feeding mode, bivalves can help maintain water quality but tend to be susceptible to pollution.

(continues)

TABLE 2-2. *Continued*

	General Features	Significance in Freshwaters
Invertebrates: crustaceans	A very large Class of animals with a jointed exoskeleton often hardened with calcium carbonate.	Include larger bottom-living species such as shrimps, crayfish, and crabs of lake margins, streams, alluvial forests, and estuaries. Also larger plankton: filter-feeding Cladocera and filter-feeding or predatory Copepoda. Many isopods and copepods are important fish parasites.
Invertebrates: insects	By far the largest Class of organisms known. Jointed exoskeleton. The great majority of insects are terrestrial, because they are air-breathing.	In rivers and streams, grazing and predatory aquatic insects (especially larval stages of flying adults) dominate intermediate levels in food webs (between the microscopic producers, mainly algae, and fishes). Also important in lake communities. Fly larvae are numerically dominant in some situations (e.g., in Arctic streams or low-oxygen lake beds) and are vectors of human diseases (e.g., malaria, river blindness).
Vertebrates: fishes	More than half of all vertebrate species are fish. These are comprised of four main groups: hagfish (marine), lampreys (freshwater or ascend rivers to spawn), sharks and rays (almost entirely marine), and ray-finned 'typical' fish (> 8,500 species in freshwaters, or 40% of all fishes).	Fish are the dominant organisms in terms of biomass, feeding ecology, and significance to humans, in virtually all aquatic habitats, including freshwaters. Certain water systems, particularly in the tropics, are extremely rich in species. Many species are restricted to single lakes or river basins. Endemic fish species are the basis of important fisheries in inland waters in tropical and temperate zones.
Vertebrates: amphibians	Frogs, toads, newts, salamanders, caecilians. Require freshwater habitats.	Larvae of most species need water for development Some frogs, salamanders, and caecilians are entirely aquatic; generally in streams, small rivers, and pools. Larvae are typically herbivorous grazers, adults are predatory.
Vertebrates: reptiles	Turtles, crocodiles, lizards, snakes. All crocodilians and many turtles inhabit freshwaters but nest on land. Many lizards and snakes occur along water margins; a few snakes are highly aquatic.	Because of their large size, crocodiles can play an important role in aquatic systems, by nutrient enrichment and shaping habitat structure. They, as well as freshwater turtles and snakes are all predators or scavengers.
Vertebrates: birds	Many birds, including waders and herons, are closely associated with wetlands and water margins. Relatively few, including divers, grebes and ducks, are restricted to river and lake systems.	Top predators. Wetlands are often key feeding and staging areas for migratory species. Likely to assist passive dispersal of small aquatic organisms.
Vertebrates: mammals	Relatively few groups are strictly aquatic (e.g., river dolphins, platypus), several species are largely aquatic but emerge onto water margins (e.g., otters, desmans, otter shrews, water voles, water opossum, hippopotamus).	Top predators and grazers. Large species widely impacted by habitat modification and hunting. Through damming activities, beavers play an important role in shaping and creating aquatic habitats.

marized in Table 2-2. The interactions of these species form complex food webs/trophic structures in lake, river and wetland ecosystems. Appendix A summarizes these trophic interactions under the section entitled Biological Composition and Interactions for each freshwater ecosystem type.

REFERENCES

Cowardin, L.M., V. Carter, F. Golet, E.T. LaRoe. 1979. Classification of Wetlands and Deepwater Habitats of the United States, U.S. Department of the Interior Fish and Wildlife Service Office of Biological Services, Washington, DC.

Dunne, T., and L.B. Leopold. 1978. Water in Environmental Planning. W.H. Freeman Co. San Francisco, CA, 818 pp.

Higgins, J.V., M.T. Bryer, M. Lammert, T.W. FitzHugh. 2003. A Freshwater Ecosystem Classification Approach for Biodiversity Conservation Planning. Conservation Biology (submitted)

Korzun, V.I., A.A. Sokolov, M.I. Budyko, K.P. Voskresensky, P. Kalinin, A.A. Konoplyantsev, E.S. Korotkevich, and M.I. L'vovitch, eds. 1978. Atlas of world water balance. USSR National Committee for the International Hydrological Decade. English translation. Paris, UNESCO. 663 pp.

Maxwell, J.R., C.J. Edwards, M.E. Jensen, S.J. Paustian, H. Parrott, and D.M. Hill. 1995. A Hierarchical Framework of Aquatic Ecological Units in North America (Neararctic Zone). General Technical Report NC-176. St. Paul, MN: U.S. Department of Agriculture, Forest Service. 72 pp.

McAllister, D.E., A.L. Hamilton and B. Harvey. 1997. Global freshwater biodiversity: Striving for the integrity of freshwater ecosystems. *Sea Wind* 11(3): 1–140p.

SSC/IUCN Freshwater Biodiversity Assessment Programme. 1998. http://www.iucn.org/themes/ssc/programs/freshwater/index.htm

World Conservation Monitoring Centre. 2000. Global Biodiversity: Earth's living resources in the 21st century. By: B. Groombridge and M.D. Jenkins. World Conservation Press, Cambridge, UK.

Chapter 3

Focusing Freshwater Conservation Efforts

Mark Bryer, David Braun, Mary Khoury, and Jonathan Higgins

OVERVIEW AND LEARNING OBJECTIVES

Limited financial and human resources as well as restricted technical and other capacity require conservation practitioners to choose where to direct their abilities to most effectively accomplish biodiversity conservation. Simply stated, what is possible is usually a subset of the challenge at hand. This chapter examines this dilemma and presents three questions that, when answered, can help practitioners determine how to focus their conservation efforts (adapted from Redford *et al.* 2003):

- What biodiversity should be conserved?
- Where should the biodiversity be conserved?
- How can the biodiversity be most effectively conserved?

This chapter also describes regional and local scale approaches for focusing freshwater biodiversity conservation efforts.

WHAT BIODIVERSITY SHOULD BE CONSERVED AND WHERE SHOULD IT BE CONSERVED?

Many agencies, organizations, and individuals engaged in the conservation of natural resources struggle to define where they need to work, how to focus their efforts at these locations, and how their local activities contribute to larger conservation efforts. The complexity of these questions increases with how broadly the net is cast or with how grandly the conservation mission is defined. Is the objective the conservation of habitat for an individual endangered species of mussel found in only one river basin, migration corridors for salmonids with large ranges, or all representative biodiversity across the planet?

Obviously, for entities that define their mission narrowly (e.g., the conservation of one or a small number of species or the conservation of all species within a limited geographic area), the answer to the question "what biodiversity should be conserved" and often the related question "where should it be conserved" are predetermined. The mission of these entities will define the particular species or group of species to conserve, in what watershed or geographic area to focus conservation efforts, or both. Geographic boundaries for these conservation efforts may be politically defined (county/district, state/province, nation) or ecologically defined (e.g., world, ecoregion, watershed, etc.). For entities that define their mission expansively (e.g., all biodiversity), determining "what biodiversity should be conserved" and "where to conserve this biodiversity" is a more complex task. Yet, neither entities with narrowly defined conservation missions nor those with broadly defined conservation missions can possibly protect all biodiversity everywhere within their spheres of interest due to financial and technical limitations. Strategic planning processes and considerations can help these entities focus their limited resources to achieve greater conservation effectiveness. Ecoregional context is one such consideration. Understanding the appropriate ecoregional context will help entities with narrowly defined conservation missions more effectively identify conservation strategies and actions at appropriate scales. Understanding the ecoregional context can help entities with broadly

defined conservation missions focus their efforts on particular clusters of biodiversity and areas within this larger landscape through priority setting processes.

Ecoregions are relatively large geographic areas of land and water that differ from each other in climate, vegetation, geology, and other ecological and environmental patterns. Examples of three commonly used ecoregional classifications are those developed by Bailey (1989), Omernik (1987), and Dinerstein *et al.* (1995). Bailey created a hierarchy of ecoregions for the world based on climate, physiography and potential natural vegetation (1989). Omernik's ecoregions, developed for the United States, also are based on climate and physiography, but additionally take into account natural and anthropogenic variability in surface water characteristics; they are widely used as a framework for water quality monitoring (Omernik 1995). Dinerstein *et al.* (1995), as part of a broader global classification by the World Wildlife Fund, defined ecoregions in Central and South America by evaluating geographically distinct assemblages of natural, terrestrially-based ecological communities.

However, because each of these three ecoregional classifications rest primarily on terrestrial classification criteria, they are not usually spatially suitable for regional freshwater biodiversity planning. This is due to the fact that freshwater biodiversity patterns and the source areas for threats to these patterns often correspond to drainage basins, whereas the borders of terrestrially-defined ecoregions often cut across basin boundaries. Freshwater planning conducted solely in the context of terrestrially defined boundaries may result in inaccurate priorities and inefficient conservation strategies that fail to consider ecological patterns, connectivity, and hydrologic issues adequately to maintain freshwater ecosystems. Recently the World Wildlife Fund (Abell *et al.* 2000) has begun to define freshwater ecoregions that incorporate drainage basins and take into account patterns in freshwater zoogeography along with patterns in climate and physiography. This initial effort for North

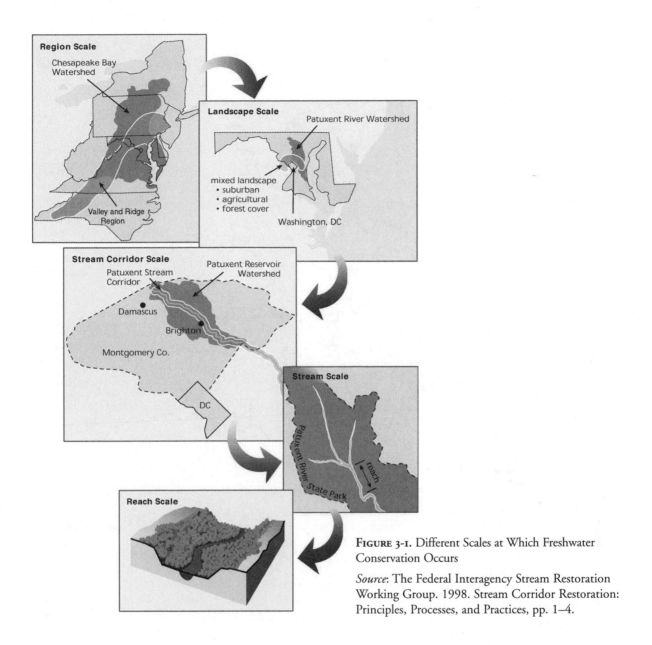

FIGURE 3-1. Different Scales at Which Freshwater Conservation Occurs

Source: The Federal Interagency Stream Restoration Working Group. 1998. Stream Corridor Restoration: Principles, Processes, and Practices, pp. 1–4.

America is being replicated across the world to create a global framework for freshwater biodiversity conservation.

Ecoregional conservation planning uses ecoregional context to set conservation priorities (Groves *et al.* 2002, Groves 2003), and it is one of a handful of approaches used by conservation organizations to answer the question of where conservation should be done (see Redford *et al.* 2003 for a full review). This process involves (1) defining the conservation targets in the ecoregion as well as mapping the distribution of their occurrences (see explanation below), (2) set-

ting ecoregion-wide goals for protecting these targets, (3) assessing the integrity of all target occurrences, (4) selecting a sufficient number of target occurrences of sufficient integrity and at the right spatial distribution to meet the goal of conserving the selected targets, and finally (5) delineating conservation areas that incorporate the selected occurrences for more focused conservation inquiry. The results of this process often include a written document, maps, databases, and partnerships between interested organizations. Each of these steps is discussed below.

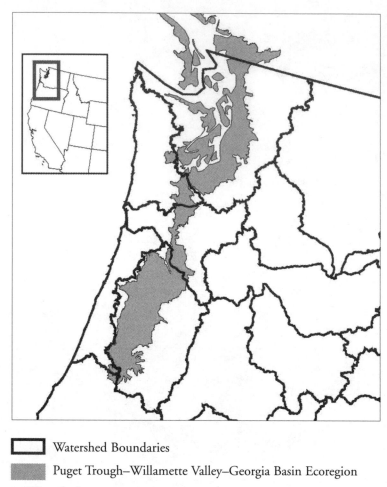

☐ Watershed Boundaries

▉ Puget Trough–Willamette Valley–Georgia Basin Ecoregion

FIGURE 3-2. Ecoregions vs. Watersheds
Ecoregion and watershed boundaries frequently do not correspond, as in this example from the Pacific Northwest of the United States.

Defining the Conservation Targets in the Ecoregion

Even focused solely on freshwater biota, an ecoregion may contain hundreds of species, communities, and ecological systems of particular conservation concern—and thousands more, both known and unknown—that are part of the ecoregion's biological richness. It would of course be prohibitively expensive and time-consuming to build a conservation plan for an ecoregion, one species, one community, or one ecological system at a time. A better approach is to select a limited number of species, communities, or ecological systems that, through their conservation, results in adequate protection of the whole. These selected species, communities, or ecological systems are termed ecoregional conservation targets.

One approach employed in ecoregional conservation planning to meet the challenge of representing all biodiversity is referred to as coarse-filter/fine filter. This approach focuses first on conserving representative examples of all ecological systems and communities in each ecoregion, the coarse-filter units, as a way to conserve the many common species contained by these systems and communities, the ecological conditions that support these species, and the environments in which these species evolve (Hunter 1991, Groves *et al.* 2002). While all available information on the distribution of freshwater ecological systems and communities should be used in selecting coarse-filter

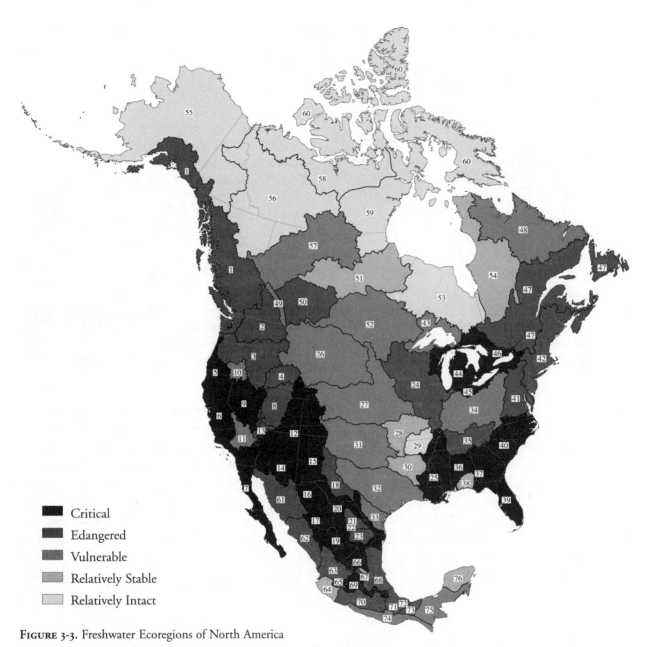

FIGURE 3-3. Freshwater Ecoregions of North America

Source: Abell, R., D.M. Olson, E. Dinerstein, P. Hurley, J.T. Diggs, W. Eichbaum, S. Walters, W. Wettengel, T. Allnutt, C. Louks, and P. Hedao. 2000. Freshwater Ecoregions of North America: A Conservation Assessment. Island Press, Washington, DC.

targets, there typically is no taxonomy of such systems and communities available for most large regions or basins. This problem may be overcome by relying on the fact that natural patterns of composition and distribution among freshwater ecosystems, communities, and species vary in response to certain consistent environmental variables (Moyle and Ellison 1991, Pflieger 1989, Maxwell *et al.* 1995, Angermeier and Winston

1999, Angermeier *et al.* 2000, Oswood *et al.* 2000, Rabeni and Doisy 2000). This relationship allows for the development of a classification that describes the types and distributions of freshwater ecosystems and communities expected to occur in an ecoregion based on abiotic factors, such as climate, geology, topography, and stream order that have been shown to influence biotic patterns. The units of this classification

The ecological system of the Apalachicola River mainstem (left, photograph by Harold E. Malde) and its associated floodplain (right, photo by Brian Richter/TNC) is an example of a coarse-filter target.

can then be mapped to permit further analysis of their individual occurrences. The Nature Conservancy employs a hierarchical classification method (Higgins *et al.* 2003) that loosely follows the model of Tonn *et al.* (1990) and Maxwell *et al.* (1995) as summarized in Box 3-1.

The selected coarse-filter targets are then complemented by a limited set of species, or fine-filter targets, to fill gaps in coverage by the ecological system and community targets and/or to adequately protect species of special concern. Fine-filter freshwater targets are selected from taxa such as fish, crustaceans, insects with aquatic lifestages, mollusks, herpetofauna, and aquatic plants. Factors considered in selecting these targets include whether the prospective target is a rare or endangered species (e.g., as defined by NatureServe, government agency declaration, the IUCN Red List, and expert interviews), a declining species or species of special concern, a wide-ranging species that is sensitive to degradation in large-scale

---

Box 3-1. Hierarchical Classification Used to Describe the Types and Distributions of Freshwater Ecosystems Based on Abiotic Factors

Regional-scale units (Freshwater Ecoregions and Ecological Drainage Units). The broadest level of the classification are Freshwater Ecoregions which are large-scale drainage basins distinguished by patterns of native fish distribution. Freshwater Ecoregions account for the geologic, climatic, and biologic history shaping present freshwater ecosystems. Regional fish distribution patterns are a result of large-scale geoclimatic processes (e.g., ice age glacial activity) and evolutionary history (Maxwell *et al.* 1995, Abell et al. 2000). Ecological Drainage Units (EDUs) account for variability within Freshwater Ecoregions and provide ecologically meaningful stratification units that can be used to help ensure that conservation targets are identified for protection across key environmental gradients. EDUs are groups of watersheds that not only share a common zoogeographic history but also share physiographic and climatic characteristics. EDUs represent patterns in taxonomic groups and likely have their own distinct set of species assemblages and habitats. Sources of data useful to create EDUs include mapped species distributions, climatic patterns, lithology, surficial geology, and other mappable physiographic information.

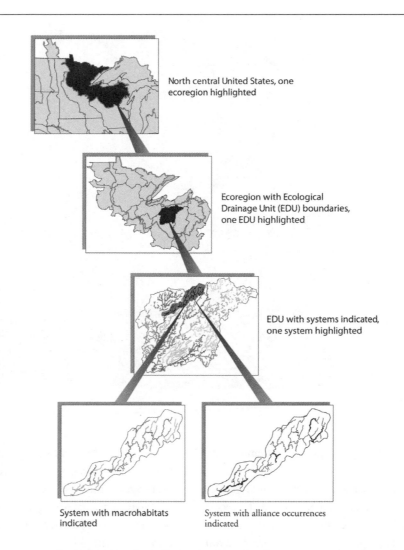

North central United States, one ecoregion highlighted

Ecoregion with Ecological Drainage Unit (EDU) boundaries, one EDU highlighted

EDU with systems indicated, one system highlighted

System with macrohabitats indicated

System with alliance occurrences indicated

Meso-scale units (Aquatic Ecological Systems). Sufficient biological information to classify or describe freshwater communities or freshwater ecosystems seldom exists. However, abiotic data can be used to describe environmental features of freshwater ecological units, and these can, in turn, be used has physical surrogates for biologically defined freshwater communities and freshwater ecosystems. Aquatic Ecological Systems represent stream, lake, and wetland networks that are distinct in terms of the nutrient flow, energy exchange, and metapopulation dynamics that influence the distributions of communities and individual species. Aquatic Ecological Systems are aggregations of Local Scale Units or Macrohabitats (see below). Aquatic Ecological Systems are characterized by distinct combinations of key ecological factors. These factors may vary by ecoregion. Aquatic Ecological Systems are not predictive units, per se. They do not define specific patterns of biodiversity but, used with biotic information, they can increase our understanding of the relationship between biota and the environment.

Local-scale units (Macrohabitats). Small to medium-sized lakes and valley segments of streams are defined by hydrology and map-based criteria (such as stream size, gradient, connectivity) to represent local environmental patterns and processes (figure on this classification). Macrohabitats are river valley segments (typically 1 to 10 km in length) and small- to medium-sized lakes or lake basins (typically <1000 hectares) that are relatively homogeneous with respect to hydrologic regime, temperature, chemistry, and morphology. Support for classifying and mapping macrohabitats is found in Seelbach *et al.* (1997) and Cupp (1989). Macrohabitats also correspond to the valley segment types defined by Paustian (1992) and lake classification methods are similar to those reviewed by Busch and Sly (1992).

The lake sturgeon, Acipenser fulvescens, *is an example of a potential fine-filter target. Photograph by Eric Engbretson/USFWS.*

connectivity within the system, or an endemic or disjunct species.

The coarse filter/fine filter approach should lead to the conservation of the greatest portion of the ecoregion's biodiversity, while keeping the final list of targets to a reasonable length. However, rarely does only one right answer exist in selecting a set of conservation targets. That is, different sets can be equally effective in representing the region's diversity of species, communities, and ecosystems, and capturing the ecological conditions that support them.

Setting Ecoregion-Wide Goals for Conservation Targets

Once a list of ecoregional conservation targets has been assembled, the next step in ecoregional conservation planning is to establish goals for each target. The purpose of the resulting ecoregional conservation goals is to define what is required to maintain full and sustainable representation of a region's native biodiversity. These goals form the foundation for identifying areas of biodiversity significance, including the necessary number, size, condition (integrity), and distribution desired for each target across the ecoregion. For freshwater conser-

vation, goals for species, community, and ecosystem targets are usually set separately for each Ecological Drainage Unit across the ecoregion (see Box 3-1).

Goals for species targets are expressed as the number of viable populations or in some cases simply the number of individuals by ecological drainage unit and are based on considerations of global rarity, distribution relative to the ecoregion, and life-history needs. Conservation goals for freshwater communities and ecological systems are typically based on their current distributions in relation to their historic distribution (if known), relative abundance, size, condition (i.e., integrity), and susceptibility to threats and stochastic processes. The minimum goal for each freshwater ecological system known or expected in an ecoregion should be to capture viable or restorable examples of that system across its entire historic or expected ecological and geographic range.

Assessing the Integrity of Ecoregional Target Occurrences

A key goal of ecoregional conservation planning is to select those areas within the ecoregion within which to concentrate conservation efforts in order to meet the objectives of conserving representative biodiversity within the ecoregion. As noted above, selecting an area for conservation simply because it harbors an example of a target community or ecological system or a population of a target species is not enough. The area selected must harbor viable populations of target species, or populations whose viability can be restored and must harbor occurrences of the target communities and ecological systems with sufficient current integrity or whose integrity can be restored, to support the continuing persistence of these targets as well. Ecoregions may contain numerous populations of target freshwater species and numerous examples of every freshwater community and ecological system. Conservation practitioners therefore must examine all such target occurrences, to rate their integrity (for simplicity, the term integrity here refers both to population viability and community/ ecological system integrity) in order to identify the best examples to include in the ecoregional conservation plan.

Practitioners can assess the integrity of individual target occurrences using a combination of qualitative and quantitative information. Natural Heritage Programs/Conservation Data Centers are critical resources for information about freshwater species targets, as many programs have already ranked occurrences according to their integrity (see Box 3-2). Other relevant biological data are often available from government agencies (e.g., recovery plans for endangered species in the U.S.) and other freshwater experts. In addition, data may exist on abiotic factors crucial to the integrity of a freshwater ecosystem, such as the quantity and quality of water. Finally, indirect measures can also be used to assess the condition of conservation targets. These measures are known to be related to freshwater ecosystem degradation and can be derived from widely available spatial data sets. Examples include the density of dams in a watershed and the percentage of impervious areas in a watershed. Information assembled from direct ratings of target biological integrity, assessments of critical abiotic factors, and assessments of indirect measures should always be reviewed by freshwater experts to develop the final assessments of target occurrence integrity.

Box 3-2. NatureServe

NatureServe is a non-profit conservation organization that provides the scientific information and tools needed to help guide effective conservation action. NatureServe represents an international network of biological inventories—known as Natural Heritage Programs or Conservation Data Centers—operating in all 50 U.S. states, Canada, Latin America and the Caribbean. These organizations collect and manage detailed local information on plants, animals, and ecosystems, and develop information products, data management tools, and conservation services to help meet local, national, and global conservation needs.

NatureServe offers a number of on-line data products with information about freshwater species. **NatureServe Explorer** (www.natureserve.org/explorer/) is an on-line source for conservation information on more than 50,000 plants, animals, and ecological communities of the United States and Canada. **InfoNatura** (www.natureserve.org/infonatura/) is a searchable database for conservation information on more than 5,500 birds and mammals of Latin America and the Caribbean. For additional information about NatureServe and its data products, go to www.natureserve.org.

Selecting Areas of Biodiversity Significance

Specific criteria used to select the individual conservation areas and the collective portfolio of areas of biodiversity significance for a region should include:

- coarse scale focus (ecosystems and communities)
- fine scale focus (individual species of concern)
- representativeness (multiple examples of all targets across environmental gradients)
- efficiency (area supports multiple targets)
- integration (opportunities to protect freshwater, marine, and terrestrial targets)

- functionality (natural range of variability is present or restorable in dominant ecological processes)
- completeness (the full portfolio captures all the targets).

Clearly, designing a portfolio of areas of biodiversity significance for a region requires a synthesis of many layers of information and is best undertaken by a team of local and regional experts. Tools, such as computer programs that optimize the selection of conservation areas, also are available to support portfolio development (e.g., Possingham *et al.* 1999). Where such programs are used,

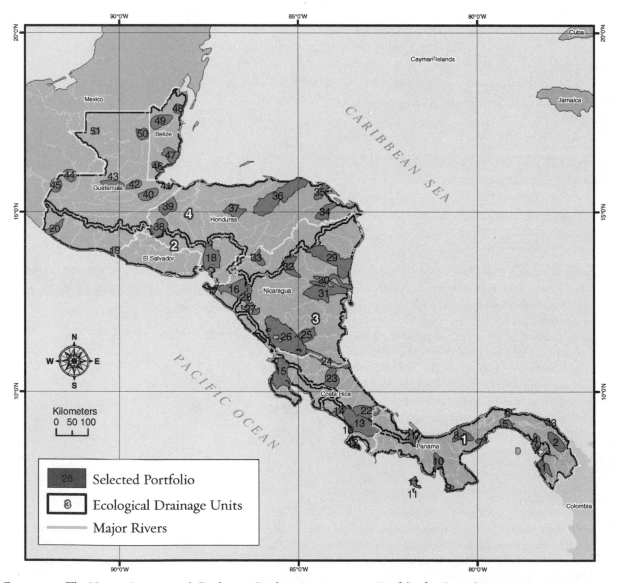

FIGURE 3-4. The Nature Conservancy's Freshwater Biodiversity Assessment Portfolio for Central America

the product should be viewed as a starting point for the experts as they consider such questions as:

- Are there missing or unwarranted targets (including a critical review of the ecosystem classification work)?
- Are there more appropriate conservation goals to set for the targets?
- Are healthy, viable populations of key species identified, and are their locations well connected to other habitats to ensure the fulfillment of all life history requirements?
- Are any areas missing that contain critical freshwater biodiversity?
- What species, communities, or ecosystems exist in the region but are not captured in the draft, and what is their viability or relative integrity?
- Have areas been selected where the freshwater biodiversity is not viable? If so, are there other areas with similar but viable targets that can be substituted?
- Are the data being used the most up-to-date and at the finest resolution?

Delineating Conservation Areas

The areas of freshwater biodiversity selected through an ecoregional conservation planning process will include stream and river reaches, ponds and lakes, wetlands, and riparian areas, arranged in clusters to capture entire portions of river basin drainage networks. The final step in ecoregional conservation planning is to identify clusters of these occurrences that can be managed together as conservation areas. Conservation areas are landscapes within which it will be possible to integrate the management of freshwater with terrestrial and, where appropriate, marine biodiversity conservation as well. Threats may be contained within this area but many will likely extend across a larger area. Similarly, the con-

servation area may or may not be contained by existing political boundaries and institutional jurisdictions.

Drawing the boundaries of conservation areas for freshwater conservation involves highly practical decisions that take into account several factors: the location of target occurrences within the hydrologic system; the patterns of ownership of land, water, and structures; the interests of potential partners and the potential resistance of other stakeholders; and the distribution of those human activities that pose threats to each cluster of occurrences.

In addition to being institutionally practicable, the map of conservation areas should meet four specific criteria that build on those used to select the target occurrences in the first place:

- Completeness—Every selected target occurrence should be assigned to a conservation area.
- Wholeness—Individual conservation areas should be delineated to encompass entire examples of these target types.
- Functionality—Each conservation area should provide the opportunity to conserve the natural dynamics of all five categories of key ecological factors.
- Integration—Whenever possible, conservation areas should be delineated to take advantage of opportunities to protect freshwater, marine, and terrestrial conservation targets at the same time.

At this point, conservation areas will be delineated by rough boundaries. It is important, however, to note that this process results only in identifying where that biodiversity lives, not necessarily what it needs to be viable. Delineating more precise conservation area boundaries and achieving conservation for the biodiversity selected can best be accomplished through conservation area planning-a process described in the following section.

HOW CAN THE BIODIVERSITY BE MOST EFFECTIVELY CONSERVED?

Setting freshwater conservation priorities across large geographic regions has three results: (1) it produces a list of freshwater species, communities, and ecological systems that are of high conservation value across the

region; (2) it produces a map of specific areas where this biodiversity exists; and (3) it defines a set of general goals for freshwater conservation across the region. However, while regional planning efforts identify areas that capture where critical biodiversity lives, they do not necessarily answer the question, "How can the biodiversity within these areas be most effectively conserved?" Even entities with more narrowly defined conservation missions, such as a predetermined focus on a particular species or geographic area, must also answer this crucial question.

Determining how best to conserve the biodiversity in an area—i.e., determining the best mixture of conservation strategies—requires careful analyses at both local and regional spatial scales. The results of these analyses are often assembled into a written document frequently termed a conservation area plan or a management plan (conservation plan). The conservation plan articulates and guides the specific management efforts that are most needed and appropriate to maintain or improve the ecological condition (integrity) of the targeted freshwater biodiversity and abate threats to it (Poiani *et al.* 1998). Conservation plans identify the challenges to freshwater biodiversity conservation in the area; and they define specific conservation goals, actions needed to achieve these goals, ways that

these conservation actions and their benefits will be evaluated, and research needed to better understand the area and its biodiversity. This information helps planners and practitioners focus their limited resources on the most important biodiversity, or the most promising options for conservation, within a particular area.

The next section briefly synthesizes the challenges behind conservation area planning for freshwater biodiversity and then outlines and explains the major components of conservation area planning.

The Science and Challenges Behind Conservation Area Planning

Conserving freshwater biodiversity at individual conservation areas requires maintaining the freshwater ecological integrity of the area, that is, the natural patterns of biological structure and composition as well as the biological processes and environmental regimes that shape these patterns over space and time (Noss 1990). Table 3-1 summarizes the most

TABLE 3-1. Critical Biological Patterns and Processes in Freshwater Ecosystems.

Biological Scale	Patterns	Processes
Species	• Genetic composition • Demographic composition • Abundance • Range	• Genetic isolation, mutation, and hybridization • Aggregation and dispersion; migration • Recruitment and mortality • Health dynamics
Assemblage	• Taxonomic composition (e.g., including dominant as well as rare and imperiled taxa) • Demographic composition • Range • Spatial patterning (1, 2, and 3 dimensions) among taxa	• Competition & exclusion
Community or Ecosystem	• Taxonomic composition (e.g., including dominant as well as rare and imperiled taxa) • Functional composition (e.g., with respect to functional guilds or keystone species) • Seral stage composition • Range • Spatial patterning (1, 2, and 3 dimensions) among taxa, functional groups, seral stages	• Succession • Predation • Herbivory • Productivity • Trophic dynamics • Biological transformation of physical and chemical habitat

common critical patterns of freshwater biological structure and composition and critical biological processes for different scales of biological organization that must be conserved to ensure the persistence of targets at these scales (after Noss 1990, Karr 1991, Karr and Chu 1999, see also Chapter 2 and Appendix A).

In practice, two challenges arise in conserving freshwater biodiversity at individual conservation areas. First, conservation area planning and management can never individually address the critical requirements of every freshwater species that an area supports. That is, documenting every species present, let alone knowing their conservation requirements is simply impossible. This shortcoming is exacerbated by the fact that freshwater ecosystems are naturally dynamic and their biological composition naturally changes and evolves over time. Second, pristine ecosystems that are devoid of human impacts no longer exist even in the harshest environments on the planet. Among many impacts, for example, human activities around the world have introduced countless species and chemical compounds into freshwater ecosystems. The ultimate question in freshwater conservation therefore is not how to prevent or eliminate human impacts but rather how to identify and manage these impacts in order to sustain the full spectrum of native biodiversity.

The solution to these challenges adopted by most conservation organizations, including The Nature Conservancy, involves two corresponding elements:

1) Focus conservation efforts on a limited number of target species, natural communities, and ecological systems, the conservation of which should serve as a safety net in protecting the whole (Noss and Cooperrider 1994, Schwartz 1999, The Nature Conservancy 2000, Poiani *et al.* 2000); and

2) Define conservation goals in relation to a functional ecosystem instead of some hypothetical natural or pristine ecosystem; that is, one that can " . . . maintain focal target species, communities, and ecological systems, along with their supporting ecological patterns and processes, within their natural ranges of variation" (Poiani *et al.* 2000; see also Noss 1990; Christensen *et al.* 1996; Balmford *et al.* 1998, Redford and Richter 1999).

Selecting Freshwater Targets for a Conservation Area

As with ecoregional targets, conservation area targets may be species, communities, or entire ecological systems. Focusing freshwater conservation efforts within a conservation area on a limited number of targets serves two crucial purposes. First, it establishes specific conservation goals for the area, framed in terms of the desired status of these specific targets. It therefore facilitates the establishment of specific measures for evaluating the success (or failure) of the conservation effort. Second, it allows the identification and prioritization of the specific conservation actions or strategies to pursue across the conservation area, based on the threats that impinge on these specific targets. This approach has an additional benefit for organizations with broadly defined conservation missions: if the targets are well chosen, the resulting suite of goals, measures, and strategies should ensure conservation of not only the targets themselves, but all native freshwater biodiversity in the area.

Consider a river that has a substantial flood-plain valley along its lowest reach characterized by a distinct aquatic community. Much of what happens ecologically along this valley reach depends on conditions and human activities both in the water and on the land across the entire contributing watershed. Efforts to conserve the integrity of the aquatic community along the valley reach therefore necessarily requires protecting the upstream watershed conditions that support the reach of concern. In other words, selecting the aquatic community of the valley reach as a conservation target provides at least part of the safety net for the conservation of upstream biodiversity.

The best way to ensure that suitable conditions occur frequently and widely enough for all native species in a freshwater ecosystem is to focus conservation efforts not only on a few species but also on the composition and structure of entire communities and encompassing ecological systems (e.g., Noss 1990 and 1996, Christensen *et al.* 1996, Karr and Chu 1999, Karr 1999, Schwartz 1999, Poiani *et al.* 2000). In addition, the best way to ensure the integrity of biological patterns and processes at several spatial scales is to explicitly include conservation targets that respond to conditions at different spatial scales (e.g., Noss

BOX 3-3. Guidelines for Selecting a Suite of Freshwater Conservation Targets for an Area

- Conservation area targets and ecoregional targets need not be identical. However, conserving the local targets should ensure conservation of ecoregional targets that occur within the conservation area.
- Conservation area targets should capture or require that the project conserve the major environmental regimes and constraints that shape overall freshwater biodiversity across the area and those that create the major differences in freshwater biota across the area at two or more spatial scales.
- Conserving one or more of the targets should ensure the connectivity of different freshwater habitat types to each other within the conservation area, and the connectivity of the entire conservation area to larger aquatic systems.
- The targets should not result in significant duplication in the kinds of efforts needed to achieve their conservation, should ensure that every threat to freshwater biodiversity in the conservation area can be addressed through conservation of at least one target, and should ensure the conservation of rare and imperiled species and communities.
- The targets must be amenable to monitoring for conservation effectiveness and should address not only ecoregional conservation goals, but also strategic or programmatic goals such as engaging the interest of a key stakeholder or potential conservation partner organization.
- There should be neither too many nor too few targets. Keeping track of large numbers of targets and pursuing individually selected strategies for each can be a management nightmare. At the other extreme, working with a very small number of targets may make it difficult to conserve unique features of the freshwater biodiversity in a conservation area, at one or more spatial scales.

1990 and 1996, Christensen *et al.* 1996, Poiani *et al.* 2000). Specifically, the key to selecting freshwater focal targets for an individual conservation area is understanding how watersheds "work" as landscapes of freshwater biodiversity, and identifying targets that will be conserved only if the watershed is working well.

Box 3-3 provides some guidelines for sorting through the alternatives to identify the best overall collection of targets for conserving the freshwater biodiversity of a conservation area.

Setting Goals for Freshwater Targets in Conservation Areas and Assessing Their Current Status

Conserving freshwater species, communities, and ecological systems means maintaining or restoring their biotic composition and their supporting ecological patterns and processes within their natural ranges of variation. More specifically, every freshwater conservation target, when found in a relatively undisturbed condition, will be associated with (1) a distinct hydro-

logic regime; (2) a distinct water chemistry regime; (3) a distinct range of physical habitat conditions and dynamics; (4) distinct requirements for connectivity; and (5) distinct biological patterns and processes-including interactions among species, and between them and the physical environment (Poff *et al.* 1997, Karr *et al.* 1986, Karr 1999, and Karr and Chu 1999). The most effective way to ensure conservation of each freshwater target in a conservation area therefore is to establish explicit conservation goals for all five of these categories of key ecological factors (Parrish *et al.* 2003). See Appendix A for an overview of key ecological factors for lakes, rivers and wetlands.

Establishing explicit conservation goals for each of the five categories of key ecological factors for each freshwater target requires two types of information. First, practitioners need to determine what specific ecological factors to consider and how they will measure the status of each of these factors, that is, what indicators they will use. Second, practitioners need to establish guidelines for the acceptable range of variation for each of these indicators. Once these steps are taken, practitioners can assess the current status of the targets, in order to determine whether each target occurrence meets conservation goals. This final step provides the crucial information for assessing threats and determining how much work is needed to restore or sustain all targets.

CHOOSING THE RIGHT FACTORS AND INDICATORS

Identifying the specific factors and indicators for the target and their acceptable ranges of variation involves developing a conceptual ecological model for the target. Even a rudimentary model is better than no model at all. This model should represent the key states of the target and the key dynamics that shape the variation in target state over time and space. Box 3-4 provides several guidelines for developing a model and Figure 3-5 represents an example of a conceptual ecological model.

Setting specific conservation goals for each key ecological factor in turn requires choosing specific indicators, for the simple reason that it is useless to set goals for something you can't measure. Indicators are, simply, measurable aspects of the key ecological factors.

The selection of appropriate indicators receives extended attention in Chapter 5 and Appendix B of this guide. Here, we merely offer a list of useful selection criteria. Indicators ideally should be: (1) scientifically relevant, i.e., provide an accurate assessment of the key factor; (2) consistently measurable, i.e., measurable by highly repeatable and preferably standardized procedures with low measurement error; and (3) cost-effective, i.e., providing the maximum amount of information per unit effort and expense. Preferably, indicators should also be (4) responsive, i.e., able to detect change as soon as it begins and able to register degrees of alteration along a single scale; and (5) institutionally relevant, i.e., valued or respected, and observable by important stakeholders or conservation partners. In addition, indicators may be needed to

---

BOX 3-4. Guidelines for Developing a Conceptual Model for a Freshwater Conservation Target and Its Key Ecological Factors

- Keep the model simple. For any of the five categories of key ecological factors for a freshwater conservation target, it will be possible to identify many specific factors that shape the target's condition and variation. Thus, it is important to try to identify the minimum number of factors necessary to characterize the target, both within and across all five categories. Increasing the number of factors in a model may add little to its accuracy and complicate the task of finding ways to monitor target status.
- Always consider which characteristics of the target, if altered (e.g., spring flood magnitudes, winter water temperature, the relative dominance of a keystone species) or missing (e.g., a migratory fish species barred from reaching the area by a downstream dam), could seriously jeopardize the target's ability to persist over time. The history of human impacts to each target or type of target—both locally and in general—serves as a broad, uncontrolled experiment that often reveals what factors matter most for any given target. Always include in the model those factors known or suspected to have a significant impact on target integrity when altered by human activity.
- Consider carefully both the scale of time and timing within which different biological dynamics unfold in the target of interest—disturbance and colonization cycles, timing of reproduction and reproductive cues, etc. Different factors will operate at different scales of time, and the model should group together factors that operate at similar scales of time. In addition, for management purposes, the model should focus on factors and time scales over which biological dynamics and threat dynamics can reasonably be assessed and managed.
- The model should be a practical tool for conservation management. Its purpose is to identify those key factors that you may need to monitor in order to keep track of the conservation status of the target or gain more knowledge of target dynamics; and those factors which, if altered, potentially could involve or lead to unacceptable changes in the target's status.

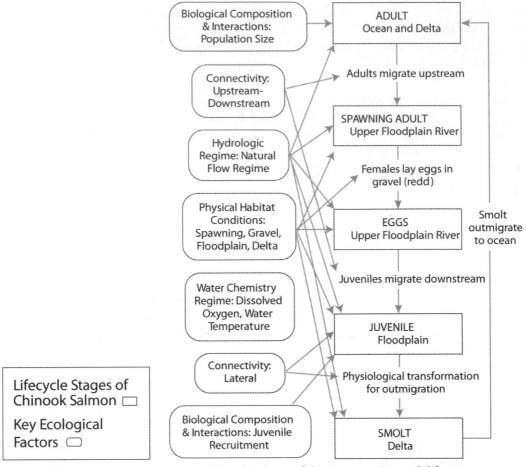

FIGURE 3-5. Key Ecological Factors for the Target Chinook Salmon of the Cosumnes River, California

address not only the natural characteristics of each key ecological factor, but characteristics that result from human interference. Indicators for biological composition and interactions, for example, may need to keep track of the effects of invasive alien species; and indicators for water chemistry may need to keep track of the contribution of chemicals that did not occur naturally in the system, such as synthetic organic compounds, industrial metals, and so forth. Indicators should always meet the first three criteria and as many additional criteria as feasible.

DEFINING THE ACCEPTABLE RANGE OF VARIATION

Conserving freshwater biodiversity, as noted above, must always involve conserving the ecological patterns and processes that shape this biodiversity within their natural ranges of variation. The natural ranges of variation in physical habitat, connectivity, biological compo-

sition and interactions, and the hydrologic and water chemistry regimes matter for two crucial reasons, also discussed in Chapter 2 and Appendix A. First, the species that occur in freshwater ecosystems are ones that have evolved adaptations to the physical environment and to the other biota of each unique freshwater ecosystem. This includes adaptations to both normal conditions in the system and to that system's natural patterns of disturbance. If these conditions and their patterns of disturbance are changed, a system may become less hospitable or even inhospitable to some species; and may become more hospitable to others that previously played little or no role in the system. Such changes at the scale of individual species could in turn have cascading effects on other species, and so forth, resulting in significant changes to the system and its biodiversity (e.g., Pace *et al.* 1999, Scheffer *et al.* 2001). Second, even within its natural range of variation, no freshwater system ever offers ideally hospitable conditions for all of its species, all of the time. Instead, as previously

Box 3-5. Range of Variation of Key Ecological Factors—The Neversink River, New York
The Neversink River is a tributary of the upper Delaware River in southeastern New York. Diadromous fish (fish that spawn in freshwater and migrate to the sea), including American shad, are one of the conservation targets selected for the Neversink watershed. A conceptual ecological model developed for this target identified the hydrologic regime, particularly during early spring through early summer due to spawning needs, as an important key ecological factor for this target. The primary cause of alteration of this key ecological factor has been the construction and operation of the Neversink Dam. Understanding the range of variation within this key ecological factor needed to maintain this target and the way in which the dam has altered this variation, as expressed in the figure below for American shad spawning needs, has helped inform restoration goals and management objectives.

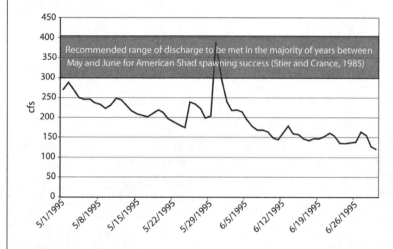

Neversink River discharge at Godeffroy, New York, May and June, 1995 (low flow year). The dark line depicts actual early spring to early summer discharge in the Neversink River for a stardard year (1995) whereas the shaded area shows the natural range of variability needed to maintain spawning conditions for American Shad. The pre-dam mean was greater than 500 cfs during this time period. The source of this illustration is Schuler.

emphasized, the species that occur in freshwater ecosystems are simply ones that find hospitable conditions there often enough to sustain their presence. The biological diversity of every freshwater ecosystem therefore changes constantly, from one year, one decade, or even one century to the next. Conserving this full spectrum of biodiversity, including its own natural variation and its potential for further natural evolution, requires conserving all of the natural processes and interactions that drive this variation (Poff *et al.* 1997).

Conservation practitioners therefore face the difficult challenge of defining the natural range of variation for each of the key ecological factors in freshwater ecosystem dynamics. In practice, this involves defining the acceptable range of variation for each of the indicators selected for these key factors. The goal of conservation, in turn, is to maintain or restore each target, so that all of its key ecological factors lie within these acceptable ranges of variation (Christensen *et al.* 1996, Parrish *et al.* 2003). For each freshwater conservation target, defining the acceptable range of variation for each key ecological factor means identifying threshold values for each indicator, which, if exceeded, would directly entail or lead to significant changes in the biological structure and composition of the target. The goal of conservation, in turn, is to maintain or restore each target, so that all of its key ecological factors lie within these acceptable ranges of variation (Parrish *et al.* 2003).

INTEGRATING REGIONAL AND CONSERVATION AREA PLANNING

So far, this chapter has treated ecoregional and conservation area planning as relatively independent, sequential steps in answering the three questions posed at the start of this chapter: (1) What biodiversity should be conserved, (2) Where should the biodiversity be conserved, and (3) How can the biodiversity be most

Conservation area plans need to take into account wide-ranging species, such as salmon (above, photograph courtesy USFWS) and threats such as dams (below, photograph by Doug Thiele/ USACE), that occur across multiple conservation areas.

effectively conserved? In practice, however, much interplay exists between these two steps. Specifically, planning at the scale of individual conservation areas provides invaluable feedback to the ecoregional plan, on such topics as the delineation of conservation area boundaries and the assessment of ecoregional target integrity. In addition, taken together, ecoregional and conservation area plans within an ecoregion can help identify threats to biodiversity that occur across multiple conservation areas. Such threats present opportunities to pursue conservation strategies across multiple areas at once. And ultimately, of course, success at the scale of the individual conservation areas should, in aggregate, lead to success in conserving the targets identified in the ecoregional plan itself.

Integrating Conservation Across Multiple Conservation Areas

Conservation area plans should not be developed independently of each other across an ecoregion. Planning at larger, multi-area scales may identify economies of scale that can be realized when taking

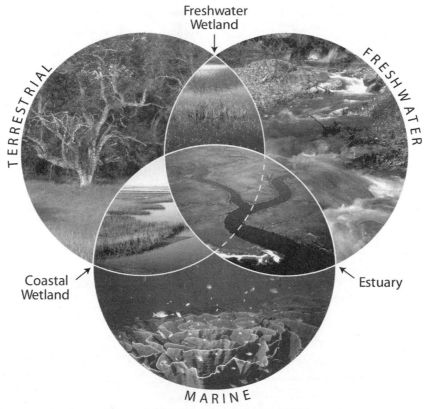

FIGURE 3-6. The Interconnectedness of Terrestrial, Freshwater, and Marine Habitats.

Photographs of terrestrial and freshwater habitat by Harold E. Malde, marine habitat by Nancy Sefton, and coastal wetland and estuarine habitat courtesy of NOAA.

conservation action. For example, many targets may occur in more than one conservation area; examples might include wide-ranging species, or species that occur in widely but sparsely distributed habitat, such as migratory fish or certain flood-dependent plants. The presence of such targets among many conservation areas makes it desirable to develop several conservation area plans together, in order to ensure that the actions taken at all of these areas contribute most effectively to the conservation of these targets. Similarly, the same threats to freshwater biodiversity may recur across multiple conservation areas, such as pollution from municipal wastewater facilities or flow alteration from dams built to generate electricity and/or manage floods. Indeed, the importance of such threats may become apparent during ecoregional conservation planning even before the development of any detailed conservation area plans. Identifying such cross-cutting threats is crucial for designing an effective mix of strategies for threat abatement across an

ecoregion. Sometimes the most effective action in the long term may be to promote changes in policy across an entire region which will help reduce the impacts of potentially harmful human endeavors on a large scale rather than one conservation area at a time.

Additionally, conserving freshwater biodiversity within and across conservation areas may also contribute to downstream terrestrial and coastal/marine biodiversity conservation. Conserving freshwater targets in a watershed, basin, or other large landscape often requires abating threats that result from human landuse practices. These practices may also pose threats to terrestrial biodiversity, for example, by changing land cover and permeability, draining wetlands, using levees to isolate floodplains from their rivers, and broadcasting harmful chemicals. In this example, conservation efforts aimed at abating threats to the freshwater biodiversity will likely also deliver benefits for terrestrial biodiversity. Similarly, the ecological integrity of all estuarine ecosystems and some marine ecosystems depends on the ecological integrity of the freshwaters that flow into them—and sometimes vice versa, as well. Thus, again, where both freshwater and coastal/marine biodiversity are at stake, there may be significant benefit in coordinating conservation efforts, to achieve the greatest benefit to both ecological spheres in the most cost effective manner. Ultimately, of course, the conservation of terrestrial, freshwater, and coastal/marine biodiversity should all be parts of one continuous conservation fabric (e.g., Groves *et al.* 2002).

The conservation of biodiversity within and across multiple conservation areas in an ecoregion should result in the achievement of ecoregional conservation success. This is the reasoning behind ecoregional conservation planning. Success at both scales in turn depends not only on developing carefully defined goals, but on accurately assessing threats, identifying the best ways and the best spatial scales for abating these threats, and implementing a well-designed monitoring and research program. These are the topics of Chapters 4 and 5.

REFERENCES

Abell, R. A, D.M. Olson, E. Dinerstein, P.T. Hurley, J.R. Diggs, W. Eichbaum, S. Walters, W. Wettengel, T. Allnutt, C.J. Loucks, and P. Hedao. 2000. Freshwater ecoregions of North America: A conservation assessment. Washington, DC: World Wildlife Fund-US, Island Press. 319 pp.

Angermeier, P.L., and M.R. Winston. 1999. Characterizing fish community diversity across Virginia landscapes: prerequisite for conservation. Ecological Applications 9: 335–349.

Angermeier, P.L., R.A. Smoger, and J.R. Stauffer. 2000. Regional frameworks and candidate metrics for assessing biotic integrity in Mid-Atlantic highland streams. Trans. Am. Fish. Soc. 129: 962–981.

Bailey, R.G. 1989. Ecoregions of the continents. Washington: U.S. Department of Agriculture, Forest Service. Map 1:30,000,000.

Balmford, A., G.M. Mace, J.R. Ginsberg. 1998. The challenges to conservation in a changing world: Putting processes on the map. In G.M. Mace, A. Balmford, J.R. Ginsburg, eds. Conservation in a Changing World. Cambridge, UK: Cambridge University Press. Pp. 1–28.

Carignan, V. and M.A. Villard. 2002. Selecting indicator species to monitor ecological integrity: A review. Environmental Monitoring and Assessment 78: 45–61.

Caro, T.M., and G. O'Doherty. 1999. On the use of surrogate species in conservation biology. Conservation Biology 13: 805–814.

Christensen, N.L., A.M. Bartuska, J.H. Brown, S. Carpenter, C. D'Antonio, R. Francis, J.F. Franklin, J.A. MacMahon, R.F. Noss, D.J. Parsons, C.H. Peterson, M.G. Turner, and R.G. Woodmansee. 1996. The report of the Ecological Society of America Committee on the Scientific Basis for Ecosystem Management. Ecological Applications 6: 665–691.

Dinerstein, E., D.M. Olson, D.J. Graham, A.L. Webster, S.A. Primm, M.P. Bookbinder, and G. Ledec. 1995. A Conservation Assessment of the Terrestrial Ecoregions of Latin America and the Caribbean. Washington, DC: World Wildlife Fund and The World Bank.

Flather, C.H., K.R. Wilson, D.J. Dean, W.C. McComb. 1997. Identifying gaps in conservation networks: Of indicators and uncertainty in geographic-based analyses. Ecological Applications 7: 531–542.

Fleishman, E., D.D. Murphy, and P.F. Brussard. 2000. A new method for selection of umbrella species for conservation planning. Ecological Applications 10: 569–579.

Groves, C.R., D.B. Jensen, L.L. Valutis, K.H. Redford, M.L. Shaffer, J.M. Scott, J.V. Baumgartner, J.V. Higgins,

M.W. Beck, and M.G. Anderson. 2002. Planning for biodiversity conservation: Putting conservation science into practice. BioScience 52: 499–512.

Groves, C.R., 2003. Drafting a Conservation Blueprint: A Practitioner's Guide to Planning for Biodiversity. Washington, DC: Island Press.

Higgins, J.V., M.T. Bryer, M.L. Khoury, and T.W. FitzHugh. In review with Conservation Biology. A freshwater classification approach for biodiversity conservation planning.

Holling, C.S. 1973. Resilience and stability of ecological systems. Annual Review of Ecology and Systematics 4: 1–23.

Holling, C.S. 1992. Cross-scale morphology, geometry, and dynamics of ecosystems. Ecological Monographs 62(4): 447–502.

Holling, C.S. and G.K. Meffe. 1996. Command and control and the pathology of natural resource management. Conservation Biology 10: 328–337.

Hunter, M.L., Jr., 1991. Coping with ignorance: The coarse filter strategy for maintaining biodiversity. In Balancing on the Brink of Extinction. L.A. Kohm, ed. Washington, DC: Island Press.

Karr J.R. 1991. Biological integrity: A long neglected aspect of water resource management. Ecological Applications 1: 66–84.

Karr, J.R. 1999. Defining and measuring river health. Freshwater Biology 41: 221–234.

Karr, J.R. and E.W. Chu. 1999. Restoring Life in Running Waters. Washington, DC: Island Press.

Karr, J.R., K.D. Fausch, P.L. Angermeier, P.R. Yant, and I.J. Schlosser. 1986. Assessment of biological integrity in running waters: A method and its rationale. Illinois Natural History Survey Special Publication No. 5. Springfield, IL: Illinois Natural History Survey.

Lambeck, R.J. 1997. Focal species: A multi-species umbrella for nature conservation. Conservation Biology 11: 849–856.

Maxwell, J.R., C.J. Edwards, M.E. Jensen, S.J. Paustain, H. Parrot, and D.M. Hill. 1995. A hierarchical framework of aquatic ecological units in North America (Nearctic Zone). General Technical Report NC-176. St. Paul, MN: USDA Forest Service, North Central Forest Experimental Station.

Moyle, P.B., and J.P. Ellison. 1991. A conservation-oriented classification system for the inland waters of California. California Fish and Game 77:161–180.

Naeem, S., F.S. Chapin III, R. Costanza, P.R. Ehrlich, F.B. Golley, D.U. Hooper, J.H. Lawton, R.V. O'Neill, H.A. Mooney, O.E. Sala, A.J. Symstad, and D. Tilman. 1999. Biodiversity and ecosystem functioning: Maintaining natural life support processes. Issues in Ecology 4, Fall 1999. Ecological Society of America.

Noss, R.F. 1990. Indicators for monitoring biodiversity: A hierarchical approach. Conservation Biology 4: 355–364.

Noss R.F. 1996. Ecosystems as conservation targets. Trends in Ecology and Evolution 11: 351.

Noss R.F, A.Y. Cooperrider. 1994. Saving Nature's Legacy: Protecting and Restoring Biodiversity. Washington, DC: Island Press.

Omernik, J.M. 1987. Ecoregions of the conterminous United States. Annals of the Association of American Geographers 77:188–125.

Oswood, M. W., J.B. Reynolds, J.G. Irons, and A.M. Miller. 2000. Distributions of freshwater fishes in ecoregions and hydroregions of Alaska. J. N. Am. Benthol. Soc. 19(3):405–418.

Pace, M.L., J.J. Cole, S.R. Carpenter, and J.F. Kitchell. 1999. Trophic cascades revealed in diverse ecosystems. Trends in Ecology and Evolution 14: 483–488.

Parrish, Jeffrey D., David P. Braun, and Robert S. Unnasch. 2003. Are we conserving what we say we are? Measuring ecological integrity within protected areas. BioScience 53: 851–860.

Poff, N.L., J.D. Allan, M.B. Bain, J.R. Karr, K.L. Prestegaard, B.D. Richter, R.E. Sparks, and J.C. Stromberg. 1997. The natural flow regime: A paradigm for river conservation and restoration. BioScience 47: 769–784.

Poiani K.A., J.V, Baumgartner, S.C. Buttrick, S.L. Green, E. Hopkins, G.D. Ivey, K.P. Seaton, R.D. Sutter. 1998.

A scale independent site conservation planning framework in The Nature Conservancy. Landscape and Urban Planning 43: 143–156.

Poiani, K.A., B.D. Richter, M.G. Anderson, and H.E. Richter. 2000. Biodiversity conservation at multiple scales: Functional sites, landscapes, and networks. BioScience 50: 133–146.

Possingham, H., I. Ball, and S. Andelman. 1999. Mathematical models for identifying representative reserve networks. Chapter 16 in S. Ferson and M.A. Burgman, eds. Quantitative Methods for Conservation Biology. New York: Springer-Verlag.

Rabeni, C.F., and K.E. Doisy. 2000. Correspondence of stream benthic invertebrate assemblages to regional classification schemes in Missouri. J. Am. Benthol. Soc. 19(3): 419–428.

Redford, K.H. and B.D. Richter. 1999. Conservation of biodiversity in a world of use. Conservation Biology 13: 1246–1256.

Redford, K.H., P. Coppolillo, E.W. Sanderson, G.A.B. Da Fonseca, E. Dinerstein, C. Groves, G. Mace, S. Maginnis, R.A. Mittermeier, R. Noss, D. Olson, J.G. Robinson, A. Vedder, and M. Wright. 2003. Mapping the conservation landscape. Conservation Biology 17 (1): 116–131.

Sanderson, E.W., K.H. Redford, A. Vedder, P.B. Coppolillo, and S.E. Ward. 2002. A conceptual model for conservation planning based on landscape species requirements. Landscape and Urban Planning 58: 41–56.

Scheffer, Marten, Steve Carpenter, Jonathan A. Foley, Carl Folke, and Brian Walker. 2001. Catastrophic shifts in ecosystems. Nature 413: 591–596.

Schwartz M.W. 1999. Choosing the appropriate scale of reserves for conservation. Annual Review of Ecology and Systematics 30: 83–108.

Simberloff, D. 1999. Flagships, umbrellas, and keystones: Is single-species management passé in the landscape era? Biological Conservation 83: 247–257.

The Nature Conservancy. 2000. The Five-S Framework for Site Conservation: A Practitioner's Handbook for Site Conservation Planning and Measuring Conservation Success. Arlington, VA: The Nature Conservancy.

Tonn, W.M., J.J. Magnuson, M. Rask, and J. Toivonen. 1990. Intercontinental comparison of small-lake fish assemblages: the balance between local and regional processes. American Naturalist 136: 345–375.

Chapter 4

Understanding Threats to Freshwater Biodiversity and Developing Effective Conservation Strategies

Nicole Silk, Kristine Ciruna, David Braun, Ronald Bjorkland,

Catherine Pringle, Rebecca Esselman, and David Allan

OVERVIEW AND LEARNING OBJECTIVES

Human survival depends on freshwater ecosystems. This chapter describes how to begin the process of unraveling the causes of freshwater ecosystem decline through a threats analysis, explains the relationship of threats to conservation targets and key ecological factors, and explores the importance of linking strategies directly to abating or preventing specific threats. This chapter also includes thorough reviews of the four primary threats to freshwater biodiversity and promising strategies for abating or preventing each of these specific threats:

- water use and management
- land use and management
- invasive alien species
- overharvesting/fisheries management

The strategies included in this chapter encompass technical, legal and institutional, and community-based approaches and all have their foundation in actual practitioner experience. Figure 4-4 at the end of this introduction to Chapter 4 explains the context of this information in relation to the entire guide.

Introduction

THREATS TO FRESHWATER BIODIVERSITY &
DEVELOPMENT OF EFFECTIVE CONSERVATION STRATEGIES

Freshwater ecosystems have lost a greater proportion of their species and habitat than terrestrial or marine ecosystems, making them arguably the most threatened of ecosystem types on Earth (McAllister *et al.* 1997). Threats to freshwater biodiversity occur in every nation and nearly every watershed throughout the world. These threats, although numerous, can be grouped into four broad categories: water use and management, land use and management, invasive alien species, and overharvesting/fisheries management. After a brief introduction that describes a number of tools for analyzing threat information and explains the process of developing and implementing conservation strategies, the remainder of the chapter focuses on these four categories of threats and specific strategies for abating or eliminating them.

Understanding Threats to Biodiversity: Identifying Stresses and Their Sources

Stresses are specific human-induced alterations of a species, community or ecosystem's key ecological factors, such as altered sediment or flow regime, or predation from an invasive alien species, which push key ecological factors toward the edge or even outside their natural ranges of variation. Sources are the specific human activities responsible for a stress. Clear articulation of stresses and associated sources of stress, facilitates the development of effective and well-focused strategies by planning teams. In essence, before a problem can be solved it must be clearly defined.

Identified stresses and sources of stress can be extensive and resources for developing and implementing strategies are often limited. Either situation makes the task of focusing conservation efforts more challenging. In these cases, prioritizing stresses and sources based on their relative impact and urgency proves useful. Ranking criteria might include: assessing the severity of impact on conservation targets; evaluating the geographic scope of damage caused by the stress; considering the irreversibility of the expected damage to be caused; determining whether the stress or source is imminent; etc. Other tools for threat assessments include: statistical analysis of hydrologic, water quality, and biological monitoring data; computer-based models of water budgets and surface flow and groundwater systems; conceptual ecological models; remote sensing; and geographic information systems and analyses (US EPA 1995; US EPA 1997a; http://www.epa.gov/owow/watershed/tools/; Richter *et al.* 1996; TNC 2000a). Of these tools, a conceptual ecological that integrates threats information is particularly powerful for illustrating relationships between key ecological factors for conservation targets and stresses and their sources. Figure 4-1 is an example of such an integrated model.

More Deeply Understanding Sources of Stress: Stakeholder Analysis

Once the critical threats (stresses and their sources) are identified for conservation targets at a conservation area or larger area, the next step is to determine the stakeholders engaged in activities identified as the sources of stress and assess the driving forces behind their actions. A situation-stakeholder diagram is a useful tool for illustrating these relationships. Developing a situation-stakeholder diagram is essentially a mapping exercise in which the relationships between the sources of stress, the stakeholders, and the forces that drive or motivate their behavior (root causes) are graphically represented. Situation-stakeholder diagrams help to identify the positive and negative cause and effect relationships between the critical threats

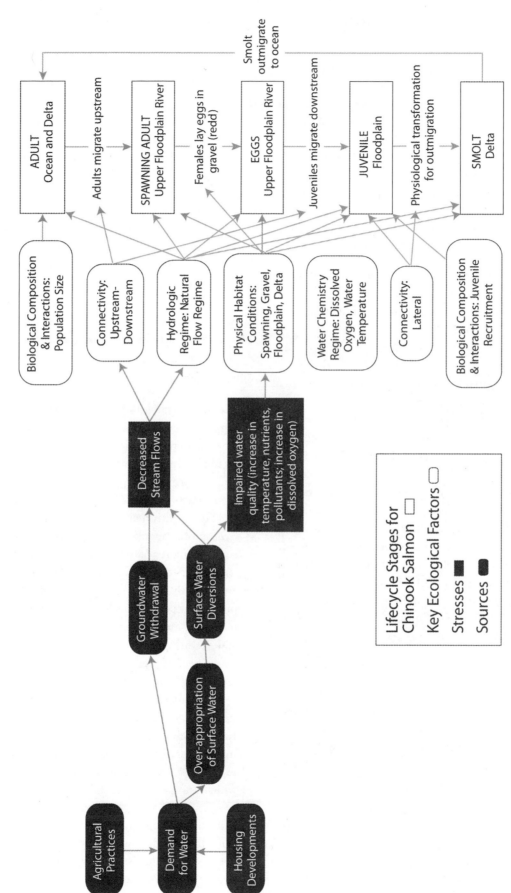

FIGURE 4-1. Conceptual Ecological Model for Chinook Salmon with Integrated Threats Information

and the stakeholders. They help map complex situations and identify stakeholders who otherwise might not have come to mind. Ultimately, the diagramming exercise can help to identify key points within these relationships where conservation action can occur in a participatory manner to improve biodiversity health and abate critical threats. Figure 4-2 integrates this information into the evolving model for chinook salmon.

The following is a brief outline of key steps for developing a situation-stakeholder diagram:

1) *Begin with one source of stress per diagram:* One diagram should be generated for each source of stress identified for the conservation area(s) or ecoregion of concern.

2) *Identify the stakeholders directly linked to the source of stress:* Who (e.g., what individuals, groups or organizations) are behind the activity causing a critical threat?

3) *Determine the motivations of each stakeholder:* Why are the identified stakeholders partaking in the activity that is a critical threat? What motivates them?

4) *Identify the controlling forces/driving forces/root causes:* Are there factors that are encouraging or facilitating the stakeholder activities? Controlling forces are factors or issues that control the extent to which a stakeholder can continue to partake in a particular activity. Often the most successful conservation strategies address controlling forces.

5) *Identify stakeholders linked to the controlling forces:* Are there specific stakeholders linked to controlling forces? These might be stakeholders who indirectly influence an activity by determining larger policy issues (a controlling force).

6) *Use the situation diagram to write well-informed strategies for each critical threat:* Remember, the purpose of the situation-diagram is to help develop effective strategies that will produce tangible results.

Whenever possible, meaningful dialogue with stakeholders should also take place, including the development of a shared vision for a project area. In some cases, stakeholder involvement may make project success more feasible.

Developing and Implementing Effective Conservation Strategies

Conservation strategies are actions carried out specifically to improve the viability of some portion of an area's biodiversity. Such actions may directly abate the threat by removing the source of the stress; restore a conservation target by the removal of relict stresses impacting the target that no longer have an active source; or change a stakeholder's activity that is the proximate cause of a particular source of stress. Figure 4-3 integrates this information into the evolving model for chinook salmon. The most effective strategies are usually those that focus on the ultimate source of stress; in other words those that are directed at changing actions or activities of a particular stakeholder.

Generally, strategies fall into one of the following three categories:

- **Technical strategies** focus on reducing or eliminating the impact of a source of stress by changing specific human activities responsible for the stress. Examples include persuading or providing incentives to farmers to apply agricultural best management practices to reduce runoff of soils and chemicals from cultivated fields; persuading reservoir or hydropower operators to change dam operations to support more natural flow regimes; convincing landscapers to stop selling invasive wetland species; and directly acquiring rights to land or water to protect important resources. Technical strategies may also include activities directed at enhancing and restoring ecosystem or biodiversity integrity using techniques such as prescribed burning, replanting native riparian vegetation, removing invasive alien species, or re-establishing historic stream channels.

- **Institutional and legal strategies** focus on working with or changing legal, social, and/or economic institutions to encourage human activities which are not detrimental to freshwater biodiversity. Examples include improving weak zoning regulations, supporting the development of institutions to provide low-interest loans to enable land owners to purchase better equipment, creating markets for ecologically sustainable products, etc.

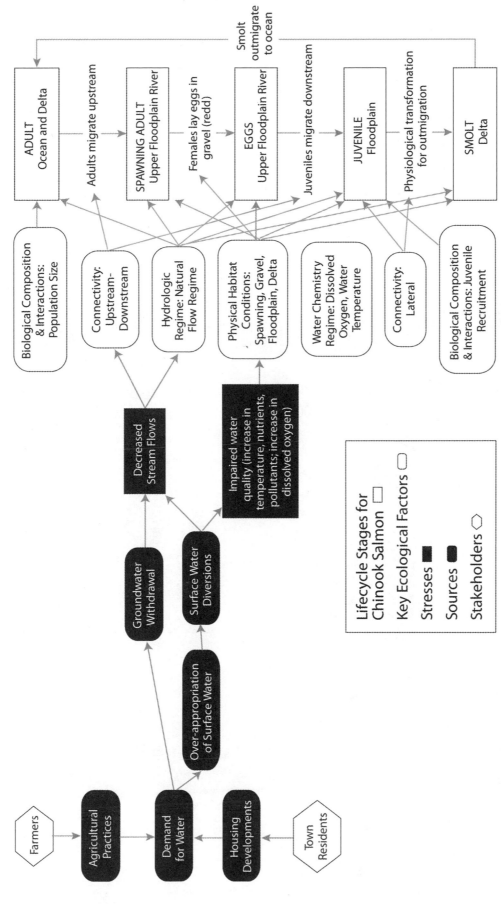

Figure 4-2. Conceptual Ecological Model for Chinook Salmon with Integrated Threats and Stakeholder Information

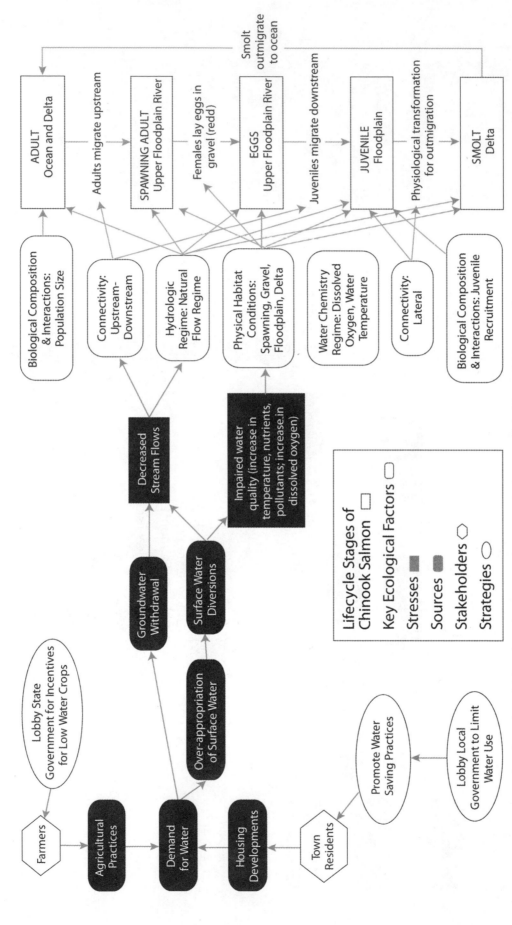

FIGURE 4-3. Conceptual Ecological Model for Chinook Salmon with Integrated Threats, Stakeholder, and Strategy Information

Global processes, including geology and climate, interact to produce...

The Watershed Context of Freshwater Ecosystems

- Location
- Waterhed vegetation cover
- Watershed elevation, gradient, and drainage patterns

which establishes the natural patterns of variation in...

The Five Key Ecological Factors of Freshwater Ecosystems

- Hydrology
- Physical habitat structure
- Water chemistry
- Connectivity
- Biological composition and interactions

which in turn can be altered by...

Human Activities

- Land use and management
- Water use and management
- Invasive alien species
- Overharvesting and fisheries management

because of the adverse effects these activities can have on...

Geophysical Conditions	**Aquatic Biological Conditions**
• Watershed vegetation cover	• Taxonomic and genetic composition
• Soil erosion rates	• Individual health
• Surface and groundwater hydrology	• Biological processes
• Soil and water chemistry	• Ecological processes
• Channel/shoreline morphology	• Evolutionary processes

which must be prevented or abated by...

Conservation Strategies

- Restoration and land/water protection
- Specific land use policies and practices
- Specific sustainable water management policies and practices
- Invasive alien species management policies and practices
- Fisheries management and harvesting policies and practices
- Etc.

and we improve our success through...

Monitoring and Adaptive Management

FIGURE 4-4.

• **Community-based strategies** include working with or empowering local stakeholders to influence practices, policies, and approaches to abate threats to freshwater biodiversity. Often, the stakeholders approach involves strategies that fall into either of the two proceeding strategy types.

Significant overlap exists between these three categories. For example, practitioners may develop community support for passing particular legislation and the legislation may provide funding to buy wetlands. This example crosses all three categories.

Effective strategies must also be applied at the right spatial and temporal scales to address the threat in question and be as efficient as possible in the use of resources and partnerships. A threats assessment is a powerful tool for helping to assess the scope and scale of the threat and thus the scope and scale of the strat-

egy most effective at abating or mitigating the particular threat.

Potential strategies should be evaluated and ranked according to three criteria: the likely benefits to biodiversity or to the identified conservation target, the feasibility of the strategy and the probability of success, and the costs of implementation. Benefits can be both direct and indirect or may provide important leverage for additional efforts. Costs include the actual human and financial resources necessary to implement the strategy as well as the potential impact or cost of failure. Identifying the specific actions necessary to implement the strategy and the areas on the ground where the specific strategies and actions must take place may also prove useful. Linking strategies to specific threats affecting specific targets ensures that resources and efforts are directed at the most critical management needs for biological conservation.

—Authored by Nicole Silk,
Kristine Ciruna, and David Braun

Water Use and Management

The amount of water withdrawn from freshwater ecosystems to meet human demands has risen 35-fold in the past 300 years and over half of that increase has occurred since 1950 (Revenga *et al.* 1998). Structural modifications—such as dams and diversions, flood control projects, channelization, and groundwater extraction—facilitate this use, but at considerable cost to the underlying ecosystem. These modifications significantly alter the dynamics of freshwater ecosystems, fragment existing systems, and join previously unconnected ones, causing declines in fish catches, loss of freshwater biodiversity, increases in the frequency and severity of floods, loss of soil nutrients in the floodplain, and increases in the incidence of diseases such as schistosomiasis and malaria (Revenga *et al.* 1998).

This subchapter examines changes to freshwater ecosystems caused by the following major water use and management related threats:

A. Dams;
B. Surface water diversions;
C. Altered bed and bank structure (channelization, dredging, armoring, and levees); and
D. Groundwater overexploitation.

For each of these threats, this subchapter also presents information about specific strategies for reducing the effects of these threats to freshwater biodiversity as well as strategies for eliminating the threats themselves.

DAMS

Introduction

Dams hold back water in rivers to serve numerous human demands including flood control, recreation in waters trapped behind the dam, and releases for irrigation, hydroelectric power generation, navigation, in-stream recreation (boating and angling), drinking water, and industrial use. Every dam is unique due to differences in design (including the dimensions of the dam, the location of the dam, available construction materials, etc.) and purpose.

In general, dams follow one of three construction designs: embankment, gravity, and arch. Rock and earth embankment dams, usually built across broad valleys, are the least costly to build and represent more than 80% of all large dams. Gravity dams consist of thick walls of concrete and are built in relatively narrow canyons with firm bedrock. Like gravity dams, arch dams are made of concrete and are located only in narrow valleys. The upstream-facing arch of the dam can absorb more pressure than a gravity dam and thus requires less construction material (McCully 2001).

Dams of the same size may vary in the amount of water they hold depending on their primary purposes. A flood control dam keeps its reservoir water level low at the onset of each flood season so that it can store river flow during storm events. Such dams are located along rivers that pose frequent threats of flooding to adjacent lands. In contrast, a water supply reservoir dam attempts to retain as much water as possible in order to meet water supply demands such as irrigation. Hydropower dams are designed to maximize hydraulic head for electricity production. Hydraulic head is the height difference between the surface of a dam's reservoir and the river below the dam. Penstocks convey water under pressure to turbines to produce electricity. In contrast to single purpose dams, some dams are operated for multiple uses. The Colorado River's Glen Canyon Dam, commissioned in 1963, was initially designed for water supply. However, financial and political pressures forced the inclusion of hydropower, downstream distribution, and recreation into the construction design and operating criteria.

In contrast to the typical dams that impound river

*There are three primary varieties of dam construction designs: **arch dam** (above, Boundary Dam, WA, photograph© Seattle City Light), **embankment dam** (above right, Red Rock Dam, IA, photograph courtesy U.S. Army Corps of Engineers), and **gravity dam** (right, Martins Fork Dam, KY, photograph courtesy U.S. Army Corps of Engineers)*

water behind them in a reservoir, weirs and barrages are considered run-of-the-river dams. They create a hydrologic head in the river for the purpose of diverting some portion of the river's flow and have no storage reservoir or only a limited poundage capacity. Weirs are generally small structures constructed to measure water flow and generally have no or minimal overall impact on rivers. In contrast, barrages are larger structures, some exceeding 20 meters in height and hundreds of meters long. They are often located on large rivers (4th order or higher) and are used in energy production and water diversion for irrigation and regulation of downstream flow. While barrages are generally smaller than typical dams, their impacts on a river ecosystem can be considerable. The Farakka Barrage on the Ganges River in eastern India diverts a portion of the water to the Bhagirati-Hoogly River that empties into the Port of Calcutta, thereby improving navigation and supplementing Calcutta's water supply. However, this project has also con-

tributed to changes in the composition and structure of riverine and estuarine biota (Sinha *et al.* 1996, Prakash 2002) and caused declines in agricultural and fisheries production, reduced water supplies, and increased tensions between India and Bangladesh (Tanzeema and Faisal 2001). A more complete glossary of dam-related terms can be found at American Rivers' websites: www.amrivers.org/tableofcontents/glossary.htm and www.amrivers.org/glossary/default.htm.

As stated in Chapter 1, over 45,000 large dams exist around the globe. China has the greatest percentage of these dams with more than 22,000 and the U.S. has almost 6,600. Other nations with significant numbers of large dams include India (4,300), Japan (2,700), and Spain (1,200). Over 140 nations have at least one large dam. In addition to these large dams, more than 800,000 smaller dams (<15 meters high) also exist worldwide, including over 100,000 in the United States (McCully 2001). Cumulatively, these

*Dams are designed for many different purposes, including **navigation** (top left, Belleville Lock & Dam, OH, photograph by Cheryl Payton, U.S. Army Corps of Engineers), **water supply** (top right, Great Salt Plains Dam, OK, photograph by Cheryl Payson, U.S. Army Corps of Engineers) **flood control** (bottom right, Otter Brook Dam, NH, photograph courtesy U.S. Army Corps of Engineers), **hydropower** and **recreation** (bottom left, Dworshak Dam, ID, photograph courtesy U.S. Army Corps of Engineers).*

dams have fragmented 60% of the world's large river basins (McCully 2001) and create barriers for migrating fish and to the natural movement of sediments, nutrients, and water. Reservoirs associated with many large dams have also significantly altered freshwater ecosystems and affected global processes. Reservoirs now have a combined storage capacity of 10,000 km^3, equivalent to about 5 times the volume of water in all the world's rivers (Chao 1995) or enough to cover the world's dry land area in water to a depth of 10 cm (Pielou 1998). Total global area inundated by reservoirs created by large dams exceeds 400,000 km^2, or an area equivalent to the size of California. The weight of the impounded water of large reservoirs has triggered earthquakes, and some geophysicists suggest

that the redistribution of weight caused by reservoirs affect the speed of Earth's rotation, angle of inclination, and the shape of its gravitational field (Chao 1991, 1995). The proliferation of dams on the world's rivers represents a significant challenge to the health and biotic integrity of watersheds.

The Effects of Dams on Freshwater Ecosystems

Differences in dam size, their location within a river drainage, and operation create a suite of local environmental effects that are often unique to each dammed body of water (Collier *et al.* 1996). Dams can also have cumulative effects at regional and even global

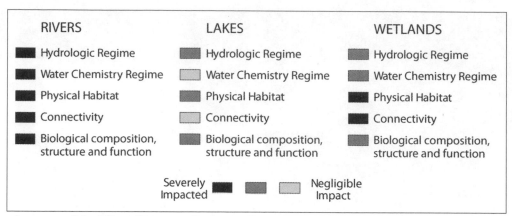

FIGURE 4-5. Summary of the Effect of Dams on Freshwater Ecosystems

scales. This section examines the effects of dams on the five key ecological factors of freshwater ecosystems: the hydrologic regime, the water chemistry regime, physical habitat conditions, connectivity, and biological composition and interactions.

THE HYDROLOGIC REGIME

The hydrologic regime is the primary driver of river ecosystems. Dams alter the hydrologic regime by controlling a river's natural flow (Rosenberg *et al.* 2000). Disruption of a river's natural flow regime changes the movement of water, nutrients, sediments, and biota longitudinally along the river and laterally between the river channel and its floodplain. This disruption depresses productivity and fisheries and jeopardizes the integrity of both the river and the floodplain (Freeman *et al.* 2003). Regulated flows, resulting in decreased productivity, loss of available habitat, and impaired water quality also effect downstream lakes and wetlands dependent on natural flow regimes.

CONNECTIVITY

Rivers have interactive pathways along three spatial dimensions: longitudinal (headwaters-estuarine), lateral (riverine-riparian/floodplain), and vertical (riverine-groundwater) (Ward and Stanford 1989). Refer to Appendix A for in-depth discussion on connectivity and its importance for freshwater biodiversity. Dams pose the most serious disruption of this connectivity, creating changes to the riparian community, the river

channel itself, and the delta, ocean, or other water body that the river flows into.

Longitudinal connectivity refers to upstream-downstream linkages in rivers (Ward 1986). Anything that tends to disrupt this connectivity threatens the ecological integrity of the river system. Altering the timing, extent, and intensity of this connectivity will also alter the river's associated connectivity with its floodplain. Dams can permanently alter the downstream passage of sediment, large woody material, fine organic material and nutrients and the upstream movement of aquatic and riparian species normally present in free-flowing streams (Tracy 2000). For example, the series of dams and other structures on the Mississippi River have fragmented river and riparian habitats, modified the flow regime, and altered sedimentation patterns, severely disrupting geomorphic processes (Delaney and Craig 1997).

Due to the connectivity between river drainages and coastal and marine environments, dams can also alter the productivity of coastal and offshore waters. For example, rivers supply more than 80% of the total input of silicate to the oceans, which stimulate the production of diatoms that in turn fuel food webs and play a critical role in carbon dioxide (CO_2) uptake. Decreased amounts of silicate in coastal areas around the world (relative to nitrate and phosphate) can translate into shifts in nutrient regimes, discouraging silicate-using diatoms and favoring nuisance algae (Justic *et al.* 1995) that negatively affect the ecological integrity of estuaries and coastal foodwebs (e.g., Turner *et al.* 1998).

Lateral connectivity includes the form and dynamics

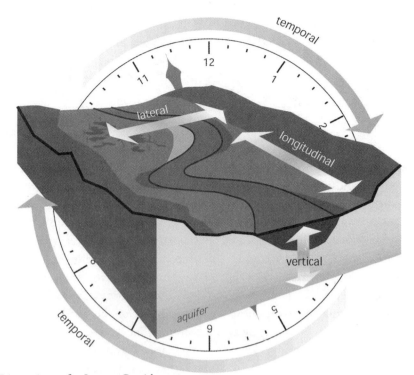

FIGURE 4-6. The Dimensions of a Stream Corridor

Source: The Federal Interagency Stream Restoration Working Group. 1998. Stream Corridor Restoration: Principles, Processes, and Practices, pp. 1–i.

of the channel itself, and the interactions between the river and its riparian zone, including its floodplain (Ward 1988). Dams disrupt the lateral transfers of water, sediment, nutrients and organisms, both upstream and downstream of the dam (Ward and Stanford 1989). The presence of a dam generally curtails the duration and often the magnitude of high flows, thereby disabling the tendency for a river to rise out of its banks and hydraulically connect with its floodplain. This results in the disconnection of river biota from critical spawning, refuge, and foraging habitat. Breaks in lateral connectivity also: alter the abundance and diversity of riverine and riparian vegetation (e.g., Dister *et al.* 1990, Keller and Kondolf 1990); desiccate wetlands located far from the river channel itself due to a lowering of the groundwater table; and decrease reproductive success of gravel-spawning fish due to changes in mixing of surface water and groundwater below dams (Curry *et al.* 1994).

Reservoirs behind dams flood out riparian areas and may create new ones. Water levels in newly flood-ed areas are regulated and do not compensate for loss of periodic flooding that naturally occurs. This change is particularly harmful for floodplain fish that are dependent upon terrestrial food sources, such as terrestrial arthropods, fruits, seeds, and flowers that fall into the water. Reservoir flooding simplifies up-stream river complexity, and the impounded water favors a shift to fish adapted to slow-moving water. Studies suggest that permanent flooding of islands and sidearms eliminates important resting and feeding sites thereby decreasing fish production (Gosse 1963, Ward 1985).

Rivers are in constant contact with groundwater, and this interaction exerts a significant influence on habitat conditions. Spatial and temporal patterns of recharge and discharge between surface and groundwater are often changed by altered surface flows (Pringle and Triska 2000). Reduced surface flows can lead to lowered levels in adjacent groundwater (Galay 1983, Golz 1994) and even slight changes in water tables can decrease the amount of available instream habitat, especially during dry periods (Welcomme

1979). Groundwater levels are also important in the productivity and composition of riparian, floodplain, and wetland vegetation (Décamps 1984).

PHYSICAL HABITAT CONDITIONS

Habitat structural changes

One obvious and striking effect of dams is on upstream terrestrial, wetland, and riparian habitat. In some cases reservoirs expand the size of already existing lakes and ponds and in other cases they create large bodies of water where none existed previously. These reservoirs transform riverine habitat to lentic (lake) habitat, which is not the preferred habitat of lotic or stream-adapted organisms. Resultant floral and faunal changes occur as stream-adapted organisms are replaced by lake-adapted (often invasive alien) species, potentially leading to cascading trophic effects throughout the entire river basin.

Instream habitat downstream of the dam is also significantly altered due to sediment reductions and associated channel morphology changes as a result of the dam. Channel substrate and pool, riffle, and run habitat change as the river adjusts to new conditions. Reduction in the transfer of coarse woody debris from

upstream to downstream as a consequence of the dam also changes physical habitat conditions for species needing cover.

Sediment regime

All rivers contain sediment, and the amount transported usually changes exponentially in relation to the river's discharge or flow (Waters 1995). Large and fast moving rivers can carry enormous amounts of sediment, particularly in arid regions where soils are loose and precipitation events are frequently flashy (Collier *et al.* 1996). For any river system, high floods carry the largest amount of sediment.

Dams trap flows from progressing downstream, and in this process facilitate the settling of sediment particles out of the water column for deposit at the bottom of the reservoir. Many of the persistent, bioaccumulating, and toxic organic contaminants are strongly associated with sediment (Miller 2001). These pollutants pose a threat to biota when intentional release, high water flows, or ice scouring events move them downstream in concentrated quantities.

By interrupting the normal transport of sediment, nutrients, and other material downstream, dams also affect downstream habitat within the stream channel,

Diatom Stephanodiscus niagarae, *common in many temperate lakes in North America. Image by Mark Edlund/Science Museum of Minnesota.*

as well as in associated floodplains, receiving deltas, and coastal areas. The channel degrades, beaches and backwaters decrease, and riparian, deltaic and floodplain habitat often reduce in size and change in morphology.

As mentioned previously, dams also block the downstream movement of coarse woody debris (CWD). CWD is an important substrate, food source, and refuge for fish. CWD also influences channel morphology by creating pools and inhibiting the movement of sediment. Loss of this material has important consequences for freshwater species, especially those closely tied to floodplain habitat (Wilson *et al.* 2001). Loss of CWD has degraded habitat quality for, and contributed to the loss of, many salmonid populations (Dooley and Paulson 2003).

THE WATER CHEMISTRY REGIME

Tailwater temperature and chemistry

Lake and reservoir water is stratified along a temperature gradient: the colder, heavier water occupies the bottom layer (hypolimnion), while the lighter surface water (epilimnion) is warmed by the sun and ambient air temperature. This thermal stratification is particularly strong during the warm months and in deep reservoirs where mixing is minimal. This stratification inhibits gas transfer between the oxygen-rich surface layers and the poorly oxygenated bottom layers. Tailwaters released from a dam may originate from either of these layers, causing significantly different effects. Water drawn from the epilimnion layer may elevate the temperature of the receiving water, causing accelerated growth rates and mistiming of life cycle stages of biota (Davies and Day 1998). Water released from the hypolimnion layer may lower the temperature of the receiving river, causing a decline in downstream productivity and a shift in biotic composition toward cold-water species (Wetzel 1983, Horn and Goldman 1994, Collier *et al.* 1996, Bednarek 2001).

Toxic material, especially organic chemicals absorbed to the sediment at the bottom of the reservoir, may be stirred up and released downstream with a hypoliminion tailwater release. This contaminant-bearing sediment and particulate matter may be ingested by fish and benthic organisms, macroinvertebrates, and other biota and passed through the food

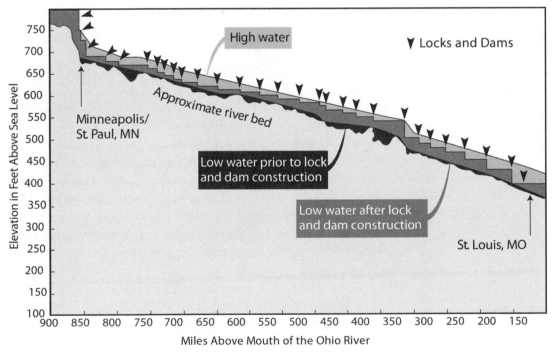

FIGURE 4-7. A profile of the Mississippi River, showing water levels before and after lock and dam construction

Source: Adapted from U.S. Army Corps of Engineers, http://www.mvr.usace.army.mil/navdata/locpic.htm.

chain where it bioaccumulates in top predators (Miller 2001). Removal of Fort Edward Dam on the Hudson River (New York) in 1973 released large quantities of polychlorinated biphenyl (PCB) contaminants downstream in river sediments. The resulting downstream contamination required extensive cleanup efforts (American Rivers 2002a).

Methylmercury

The creation of reservoirs (and the elimination of wetlands) increases the mobility of organic and inorganic matter, including both natural and anthropogenic sources of mercury (U.S. EPA 1999). Conditions often exist in reservoirs that stimulate the transformation of inorganic mercury into toxic methylmercury (i.e., the hypolimnion of many stratified reservoirs which support sulfate-reducing bacteria that take up inorganic mercury and transform it into methylmercury). Methylmercury in water is absorbed readily into living tissue via bioaccumulation, resulting in the build-up of concentrations in large fish to levels millions of times higher than the surrounding water. Methylmercury is a significant problem as indicated by the number of fish consumption advisories. As of July 1999, 40 states in the U.S. had issued 1,931 fish advisories for mercury (most in the midwestern and eastern USA).

Greenhouse gases

Reservoirs created by dams can also be a significant source of greenhouse gases (GHG). The rotting vegetation in flooded reservoirs emits carbon dioxide (CO_2) and methane (CH_4), two heat-trapping, or greenhouse, gasses. Studies of GHG released from the reservoirs of the hydropower Balbina and Tucurui Dams in Brazil showed high initial pulses followed by a gradual decrease, especially for carbon dioxide, as the vegetation decayed. Methane emissions tended to remain constant as a function of the slow but continuous decay of aquatic vegetation. GHG from the Balbina Reservoir has a 26 fold greater impact on global warming than the emissions from a coal-fired power station that produces an equivalent amount of electricity (McCully 2001). Studies in other parts of the world show similar trends of GHG release from reservoirs. However, lower amounts of GHG are reported for deeper and colder reservoirs, such as those in the higher latitudes including the northern United States, Canada, and Europe.

BIOLOGICAL COMPOSITION AND INTERACTIONS

Dams substitute extreme conditions with average conditions, thereby altering water quantity and water quality as well as the character and composition of the materials that create the bed and banks of freshwater ecosystems. In turn, these changes modify the structure, function, and biotic integrity of freshwater ecosystems.

Structure

As a physical barrier, dams disrupt the movement of species. Decreased species mobility contributes to significant changes in species composition as well as species loss. Overall trends of biotic impoverishment caused by dams include: (1) extirpation or imperilment of migratory fish (from anadromous salmonids to many other fish taxa with different migratory strategies); (2) faunal range fragmentation and population isolation; (3) extinction or imperilment of geographically restricted taxa dependent on uniquely riverine habitats; (4) reduction in abundance of flood-dependent taxa, as well as taxa dependent on freshwater inflows to estuarine habitats; and (5) increases in lentic and nonnative taxa (summarized in Pringle *et al.* 2000). In tropical South America and Asia, much less published information exists regarding the effects of dams on the biotic integrity of freshwater ecosystems. However, neotropical rivers are ecologically vulnerable to increasing hydropower development given the degree of endemism of freshwater biota, the extent of migratory behavior of fish, the importance of seasonal inundation of floodplains for fish migrations, and the adverse physical or chemical conditions often created in tropical reservoirs or tailwaters (summarized by Pringle *et al.* 2000; Dudgeon 2000). Dams have also caused global scale ecological changes in riparian ecosystems (summarized by Nilsson and Berggren 2000) that are particularly sensitive to variation in the hydrological regime. Eliminating or reducing flood

A flood in river red gum forest along the Murray River floodplain, Australia. Photograph by Amy Jansen.

disturbances changes the species composition of streamside vegetation to that of forest types characteristic of unflooded upland areas (Décamps *et al.* 1988).

Function

Migratory fish and other organisms influence the structure and function of local habitats and communities through their contributions of nutrients and energy to freshwater systems from the sea (Ben-David *et al.* 1998, Gresh *et al.* 2000). Other less-studied taxa that migrate between distinct portions of riverine systems (e.g., acipencerids, catostomids, prochilodontids) may provide similar inputs (Hall 1972). Dams disrupt these contributions through changes to species distribution patterns and abundance within freshwater ecosystems. Furthermore, depletion of amphidromous shrimp and potamodromous fish on benthic organic matter and algal and invertebrate communities above dams is likely to significantly affect ecosystem processes, such as primary production and detrital processing (Flecker 1997). As a result of a dam, algae once restricted to an attached layer, or biofilm, on the stream bottom may become part of a larger planktonic community of floating algae within the reservoir. In the reservoir, low turbidity levels coupled with polluted runoff can result in high primary production and nuisance growths of this planktonic algae. Tropical and subtropical reservoirs are often plagued with nuisance growths of invasive alien floating aquatic macrophytes, such as water hyacinth (*Eichornia crassipes*), which create anoxic conditions (deleterious to other aquatic biota) as these species die and decompose. Finally, the decline of freshwater mussels isolated by dams from their migratory fish hosts can negatively affect stream water quality and benthic stability (Strayer *et al.* 1994, Kowalswski *et al.* 2000).

The decline of the duration and magnitude of flood events caused by dams also affects the natural productivity of floodplains, riparian areas, deltas, and wetlands. Many species that inhabit these areas require periodic flooding to supply them with nutrients, connect them to the river channel, and recharge shallow groundwater reserves upon which they depend. Seed regeneration of the eucalyptus forests of the Murray floodplain, Australia, is dependent upon the natural flooding cycle. Dams now impound these floodwaters, thereby curtailing regeneration. Conversely, releases of water at the wrong time threaten the destruction of the *Acacia xanthophloea* forest below the Pongolapoort Dam in South Africa (WCD 2000). Deprived of the natural supply of silt, nutrients, and moisture, these floodplains are subjected to morphological changes, resulting in cascading affects to resident native species and an increased incidence of invasion by alien species.

Strategies for Mitigating/Abating the Effect of Dams on Freshwater Ecosystems

Dams are a notorious as well as an obvious culprit of harm to freshwater ecosystems. Perhaps because of this, a wide variety of stakeholders have developed and applied a considerable range of strategies to abate the effect of dams on these ecosystems. The strategies applied include an assortment of technical, legal and institutional, and community-based efforts at modifying plans for, changing the operation of, or applying efforts to remove, dams. This section attempts to synthesize these efforts into a coherent toolbox.

TECHNICAL STRATEGIES

Technical strategies to improve flow patterns of regulated rivers include: modifying dam operations, decommissioning and removing dams, and reengineering systems through modifications of channels and other water management structures. Each of these strategies are discussed below.

Modifying dam operations

While the natural flow in some rivers may be reestablished through dam removal (this strategy is described in greater detail below), most large dams will remain in place for the near future. However, flow releases from a dam may be brought into closer alignment with a river's natural flow regime through modifications to the structure and operations of the dam. The best time to implement such modifications is often when dam operations undergo scheduled maintenance, repair, or administrative review. However, significant interaction with water managers and other stakeholders or engagement in administrative procedures will usually be necessary in order to make the most of such critical junctures. For example, the

Federal Energy Regulatory Commission (FERC) is the primary agency responsible for licensing most small hydroelectric power projects in the U.S. FERC issues a license authorizing construction and/or continued operation of existing projects for limited time periods, and dam operators must seek a new license at the end of this period. This relicensing offers a unique opportunity to significantly influence dam operations. Stakeholders can influence the decision-making because the commission is required to "provide the same level of consideration to the environment, recreation, fish and wildlife, and other non-power values that it gives to power and development objectives in making a licensing decision" (FERC 2002a). Linking improved flow releases to relicensing can be a powerful tool in stream restoration (Haeuber and Michener 1998). Strategies to influence FERC decision-making and suggested points of contact are discussed in more detail below.

Dam reoperation to simulate natural flows

Scientists and water resource managers are trying new operational strategies and improved designs in dams to minimize negative impacts of dams and dam operations on flow and aquatic and riparian biota. These approaches attempt to improve the pattern of a dam's releases for the downstream freshwater ecosystem.

The high profile *Beach Habitat Rebuilding Flow* experiment in 1996 demonstrated the potential restorative powers of short-term release of water. This trial simulation of a spring flood involved the release 1274 m^3 (45,000 ft^3) per second of water into the Colorado River from the Glen Canyon Dam (Poff *et al.* 1997, Collier *et al.* 1997, 1996). This amount is several times the regulated dam outflow volume but only 35% of the volume of historical average annual spring floods. The overall goal of this experiment was to learn about the potential of river restoration through management of releases that more closely match natural patterns. Specific goals were to: (1) redeposit high elevation sand bars; (2) preserve and restore camping beaches; (3) flush non-native fish; (4) rejuvenate backwater habitat for native fish; (5) scour new high water zones; and (6) provide water to established riparian vegetation at the old high water zone. Perhaps the most important outcome of this experi-

A young villager celebrates the opening of the sluice gates of the Pak Mun Dam, Thailand, in June 2001. Photograph courtesy of the Assembly of the Poor, Thailand.

ment was a political success: legitimizing managed increased flows for river restoration. Smaller-scale controlled releases for river restoration have also been used on other rivers in the U.S. and internationally (summarized by Freeman 2002 and by the flow restoration database available through www.fresh waters.org). A recent trial release from the Pak Mun Dam (Thailand) was initiated by pressure from communities affected by decreased fish catches and significant economic hardship. After the gates of this dam were open a year, reservoir water levels returned to normal, more than 152 species of fish returned to the river reach below the dam (including 145 indigenous species), and riparian vegetation began to recover (RWESA 2002).

Sometimes altering management patterns can both provide improved ecological conditions and also serve downstream human water uses. One approach developed by staff at The Nature Conservancy includes a framework, entitled ecologically sustainable water management (ESWM), that can be used to achieve such seemingly opposing management objectives. ESWM involves six steps:

- **Step 1: Estimate Ecosystem Flow Requirements.** Develop initial numerical estimates of key aspects of river flow necessary to sustain native species and natural ecosystem functions.
- **Step 2: Determine Human Influences on the Flow Regime.** Account for human uses of water, both current and future, through development of a computerized hydrologic simulation model that facilitates examination of human-induced alterations of river flow regimes.
- **Step 3: Identify Incompatibilities between Human and Ecosystem Needs.** Assess incompatibilities between human uses and ecosystem needs with particular attention to their spatial and temporal character.
- **Step 4: Collaboratively Search for Solutions.** Explore options for reducing or eliminating conflicts between human and ecosystem needs through an open dialogue that helps clarify values, share information, and build trust between stakeholders.
- **Step 5: Conduct Water Management Experiments.** Resolve critical uncertainties that frustrate efforts to integrate human and ecosystem needs through

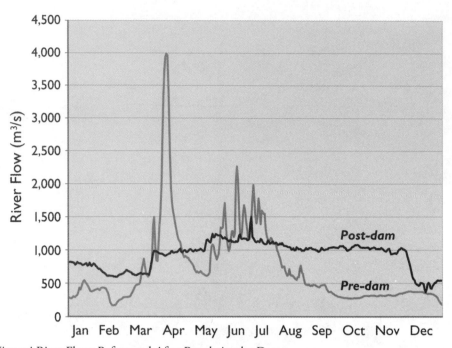

FIGURE 4-8. Missouri River Flows Before and After Regulation by Dams

Source: Postel, Sandra and Brian Richter. 2003. *Rivers for Life: Managing Water for People and Nature*, (Washington, DC: Island Press) p. 126.

research, monitoring, and science-based experimentation.

- **Step 6: Design and Implement an Adaptive Water Management Plan.** Define mutually acceptable goals related to ecosystem health, economic benefits, and other societal needs; institute a monitoring program to track progress toward meeting these goals; and establish a process for refining water management based on new information.

The first step in this process involves determining how much water a river needs and describing this flow pattern using the five fundamental elements of the hydrologic regime: (1) magnitude of water at any given time; (2) timing of occurrence of a given water condition; (3) frequency of occurrence of a given water condition; (4) duration of time over which specific water condition exists; and (5) rate of change in water conditions. Determining the timing, duration, frequency, magnitude, and rate of change for high flow pulses, low flow periods, and flood flow events also proves exceedingly useful. The Indicators of Hydrologic Alteration, a software program also developed by staff at The Nature Conservancy, uses a large

suite of parameters to characterize such flow patterns. These same tools can be used to explore the degree of deviation from these patterns caused by human uses of water. A more complete discussion of how to use this tool can be found in Richter *et al.* (1996).

Embedded in this approach is consideration of how much alteration of (natural) flow conditions would be too much to ensure continued river health and integrity. A newly emerging strategy for addressing this question assembles data on the hydrologic, physical, chemical, habitat, and biotic characteristics of a river to develop a holistic profile in a scientifically sound way (Postel and Richter 2003). Several techniques for collecting and assembling the data have evolved recently, including the Building Block Methodology (BBM) (Tharme and King 1998), the Holistic Approach (Arthington 1998) and the Benchmarking Methodology (Brizga *et al.* 2002). While these methodologies use similar data, they may produce different conclusions depending on differences in ecological goals. For example, are the goals maximum human use and protection of ecosystem functions and native species or protection of the system in its natural state?

Once practitioners identify the flow patterns that they seek to improve, this information can form the basis of discussions with other stakeholders about solutions to water management challenges. Where uncertainties remain, modeling, experimentation, and monitoring can inform improved versions of management plans. This approach is gaining acceptance as more projects succeed in adjusting existing water management plans resulting in significant ecological benefits with minimal impact on water supply available for human populations and institutions.

Dam modifications for improved fish passages

The primary purpose of fish passage facilities is to permit the movement of migratory fish around a dam. These facilities are built into the dam complex either during initial construction or in subsequent modifications.

Fish passages include the following types of facilities and operations:

- **Fish ladders** consist of a series of interconnected sloping channels with pools created by weirs or baffles over which water flows. They provide a passageway for fish from the river to the reservoir. There are many designs of this type of facility to meet specific environmental considerations and species needs. For example, some weirs are now designed with bottom orifices to allow passage of fish and bedload and to improve flow regulation. However, efficiency for even modest fish ladders of the pool and weir type can be as little as 2%. Key factors affecting success of the fish ladders are: (1) adequate water flow to attract fish to the passage entrance, (2) correct flow in the passage as the gravitational head changes, (3) channel slope, and (4) absence of obstructions such as debris (World Bank 2002).

- **Lock and lift systems** are operated in much the same manner as locks for barges and boats. Fish are attracted or crowded into a chamber. When the chamber is full, it closes and transports the fish (and water) to the next level up or down. When the chamber reaches the next level, it opens and the fish are released.

- **Denil and vertical slotted fishways** consist of a sluice with a series of vertical baffles through which water passes. The design facilitates self-flow regulation, resting areas for fish, and bedload transportation.

- **Trapping and transport** occurs when fish are caught and transported by tram, barge, or truck around the dam or relocated to another river. Fish transported

Adult fish ladder from the Ice Harbor Lock and Dam, Snake River, WA. Photograph courtesy U.S. Army Corps of Engineers.

long distances may require refrigeration. This type of transport is expensive and success rates of returning fish may be less than 0.5% (Lovett 1999).

Unfortunately, fish passage facilities can be very costly to install and maintain, particularly if added after the original construction of the dam is complete. For example, installing lifts for sea-run species such as alewives, American shad, and Atlantic salmon on the Sebasticook River, Maine (IRN 2002a) cost an estimated $3 to $4 million. The Yacyreta Dam on the Parana River in South America was outfitted with fish lifts that cost $30 million and were unsuccessful in facilitating fish migration (McCully 2001).

Additionally, fish passage facilities are not always effective in facilitating the migration of fish due to inappropriate design and operation (Jobin 1998). Many fish passages are based on the salmon model that assumes species are powerful swimmers and move upstream in fast-moving water to spawn (McCully 2001). Such models are not suitable for species that have other migratory patterns and needs such as catadromous (species that live in the rivers and spawn in the estuaries and coastal waters), amphidromous (species that spawn and mature in both salt and fresh water), and potamodromous (species that migrate entirely in freshwaters) fish or species that require slow-moving water (Pringle et al. 2000, Dudgeon 2000). The native potamodromous silver perch in south-eastern Australia have declined by more than 90% since the 1940s despite the presence of fish ladders modeled after those on North American and European rivers, and the species is now listed as threatened (McCully 2001). Some of the more than 250 known species in the Parana River in South America migrate the river in both directions several times during their lifecycle, and the fishlifts at the Yacyreta Dam are designed only for upstream migration (McCully 2001); downstream migration needs remain unmet. Additionally, the needs of climbing aquatic taxa, such shrimps, gobies, and snails have not been addressed until recently (March et al. 2003). For more information on fish passages see Odeh (1999, 2000).

Dam removal

Dam removal is another option available to mitigate negative effects of dams on freshwater ecosystems. Additional justifications for dam removal include: safety concerns, growing demand for recreation, and new options for meeting the needs for which they were originally commissioned (e.g., power, municipal water supplies, flood control, navigation, movement of logs downstream (Gleick 2000)). Removal may be a sound solution for a functioning dam where the dam's benefits are outweighed by the environmental damage it causes (Maclin and Sicchio 1999). These additional environmental justifications may prove key when trying to influence dam removal.

Since 1912, about 500 dams have been removed in the U.S. (Poff and Hart 2002, Maclin and Sicchio 1999, Flavin et al. 2002) and about half of these occurred during the 1990s, with the state of Wisconsin leading the charge with 73 dams removed. Whereas the largest dam removed was the 19-meter Grangeville Dam on the Clearwater River, Idaho (1963 removal to restore salmon runs), the vast majority of dams removed have been small with an average height of only seven meters and these removals represent only about 0.5% of the total stock of dams greater than 2 meters in height. Examples also exist of dam removal outside the U.S., including two small dams in France in 1998 to restore salmon habitat (IRN 2002b) and one in Latvia in 2002 to improve fisheries (IRN2002c); a small dam in the Czech Republic in 1991 to restore riparian and woodland habitat; a large dam in Australia in 2000 and an additional nine in the near future to restore streamflow and water quality (River Alliance of Wisconsin 2002).

Advocates for dam removal may also point to a particular dam's life expectancy. In the U.S., more than 25% of all dams are older than their 50-year life expectancy and by 2020 that number will reach 85%. Many aging and silted dams are uneconomical to operate and pose hazards to public safety. The National Dams Inventory (USACE 2002b) notes that 32% of dams have a high or significant downstream hazard potential and the majority of these do not have an emergency action plan in the event of failure or negligent operation. As dams age, public safety

Removal of a dam near the village of Saint-Etienne du Vigan on the Allier River, a tributary of the Loire River in France: before demolition (above left), during demolition (below left), and eight weeks after decommissioning in 1998 (above right). Photographs courtesy ERN European Rivers Network/SOS Loire Vivante.

becomes a key concern. Additionally, maintenance and operational costs increase significantly after 25–35 years of operation, and for many dams these expenses exceed economic benefits. Repairing or retrofitting dams to keep them operational and economical is often much more costly than removing them (McCully 2001, Maclin and Sicchio 1999).

Results from most dam removal projects have demonstrated significant benefits to the river ecosystem, riparian communities, and the dam owners and operators. Although dam removal may result in some undesirable ecological consequences (e.g., removal of barriers blocking the movement of invasive alien species upstream and the release of sediments and pollutants down-stream), often the long-term river restoration benefits outweigh the costs. These benefits include:

- Restoring river habitat
- Improving water quality
- Reestablishing fish passage upstream and downstream

- Restoring threatened and endangered species
- Improving riparian and floodplain habitat
- Removing dam safety risks and associated liabilities
- Saving taxpayer dollars
- Eliminating dam maintenance and operational costs
- Improving aesthetics
- Improving fishing opportunities
- Improving boating recreational opportunities
- Improving public access to the river, upstream and downstream
- Recreating new land for the public and landowners
- Improving riverside recreation
- Improving tourism opportunities

(List modified from: Maclin and Bowman 2002.)

Cost of dam removal varies considerably and depends upon numerous factors such as size, complexity of structure, and characteristics of the river. Costs range from as little as $1,500 (dam on the Muddy

BOX 4-1. Case Study: Removal of Edwards Dam on the Kennebec River, Maine

The Kennebec River in Maine historically supported large populations of commercially important migratory fish such as Atlantic salmon, shad, sturgeon, and striped bass. In 1837, the Edwards Dam was constructed to provide mechanical power, and later electrical power, to support saw, grist, and textile mills despite local opposition from citizens concerned about its effect on fish. After construction of the dam, fish landings dropped precipitously. Prior to the dam's construction, an individual fisherman could catch 500 salmon in a season, four men caught 6,400 shad in a single day, and 1,000 striped bass were taken from a one weir during a single high tide event. By 1880 the sturgeon industry supported only 12 fishermen and the annual catch shrank from 66,000 kilograms to 2,500 kilograms.

Edwards Dam, Kennebec River, Maine, February 1999. Photograph courtesy Maine State Planning Office.

The Kennebec Coalition was formed in 1989 to secure the removal of Edwards Dam and restore the river. In November 1997, the Federal Energy Regulatory Commission refused to relicense the operation of the dam, the first time the agency had ever exercised this option. In May 1998 the Kennebec Coalition, stakeholders, business interests, the dam owner, and several federal and state agencies announced a settlement that provided for funding to remove the dam and assist with fisheries restoration programs. Numerous businesses, foundations, organizations, and individuals contributed financial and in-kind services to accomplish the goal of improving and protecting the Kennebec River and its rich biotic community. The total $3 million cost for removal, including $2.1 million for dam destruction and more than $800,000 for engineering and permitting costs, were paid by upstream dam operators and a downstream shipbuilder. As part of the overall agreement, upstream operators were granted a delay in implementing a $9 million fish restoration project and the shipbuilder was approved to expand its facilities. Total costs were less than one-third the expense of proposed installation of fish passage system. The owners and local, state and federal government agencies paid the costs (American Rivers 2002c, d, IRN 2002d).

Edwards Dam during removal, with a channel cut through the remains of the dam. Photograph courtesy Maine State Planning Office.

Dam removal occurred in stages over a 5-month period beginning in July 1999. Gravel cofferdams[1] were constructed to facilitate removal of the main dam by heavy equipment Once the dam was removed these temporary cofferdams were breached and the river allowed to stabilize. Demolition debris was used to fill the power canal (on the west bank) and other locations.

The removal marked the first time in more than 160 years that migratory fish species in the Kennebec River—including Atlantic salmon, Atlantic sturgeon, short-nosed sturgeon, blue-back herring, rainbow smelt, striped

---

[1] Cofferdams are temporary barriers for excluding water from an area that is normally submerged. Commonly made of wood, steel, or concrete sheet piling, they are used in constructing foundations of dams, bridges, and similar subaqueous structures and for temporary drylocks.

bass, and alewife—could travel another 27 kilometers beyond the dam site to Waterville. Within a few months of the dam's removal, wildlife sightings and aquatic insect populations have improved significantly. Return of the fish has already led to increased numbers of other riverine animals, such as osprey, bald eagle, kingfishers, great blue heron, sand pipers, and comerants. Within weeks of the breaching volunteer vegetation had colonized the banks of the former reservoir.

The local and regional economy has also benefited from the dam removal through improvements to water quality, fisheries, and the tourism sector of the economy. This continuing and cooperative effort among multiple parties is a model of community involvement toward improving environmental conditions while benefiting a wide sector of the local community (Kennebec Coalition 1999).

Following the removal of the Edwards Dam, and the return of long-absent migratory fish species, osprey and other wildlife returned to the Kennebec River. Photograph by Marian McSherry.

Creek, PA) to $3.2 million (Two Mile River, Santa Fe, New Mexico). To date, a variety of entities have paid for the removals including local, state/provincial and federal governments; dam owners; private citizens and corporations. Often costs are shared across a number of entities. Funding sources may come from public general coffers. They may be integrated into licensing fees (as proposed by the Hydropower Reform Coalition for FERC licensed facilities), or can be creatively generated from license plate sales and mitigation funds for continued operation of other dams on the river.

Steps to dam removal

Dam removal is a major undertaking and should be pursued only after careful consideration of benefits and liabilities. Unlike dam building, removal is a new and emerging strategy. Dam removal efforts are often bogged down by inadequacies in the decision-making process, incomplete and inaccurate information, and emotionally charged and divisive atmospheres. Possible scenarios should be examined in an open and constructive atmosphere. Scientists and water managers recognize the need to improve decision-making and are beginning to apply social science concepts and principles to help achieve outcomes that are both ecologically sustainable and are in the public interest (Johnson and Graber 2002).

Each dam removal project is unique, requires its

own formula for effective action, and frequently takes years or decades to complete. Experience has demonstrated that dam removal decisions must take into account the needs of multiple interested parties and administrative, political, social, economic and environmental issues. These needs can be best met through an overall strategy that includes information gathering, communication, organization and support building, and identification of available institutional, legal and other implementation tools. The following process provides a basic structure for informed decision-making that can be applied in most situations:

Step 1: Establish goals and objectives

Step 2: Identify major issues of concern

Step 3: Collect data and make assessments

Step 4: Make decisions

(If a decision is made to remove the dam, the following steps are also included)

Step 5: Remove dam

Step 6: Collect data, make assessments, and conduct post-removal monitoring

Each of these steps is discussed in considerable detail within a 2002 publication by the Heinz Center titled "Dam Removal: Science and Decision Making." This document is available free upon request or the

PDF file can be downloaded from the internet at http://www.heinzctr.org/publications.htm (Heinz Center 2002).

Please refer to the following publications for more detail and descriptions of dam removal examples, issues, and considerations:

Bolling, D.M. 1994. How to Save a River. A Handbook for Citizen Action. River Network.

Echeverria, J.D., P. Barrow, and R. Roos-Collins. 1989. Rivers at Risk. The Concerned Citizen's Guide to Hydropower. American Rivers.

The Aspen Institute. 2002. Dam Removal. A New Option for a New Century. 81 pp. http://www.aspeninst.org/eee/pdfs/damremoval option.pdf.

Trout Unlimited Small Dams Campaign. Multiple publications, and some may be downloaded free through http://www.tu.org.

- Dam Removal Success Stories: Restoring Rivers Through Selective Removal of Dams that Don't Make Sense (December 1999)
- Dam Removal: A Citizen's Guide to Restoring Rivers (November 2000)
- Taking a Second Look: Communities and Dam Removal (December 2000)
- Small Dam Removal: A Review of Potential Economic Benefits (October 2001)
- Exploring Dam Removal: A Decision-making Guide (Spring 2002)
- Removing Small Dams: A Practical Guide to Engineering and Other Scientific Considerations (Fall 2002)

Influencing the establishment of dams

Increasingly stringent environmental and safety protection laws have provided practitioners with tools to influence the building of future dams. Essentially, two points of entry exist for practitioners: educating water managers and technical staff regarding the establishment of a new dam or dams and using existing policies to influence the approval for future dams.

Many stakeholders, including conservation groups, would argue that engineers and managers should develop sustainable projects that are adaptable to changing environmental conditions and human communities. However, the current education

that dam designers and water resource managers receive does not provide significant instruction related to alternative dam structures and operational schemes to adequately prepare them to meet this challenge adequately. Broadening and modifying engineering curricula coupled with continued experiments to develop appropriate design and operation models would help provide more complete education in these areas (Jobin 1998). The establishment of dams may also be influenced by stakeholder participation in the: review of existing dams for compliance with relevant laws and achievement of established goals; preliminary assessments of the demand for a particular dam; permitting applications for future projects; and the establishment of monitoring criteria and the collection of data for evaluating project proposals and performance of existing dams. Stakeholders should also consider encouraging the review and acceptance of guidelines for new dams established by the World Commission on Dams (adapted from WCD 2000).

INSTITUTIONAL AND LEGAL STRATEGIES

Practitioners can work with or influence a wide range of institutions and legal authorities to safeguard and improve stream flow. These institutional and legal authorities are available at all levels of governance, from local to international. For example, local zoning ordinances and land use plans can be crafted to ensure adequate flows to protect riparian areas and wetlands. State and federal environmental and safety regulations have been used successfully to deny dam relicensing or require improved reoperation procedures. An increasing number of binational and international environmental agreements offer limited guidelines on safeguarding shared national water resources. While several watercourse treaties (e.g., United Nations Convention on the Law of the Non-navigational Uses of International Watercourses) refer to regulation of flows, the provisions focus on the role of flow for production, protection of commercial fisheries, and protection against flooding. No treaty yet addresses stream flow regulation for the protection of chemical, physical, and ecological integrity of the river system (IUCN 2002).

However, preliminary to developing specific institutional or legal strategies to abate the effects of a particular dam, practitioners should first ask and answer the following of basic questions about the dam:

What are the problems or issues of concern?

- Dam construction
- Dam reoperation
- Dam decommissioning

What are the goals of proposed activity (dam building, reoperation)?

- Economic development (irrigation, hydropower, industrial)
- Improved efficiency of dam operations
- Expansion of operations (e.g., increasing reservoir capacity)
- Improved safety operation
- Compliance with regulations (environmental, safety, other)

What are the goals of the stakeholders?

- Environmental (species protection, riparian and wetlands preservation)
- Economics (recreational opportunities, tourism, angling)
- Cultural preservation
- Safety considerations

What are the immediate threats?

- Habitat inundation
- Inadequate water for downstream wetlands
- Blockage of migratory passage for fish
- Water quality
- Increased salinization

What are the agencies/parties responsible for operation and maintenance of the dam?

- Private owner
- Municipality
- Water authority
- State or federal government agency

What are the instruments that can be utilized to change decision-making?

- Zoning regulations
- Hazard and safety laws
- Environmental protection laws
- Historical and cultural preservation laws
- Tribal protection laws
- Binational and international treaties and agreements

What institutions can be influenced?

- (Basin) commissions
- Water authorities
- Government agencies (local, regional, federal)
- International bodies (lending institutions such as the World Bank, IMF, Asian Development Bank; entities with responsibility for enforcing treaty conventions, environmental protection agencies, such as the United Nations Environment Program
- Dam owners and operators
- Public officials and community leaders

What is the timeframe of proposed action?

- Immediate
- Long-term

Is proposed activity part of a larger project?

- Regional flood control
- Regional water or power supply
- Restoration efforts
- Regional development

What type of strategy is most effective for influencing decision-makers?

- Lobbying public officials
- Lobbying agency officials
- Participation in information and public comment sessions
- Public information campaigns using media, rallies, meetings

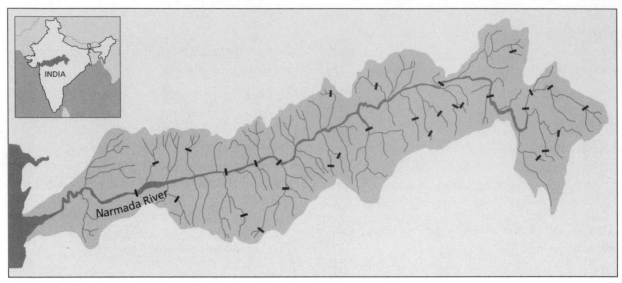

FIGURE 4-9. The thirty dams proposed, many of them already constructed, along the Narmada River, India

- Legal tools, including condemnation of facility and suits and appeals to higher court levels on basis of environmental, historical, cultural, and safety concerns and using existing instruments, such as the Endangered Species Act and the Clean Water Act in the U.S.
- Collaborative or cooperative compromises
- Designation as protected areas or areas of special concern (e.g., Wild and Scenic Rivers Act in the U.S.)
- Buyout of facility or land

Additional challenges may also exist, including the existing institutional structure does not facilitate participation in decision-making; environmental protection, safety and cultural as well as historical preservation laws are absent, inadequate, or insufficiently enforced; financial resources to pursue activities and legal challenges are lacking; data availability impedes abilities to assess current conditions, predict the impacts of proposed activities, and develop alternatives; etc. (WCD 2000). For example, the Indian government continues construction of multiple dams in the Narmada River Basin despite widespread local and international criticisms based on environmental, economic, safety, and human rights (e.g., displacement of

a large population and inadequate compensation) concerns and the withdrawal of World Bank funding (Friends of the River Narmada 2002).

The following section reviews in greater detail how some U.S. and international institutions and legal authorities can be used to affect policies regarding construction, relicensing, and decommissioning of dams.

U.S. institutions and legal authorities

Working with or influencing the Federal Energy Regulatory Commission

The Federal Energy Regulatory Commission (FERC) is an independent agency within the U.S. Department of Energy that regulates private, municipal, and state hydroelectric projects.[2] The FERC currently has authority over about 100 licenses and almost 600 exemptions, or approximately 96% of all private and publicly owned, non-federal hydropower dams; these totals represent approximately 43% of all hydropower facilities operating in the United States. FERC oversight includes the issuance of licenses for construction and continued operation of dams. It can issue licenses for periods up to 50 years after reviewing the engineering, environmental, and economic aspects of the pro-

---

[2] In contrast, the Bureau of Reclamation, U.S. Army Corps of Engineers, and the Tennessee Valley Authority have jurisdiction over federal hydropower facilities.

posal. The review process considers: (1) recommendations to mitigate adverse effects, (2) comments and recommendations submitted by other government agencies and stake-holders, and (3) proposals best adapted to a comprehensive plan for improving or developing a waterway for beneficial public uses. (FERC 2002b).

FERC policies and procedures permit public involvement with dam operations and construction and establish guidelines for mitigating negative impacts of dams. Specifically, they: (1) include opportunities for stakeholders to participate in the (re)licensing process, (2) require that its recommendations for mitigating adverse effects of a licensing proposal be based on the recommendations of federal and state fish and wildlife agencies and to negotiate with the agencies if disagreements occur, (3) require the same level of consideration to the environment, recreation, fish and wildlife, and other nonpower values as that given to power and development objectives in making a licensing decision, (4) prohibit licensees from using the right of eminent domain in parks, recreational areas, or wildlife refuges established under state laws, and (5) requires license applicants to fund environmental impact statements and other related studies.

As the original license expires, the relicensing becomes an unprecedented opportunity to promote river protection and flow mitigation plans. It allows agencies and stakeholders opportunities to examine the best hydropower operations and management for each project, taking into account current social and scientific knowledge. Since 1993, more than 150 projects have been relicensed and an additional 250 licenses will expire by 2010 (American Rivers 2002b). In its evaluation of environmental impacts, FERC is obligated to prepare an Environmental Impact Statement (EIS) or Environmental Assessment (EA), investigative reports that assess environmental consequences of a proposed hydropower project and compare the impacts with those of alternatives.

Opportunities for involvement and influence in hydropower dam operations are well articulated in American Rivers's *Hydropower Dam Reform Toolkit.* This Toolkit, which summarizes the 14-stage FERC hydropower dam relicensing process, can be found at http://www.amrivers.org/hydropowertoolkit/relicensing 14steps.htm.

In addition to the toolkit, the Hydropower Reform Coalition (HRC), a river conservation NGO,

published a guidance handbook in 1997 *Relicensing Tool Kit: Guidelines for effective participation in the FERC relicensing process.* HRC also supports local groups and may intervene in relicensings proceedings as a technical or legal consultant or organizer of community efforts. Additional information about improving river flows through relicensing can be found in *River Renewal: Restoring Rivers Through Hydropower Dam Relicensing,* by Rivers, Trails and Conservation Assistance Program, National Park Service, and American Rivers, 1996. Finally, interested parties seeking more information should consult the official and complete guidance listed in the *Federal Power Act 16 USC 791–828c* and its implementing regulations found at *18 CFR Parts 4 and 16.*

Working with or influencing the U.S. Army Corps of Engineers

The U.S. Army Corps of Engineers (the Corps) is the nation's largest water resource developer and the primary manager of some of the largest rivers in the U.S. including the Columbia, Illinois, Mississippi, Missouri, Ohio, and Snake Rivers. The Corps is responsible for managing numerous dams and other water regulation structures throughout the country that have severely disrupted hydrologic connectivity, destroying habitat and putting at risk hundreds of species. However, changing operation toward greater ecological sustainability has become of greater interest to the Corps as evidenced by the Sustainable Rivers Project (SRP). For more information about the SRP see http://www.freshwaters.org/eswm/sustrivs.

Working with or influencing the U.S. Bureau of Reclamation

As a water management agency, the Bureau of Reclamation (the Bureau) has constructed and manages more than 600 dams and reservoirs including Hoover Dam on the Colorado River and Grand Coulee on the Columbia River in the 17 western states. These projects are major sources of irrigation water, electric power, and recreation for the region, and like the Corps', these dams and water regulation structures have significantly altered natural flow regimes and contributed to the dramatic decline of

BOX 4-2. Case Study: Dam Reoperation on the Green River, Kentucky

The Green River is one of the crown jewels of freshwater biodiversity of the Southeast. It supports 151 freshwater species, including 12 endemic fish, 59 mussels, and an unparalleled collection of cave flora and fauna. Threats to the river include nonpoint source pollution from agriculture, competition and predation from exotic species, and land development. However, the predominant threat is hydrologic alteration, and the primary source is the U.S. Army Corps of Engineers operated Green River Dam in the river's headwaters. For more than thirty years the Corps has strictly regulated lake levels, down-stream flows, and water temperatures for recreation, irrigation, and flood control. As a result, there is rarely enough flow when the river should be flooding, far too much when it should be trickling, and the water is almost always too cold for its native inhabitants. Changing the operation of the Green River Dam was obviously critical to improving conditions for biodiversity.

The Nature Conservancy had been engaged in conservation efforts within the Green River watershed for some time. Although influencing the dam's operation was a great goal, staff had little experience to date in working with Corps staff to accomplish such a goal. When asked by the Corps "what would you like to see happen out there?" Conservancy staff began introducing the concept of natural flow regimes and efforts to reintroduce them in other parts of the country. Immediately, the engineer seemed to understand and sketched out feasible changes to the dam's release schedule which still met the Corps' flood control and recreation objectives and modified thirty years of standard practice. The Corps was also willing to modify water temperatures discharged from the reservoir to restore a more natural temperature regime. Important lessons that emerged from the initial Corps-TNC meeting were: (1) asking key questions is the first step in conserving freshwater biodiversity and (2) multiple stakeholders can work together cooperatively to meet multiple demands.

The experience on the Green River provides a platform for demonstrating that dams can be managed in a way that is ecologically sustainable. In 2002 the Corps launched the *Sustainable Rivers Project (SRP)*. Beginning with 12 dams from across the country, SRP will export lessons learned from the Corps-TNC collaboration on reoperating the Green River Dam. This will provide a broader basis for analyzing successes, problems, and solutions for reoperating Corps dams and is the next step toward achieving more ecologically sustainable flows at other Corps dams.

The Green River, Kentucky. Photograph by Lynda Richardson.

The Potomac River, here at Great Falls National Park, flows between the states of Maryland and Virginia. Photograph courtesy of the National Park Service.

many fish species, such as salmon (Brec 2002). As a public institution, the Bureau's decision-making process regarding facility operation can be influenced through public participation, such as open meetings and contact with elected and agency officials.

Working with or influencing river basin commissions

River basin commissions around the world provide guidance and set policies for management and development of particular river basins and are instrumental in providing information to communities and officials. Stakeholders in the United States can influence these commissions by participating in public meetings or working through commissioners and citizen advisory groups. Objectives of commissions include: (1) manage river compacts or agreements among regional, inter-state, or international parties, (2) provide a forum to study, discuss, and develop regional policies concerning water and related land resources, (3) coordinate water and land resources planning, (4) provide representation of regional interests before local, regional, and federal agencies, (5) investigate, study, and review water related problems and issues of interest to the member states, and (6) contribute to national and international water policies. Commissions may also form partnerships among interstate governmental organizations and other stakeholder organizations. For example, the Pecos River Compact Commission agreed in 2002 to augment Pecos River flow by pumping artesian aquifer water and to implement water supplies through removal of exotic salt cedars (State of New Mexico 2002), and the Potomac River Basin Commission sets standards, negotiates for loans, grants, etc., and institutes actions (PRBC 2002). In order to implement their goals, the Ohio River Basin Commission conducts studies, conferences, workshops, and information exchange as well as initiate policies (ORBC 2002). The Apalachicola-Chattahoochee-Flint River Basin Commission (ACF) was established 1997 to oversee development and implementation of a water use compact between Alabama, Georgia, and Florida including monitoring support and funding (Richter *et al.* 2003, Kerr and Reheis 2002).

International institutions and legal authorities

Internationally, numerous agreements exist regarding the utilization of waters in and other resources of rivers shared by two or more nations. More than one half of the 261 transnational river systems have commissions that monitor agreements and projects through the riparian states (DSE 1998). The

BOX 4-3. The Establishment of the Mississippi Headwaters Board

In the late 1970s, 650 km of the upper Mississippi River were identified as eligible for protection under the federal Wild and Scenic Rivers Act. Concerned about federal jurisdiction over more land in Minnesota, the state legislature created and funded the Mississippi Headwaters Board (MHB) to protect and preserve the natural, cultural, scenic, scientific, and recreational values of the headwaters. Formed in 1980 as an alternative to designation under the Wild and Scenic Rivers system, MHB includes representatives from the first eight counties that the Mississippi River flows through. MHB agreed to develop a river management plan to protect the river against development and pollution.

Since most of the land in this part of the Mississippi River is privately owned, MHB achieves its goal of river protection through cooperative land use planning, research, and stewardship and supports efforts of local citizens, government and NGOs to protect the river (MHB 2002). Working with the National Park Service, MHB developed and implemented protection and management plans and it was eventually recognized as a state authority.

Currently overseeing the longest stretch of protected river in the United States, MHB provides guidance to participating counties, insures compliance with regulations throughout the region, and acts as a safety valve for challenges to regulations by individuals and

The Mississippi River, near the Crow Wing River, Minnesota. Photograph courtesy of Parks and Trails Council of Minnesota.

businesses. As a state authority it can take action against major activities that have significant impacts on the river. MHB's primary tool is the establishment of minimum standards for residential lot sizes, building setbacks, sewage system design and placement, and cutting of vegetation, and it utilizes three strategies to carry out its responsibilities: regulation, monitoring, and stewardship. MHB relies on strict adherence to local land use regulations instead of employing federal regulations. Other local river protection groups have since emerged, including the Mississippi Headwaters River Watch, a citizen water quality monitoring program, and the Headwaters Heritage, a program of river stewardship activities designed to foster a philosophy of river protection.

Environment Program of the Mekong River Commission (Cambodia, Lao PDR, Thailand, and Vietnam) monitors the Basin's environmental health, develops policies and legislation, encourages cooperation among the riparian countries, and works to increase the public's environmental awareness (MRC 2002). The Mekong River Commission is responsible for adopting guidelines for the location and levels of flows and developing a mechanism to oversee interbasin diversions from the mainstem (IUCN 2002). Examples of other international commissions include the Rhine Basin Commission (Europe), Indus River Basin Commission (India, Pakistan), the Chad River Basin Commission (Cameroon, Central African Republic, Guinea, Mali, Chad, Niger, and Nigeria), Bermejo River Commission (Argentina and Bolivia), and the trinational Pilcomayo Commission (Argentina, Bolivia, and Paraguay).

These laws and treaties, as well as others summarized below, may prove instructive to those seeking guidance from the international arena. Although this section does not attempt to explore institutional and legal authorities surrounding dam removal and reoperation on a country-by-country basis, it does provide a list of useful resources, including important literature summarizing experience from around the world (see Table 4-1).

TABLE 4-1. International Institutions and Legal Authorities

International

Convention Relating to the Development of the Hydraulic Power of International Affecting More Than One State, and Protocol of Signature. Done in Geneva, 9 December 1923

UN Convention on the Law of the Non-navigational Uses of International Watercourses (May 1997)

Helsinki Rules on the Uses of the Waters of International Rivers, International Law Association (1966)

Madrid Declaration on Int'l Regulations Regarding the Use of Int'l Watercourses for Purposes other than Navigation, Institute of International Law, 24 Annuaire de l'Institut de Droit International (1911)

General Comment No. 15 (2002). The Right to Water, Substantive Issues Arising in the Implementation of the International Covenant on Economic, Social and Cultural Rights, U.N. (Economic and Social Council, E/C.12/2000/11 (26 November 2002)

Dublin Statement on the Water and Sustainable Development

UN Conference on Environment & Development (Rio de Janeiro/Brazil, June 1992), Chapter 18 - Protection of the Quality and Supply of Freshwater Resources: Application of Integrated Approaches to the Development, Management and Use of Water Resources

Agenda 21, Chapter 18: Protection Of The Quality And Supply Of Freshwater Resources: Application Of Integrated Approaches To The Development, Management And Use Of Water Resources

Dams and development: A New Framework for Decision-Making, The World Commission on Dams (2000)

Arechaga, F.J., International Legal Rules Governing Use of Waters from International Watercourse, 2 Inter-Am. L. Rev. 329 (1960)

Arechaga, F.J., International Legal Rules Governing Use of Waters from International Watercourse, 2 Inter-Am. L. Rev. 329 (1960)

Bradlow, D., Eckstein, G. *et al.*, Report on International and Comparative Water Law Applicable to Large Dam Construction, submitted to The World Commission on Dams as background for Dams and Development: A New Framework for Decision-Making Garretson, *et al.*, eds., The Law of International Drainage Basins (1967)

Lee, Terence R., Water Management in the 21st Century: The Allocation Imperative (Edward Elgar 1999)

Legge, D. The Sustainability of the Water Industry in a Regulated Environment, 12 J. Envtl. L. 3 (2000)

McCully, Patrick, Silenced Rivers: The Ecology and Politics of Large Dams (London: Zed Books 1996)

Palmieri, A., Bradlow, D. & Salman, S.M.A., Regulatory Frameworks for Dam Safety: A Comparative Study, World Bank (2002)

United Nations Food and Agriculture Organization, Systematic Index of International Water Resources: Treaties, Declarations, Acts and Cases, by Basin. Volume II. Legislative Study #34 (1984)

United Nations Food and Agriculture Organization, Systematic Index of International Water Resources: Treaties, Declarations, Acts and Cases, by Basin. Volume I. Legislative Study #15 (1978)

United Nations Food and Agriculture Organization, Sources of International Water Law, Legislative Study # 65 (1998)

Utton, Albert E. & Utton, John, International Law of Minimal Stream Flows, 10 Colo. J. Int'l Envt'l L. & Pol'y 7 (1999)

Sevette, Legal Aspects of Hydro-Electric Development of Rivers and Lakes of Common Interest, U.N. Doc. E/ECE/136 (1952)

Europe

Treaty for the International Commission for the protection of the Meuse and Scheldt Rivers (French) (German) (Dutch)

Convention on the International Commission for the Protection of the Oder. Done in Wroclaw, 11 April 1964

Vinogradov, Sergei & Langford, Vance P.E., Managing Transboundary Water Resources in the Aral Sea Basin: In Search of a Solution, 1 Int'l J. Global Envt'l Issues 345 (2001)

Pichyakorn, Bantita, Sustainable Development and International Watercourse Agreements: The Mekong and the Rhine, International(Union for the Conservation of Nature (Draft 30 June 2002)

(continues)

TABLE 4-1. *Continued*

Europe *continued*

Bostian, I.L., Flushing the Danube: The World Court's Decision Concerning the Gabcikovo Dam, 9 Colo. J. Int'l Envtl. L. & Pol'y 401 (1998)

Food and Agriculture Organization of the United Nations, Land and Water Legislation Section, Water Laws in Selected European Countries (1975)

Schwabach, Aaron, From Schweizerhalle to Baia Mare: The Continuing Failure of International Law to Protect Europe's Rivers, 19 Va. Envtl. L.J. 431 (2000)

Williams, Paul R., International Environmental Dispute Resolution: The Dispute Between Slovakia and Hungary Concerning Construction of the Gabcikovo and Nagymaros Dams, 19 Colum. J. Envtl. L. 1 (1994)

Middle East

Baim, Karen A., Come Hell of High Water: A Water Regime For the Jordan River Basin, 75 Wash. U. L. Q. 919 (1997)

Batstone, The Utilization of the Nile Waters, Int'l & Comp. L.Q. 523 (1959)

Caponera, Dante, Water Laws in Moslem Countries (1954)

Caponera, Dante, Water Laws in Moslem Countries (1973–78)

Carroll, C.M., Past and Future Legal Framework of the Nile River Basin, 12 Geo. Int'l Envt'l L. Rev. 269 (1999)

Chenevert, Donald J., Jr., Application of the Draft Articles on the Non-Navigational Uses of International Watercourses to the Water Disputes Involving the Nile River and the Jordan River, 6 Emory Int'l L. Rev. 495 (1992)

Cohen, Jonathan E., International Law and Water Politics of the Euphrates, 24 J. Int'l. L. & Pol. 503 (1991)

Kasimbazi, E., The Relevance of Sub-Basin Legal and Institutional Approaches in the Nile Basin 5 S. Afr. J. Envtl. L. & Pol'y (1998)

Kibaroglu, Aysegül, Building a Regime for the Waters of the Euphrates-Tigris River Basin, International and National Water Law and Policy Series: Volume 7 (Kluwer Law 2002)

North America

Treaty relating to cooperative development of the water resources of the Columbia River Basin (with Annexes), Done 17 January 1961

Treaty between the United States of America and Canada relating to the uses of the waters of the Niagara River. Signed at Washington, 27 February 1950; in force 10 October 1950

Colorado River Storage and Interstate Release Agreement among the United States of America, acting through the Secretary of the Interior; the Arizona Water Banking Authority; the Southern Nevada Water Authority; and the Colorado River Commission of Nevada

International Boundary and Water Commission, United States and Mexico, Minute 242, Permanent and Definitive Solution to the International Problem of the Salinity of the Colorado River, 30 August 1973

Treaty between the United States of America and Mexico relating to the utilization of the Waters of the Colorado and Tijuana Rivers and of the Rio Grande, signed at Washington February 3, 1944; protocol signed at Washington November 14,1944, Entered into force November 8,1945, 59 Stat. 1219; Treaty Series 994

Agreement between U.S. and Mexico, Re-diversion, Allocation and Equitable Division of the Waters of Rio Grande (May 21st, 1906) Consolidated Treaty Series, vol. 201 (1906); A.J.I.L., I, 281; U.S. stat, XXXIV, 2953; Mex. Tr. 1909, I, 318.

Treaty to Resolve Pending Boundary Differences and Maintain the Rio Grande and Colorado River as the International Boundary Between Mexico and the United States, 23 November 1970. 23 U.S.T. 371, T.I.A.S. No. 7313.

Fort, D.D., Restoring the Rio Grande: A Case Study in Environmental Federalism, 28 Envtl. L. 15 (1998)

Lopes, M., Border Tensions and the Need for Water: An Application of Equitable Principles to Determine Water Allocation from the Rio Grande to the United States and Mexico, 9 Geo. Int'l. Envtl. L. Rev. 489 (1997)

Central and South America

Treaty for Amazonian Co-operation. Done at Brasilia, 3 July 1978.(Bolivia, Brazil, Colombia, Ecuador, Guyana, Peru, Suriname, Venezuela

Argentina-Brazil-Paraguay: Agreement on Paraná River Projects (1979)

Treaty Between the Federative Republic of Brazil and the Republic of Paraguay Concerning the Hydroelectric Utilization of the Water Resources of the Paraná River Owned in Condominium by the Two Countries, From and Including the Salto Grande de Sete Quedas or Salto Del Guaira, to the Mouth of the Iguassu River (1973)

Agreement Between The Argentine Republic and the Republic of Paraguay Concerning a Study of the Utilization of the Water Power of the Apipe Falls, Done at Buenos Aires, 23 January 1958

Dourojeanni, Axel, Water Management at the River Basin Level: Challenges in Latin America, Serie Recursos Naturales e Infraestructura No. 29, LC/L.1583-P, (August 2001)

Legislacion de Aguas en Los Paises del Grupo Adino. (Water Legislation in the Andean Pact Countries)

Africa

Caponera, Dante, Water Law in Selected African Countries (Benin, Burundi, Ethiopia, Gabon, Kenya, Mauritius, Sierra Leone, Swaziland, Upper Volta, Zambia) (1979)

Chenevert, Donald J., Jr., Application of the Draft Articles on the Non-Navigational Uses of International Watercourses to the Water Disputes Involving the Nile River and the Jordan River, 6 Emory Int'l L. Rev. 495 (1992)

Kasimbazi, E., The Relevance of Sub-Basin Legal and Institutional Approaches in the Nile Basin 5 S. Afr. J. Envtl. L. & Pol'y (1998)

Lebotse, K.K., Southern African Community Protocol on Shared Watercourses: Challenges of Implementation, 12 Leiden J. Int'l L 173 (1999)

Leestemaker, Joanne Heyink, An analysis of the new national and sub national Water Laws in Southern Africa: Gaps between the UN-Convention, the SADC protocol and national legal systems in South Africa, Swaziland and Mozambique

Asia

Browder, Greg & Ortolano, L., The Evolution of an International Water Resource Management Regime in the Mekong River Basin, 40 Nat. Resources J. 499 (2000)

Caponera, D.A., The Legal Aspects of Mekong River Projects, 16 Indian J. Power & River Valley Devel. 35 (1966)

Desai, B., Sharing of International Water Resources: The Ganga and Mahalaki River Treaties, 3 Asia Pac. J. Envt'l Law 172 (1998)

Gheleta, M.A., Sustaining the Giant Dragon: Rational Use and Protection of China's Water Resources in the Twenty-First Century 9 Colo. J. Int'l. Envtl. L. & Pol'y 221 (1998)

Imhoff, Aviva, Power Struggle: The Impacts of Hydro-Development in Laos, in Conference on the Mekong River at Risk: The impact of development on the river, her delta, and her people, MekongForum (May 8, 1999)

Institute for the Development of Indian Law, Indian Water Rights (1984)

Salman, S.M.A. & Uprety, K., Conflict and Cooperation on South Asia's International Rivers, International and National Water Law and Policy Series: Volume 8 (Kluwer Law 2002)

Salman, S.M.A. & Uprety, K., Hydro-Politics in South Asia: A Comparative Analysis of the Mahakali and the Ganges Treaties, 39 Nat. Res. J. 395 (1999)

COMMUNITY-BASED STRATEGIES

Local citizen group efforts can be effective in river protection. While some communities depend on federal or state legislation to implement river conservation plans, others use local or regional mechanisms to organize and motivate officials and citizenry to develop alternative strategies.

Many communities struggle with decisions about whether to repair or remove old and obsolete dams, and some feel that the issues are too complex and require professional assistance and resources. Numerous local, regional, and national groups exist to help stakeholders develop and implement alternative strategies. Trout Unlimited and the Hydropower Reform Coalition are just two examples. Their activities include public education, organization, research, advocacy, project fundraising, and technical consulting.

Please refer to the following websites for information about other NGOs working on dam removal and reoperation strategies:

- International Rivers Network (IRN) strategy of communicating water-related threats to the international community
  http://www.irn.org/index.html
- American Rivers/Hydropower Reform Coalition
  http://www.americanrivers.org/
- Oregon Water Watch-instream flow rights acquisition
  http://www.waterwatch.org/
- American Whitewater (presents annual 'lemon' award—i.e., 'Hydromania Award' to call attention to environmentally detrimental hydropower projects)
  http://www.americanwhitewater.org/
- World Resources Institute
  http://www.wri.org
- IUCN Water and Nature Program
  http://www.iucn.org
- Global Water Partnership Program
  http://www.wsp.org/english/partnerships/gwp.html
- Inter-American Water Resources Network
  http://www.iwrn.net/mainenglish.html

SURFACE WATER DIVERSIONS

Introduction

Surface water diversions are structures—such conduits on dams or networks of drainage channels—that redirect water from a river, lake, or wetland for a multitude of purposes, including irrigation, domestic water supply, hydropower generation, transportation, flood control, and recreation. Surface water diversions for agriculture and other human demands in the United States contribute to the endangerment of fish species and other wildlife, especially in arid regions of the western states. Recent examples of species adversely affected by such diversions in the United States include the silvery minnow (*Hybognathus amarus*) in the Rio Grande River, Colorado pikeminnow (*Ptychocheilus lucius*) and Razorback sucker (*Xyrauchen texanus*) in the Colorado River, migratory and shorebird species in the Stillwater National Wildlife Refuge

wetlands, and Tui chub (*Gila bicolor*) and Lahontan cutthroat trout (*Oncorhynchus clarki henshawi*) in Walker Lake. Diversion of the Owens River (from Owens Lake to Los Angeles, California) in the early part of the 20th century for municipal supply resulted in near complete dewatering of the lake system and loss of freshwater biodiversity. The dry lakebed currently is the largest single source of fugitive dust[3] (including arsenic) per unit area in the United States, with production estimates ranging up to millions of tons annually (Cahill 1996).

Significant effects from diversions are not limited to the United States. Diversion of the Amu Dar'ya River and Syr Dar'ya River in Russia for agriculture caused the surface area of the Aral Sea to drop by more than 40%, the volume to shrink by 60%, and salinity concentration to increase threefold in less than 40 years. All 24 native fish species from the sea have been

---

[3] Fugitive dust is a type of nonpoint source air pollution consisting of small airborne particles that do not originate from a specific point such as a gravel quarry or exhaust. It originates in small quantities over large areas.

The Sierra Nevada to the West and the Inyo Mountains to the east frame a dried salt flat in the center of the photograph that used to be Owens Lake. In 1913 the Owens River, seen traversing the image from north to south, was diverted to the Los Angeles Aqueduct and Owens Lake quickly dried up. Image courtesy NASA Earth Sciences and Image Analysis Laboratory, Johnson Space Center.

extirpated, and the annual commercial fish harvest has been reduced from 40,700 metric tons to zero (Postel 1997). Dojran Lake, with a surface area of 42.5 km² and located on the border of Macedonia and Greece, likewise is shrinking as a result of direct extraction and diversion of streams that supply it. The lake has already dropped 2.5 meters from the minimum water level stipulated in a 1956 bilateral accord, destroying the historically productive fisheries and changing the lake system into marshlands (ENS 2001).

The harmful effects of surface water diversions are now reaching wetter regions of the world as well. For example, in the United States rapid metropolitan growth and increased dependency on irrigation agriculture have exacerbated interstate competition between Alabama and Georgia for the waters of the Alabama-Coosa-Tallapoosa, and between Alabama, Florida and Georgia for the waters of the Apalachicola-Chattahoochee-Flint Rivers. In the Great Lakes region, cumulative effects of five major

water diversions have changed lake levels. If constructed, the Chitose River diversion channel would harm Lake Utonai in Japan, a Ramsar Convention designated wetland (Ono 1996). Increased diversions of the Hadejia and Jama'are Rivers in Northern Nigeria have dramatically changed flooding episodes within the floodplains and threaten biodiversity of the wetlands (Acharya 1997). In the Amazon basin, lowered water levels resulting from extraction in tributaries have stranded Amazon River dolphins in drying pools, and many streams in the Caribbean National Forest (Puerto Rico) have no flowing water below municipal water supply intakes for up to several weeks, threatening the biotic integrity of the rivers and streams and causing significant mortality of shrimp and fish migrating between headwaters and coastal estuaries (Pringle 1997, Pringle *et al.* 2000, March *et al.* 1998, Benstead *et al.* 1999). The surface level of the Dead Sea (in the Middle East and shared by Jordan and Israel) is dropping by 50–70 cm annually as a result of water diversions for agricultural and industrial needs,

Caernarvon Freshwater Diversion Structure, just south of New Orleans on the Mississippi River, Louisiana. Photograph by Arthur Belala/USACE.

and in 40 years its length shrunk from 80 km to 50 km. There are proposals for a $1 billion project to pipe water from the Red Sea to the Dead Sea to stem the rapid shrinkage (BBC News 2002, UNDESA 2002).

Conflicts over water diversions also jeopardize relations between neighboring countries. Recently completed diversion projects on the Euphrates River in Turkey threaten to eliminate water for agriculture in downstream states of Iraq and Syria (Jehl 2002), and Lebanon's recent decision to pump water from the Wazzani River, a tributary to the south-flowing Jordan River, has exacerbated tensions between Israel and its neighbors (ENN 2002).

Interbasin water transfers (IBWT) are a specific form of surface water diversions involving the physical transfer of water from one geographically distinct watershed to another through conveyance systems (e.g., canals, pipes, tunnels), pumping, and storage facilities (Davies and Day 1998). Some transfer systems also use naturally occurring river and lake systems (and aquifers) as principle transit corridors or storage facilities. IBWT are often part of complex water management schemes with multiple objectives. Importantly, these transfers permit urban growth and agriculture in areas that would otherwise be constrained by insufficient water supply. IBWT, particu-

larly useful in arid areas, have been practiced for hundreds of years and today are essential aspects of water management in many countries and regions of the world, including much of Asia (especially India, China, and Russia), the Middle East, parts of Africa (especially southern Africa), and the United States (UNESCO 1999).

The Effects of Surface Water Diversions on Freshwater Ecosystems

Diversion channels reduce water flow in the main channel and direct it to an alternative channel or artificial canal. Water diversions affect river systems at scales ranging from an individual stream reach to entire water basins. Decreased water supply in rivers in the headwaters directly threatens aquatic, riparian, and wetland communities. These threats include changes to food supply, habitat availability, nutrient cycling, sediment loads, and water quality. As a result of reduced flushing capacity of the river, downstream deltas and estuaries become hypersaline and starved of sediments and important nutrients, seriously affecting local fisheries. Increasingly, waters of the Rio Grande River and the Colorado River do not reach their historic deltas and receiving bays due to diversions, offstream consumption, and drought conditions. In

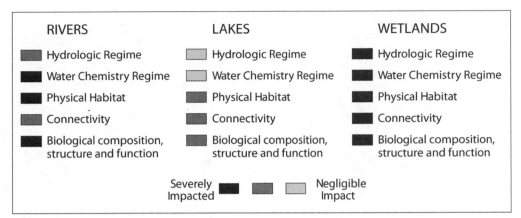

FIGURE 4-10. Summary of the Effect of Surface Water Diversions on Freshwater Ecosystems

some projects part of the diverted water is returned to the mainstem downstream from the diversion. Frequently, the water quality of this return flow is degraded from chemical pollution, pathogens, and sediment, making it unsuitable for freshwater organisms downstream.

The primary ecological threats of diversions are similar to those caused by dams. Please see the previous section on dams for a review of these impacts. The following subsections identify some of distinct effects of surface water diversions on specific key ecological factors of freshwater ecosystems, including the hydrologic regime, physical habitat conditions, the water chemistry regime, and biological composition and interactions.

Among surface water diversions, IBWT exert the most significant ecosystem changes, including the creation of new ecosystems very different from the natural systems they replace. Risks associated with such transfers of water include loss of biogeographic integrity and endemic biota, disruption of the hydrologic regime, impairment of water quality, spread of invasive alien species and diseases, and disruption of significant ecological processes (Davies *et al.* 1992, Arthington and Welcomme 1995). IBWT schemes facilitate the mixing of previously isolated biota, communities, and populations and seriously compromise the native freshwater biodiversity in these systems. For example, Spain's National Hydrological Plan will significantly change the aquatic environments of more than five river basins as well as the Ebro River delta, a Ramsar site and the third most important wetland in Spain (WWF 2001, Rivernet 2002). Figure 4-10 sum-

marizes these impacts of surface water diversions by freshwater ecosystem type.

THE HYDROLOGIC REGIME

Most diversion projects affect the hydrologic regime similarly to dams. Diversion projects regulate the amount and timing of water flow in a river. In many cases, floodplains are deprived of adequate water to support native vegetation and animal communities. Recent studies of four Ramsar-designated floodplains in Australia showed water diversion projects significantly altered the natural hydrology. These changes threaten biodiversity by reducing native aquatic vegetation cover and health, limiting suitable feeding and breeding habitat, and causing changes in water quality (Kingsford 2000).

The effects of water-level manipulation through surface water augmentation and diversion can also starve lakeside beaches. As a general rule, waves move sand onshore in summer and move sand offshore during winter storms. When lake levels are artificially increased (to augment water storage), sediments of drowned beaches are too deep to be carried to shore and wave action erodes material from newly created lake edges. This erosion releases soil organics, minerals, and nutrients into the lake, promoting water quality changes. When the lake level is artificially lowered, roots of near shore vegetation are exposed or deprived of adequate water, causing stress or dieback of vegetation. Loss of root mass can lead to increased soil erosion or collapse of undercut bank edges.

Salt build-up on a field in Colorado. Photograph by Tim McCabe/USDA NRCS.

IBWTs are particularly harmful to the hydrologic regime of both donor and receiving freshwater ecosystems since these transfers can affect all characteristics of the hydrologic regimes, and particularly flow, magnitude, timing, and frequency. Impacts of a transfer are location specific, may vary greatly over short distances, and are often relatively permanent. In donor systems, assuming a transfer of all water, the hydrologic regime will be completely eliminated for the stream reaches immediately downstream of the extraction point. The recipient system will experience greater magnitude of flow below the point of entry of the transferred water. Water transfers tend to stabilize flows along the transfer route, thereby reducing the magnitude and extent of the water-land interactions (e.g., periodic flooding).

CONNECTIVITY

Rivers with numerous diversion structures exhibit significant changes in connectivity. Surface water diversions, particularly when numerous, may decrease lateral connectivity between rivers and their floodplains, and the reduced flow as a result of the diversions may also harm longitudinal connectivity. These changes harm native fish breeding and migration patterns.

PHYSICAL HABITAT CONDITIONS

Surface water diversions affect physical habitat conditions by increasing the sediment load contributed to freshwater ecosystems by diversion-related return flows. This contribution is usually most significant the first time water passes through the structures or when the discharge is increased dramatically. Additionally, dewatered river reaches frequently erode following the establishment of a diversion channel as the river begins to degrade to a new equilibrium. In rivers where a structure diverts a significant portion of the flow, the capacity of the river to transport sediment below the structure declines as a result of decreased flows, causing increased deposition of fines (Glasser 2000). This condition can lead to burial of fish eggs and food sources and increased injury to fish resulting from abrasions to gills.

THE WATER CHEMISTRY REGIME

Pollution

Reduced flow as a result of surface water diversions increases pollutant concentrations, some of which migrate into groundwater supplies and move vertically into wetlands and riparian areas. Acidity often increases (lowering pH), thereby changing the solubility of metals and rates of chemical reactions in the water column (Glasser 2000).

Temperature

Water temperatures below diversions may increase during summer periods as a result of reduced flow. In regions of winter freezing, water bodies with reduced flows are subject to icing, creating problems for birds and other fauna dependent upon open-water feeding.

Salinization and Other Mineral Deposits

Decreased flows caused by diversions may elevate salinity levels in the floodplains and main channel, stressing riparian vegetation and aquatic biota below the diversion. Heightened salinity levels are unfavorable to many terrestrial and freshwater plants, causing dieback of native vegetation and invasion by salt tolerant species, such as *Tamarix spp.* (salt cedar). Salinization in heavily irrigated regions of the western U.S., as well as other arid regions of the world, has also resulted in the build-up of toxic elements naturally present in soils, such as boron (Lemly *et al.* 1993). The harm caused by these elevated concentrations may not be limited to the waterbody itself since these materials may blow onto adjacent land, including land used for agriculture. For example, water diversion dams have cut off most of the incoming freshwater to the Aral Sea in Kazakhstan and Uzbekistan. The resulting waterbody is shallower, less surface area, and has a high degree of salinization. In fact, today the water is saltier than seawater and salts exposed along the receding shoreline blow into adjacent agricultural areas, resulting in enormous losses in productivity (Nilsson and Berggren 2000).

Water Mixing Through IBWT

Alterations in flow regime and mixing of waters as a result of IBWT schemes also modify water quality. Changes include major ion and nutrient concentrations, thermal characteristics, pH, and transport and retention characteristics (Snaddon *et al.* 2000).

BIOLOGICAL COMPOSITION AND INTERACTIONS

Changes in channel morphology as a result of diversions alter aquatic and riparian community structure by contributing to the establishment of invasive alien vegetation and fish species (NSWEPA 2002) and contributing to the decline of numerous native fish species (Golladay and Hax 1995). Reduced inflows into bays are also responsible for reducing the recruitment of numerous estuarine and nearshore fauna such as shrimp, snook, and redfish; lowering reproductive success of pisciverous birds (e.g., ospreys and herons); and changing the distribution in mammals (e.g., West Indian manatees), reptiles (American crocodiles), and wading birds that nest in estuaries (McIvor *et al.* 1994).

IBWT significantly alter biological composition and interaction in river ecosystems by providing invasion routes for species (e.g., invasives, parasites, and diseases) into both donor and recipient catchments. This threat is particularly strong for river systems that have a high degree of endemism[4] or biodiversity. For example, invasive alien fish introduced to the Mekong River system through IBWT now threaten the inland fishing industry (Coates 2001). Fish introduced in the Mekong Basin in China are now appearing in Thailand (Vidthayanon and Kottelat 1995). In North America, nine species native to the Missouri River are expected to invade Lake Winnipeg (Manitoba, Canada) through the Garrison Diversion Project, a planned IBWT project in North Dakota. For an in-depth review of the effects of invasive alien species on freshwater ecosystems and strategies for abating these threats, please refer to the invasive alien species section of this subchapter that is dedicated to this topic.

Relatively small changes in velocity may interfere with behavior and life cycles of native species, and reduce the abundance of flow sensitive taxa (e.g., *Ephemeroptera heptagenii* (mayflies) and *Trichoptera leptocerid* and *Micronecta poweri* (caddisflies)) (Gibbins *et al.* 2000, Snaddon and Davies 1998). Reduced water flows can also interfere with the stimulus required for breeding migrations by diadromous fish. Increased sediment loads of the recipient river will reduce photosynthesis and zooplankton production, reducing overall food sources for fish stock (Yu 1983).

---

[4] Endemism describes species that are locally evolved within a particular geographic area and are found nowhere else on Earth. Endemism usually occurs in geographically isolated areas.

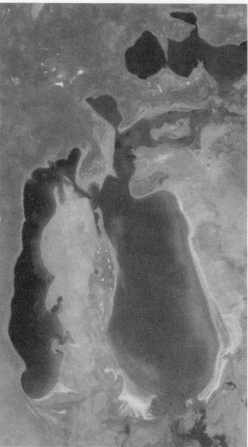
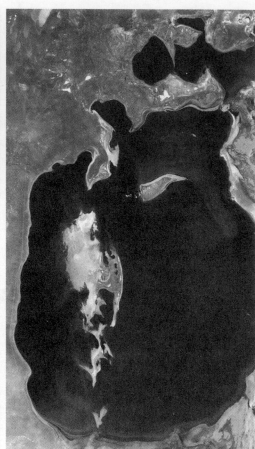

The Aral Sea, of Kazakhstan and Uzbekistan, in 1989 (right) and 2003 (left). Once the fourth largest lake in the world, the Aral Sea has shrunk in recent decades due to diversions for agriculture from the rivers that feed the lake. The exposed salty soils are blown into the surrounding lands, contaminating the soil. Images courtesy NASA Earth Observatory (http://earthobservatory.nasa.gov/).

Strategies for Mitigating/Abating the Effect of Surface Water Diversions on Freshwater Ecosystems

The following section identifies some strategies that have been used successfully to abate the effects of surface water diversions on freshwater ecosystems. These strategies include technical and legal or institutional efforts to promote more efficient water use, maintain natural flow patterns, and integrate technological features and operational procedures.

TECHNICAL STRATEGIES

Technical strategies to abate threats to freshwater ecosystems from surface water diversions include diverting or reallocating water back to natural areas, implementing less environmentally damaging diversion structures, promoting water conservation measures, and restoring, enhancing, and creating wetlands.

These strategies often develop in response to market forces and legal challenges to water rights.

Diverting water from irrigation projects back to natural areas

Irrigation water may be reallocated to natural areas, such as wildlife refuges or rivers, to protect biodiversity. Reallocation to these areas involves solving complex legal, administrative, and technical issues. The process is complicated in part because every political area has its own policies and laws governing water rights, transfers, and uses. Additionally, water rights laws may create obstacles or limit water allocation for instream use.

Reallocating more water and reestablishing the natural flow to such natural areas can improve habitat, food supply, water quality, and reproductive success of aquatic and riparian wildlife. For example, the U.S. Central Valley Project Improvement Act of 1992 increased water allocation to wetlands and wildlife refuges in the Central Valley of California annually by 413,219,000 m³ and provided for additional purchases of water from willing sellers. The dedicated yield provision of the legislative mandate also increased instream flows in California's Trinity River and Central Valley rivers. Results have been encouraging: decreased selenium concentrations, increased food production for migrating birds and other wetland-dependent wildlife, and vastly improved stocks of Chinook salmon and other anadromous fish populations (NRLC 1997).

Water reallocation projects may be carried out on both public lands and private holdings. However, in the United States as well as other countries, large scale changes in water allocation involving government projects may trigger the need to comply with national and state requirements, including environmental assessments and consideration of alternatives. See for example the National Environmental Policy Act, or the state equivalents, in the United States.

Some of the most successful reallocation efforts result from buyouts of water rights from willing sellers. This approach has the dual benefit of providing economic incentives to the seller as well as establishing a minimum instream flow for conservation purposes. In some cases, irrigators may realize that their operations will not be adversely affected by reduced water delivery as a result of efficiencies in operation, changes to crops requiring less water, or reduced acreage of irrigated crops. In other cases, the economics of irrigated cropland may create unfavorable conditions for farmers and they may elect to retire the land from crop production, possibly freeing up water for reallocation back to the stream.

Implementing less environmentally damaging diversion structures

Low head diversion dams can be formidable barriers to a wide range of migratory species, causing high rates of mortality of some aquatic species, particularly during low flow periods (Benstead 1999). The french tile drain system offers an alternative to these dams. It consists of a series of risers that siphon off river water and convey it to a point outside the streambed. The water is then transferred through a pipe by gravity feed or pumping facility for storage to a reservoir constructed outside the immediate vicinity of the river. The reservoir may be equipped with a sediment pond to prevent the build-up of sediments. This type of water withdrawal and storage facility has the advantage of: (1) creating minimal alteration of channel morphology, (2) providing continuous water flow in stream channel, (3) providing maximum control of water intake (to protect against entrainment of larvae and to trap sediment), and (4) reducing reservoir construction and maintenance costs (because it eliminates the need for a temporary diversion of the river water). A successful 5.5-million m³ reservoir prototype was constructed off of the Río Fajardo, Puerto Rico (March *et al.* 2003).

The Upper Colorado Recovery Implementation Program (Recovery Program) is an example of changes in structural design and procedure to minimize operational spills that currently pass through the Government Highline (diversion) Canal in Colorado. The project was designed to reduce water diversion demand by 11–20 m³ per second, thereby saving water in the mainstem. Prior to this restoration project, river flows below the diversion were significantly reduced and 40 km of critical river habitat were significantly altered, threatening fish stocks, including the endangered *Ptychocheilus lucius* (Colorado pikeminnow) and *Xyrauchen texanus* (razorback sucker). The Recovery Program includes: (1) construction of new check dams and expansion of existing ones, (2) addition of a pumping station and pipelines, (3) installation of monitoring and control equipment and software for improved management of water flow through the canal, and (4) changes in operational procedures. The $2–$3 million for the infrastructure improvements was funded primarily by direct federal and state appropriations and hydropower user fees. This project was a multi-stakeholder, consensus-based collaborative effort in which complex legal issues of water rights and instream flows were addressed and the agricultural community retained access to water (USFWS 2002a; Tom Iseman, The Nature Conservancy, *personal communication*). Additional information about the recovery program for endangered fish on the Colorado River is found at the following web site: http://mountain-prairie.fws.gov/coloradoriver/Index.htm.

The Government Highline Canal at Camp 7 headgate near Grand Junction, Colorado. Photograph by Joe Sullivan/USGS.

Promoting water conservation measures

Water is wasted in every sector of society. By implementing water conservation strategies, water demand to meet human needs can be reduced and sometimes additional supplies provided to meet ecosystem needs. This nonstructural approach to water management incorporates water efficiency technologies, appropriate economic incentives, and institutional tools (Gleick 2000). Estimates suggest that in the agricultural sector, producers can cut water consumption by more than 50% without any change in economic output or change in lifestyle. Water use can be cut 40–90% in the industrial sector and by more than 30% for domestic and municipal consumption (Postel 1997).

Water conservation involves changes to engineering practices (e.g., modifications to plumbing, fixtures, or water supply operating procedures) and behavioral practices (e.g., modifications in water use habits). Both policy and technology are necessary for conservation strategies to be effective. Policy efforts include pricing structures that reflect actual total costs in water delivery, incentives (e.g., financial) to encourage conservation, national standards for water delivery

and consuming appliances and machinery, availability and distribution of water-saving devices (e.g., low-flush toilets, low flow shower heads), accounting systems to ensure compliance with water conservation goals, and educational campaigns. Technology inputs include improved water conveyance systems and monitoring of losses; improved appliances, machinery, and manufacturing processes; and allocation strategies. The following section highlights engineering and behavioral practices that can be implemented to achieve higher water use efficiency in agricultural and urban sectors.

Agriculture

Many irrigation systems are very inefficient. In fact, often less than half the water diverted for irrigation actually benefits crops. Inefficiencies result as water (1) seeps out of unlined canals as it is transported to fields, (2) evaporates from canals and soil, (3) evaporates as its being applied, (4) is delivered to plants on a fixed schedule that does not match the plants' needs, and (5) evaporates from between plant rows (WWI 2002).

Additionally, many water management systems encourage wasteful practices. The cost of water is relatively cheap in some parts of the world (e.g., the U.S.), and in other parts (e.g., India and Pakistan), the government subsidizes these costs. Current water rights legislation in many parts of the U.S. promotes inefficient water use since the rights tend to work on a "use it or lose it" basis: if full allocation is not used in one year, the amount allotted in subsequent years may be reduced. Inefficiencies in water management and cultivation of water intensive crops (e.g., cotton, alfalfa, corn) in semi-arid areas require large amounts of water which often is applied to fields in excess amounts. Excessive irrigation also degrades soil fertility through salinization or waterlogging seriously limiting production.

Efficient water management can substantially improve agricultural productivity while minimizing water use. Reduced demand is transferred up the system and results in less water being diverted from a river or extracted from a lake. The saved water can be used to (1) replace return flow, (2) reallocate for other farm or domestic uses, (3) sell at a price that reflects the value of water (not just the cost), and (4) reduce the environmental impacts of irrigation including issues of quantity and quality (Clyma and Shafique 2001). Saved water has an effective value much greater than the actual value of the return flows because of its low concentrations of dissolved mineral salts as well as other potential benefits.

Efficient use technologies have been developed to go hand-in-hand with improved management practices. Some technologies include:

- check structures to improve control of water supply;
- regulation reservoirs for short term storage of water during periods of high water supply;
- pressurized pipelines to replace dirt laterals (irrigation ditches);
- sprinkler and drip irrigation to replace fill and furrow irrigation;
- lining the canal system with concrete to minimize leakage;
- laser leveling of fields; and
- improved accuracy to measure water released and consumed.

Urban use

Significant gains have been made in urban water use efficiency in the past decade. Engineering practices for improved conservation include:

- Installation of low-flow showerheads (9.5 liters per minute);
- Installation of low-flush toilets (6 liters). (A water conservation project in Mexico City involving the replacement of 350,000 toilets has saved enough water to supply 250,000 additional residents (Postel 1997));
- Installation of faucet aerators, reducing water needs by 60% while maintaining a strong flow; and
- Installation of pressure reduction mechanisms.

Improvements to industrial processing or manufacturing (e.g., metals, chemical, paper) result in large water use reductions. For example, steel making today requires 10 to 16 times less water than it did 70 years ago (Gleick 2000). Aluminum and plastics, which require less water to manufacture, are now commonly used as replacement materials for steel.

Water is also lost through evaporation and seepage from storage and conveyance structures. Estimates of the amount of water lost vary depending on structure design, material used for storage and conveyance structures, climatic conditions, and operation of the facilities. Average amount of water lost through evaporation in the U.S. West is six percent; however, in some reservoirs it may exceed 40%. Methods for controlling evaporation loss include surface-area reduction, reflective coatings, surface films, and mechanical covers. Seepage occurs through the sides and bottom of reservoirs and the canal system. The amount lost through seepage is estimated at about five percent in the western U.S. Seepage control is easier and less costly than evaporation control and currently includes use of rigid surface linings (e.g., concrete, asphalt, etc.), membranes, and soil sealants on the bottoms and sides of the canal and reservoir system (OTA 1983).

Treated wastewater is another valuable water source. An increasing number of communities use recycled water to recharge aquifers, supply industrial processes, maintain public gardens and space, irrigate certain crops, augment potable water supply, and

Drip irrigation waters young grape vines in California's Imperial Valley. Drip irrigation's efficiency comes from delivering small amounts of water over long periods of time, reducing water loss to evaporation. Photograph by Tim McCabe/USDA NRCS.

supplement natural flow in rivers and wetlands. The advantages of wastewater are that it offers a reliable supply of a known quality and is usually located near centers of demand (Gleick 2000).

For more information on how to conserve water and use it effectively, please see http://www.hireskip.com/enviro/keyissues2c.htm-conserve.

Restoring, enhancing, and creating wetlands

Surface water diversions significantly diminish wetland acreage, although wetlands have also been reduced as a result of hydrologic alteration from dams and land conversion to other uses. Accordingly, wetland restoration is also a relevant technical strategy appropriate for other sections of this module as well. Wetland restoration may contribute to improved surface flow hydrology and water quality, wildlife enhancement, wastewater treatment, mine drainage, and stormwater retention and control (Mitsch and Gosselink 1993). Wetland restoration measures include reestablishing former wetlands and/or repairing damaged ones. The former leads to a net gain in wetland acreage while the latter restores or improves the functional capacity of damaged systems. Additionally, wetlands may be enhanced or created.

Enhancement involves changing the condition of an existing wetland to strengthen or favor one or more of its functions, such as benefiting waterfowl or shorebirds. Creation involves building a wetland where one never existed (Tiner 1998). This is often attempted as a mitigation or compensatory effort to satisfy regulations governing wetlands protection. For example, provisions under the U.S. federal wetlands protection acts require the creation of wetlands as a substitute or mitigation for unavoidable loss of wetlands to other land uses. The Ramsar Convention likewise requires participating countries to provide compensatory measures, including habitat recreation or restoration, for loss of designated wetlands under the convention (DEFRA 2002).

Restoring the hydrologic regime, establishing hydric soils and nutrient flux, having an available seed source, and minimizing the impact of exotic plant species all contribute to the success of wetland restoration, enhancement, and creation efforts. Prior land use is also an important factor for success. Restoration is usually more successful than wetland creation for the following reasons: (1) the site is a former wetland and therefore can support desired functions, (2) soils are frequently in place, (3) the original hydrology can often be restored, and (4) it usually has

A restored wetland in Iowa. Photograph by Lynn Betts/USDA NRCS.

a natural seed-bank of hydrophytes to facilitate reestablishment of the plant community (Tiner 1998). The efforts of the Chilika Development Authority (State of Orissa), India, are an example of repairing damaged wetlands. A major component of the project was restoration of natural water flow and salinity levels in the 116,500-ha Chilika Lake, a Ramsar Site.

For more detail and descriptions on the ecology of wetlands and planning, implementation, monitoring, and management of wetland restoration and creation projects, please refer to the following publications and websites:

1. Interagency Working Group on Wetlands Restoration (National Ocean and Atmospheric Administration, Environmental Protection Agency, Army Corps of Engineers, Fish and Wildlife Service, and the Natural Resources Conservation Service). 2003. "An Introduction and User's Guide to Wetland Restoration, Creation, and Enhancement." Washington, DC http://www.epa.gov/owow/wetlands/finalinfo.html.

2. Tiner, R. 1998. In Search of Swampland. A Wetland Sourcebook and Field Guide. Rutgers University Press, New Brunswick, NJ.

3. Mitsch, W.J. and J.G. Gosselink. 1993. Wetlands. 2nd edition. VanNostrand Reinhold, New York, NY.

4. The Ramsar Convention on Wetlands. The Ramsar Convention's Resources on Wetland Restoration http://www.ramsar.org/strp_rest_index.htm.

5. Kentula, M.E. 1999. Restoration, Creation, and Recovery of Wetlands. Wetland Restoration and Creation. National Water Summary on Wetland Resources. U.S. Geological Survey Water Supply Paper 2425. http://water.usgs.gov/nwsum/WSP2425/restoration.html.

6. Northern Prairie Science Center and Midcontinent Ecological Science Center. 1996. Wetland restoration bibliography. (Version30SEP2002) http://www.npwrc.usgs.gov/resource/literatr/wetresto/wetresto.htm.

INSTITUTIONAL AND LEGAL STRATEGIES

Understanding the legal framework governing water rights, transfers, and allocation is important to work effectively with institutions and develop mitigation strategies for surface water diversions. The following is a summary of institutional and legal strategies for

A Chilika Lake, India, a fisherman shows off his catch. Photograph by Najam Khurshid/Ramsar.

IBWTs as well as more generalized strategies for the abatement or mitigation of surface water diversion threats in the U.S. as well as abroad.

U.S. institutional and legal authorities

In the United States, property rights in water are usually governed under state law according to one (or a combination of)[5] the following two legal regimes: Riparian Doctrine and Prior Appropriation Doctrine. Where water is relatively abundant in the U.S., such as in most of the eastern states, water allocation laws are grounded in the Riparian Doctrine. This system recognizes the right of a riparian owner to make reasonable use of the stream's flow. Reasonable use of water generally implies that landowners may use all the water they need for drinking, household purposes, and watering livestock, and this right is not lost by nonuse. Many states have modified the Riparian Doctrine by regulating use through issuance of permits for specified amounts of water and by restricting use in certain areas.

The Doctrine of Prior Appropriation governs the use of water in many western states where water is scarce, such as in the Southwest and Rocky Mountains. It operates from the fundamental principle first in time, first in right and is based on use rather than land ownership. By law, the waters of a state belong to the public, but individuals are granted permanent rights to take water out of a river regardless of instream needs as long as the water is put to "beneficial use" without waste. Additionally, the first party to use water (called a senior appropriator) acquires the right (called a priority) to its future use as against later users (called junior appropriators). Because this legal regime conveys rights to water due to actual use, it includes little inherent incentive for protecting instream water uses. States can address this deficiency and create incentives and a framework for protecting instream flows through legislation, judicial decisions, and agency actions. They may also consider purchasing or leasing senior water rights to augment instream flow as discussed below (Castle 1999, Shane 2001, WaterWatch 2002).

Surface water diversions take on an international dimension for water basins that cross international

---

[5] California, Texas, and Florida recognize both the Prior Appropriation Doctrine and the Riparian Doctrine.

boundaries. However, with the exception of the Agreement on the Cooperation for the Sustainable Development of the Mekong River Basin (between Cambodia, Lao PDR, Thailand, and Vietnam), there are no international treaty practices that expressly guarantee environmental flows. The United Nations Convention on *Law of the Non-Navigational Uses of International Watercourses* addresses the issue of equitable water allocation among riparian states but does not specifically identify instream flow; it commits participating states to protect the international watercourses and their ecosystems.

Returning water to streams through the acquisition of water rights

In the U.S., water rights may be obtained by a variety of mechanisms, including purchase or lease. These approaches are particularly important for protecting streams from drying up completely during low flow periods. In addition to states purchasing such rights, precedent also exists for federal water rights purchases.

Some private organizations, including The Nature Conservancy and the Audubon Society, have been actively protecting instream flow through market arrangements as well. Private sector involvement, especially by nonprofit organizations, has become more common in response to the unpopularity of the federal involvement in state water matters. However, this opportunity is limited by statutory regulations. Adhering to the generally strong stance of defenders of private property rights of water, many western states do not permit private parties to apply for, purchase, or own water rights for instream purposes; some states extend this prohibition even to public entities when the purpose is instream flow augmentation. In Idaho, Kansas, and Utah, instream appropriations or minimum flows that are recommended by state agencies must be approved by the state legislature (Gillilan and Brown 1997).

Water rights have been leased as a temporary solution to instream flow problems or as part of a larger, habitat protection effort. For example, in the winter 1988–89, The Nature Conservancy and the Trumpeter Swan Society each rented 3,947,142 m^3 (3,200 acre-feet) of water from a water bank. Supplemented by a 12,334,818 m^3 (10,000 acre-feet)

donation from the Snake River Water District 1, the water was released into Henry's Fork of the Snake River to help break up ice that had formed over the river and prevented birds from accessing their aquatic food supply. Another purchase of water rights was initiated to assess the effects of improved winter streamflow on fisheries of the North St. Vrain Creek in Colorado. A consortium of interest groups (e.g., Trout Unlimited, the local water conservancy district, and local municipalities) used primarily public funds to purchase 740,000–1,233,500 m^3 per year for the five-year study at an annual cost of $8,000 to $14,000.

Returning water to streams through the application of statutory laws

Laws—including statutes and judicial decisions, international treaties, and legislative mandates—are effective instruments for protecting freshwater systems threatened by diversions. Statutory laws in the U.S., such as the Endangered Species Act (ESA), have successfully challenged proposed water projects or required implementation of mitigation strategies. For example, six national, regional, and local conservation groups filed a lawsuit claiming federal water managers failed to recover the endangered Rio Grande silvery minnow and southwestern willow flycatcher in violation of the federal Endangered Species Act (ESA) and the National Environmental Policy Act (NEPA). The ESA was also used to increase instream flow in the Klamath River Basin.

The Boundary Waters Treaty of 1909 is a precedent-setting international agreement between the U.S. and Canada regulating diversions that affect the hydrology and water quality of the Great Lakes. It stipulates that "no further or other uses or obstructions or diversions, whether temporary or permanent, of boundary waters on either side of the line, affecting the natural level or flow of boundary waters on the other side of the line shall be made except by authority of the United States or the Dominion of Canada within their respective jurisdictions and with the approval, as hereinafter provided, of a joint commission, to be known as the International Joint Commission" (CGLG 2002). The U.S. Supreme Court upheld this treaty in a 1967 challenge seeking increased flows through the Michigan Diversion.

A diversion structure on North St. Vrain Creek, Colorado. Photograph by Nicole Rousmaniere.

Decreasing the need for diversions through improved efficiencies and decreased demand

Construction and maintenance costs of most major water diversion projects are publicly financed and the cost of such "improvement" is usually not or is only minimally passed on to consumers. Absence of market forces in water projects is a legacy of an earlier era of federally sponsored reclamation projects that fostered agricultural development in the western states. Such policies often encourage overuse of water and inefficiencies in the system. For example, in many western states, water policies promote rapid extraction and excessive use of water (MacDonnell and Bates 1993). There are signs that this mindset is changing through modification of water use policies, advances in technology, and improved collaboration among interested parties. As a result of dwindling financial resources and increased awareness of environmental impacts, there is less political will and community support to develop new water diversion projects, and existing ones are under increased scrutiny to improve efficiency (MacDonnell 1999, MacDonnell and Bates 1993).

Water regulators themselves may implement programs to improve the efficiency of current water uti-lization. For example, during a drought period in the mid-1990s, the Roza Water District in the Yakima watershed (Washington) initiated programs that encouraged conversion from low-value, water intensive, agricultural crops (e.g., alfalfa) to high value crops (e.g., fruit). In an effort to minimize diversions from the Truckee River (Nevada), the Truckee-Carson Irrigation District: (1) established targets for project efficiency[6] at the individual farm level; (2) employed a penalty system for failure to meet them; (3) made changes in use of the existing system of regulatory reservoirs; and (4) shortened the irrigation season. However, sometimes such imposed efficiencies have unintended negative effects when the ecology of the system is not fully understood. The efforts described above associated with the Truckee-Carson Irrigation District led to less water being available for the Stillwater Wetlands located at the terminus of the reclamation project managed by the District.

Improved cooperative efforts and resource sharing are also gaining acceptance. Cooperative management processes involving multi-party interests increasingly shape water use policies. For example, in 1995 the adjacent Roza and Sunnyside Water Districts (Washington) agreed to form a Board of Joint Control under which

---

[6] Project efficiency is defined as the water delivered at the farm headgates divided by the total project diversion

they shared some functions and employees while remaining independent entities. In this arrangement, the Roza District funds improvements for the Sunnyside District in return for a share in the conserved water (MacDonnell 1999). Citizen groups engaged in watershed protection also fulfill similar purposes.

Finally, water conservation strategies can result in a significant reduction of current water demand. The broad policy objective of water conservation is to reduce unneeded uses of water for expansion of service, or to minimize the amount diverted from streamflow. In order to achieve this objective some states are beginning to adopt laws encouraging water conservation. However, policy reforms that emphasize demand

reduction can be carried out at local, state and federal government levels. These reforms include:

- Regulatory tools
  - **permitting**—implement new legislation calling for effective and appropriate permitting systems.
  - **enforcement**—improve enforcement of laws by providing adequate resources and eliminate redundancies in the enforcement system.
  - **market creation**—establish legal frameworks designed to let free-market forces effect changes. Water markets are becoming increasingly popular and can help manage water demands within the existing supply system.

Box 4-4. Stillwater National Wildlife Refuge, Carson and Truckee Rivers, Nevada

The Stillwater National Wildlife Refuge complex is an important oasis for wildlife in the arid western U.S. It encompasses a great diversity of habitats, including freshwater marshes and rivers, brackish-water marshes, alkali playas, extensive salt desert shrublands, desert lake and island subunit, and a 40 km long sand dune complex. This diversity of habitats

Photograph by George Gentry/USFWS.

supports nearly 400 species of vertebrates including more than 260 resident and migratory bird species. The associated wetlands are critical to Pacific Flyway waterfowl and shorebirds. In 1988 the Stillwater National Wildlife Refuge complex was dedicated as a Western Hemisphere Shorebird Reserve in recognition of its importance to migratory shorebirds and waterfowl. It is a stopover for as many as 350,000 ducks and an equal number of shorebirds. Located about 113 km east of Reno, Nevada, in the Carson Desert of the Great Basin, this 66,367-hectare conservation area includes the Stillwater National Wildlife Refuge (NWR), Stillwater Wildlife Management Area (WMA), Fallon NWR, and the Anaho Island NWR. This complex has no outflow.

The Truckee and the Carson Rivers historically provide the main source of river water flowing into the complex, but these rivers have been significantly altered for irrigation and other uses. Since the Stillwater complex is an aquatic system with no outflow and a high evaporation to precipitation ratio, the wetlands are particularly susceptible to water quality degradation from irrigation return flow. Incoming contaminants in the water are trapped and accumulated, thus exposing wildlife to elevated concentrations (summarized by Pringle 2000). These conditions were responsible for high rates of mortality among birds, fish, and invertebrate taxa in 1986–1987.

In an effort to improve water quality and habitat in Stillwater NWR complex, The Nature Conservancy, in partnership with the Nevada Waterfowl Association and the State of Nevada, began purchasing water rights for the refuge in 1989. The purchased water was allowed to return to the wetlands through the irrigation system. Subsequently, the Water Settlement Act of 1990 authorized a federal agency to purchase water rights to decrease the agricultural demand and consequently support wetland needs. This precedent setting action illustrated the potential of transferring water rights from agriculture for environmental needs. The federal policy specified that 154,185,230 m^3 of water was needed annually to sustain 10,117 hectares of Lahontan Valley wetland habitat over the long term. As of September 2001, approximately 39,964,811 m^3 of water rights had been acquired from willing sellers (USFWS 2002b) through a partnership with the State of Nevada, The Nature Conservancy, the Bureau of Reclamation, and the Bureau of Indian Affairs. Communities affected by reduced irrigation waters, namely Churchill County and the City of Fallon, have repeatedly challenged these purchases in court in an attempt to gain increased water diversions.

- Financial assistance
  - **research funding**—for improved technologies and management strategies.
  - **producer payments**—use of payment subsidies as incentives for water users to adopt better water management practices.
  - **taxbreaks and business incentives**—to encourage initiatives geared toward increased water efficiencies.

- Education
  - **technical advice and oversight**—informational resources, including clearinghouses, to aid in creation and operation of water management initiatives.
  - **educational programs**—for water consumers to implement Best Management Practices.
  (Adapted from Covalla *et al.* 2001)

Using existing government incentives to diminish surface water diversions to protect wetlands

Wetlands may be intentionally destroyed through draining or indirectly altered through modifications to a river's natural flow as a result of surface diversions. Examples of wetland destruction as a result of changes to a river's flow patterns include upper Klamath Basin (TCWN 2002), Mono Lake Basin (Living Lakes 2003), Murrumbidgee River (Kingsford and Thomas 2001), and the Colorado River (Nabhan and Holdsworth 1998). In response to the significant loss of wetlands in the United States, the federal government offers incentives programs to protect and rehabilitate wetlands on private holdings through the Farm Bill. The recently passed 2002 Farm Bill maintains and expands these wetland protection programs:

- The Farmable Wetlands Pilot Program to help producers improve the hydrology and vegetation of farmable wetlands and associated buffers.
- Wetlands Reserve Program (WRP) provides payments for restoring and protecting wetlands.
- Desert Terminal Lakes program provides funding for at-risk desert lakes including associated wetlands.
- The Environmental Quality Incentives Program (EQIP) provides support for surface and ground-

water conservation efforts such as improvements to irrigation and conversion to less water intensive crops through cost-sharing, incentive payments, and loans.
(NRCS 2002)

Legislation creating economic disincentives for wetland conversion have also proved useful. In the U.S., the Swampbuster provision of the 1985 Food Security Act denies federal farm program benefits to landowners or farmers who drain protected wetlands. Under this Act, $11 million of benefits were denied to producers representing 6,070 hectares. Additionally, the Tax Reform Act of 1986 eliminated a provision that allowed capital investment in drainage and land clearing to be treated as annual expenses and preferential tax treatment for capital gains (Heimlich *et al.* 1998).

Section 404 of the Clean Water Act is the nation's primary wetlands regulatory authority, which the U.S. Army Corps of Engineers (the Corps) is responsible for administering. The Corps also administers the Rivers and Harbors Act of 1899. Both the Clean Water Act and the Rivers and Harbors Act can be used to protect wetlands by regulating activities that involve the discharge of dredged material. Before such a project begins, the Corps must first issue a permit. A public notice and comment period may be requested before the permit is issued, and this mechanism allows interested parties to present concerns and identify alternatives (USACE 2003, USEPA 2003a, b).

International institutional and legal authorities

Many developed and developing countries around the world share the same degree of complexity in national and sub-national governing policies and regulatory frameworks surrounding surface water diversions as the U.S. Although this section does not attempt to explore institutional and legal authorities pertaining to surface water diversions on a country-by-country basis, it does provide a list of useful resources, including relevant international laws and treaties and important literature, summarizing experience from around the world (Table 4-2).

TABLE 4-2. International Instutions and Legal Authorities

International

UN Convention on the Law of the Non-navigational Uses of International Watercourses (May 1997)

Ramsar Convention on Wetlands of International Importance especially as Waterfowl Habitat, Done at Ramsar, Iran, 2 February 1971

Helsinki Rules on the Uses of the Waters of International Rivers, International Law Association (1966)

Madrid Declaration on Int'l Regulations Regarding the Use of Int'l Watercourses for Purposes other than Navigation, Institute of International Law, 24 Annuaire de l'Institut de Droit International (1911)

General Comment No. 15 (2002), The Right to Water, Substantive Issues Arising in the Implementation of the International Covenant on Economic, Social and Cultural Rights, U.N.(Economic and Social Council, E/C.12/2000/11 (26 November 2002)

Dublin Statement on the Water and Sustainable Development UN Conference on Environment & Development (Rio de Janeiro/Brazil, June 1992). Chapter 18 - Protection of the Quality and Supply of Freshwater Resources: Application of Integrated Approaches to the Development, Management and Use of Water Resources

Arechaga, F.J., International Legal Rules Governing Use of Waters from International Watercourse, 2 Inter-Am. L. Rev. 329 (1960)

Bains, The Diversion of International Rivers, 1 Indian J. Int'l L. 38 (1960-61)

Bergkamp, Ger & Pirot, Jean-Yves, The Freshwater Challenge: Drain or Gain?, World Conservation 3 (May 1999)

Agenda 21, Chapter 18: Protection Of The Quality And Supply Of Freshwater Resources: Application Of Integrated Approaches To The Development, Management And Use Of Water Resources

Caponera, Dante A., Patterns of Cooperation in International Water Law: Principles and Institutions, 25 Nat. Res. J. 563 (1985)

Dellapenna, Joseph W., Forward: Bringing the Customary International Law of Transboundary Waters into the Era of Ecology, 1 Int'l J. Global Envt'l Issues 243 (2001)

Dellapenna, Joseph W., The Customary International Law of Transboundary Fresh Waters, 1 Int'l J. Global Envt'l Issues 264 (2001)

Dellapenna, Joseph W., Treaties as Instruments for Managing Internationally-Shared Water Resources: Restricted Sovereignty vs. Community of Property, 26 Case W. Res. J. Int'l L. 27 (1994)

Garretson, et al., eds., The Law of International Drainage Basins (1967)

Lee, Terence R., Water Management in the 21st Century: The Allocation Imperative (Edward Elgar 1999)

Legge, D. The Sustainability of the Water Industry in a Regulated Environment, 12 J. Envtl. L. 3 (2000)

Simsarian, The Diversion of International Waters (1939)

United Nations Food and Agriculture Organization, Systematic Index of International Water Resources: Treaties, Declarations, Acts and Cases, by Basin. Volume I. Legislative Study #15 (1978)

United Nations Food and Agriculture Organization, Systematic Index of International Water Resources: Treaties, Declarations, Acts and Cases, by Basin. Volume II. Legislative Study #34 (1984)

United Nations Food and Agriculture Organization, Sources of International Water Law, Legislative Study #65 (1998)

Utton, Albert E. & Utton, John, International Law of Minimal Stream Flows, 10 Colo. J. Int'l Envt'l L. & Pol'y 7 (1999)

Brunnée, J. & Toope, S.J., Freshwater Regimes: The Mandate of the International Joint Commission, 15 Ariz. J. Int'l & Comp. L. 273 (1998)

Europe

UN/ECE Convention on the Protection and Use of Transboundary Watercourses and International Lakes, done at Helsinki, 17 March 1992.(31 I.L.M. 1312 (1992)

Convention on Cooperation for the Protection and Sustainable Use of the Danube River. Done in Sofia, 29 June 1994

Convention on Cooperation for the Protection and Sustainable Use of the Danube River. Done in Sofia, 29 June 1994

(continues)

TABLE 4-2. *Continued*

Europe

Treaty for the International Commission for the protection of the Meuse and Scheldt Rivers (French) (German) (Dutch)

Convention on the International Commission for the Protection of the Oder. Done in Wroclaw, 11 April 1964

Convention on the Protection of the Rhine. Done at Rotterdam, January 22, 1998. Federal Republic of Germany, France, Luxembourg, the Netherlands, Switzerland, and the European Union

Agreement regulating the withdrawal of water from Lake Constance (with Final Protocol). Signed at Berne, on 30 April 1966. Came into force on 25 November 1967. Switzerland, Austria and Federal Republic of Germany

Agreement Between the Government of the Czechoslovak Republic and the Government of the Polish People's Republic Concerning the Use of Water Resources in Frontier Waters; signed at Prague 212 March 1958; in force 7 August 1958

Agreement Between the government of the Polish People's Republic and the Government of the Union of Soviet Socialist republics Concerning the Use of the Water Resources in Frontier Waters. Signed at Warsaw, 17 July 1964; in force, 16 February 1965

Agreement Between the Peoples Republic of Bulgaria and the Republic of Turkey Concerning Co-operation in the Use of the Waters of Rivers Flowing Through the Territory of Both Countries (Maritsa/Marica, Tundzha, Veleka, Rezovska Rivers), Done on 23 October 1968

European Commission, Towards sustainable water resources management - A Strategic Approach, Comprehensive Guidelines for water resources development co-operation (available in English, French and Portuguese

Vinogradov, Sergei & Langford, Vance P.E., Managing Transboundary Water Resources in the Aral Sea Basin: In Search of a Solution, 1 Int'l J. Global Envt'l Issues 345 (2001)

A-Khavari, Afshin & Rothwell, Donald R., The ICJ and the Danube Dam Case: A Missed Opportunity for International Environmental Law? 22 Melbourne U. L. R. 507 (1998)

A-Khavari, Afshin, The Danube Dam Case: The World Court and the Development of Environmental Law, 3 Asia Pac. J. Envtl. L. 101 (1998)

Pichyakorn, Bantita, Sustainable Development and International Watercourse Agreements: The Mekong and the Rhine, International(Union for the Conservation of Nature (Draft 30 June 2002)

Food and Agriculture Organization of the United Nations, Land and Water Legislation Section, Water Laws in Selected European Countries (1975)

Schwabach, Aaron, From Schweizerhalle to Baia Mare: The Continuing Failure of International Law to Protect Europe's Rivers, 19 Va. Envtl. L.J. 431 (2000)

Vinogravov, S.V. & Wouters, P.K., The Caspian Sea: Quest for a New Legal Regime, 9 Leiden J. Int'l L. 87 (1996)

Middle East

Baim, Karen A., Come Hell of High Water: A Water Regime For the Jordan River Basin, 75 Wash. U. L. Q. 919 (1997)

Batstone, The Utilization of the Nile Waters, Int'l & Comp. L.Q. 523 (1959)

Caponera, Dante, Water Laws in Moslem Countries (1954)

Caponera, Dante, Water Laws in Moslem Countries (1973-78)

Carroll, C.M., Past and Future Legal Framework of the Nile River Basin, 12 Geo. Int'l Envt'l L. Rev. 269 (1999)

Chenevert, Donald J., Jr., Application of the Draft Articles on the Non-Navigational Uses of International Watercourses to the Water Disputes Involving the Nile River and the Jordan River, 6 Emory Int'l L. Rev. 495 (1992)

Cohen, Jonathan E., International Law and Water Politics of the Euphrates, 24 J. Int'l. L. & Pol. 503 (1991)

Kasimbazi, E., The Relevance of Sub-Basin Legal and Institutional Approaches in the Nile Basin 5 S. Afr. J. Envtl. L. & Pol'y (1998)

Kibaroglu, Aysegül, Building a Regime for the Waters of the Euphrates-Tigris River Basin, International and National Water Law and Policy Series: Volume 7 (Kluwer Law 2002)

Agreement of the Republic of Kazakhstan, Republic of Kyrgyzstan, Republic of Tajikistan, Tuskmenistan, and Republic of Uzbekistan on joint activities in addressing the Aral Sea. Signed 26 March 1993

Agreement Between the Republic of Syria and the Hashemite Kingdom of Jordan Concerning the Utilization of the Yarmouk Waters. Signed at Damascus, 4 June 1953; in force 8 July 1953

The Syrian-Iraqi Agreement on the Utilization of the Euphrates Waters, signed April 1990

North America

Treaty relating to cooperative development of the water resources of the Columbia River Basin (with Annexes), Done 17 January 1961

Treaty between the United States of America and Canada relating to the uses of the waters of the Niagara River. Signed at Washington, 27 February 1950; in force 10 October 1950

Colorado River Storage and Interstate Release Agreement among the United States of America, acting through the Secretary of the Interior; the Arizona Water Banking Authority; the Southern Nevada Water Authority; and the Colorado River Commission of Nevada

International Boundary and Water Commission, United States and Mexico, Minute 242, Permanent and Definitive Solution to the International Problem of the Salinity of the Colorado River, 30 August 1973

Treaty between the United States of America and Mexico relating to the utilization of the Waters of the Colorado and Tijuana Rivers and of the Rio Grande, signed at Washington February 3, 1944; protocol signed at Washington November 14,1944, Entered into force November 8,1945, 59 Stat. 1219; Treaty Series 994

Agreement between U.S. and Mexico, Re-diversion, Allocation and Equitable Division of the Waters of Rio Grande (May 21st, 1906) Consolidated Treaty Series, vol. 201 (1906); A.J.I.L., I, 281; U.S. stat., XXXIV, 2953; Mex. Tr. 1909, I, 318.

Treaty to Resolve Pending Boundary Differences and Maintain the Rio Grande and Colorado River as the International Boundary Between Mexico and the United States, 23 November 1970. 23 U.S.T. 371, T.I.A.S. No. 7313.

Fort, D.D., Restoring the Rio Grande: A Case Study in Environmental Federalism, 28 Envtl. L. 15 (1998)

Jones, Patricia, The U.S. Mexico Boundary Waters Regime and North American Environmental Agreements: What Lessons for International Water Agreements' Compliance Mechanisms?, CEPMLP Annual Review 1999

Lopes, M., Border Tensions and the Need for Water: An Application of Equitable Principles to Determine Water Allocation from the Rio Grande to the United States and Mexico, 9 Geo. Int'l. Envtl. L. Rev. 489 (1997)

Central and South America

Treaty for Amazonian Co-operation. Done at Brasilia, 3 July 1978. Bolivia. Brazil, Colombia, Ecuador, Guyana, Peru, Suriname, Venezuela

Argentina-Brazil-Paraguay: Agreement on Paraná River Projects (1979)

Dourojeanni, Axel, Water Management at the River Basin Level: Challenges in Latin America, Serie Recursos Naturales e Infraestructura No. 29, LC/L.1583-P, (August 2001)

Legislacion de Aguas en Los Paises del Grupo Adino. (Water Legislation in the Andean Pact Countries)

Africa

African Convention on the Conservation of Nature and Natural Resources. Done in Algiers, 15 September 1968. Gambia River Basin

Convention Relating to the Creation of the Gambia River Basin Development Organisation. Signed at Kaolack, 30 JUNE 1978

Revised Protocol on Shared Watercourses in the Southern African Development Community, Done August 7, 2000

Caponera, Dante, Water Law in Selected African Countries (Benin, Burundi, Ethiopia, Gabon, Kenya, Mauritius, Sierra Leone, Swaziland, Upper Volta, Zambia) (1979)

Chenevert, Donald J., Jr., Application of the Draft Articles on the Non-Navigational Uses of International Watercourses to the Water Disputes Involving the Nile River and the Jordan River, 6 Emory Int'l L. Rev. 495 (1992)

Hitchcock, Robert K., The Kavango Basin: A Case Study

Kasimbazi, E., The Relevance of Sub-Basin Legal and Institutional Approaches in the Nile Basin 5 S. Afr. J. Envtl. L. & Pol'y (1998)

Lebotse, K.K., Southern African Community Protocol on Shared Watercourses: Challenges of Implementation, 12 Leiden J. Int'l L 173 (1999)

Leestemaker, Joanne Heyink, An analysis of the new national and sub national Water Laws in Southern Africa: Gaps between the UN-Convention, the SADC protocol and national legal systems in South Africa, Swaziland and Mozambique

Rothert, Steve, Meeting Namibia's Water Needs While Sparing the Okavango

TABLE 4-2. *Continued*

Asia

Agreement on the Cooperation for the Sustainable Development of the Mekong River Basin. Done in Chiang Rai, 4 April 1995. Cambodia, Lao People's Republic, Thailand and Viet Nam

Pichyakorn, Bantita, Sustainable Development and International Watercourse Agreements: The Mekong and the Rhine, International(Union for the Conservation of Nature (Draft 30 June 2002)

Browder, Greg & Ortolano, L., The Evolution of an International Water Resource Management Regime in the Mekong River Basin, 40 Nat. Resources J. 499 (2000)

Caponera, D.A., The Legal Aspects of Mekong River Projects, 16 Indian J. Power & River Valley Devel. 35 (1966)

Desai, B., Sharing of International Water Resources: The Ganga and Mahalaki River Treaties, 3 Asia Pac. J. Envt'l Law 172 (1998)

Gheleta, M.A., Sustaining the Giant Dragon: Rational Use and Protection of China's Water Resources in the Twenty-First Century 9 Colo. J. Int'l. Envtl. L. & Pol'y 221 (1998)

Institute for the Development of Indian Law, Indian Water Rights (1984)

Salman, S.M.A. & Uprety, K., Conflict and Cooperation on South Asia's International Rivers, International and National Water Law and Policy Series: Volume 8 (Kluwer Law 2002)

Salman, S.M.A. & Uprety, K., Hydro-Politics in South Asia: A Comparative Analysis of the Mahakali and the Ganges Treaties, 39 Nat. Res. J. 395 (1999)

Salman, S.M.A., Co-Management of Resources: the Case of the Ganges River, Conference-Water: Dispute Prevention & Development, Center For the Global South, October 12–13, 1998, Washington College of Law, American University, Washington, DC

Institutional and legal strategies related to addressing IBWT

Interbasin transfer schemes are inherently complex and generate controversy. Institutional models may be (1) commercial enterprise; (2) joint venture benefiting both partners; or (3) a unifying element, linking a water-deprived region with a water-rich region. The complexity of institutional structure and legal authority increases with the number and variety of administrative and political jurisdictions involved; this is particularly critical for international transfers where parallel and overlapping governance may confound project administration (UNESCO 1999).

In the United States, regulatory considerations and limitations pertaining to IBWTs include: (1) extant treaties and restrictions (e.g., 1944 Utilization of Waters Treaty for the Rio Grande, Colorado, and Tijuana River waters); (2) protection status under federal or state statutes (e.g., federal Wild and Scenic Rivers Act, Endangered Species Act); (3) federal and state statutory prohibitions against transfers; (4) vested water rights of the source body of water; (5) allocations under interstate compacts; (6) uncertainties concerning federal reserved water rights and indigenous peoples water rights; (7) lack of comprehensive, multi-purpose, current regional planning; (8) lack of local, regional or national water plans (in many states) including projected future water needs; and (9) public opposition to IBWT schemes (especially in source regions) (OTA 1983). A newly emerging issue of water transfer and governance is how trade laws and principles are applied (e.g., guidelines and principles of the World Trade Organization).

Similar regulatory considerations and limitations concerning IBWTs in other countries may or may not exist. However, UNESCO suggests the following four criteria when evaluating IBWT proposals:

- **Economic productivity impact**—recipient area must face substantial water deficit and its development constrained by this shortage. Conversely, donor area must have adequate water to meet its current and projected needs;
- **Environmental quality impacts**—environmental impacts must be minimized in the recipient, donor and transit area and compensation made to offset environmental injury;

Box 4-5. Meeting Human Needs in Boston: the Connecticut River

In the 1980s, the Boston Metropolitan Area's water demands were 330 million gallons per day while available supplies were only 300 million gallons per day. The Massachusetts Water Resources Authority (MWRA) began exploring options for meeting this need. One option considered was the diversion of the Connecticut River into the Quabbin Reservoir to provide a greater water supply. However, resulting public concern led to the passage of the Interbasin Transfer Act (ITA). The ITA requires that water transfers between any of 27 watersheds within Massachusetts be approved by the state's water resource commission and must also include an examination of alternative water sources, consideration of

A view over tanker piers toward downtown Boston. Photograph courtesy of NOAA.

conservation measures, and implementation of leak detection and correction measures. As a result of ITA, the MWRA began a comprehensive leak detection and repair program. Consequently, the MWRA dropped its average day demand to 245–250 million gallons per day, well below 300 million gallons per day which the system could deliver—a savings of almost 25%! Other water conservation efforts (toilet replacement programs, etc.) would drop water demand even further. As a result, the transfer from the Connecticut River was no longer considered as an option for increasing the water supply available for serving the Boston Metropolitan Area.

- **Socio-cultural impacts**—socio-cultural impacts must be minimized in the recipient, donor and transit area and compensation made to offset environmental injury;
- **Benefit distribution**—net benefits to recipient, donor and transit areas. (UNESCO 1999)

COMMUNITY-BASED STRATEGIES

Community members are increasingly involved in water management and related institutional reforms. Resource managers, government officials, and community members must work together to address environmental, social and economic issues in order to understand and develop effective water management plans. The following guidelines can help evaluate new water management proposals for large-scale surface water diversions (and specifically IBWTs). The process for evaluating the suitability of new proposed surface water diversions includes:

- Ample and effective opportunities for informed public participation in the formulation and analysis of proposed projects;
- Evaluation of economic, social, and environmental impacts in the basin of origin, the receiving area and any area through which the diversion must pass, so that decision makers and the public have adequate information on which to base a decision;
- Examination of all short- and long-term economic costs including, but not limited to, construction, delivery, operation, maintenance, and market interest rate;
- Examination of alternative supply options, such as water conservation, water pricing and reclamation;
- Participation and review by all affected governments;
- Procedures for resolution of intergovernmental conflicts;
- Accord with international treaties (where applicable);

BOX 4-6. Two Chinese Interbasin Water Transfers

A rapidly expanding economy, falling water tables, and a prolonged regional drought have prompted Chinese officials to begin construction of two new major water transfer schemes to augment supplies in the arid northern regions of the country. The Wanjiazhai Water Transfer Project (WWTP), a $1.4 billion interbasin water transfer scheme will divert water from the Yellow River northward to Taiyuan, Datong, and Shouzhou. The scheme will transfer 1.2 billion m³ of water per year through a 285 km tunnel and canal system (CNS 2002, CDG 2002). Other components of the WWTP include institutional resource reform (e.g., water pricing liberalization, institutional autonomy) and water pollution control and industrial waste management (including equipment, training, pollution prevention programs). The World Bank supported this project through a $400 million loan (World Bank 1997).

    The second IBWT scheme, the South-to-North Water Diversion Project will transport 38 billion to 45 billion m³ of water annually from the lower, middle, and upper reaches of the Yangtze River through three interconnected routes (eastern, central, western) to northern China (People's Daily 2001). The western route will transfer water from the upper reach of Yangtze River to the Yellow River to address water shortages caused by frequent droughts in Northwest and North China; the central route will deliver water to Beijing, Tianjing and North China, providing 6.4 billion m³ additional water for urban and industrial use and 3 billion m³ for agricultural use; the eastern route will provide 14.33 billion m³ of water for agricultural, industrial, domestic, and shipping use in major northeastern urban centers (e.g., Hebei and Tianjing). Project costs include a price tag exceeding $59 billion and relocation of almost 370,000 people along the path of construction (Chang 2002, US Water News 2003).

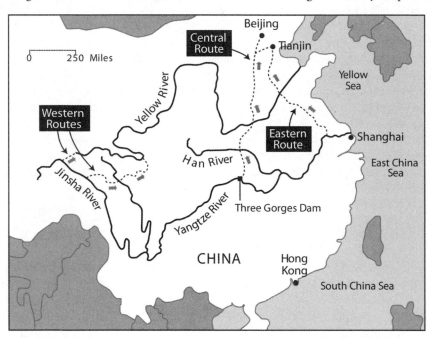

• Provisions to ensure that responsibility for funding is borne primarily by the user with no federal subsidy, loan guarantees, or use of the borrowing;
• Enforceable intergovernmental agreement with supervision separate from implementation and with assurances that any mitigation offered to alleviate any adverse impacts be financed;
• Inclusion of water conservation as a goal of all concerned government entities;
• Establishment of water accounting systems and adoption of water use plans as a basis for management strategies;

• Strengthening multi-government commissions and task forces; this is especially important for multinational water resources (e.g., transnational water resource agreements such as the 1909 Boundary Waters Agreement between the U.S. and Canada on shared waters of the Great Lakes and the 1944 Utilization of Waters Treaty between the U.S. and Mexico on the shared waters of the Colorado, Rio Grande, and other rivers);
• Cooperative management of resources between participating political entities (e.g., states or countries). (adapted from the League of Women Voters 2002)

San Marcos River, Texas. Photograph by Jerry Touchstone Kimmel.

In addition to stakeholders groups and public participation in all meetings, water policy makers should establish working bodies that offer a real and substantive opportunity for interested parties to participate in the management of the basins. Additionally, governing agencies should make available to the public any information, including monitoring data, relevant to management of the basins (Florida Wildlife Federation 2002).

Active public participation can provide critical input into water management issues. In Georgia, for example, the state legislature created two citizen group committees to develop a comprehensive state water plan. The committees (1) study current water issues including quantity and quality; (2) consider extant water management policies, laws, rules, and programs; (3) recommend process and schedule for development of comprehensive plan; (4) develop principles for the plan; and (5) recommend action and draft legislation where needed. Committees consist of members of the scientific, business, agricultural, fisheries, recreation, and academic communities and environmental advocacy groups, water professionals, and citizen groups (CVIOG 2001).

Some communities resolve water allocation issues

through non-confrontational mechanisms, such as applying for water rights and developing water management strategies. Local concern over imposition of federal law or threat of lawsuits by interested parties, such as conservation groups, can be the motivation for the involved parties (e.g., water districts and individual farming interests), to voluntarily develop plans to restore instream flow.

Efforts of the San Marcos River Foundation (SMRF) demonstrate how a local community can challenge traditional resource allocation practices by using existing water rights laws. Decreased inflows of freshwater from the Guadalupe River system have increased salinity concentrations and produced eutrophic conditions in the Guadalupe Bay and Estuary, significantly harming fisheries and shrimp nurseries. Loss of productivity in the Bay is reflected by 12% mortality of the highly endangered whooping cranes that overwinter in the region and reduced commercial catch of saltwater fish and shrimp. Should the commercial fishery supported by this system collapse, the economy would loose a $20 million/year industry plus a significant decline in local tourism-related activities (estimated at $6 million per year). Concerned about the effects of dwindling freshwater supplies reaching the Gulf of Mexico on the area's wildlife and fisheries, a small group of citizens applied for a water rights permit following procedures under Texas state water law. The application petitioned 1,418,510,000 m³ of water per year and, if approved, SMRF proposes to donate the rights to a state water trust for management with the reservation that it is used exclusively for maintenance of instream flow. The petition for rights to such a large amount of water is a novel approach in Texas and has caused considerable controversy. Water user groups, including state water authorities and rapidly growing metropolitan areas (e.g., San Antonio), have proposed numerous dams, diversions, and pipelines that would further decrease instream flow and the amount of water reaching the Bay. These groups strongly oppose

granting of the permit, and some have filed a motion to dismiss the application. However, less than two years after initiating the application, a review panel recommended a permit for 1,233,490,000 m³ of water. Although the final decision will likely be challenged, this precedent-setting use of existing water rights demonstrates the ability of a small group to address the protection of an entire riverine system. Already this action has garnered the support of more than 150,000 residents in the affected area as well as the attention of national environmental organizations, such as the American Rivers, Sierra Club, and the Environmental Defense Fund (American Rivers 2002, Texas Observer 2002, Dianne Wassenich-San Marcos River Foundation, *personal communication*).

ALTERED BED AND BANK STRUCTURE
(channelization, dredging, armoring, and levees)

Introduction

River channels are commonly modified to provide flood control, improved land drainage, adequate conditions for barge and boat traffic, and reduction in bank erosion. Estimates for the U.S. suggest that modified channels exceed one million km (NRC 1992), although some states have particularly high rates (e.g., by 1972, 27% of Illinois streams were channelized) (Lopinot 1972). Totals are higher in parts of Europe where river channels in the majority of lowland rivers have been modified (e.g., 89% of the streams in Denmark and 98% of streams in lowland areas of Britain have been channelized (Brookes and Shields, Jr. 1996). Efforts to stabilize shoreline areas of lakes to reduce erosion and to install structures to facilitate human use of lakes and nearby areas (e.g., construction of docks, management of water levels, etc.) also degrade unique habitat and contribute to the decline of many freshwater species. For example, juvenile sockeye rear for one or two years in lake habitats before migrating to sea. Increased shoreline erosion as a result of removal of native vegetation negatively affects their food production and hence their growth

rate, as well as their reproductive rate due to loss of nearshore spawning habitat resulting in an overall decrease in their survival rate.

Modifications to alter bed and bank structure include:

- physically removing material and changing the shape of a stream or channel to increase its conveyance of water or navigability (termed channelization)
- adding material (stones, pre-cast blocks, or molded concrete) to protect river and lake banks from collapse (termed armoring)
- building levees to prevent flooding in low-lying areas and generally creating more significant boundaries between rivers and their associated riparian or floodplain areas, and
- building other structures at or near shorelines to change flow patterns and the natural patterns of interactions of water with land (bulkheads, breakwaters, and groins).

The following section briefly explores threats to freshwater ecosystems caused by altered bed and bank structure.

The Effects of Altered Bed and Bank Structure on Freshwater Ecosystems

The effects of altered bed and bank structure on rivers, lakes, wetlands and riparian areas vary spatially and temporally due to factors such as climate, soil, channel morphology, flow patterns, drainage basin characteristics, vegetation, and land use. However, in many cases these structural changes permanently alter flow patterns and water quality, resulting in habitat loss, habitat fragmentation and isolation, increased erosion, reduced structural diversity, decreased species diversity, and increased downstream flooding (Brookes 1988, USEPA 2002a).

Similarly, efforts to stabilize lakeshores affect habitat and biota, though the significance of these effects varies with strategies employed and characteristics of the lake itself. The natural balance of sediment deposition and removal from shore areas is maintained primarily by wave action. Most structural options offer only temporary protection against erosion or collapse of the shore, and some may actually accelerate these processes.

The following is a summary of the effects of altered bed and bank structure on the key factors driving freshwater ecosystems.

THE HYDROLOGIC REGIME

Normal, meandering rivers tend to flood adjacent riparian areas following precipitation events, and these areas act as buffers against stormwater surges. Channelization facilitates movement of surface water draining the land and accelerates water flow in the

Examples of channel modifications include levees, as in the West Atchafalaya Basin, Louisiana (above left, photograph by Michael Maples/USACE); streambank lining, as on the River Rouge in southeast Michigan (top right, photograph courtesy of the USACE); and floodwalls and bank stabilization with riprap, as along the Ararat River in Mt. Airy, North Carolina (bottom right, photograph by Bud Davis/USACE).

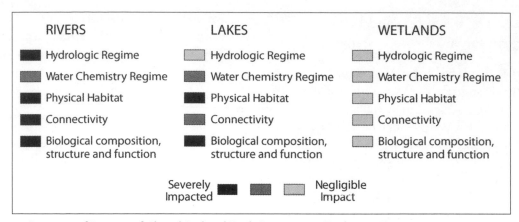

FIGURE 4-11. Summary of Impacts of Altered Bed and Bank Structure on Freshwater Ecosystems

mainstem and tributaries. By removing meanders, channelization reduces channel length and width, increases channel gradient, and alters flow regimes. Channelization of the Missouri River below Sioux City (Iowa) has reduced river width by two-thirds and shortened length by more than 204 km. River channels constricted by channelization and levees accentuate impacts of flowing water energy (e.g., streambed scour, bank collapse, erosion). Some channelization (e.g., Florida Everglades) decreases seasonal fluctuations in water levels and substitutes more stable water levels. However, other river systems experience the opposite effect. Although channelization generally reduces natural flood frequency and intensity upstream, it can significantly increase downstream flood potential, especially when the mainstem and tributary flood peaks are synchronized (Brookes 1988, Shankman and Samson 1991, Wyzga 1993). For example, extensive land drainage in Ireland increased flood discharge in seven of twelve catchment areas by 57–65% (Bree and Cunnane 1980). Straightened channels and levees force water to bypass energy dissipating floodplains and wetlands. In Massachusetts more than 17 million m³ of water are retained by the floodplains of the naturally flowing Ipswich River, thereby reducing downstream floodpeaks (Sammell *et al.* 1966).

Channel modification also disrupts groundwater recharge, generally lowering water table levels. These impacts radiate beyond the immediate area of channel modification. Groundwater is lower even in areas where headcutting occurs, a geomorphological process common in channelized areas.

PHYSICAL HABITAT CONDITIONS

Sediment regime and erosion

Channelization alters sediment characteristics including composition and rates and paths of erosion, transport, and deposition. Overland transport of sediments (from agricultural fields, logging operations, construction sites, etc.) as well as headcutting, and lateral bank failures of channelized tributaries, lead to channel aggradations and the formation of valley plugs in the mainstem of rivers. Channel blockages, in turn, increase depth, area and duration of seasonal flooding, alter sediment deposition patterns and impact vegetation composition over extensive areas of adjacent valley bottoms. Modified river channels are prone to frequent disturbances including eroding banks. These natural adjustments frequently require rechannelization or redredging and reconstruction of the levees on stream reaches for hydrologic management.

Habitat

Channelization converts naturally heterogeneous reaches into a simplified, uniform system, reducing habitat diversity. These disturbances extend from the river's channel to its bank and are propagated upstream and downstream. Channelization also reduces river sinuosity, removing unique habitat and changing the riffle-pool configuration. The downstream deposition of sediment eliminates pool habitat and may cause the riverbed to rise, making the water depth too shallow for fish. Boulders and snags are

Paddlefish (Polydon spathula) *are endangered by the loss of floodplain habitat in the Midwest United States. Illustration by Timoth Knepp/USFWS.*

frequently removed as part of channel modification, eliminating these colonization sites (NRC 1992). Additionally, floodplains isolated from the channel are not available to species dependent on this connection for feeding, spawning, rearing, and refuge (e.g., paddlefish[7] and pallid sturgeon[8]).

Streambed and streambank modifications (e.g., channelization, levees) also disrupt the connectivity between the channel and floodplains. These modifications regulate the extent and timing of natural occurrences of floodplain inundation, impacting community composition and ecological processes in the floodplain. Floodplains and off-channel wetlands are important habitats for many resident and migratory aquatic, bird, and terrestrial taxa. They serve as breeding and spawning grounds and are a rich source of

nutrients for instream ecological processes. The severe losses of floodplains in the Midwest of the U.S. have endangered many neotropical migratory birds (e.g., Swainson's Warbler, *Limnothlypis swainsonii*) and endemic fish, such as the paddlefish (*Polyodon spathula*) that are dependent on these environments.

Armoring simplifies shorelines and reduces the amount, quality, and diversity of habitat in the littoral zone[9] of lakes. These transitional areas are highly productive. The shallow water, abundant light, and nutrient-rich sediment are ideal for plant growth. In turn these aquatic plants provide food and habitat for many animals, such as fish, frogs, birds, muskrats, turtles, insects, and snails. Traditional armoring (e.g., retaining walls) disconnects nearshore habitat from the lake resulting in decreased input of nutrients and

---

[7] Paddlefish (*Polyodon spathula*) is now state listed as threatened in many states of its range. Damming and channel modifications of large rivers has controlled spring flooding and kept water within river banks, thereby eliminating much of the paddlefish's spawning habitat.

[8] Pallid sturgeon (*Scaphirhynchus albus*) is an endangered species and is federally listed throughout its range in the Missouri and Mississippi River drainages. Primary cause of the rapid decline in population is habitat modification through river channelization, construction of impoundments, and related changes in water flow. These changes have blocked the pallid sturgeon's movements, destroyed or altered its spawning areas, reduced its food sources or its ability to obtain food, and altered water temperatures and other environmental conditions.

[9] Littoral zone is the shallow transition zone between dry land and the open water area of the lake to a depth to which light ceases to reach the bottom of the lake thereby inhibiting plant growth. The width of the littoral zone will vary within a lake and among lakes. In places where the slope of the lake bottom is steep, the littoral area may be narrow, extending several feet from the shoreline. In contrast, if the lake is shallow, the littoral zone may be quite extensive.

Dredging the ship channel of the Sacramento River, California. Photograph by Michael Nevins/ USACE.

substrate (e.g., woody debris, decaying leaves, and other vegetation), and decreased 'filtering' capacity of the shoreline to intercept sediment and contaminants flowing to the waterbody. Impact of these shoreside activities extends into nearshore areas of waterbodies. Additionally, reducing structural complexity can remove prey refuges and subject prey to high risk of predation as well as significantly decreasing species richness (Cooper and Crowder 1979).

Water Chemistry Regime

Channelization changes the physical and chemical regime of surface water, including turbidity, salinity, temperature, nutrients, dissolved oxygen, oxygen demand, and contaminants. Loss of bank vegetation exposes the water to increased sunlight resulting in warmer water temperatures and higher instream plant and algae growth. Removal of organic material from the stream channel and increased velocity and turbulence in the flow can increase dissolved oxygen levels. However, if too much of the material (including substrate, sediment, and buried organic material) is exposed by dredging, oxidation of the newly exposed material may deplete dissolved oxygen reserves. Dredging may also release or re-suspend toxic materials, such as hydrogen sulfide, methane gas, organics,

heavy metals, pesticides, other chemical pollutants and biological pathogens (e.g., fecal coliform) (Grimes 1975). Additionally, where channelization promotes erosion, nutrients (e.g., nitrogen, phosphorous), organic material, and contaminants flow off the land into the river, modifying water chemistry. Levees disrupt the natural flushing action of overland flow of freshwater through coastal wetlands, causing an increase in salinity and intrusion of saltwater inland. These changes in water chemistry threaten trees, wetland vegetation, shellfish, and fish (U.S. EPA 2002b).

Biological Composition and Interactions

Bed and bank modification eliminates and modifies habitat for aquatic life. Organisms that use sandbars, undercuts, oxbows, pools and riffles, and floodplain pools disappear when channels are stabilized and developed (NRC 1992). Modification of substrate threatens feeding opportunities and may cause behavioral changes (e.g., spawning). Salmonids require gravel of various grain sizes, whereas female darters deposit their eggs in fine gravel. Members of the cottid or sculpin family lay eggs on gravel slabs or shingled rocks and crevice spawners need crevices or cracks in rocks for egg laying (Simpson *et al.* 1982). Mollusks and aquatic insects (e.g., dragonflies and stoneflies)

Aquatic insects, such as this green darner dragonfly, decline in population and diversity following channelization of a stream. Photograph by Janet Haas.

decline in population and diversity following channelization. Invertebrate species less sensitive to the disturbances (e.g., chironomid midges and blackflies) may dominate the aquatic invertebrate community immediately after channelization. Effects on community composition and function can be long lasting; depressed biomass, productivity, diversity and numbers of macroinvertebrates were noted for the Luxapalila River (Mississippi) more than 52 years after channelization. These long-lasting declines were attributed to change of substrate from pebbles to the fine sand of the channelized reach (Arner *et al.* 1975, 1976). Drift rates[10] are also likely to be higher in unchannelized river reaches where dominant macroinvertebrates are riffle species (e.g., Hydropsychids, Heptageniids). In channelized rivers, dominant species are more likely to be burrowing forms adapted to living in soft substrate in slow-moving water (e.g., Oligochaetes and Chironmids) (Brookes 1988). Construction of levees also eliminates backwaters, decreasing habitats and restricting movement between mainstem channel and floodplains (Funk and Robinson 1974).

Bed and bank modification in lakes and rivers also affects amphibians, reptiles, birds, and mammals. Loss of habitat reduces amount of food and shelter, restricts access to breeding grounds, and exposes wildlife to increased predation. For example, as a result of lost habitat in the lower reaches of the Missouri River, the pallid sturgeon (*Scaphirhynchus albus*) and interior least tern (*Sterna antillarum*) are listed under the federal Endangered Species Act. Studies show population size and species diversity of riverside mammals in channelized rivers decreased following channelization. However, population and diversity increase as the riparian area recovers from the initial disturbance and more heterogeneous habitat develops (Simpson *et al.* 1982, Mason 1995). Lastly, alterations to stream and lake shorelines reduce shallow areas and limit important breeding and feeding areas for aquatic macroinvertebrates (e.g., dragonflies) and fish. Loss of this area also exposes many fish to increased predation as the littoral zone of a lake acts as a warm water refuge for small-bodied fish and juveniles (Close and Lieschke 2002).

Connectivity

Channelization and levees serve to isolate floodplains from rivers. Channelization disrupts the natural process of periodic overbank flooding which supplies wetlands and riparian areas with nutrients and organic matter,

---

[10]Drift rate refers to the downstream transport of aquatic organisms in the current.

removes contaminants, and recharges groundwater supplies. Land adjacent to channelized rivers is drained of surface water and levees constrict lateral movement of water across the floodplains. These hydrologic modifications exacerbate changes in ecosystem structure and function by limiting exchange of matter and energy and limit movement of wildlife, fish, and invertebrates. Additionally, both channelization and levees decrease groundwater recharge, causing water tables in floodplains to drop and dramatic changes in vegetation and wildlife. Armoring lake shorelines isolates freshwater from marine and terrestrial influences, and reduces the supply of nutrients, sediments, and coarse woody debris into the lake system as well as impedes terrestrial nearshore species from using the lake for drinking water and food supply.

Strategies for Mitigating/Abating the Effect of Altered Bed and Bank Structure on Freshwater Ecosystems

The harmful effects of conventional methods[11] of modifying streambed and bank structure have encouraged a new breed of stream management plans that emphasize working with a river (Brookes 1988). While the conventional methods or structural management approaches in some river environments are still important in many environments (e.g., urban areas), greater attention is now focused on integrated river-basin management. This approach emphasizes improved and integrated land use management, along with greater attention to incorporate a river's naturally occurring characteristics. The following section briefly discusses these approaches.

TECHNICAL STRATEGIES

Many types of technical strategies may be used to improve stream channel and lakeshore management. This section examines three types of strategies commonly used: channel restoration, integrated floodplain management, and lakeshore protection.

Channel restoration

Scientists and managers recognize that effective engineering and management techniques must be developed to mitigate damages caused by channel modification (Ward et al. 2001). Legal requirements to mitigate damage to riverine habitats are largely responsible for the expanding interest and funding in restoring river channels. Re-establishing the natural hydrology and geomorphology is critical to successful restoration (NRC 1992). However, legislation, availability of funding, and multiple land use activities continue to constrain river restoration (Brookes 1996).

Channel restoration goals usually include (1) restoring or enhancing aquatic and riparian habitat, (2) providing functional recreational corridors in urban areas, and (3) improving water quality. Restoration strategies include (1) recreating meander bends, (2) changing the shape of channel bed and bank slopes, (3) creating habitat for fish and other wildlife, (4) stabilizing banks by planting vegetation and structural changes, and (5) creating open channels in streams formerly encased in underground culverts (Kondolf 2002). Channel restorations may involve merely removing the disturbance (e.g., fencing out livestock from a river). In these cases natural vegetation regrowth will stabilize streambanks providing the ecological benefits to the stream. However, the recovery process may be slow. Highly degraded streams will require engineering efforts to reshape river channel and bank to its original shape.

Channel restoration consists of three basic steps: (1) assessment and evaluation, (2) data synthesis and design, and (3) implementation. Assessment and evaluation involves multi-scale data collection to quantify both current and historic channel characteristics (e.g., shape, pattern, and gradient), flow regime, riparian and instream habitat, and fish and wildlife census. Data synthesis and design integrate information into design plans that include multiple tasks, such as constructing floodplains, revegetating streambanks and riparian areas, creating habitats, and modifying current flow patterns. Design plans should mimic a stream in dynamic equilibrium with its watershed and

---

[11] Conventional methods may include straightening, deepening and broadening stream channel, removal of vegetation, constructing bulkheads, and armoring streambanks and lakeshores.

provide a diverse and complex river system channel capable of conveying flows, transporting sediment, and integrating essential habitat features and ecological processes related to recovery of fish and other aquatic animals and flora. Implementation should incorporate the use of locally obtained material to minimize costs and avoid introducing of exotic species. Additionally, meeting restoration goals requires follow-up monitoring, maintenance, and evaluation (Brown *et al.* 2002).

Although numerous channel restoration projects have been attempted, results of many are mixed and a high proportion fail (Lockwood and Pimm 1999). Most restoration projects to date are small in scale (e.g., involving stream reach). However, a pilot project in the Kissimmee-Okeechobee-Everglades (KOE) ecosystem in south Florida is attempting watershed scale restoration. Channel modification of the Kissimmee River in the 1960s eliminated more than 75 km of river and 12,000–14,000 ha of wetland habitat. Objectives of the current restoration efforts are to restore the natural flow regime and most of the lost floodplains. Restoration strategies for the Kissimmee River include recreation of meanders, reshaping the river channel, elimination of some water-control structures and associated levees, and backfilling portions of the channelized river. Habitat restoration is expected to benefit more than 32 species of fish and wildlife (Koebel 1995).

The following publications provide more information about useful restoration techniques for readers seeking additional resources:

- Federal Interagency Stream Restoration Working Group (FISRWG). 1998. *Stream Corridor Restoration: Principles, Processes, and Practices.* Washington, DC. Website links: http://www.usda.gov/stream_restoration.
- Riley, A. L. 1998. *Restoring Streams in Cities: A Guide for Planners, Policy-makers, and Citizens.*
- Shields, F. D. (ed.). 1996. *River Channel Restoration: Guiding Principles for Sustainable Projects.*
- Williams, J.E., C.A. Wood, and M.P. Dombeck (eds.). 1997. *Watershed Restoration: Principles and Practices.*
- Resources and Abstracts on Adaptive Management, at: http://www.iatp.org/AEAM/abstracts.htm, especially Anecdotal History: A Tool for the Kissimmee River Restoration Project by Kent Loftin, Earth-Tech, Inc. for Kissimmee R. restoration project specific, at http://www.iatp.org/AEAM/anecdote.htm.

Integrated floodplain management

The disconnection of a floodplain from its river and the urban and rural development of floodplains have highlighted the need for improved floodplain management. The challenge of floodplain management is to provide an acceptable degree of protection against

Kissimmee River Restoration Project, Florida. Photograph by Tony Santana/USACE.

BOX 4-7. Levee Removal and Reconnection of the River with its Floodplain: the Cosumnes River

The 3,000 km² Consumnes River watershed empties into the Mokelumne River and forms an integral part of the Sacramento Bay Delta ecosystem. Fertile floodplain, extensive wetlands, and stream riparan habitat occupy the lower watershed. Vernal pools and lagunitas contain rare plants and animals, and the river and floodplain support numerous native fish species, including chinook salmon. Remnant stands of valley oak, Oregon ash, box elder, and willow form a unique winter-deciduous forest.

Historically, periodic floods of the Consumnes River left behind rich alluvial soils that now support extensive farms and cattle ranches. Watershed development over the last 100 years including a system of levees effectively cut off the river from its floodplain, forcing it to remain in a single channel. By restricting floodwaters to the channel, levees increased the erosive power of the river, causing the channel bed to drop by more than three meters in 40 years. The deeper river also created vertical streambanks devoid of vegetation.

In early 1997, a severe flood caused more than $35 million of property damage (MCWA 2002). This event also provided the catalyst for a major review and overhaul of floodplain management policy. As a result, the Consumnes Task Force was established to "develop a long term strategy that will encourage restoration of watershed health and improve flood management." The Task Force has broad-based representation: federal and state agencies, conservation districts, and NGOs. To be successful, the management plan must include a process that recognizes the fragile nature of the watershed, the needs and input of local landowners, the need for protection of the public trust, and economic feasibility.

Two years before this flood event, The Nature Conservancy initiated an intentional levee breach demonstration project to restore and show the importance of the floodplain. As a result of the project, flood waters delivered sand, nutrients, and seeds to agricultural fields. The sand splays and vegetation added roughness that promoted additional sand deposition, scour and increased residence time of sediment, nutrients, and water in the floodplain.

Based on the success of the levee breach demonstration project, the Consumnes Task Force developed a draft management plan that includes recommendations for setting the levees back from the river's edge. This setback will reconnect the river to the floodplain and should help dissipate peak flow energy and water, reducing the potential for downstream flood hazards. Additionally, it should provide valuable ecosystem services including groundwater recharge, nutrient transport, floodplain enrichment, and flushing of contaminants.

Cosumnes River, California. Photograph by James A. Martin.

floods by physical infrastructure and alternative means of risk reduction against floods. In order to make informed resource management decisions, planners, and managers need to understand the environmental, social, and economic importance of floodplains. Fundamental components of an integrated floodplain management plan are information management (collection, analysis, synthesis, and integration) and public awareness of the impact of land use activities in floodplains (ARMCANZ 2000).

Integrated floodplain management considers the total catchment, the integration of roles and responsibilities between government agencies and other stakeholders, and information about the behavior of floodplains. Consideration of the entire catchment is necessary to avoid moving impacts from one point to another by inappropriately designed management measures. For example, construction of levees may reduce the flooding on one parcel of land, but increase flooding on upstream or downstream properties. Integration of roles and responsibilities is necessary to ensure that the various technical elements and planning tools (e.g., emergency flood planning and relief efforts, multiple land use practices) come together to form a workable management plan.

Contemporary integrated floodplain management plans are site and goal specific, but they frequently include the following elements and steps:

- **Planning**—Involve stakeholders in a process of collecting and analyzing information, defining options and assessing impacts associated with these options, and making decisions about floodplain and watershed-related resource management that views the area as an integrated unit that has interacting economic, social, and environmental components.
- **Implementation**—In addition to a strategy for implementing the plan, also establish an effective monitoring and evaluation framework, establish coordination mechanisms, define responsibilities of involved institutions, and develop management instruments.
- **Institution building**—Develop opportunities for community participation during all phases of the management scheme, including communication strategies and methods to keep everyone informed, strengthening NGO institution capacity in planning and management, and outreach and education for the community at large regarding floodplain planning and management.
- **Financing floodplain development**—Develop strategies for diversified sources of income to reduce risk, including private, foreign and local and state governments.

(adapted from IUCN 2002).

Since its emergence in the mid-1960s in the U.S., nonstructural strategies of floodplain management have been used with increasing frequency, replacing traditional strategies of levees, dams, and channelization. The goal of nonstructural strategies is to adjust the use of floodplains to the flood threat rather than modifying natural flow regime of the rivers. These strategies include flood warning and evacuation systems, land use regulations (e.g., zoning, setback criteria, designated uses), and land acquisition by government agencies and conservation organizations. Financial disincentives (e.g., elimination of subsidized flood insurance, reduced federal payments for flood control structures) are used to discourage floodplain development. Additionally, federal and state wetlands protection laws operate under the "no net loss" principle, further encouraging an integrated approach to floodplain management. For example, the Corps is directed to "enhance existing environmental values of projects and to carry out wetland restoration and create demonstration projects" (NRC 2002).

Lakeshore protection

Natural lake level fluctuations, storm events, and other natural processes continuously reshape the lakeshore zone through wave action, flooding, and erosion. These processes are an integral part of the ecosystem and it is neither economically feasible nor environmentally desirable to limit these processes. The most efficient strategies recognize that shoreline processes are dynamic and must be protected to ensure protection of ecological functions of shores, including water-quality protection, beach nourishment, and maintenance of aquatic and littoral habitats. Lakeshore development and rehabilitation must ensure: (1) longshore drift is not impeded, (2) wave energy is not amplified by the treatment, (3) downdrift[12] properties are not degraded by upshore treatments, and (4) shore-zone processes can operate at expected magnitudes for diurnal, seasonal, annual, and periodic events. Strategies often integrate structural solutions with Best Management Practices (BMPs)[13] such as required setbacks, vegetative buffers, limitations on hard and impervious surfaces, and requirements for restoration of the littoral zone.

Nonstructural options usually are less expensive to install and maintain than structural approaches and

---

[12] Downdrift is the direction of predominant movement of littoral material.

[13] Best Management Practices are prescribed activities, their schedules, prohibitions of practices, maintenance procedures, and other management options implemented to produce the desired environmental benefit.

do not have such harmful side-effects if applied properly. Examples are:

- **Revegetation** to establish desired species for bluff and beach stabilization. While it is among the least expensive of all protection measures, it alone is not effective under conditions of heavy waves or fast moving water. A variety of groundcover, (e.g., grasses, sedges), shrubs and trees trap sand particles and stabilize shoreline areas. Additionally, extensive coastal wetlands can effectively dissipate wave forces on adjacent beaches.
- **Bluff drainage** addresses seepage problems common to clay or composite bluffs. Seepage contributes to bluff instability when upper layers are saturated, slough off, and are ultimately carried away by wave action. Tile drains help resolve shallow groundwater drainage problems and pumps can be used for deeper drainage problems.
- **Slope re-grading** changes the bluff or shore edge to a more gradual slope. This option is often coupled with revegetation.
- **Beach nourishment** is placing sand, gravel, or stone on the shoreline (by overland hauling or nearshore pumping). The deposits serve as a buffer zone that slows erosion. Wave action carries the material off-shore where it forms sand bars that may cause waves to break farther from the beach. The useful life of a nourished beach depends upon the size and quantity of materials placed on the beach as well as the frequency and severity of storms that erode the deposits; use of larger and heavier deposits than naturally occur may reduce the ability of wave action to carry away the supplemental material.
- **Relocation** is the removal of structures vulnerable to damage from flooding and erosion. This option recognizes that erosion and shoreline recession is a natural process and may be impossible to stop entirely. This option is often more cost-effective and reliable in the long-term than most structural options. (adapted from MCCIS 2003)

INSTITUTIONAL AND LEGAL STRATEGIES

Effective solutions to environmental problems associated with bed and bank alterations require participation and coordination of efforts of all stakeholders: water and resource managers, community residents (especially those that have stream and lakeside investments), the business community, and government officials. The most successful and cost-effective solutions

Beach nourishment project at St. Joseph, Michigan, on Lake Michigan. Photograph courtesy USACE.

address the range of forces acting on streams and shore-lines and consider the long-term investments of alternatives and costs avoided by making the investments. Stream and lakeshore zoning codes, ordinances, and development standards at local to federal government levels can be promoted to protect and upgrade these environments. Laws protecting resources, such as the Endangered Species Act and the Clean Water Act, may also be used. For example, management plans and protection instruments may be developed in response to listing of aquatic or riparian-dependent species or to comply with water quality and health statutes. Federal and state programs, including tax incentives, financial support, and buyouts of sensitive areas have also been used successfully to protect streams and shore areas.

The following sections present some of these tools and efforts implemented through U.S. land use regulations and international policies.

U.S. institutional and legal authorities

Utilizing the tools and programs of the Natural Resources Conservation Service

More than 70% of the land in the U.S. is privately owned, and much of this is used for agricultural production. Considering the enormous effect these stakeholders have on the landscape and associated freshwater ecosystems, conservation efforts must include appropriate guidance and help to these stakeholders. The Natural

---

Box 4-8. Integrated Floodplain Management: the Pantanal

South of the Amazon Basin, the Pantanal extends over 130,000 km² of central-western Brazil, eastern Bolivia and eastern Paraguay. The diverse habitats of the Pantanal include flooded forests, semi-deciduous forests, and dry savannahs. One of the world's largest and most significant remaining wetlands, the Pantanal is home to nearly 300 species of fish, 650 species of birds, 100 species of mammals, 180 species of reptiles, and 3,500 species of plants. The Pantanal also supplies water for agriculture and other human uses, provides transportation corridors for goods and services, and supplies a range of other goods (fish, timber, peat, wildlife) which benefit millions of inhabitants. The Pantanal's environmental services also include moving sediments, removing pollutants, dampening seasonal flooding, and delivering nutrients to the land. Both Brazil and Bolivia have designated sections of the Pantanal as Ramsar sites.

One of the major pending threats to the Pantanal and its biodiversity is hydrologic alteration as a result of the proposed Paraná-Paraguay Waterway Megaproject (also called the Paraguay-Paraná Hidrovia project). Promoted by the La Plata basin countries (Argentina, Bolivia, Brazil, Paraguay, and Uruguay) this project would create a 3,442 km shipping canal through the Pantanal. It will promote regional development and exports, expand agribusiness and mining, and encourage political integration of the region. However the direct and indirect costs of this project are expected to be substantial and include disruption of the natural hydrology and flooding patterns of much of the river basin and destruction of wetlands in the Chaco region of Paraguay.

Due to conflicts over the ecological effects of this project on the Pantanal, Brazil stopped construction on its portion of the waterway in 1998 and implemented smaller, non-structural improvements. This decision was part of a larger water policy passed in 1997 designed to support sustainable water development. The government has also established a series of conservation easements on private land to protect critical wetland habitats.

Minor changes to the level of the Paraguay River in the Pantanal could disconnect the river from its floodplain, resulting in the loss of wetlands equal to an area the size of the Florida Everglades. Photograph by David Harrison.

Resources Conservation Service (NRCS) of the U.S. Department of Agriculture provides assistance for land management planning and conservation measures on private farmland in the United States. The mission of NRCS is to provide "leadership in a partnership effort to help people conserve, maintain, and improve our natural resources and environment." NRCS provides technical assistance on natural resource management and agriculture on a voluntary basis to private landowners, policymakers, and local, state and federal agencies. NRCS reaches stakeholders through 3,000 conservation districts, representing almost every county in the U.S. It works with partner agencies and stakeholder groups[14] to: (1) serve the customers' local resource conservation needs, (2) foster economically viable environmental policies, (3) advocate a total natural resources approach to conservation, and (4) maintain and advocate grass roots conservation delivery systems.

NRCS manages programs that offer landowners financial, technical and educational assistance to implement conservation practices. These cost-share programs focus on soil erosion control, water quality improvement, and habitat protection as summarized below:

- **Wetlands Reserve Program (WRP)**—provides funds for wetland protection and restoration through cost-sharing and acquisition of easement rights.
- **Wildlife Habitat Incentives Program (WHIP)**—provides financial incentives through cost-share assistance to develop habitat for fish and wildlife on private lands.
- **Conservation Reserve Program (CRP)**—encourages farmers to convert highly erodible cropland or other environmentally sensitive acreage to vegetative cover to reduce erosion and provide wildlife habitat. Farmers receive annual rental payments, and cost sharing is provided to establish the vegetative cover practices.
- **Environmental Quality Incentives Program (EQIP)**—incentive payments and cost sharing for conservation practices, such as manure management systems, pest management, erosion control, and other practices to improve and maintain the health of natural resources. Priority is given to projects that help meet water quality objectives.

- **Farmland Protection Program (FPP)**—provides funds to help purchase development rights to keep productive farmland in use and to acquire conservation easements or other interests from landowners.
- **Emergency Conservation Program (ECP)**—funds emergency water conservation measures and restoration of conservation installations (e.g., terraces, permanent fences, debris removal) following natural disasters.
- **Emergency Watershed Protection (EWP)**—provides assistance for a variety of projects to stabilize watersheds following natural disasters; projects removing and establishing vegetative cover, gully control, installing streambank protection devices, and removing debris and sediment. Funds may also be used to purchase floodplain easements. (NRCS 2002)

Working with NRCS staff or receiving NRCS support through these programs is often an effective strategy for abating the effect of altered bed and bank structures or protecting freshwater ecosystems from the establishment of such alterations in the first place.

Applying local land use planning processes and regulations

Recognizing the importance of protecting waterbodies, many local communities have enacted a full range of codes, ordinances and other regulations to protect and manage floodplains and river corridors. Although state and federal laws govern some aspects of land use and protection for water resources (e.g., Clean Water Act), many local communities have adopted regulations that go beyond these controls. Local regulations include zoning codes, building codes, and subdivision regulations that prohibit construction in flood-prone areas or allow some construction under certain conditions. Outright purchase of land and easements on private holdings is another strategy local communities use to protect rivers, floodplains, and wetlands. Purchase of land has the benefit of local government control over use and providing recreational amenities to residents.

Local land use regulations are most effective if they are part of a community development strategy that

---

[14] These groups include: (1) conservation districts, (2) local communities, (3) state and federal agencies; (4) agricultural and environmental groups, (5) professional societies, (6) academic institutions, (7) conservation organizations, (8) agribusiness, (9) NRCS Earth Team volunteers, and (10) research conservation and development councils.

Terraces, buffers, and conservation tillage are among the practices being used by farmers in Shelby County (IA) in an NRCS water quality improvement project to benefit a nearby lake. Photograph by Tim McCabe/NRCS.

integrates the various sectors. Recommended elements of waterbody and wetland protection ordinances include: (1) prohibit damaging modifications such as channelization, straightening, filling, impoundment, draining, and armoring, (2) require mitigation for unavoidable disturbances, (3) protect natural buffer zones along the edge of waterbodies and wetlands, (4) require setbacks for buildings and pavement, and (5) prohibit direct discharges of untreated stormwater into existing wetlands (NIPC 2002).

International institutional and legal authorities

As discussed in the previous section on U.S. land use regulations, regulatory and policy-related strategies for dealing with altered bed and bank structure in freshwater ecosystems is most effectively dealt with a local and regional scales. The following list summarizes relevant international laws and treaties as well as important literature describing experience from around the world (Table 4-3).

TABLE 4-3. International Institutions and Legal Authorities

International
Helsinki Rules on the Uses of the Waters of International Rivers, International Law Association (1966)
Madrid Declaration on Int'l Regulations Regarding the Use of Int'l Watercourses for Purposes other than Navigation, Institute of International Law, 24 Annuaire de l'Institut de Droit International (1911)
General Comment No. 15 (2002), The Right to Water, Substantive Issues Arising in the Implementation of the International Covenant on Economic, Social and Cultural Rights, U.N. Economic and Social Council, E/C.12/2000/11 (26 November 2002)
Dublin Statement on the Water and Sustainable Development UN Conference on Environment & Development (Rio de Janeiro/Brazil, June 1992), Chapter 18 - Protection of the Quality and Supply of Freshwater Resources: Application of Integrated Approaches to the Development, Management and Use of Water Resources

Europe
Third Protocol amending the Convention on the canalization of the Mosel. Done in Trier, 12 May 1987; in force, 1 January 1988
Convention on the International Commission for the Protection of the Oder. Done in Wroclaw, 11 April 1964
Convention on the Protection of the Rhine. Done at Rotterdam, January 22, 1998. Federal Republic of Germany, France, Luxembourg, the Netherlands, Switzerland, and the European Union

COMMUNITY-BASED STRATEGIES

Watershed management strategies increasingly involve and require public participation. However, sustaining public interest and commitment can be challenging. Successful management efforts involve watershed projects built from the bottom-up by local citizens who are concerned and willing to take action to manage water resources (Mullen and Allison 1999). Public involvement currently is "experiencing a paradigm shift from adversarial, top-down, public meeting approach to a collaborative, bottom-up, citizen led and citizen organized approach" (Griffin 1999). The growing number of watershed councils attest to this shift in community involvement. Watershed councils are groups formed to participate collaboratively in the management of natural resources at the watershed level. These councils consist of government agencies, stakeholders, and practitioners.

Watershed councils differ widely in their goals, composition, strategies, and role in decision-making. While the goal of most councils is improved water management (e.g., flood control, reliable water supplies), other councils have broader goals (e.g., increased local control over natural resources, integrated resource planning and management).

Natural catastrophes (e.g., floods) or human mismanagement of resources (e.g., species and habitat loss) often propel communities and stakeholders into action. For example, stakeholders and local officials were proactive in modifying mitigation plans following the 1986 floods of the Napa River (California). The original plan proposed by the Corps followed a more traditional approach of enlarging the existing channel and constraining the river to its main channel. Major concerns were salinity intrusion due to channel deepening, degradation of water quality in the river, disposal of contaminated dredge material, and the general environmentally insensitive nature of the project. To foster community consensus and support for a flood protection plan, the conservation district initiated a community-wide coalition process to develop alternatives. Stakeholders supported a living river concept or a river system with the physical, chemical, and biological components that function together to produce complex, diverse communities of plants and animals. In order to achieve this goal, restoration strategies to abate bed and bank structure alterations were included in project design (USACE 2002b).

GROUNDWATER EXPLOITATION

Introduction

Groundwater is subsurface water located in the spaces between soil particles and within rock cavities. Rocks and soils that have the ability to hold a lot of water and allow this water to pass easily through them are called aquifers. The water table (the top of the uppermost aquifer) may be only a foot below the ground's surface or hundreds of feet down. Groundwater is intimately connected hydrologically, chemically, and biologically with surface freshwater ecosystems—rivers, lakes, and wetlands. Please see Chapter 2 of this guide for an in-depth overview of groundwater.

Groundwater provides the largest reserve of active freshwater for human needs. Groundwater volume is estimated at 6,000 times the instantaneous flow of all rivers and streams in the world. The amount of groundwater globally is approximately 11×10^6–60×10^6 km^3 (or 0.61% of all water on the planet) (Davies and Day 1998, Gleick 1993, Freeze and Cherry 1979). Nearly 2 billion people globally rely almost completely on groundwater for drinking water, including residents of some of the largest cities in the developing world, such as Jakarta, Dhaka, Lima, and Mexico City (Sampat 2000). About 20% of global water withdrawals (approximately 600–700 km^3 per year) come from groundwater sources (Shiklomanov 1997). In the U.S., groundwater accounts for 22% of all freshwater withdrawals. More than 37% of irrigation water, 38% of total public water supply, and 62% of potable water comes from groundwater reserves (USGS 1999a, NRC 2000). About 60% of Arizona's annual water usage comes from groundwater reserves (Saliba and Bush 1987). The Biscayne aquifer in

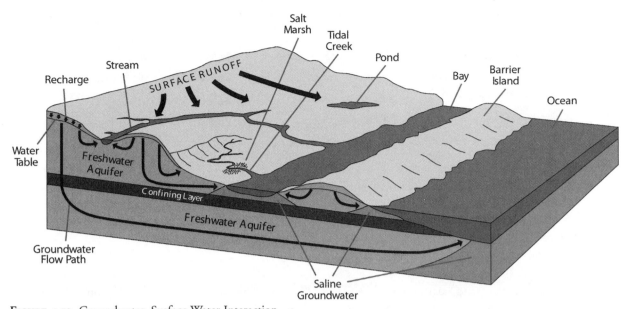

FIGURE 4-12. Groundwater–Surface Water Interaction

Adapted from Paul M. Barlow. 2003. USGS Circular 1262, Groundwater in Freshwater-Saltwater Environments of the Atlantic Coast. Available at http://water.usgs.gov/pubs/circ/2003/circ1262/index.html.

Florida is the only source of drinking water for more than three million residents of the Miami area, and the Edwards Aquifer is the primary water supply for San Antonio, Texas (NRC 2000). In South Africa, 50% of the total population relies on groundwater (SADC 2002), and 90% of the water consumed in urban areas of northern China comes from groundwater sources (Lierong 2002). In Libya 87% of the water used comes from fossil aquifers in the Sahara Desert (Lopez and Morales 2002). In contrast, groundwater supplies only 10% of Russia's drinking water supply (World Water Forum 2000) and only 20% of Australia's water supply (National Land and Water Resources Audit 2001).

Not surprisingly, given these current levels of extraction, groundwater sources are declining in areas of the world where the rate of water withdrawal or extraction is greater than the rate of recharge (called overdraft). Globally, aquifers are shrinking by more than 160 billion m³ per year (Postel 1999). Additionally, human activities are polluting some aquifers with toxic chemicals and pathogens as well as through excessive pumping that allow seawater to intrude into the aquifer. These contaminated waters are unsuitable for most human needs. Regions of the world experiencing serious overdraft rates include China, India,

the Middle East, North Africa, and portions of the United States and Russia. The ratio of withdrawal to recharge in some aquifers around the world reflect the widespread nature of this problem: the Saq aquifer in Saudi Arabia, 4.8:1; Coastal aquifer in the Gaza Strip, 1.6:1; Ogallala aquifer in the U.S., 3.2:1; the Sana'a Basin (Yemen), 5.3:1; and in parts of Arizona 10:1 (Ayelel and Al Shadily 2000). In the Jefara plain of northern Libya intensive development and population growth have resulted in severe mining of aquifers; this is reflected in declining water tables, exhaustion of accessible aquifers, seawater intrusions, deterioration of water quality, reduced land production, and diminishing biodiversity (Alghariani 1999).

The following section presents some of the deleterious consequences of groundwater overdraft on freshwater ecosystems and strategies to abate these effects.

The Effects of Groundwater Withdrawals on Freshwater Ecosystems

Groundwater and surface water are intimately linked. Their interactions involve the transfer of water, physical and biological matter, and energy across numerous spatial and temporal scales (Winter *et al.* 1998). These interactions occur in river and lake systems,

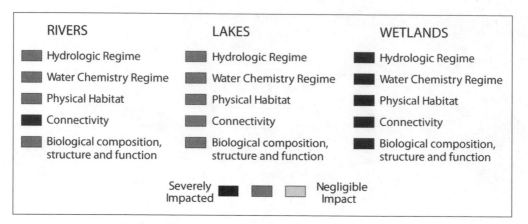

FIGURE 4-13. Summary of the Impact of Groundwater Overexploitation on Freshwater Ecosystems

wetlands, estuaries, bays, and coastal areas. Aquifers are like giant sponges, and pumping may affect water supplies outside the immediate area of withdrawal. Current water management schemes frequently fail to acknowledge this spatial connectivity. For example, the pumping of groundwater has resulted in the rerouting and/or desiccation of numerous river systems (Reisner 1993). Pumping an aquifer is like drinking a beverage through a straw: only a few wells or straws are needed to lower the reserve quickly, even for larger aquifers. The issue of water rights and groundwater withdrawal under adjacent land are at the core of ongoing litigation in some western states in the U.S. The following sections identify some of distinct effects of groundwater exploitation on specific key ecological factors of freshwater ecosystems.

CONNECTIVITY

In most watersheds, surface water and groundwater are interconnected. Groundwater pumping initially causes a localized decline in water tables, and that decline, or cone of depression, propagates progressively outward until it encounters hydraulically connected surface water bodies. These surface water bodies are subsequently depleted as a result of the pumping (Johnson *et al.* 1998). Since groundwater provides the baseflow for most rivers, lowering the water table reduces instream flow. When high capacity wells were put into operation along the Tanque Verde Creek in Arizona, the water table dropped 3.7–6.5 meters per year near the pumps and 0.5–1.5 meters per year in areas further

removed from the pumping stations (Stromberg 1992). The groundwater level in the Ogallala aquifer, which lies beneath parts of the U.S. Great Plains, dropped 16–50 meters over the past 60 years as a result of heavy reliance on groundwater for agricultural crops. Net cumulative depletion of water through 1999 is estimated to be 271,368,000,000 m^3 (USGS 2002). Groundwater levels may also affect the estuaries of rivers entering bays and coastal waters. As a result of heavy use of groundwater in South Africa, many estuaries are becoming shallow and silt-laden and the mouths are frequently closed by the deposits because of decreased instream flows (Davies and Day 1998).

PHYSICAL HABITAT CONDITIONS

In addition to effecting streamflow and water tables, large-scale pumping can cause regional subsidence. As water is withdrawn, aquifers collapse and the soil becomes compacted, resulting in irreversible loss of underground storage capacity. More than 50% of the pre-development saturated thickness has been dewatered in the central and southern regions of the Ogallala aquifer in the U.S. This volume represents more than 40% of the combined storage capacity of human-made reservoirs in the region. In California's San Joaquin Valley, more than 13,500 km^2 of irrigable land subsided 30 cm or more by 1972 as a result of groundwater pumping for irrigation (Poland *et al.* 1975). Massive groundwater withdrawals in areas just to the south of San Francisco, California, have caused substantial land subsidence in the Santa Clara Valley. Land in downtown

Low-lying land is frequently flooded in the Chesapeake Bay region due to sea level rise and subsidence caused by increasing water demand and lowering water tables. Photograph by Mary Hollinger/NOAA.

San Jose (California) subsided more than four meters in an 85-year period beginning in 1910. Lands adjacent to the southern part of San Francisco Bay sank an average of 0.6 to 2.4 meters between 1910 and 1969, putting 44 km² of dry land below the high-tide level. Other areas in the U.S. showing significant subsidence include Houston-Galveston (Texas), Baton Rouge (Louisiana), and Phoenix (Arizona). Smaller areas of subsidence are also common in the southeast (particularly Florida), where pumping from carbonate aquifers has caused numerous sinkholes (USGS 1999b).

THE WATER CHEMISTRY REGIME

Saltwater intrusion

Freshwater aquifers can become contaminated by saline water when the hydraulic head[15] of a freshwater aquifer is reduced by pumping, allowing the movement of saltwater into it. Many Atlantic Ocean coastal communities in the U.S. are plagued by saltwater intrusion resulting from groundwater extraction. Aquifers in Brooklyn, New York were destroyed in the 1930s when pumping lowered the water table by 9–15

meters below sea level (Fetter 1994). Eighty percent of the drinking water for Dakar (capital of Senegal) comes from groundwater, but overdraft has caused significant saltwater intrusion into the aquifer and threatens to make the water unsuitable for human use by the middle of the 21st century; saltwater is contaminating the aquifer at the rate of 40 m per year (Potworowski 1990). Some aquifers in interior regions also contain saline water, and pumping activities of freshwater aquifers that overlay them increases the potential of saltwater intrusion from below. For example, groundwater withdrawal from an alluvial aquifer in Arkansas causes upward movement of saline water into a freshwater source (Morris and Bush 1996).

Salinization and other chemical changes

As groundwater is pumped, shallow bodies of surface water (e.g., wetlands, lakes) dry out, exposing and concentrating mineral salts (e.g., sodium, magnesium, potassium, calcium, and sulfates) in upper soil layers. Additionally, when the water table reaches a critical depth below the ground surface (e.g., 2 m in Australia), evaporation of water can occur via capillary rise,

---

[15] Hydraulic head is an indicator of total energy available to move groundwater through an aquifer. Hydraulic head is measured by the height to which a column of water will stand above a reference elevation, such as mean sea level. Groundwater flows from locations of higher hydraulic head to locations of lower hydraulic head. Change in hydraulic head over a specified distance in a given direction is called the hydraulic gradient.

Box 4-9. San Pedro Riparian National Conservation Area, Arizona

The San Pedro National Conservation Area (SPNCA), designated by Congress in 1988, encompasses 23,471 ha of a unique desert riparian ecosystem, the star of which is the San Pedro River. The perennial, north flowing San Pedro River supports remnant communities of riparian vegetation (e.g., cottonwoods, willows, ash, walnut, netleaf, and hackberry) while Chihuahuan desert-scrub communities (e.g., tarbush, creosote and acacia) dominate drier reaches. SPNCA supports over 350 species of birds, 80 species of mammals, two native and several introduced species of fish, and more than 40 species of amphibians and reptiles. The groundwater found beneath the Conservation Area not only keeps the riverbed wet during low flow periods, but also provides water to the growing town of Sierra Vista, the Fort Huachuca Army Base, and the surrounding area. However, the ability of this unique system to continue supporting this diverse array of plants and animals as well as human water needs is now in question. Groundwater pumping in the Sierra Vista/Fort Huachuca area has lowered water tables, thereby reducing annual base flow into the San Pedro River by 30%. Annual groundwater overdraft currently is more than 8.6 million m^3 and is predicted to exceed more than 16 million m^3 within 30 years.

Recognizing the need for an adequate and continuous supply of water to maintain the ecosystem, a group of 17 local, state, and federal agencies and organizations formed The Upper San Pedro Partnership to develop a conservation plan. The goal of that plan is to "assure that an adequate long-term groundwater supply is available to meet the reasonable needs of both the area's residents and property owners (current and future) and the San Pedro Riparian National Conservation Area" (TNC 2000). Efforts across this diverse array of partners include water conservation, groundwater recharge enhancement, and community education and support initiatives, a few of which are described below:

- Fort Huachuca plans to reduce their water consumption by more than 325,500 m^3 per year through water conservation efforts. These efforts include leak detection and repair, installation of low-flow and waterless fixtures, and implementation of a high-visibility water conservation education program (FEMP 2003).

- The City of Sierra Vista plans to replace 3.0–3.7 million m^3 of water into this system annually by recharging threatened wastewater to the ground as part of the Sierra Vista Wastewater Recharge Project (DOI 2000). This joint federal, state and local cost-sharing agreement commits $7.5 million for construction of a water reclamation facility, a 4-ha lagoon system, a 20-ha wetlands complex, and 12-ha groundwater recharge basins complex to increase groundwater recharge.

- The Nature Conservancy hopes to decrease water demand by purchasing agricultural land and either converting this land to native grassland habitat or retiring it from agriculture (TNC 2002).

San Pedro River, Arizona. Photograph by Harold E. Malde.

BOX 4-10. Mexico City's Falling Water Table and Subsidence

Mexico City extends over 3,773 km² and with more than 18 million residents, it is the world's third largest city. Historically, the city depended primarily on groundwater pumped from the underlying Mexico Basin aquifer to meet its needs, supplemented by small amounts from surface supplies. To meet current water demands, 4.8 million m³ of water per day is pumped from the main aquifer, accounting for about 72% of total needs. Natural recharge of the Mexico Basin aquifer is 2.4 million m³ of water per day. Although overdraft of the aquifer has occurred since the early 1900s, the problem has intensified recently. Groundwater level is sinking by about one meter each year, and between 1986 and 1992, it dropped six to ten meters in heavily pumped zones. Although water is imported from the Lerma and Cutzamala basins to make up for the make up the shortfall as well provide water for recharging the aquifer, it only partially addresses the problem.

As a result of overdraft, Mexico City suffers from severe land subsidence. Over the past 100 years, the central area of the Mexico City has fallen an average of 7.5 meters; current rates are now about six cm per year (Morgan 2002). Direct impacts include structural damage to buildings and other facilities (e.g., sewer systems, water and gas pipes) and persistent flooding during periods of heavy rainfall. Damage from earthquakes which the area is also prone to can be significantly exacerbated by this subsidence. In 1900, the bottom of Texcoco Lake was three meters lower than the average level of the city center; by 1974 the lake bottom was two meters higher than the city. The aquifer is also at risk from contamination and saltwater intrusion. Currently, 90% of municipal and industrial liquid wastes from the metropolitan area are discharged untreated into the sewer systems, some of which are damaged by subsidence. Industries alone generate an estimated three million metric tons of hazardous wastes per year, and in many areas, this wastewater travels in unlined drainage canals (WRI 1997, Hunt 1990).

A satellite image of Mexico City, Mexico by METI/ERSDAC.

Although the city's location (2,300 m) and geographic setting (closed basin) present unique challenges for importing water (e.g., water transfers from distant sources are expensive and technologically challenging), Mexico City is pursuing strategies to slow demand and increase water conservation, including repairs to distribution systems, replacing toilets with low-flow models, and installing meters on all users. Officials also instituted a new pricing system that includes full cost of urban water use (e.g., cost of developing sewage systems, wastewater treatment facilities, price of water). Currently, only 10% of the marginal cost of supplying water is collected. The new rate structure will charge more per unit as consumption levels increase. The goal is to provide metered industries with incentives to conserve water, eventually leading to full cost recovery (WRI 1997).

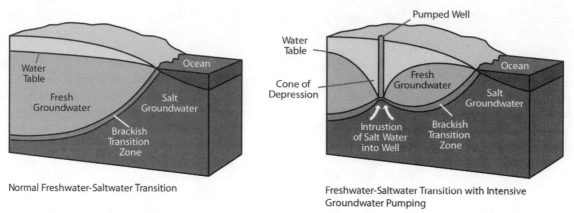

FIGURE 4-14. Saltwater Intrusion Can Occur with Intensive Groundwater Pumping.

transporting soluble salts with it to the soil surface. While mineral salts in low concentrations are important for plant growth, high concentrations are harmful to most vegetation and animals. Salinization is widespread in arid regions and is a serious problem for native vegetation and crop and pasture production (Yahyaoui and Ouessar 1999, Seiler and Lindner 1995).

Paradoxically, many places in Australia (one of the most arid places in the world) are experiencing increased soil salinity levels as a result of rising water tables. Replacement of deep-rooted native vegetation with shallow-rooted annual crops and pastureland has caused water tables to rise, concentrating salts near the soil surface. Additionally, hydrologic changes (e.g., caused by the construction of dams and diversions) have eliminated the flushing capacity of natural flows, leaving salts concentrated near the surfaces. Increased salinization can have enormous social and economic costs: within 50 years drinking water supplies in Adelaide (Australia) are predicted to be unsuitable and 15–19 million hectares will be only marginally productive (Planet Ark 2000).

BIOLOGICAL COMPOSITION AND INTERACTIONS

Structure

Effects of groundwater pumping on community structure are most apparent in arid regions where surface water supplies and precipitation are limited. Ground-water extraction affects the structure of surface water and hyporheic[16] communities by limiting available food and habitat. Water flowing through the hyporheic zone on its way to the river carries organic matter that supports food webs. Bacteria, protozoans (i.e., amoebae and paramecium), and meiofauna (very small insects, worms, and crustaceans) that live in this zone absorb the matter, and in turn they are a food source for small, bottom-feeding fish, amphibians, and aquatic invertebrates. Groundwater pumping reduces or eliminates waterflow through this zone, imperiling biota dependent upon these resources for food. Overdraft also causes desiccation of aquatic plants in stream channels, riparian areas, floodplains, and wetlands through lowered water tables. For example, the range of the riparian cottonwood-willow habitat of the San Pedro River (Arizona) which supports the endangered southwestern willow flycatcher (*Empidonax traillii extimus*) and the Huachuca water umbel (*Lilaeopsis schaffneriana ssp. recurva*), a listed herbaceous, semiaquatic perennial plant, has been significantly reduced from historical levels by declining water tables. Likewise, cottonwood stands along the lower Verde River (Arizona) have declined as a result of groundwater pumping (Stromberg 1992). Additionally, increased soil salinity, resulting from groundwater overdraft, favors opportunistic invasive alien species (e.g., salt cedar (*Tamarix aphylla*)), further increasing competition with native flora. Where groundwater pumping reduces freshwater flows into estuaries and bays, community structure shifts to more saline tolerant species.

---

[16] Hyporheic zone is the saturated sediment beneath and beside streams where groundwater and surface water mix. It is a hotspot of biological diversity and contains active physical and chemical gradients.

Increased soil salinity, resulting from groundwater overdraft, favors opportunistic invasive alien species like the tamarisk lining the banks of this stream. Photograph by Scott T. Smith.

In the Edwards Aquifer (Texas) over-pumping of groundwater threatens aquatic species that live in water-filled caverns beneath the surface as well as river and estuary taxa. Dewatering, intrusion from saline water zones, direct mortality due to pumping, and contamination from human activities over the aquifer threaten the widemouth blindcat (*Satan eurystomus*), toothless blindcat (*Trogloglanis pattersoni*), and more than 40 species of macroinvertebrates. The two fish species are endemic, have a very limited range, and are found at depths of 400 to 600 meters (TSHA 2002). Pumping from the aquifer has also lowered amount of water supplying surface streams and spring, jeopardizing water quality and aquatic habitat.

THE HYDROLOGIC REGIME

Groundwater extraction alters a freshwater ecosystem's hydrologic regime to the extent that such extraction affects base flow levels. Rivers, lakes, and wetlands whose source of water is largely if not exclusively groundwater sources will logically face the highest degree of alteration to this regime caused by groundwater extraction. In many areas of the world, rivers and streams depend almost entirely on groundwater to maintain their base flows, often the only source of water during times with no precipitation or runoff. However, these effects are very closely linked to the issues described above with **connectivity**. Please refer to this discussion above for more information.

Strategies for Mitigating/Abating the Effect of Groundwater Extraction on Freshwater Ecosystems

Groundwater resources are a valuable supply of freshwater to meet human uses and serve ecosystem needs. Yet, the extent of the effect of groundwater extraction on the integrity of freshwater ecosystems is often not examined by decision makers when weighing various management options. Additionally, extraction activities frequently are inadequately regulated, and where regulations exist, they tend to be independent of surface water needs and rights. Social, economic, and environmental concerns are seldom integrated in decision-making on groundwater (Kidd 2002). The following section identifies some strategies that have been used

*The widemouth blindcat (*Satan eurystomus*), an endemic species found in Edwards Aquifer, Texas, is threatened by over-pumping of groundwater. Photograph by Garold W. Sneegas.*

successfully to mitigate the effects of groundwater overexploitation. Because groundwater is underground and cannot be seen, special attention should be paid to understand this resource and assess the effectiveness of any strategy, e.g., developing aquifer maps and monitoring groundwater quantity and quality, etc.

TECHNICAL STRATEGIES

Water management sensitive to ecosystem needs should include protection against groundwater overexploitation given the strong linkage between surface water and groundwater resources. Technical strategies for protecting groundwater include restricting groundwater over-pumping and enhancing groundwater recharge by protecting key recharge areas or through the injection of additional waters into groundwater reserves. This section briefly discusses these strategies.

Restricting groundwater overpumping

Demand reduction is an approach to protect against overdraft of aquifers. This strategy has both technical and management considerations. It involves decreasing demand on groundwater supplies by using alternative sources and overall reduction in consumption through efficiency. It is estimated that urban per-capita demand can be reduced by 46% by increasing efficiency and the use of reclaimed water (Haasz 1999). In Monterey County (California), a $75 million project will deliver 200,000 m³ of recycled water annually to 5,000

hectares of farmland, thereby relieving pressure on coastal aquifers for water (Gleick 2000). Another strategy is use of desalinized water to supplement water supplies. The Tampa Bay Water District (Florida) built a 95,000 m³ per day reverse osmosis desalinization plant in order to stop degradation of coastal wetlands and seawater intrusion resulting from groundwater overdraft. The facility is integrated into a nearby energy cogeneration plant to utilize waste heat. At $0.55 per m³, the desalinized water is 20–25% of the cost from similar facilities in other parts of the world (e.g., Singapore, Cyprus, and Trinidad). Some environmental concerns associated with this project are the effects on local ecosystems of water withdrawals and disposal of the brine after desalinization (Gleick 2000). Other strategies to relieve pressure on local groundwater sources include transfer of water through canals and pipes from other underground supplies or surface sources (e.g., reservoirs, lakes and rivers). There are numerous examples of such water transfer schemes, such as the Central Arizona Project and the Central Valley Project of California. However, these water transfers projects present their own unique set of environmental risks.

Promoting/enhancing groundwater recharge by limiting development of impervious surfaces in key recharge areas

The amount of impervious surface reflects the degree of urbanization and strongly affects both replenishment and the quality of groundwater. Rapid growth of urban areas throughout the world results in lost groundwater recharge unless water management plans guide development. For example, annual recharge loss rates between 1982–1997 in Atlanta (Georgia) are estimated at 215,390,000 m^3–502,703,000 m^3 and in Seattle (Washington) 39,746,800 m^3–93,121,100 m^3 (Smart Growth America 2002).

Land use planning that safeguards the integrity of recharge zones is critical in protecting groundwater sources. There is growing awareness of the need for smart growth[17] that protects the environment and meets human needs. Key elements of this type of land use planning include:

- Allocation of adequate resources to identify and protect open space and critical aquatic areas;
- Implementation of sound growth management by strong, comprehensive legislation that includes incentives for smart growth and designated growth areas;
- Integration of water supplies into planning efforts through coordination of road-building and other construction projects with water resource management activities;
- Investment in existing communities by rehabilitating infrastructure before building new structures (a fix it first strategy of development);
- Fostering compact development that mixes retail, commercial, and residential development;
- Management of stormwater using natural systems; where possible use low-impact development techniques that foster local infiltration;
- Allocation of resources to research and analyze impact of development on water resources; and
- Public access to research and analysis information. (Adapted from *Smart Growth America 2002*).

Please see the urbanization and industrialization section of the land use and management subchapter for more information about smart growth practices.

Groundwater protection may be guided by regulatory policies, voluntary guidelines, and incentive-based programs. As an example of regulatory policies, Massachusetts state law requires municipalities to adopt an impervious surface control; regulations prohibit "land uses that result in the rendering impervious of more than 15% or 232 m^2 of any lot, whichever is greater, unless a system for artificial recharge of precipitation is provided that will not result in the degradation of groundwater quality" (Massachusetts 1999). Local or state regulations may also prohibit or restrict building on areas critical to surface water flow and infiltration, such as flood-plains and wetlands.

Enhancing groundwater resources through artificial injection

Artificially injecting water into existing groundwater is another approach used by a number of municipalities and others who are concerned over declining water tables. Obviously, high quality water should be used for such purposes since contamination is a concern. One advantage of this approach is that it can help reduce the expansion of any "cone of depression" (see Boxes 4-9 and 4-10), stop the decline of baseflow levels in streams, and maintain the connection between surface waters and groundwater. Artificial injection has also been used to prevent the intrusion of saltwater into groundwater aquifers in coastal areas.

Recycled water (treated and disinfected wastewater), as well as potable water, is often used for artificial injection. Although contamination of aquifers by using reclaimed water remains a health and ecological concern, this problem can be addressed by monitoring and pretreatment of the water before it is released for recharge. In southern California, water and waste treatment agencies have worked cooperatively recharging the Central Basin aquifers with treated effluents since the 1960s. In Israel, treated wastewater already accounts for 30% of the water supply, and this amount is expected to increase to almost 80% by 2025 (Postel 2001). Discussion of the potential ecological concerns of this approach are similar to the description of ecological effects included below within the surface water diversions section under interbasin water transfers.

---

[17] Smart growth is well-planned development that protects open spaces and farmland, revitalizes communities, maintains 'affordable' housing, and provides more transportation choices.

INSTITUTIONAL AND LEGAL STRATEGIES

In the U.S., as well as most of the world, property rights in underground water resources are usually determined from surface land ownership immediately above the groundwater. Use of these resources tends to be governed by an examination of whether the use is reasonable rather than whether the groundwater is used within recharge areas for the groundwater resource. In many instances, this is the extent of regulatory control. Most government regulation of groundwater resources (1) does not protect groundwater from land use changes, (2) does not take an ecosystem approach, (3) varies widely across levels of government and political entities and therefore the regulatory regime is patchwork, (4) lacks adequate transboundary mechanisms of governance, (5) is often driven by the principle of supply management, and (6) is hampered by large gaps in knowledge of groundwater resources (e.g., assessment of reserves, recharge rates, groundwater-surface water interaction) (Kidd 2002). Historically, groundwater has avoided significant regulatory control because it is not visible, due to the changes of monitoring water quantity and quality, and because little was known about its linkage with surface features and processes.

U.S. institutional and legal authorities

Working with state agencies to establish regulations on groundwater overpumping

Key elements of groundwater protection programs are legal instruments, information, and resource support. Specifically, they include:

- Legislation including establishment of protection regulations;
- Inter- and intra-agency coordination with surface water and other programs;
- Groundwater mapping and classification;
- Monitoring of ambient groundwater quality;
- Comprehensive data management systems;
- Prevention and remediation programs for contaminated sites;

- Adequate resources to develop and implement BMPs
(adapted from USEPA 1999).

Introducing legislation at national, regional, and local levels to encourage sound management of groundwater resources offers one option for improving regulatory control. The right of an institution (e.g., government authority, other body) to regulate groundwater extraction and its use should be recognized by legal documents or other instruments. Additionally, establishment of ownership (e.g., public, private) and conditions of transfer, modification or abolition of use rights is necessary to promote equitable and effective groundwater protection strategies (UN 1989). Limiting over-pumping and carefully managing both well placement and extraction from these wells can minimize the effects of pumping on associated freshwater ecosystems. Deeper wells or wells located farther from rivers are less likely to be hydrologically linked to these resources or may result in a longer delay between extraction activities and impacts to surface waters. Allowing wells to periodically rest provides an opportunity for groundwater levels to recover, which may, in turn, provide more water to wetlands and rivers. Resting wells is often common practice for water supply wells in order to maintain consistently high quality in extracted water—overtaxed wells may result in increased concentrations of naturally occurring chemicals and pollutants from human activities. Developing operation plans that take into account ecological needs can significantly reduce the impacts of groundwater extraction on freshwater ecosystems.

One of the most important considerations in groundwater management is safeguarding the quantity and quality groundwater supplies. This involves assuring a continued supply of high quality recharge water, protecting critical recharge areas from development, and preventing contaminants from reaching groundwater:

- Assuring a continued supply of high quality recharge water proves increasingly difficult as land use changes alter soil infiltration patterns and capacity. Also, where groundwater supplies are augmented by artificial recharge (e.g., through treated

TABLE 4-4. International Institutions and Legal Authorities

International

International Law Commission, Resolution on Confined Transboundary Groundwater, 2 Y.B. Int'l L. Comm'n 135 (1994)

Seoul Rules on International Groundwaters, International Law Association (1986)

Resolution VIII.40, Guidelines for rendering the use of groundwater compatible with the conservation of wetlands: "Wetlands: water, life and culture." 8th Meeting of the Conference of the Contracting Parties to the Convention on Wetlands (Ramsar, Iran, 1971) Valencia, Spain, 18–26 November 2002

Transboundary Groundwaters: The Bellagio Draft Treaty, available at: 29 Nat. Resources J. 676 (1989)

Matsumoto, Kyoko. 2002. "Transboundary Groundwater and International Law: Past Practices and Current Implications." Oregon State University. Master's paper

Barberis, Julio, International Groundwater Resources Law, in U.N. Food and Agriculture Organization Legislation Study No. 40 (1986)

Groundwater and its Susceptibility to Degradation: A Global Assessment of the Problem and Options for Management (United Nations, May 2003)

Guidelines on Monitoring and Assessment of Transboundary Groundwaters, UN/ECE Task Force on Monitoring and Assessment (2000)

Internationally Shared (Transboundary) Aquifer Resources Management, Int'l Assoc. of Hydrogeologists and UN Econ., Social., and Cultural Org. (2001)

Barberis, Julio, The Development of International Law of Transboundary Groundwater, 31 Nat. Res. J. 167 (1991)

Hayton, Robert D. & Utton, Albert E., Transboundary Groundwaters: The Bellagio Draft Treaty, 29 Nat. Resources J. 663 (1989)

Hayton, Robert D., The Law of International Aquifers, 22 N.R.J. 71 (1982)

Teclaff, Ludwik A. & Utton, Albert E., eds., International Groundwater Law (1981)

Llamas, R. & Custodio, E., Intensively Exploited Aquifers: Main Concepts, Relevant Facts, and Some Suggestions, IHP-VI, Series on Groundwater No. 4, UNESCO (2002)

Europe

Council Directive 80/68/EEC of 17 December 1979 On the Protection of Groundwater Against Pollution Caused by Certain Dangerous Substances

UN/ECE Charter on Ground-Water Management, U.N. Doc. E/ECE/1197, ECE/ENVWA/12, U.N. Sales No. E.89.II.E.21 (1989)

Arrangement relatif a la Protection, a l'Utilization et a la Realimentation de la Nappe souterraine franco-suisse du Genevois (Arrangement on the Protection, Utilization and Recharge of the Franco-Swiss Genevese Aquifer) (Sept. 1977) (Unofficial English Translation)

Food and Agriculture Organization of the United Nations, Legislative and Research Branch, Groundwater Legislation in Europe (1964)

Lefevere, J., Integrating Groundwater Quality Control into European Community Water Policy, 8 Rev. Eur. Community & Int'l Envtl. L. 291 (1999)

Eckstein, Gabrid, Application of International Water Law to Transboundary Groundwater Resources, and the Slovak-Hungarian Dispute Over Gabcikovo-Nagymaros, 19 Suffolk Transnt'l L.R. 67 (1995)

Middle East

Feitelson, Eran & Haddad, Marwan, Identification of Joint Management Structures for Shared Aquifers: A Cooperative Palestinian-Israeli Effort, World Bank Technical Paper No. 415 (1998)

North America

Anderson, T.L., & Snyder, P.S., A Free Market Solution To Groundwater Allocation In Georgia

Chavez, O. E., Mining of Internationally Shared Aquifers: The El Paso-Juarez Case, 40 Nat. Resources J. 237 (2000)

Ingram, Helen, Transboundary Groundwater on the U.S.-Mexico Border: Is the Glass Half Full, Half Empty or Even on the Table?, 40 Nat. Resources J. 198 (2000)

Mumme, P. Stephen, The La Paz Symposium on Transboundary Groundwater Management on the U.S.-Mexican Border, 40 Nat. Resources J. 435 (2000)

Arias, Hector M. International Groundwaters: The Upper San Pedro River Basin Case, 40 Nat. Resources J. 199 (2000)

wastewater injection and infiltration ponds), controls must be in place to assess the quality of this water (see previous information on enhancing groundwater resources through artificial injection included within technical strategies related to groundwater for more information).

- Strategies for protecting critical recharge areas include land acquisition of such areas by local governmental agencies (as well as by NGOs) and the implementation of local government controls such as land use planning and zoning as well as other regulatory instruments.

- Preventing contaminants from reaching groundwater requires identifying a potential source of contamination before it leaches into the groundwater and implementing appropriate strategies to reduce or eliminate the contaminant before it causes harm. The most common sources of contaminants for groundwater extend from agriculture and fuel or chemical storage facilities. The Groundwater Foundation has developed a useful resource, entitled *Using Technology to Conduct a Contaminant Source Inventory: A Primer for Small Communities* (available for download from http://www.groundwater.org/pe/actt/actt.html), that explains s the threat posed by various contaminants, describes approaches for assessing their extent, and presents strategies for abating these threats (GF 2002b).

Finally, reducing demand for groundwater through water conservation efforts (see the Surface Water Diversions section of this subchapter for more information) also offers an opportunity to reduce stress to this important resource.

International institutional and legal strategies

Table 4-4 summarizes international laws and policies and important literature examining useful approaches from around the world relevant to groundwater management.

COMMUNITY-BASED STRATEGIES

Local strategies may provide practical and better alternatives than the large-scale, centralized, and capital-intensive approaches that have dominated water management in the past. Numerous examples in both developed and developing nations have shown that local strategies can provide invaluable complements to comprehensive water-management policies and projects. Addressing the needs of local groups and incorporating their suggestions/strategies can produce the best results in terms of efficiency of resource use and minimized negative environmental impacts. In order for local communities to be effective, close collaboration between local communities and governments is needed. Governments can provide local communities with a knowledge base and instruments to influence policies as well as ensure a more secure source of support and continuity in policy (Brooks 2000). The following section discusses a few locally based efforts that address issues of groundwater exploitation through education and policy initiatives.

Numerous government, university, and NGO programs exist that provide education, technical assistance, and capacity enhancement aid to community-based programs engaged in groundwater protection. The majority offer educational services and a few provide financial support for enhancement programs. For example, the Blue Planet Foundation (2002) funds water-related educational projects that focus on a variety of water-related environmental issues (e.g., water conservation, recycling, treatment, quality, or water issues related to politics or the economy). The state of Wisconsin sponsors a program that interprets drinking water test results, shares groundwater data, and provides access to groundwater flow models. The Groundwater Foundation provides a range of services and publications for citizens and communities seeking to protect groundwater quality and quantity. For more information on the Groundwater Foundation's programs, please see their website at http://www.groundwater.org/.

—Authored by Ronald Bjorkland and Catherine Pringle

Land Use and Management

Humans use land for a variety of purposes including urban development, recreation, food and timber production, and mineral and metal extraction for energy production and as raw materials for a wide range of products. These activities have been costly for freshwater ecosystems, contributing to the decline and alteration of water quantity in many ecosystems, the elimination of riparian and wetland areas, and the significant loss of biodiversity supported by these ecosystems. As human population grows, conversion of undeveloped land continues to expand, thereby magnifying these effects.

This subchapter examines changes to freshwater ecosystems caused by five land use practices:

A. Agriculture;
B. Urbanization and industrialization;
C. Forestry;
D. Mining; and
E. Recreation.

For each of these threats, this subchapter also presents information about specific strategies for reducing the effects of these threats on the underlying conservation goals and targets as well as strategies for eliminating the threats themselves.

AGRICULTURE

Introduction

Agriculture currently occupies 23% of global land (excluding Antarctica and Greenland), dramatically more than any other land use activity. Almost half of the one billion hectares of land in the contiguous United States has been cultivated or grazed by livestock (U.S. Bureau of the Census 1990) and 60% of Western Europe is in agricultural production (Thompson and Polet 2000). Agriculture includes both crop production and animal husbandry:

- Cultivated (e.g., tilled) and non-cultivated land are both used to grow crops. Crop production on non-cultivated lands includes orchards, vineyards, and other tree plantations such as coffee, rubber, and palm oil. Crop production on cultivated lands predominates in some regions of the world. For example, cultivated lands are used for 90% of crops grown in Asia (WRI 2000).
- Animal husbandry produces meat, eggs, milk, and fur. Animals may be raised on pasture or rangeland or in animal feeding operations (AFOs). As defined by the U.S. Environmental Protection Agency

(EPA), an AFO has animals that are stabled or confined and fed or maintained for a total of 45 days or more in any 12-month period and contains no crops, vegetation, forage growth, or post-harvest residues over any portion of the lot or facility. When the density of individuals exceeds a designated number (depending on the animal) an AFO becomes a Concentrated Animal Feeding Operation (CAFO), considered a point source of pollution.

Agriculture harms freshwater ecosystems by extracting water from and contributing pollutants to these ecosystems. Approximately two-thirds of global water use is extracted from either groundwater or surface water sources for agricultural purposes (Postel 1993). Most of this water is returned to the atmosphere by evaporation and does not replenish surface supplies. In addition to water quantity declines, irrigation results in significant water quality declines by contributing return flows or runoff back to freshwater ecosystems that is tainted with inputs to increase agricultural production and eroded soils. Major pollutants

BOX 4-11. Conversion of Everglades Wetlands for Agriculture

Conversion of the vast Everglades wetland complex began in the late 1800s. By 1948, the complex infrastructure of canals, levees, pumps, and control structures resulted in the conversion of 800,000 acres of wetlands for agriculture. In addition to these losses, altered hydrology and accelerated eutrophication from farm runoff have impaired the quality, function, and biological integrity of remaining wetland areas (McPherson and Halley 1997).

East Everglades Agricultural Area in Florida, once wetlands that were diked and drained. Photograph by Gary M. Stolz, U.S. Fish and Wildlife Service.

in freshwater ecosystems due to agricultural land uses are sediment, nitrogen, phosphorus, chemicals in pesticides, bacteria and synthetics. Agriculture causes approximately 60% of the pollution in lakes and rivers in the United States (Carey 1991) (USEPA 2000).

Agriculture also harms freshwater ecosystems by directly converting these ecosystems to agriculture. Although agricultural land area has continued to increase slowly over the past 30 years, this trend masks region-specific changes (FAO 2000). For example, although the United States, Western Europe, and Oceania have actually decreased agricultural acreage over the past few decades, agricultural expansion in developing nations has vastly exceeded that global average (National Research Council Committee on Sustainable Agriculture and the Environment in the Humid Tropics 1993).

Lands converted to agriculture are most commonly wetlands and riparian areas. In the 48 continental U.S. states, only half of the pre-settlement wetland area remains (National Research Council 1995) and agriculture accounts for the majority of those losses (Brinson and Malvarez 2002). In Europe, only those wetlands that occur in difficult environments, such as rugged terrain within major river floodplains or along lake margins, persist. While the loss of wetland area

has slowed dramatically in the U.S. and Europe, developing nations are rapidly losing wetland area to agricultural development. Estimates of total riparian vegetation loss due to conversion for agriculture are also high (e.g., 70–90% within the United States (Palmer 1994)). These lands are highly valued as they tend to offer nutrient rich soils due to regular alluvial deposits.

The Effects of Agriculture on Freshwater Ecosystems

Agricultural activities have impaired or are impairing most freshwater ecosystems. Intensive agriculture often leads to the eutrophication of freshwater ecosystems, resulting in deoxygenation of water, production of toxins, and a general decline in freshwater biodiversity. Over 46% of Ramsar lake sites in Europe have suffered a decline in water quality, largely as a result of eutrophication (EEA 2001). Agricultural development has eliminated vast expanses of wetlands around the world. In Spain alone, more than 60% of all wetlands disappeared during a 25 year period (Casado *et al.* 1992). In North America, one-half of its original wetland habitat has been lost with agricultural expansion responsible for between 85–87% of the losses

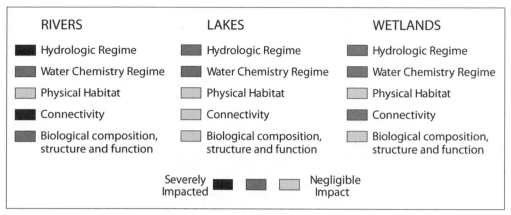

FIGURE 4-15. Summary of Impacts of Agriculture on Freshwater Ecosystems

(NRC 2001). The following text describes in greater detail the effects of agricultural practices on freshwater ecosystems by examining specific key ecological factors.

THE HYDROLOGIC REGIME

Agriculture changes the hydrologic regime of associated freshwater ecosystems primarily through altering the area's soil structure by compaction due to heavy machinery and trampling by livestock. These soil changes decrease infiltration capacity and the potential for soil to store water, thus affecting the balance of infiltration, percolation and overland flow of water. Runoff from lands converted from wetlands to farmland is 200–400% higher (Administration Floodplain Management Task Force 1994). Additionally, structures installed by humans to prepare land for crops and livestock or facilitate the delivery of water for agriculture affect the hydrology of watersheds by increasing the frequency, severity, and unpredictability of flood flows and prolonging low flow and drought conditions.

The hydrologic regime is also affected by direct withdrawals of water for agriculture as described by the Water Use and Management subchapter. Globally, 70% of all water withdrawn for human use is for irrigation (WRI 2000). In the U.S. in 1995 63% of the water withdrawn for irrigation came from surface water sources, except for in the south and southwest where groundwater sources are more heavily utilized (Solley *et al.* 1995). As stated within the Water Use and Management subchapter, the problem with water

withdrawals is that they alter the flow pattern and water levels in freshwater ecosystems. Where the extraction of surface water or groundwater lowers water levels at already low flow times of the year, consequences for biodiversity can be tragic. Alternatively, in wetter regions, irrigation infrastructure such as canals and reservoirs can tip the balance of the hydrologic cycle toward too much water, with equally dire consequences for resident biodiversity (Prasad 1994).

THE WATER CHEMISTRY REGIME

The major chemical inputs to freshwater ecosystems from land under crop production are fertilizers, herbicides, and pesticides. The major chemical inputs to freshwaters from land used for raising animals are manure and pharmaceuticals including pesticides and hormones. Most chemical pollution flows to freshwater ecosystems as runoff, from point sources, or through subsurface flow. Agricultural pollutants can be classified as nutrients, biodegradable organic matter, heavy metals, synthetic organic chemicals, salts, and bacteria (Clapham *et al.* 1998).

Nutrients

Nutrient enrichment, from nitrogen and phosphorus, is the leading pollution problem for lakes and the third most important pollution source for streams and rivers in the United States (USEPA 2000). Nutrient pollution accelerates the eutrophication process causing algal blooms followed by bacterial population explosions fed

A small wetland in Iowa farmland. Photograph by Tim McCabe/NRCS.

by algal decomposition. Bacterial decomposition depletes available oxygen, thereby harming other aquatic life.

Nutrient enrichment from agriculture can be attributed to two sources: fertilizer application and manure production. Historically, manure and other organic waste were the primary forms of fertilizer used for crop production. Crop rotation was also used to replenish necessary elements in the soil. Synthetic chemical fertilizers are more heavily used today. Superphosphates, urea, anhydrous ammonia and others are replacing natural fertilizers because they are available at low cost and often produce higher yields, allowing farmers to produce more with less acreage (Uri 1999). Typically, fertilizer is applied at rates that exceed the uptake potential of the crop. This leaves a surplus of available nutrients in the soil that will move through the environment and reach freshwater ecosystems.

As with surface waters, nitrate pollution is one of groundwater's most serious threats. In general, the risk of nitrate pollution for groundwater supplies is directly related to the amount of fertilizers or other nitrogen inputs to the land, as well as the permeability of the soil. For example, half of the groundwater samples in a heavily fertilized region of northern China contain nitrate levels above the safe limit for drinking water (Zhang *et al.* 1996).

Biodegradable organic matter

Animal waste associated with animal husbandry also contributes detrimental levels of nutrients to surface and ground waters (de Haan *et al.* 1997). Pastures are commonly located near small streams or on steeper slopes making manure runoff potential great (Line *et*

Box 4-12. Release of Nutrients into Watersheds by Flooding from Hurricane Floyd

In 1999, Hurricane Floyd caused severe flooding in North Carolina. Some of the hardest hit areas coincided with hot spots for hog production. Farms located within the 100-year floodplain lost untreated manure and urine waste stored in waste lagoons and on land as this material was flushed to the rivers and ultimately to coastal zones. As a result, these systems were saturated with nutrients, organic matter, antibiotics, hormones, and other synthetics causing severe deoxygenation, bacterial and algal blooms (including the highly toxic *Pfiesteria piscicida*), massive fish kills, and increased levels of synthetic contaminants (Floegel 2000) [news article "The Dirt on Factory Farms: Environmental and Consumer Impacts of Confined Animal Feeding Operations" Volume 21, Number 7 and 8].

Hogs swimming in North Carolina floodwaters following Hurricane Floyd. Photograph courtesy of the North Carolina Division of Emergency Management.

al. 2000). Feeding operations with high densities of animals have difficulty disposing of the enormous amounts of waste produced. Animal wastes contribute nitrogen and phosphorus to freshwater ecosystems and are a major source of organic material. Over half of reported agricultural pollution incidents from 1985–89 in England and Wales were related to cow slurry and an additional 20% with silage effluent (Thompson 1996). Wastes from animal operations can be 100 to 200 times more potent in terms of biological oxygen demand (BOD) than human effluent (Thompson 1996), yet animal waste disposal remains far less regulated than human waste disposal. Water bodies with BOD values exceeding 10 mg/l are considered impaired and require oxygen-consuming bacterial decomposition (Thorton *et al.* 1999). Other sources of organic material include animal mortality, processing plant wastewater, and crop harvest refuse.

Heavy metals

Contributions of heavy metals from agricultural lands are less significant than with other land uses including urbanization and mining. However, some synthetic fertilizers and pesticides contain zinc, copper, cadmium, and mercury. Other sources of heavy metals include insecticides that contain lead and livestock feed that sometimes contains copper and zinc (Clapham *et al.* 1998; de Haan *et al.* 1997). Excess heavy metals accumulate in soils, subsequently moving to freshwater ecosystems in runoff or by leaching through soils. In arid regions, the effects can be particularly significant as irrigation runoff can become trapped above an impervious clay layer in the soil, saturating the root zone and drowning crops. To address this effect, farmers drain subsurface waters into local waterbodies. Because these wastewaters can be highly contaminated with trace elements—including mercury, selenium, boron, molybdenum, lithium, and arsenic—they can be extremely toxic to waterfowl causing deformities, reproductive impairment, and death in many bird species. Irrigation runoff or drainwater contamination is a global issue having been identified in the Western United States, Australia, Central Asia, Mexico, and elsewhere (Lemly *et al.* 2000).

Runoff from heavy rain carries topsoil, agricultural chemicals, and potentially other pollutants that will end up in streams and lakes. Photograph by Lynn Betts/NRCS.

Synthetic organic chemicals

Chemicals that pose the most serious threat to freshwater ecosystem integrity include those that are highly toxic and can therefore cause damage even at very low levels and those that persist and accumulate in aquatic environments (Clapham *et al.* 1998). Chemical movement and fate can be deduced by the tendency of these substances to adhere to soil particles and the time it takes for these substances to breakdown. Chemicals likely to leach into groundwater tend not to adhere to soil particles, do not breakdown quickly, and are highly water-soluble. Those likely to end up in surface waters and in runoff readily adhere to soils. Soil properties, site conditions, and management practices also influence the effect of these substances on freshwater ecosystems (National Research Council Committee on Long-Range Soil and Water Conservation 1993).

Most synthetic organic chemicals come from pesticide application. In the USGS National Water Quality Assessment (NAWQA) study, 95% of all streams and 60% of all sampled groundwater wells contained a minimum of one pesticide. In agricultural areas, most sampled locations contained a minimum of five different pesticides. The most common herbicides detected in agricultural areas were atrazine, metolachlor, cyanazine, and alachlor. The most common insecticide was DDT, followed by dieldrin and chlordane. All of these insecticides had heavy restrictions on their use by the 1980s (USGS 2001). Pharmaceuticals including antibiotics, steroids, and hormones frequently used for animal husbandry are another source of synthetic organics in aquatic environments. The effects of most of these chemicals on aquatic life and human health remain uncertain. Concerns include abnormal physiological processes and reproductive impairment, increased cancer rates, development of antibiotic resistant bacteria, and increased toxicity from chemical synergies (Kolpin *et al.* 2002). Some of these synthetic organic chemicals have already been linked to birth defects, physical deformities, immune deficiencies and impairment of reproductive success (Colborn and Thayer 2000).

Salts and bacteria

Salts and bacterial inputs to freshwater ecosystems further alter chemical regimes of these systems. The salts are concentrated in ground and surface waters and reduce the dilution potential, accelerate leaching from soils, and induce erosion of soils (Clapham *et al.*

This image shows the large sediment plume released from the mouth of the Yangtze River, China, into the South China Sea. Image by Jacques Descloitres, MODIS Land Science Team, NASA.

1998). This phenomenon is most common with irrigated lands in arid regions. Manure in runoff can vector toxic bacteria to surface waters, increasing disease and biological oxygen demand.

PHYSICAL HABITAT CONDITIONS

Soil erosion and the resulting sedimentation of lakes, rivers and wetlands is the most significant cause of the degradation of physical habitat conditions from agricultural activities. Erosion of agricultural soils is exacerbated by: large-scale mechanical cultivation; continuous cropping rather than crop rotation; shortening or eliminating fallow periods; extending cultivation onto more erosive land; destruction of forest cover, grasslands, and windbreaks; and overgrazing of pasture lands (Harris 1990).

In 1987, approximately 25% of cropland, 8% of pastureland, and 13% of rangeland in the U.S. was actively eroding (National Research Council Committee on Long-Range Soil and Water Conservation 1993). Russia experiences similar rates. Erosion rates in India and China are more than twice as severe. These four nations contain more than half of the total global cultivated lands (Harris 1990). Soil erosion and resultant sedimentation problems are also severe in the tropics where soils are shallow and rainfall is high (National Research Council Committee on Sustainable Agriculture and the Environment in the Humid Tropics 1993). Much of this eroded sediment is deposited in freshwater ecosystems. One study reports that sediment delivered to oceans has increased from 9 billion tons annually to between 23 and 45 billion tons annually (National Research Council Committee on Long-Range Soil and Water Conservation 1993).

Extensive sediment can significantly reduce water storage capacity in lakes. Sediment settling to the bottom of the water column may cover over valuable fish spawning habitat. Sediments suspended in the water column reduce the ability of light to penetrate into lotic waters, limiting plant growth potential, which reduces cover and substrate for aquatic organisms and a food source (National Research Council Committee on Restoration and Aquatic Ecosystems 1992). When deposition exceeds transport, sedimentation begins to cause problems in flowing waters. Fine sediments settle into pore spaces of the hyporheic zone, clogging valuable habitat for aquatic invertebrates (Hancock 2002). Sediments will also cover diverse substrates such as cobbles, boulders, woody debris and leaf litter to the detriment of larger aquatic organisms that use these substrates for cover, feeding and spawning.

Channelization, riparian clearing, and bank erosion are other alterations to freshwater habitats commonly associated with agricultural land uses. Riparian clearing and heavy grazing reduce riparian shading, thereby increasing summer maximum daily temperatures (Karr and Schlosser 1978; Quinn et al. 1992). Grazing along stream banks and planting crops up to channel margins increase bank failures and sediment delivery, leading to channel widening, aggradations and base flow lowering. Rivers become warmer, shallower, and with more uniform substrates (National Research Council Committee on Restoration and Aquatic Ecosystems 1992). The practice of straightening rivers is commonly associated with agricultural development and simplifies river habitat structure, reducing available habitat types: riffle-pool habitat sequences are lost, sinuosity is reduced, substrate is altered, and flow velocities, suspended sediments and water temperatures all increase (National Research Council Committee on Restoration and Aquatic Ecosystems 1992).

BIOLOGICAL COMPOSITION AND INTERACTIONS

Agriculture has contributed to significant changes in aquatic biota. In the U.S. EPA's 1998 report to Congress on the quality of the nation's water, 41% of all rivers and streams and 42% of all lake, reservoir, and ponds assessed did not fully support aquatic life. In both cases impairment of a system to support aquatic life was more common than impairment of all

other valued uses (e.g., drinking water, swimming, recreation, etc.). The major source of impairment was agriculture (USEPA 2000). Much research has been directed at determining how agricultural land use alters the biological composition of freshwater ecosystems. This body of literature indicates that as agricultural land use in a basin increases, a decrease in the integrity of both invertebrate and fish communities follows (Roth et al. 1996; Lammert and Allan 1999; Cuffney et al. 2000). The specifics of this loss of integrity, and its detailed causes, are less well understood.

In flowing waters, habitat loss is the greatest cause of biological impairment (Allan and Flecker 1993). Sedimentation from field erosion not only alters water quality but also alters habitats required for many species. Combined with the loss of woody debris and the increase in water temperatures caused by riparian forest removal, invertebrate richness (Richards and Host 1994), fish species distributions (Allan 1995), and the integrity of mollusk populations (Diamond et al. 2002) all suffer. Seventy-one percent of all freshwater mussels in the United States and Canada are considered endangered, threatened or of special concern (Williams et al. 1993). Agricultural streams have been shown to experience a shift in the dominance of species, a loss of intolerant taxa, an increase in tolerant taxa richness, and a shift from a fall peak in abundance to a summer peak in abundance (Lenat and Crawford 1994), illustrating a dramatic alteration of community structure and function.

For ponds, lakes and wetlands, nitrogen and phosphorus in runoff from fertilized agricultural fields and animal waste increases eutrophic conditions. Nuisance algal blooms and macrophyte plant growth alter natural conditions, decreasing light availability and dissolved oxygen and resulting in alterations to the food web's structure (National Research Council Committee on Restoration and Aquatic Ecosystems 1992). Blooms of certain types of algae can be toxic, causing fish kills. Cyanobacterial (blue-green) algal blooms release neuro- and hepatoxins that are highly toxic to both humans and livestock (Lawton and Codd 1993). Damming outlets for flood control and irrigation stabilizes water levels, affecting fish reproduction by regulating access to spawning areas in the littoral zone and marginal wetlands. Canals and diversions open

Algae takes over a lake in Iowa. Photograph by Lynn Betts/NRCS.

otherwise isolated basins with unique biota to invasion by alien species (Naiman *et al.* 1995).

CONNECTIVITY

Lateral, vertical, and longitudinal connectivity are crucial to the maintenance of freshwater ecosystem function. Flood control measures and the common practice of developing floodplains for agricultural production has disconnected lotic waters from their floodplains in nearly all major rivers with the exception of some tropical systems (Allan and Flecker 1993). River-floodplain connectivity is essential to the maintenance of biodiversity (Welcomme 1979). When floodplain wetlands are left intact, they require overflow from adjacent lakes and rivers to replenish water and sediment. When these wetlands are drained or filled in order to be cultivated, valuable within catchment connectivity is lost. Floodplains become less effective at or can no longer provide a mechanism for dissipating upland and upriver flood flows. They also become less able to provide groundwater recharge. Finally, as stated previously, extraction of surface and groundwater for irrigation can lower base level conditions in surface waters.

The connection between surface water and groundwater allows for the exchange of contaminants, making both vulnerable even if only one is directly receiving heavy pollutant loads. Agricultural development in the headwaters of a catchment has resounding implications for water bodies lower in the catchment because of the longitudinal connectivity of freshwater ecosystems. High sediment and nutrient loads in source streams feeding a lake will ultimately be delivered to that lake contributing to eutrophication and habitat loss even if much of the land area near that lake remains undeveloped. Small dams constructed as a source of irrigation or for watering of livestock inhibit the movement of organisms, affecting migratory populations. In general, any structures within a freshwater ecosystem—such as culverts, dams, bridges and diversions—may alter connectivity within and between freshwater ecosystems.

Strategies for Mitigating/Abating the Effect of Agriculture on Freshwater Ecosystems

Strategies for mitigating or abating the effects of agriculture on freshwater ecosystems relate to either reducing the conversion of freshwater ecosystems to agricultural land uses or to improving agricultural practices so that they are not as harmful to freshwater ecosystems. A wide range of Best Management Practices (BMPs) exist and a broad range of laws influence the adoption of such practices. Because of the importance of reducing conversion as well as improving agricultural practices, this section will include strategies related to both these topics.

TECHNICAL STRATEGIES

Technical strategies for mitigating/abating the effects of freshwater ecosystem conversion for agriculture

Technical strategies for abating the effects of ecosystem loss due to conversion for agriculture center on efforts to restore these ecosystems, including wetlands and riparian areas. Strategies vary with the type and location of the area to be restored. For both wetland and riparian restoration, the level of success achieved will depend on the larger context. For example, isolated restoration activities will be more sustainable when associated eco-system processes (e.g., flooding) are also intact. Watershed scale and national level strategies for the restoration of freshwater ecosystems should be developed to guide small-scale restoration and ensure the success of these efforts (National Research Council Committee on Restoration and Aquatic Ecosystems 1992).

Wetland restoration efforts have improved surface flow hydrology and water quality, wildlife enhancement, wastewater treatment, mine drainage, and stormwater retention and control (Mitsch and Gosselink 1993). Wetland restoration measures include re-establishing former wetlands and/or repairing damaged ones. The former leads to a net gain in wetland acreage while the latter restores or improves functional capacity of damaged systems. Additionally, wetlands may be enhanced or created. Enhancement involves changing the condition of an existing wetland to strengthen or favor one or more of its functions. Creation involves building a wetland where one never existed (Tiner 1998). This is often attempted as a mitigation or compensatory effort to satisfy regulations governing wetlands protection. For example, provisions under the U.S. federal wetlands protection acts require the creation of wetlands as a substitute or mitigation for unavoidable loss of wetlands to other land uses. The Ramsar Convention likewise requires partic-

ipating countries to provide compensatory measures, including habitat recreation or restoration, for loss of designated wetlands under the convention (DEFRA 2002).

The National Research Council Committee on Mitigation Wetland Losses recommends these ten considerations to encourage successful mitigation of wetland loss (National Research Council 2001):

- Consider the hydrogeomorphic and ecological landscape and climate. Locate the mitigation site in a similar setting duplicating the features of the reference wetland.
- Adopt a dynamic landscape perspective. Give consideration to current and future hydrologic conditions and avoid areas that are likely to be subjected to extreme disturbance. Maintain wide buffers and connectivity to other freshwater bodies.
- Restore or develop naturally variable hydrologic conditions. Enable fluctuations in water level and flow to mimic natural duration and frequency of fluctuations. Re-establish the natural hydrologic regime when possible and utilize artificial infrastructures as a last alternative.
- Whenever possible, choose wetland restoration over creation. It is far more feasible and sustainable than the creation of wetlands.
- Avoid over-engineered structures in wetland design. Minimal maintenance is preferable.
- Rely on native seed bank when possible. Pay particular attention to appropriate planting elevation, depth, soil type, and seasonal timing. Select appropriate genotypes to ensure survival of vegetation.
- Provide appropriately heterogeneous topography. This will allow for the establishment of a diversity of plants and animals adapted to specific hydroperiods.
- Pay attention to subsurface conditions, including soil and sediment geochemistry and physics, groundwater quantity and quality, and infaunal communities. Determine soil permeability, texture and stratigraphy, the general chemical structure of soils and water. These are important to wetland function.
- Consider complications associated with creation or restoration in seriously degraded or disturbed sites. These sites may require more active management

Wetland restoration, Pelican Island National Wildlife Refuge, Florida. Photograph by George Gentry/USFWS.

but may be valuable for certain mitigation goals such as water or sediment quality improvement, or habitat in an otherwise disturbed landscape.

- Conduct early monitoring as part of adaptive management. A thorough monitoring program will identify potential problems and allow for corrective actions. Monitor processes (water level fluctuations, bird nesting, etc.) and invasive alien species in addition to structure (vegetation, sediments, nutrients, etc.).

Most wetland restoration in agricultural areas involves the cessation of planting crops or the exclusion of domestic animals, breaking drainage tiles, filling in drainage ditches, and removing flood control structures. Sediment removal may be necessary if the original elevation of a wetland has been altered due to erosion and sedimentation. Re-establishment of topography consistent with natural surface and subsurface hydrology is also important, requiring the removal of material from filled wetlands and the addition of material in the case of dredged wetlands. Finally, the control of contaminant loads is necessary for successful wetland restoration (National Research Council Committee on Restoration and Aquatic Ecosystems 1992). Usually, the native seed bank will provide the basis for the re-establishment of a native community, though not all species will return and the

likelihood of invasion by alien species is high. Animals will return, though many factors determine the extent to which the restored animal community resembles the historic community, such as proximity to a source population and the quality of the wetland restoration.

Wetland restoration and creation is a new science and long-term success has not yet been determined. However, wetland restoration is usually more successful than wetland creation for the following reasons: (1) the site is a former wetland and therefore can support desired functions, (2) soils are frequently in place, (3) the original hydrology can often be restored, and (4) it usually has a natural seedbank of hydrophytes to facilitate re-establishment of the plant community (Tiner 1998). The efforts of the Chilika Development Authority (State of Orissa), India, is an example of repairing damaged wetlands. A major component of the project was restoration of natural water flow and salinity levels in the 116,500 ha Chilika Lake, a Ramsar site. This was accomplished by removing silt in a channel connecting lagoons to the sea and resulted in improved fisheries in the lagoon and reduction of invasive alien freshwater plant species.

For more detail and descriptions on the ecology of wetlands and planning, implementation, monitoring, and management of wetland restoration and creation projects, please refer to the following publications and websites:

- Interagency Working Group on Wetlands Restoration (National Ocean and Atmospheric Administration, U.S. EPA, Army Corps of Engineers, Fish and Wildlife Service, and the Natural Resources Conservation Service). 2003. "An Introduction and User's Guide to Wetland Restoration, Creation, and Enhancement". Washington, DC. http://www.nmfs.noaa.gov/habitat/habitatconservation/publications/index.htm.
- Tiner, R. 1998. In Search of Swampland. A Wetland Sourcebook and Field Guide. Rutgers University Press, New Brunswick, NJ.
- Mitsch, W.J. and J.G. Gosselink. 1993. Wetlands. 2nd edition. VanNostrand Reinhold, New York, NY.
- The Ramsar Convention on Wetlands. The Ramsar Convention's Resources on Wetland Restoration http://www.ramsar.org/strp_rest_index.htm.
- Kentula, M.E. 1999. Restoration, Creation, and Recovery of Wetlands. Wetland Restoration and Creation. National Water Summary on Wetland Resources. U.S. Geological Survey Water Supply Paper 2425 http://water. usgs.gov/nwsum/WSP 2425/restoration.html.
- Northern Prairie Science Center and Midcontinent Ecological Science Center. 1996. Wetland restoration bibliography. (Version30SEP2002) http://www.npwrc.usgs.gov/resource/literatr/wetresto/wetresto.htm.

Technical strategies for mitigating/abating the effects of agricultural practices on freshwater ecosystems

Technical mitigation and abatement strategies for agricultural threats to freshwater ecosystems attempt to reduce net losses of energy, nitrogen, phosphorus, pesticides, soil, salts, and trace elements from agricultural land (National Research Council Committee on Long-Range Soil and Water Conservation 1993). Because sources of agricultural pollution are predominantly surface runoff, or diffuse sources, most strategies aim to improve the management of agricultural lands. These strategies are often referred to collectively as agricultural Best Management Practices (BMPs).

Agricultural BMPs generally are voluntary practices that fall into one of four categories: source, structural, cultural or managerial. Some examples of agricultural BMPs by category include (Waskom 1994):

- Source Controls:
  - Voluntary restriction of a labeled pesticide by manufacturer
  - Mandatory label restrictions by EPA
  - Local restriction of nitrogen fertilizer application
- Structural Controls:
  - Grass waterways and filter strips
  - Drip and surge irrigation systems
  - Chemigation backsiphon devices
  - Irrigation tailwater recovery systems
- Cultural Practices:
  - Conservation tillage
  - Cover cropping
  - Crop rotation
  - Application techniques, such as split nitrogen application
- Management Practices:
  - Integrated Pest Management (IPM)
  - Irrigation scheduling
  - Soil and water analysis
  - Recordkeeping of pesticide and fertilizer use

The Colorado State University's Cooperative Extension service summarizes nine guiding principals to help protect water resources from agricultural land use threats. Presented in abridged form here, further details can be found at http://www.colostate.edu/Depts/SoilCrop/extension/WQ/WQPubs. html:

- Manage nitrogen applications to maximize crop growth and economic return while protecting water quality. Proper fertilizer selection, rates of application, and timing of use are the keys to maximizing plant uptake and minimizing losses. Use slow release fertilizers and, apply in small amounts several times rather than large quantities a few times, and avoid fall applications.
- Manage irrigation to minimize transport of chemicals, nutrients, or sediments from the soil surface or immediate crop root zone. Avoid runoff and encourage percolation by upgrading equipment and scheduling irrigation according to crop needs. Avoid deep percolation following pesticide application.
- Collect, store and apply animal manures to land at agronomic rates to ensure maximum crop growth and economic return while protecting water quality.

Contour farming, terraces, and grass buffer strips help reduce impacts to water quality in agricultural areas. Photograph by Jeff Vanuga/NRCS.

Although incorporation of manure into soils is beneficial, reduce nitrogen fertilizer applications to account for nitrogen in manure applications and do not apply manure to saturated soils.

• Manage phosphorus requirements for crop production to maximize crop growth and economic returns while minimizing degradation to water resources. Phosphorus generally moves with eroding soil, therefore control of phosphorus levels reaching water is intimately tied to soil erosion control.

• Use an Integrated Pest Management (IPM) approach in pest control decisions. Use proper pesticide at the time of maximum pest susceptibility. Combine chemical with biological controls. Plant appropriate crops resistant to common pest pressures and accept a minimal amount of damage. Also consider crop rotation and spot treatments.

• Apply pesticides only when needed and use in a manner that will minimize unintended effects. Train and certify all chemical applicators. Choose chemicals best suited to site conditions such as soil type, depth to groundwater, and erosion potential. Minimize waste and storage.

• Maintain records of all pesticide and fertilizers applied. Record irrigation water analysis, subsoil nitrate, yield goals versus actual yields, application timing and rates of chemical and water use.

• Protect groundwater from contamination due to spills or leaks from facilities that store, mix, and load pesticides and fertilizers. Store in locked building with cement floors at least 100 feet from water supply and equipped with secondary containment dikes to contain spills.

• Protect wellheads from potential sources of contamination. Maintain wells. Install backflow prevention devices. Keep chemicals far from wellheads. Monitor well water quality (Waskom 1994).

In addition to the principles listed above, similar protections should be considered for reducing pollution from animal husbandry operations. Here BMPs should abate harm caused by feeding and watering operations, disposing of dead animals, controlling runoff, and manure management. While implementation of BMPs varies widely, the main focus for mitigating the impacts of animal husbandry activities on freshwater ecosystems include (Warrington 2000):

• Prevent animal access to streams, lakes and riparian areas

• Keep feeding area well away from the high water mark (floodplain) of a waterbody

Young corn plants grow in the residue of last year's soybean crop. This method of conservation tillage helps retain moisture in and reduce erosion of the soil. Photograph by Tim McCabe/NRCS.

- Divert clean runoff from passing through livestock area. Prevent runoff from livestock area.
- Provide several feed and watering locations to disperse manure. Keep these locations far from surface waters.
- Store feed in a contained and dry area away from surface water. Feed animals from containers, not on bare ground.
- Render dead animals as soon as possible and not more than 48 hours after death.
- When rendering service is unavailable locate burial pits as far from wells, water intakes, and surface waters as possible and a minimum of 1.2 meters above highest seasonal water table depth. Disperse pits.
- Keep compost piles off of permeable soils and away from surface and groundwater.
- Prevent runoff from manure storage, wet or dry, from entering surface waters directly. Provide a berm or trenches adequate to hold the entire contents of the liquid manure storage facility in case of a spill or leakage.
- Do not apply manure onto land under conditions that encourage rapid delivery of waste to surface or ground waters.

- Find an alternate market or disposal site for any excess manure generated.

Many states, agencies and organizations have guides to agricultural BMPs well suited to their particular geographic region. These can often be found either with state environmental agencies or university extension offices. For example:

- Colorado: Best Management Practices for Colorado Agriculture. Available through Colorado State University Cooperative Extension and Colorado Department of Agriculture and on-line at http://www.colostate.edu/Depts/SoilCrop/extension/WQ/WQPubs.html
- North Carolina: BMPs for agriculture in the Tar-Pamlico Basin are available through the Department of Environment and Resources at http://www.enr.state.nc.us/DSWC/pages/tar-pamlicoBMP.html

In addition, guidance on BMPs is also available through the EPA's National Management Measures to Control Nonpoint Source Pollution from Agriculture, accessible on-line at http://www.epa.gov/owow/nps/agmm/index.html.

Additionally, Purdue University's Core 4 program,

BOX 4-13. Development of Alternatives to Organophosphate Pesticides

Organophosphate pesticides (diazinon and chlorpyrifos) used in orchards located in California's Sacramento and San Joaquin River watersheds were reaching the Sacramento and San Joaquin Rivers and killing aquatic inverte-brates and likely other species as well. In response, these rivers were placed on the Clean Water Act 303(d) list of impaired waterbodies and limits were set on the daily allowable loads of these pesticides. The University of California identified viable pest control alternatives including pheromone mating disruption with biological con-trols, alternate-year dormant applications, and more benign dormant spray chemicals. They also developed a Dormant Spray Alternatives Calculator to help growers compare costs associated with various alternatives on their land. Growers and industry organizations helped publish and distribute literature on IPM alternatives to organophosphate (OP) sprays (UCIPM 1999). Over the period of 1992–1997, reports show a 22–57% reduc-tion in the mass of OPs applied on almond orchards (the major industry using OPs) corresponding to a 30–48% decrease in the number of growers using these chemicals and a significant increase in growers using reduced-risk methods (Epstein *et al.* 2001).

---

also promoted by the EPA and U.S. Department of Agriculture's Natural Resource Conservation Service, provides useful information about BMPs. The Core 4 program (http://www.ctic.purdue.edu/Core4/Core4.html) is a partnership composed of more than 60 farmer-led organizations, agricultural businesses, state and federal government agencies, universities, and other agricultural leaders. The emphasis of this pro-gram is to promote the wide installation of four key BMPs which are projected to reduce water pollution from cropland by 80%: conservation tillage, nutrient management, pest management, and conservation buffers:

- **Conservation tillage.** Conservation tillage involves covering 30% or more of the soil surface with crop residue to reduce soil erosion by water. The types of conservation tillage include: no-till/strip-till where soil is not disturbed between harvest and next planting or only disturbed in small strips; ridge-till where narrow strips are used on ridges but residue is left between tilled ridges; and mulch-till where tilling disturbs the entire soil surface but is done just prior to, or during planting.

- **Nutrient management.** The goal of nutrient man-agement is to maximize efficiency of nutrient addi-tions to crops thereby reducing excess nutrients that runoff and pollute freshwaters. Documents, soft-ware packages and agency employees are available to help farmers create nutrient management plans.

See *A Step-by-step Guide to Nutrient Management* by R. P. Wolkowski at http://ipcm.wisc.edu/pubs/pdf/stepbystep.pdf and the Nutrient Management Planner for Minnesota software program available through Minnesota Extension Service at http://wrc.coafes.umn.edu/EQIP/software.htm for quality examples. The process can be briefly summarized by the following steps: create a field map; test soil for nutrients, pH, and organic matter; evaluate previ-ous crop sequence and its relationship to soil and crop nutrient content; accurately estimate expected yields based on historic yields; determine the sources and forms of nutrients (i.e., nutrient con-tent of manure, nitrogen fixation by cover crop, etc); identify sensitive areas that need special con-sideration in management plans; determine optimal rates, timing and methods of application of nutri-ents; include all of this information in the nutrient management plan; and annually review and update any management plans developed.

Animal husbandry has its own unique set of nutrient management considerations. In 2002, the EPA developed a final rule requiring all Concen-trated Animal Feeding Operations be permitted under the Clean Water Act requiring comprehen-sive nutrient management plans (CNMPs) before permit issuance. In addition to assistance and guid-ance provided through many state programs, the U.S. Department of Agriculture Natural Resource Conservation Service helps those with animal feed-

BOX 4-14. The Gulf of Mexico "Dead Zone"

Each summer, a dead zone of severely depleted oxygen, or hypoxia occurs in the Gulf of Mexico and causes severe stress of organisms, emigration, and death. In 1999 the size of this dead zone was 20,000 km². The primary cause of this condition in the Gulf of Mexico is the high level of nutrients running off of agricultural lands throughout the Mississippi drainage basin. Excess nutrients accelerate the eutrophication process. Higher levels of phosphorus and nitrogen encourage algal blooms; as algal blooms die off, bacterial populations explode; high bacteria levels consume more oxygen leaving less in the water for other consumers; low oxygen levels make waters uninhabitable for most aquatic life. As a result of the size of the affected area and the severity of impact on both the ecosystem and citizens' livelihoods, a national initiative is underway led by the EPA.

Most of the nitrogen reaching the Gulf of Mexico has been traced to farm fields in Minnesota, Iowa, Illinois, Indiana and Ohio (Mississippi River/Gulf of Mexico Watershed Nutrient Task Force 2001). Extensive channelization and conversion of riparian areas and wetlands at the mouth of the Mississippi River have eliminated the ability of this system to naturally filter these contaminants before reaching the Gulf of Mexico.

The Mississippi Basin.

The most cost-effective approach for farmers to help contribute to the reversal of the dead zone in the Gulf of Mexico is to implement BMPs (e.g., no fall fertilizing, install stream buffers, etc.). The EPA is using existing legislation and funding sources to encourage and assist farmers in improving the management of nutrients on their lands. The World Resources Institute found nutrient trading to be the most promising policy approach to reducing nitrogen loads in the Mississippi River Basin. While other options such as taxing nitrogen fertilizers and subsidizing farmers using conservation tillage practices promised a reduction in nitrogen loads, they also came with a loss in farm income (Greenhalgh and Sauer 2003). For farmers contributing to this problem, it is unclear whether they can reduce nutrient inputs sufficiently to help diminish the dead zone and still remain economically viable. One study found that farmers can reduce nitrogen only 20% before affecting production, profits, and food costs (Doering *et al.* 1999).

Although each state contributing to the hypoxia problem in the Gulf of Mexico has its own approach to reducing nutrient loads, efforts in Minnesota demonstrate how important outreach can be to the success of such efforts. At the Zumbro River watershed, intensive one-on-one landowner education led to dramatic changes in agricultural practices among farmers, including a reduction in the use of nitrogen by up to 50 pounds per acre. Although it will take time before activities on land will be reflected in the condition of the Gulf of Mexico, a combination of federal and state regulatory programs and non-regulatory initiatives, including financial aid, outreach, education, and technical assistance catered to the needs of individual states and communities show promise for nutrient level reductions in the waters of the Mississippi basin.

ing operations produce Comprehensive Nutrient Management Plans (CNMP) and the National Association of State Departments of Agriculture Research Foundation provides training workshops. Information on their CNMPs training can be found at http://www.nasdahq.org/nasda/nasda/Foundation/CMNP.

- **Pest management.** Integrative pest management (IPM) is the wise use of conventional, cultural, and biological practices to manage pests and invasive alien plant species with minimal impact to the environment, nontarget organisms and human health. Guiding principles of IPM are to eliminate pest problems, not all pests; to apply chemicals and irrigation only when benefits outweigh the cost; and to consider all management options including biological and cultural controls. Monitoring is the key to the success of an IPM program so that appropriate action can be initiated once key thresholds are met. Some alternative methods to controlling pests utilized in IPM include natural predators, resistant crop varieties, habitat manipulation and modification of cultural practices. For more information on IPM, please refer to the IPM Almanac (http://www.ipmalmanac.com/) and the University of California IPM Online (http://www.ipm.ucdavis.edu/).

- **Conservation buffers.** A conservation buffer is any strip of permanent vegetation which slows runoff; reduces nutrient, contaminant, and sediment loads to surface water; and stabilizes the banks and shores of freshwater ecosystems. Various types of buffers include contour buffer strips, field borders, filter strips, grassed waterways, living snow fences, riparian buffers, shelterbelts/windbreaks, (grass, shrubs and trees), and wetlands. Factors such as topography, drainage density, soils and climate will determine the effectiveness of buffers as a pollution prevention practice and should be used to design efficient buffers (Lowrance *et al.* 1997). Although conservation buffers may be expensive to install and result in less land under cultivation for farmers, their benefits for improved water quality extend to society as a whole (Stonehouse 1999).

Given the huge demand for water by agriculture and the effect of agriculture on water quality, technical strategies related to water conservation should also be considered. Increasing irrigation efficiency can improve water quality by: (1) reducing volume of surface runoff and subsurface drainage; (2) reducing pollutant loads of subsurface drainage; (3) allowing more efficient use of agricultural chemicals; and (4) limiting irrigation-induced erosion and sedimentation (Cohen, 1998). Many technological solutions have been developed to increase irrigation efficiency. Solutions shown to effectively reduce water use include soil moisture monitoring, canal automation, tailwater recovery/reuse, microirrigation, surge flow, laser leveling of machinery to even grade of fields, low energy precision application (LEPA) sprinkler systems, limited irrigation/dry farming, gated pipes and canal lining (Cohen, 1998). Details about irrigation efficiency technologies can be found in the following publications:

- Environmental and Energy Study Institute (1997). The role of improved irrigation technologies in helping farmers meet environmental and economic challenges. Washington, DC., Environmental and Energy Study Institute.
- Negri, D. and J. Hanchar (1989). Water conservation through irrigation technology. Washington, DC, United States Department of Agriculture, Economic Research Service. Agriculture Information Bulletin Number 576.

Please also see the technical strategies included within the Surface Water Diversion section of the Water Use and Management subchapter for more information about water conservation strategies.

Also important to consider are sustainable agriculture and organic farming, two approaches to production that fall outside the realm of conventional farming yet hold significant promise for protecting of freshwater ecosystems from the impacts of agriculture. The definition of sustainable agriculture is elusive though most definitions incorporate several or all of the following components: discriminating use of land resources, conservation and enhancement of natural resources, economic viability, increased and stabilized productivity, enhanced quality of life, intergenerational equity, and buffering against risks (Eswaran 1991). In developing countries where rapid soil degradation leads to field abandonment and continued clearing of new lands, providing education about and encouraging the expansion of sustainable agriculture practices is particularly pertinent. The Sustainable Agriculture Research Education (SARE) program of the U.S. Department of Agriculture offers grants for research and education and has a website (http://www .sare.org/) containing useful information about this topic. A good non-governmental source of information about sustainable agriculture is National Campaign for Sustainable Agriculture, Inc. (http:// www.sustainableagriculture.net/). Organic farming takes sustainable agriculture further to exclude the use of all synthetic pesticides or fertilizers. Organic agriculture is the fastest growing sector of agriculture with sales growing by 20% per year for the past 10 years. The National Sustainable Agriculture Information Service is an excellent resource for farmers interested in growing crops organically and includes details for individual crop types and regarding specific pest problems (http://attra.ncat.org/organic.html).

INSTITUTIONAL AND LEGAL STRATEGIES

While technical strategies to abate the effects of land conversion center on restoration of lost ecosystems, institutional strategies generally work to protect remaining ecosystems from further losses. The following subsections discuss both U.S. and international institutions and legal authorities related to mitigating or abating the effect of freshwater ecosystem conservation to agriculture as well as the effect of agricultural practices on freshwater ecosystems.

U.S. institutions and legal authorities related to mitigating/abating the effects of freshwater ecosystem conversion for agriculture

Defending a wetland from development using Section 404 of the CWA

In the United States, the institutional framework to protect remaining wetlands exists through Section 404 of the Clean Water Act. This law requires that a permit be issued by the U.S. Army Corps of Engineers for all activities that might result in wetland destruction or alteration. Section 404 requires, first, that the applicant take all possible steps to avoid developing in

the wetland; second, the minimization of unavoidable damages to the wetland; and finally, the construction or restoration of a wetland of equal or greater area and of the same type to that which was eliminated. A public notice and comment period is also part of this section, allowing opportunities for practitioners and others to influence decisions.

Despite this legislation, numerous loopholes exist allowing for continued wetland loss in the United States. For example, wetlands may be filled for agricultural purposes if filling increases productivity or allows for the construction of farm buildings. According to the Sierra Club, "this permit is easily abused as the back door means to convert wetlands and relocate streams for development purposes" (Sierra Club 2002). Furthermore, the National Academy of Sciences and the General Accounting office found compensatory mitigation of wetlands under Section 404 to not meet the "no net loss" goal set forth by the legislation (USEPA 2003). Due to these inconsistencies, many advocate legal reform of Section 404 permit issuance.

Utilizing federal legislation to encourage protection of wetlands and riparian areas

The Conservation Reserve Program (CRP) and the Wetland Reserve Program (WRP), administered by the U.S. Department of Agriculture's Natural Resource Conservation Service (NRCS), offer long-term conservation easements and payments to landowners who restore or protect wetlands or riparian habitats. The Partners for Wildlife program through the U.S. Fish and Wildlife Service provides financial and technical assistance to land owners for projects designed to protect, restore or enhance wetlands and riparian area. The Swampbuster program excludes those who convert wetlands to cultivated land from eligibility for many U.S. Department of Agriculture program benefits. Major roadblocks preventing farmers from making use of such programs include lack of awareness of the programs and inadequate support for the application process to participate in such programs. Information about these programs can be found at:

- The U.S. Department of Agriculture's Farm Service Agency provides support to farmers and presents a summary of conservation opportunities available to farmers and describes how to utilize these opportunities. http://www.fsa.usda.gov/dafp/cepd/crpinfo. htm

- The Farm Bill Network provides links to organizations and state agencies that provide local support for CRP and WRP. http://www.fb-net.org/index. html

- USDA's Cooperative Extension Service provides technical and practical help with these programs and is linked to land-grant universities who provide local assistance. http://www.csrees.usda.gov/

- FWS's Partners for Fish and Wildlife Program homepage contains details on the program and application process. http://partners.fws.gov/

Utilizing state programs and legislation to encourage protection of wetlands and riparian areas

Numerous states also have programs providing incentives to encourage or even mandate wetland protection. Some states reduce property taxes for wetland areas protected by conservation easements. Others reduce property tax for farmers who manage for habitat including the restoration or protection of wetland and riparian areas. The Association of State Wetland Managers has developed model legislation for protecting wetlands, "The SWANCC Decision: State Regulation of Wetlands to Fill the Gap," available at http://www.aswm.org/swp/states.htm. Also available on this website is a list of states that currently have

---

Box 4-15. National Pollution Discharge Elimination System

CAFOs must obtain a National Pollution Discharge Elimination System (NPDES) permit under Section 502(14) of the Clean Water Act. Under this scheme, the U.S. Department of Agriculture will provide technical and financial assistance to operators through the existing Environmental Quality Incentives Program (EQIP) and other Farm Bill programs (USEPA 2002). CAFO operators must develop and submit annual reports and develop and follow manure and wastewater management plans open for public review. Additionally, the EPA and U.S. Department of Agriculture have agreed that all AFOs have Comprehensive Nutrient Management Plans (CNMP's) by 2009, with operations contributing more to water quality degradation

A farm that has not implemented manure and wastewater management plans. Photograph by Tim McCabe/NRCS.

receiving higher priority for compliance (e.g., those with high manure production, facilities that discharge waste directly to receiving waters, and those that significantly contribute to water quality impairment and the non-attainment of a designated use (drinking water, aquatic life support, etc.)) (USDA and USEPA 1999). A guide on how to get involved with the NPDES process is available through The Clean Water Network entitled Permitting an End to Pollution: How to scrutinize and strengthen water pollution permits in your state which can be downloaded at http://www.cwn.org/docs/publication/permit/permithandbook.html. The report entitled *America's Animal Factories: How States Fail to Prevent Pollution From Livestock Waste* details the failure of pollution prevention from livestock farms for 30 U.S. states and can be ordered at www.cwn.org.

wetland protection legislation. Also useful is a document published by Defenders of Wildlife, entitled *Conservation in America: State Government Incentives for Habitat Conservation* (Defenders of Wildlife 2002 #575) and found at found on-line at: http://www.biodiversitypartners.org/pubs/CinAReport/Intro.html, provides a comprehensive overview of ways that state governments can encourage or require habitat protection including wetlands and riparian areas.

Utilizing mitigation banking for wetland protection

Mitigation banking is the creation or restoration of wetlands, which are then sold as credits to developers as a way to meet the requirements of the Clean Water Act. Critics of this approach argue that (1) failure is common, (2) restored or created wetlands are difficult to maintain in the long-term, (3) measuring and replacing wetland function are difficult and unreliable, (4) the legal framework does not exist that will ensure the protection of these wetlands into perpetuity, and (5) credits are often issued before creation activities can be deemed successful (Goldman-Carter and McCallie 1996). On the other hand, banking is supposed to take the mitigation task out of the hands of those who know little about wetland creation and place it into the hands of knowledgeable restorationists, make compliance easier and therefore more frequent, theoretically at no cost to the public (Albrecht and Wenzel 1996). Wetland banking may prove most useful for private land owners since this land contains much of the remaining wetlands in the United States. Existing legislation makes it difficult for wetland owners to sell land. If a landowner can sell wetland credits, a wetland will be protected and a landowner can feel they have contributed to conservation and make a profit. Farmers may consider restoration a viable alternative to continued cultivation if acreage could be sold as banking credit (Albrecht and Wenzel 1996).

U.S. institutions and legal authorities related to mitigating/abating the effects of agricultural practices on freshwater ecosystems

The U.S. has extensive governmental involvement in the business and practice of agriculture largely through the U.S. Department of Agriculture. The National Resource Conservation Service (NRCS) is the agency created within the U.S. Department of Agriculture to manage natural resource issues affected by agriculture. Other federal agencies involved with freshwater conservation issues that also play a role in shaping the agriculture industry include the EPA, FWS, and the Bureau of Land Management. Major federal legislation fostering the protection of lakes, rivers, wetlands and groundwater from agricultural threats are the Clean Water Act and the Farm Bill.

Protecting freshwater ecosystems from agricultural practices through application of various provisions of the Clean Water Act

Under the Clean Water Act both point and nonpoint sources of pollution are partially regulated. Section 402 requires all point source discharges to be issued a National Pollution Discharge Elimination System (NPDES) permit. Permits are reviewed every five years. Recently, CAFO's were classified as point sources of pollution and are now regulated by specific legislation.

Agriculture contributes the majority of its pollution via nonpoint sources to freshwater ecosystems. The sections of the Clean Water Act dealing with nonpoint source pollution include Sections 303 and 319, which require states to identify all impaired waterbodies and, for each, prepare a clean-up plan which must be approved at the federal level by EPA. Section 319 grants are then available to help fund the implementation of clean-up plans. Clean-up plans are currently centered around the concept of TMDLs or Total Maximum Daily Loads. According to the EPA, a TMDL is defined as the amount of pollutant (e.g. phosphorus, sediment), or property of a pollutant (e.g., biological oxygen demand), from point, nonpoint, and natural background sources, that may be discharged to a water quality-limited receiving water. Any pollutant loading above the TMDL results in a violation of applicable water quality standards (EPA glossary). Designated state agencies, such as a department of environmental quality, determine appropriate TMDLs by a process open to the public and through which conservationists and concerned community members may influence the determination of these loads and ensure appropriate stringency.

Protecting freshwater ecosystems from agricultural practices through the Coastal Zone Act

Section 6217 of the Coastal Zone Act Reauthorization Amendments (CZARA) of 1990 requires the use of management measures to prevent nonpoint pollution from reaching coastal waters and requires coastal states to submit Coastal Nonpoint Pollution Control Programs to the EPA and the National Oceanic and Atmospheric Administration. To assist implementation of management measures that protect coastal waters, the EPA has written "Guidance Specifying Management Measures for Sources of Nonpoint Pollution in Coastal Waters" which includes information specific to agriculture and can be read at www.epa.gov/owow/nps/MMGI.

Protecting freshwater ecosystems from agricultural practices through application of various provisions of the Farm Bill

In 2002, the newest U.S. Department of Agriculture Farm Bill, revised approximately every six years since the 1920s, was adopted. Title II, the conservation title, amended several existing programs, and created new programs, relevant to the protection of freshwater ecosystems. Farm Bill provisions are an excellent source of funds, technical support and information for freshwater conservation activities on agricultural lands. Detailed information on the 2002 Farm Bill Provisions can be found at http://www.usda.gov/farmbill. Major provisions include:

- Conservation of Private Grazing Land (CPLG) provides technical assistance and separate funding solely for conservation of private grazing lands
- Conservation Reserve Program (CRP) provides annual rental payments and cost-share assistance are available to establish long-term, resource conserving, vegetative cover.
- Conservation Security Program (CSP) rewards stewardship and provides incentives for activities addressing resource concerns on agricultural land.
- Environmental Quality Incentives Program (EQIP) provides funding and cost-share opportunities with priority on projects that reduce nonpoint pollution (especially in watersheds where TMDLs are exceeded), emissions and soil erosion and sedimentation (especially on highly erosive land), and promote recovery of at-risk species habitat.
- Ground and Surface Water Conservation is a special initiative within EQIP that institutes cost-share payments, incentive payments and loans to producers implementing eligible water conservation activities.
- Resource Conservation and Development Program (RC&D) is a voluntary community development program where a local council is created to plan and implement improvement projects which can include water protection.
- Wetlands Reserve Program (WRP) is an existing program with increased enrollment potential allowing landowners to restore and protect wetlands through the use of conservation easements or restoration cost-share agreements.
- Other significant provisions include Great Lakes Basin Program for Soil Erosion and Sediment Control, Desert Terminal Lakes, Small Watershed Rehabilitation and Grassroots Sourcewater Protection.

Utilizing federal and state funding and incentive programs to protect freshwater ecosystems

Often, costs of conservation practices are front loaded, meaning high start-up costs and low maintenance costs. Some practices require a continual small loss in profit when, for example, acreage is lost to wetland restoration or riparian buffer widening. The following strategies incorporate some of the more widely used programs to encourage farmers to adopt practices or pursue activities supportive of freshwater ecosystems:

- **Conservation easements.** Conservation easements are voluntary, legal agreements where a landowner chooses to relinquish certain land rights, such as the right to subdivide or farm or harvest timber, to protect a critical area for conservation purposes. These rights can be sold or donated to a qualified easement holder (e.g., government agency, land trust) and retired in perpetuity to guarantee the protection of the land. The landowner still holds the title and does not give up his or her right to sell the property. Conservation easements can be a cost-effective way to retain riparian buffers, wetlands

H2-O Ranch in Montana, before restoration (top) and during restoration of the oxbow wetlands (bottom). The Partners for Fish and Wildlife Program purchased an easement that enabled the restoration. Photographs by Greg Neudecker/USFWS

and other critical areas for the mitigation of agricultural impacts by retaining nutrients, dissipating surface flow and recharging groundwater. While motivation for placing land under a conservation easement is often altruistic, the donation is often tax deductible and reduces estate and property taxes. The Partners for Fish and Wildlife program through the FWS purchases and manages easements for conservation objectives. At the H2-O Ranch in Montana a purchase of 3,800 acre area easement through the Partners for Fish and Wildlife program enabled the restoration of 35 drained oxbow wetlands and the enhancement of 15 additional wetlands. For details on the Partners program visit http://partners.fws.gov/. For details on the program's use of conservation easements visit the "techniques" page of the FWS Mountain-Prairie Region web site at http://mountain-prairie.fws.gov/.

- **Cost sharing.** Cost sharing is a common agency tactic whereby the agency will finance a portion of the implementation of a conservation strategy and the landowner will pay the remainder. Cost-sharing makes capital expenditures for equipment or new practices more feasible for farmers or ranchers. For example, the state of Virginia has developed a cost share program to support farmers using BMPs to protect water quality. The program is administered by local soil and water conservation districts. Standardized applications are submitted and funding distribution places priority on those projects that will do the most to protect water quality.

- **Nutrient trading.** Nutrient trading programs allow for flexibility in how water quality standards are met within a drainage basin. This is a common way of dealing with TMDL limits. Each polluter within that basin will be issued a share of the total acceptable load. Polluters can purchase or sell shares. Those that can implement control methods inexpensively can then sell surplus shares to polluters where the cost of control is more expensive than the cost of purchasing shares. Nutrient trading programs are administratively cumbersome but work well in situations where there are a combination of point and nonpoint sources of nutrient pollution and where costs of control are excessive for point source polluters. For an example of an executed nutrient trading program investigate the Tar-Pamlico River Basin Nutrient Reduction Trading Program at http://h20.enr.state.nc.us/nps/tarpam. htm.

- **Subsidies.** Subsidies—such as grants, loans, tax allowances, charge exceptions or rebates—can be used to discourage pollution and encourage protection of freshwater ecosystems (Clapham 1998). However, subsidies can also be a root cause of harmful practices. For example, subsidized fertilizers, pesticides and machinery promoted by the District Agricultural Authorities in Greece are cited as responsible for much of the wetland deterioration from farming practices in this area, home to several RAMSAR wetlands (Pyrovetsi and Daoutopoulos 1999). Removal or revising of these subsidies could go a long way to reducing the environmental impacts of agriculture.

- **Use fees.** Public land grazing fees could be adjusted to benefit ranchers who improve operations and penalize those who continue degrading practices.

While taxation, regulation, and subsidization can be effective institutional strategies for influencing agricultural production in wealthy countries, these strategies are less appropriate for lower income countries. Where institutions are weak, rendering regulation ineffective, market instruments can curb environmental damage. Policy reform should promote increased efficiency and alleviation of poverty (Steinfeld *et al.* 1997). Local empowerment is necessary for success.

Reviewing existing policies may reveal driving forces behind destructive practices such as tax incentives or instability of land tenure. Initiatives to develop and increase capacity of natural resource management agencies is critical as their agents are responsible for outreach and capacity building among agriculturalists. Incentives should be developed that encourage investments in land improvement, the rehabilitation of abandoned lands and create markets for sustainably produced products (National Research Council Committee on Sustainable Agriculture and the Environment in the Humid Tropics 1993).

International institutions and legal authorities

This section summarizes important international laws and treaties as well as presents information on interesting regional approaches and national laws related to protecting freshwater ecosystems from harm caused by agricultural practices. Many countries share similar degrees of complexity in national and sub-national governing policies and regulatory frameworks that protect freshwater ecosystems from land use practices.

Europe

The 1992 UNECE Convention of the Protection and Use of Transboundary Watercourses and International Lakes strengthens national measures, obliging parties to prevent, control and reduce water pollution from point and non-point sources. Transboundary initiatives within Europe to improve water quality include the Convention on Cooperation for the Protection and Sustainable Use of the River Danube and the new

Convention for the Protection of the Rhine. The Danube Convention pledges the signatories to work together to conserve, improve and rationally use the surface and groundwaters in the Danube watershed and to contribute to reducing the pollution loads of the Black Sea from sources in the watershed. The Rhine Convention adopted in 2001 will be the basis for international cooperation of the riparian countries and the EU, replacing the Agreement on the International Commission for the Protection of the Rhine against Pollution (Bern 1963) and the 1976 Convention for the Protection of the Rhine against Chemical Pollution. The new convention fixes targets for international cooperation for sustainable development of the Rhine, further improvement of its ecological state, and holistic flood protection. In addition to aspects of water quality and quantity, groundwater problems in relation to the Rhine will in future be included in the convention's provisions (ICPR 2001).

Latin America

The Sustainable Agriculture Network is a coalition of nonprofit conservation groups dedicated to promoting tropical conservation and changing the face of commercial agriculture in the topics. The Rainforest Alliance, an international conservation organization, serves as the Secretariat for the Network. The Network recognizes that the well-being of societies and ecosystems is dependent on agriculture that is environmentally sound, socially equitable, and economically viable. Since 1991, the Network has developed guidelines for the responsible management of export agriculture, certifying bananas, coffee, cocoa, citrus, and flowers and foliage according to environmental and social standards, in a process that is participatory, transparent, and independent Farms that meet the Sustainable Agriculture Network standard are certified and may use the Rainforest Alliance-certified label in marketing their products, gaining the reward of a marketplace that increasingly demands responsible farm management practices. For more information please refer to: www.rainforest-alliance.org.

International Organic Agriculture

The International Federation of Organic Agriculture Movement (IFOAM)'s mission is to lead, unite and assist the organic movement in its full diversity. Its goal is the worldwide adoption of ecologically, socially and economically sound systems that are based on the principles of Organic Agriculture. IFOAM has a list of basic standards that have provided a framework for almost all of the national regulations and for the international WHO/FAO Codex alimentarius on organic agriculture and are used by organic farmer

The Kafue Flats is a wetland complex in Zambia that is home to the endangered Kachue Lefwe and wattled crane. The World Wildlife Zambia Wetlands Project is a community-based project designed to fit within the existing social framework, rely on local input and leadership and promote sustainable development of these and other Zambia wetlands. Photograph © WWF/Canon/Black.

organizations all over the world as a common platform. The facilitated international recognition of certification programs, IFAOM has established the IFAOM International Organic Accreditation Services Inc. (IOAS). The IOAS aims to ensure that certification programs meet accreditation criteria in addition to IFOAM basic standards, thus ensuring global consistency and compatibility. For an in-depth overview of IFOAM please refer to www.ifoam.org.

COMMUNITY-BASED STRATEGIES

The community is a vital source of information, support, and resources for independent producers. These producers rely heavily on their local cooperative extension agent, information included in farm magazines and newsletters, and knowledge shared with other farmers or family members (Molnar *et al.* 2001). This holds true for small farmers around the world. In rural Greece those farmers that used the most intense agricultural practices were also those with the lowest level of awareness about the impacts of agriculture to the environment Knowledge of water quality was particularly low even though farming took place adjacent to several Ramsar wetlands, protected by international conservation policies. Local training, education and incentive programs in rural areas are vital to the protection of freshwater resources and should not be overlooked (Pyrovetsi and Daoutopoulos 1999). The Food and Agriculture Organization encourages public administration agencies not only to implement specific conservation programs but also to facilitate, promote, guide and make possible broader participation in applying more sustainable forms of land use among rural communities (FAO 1988). Because of the voluntary nature of most agriculture programs that provide freshwater protection, farmer and community buy-in is critical. Programs must cater to the needs of a diversity of farmers. A study of a voluntary environmental protection program in Wales concluded that there can be a large pool of potential participators who are conservation-minded but fall through the cracks of the current program structure due to falling below a minimum required farm size, or losing money due to a compensation plan that is profitable to large producers but not for small producers. An analysis and revamping of existing policy can increase participation (Wilson 1996).

Community members, whether involved in the agriculture industry or not, can work together to defend freshwater ecosystems from damage as industrial agriculture expands. Creating local markets for organically or sustainably produced goods is a great way to encourage more benign agricultural production within a community. The use of partnerships, education, and promotion can be used to create markets. Growers may be interested in farming alternatives but fearful of financial instability avoided if a producer had a secure buyer say for the production of specialty foods. Developing outreach programs is another way to influence the community at large. An assembly of well informed citizens can go a long way toward effecting change by informing stake-holders, elected officials and those contributing to water quality degradation about problems, causes and potential solutions. A useful guide to outreach is *Getting in Step: A guide to effective outreach in your watershed* and is available on-line through EPA's Watershed Academy Web at http://www.epa.gov/watertrain.

TABLE 4-5. International Institutions and Legal Authorities

International

International and Interstate Regulation of Water Pollution Proceedings by the Conference on International and Interstate Regulation of Water Pollution (1970)

Agenda 21, Chapter 18: Protection Of The Quality And Supply Of Freshwater Resources: Application Of Integrated Approaches To The Development, Management And Use Of Water Resources

Nollkaemper, Andre, The Legal Regime for Transboundary Water Pollution: Between Discretion and Constraint (Dordrecht: Martinus Nijhoff/Graham & Trotman, 1993)

Dobbert, J.P., Water Pollution and International River Law, 35 Y.B. of the A.A.A. 60 (1965)

Nollkaemper, Andre, The Legal Regime for Transboundary Water Pollution: Between Discretion and Constraint (Dordrecht: Martinus Nijhoff/Graham & Trotman, 1993)

(continues)

TABLE 4-5. *Continued*

Africa

African Convention on the Conservation of Nature and Natural Resources. Done in Algiers, 15 September 1968.

Revised Protocol on Shared Watercourses in the Southern African Development Community, Done August 7, 2000

Middle East

Agreement of the Republic of Kazakhstan, Republic of Kyrgyzstan, Republic of Tajikistan, Tuskmenistan, and Republic of Uzbekistan on joint activities in addressing the Aral Sea. Signed 26 March 1993

The Syrian-Iraqi Agreement on the Utilization of the Euphrates Waters, signed April 1990

Asia

Agreement on the Cooperation for the Sustainable Development of the Mekong River Basin. Done in Chiang Rai, 4 April 1995. Cambodia, Lao People's Republic, Thailand and Viet Nam

Hills, P.R., et al., Transboundary Pollution Between Guandong Provinbce and Hong Kong: Threats to Water Quality in the Pearl River Estuary and their Implications for Environmental Policy and Planning, 41 J. Env't Plan & Mgmt. 355 (1998)

Railton, W. Scott, June, The Rhetoric and Reality of Water Quality Protection in China, 7 Pac. Rim L. & Pol'y 859 (1998).

Europe

Convention on Cooperation for the Protection and Sustainable Use of the Danube River. Done in Sofia, 29 June 1994

Protocol concerning the establishment of an International Commission to Protect the Mosel against Pollution. Signed at Paris on 20 December 1961; Came into force on 1 July 1962. France, Federal Republic of Germany, and Luxembourg

Agreement on the International Commission for the protection of the Rhine against pollution (with protocol of signature). Signed at Bern on 29 April 1963; Came into force on 1 May 1965. Switzerland, Federal Republic of Germany, France, Luxembourg and Netherlands

Agreement for the protection of the Rhine against chemical pollution (with annexes). Signed at Bonn on 3 December 1976 Came into force on 1 February 1979. 16 I.L.M. 242 (1976). Switzerland, European Economic Community, Federal Republic of Germany, France, Luxembourg and the Netherlands

Convention on the Protection of the Rhine. Done at Rotterdam, January 22, 1998. Federal Republic of Germany, France, Luxembourg, the Netherlands, Switzerland, and the European Union

Convention on the Protection of Lake Constance Against Pollution, UN Legislative Texts, UN Doc. ST/LEG/SER.B./12 438 (1960)

Convention Concerning the Frontier Waters Against Pollution, 1972. Rev. Gen. de Droit Int'l Publ. 265 (1975). Switzerland and Italy

van Dunne, Jan M., ed., Non-Point Source River Pollution - The Case of the River Meuse: Technical, Legal, Economics and Political Aspects (Kluwer Law Int'l 1997)

Schwabach, Aaron, The Sandoz Spill: the Failure of International Law to Protect the Rhine from Pollution, 16 Ecology L.Q. 443 (1989)

Vinogravov, S.V. & Wouters, P.K., The Caspian Sea: Quest for a New Legal Regime, 9 Leiden J. Int'l L. 87 (1996)

North America

Great Lakes Water Quality Agreement, Canada & United States of America, 30 U.S.T.S. 1383, T.I.A.S. 9257, amended 1983, T.I.A.S. 10798 (1978)

URBANIZATION AND INDUSTRIALIZATION

Introduction

Urbanization includes commercial, industrial, and residential development, transportation corridors, and landscaping associated with all of the above (The Heinz Center 2002). The intensity or density of commercial, industrial, and residential land uses generally directly relates to their effect on freshwater ecosystems and biodiversity: densely developed urban areas tend to contribute more contaminants to and modify freshwater ecosystems more dramatically than suburban and exurban areas of less intense development.

Although urban areas occupy only one percent of global land, urban development is often considered a greater threat to the integrity of freshwater ecosystems than agriculture and other land use practices. A major distinguishing attribute is reversibility. Once land is built on or paved over, only active removal of that infrastructure will allow abandoned development to be replaced by a natural system. In comparison, when abandoned, land once under agricultural use will eventually return to a more natural state and vegetative cover. For example, the north-eastern United States is a largely forested landscape, the product of reforesta-

tion following a period of farm abandonment beginning in the late 1800's (Foster *et al.* 1998). Urban development should be carried out deliberately, with a comprehensive understanding of consequences to the quality and functionality of ecosystems.

In 2000, 47% of the world's population, amounting to 2.9 billion people, lived in urban areas. By 2030, projections estimate that five billion people, 60% of the total population, will live in urban areas. Of the 2.2 billion persons expected to be added to the world in the next 30 years, 2.1 billion of those will be added to urban areas (UNPD 2002). Over that same 30 year period, it is projected that the number of urban dwellers in developing countries will double (UNPD 2002). Exacerbating the effect of growth of urban centers in developing countries is the fact that this growth is likely to occur more rapidly than will the infrastructural capacity necessary for freshwater ecosystem protection (Gleick 1993).

Patterns of urban growth are also problematic across developed nations. In many developed nations, urban populations are moving into suburban and exurban areas and to small or intermediate sized cites (World Resources Institute *et al.* 1996). This urban sprawl has

Cityscape of New Orleans. Photograph by Michael Maples/USACE.

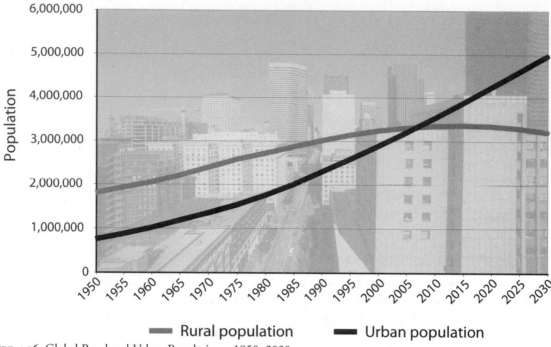

FIGURE 4-16. Global Rural and Urban Populations, 1950–2030

Data Source: Population Division of the Department of Economic and Social Affairs of the United Nations Secretariat. World Population Prospects: The 2002 Revision and World Population Prospects: The 2003 Revision. http://www.esa.un. org/unup. Photograph by Gary Wilson/NRCS.

significant detrimental consequences for freshwater ecosystems as it leads to greater amounts of land per person (USGS 1999), more infrastructure, excessive energy consumption, and pollution (World Resources Institute *et al.* 1996), thereby further exacerbating the impacts of urban development on water resources. Also relevant in developed countries is the significant recent increase in per capita water use as described within the Water Use and Management subchapter. Placed in the global context, average domestic water use per family in the United States (1300 L/d) far exceeds that of the developing world (300 L/d) (Naiman and Turner 2000).

The location of urban development also affects the severity and character of its threat to freshwater ecosystems and biodiversity (World Resources Institute *et al.* 1996). On a local scale, urban development tends to be more detrimental to natural resources when it displaces prime farm land, when it occurs on or near fragile ecosystems or when it occurs in areas with significant topographic relief, leading to severe erosion and sedimentation problems. The nature of the threat posed by urbanization also varies regionally. Urban development in arid regions may

contribute to significant water quantity declines whereas in tropical regions soil erosion, sedimentation, and contaminant mobilization may pose the major threat to freshwater ecosystems. In wealthy regions, suburban sprawl is associated with high levels of synthetic chemical pollution from lawns and roads. In poorer regions, high density cities produce more sewage than treatment facilities can process.

Most often found in urban areas, industry is a major contributor of pollution to freshwater ecosystems. Major global industries include paper product manufacturing, metal fabrication, petroleum refinement, and power generation. In the U.S., the paper industry is heavy in the Southeast and Pacific Northwest regions, metal is the intensive industry of the Great Lakes region, and petroleum extraction and refineries predominate in Texas with other dense regions being California, the lower Mississippi and the Mid-Atlantic (Kollar and Macauley 1980). Industry poses several threats to freshwater ecosystems: water withdrawal and consumption, effluent discharge, increased risk of chemical spills and accidents, and atmospheric pollution. Industry currently accounts

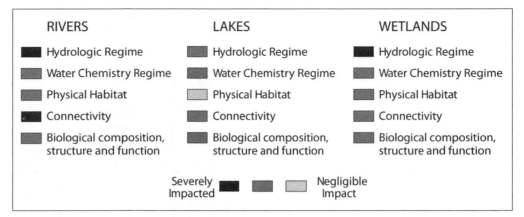

FIGURE 4-17. Summary of Impacts of Urbanization and Industrialization on Freshwater Ecosystems (can be highly variable)

for 20% of total freshwater use globally, and 7% of use in the United States. Of the freshwater used in the United States for industry, 82% is from surface water sources, 18% from groundwater, and only one percent from reclaimed wastewater (Solley *et al.* 1995). Industrial water use and pollution production is expected to increase four-fold by 2025 making the use of less-polluting technologies essential (United Nations Commission on Sustainable Development 1997). Industrial development tends to be greater across developing nations, perhaps because international companies may be attracted to locate in these countries due to the cost savings associated with less stringent environmental laws. Although local companies and governments operating industries in these nations may have a vested interest in maintaining water quality, they may lack the economic capacity to install clean technologies (Gleick 1993). Atmospheric pollution caused by industry (e.g., emissions from coal-fired generators, nonferrous metal smelters, petroleum refineries, iron and steel mills, pulp and paper mills, and motor vehicles) returns to the earth's surface and enters freshwater ecosystems as rain, snow, and fog and can also have serious consequences for freshwater ecosystems (Soares 1999).

The Effects of Urbanization/Industrialization on Freshwater Ecosystems

After agriculture, the next three top sources of alteration to freshwater ecosystems—hydro-modification, urban runoff/storm sewers, and municipal point sources—largely originate from urban environments

(USEPA 2000b). Flood control infrastructure, culverts, the in-filling of small streams, and the draining of wetlands, all activities associated with urbanization, modify the connection between land and water. Urban land use can dramatically alter the chemical and hydrologic character of freshwater ecosystems as well as affect other key ecological factors of freshwater ecosystems as described below.

THE HYDROLOGIC REGIME

Urban development dramatically changes the natural hydrologic cycle of any freshwater ecosystem. Altered hydrology from urban development often lowers baseflows, changes flood regimes, alters sediment regimes and available habitat, increases temperature and impairs biological communities (USEPA 1997). Three major elements of urbanization are responsible for these changes: impervious surface cover with the resultant stormwater delivery; water withdrawals for use and discharge of wastewater; and physical manipulation of the stream/river channel, lake basin or wetland to efficiently convey water off the land and into river systems. Changes to freshwater hydrology due to urban development extend far beyond the developed area due to the interconnectedness of the hydrologic cycle within a watershed.

Impervious surfaces

An impervious surface is any material that resists infiltration. Roads, parking lots, and roof-tops all contribute to the total impervious surface cover in an urban area,

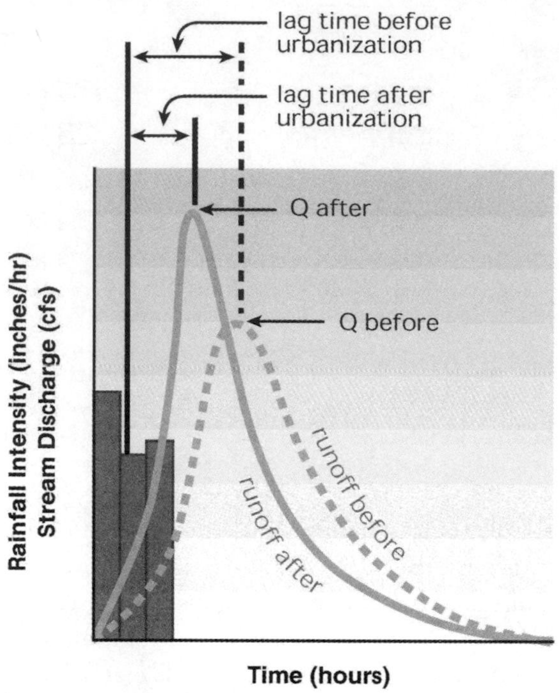

FIGURE 4-18. A Comparison of Hydrographs Before and After Urbanization

Source: The Federal Interagency Stream Restoration Working Group. 1998. Stream Corridor Restoration: Principles, Processes, and Practices.

minimizing water infiltration into soil. These effects begin when as little as 5% of the land cover in a watershed is impervious (Couch and Hamilton 2002).

As impervious surface cover increases, stormwater moves through a watershed and to a freshwater body with greater velocity and surface runoff volumes increase because of the loss of soil infiltration capacity (Dunne and Leopold 1978). This increased surface flow, coupled with traditional methods of stormwater management, results in the alteration of timing, duration, frequency, and magnitude of flood flows in rivers and streams. In lakes and wetlands, water levels and their fluctuations likewise are subject to alteration (for further details see Appendix A). Baseflow levels of all freshwater ecosystems can be reduced as flow pathways shift from infiltration to surface runoff, reducing groundwater recharge, lowering water tables, and resulting in decreased base levels in surface waters. Comparing the hydrographs of an urban stream and a forested stream, floods in urban areas occur with an abbreviated lag time (time until peak discharge) following a rain event, and exhibit higher peak discharges with shorter durations.

Water withdrawals associated with wastewater

Excessive withdrawals of water to fulfill domestic, commercial, and industrial demands in urban areas

modify the hydrologic regime of freshwater ecosystems by lowering baseflow levels in the area of extraction and potentially augmenting baseflow levels during naturally low flow periods in the area of recharge or release. For example, in the South Platte River downstream of Denver, Colorado, wastewater can account for 69–100% of the river's flow (Dennehy *et al.* 1998).

Physical manipulation of freshwater ecosystems

Engineered structures associated with urbanization or urban water use—including drains, piping, retention and detention ponds, stream channelization, levees, and dams—further alter hydrologic regimes in freshwater ecosystems. This is most marked in lotic waters. More rapid water delivery and increased flood severity result in unstable banks, channel widening and channel bed lowering (Gregory *et al.* 1992). Many engineered structures are created to retain and delay delivery in order to mitigate flood impacts. This can lead to the reduction of peak flows, water fluctuations, and over-bank flooding, all necessary for the maintenance of both instream and riparian health (Gregory *et al.* 1991; Allan 1995).

Wetlands are often removed or altered to make room for, or as a result of, urbanization. In Portland, Oregon,

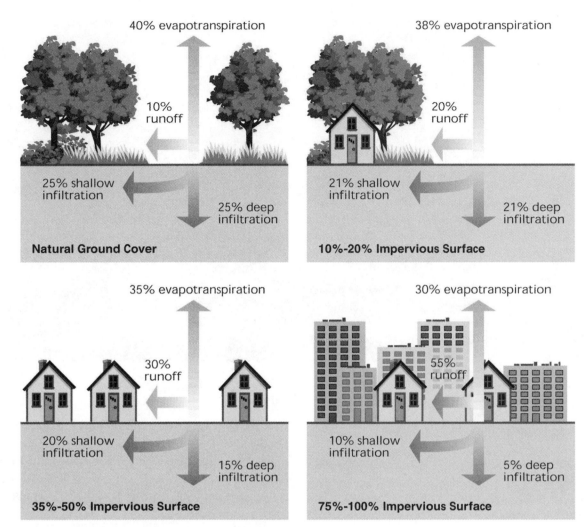

FIGURE 4-19. Relationship between Impervious Surfaces and Surface Runoff

Source: The Federal Interagency Stream Restoration Working Group. 1998. Stream Corridor Restoration: Principles, Processes, and Practices.

by 1992, 40% of the wetlands identified in 1981 had been destroyed due to human activities and drought. The remaining wetlands were degraded due to indirect effects of urban land use activities (e.g., construction, nearby excavation, etc.) (Holland *et al.* 1995). As stated previously, wetland elimination also results in the loss of other environmental services, such as flood control.

Finally, dams are common on rivers flowing through urban areas for hydroelectric power generation, flood control, and for domestic water supply. Impoundments and reservoirs impact freshwater hydrologic regimes in numerous ways. Please refer to the Water Use and Management subchapter for a more complete description of these effects.

PHYSICAL HABITAT CONDITIONS

Urban development results in both direct and indirect changes to freshwater habitat. Direct modifications include removing riparian vegetation; installing road crossings, levees, and stream enclosures; draining wetlands; changing the stream bed through channelization; and physically removing substrate (e.g., cleaning out woody debris, dredging, etc.). Habitat is modified indirectly by processes such as erosion and sedimentation and altered by hydrologic and physiochemical regimes to the extreme that areas become uninhabitable to some or most of their native biota.

Removal of riparian vegetation means the loss of valuable habitat, streambank stabilizers, and sediment filters. Photograph courtesy of NRCS.

Direct modification of freshwater habitat

The most dramatic alteration of freshwater habitat occurs with the construction and placement of structures relevant to water use and management. The effect of these structures is discussed in greater detail within relevant portions of the Water Use and Management subchapter.

Indirect modification of freshwater habitat

Sediments are the primary contaminant found in urban stormwater runoff (Clapham 1999). These sediments extend from erosion exacerbated by urban development and construction. These effects are particularly pronounced in watersheds of the humid tropics where development often occurs on steep slopes (Harper and Brown 1998). Construction activities can double the pre-construction sediment loss of a site (Guy 1965). Erosion of soils transported to streams and rivers embed substrate in fine sediment, reducing habitat diversity to uniform depositional habitats (Pedersen and Perkins 1986). Erosion of soils transported to wetlands and lakes contributes to the siltation of basin bottoms and increased turbidity,

effectively reducing littoral zone habitat (Horne and Goldman 1994). Excess nitrogen and phosphorus may be carried along with sediments inducing algal blooms and plant growth, effectively reducing the extent of photic zone habitat (Jeppesen et al. 1998).

THE WATER CHEMISTRY REGIME

Freshwater contaminants that alter the water chemistry regime of freshwater ecosystems extend from nonpoint sources (e.g., surface runoff) or from point sources (e.g., pipe discharge). Contaminants associated with nonpoint sources include pollutants that collect on or near the soil surface and are carried to freshwater ecosystems by runoff and stormwater drainage. Although the effects of nonpoint sources can be significant and are prevalent everywhere, the sources of these contaminants can be difficult to ascertain, making management or abatement more difficult (Rast 1998). Contaminants associated with point sources enter receiving waters through a pipe, most often discharging water from industrial sites, wastewater treatment facilities, or stormwater drains. Landscaping fertilizers, unsewered developments, and construction sites are major nonpoint nutrient contributors to urban freshwaters. Categories of major contaminants extending from point and nonpoint sources found in urban waterways include water temperature, nutrients (namely nitrogen and phosphorus), heavy metals, biodegradable organic material, hormones and pharmaceutical chemicals, and synthetic organic chemicals. (Clapham *et al.* 1998a).

Water Temperature

Industrial discharges, removal of riparian vegetation, reduced baseflows, and urban runoff all contribute to thermal pollution in surface waters. Industrial cooling waters are often discharged into receiving waters and increase water temperatures near and downstream of the discharge pipe. Urban storm runoff from heated impervious surfaces can create temperature pulses in streams 10–15°C above the temperature of storm pulses in forested areas (Pluhowski 1970). Temperature changes, whether localized or spread throughout the waterbody, alter the availability of habitat to organisms sensitive to temperature change. Temperature also influences chemical factors such as dissolved oxygen levels and pH further altering environmental conditions.

Nutrients

Nitrogen and phosphorus are the two nutrients most utilized by plants for growth and development. While necessary for plant and animal life, and beneficial in many circumstances, elevated concentrations of these nutrients degrade freshwater ecosystems. Sources of nitrogen and phosphorus in urban environments include fertilizers, effluent from wastewater treatment plants and other industrial activities, animal waste, decaying organic matter, soils, atmospheric deposition, and underlying geology. The USGS's National Water-Quality Assessment Program (NAWQA) reports the highest levels of total phosphorus in freshwaters associated with urban areas. While nitrogen is most problematic in agricultural watersheds, many sources of nitrogen exist in and extend from urban environments, including atmospheric deposition of nitrogen oxides produced by car exhaust and coal-fired power plants.

Excessive nutrients contribute to the eutrophication of aquatic systems. Abundant nutrients encourage excessive plant growth, often in the form of algal blooms of cyanobacteria (blue-green algae). These algae may release toxins harmful to wildlife, livestock, and humans (Lawton and Codd 1993). Additionally, as algae decompose, microbes consume oxygen, which may result in anoxic conditions and ultimately in die-offs of aquatic organisms. Eutrophication is responsible for nearly 50% of lake area and 30% of all river reaches that do not meet designated use standards or that are considered impaired in the United States (USEPA 2000b). Nutrient impairment is particularly problematic for urban areas in arid regions where effluent discharge may make up a significant proportion of total flow. Please refer to Appendix A for a more detailed discussion of the role of nitrogen and phosphorus in freshwater ecosystems.

Heavy metals

Soil and rock weathering are natural sources of metals in freshwaters. However, in urban areas, heavy metal concentrations far exceed normal background levels.

BOX 4-16. Effects of Nutrient Input to Lake Trummern, Sweden

Lake Trummen in Sweden received excessive nutrients from the sewage of a growing town and the effluent of a flax factory during the middle of the 20th century. These inputs significantly changed the water chemistry of the lake, resulting in its conversion from an oligotrophic to a hypertrophic system. Ten years after the cessation of wastewater discharges to the lake, improvement of the condition of the lake was minimal. Nutrients had been deposited in a thick layer of bottom sediments and internal cycling was responsible for the perpetuation of eutrophic conditions even when sources of stress were effectively removed (Bjork 1994).

For example, within the Seine River basin in France, an eight-fold increase in population between rural headwaters and the mid-reaches resulted in a doubling of metal concentrations (Horowitz *et al.* 1999).

Common metals found in waters affected by urban development include lead, zinc, copper, iron, chromium, cadmium, nickel, mercury, and manganese. The first three account for most of the total metal concentration in the stormwaters of many urban areas (Clapham 1998). Many non-industrial sources of heavy metal pollution in urban areas extend from the operation and maintenance of motor vehicles (Mielke *et al.* 2000). Leachate and runoff from landfills and hazardous waste dumps also deliver metals to surface waters and groundwater sources.

Metals contributed to freshwater ecosystems by industry and industrial processes are numerous. Effluent from metal industries, such as foundries and iron and steel manufacturing, contain high concentrations of many metals. Foundries can produce 20 m^3 of wastewater per metric ton of molten metal, which may contain high levels of copper, lead, chromium, and nickel. Steel manufacturing can create up to 80 m^3 of wastewater per metric ton of steel produced. This wastewater contains lead, chromium, cadmium, and zinc. Petroleum refineries also discharge certain metals in wastewaters (World Bank Group 1998). Metals may also enter freshwater ecosystems as air emissions from industry. For example, atmospheric deposition of mercury is the main pathway by which this metal reaches Lake Michigan in the United States. (Landis *et al.* 2002). Major sources of mercury emissions include fossil fuels, utility boilers, waste incinerators, iron, steel, coke and lime production, hazardous waste recycling facilities, and copper and petroleum refineries. Global emissions of mercury are 2,000–6,000 tons per year, including 158 tons from the United States (Hanisch 1998). Although most mercury settles out locally, some forms reside in the air for an average of one year, allowing it to travel great distances (Lindqvist and Rodhe 1985). Factors controlling the fate of metals in freshwaters include the organic matter content, pH, sediment characteristics, and geomorphology. High levels of particulate organic matter result in high concentrations of metals as metals readily bind to organic matter. Metals have been associated with finer sediments and in slow mov-

ing or stagnant water (Wilber and Hunter 1979; Rhodes and Cahill 1999). Metals are found to bioaccumulate in the tissues of aquatic organisms and can lead to alterations of community structure and reduced abundances (Moraes *et al.* 2003). Over the past two decades a decline in heavy metal concentrations has been documented, and likely is due to increased regulation of point source discharges. Most recently, however, runoff from urban areas is increasing in metal concentrations (Foster and Charlesworth 1996).

Biodegradable organic matter

The bacteria typically associated with sewage effluent are faecal coliforms. At elevated levels, these bacteria can cause illness. They can also serve as an indicator of other disease-causing organisms including viruses. Bacterial contamination is a serious problem in developing countries where inadequate sewage disposal and treatment infrastructure allows raw sewage to enter freshwater ecosystems either through pipe discharges or in stormwater runoff. Where infrastructure exists but cannot support a growing population, combined sewer overflows can result in harmful levels of bacteria. In South Africa, faecal coliform counts in runoff from large settlements with limited infrastructure for the disposal of sewage were measured at levels nearly as high as those measured in point source discharges (Jagals 1997). In 1998, some 240 restrictions to recreation areas arose in the United States from bacterial contaminations attributable to urban sources (USEPA 2000b).

Hormones and pharmaceutical chemicals

Hormones and pharmaceuticals pass through humans and enter freshwater ecosystems with sewage from urban areas. These by-products of human consumption bioaccumulate in aquatic food webs and are known to be carcinogens, endocrine disruptors, and the cause of widespread injury to aquatic organisms (Ludwig *et al.* 1993). In addition to die-offs of aquatic organisms, health problems such as tumors, birth defects, immune system dysfunction, and reduced or absent reproductive capacities have been attributed to natural and synthetic toxic substances (Rolland 2000).

Synthetic organic chemicals

The most common source of synthetic organic chemicals in an urban environment are household chemicals. Detergents, cleaning supplies, fertilizers, pesticides, paints, and oils become part of the runoff of driveways and lawns. Pathways to surface waters include runoff, stormwater drains, sinks, and toilets. Atrazine is the most popular herbicide for non-agricultural uses, including the maintenance of roadway right-of-ways (Aldous and Turrell 1994). DDT, now banned in the United States, is used in developing countries to control pests that pose serious health risks to humans such as the malaria virus vectored by mosquitoes. The conflict between ecosystem health and public health continues to be an issue in many parts of the world (Ryding and Thorton 1998). Many of these substances also are detected in groundwater below urban areas (Aldous and Turrell 1994; Bourgine *et al.* 1994; Bamford *et al.* 2002).

Another source of synthetic organic chemicals is commercial and industrial operations within urban areas. Two of the best known synthetic contaminants are PCB's (polychlorinated biphenols) and PAH's (polynuclear aromatic hydrocarbons). Intentionally created for industrial uses, these substances are highly toxic carcinogens disposed in effluent that persist in the sediment of freshwater ecosystems. PCB's and PAH's also move readily through the atmosphere and in doing so can reach waters far from the original source (Offenberg and Baker 2000; Bamford *et al.* 2002). Oil pollution from equipment failure in the petroleum industry, such as pipeline leaks and tanker ship spills, can be devastating to water chemistry regimes in freshwater ecosystems. Oils and grease are common elements in effluent of most manufacturing industries. The Cuyahoga River in Ohio and Hudson River in New York have burned as a result of oil pollution. Petroleum refineries also release highly toxic volatile organic compounds such as benzene, toluene, and xylene. The paper pulp industry produces toxic and non-biodegradable chlorinated organics, including dioxins and furans (Clapham *et al.* 1998a; World Bank Group 1998). Most synthetics are difficult and expensive to remove via standard treatment processes and even intensive treatment may only be marginally effective at

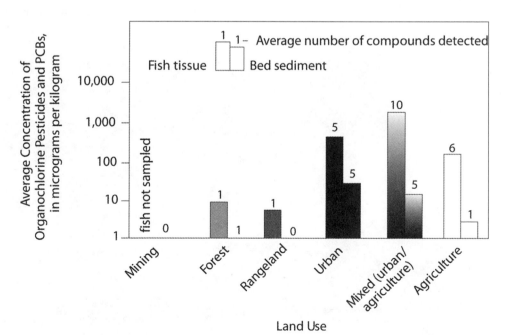

FIGURE 4-20. Concentrations of PCBs and Organochlorine Pesticides Are Highest in Urban and Mixed (urban/agriculture) Land Use Areas.

Source: Dennehy, K.F., D.W. Litke, C.M. Tate, S.L. McMahon, P.B. McMahon, B.W. Bruce, R.A. Kimbrough, and J.S. Heiny. *Water Quality in the South Platte River Basin, Colorado, Nebraska, and Wyoming, 1992–1995.* U.S. Geological Survey Circular 1167. http://water.usgs.gov/pubs/circ/circ1167.

removing these pollutants from wastewater and air emissions (Clapham *et al.* 1998a).

Connectivity

Constructed barriers common in urban areas such as dams, levees, culverts, and diversions, as well as bank stabilization materials and associated rip-rap, pose the most significant threat to the connectivity of freshwater ecosystems in urban areas as discussed in detail in the Water Use and Management subchapter.

Withdrawal of groundwater and surface water for municipal, commercial, and industrial purposes in urban areas can result in periods of dewatering for a river channel, lake basin, or wetland. The effects of such withdrawals are exacerbated by drought, a common occurrence in many urban centers located in arid regions. Furthermore, increased imperviousness of urban areas severs the vertical connection between rainfall and groundwater. The paving over of recharge zones also exacerbates low water levels in freshwater ecosystems.

Anoxic or toxic dead zones, where a portion of an aquatic system becomes uninhabitable, can create longitudinal disconnects. Anoxic conditions are created when bacterial and algal production consumes all available oxygen, rendering the environment uninhabitable for most aquatic life. These blooms occur in urban areas following nutrient enrichment from runoff or effluent discharge, as stated previously. Areas receiving untreated effluent from sewers or commercial activities can become so toxic the area is temporarily or more permanently unable to support life. When organic loading from effluent discharges exceeded ca. 10 mg/L BOD in the Yarqon stream of Israel, nearly all fish avoided the area (Gafny *et al.* 2000). Industrial point sources located in headwaters can be particularly detrimental because of the low dilution potential (Mainstone and Parr 2002). Whether the result of dewatering or severe contamination, loss of connectivity within a freshwater ecosystem impedes organism movement and is particularly problematic for anadromous fish and other migratory species.

Biological composition and interactions

The United States Environmental Protection Agency (EPA) lists elevation of temperature, depletion of dissolved oxygen, and increase in sedimentation as the three most common causes for changes in the structure of aquatic communities in urban settings (USEPA 2000b). Species life histories and behavioral

In 1952 the Cuyahoga River in Ohio caught on fire as the result of oil pollution. Photograph by James Thomas © The Cleveland Press Collection.

A fish kill resulting from water pollution. Photograph by W.L. French/USFWS.

traits correspond to such abiotic factors as sediment, substrate, habitat, and hydrology (Richards *et al.* 1997), all of which are altered by activities within an urban environment. At the community level, alteration of freshwaters due to urban land use results in shifts in the dominance, diversity and abundance of aquatic organisms. Sensitive species generally decline and tolerant species increase (Lenat and Crawford 1994), though tolerant species may include invasive alien species as described in the IAS subchapter. The South Platte River of Colorado, Nebraska, and Wyoming realized a shift in dominant fish families and an overall decrease in the number of invertebrate taxa within and downstream of Denver. Trout were dominant in forested streams whereas suckers, sunfish, and largemouth bass became the dominant families in urban streams (Dennehy *et al.* 1998).

Even relatively small changes in water temperature can affect species and communities. Temperature determines metabolic rates, food requirements, and the developmental process (Naiman and Turner 2000). For example, eggs may hatch early or late without the appropriate temperature cues (Beacham and Murray 1990). In addition to temperature shifts, removal of native riparian vegetation eliminates the main source of external carbon, which results in cascading effects throughout the biological community

(France *et al.* 1996). As more solar radiation reaches the water surface, primary producers thrive (Gregory *et al.* 1991), algal biomass increases, and the ecosystem's metabolic processes change (France *et al.* 1996). This is particularly problematic in headwater streams, wetlands and small lakes where much of the surface area of the waterbody would be under forest cover in an undisturbed setting.

Increased imperviousness and the presence of networks of sewers and drains hasten runoff following rainstorms, making recipient rivers more flashy. The consequences of these altered urban flood patterns are numerous. Reduced habitat diversity, disconnection from floodplain, and an increase in suspended sediments are three major factors influencing biological communities within lotic systems (Stranko and Rodney 2001). Fish communities become dominated by generalists rather than a diversity of habitat specialists. Altered hydroperiods and reduced recharge in urban wetlands have resounding implications for biological communities. Changes affect not only aquatic organisms but also local vegetation adapted to certain water level fluctuations, wading birds and amphibians (Holland et al. 1995; Mcpherson and Halley 1997).

Nutrients and toxins affect sensitive species first. However, all organisms are at risk to extreme levels of contamination. Low dissolved oxygen levels, often induced by nutrient enrichment, are known to stress freshwater mussels (Sparks and Strayer 1998). Mussels are regularly used as indicators of toxic contamination as they readily accumulate these substances in their tissues (Chafik *et al.* 2001). Persistent chemicals such as mercury and PCB's bioaccumulate in the body tissues of fish and mussels, posing health threats to humans and other organisms that consume contaminated tissues. When oxygen levels bottom out or toxins are released in lethal doses, massive fish kills and local extirpations, especially of mussels, are known to occur (Gafny *et al.* 2000; Diamond *et al.* 2002).

Recently, a group of contaminants known as the organochlorine chemicals, often a by-product of industrial processes, have been found to interfere with the natural chemical messengers that control normal development and reproductive function in wildlife (Colborn and Thayer 2000). These compounds are ubiquitous throughout aquatic environments and have been associated with birth deformities, demasculinization and feminization of male fishes, and defeminization and masculinization of female fishes (Colborn and Clement 1992). Additional visible impacts of persistent chemicals to freshwater biota include lesions, growths and eroded fins (USEPA 2000a). In addition to the biological effects of industrial discharges, water withdrawals for industrial purposes, namely for cooling waters, can kill or stress organisms near intake pipes (e.g., large numbers of fish and their eggs are sucked through or against these intake pipes which deliver water into the cooling systems of power plants, paper products manufacturers, petroleum refineries, and chemical and metal manufacturing facilities).

Strategies for Mitigating/Abating the Effects of Urbanization and Industrialization on Freshwater Ecosystems

Urbanization and industrialization contribute contaminants to freshwater ecosystems, thereby changing water chemistry and hydrologic regimes of these systems as well as other key ecological factors. However, complete elimination of urbanization and industrialization as a source of harm for freshwater ecosystems is neither feasible nor realistic. Therefore, strategies to abate this threat focus on management once development is in place and on intentional planning and policy implementation to guide future development.

TECHNICAL STRATEGIES

Numerous specific and effective technical strategies exist for reducing the effects of urban land uses on freshwater ecosystems. These strategies typically relate to improving the quality or quantity of stormwater drainage or other types of discharge from urban areas or they pertain to physical restoration of the affected freshwater ecosystem. Technical solutions generally either control discrete pollution discharges to a water body (point sources) or control diffuse pollution sources (nonpoint sources) through the use of best management practices (BMPs).

Technical strategies for abating the effect of urbanization and industrialization on freshwater ecosystems include BMPs related to improving stormwater discharges, improving non-stormwater discharges, and engaging in physical restoration as described below. The level of pollution control attained by the implementation of a given BMP will depend on several factors, including (USEPA 1999b):

- The number, intensity and duration of wet weather events;
- The pollutant removal efficiency of the BMP;
- The water quality and physical conditions of the receiving waters;
- The current and potential use of the receiving waters; and
- The existence of nearby substitute sites of unimpaired water.

Physical factors (such as soil type, slope, drainage area and depth to groundwater) and social factors (such as land availability, safety, and accessibility for long-term maintenance) should influence BMP selection. However, BMP selection and implementation should not take place in the absence of a more comprehensive watershed plan, because changes in hydrology and water quality at one location will impact the entire watershed and random installation may actually lead to an overall increase in nonpoint source pollution problems (Peterson *et al.* 1998).

Box 4-17. Application of BMPs at Indian River Lagoon, Florida

In Brevard County, Florida, urban stormwater pollution was responsible for the adverse impacts to the nationally significant Indian River Lagoon. Several urban sub-basins were targeted for implementation of BMPs that would help remove pollutants before reaching this lagoon. BMP implementation was funded by Clean Water Act Section 319 grants and a water utility fee. Sediment boxes were installed at the end of storm drain pipes to capture sediment before it was discharged to the lagoon. Boxes required cleanouts up to six times per year and removed 202 m³ of sediment over a three-year period. Also, an exfiltration trench and wet detention system were constructed and planted with vegetation for nutrient removal purposes and erosion control. Monitoring indicates that this system is removing 60% of the pollutants contained in the stormwater of a 120 acre residential area otherwise bound for the lagoon (USEPA 2002a).

Improving stormwater discharges

Changes in stormwater delivery via surface runoff can dramatically alter the hydrology and connectivity of, and vector pollutants to, freshwater bodies, collectively resulting in altered hydrologic regimes, chemical regimes and biological communities. Strategies here are logically related to either improving the quantity or quality of the stormwater discharge itself or reducing the major sources of contamination to stormwater: home and lawn care products, construction materials, and related pollution.

Managing stormwater runoff

BMPs related to managing stormwater runoff attempt to reduce stormwater flow, reduce pollutants contained by stormwater, and reduce stormwater pollution sources (Clapham et al. 1998b, USEPA 1999b). The major categories of these BMPs include (USEPA 1999b):

- Structural BMPs:
  - Infiltration systems such as infiltration basins and porous pavement
  - Detention systems such as basins and underground vaults
  - Retention systems such as wet ponds
  - Constructed wetland systems
  - Filtration systems such as media filters and bioretention systems
  - Vegetated systems such as grass filter strips and vegetated swales
  - Minimizing directly-connected impervious surfaces
  - Miscellaneous and vendor-supplied systems such as oil/water separators and hydrodynamic devices

- Non-structural BMPs:
  - Automotive product and household hazardous material disposal
  - Commercial and retail space good housekeeping
  - Industrial good housekeeping
  - Modified use of fertilizers, pesticides and herbicides
  - Lawn debris management
  - Animal waste disposal
  - Maintenance practices such as catch basin cleaning, street and parking lot sweeping, road and ditch maintenance
  - Illicit discharge detection and elimination
  - Educational and outreach programs
  - Storm drain inlet stenciling
  - Low-impact development and land use planning

While it may seem counterintuitive to manage stormwater in areas with low annual rainfall, stormwater management in arid and semi-arid regions is particularly important largely because of low dilution potential in streams. In these regions, selection of stormwater management practices should emphasize the following principles (Caraco, 2000 #386):

- Careful selection and adaptation of stormwater practices to arid watersheds
- Minimization of irrigation needs for stormwater practices
- Protection of groundwater resources and encouragement of recharge

• Reduction of downstream channel erosion and protection from upland sediment.

Extended detention dry ponds, sand filters, and the use of rooftop catchment devices for plant irrigation and drinking water are highly recommended for use in drier environments. Typical management techniques that are successful in humid regions that become impractical or ineffective in drier areas include wet ponds, stormwater wetlands, and swales (Caraco 2000).

A lengthy discussion of specific stormwater management practices is beyond the scope of this document because of the wealth of information on this topic, the diversity of BMPs being used, and the technical nature of BMP implementation. Useful resources on this topic include:

• The Center for Watershed Protection's Stormwater Managers Resource Center, http://www.stormwater center.net
• *Controlling Urban Runoff: A Practical Manual for Planning and Designing Urban BMP's* (Schueler 1987)
• Stormwater Strategies: Community Responses to Runoff Pollution, produced by NRDC at http://nrdc.org/water/pollution/storm/stoinx.asp

• EPA's NPDES Phase II National Menu of Best Management Practices for Storm Water Phase II http://cfpub.epa. gov/npdes/stormwater/menuof bmps/menu.cfm
• Preliminary data summary of urban stormwater best management practices (USEPA 1999b)
• Texas Nonpoint SourceBOOK: stormwater management guide, www.txnpsbook.org

Reducing contaminants from construction

Construction related to urbanization and industrialization can directly contribute sediment, chemicals, and other contaminants to freshwater ecosystems through runoff through stormwater drains and sewers. However, management practices can mitigate these effects. Before any construction activities occur, a stormwater and sediment and erosion control plan should be developed, giving consideration to factors such as soil type, grade and proximity to surface water. Many states require the submission and approval of these plans prior to commencing work. Comprehensive guidelines are available through EPA report 832-R-92-005: *Stormwater Management for Construction Activities: Developing Pollution Prevention Plans and Best Management Practices.*

Many communities are now labelling storm sewer drains to discourage the public from dumping materials that might pollute the water. Photograph by Amy Smith/NRCS.

Reducing contaminants from home and lawn care

Home owners and residents may intentionally or unintentionally contribute contamination to stormwater discharge when they spill cleaning products into drains and gutters adjacent to their homes. Public education campaigns usually effectively diminish such practices. However, the more significant contribution of contaminants from private citizens extends from lawn and garden care practices and products. Approximately 70% of all homeowners in the U.S. fertilize their lawns a minimum of once a year, and two-thirds of these apply treatments themselves at highly variable rates (CWP 2000). The remaining one-third rely on lawn services that offer base packages including fertilizer and pesticide application six to eight times a year. Nitrogen application rates often exceed 200 lbs/acre/year, a rate greater than that applied to golf course greens (Klein 1990). Soil compaction and proximity to impervious surfaces increase the likelihood that these nutrients and pesticides will reach a surface water body via stormwater runoff. Several management alternatives reduce this potential as summarized by the following eight key steps (CWP 2000):

- Lawn conversion: reduce lawn area by replacing grass with lower maintenance landscaping

- Soil building: test soils to assess nutrient needs and pH, aerate soils
- Grass selection: choose hardy grass well suited to the region
- Mowing and thatch management: leave clippings after mowing, increase mow height and reduce mowing frequency
- Minimal fertilization: only fertilize if soil test indicates a deficiency, use lower impact fertilizers such as encapsulated nitrogen or organic compost
- Weed control and tolerance: use of alternative control methods such as cultivation and burning, allowing some weed growth
- Integrated pest management: healthy lawns should resist pest, use low impact methods like insecticidal soaps and biocontrols
- Sensible irrigation: water infrequently, to a depth of six inches, early in the morning, consider sloping walkways toward lawns to harvest rainfall for irrigation purposes.

Many of these concepts form the underlying framework of a landscaping technique called xeriscaping (the wise selection and placement of landscape plantings to minimize maintenance and necessary inputs based on factors such as climate, soils and exposure). Reducing

Lawn fertilizers and pesticides from homes can enter surface waters via stormwater runoff. Photograph by Lynn Betts/NRCS.

inputs of fertilizer, water and pesticide associated with residential area will lower pollution loads in runoff and the amount that infiltrates to groundwater as well as reduce municipal water use. Because xeriscaping is region-specific, information can be sought out from a local extension agency. Much of the above also applies to commercial developments.

Improving non-stormwater discharges

Non-stormwater discharges (e.g., effluent from septic systems, sewers, and industries) also contribute contaminants to and alter flows in freshwater ecosystems. Septic systems are most problematic in exurbanizing regions or low-density developments surrounding medium to small towns. Strategies to reduce the cumulative impacts of individual septic systems include reducing failure rates, proper siting, and installation of more effective technologies. Specifications for siting of septic systems are determined at the state level. Sanitary sewers convey wastewater from urban lands to treatment facilities but sometimes release their contaminants before reaching these facilities due to the effects of storm events, overflows, and illicit connections to drain network. In the United States, some sewage systems still release harmful levels of pollutants to receiving waters. In developing countries, sewage infrastructure often does not exist or is inadequate and cannot keep up with growth in most city centers.

Techniques for treatment of sewage wastewater are well developed and generally begin with gravity separation of solids and either chemical or biological breakdown of organics in anaerobic settling tanks. Waste is then oxidized in retention ponds and sterilized with chlorine (Pereira 1973). Pollutant discharge levels may be further reduced by installing upgrades that provide for nitrification (converting toxic forms of nitrogen to nitrate), denitrification (converting nitrate to molecular nitrogen), and physical-chemical treatments (removing dissolved metals and organics) (USEPA 1999a).

Industrial effluent discharges are unique given the chemical complexity of their effluent. The Clean Water Act requires the pre-treatment of most industrial effluent before discharge to publicly owned treatment works (POTW) since municipal treatment facilities often cannot effectively remove the variety of contaminants produced by the industrial sector (USEPA 1999a). This places the burden of clean-up on the pollution producers. Technologies have been developed to clean wastewater from most industrial applications, though financial restraints or neglect may keep industries operating without infrastructure improvements for pollution control.

Selected recommendations for a few major industries illustrate the range of possibilities for the abatement and mitigation of industrial pollution to freshwater ecosystems (World Bank Group 1998):

- Steel manufacturing operations can recycle wastewater thereby reducing discharged quantities from $80m^3/t$ to less than $5m^3/t$ of steel manufactured and preferable less than $1m^3/t$. Heavy metals in remaining wastewater can be further reduced using a sedimentation process to settle out solids and precipitate heavy metals followed by filtration.

- Petroleum refining operations can reduce wastewater production by reusing both cooling waters and wastewater; recovering and reusing phenols, caustics and other toxic solvents; and using dry sweeping instead of washdown techniques. Emission controls also warrant attention since significant freshwater pollutants originate in refinery air emissions.

- Paper and pulp industries can reduce the pollutants contained in their wastewater by producing less bright products, since chlorine-based compounds, used to make brighter products, contribute greater pollutants to freshwater ecosystems. Paper products that aren't so bright can also incorporate recycled fibers. Total recycling of wastewaters is possible. Reduction of effluent volumes and concentrations can be achieved by using a dry debarking process, burning pulping chemicals in a recovery furnace and using high-efficiency washing and bleaching equipment. A typical wastewater treatment system may include neutralization, screening, sedimentation, and floatation to remove solids, and biological treatment to reduce organic content and destroy toxic organics. Biological treatments include activated sludge, aerated lagoons, and anaerobic fermentation.

The World Bank has developed a series of reports on pollution prevention and abatement for specific

A paper mill in Bucksport, Maine. Photograph by Casey Theberge/NOAA.

industries. These can be found at http://lnweb18. worldbank.org/essd/envext.nsf/51ByDocName/Pollut ionPreventionandAbatementHandbookIndustrySecto rGuidelines. Each report proposes recommended contaminant levels and ways to achieve these levels, through pollution prevention and treatment technologies, in the effluent of these industries.

Additional useful resources related to improving industrial practices and their effects on freshwater ecosystems include:

- MaESTro Environmentally Sound Technologies http://www.unep.or.jp/maestro2/
- The International Environmental Technology Centre http://www.unep.or.jp/
- Cleaner Production.Com at www.cleaner production. com, is a clearinghouse for pollution prevention and cleaner production. Available to order at this site is The CD-ROM *Digital Library for Cleaner Production and Pollution Prevention* Edition 2002, Burton Hamner, Editor.
- The World Bank Group's *Pollution Prevention and Abatement Handbook: Toward Cleaner Production,* 1998, provides pollution prevention strategies for over 50 industries and is available in hard copy and can be downloaded at http://lnweb18.worldbank. org/ESSD/envext.nsf/51ByDocName/Pollution PreventionandAbatementHandbook.

Engaging in physical restoration

The three most common types of restoration used to mitigate effects of urban development on freshwater ecosystems are the restoration of wetlands, riparian vegetation, and stream channel geometry. Not only do these activities restore a portion of the natural environment, but wetlands and riparian zones also buffer the effects of development. For example, a healthy wetland will filter out contaminants and slow the release of stormwater to a river, a functioning riparian forest will take up nutrients and dissipate energy from urban flood flows, and restored stream meanders will prevent downstream erosion and encourage the natural development of habitat diversity. Restoration work is also done to reverse or slow the eutrophication of lakes and to create instream habitat lost to sedimentation or channelization. Each of these highly technical, site-specific endeavors may involve teams of scientists and engineers. A wealth of information exists on the topic of aquatic restoration. Useful resources related to restoration include:

- *National Research Council Committee on Restoration and Aquatic Ecosystems* (National Research Council Committee on Restoration and Aquatic Ecosystems 1992)
- *Restoration and Management of Lakes and Reservoirs* (Cooke *et al.* 1993)
- *Restoring Streams in Cities: A Guide for Planners, Policymakers, and Citizens* (Riley 1998)

INSTITUTIONAL AND LEGAL STRATEGIES

One of the most effective ways to contribute to the protection of freshwater ecosystems is to influence legislative decisions made at the national, state, and local levels. Understanding the defining legislation and resulting complexion of environmental decision-making that exists within the area of interest is a critical first step. Also critical is understanding who or what agency is responsible for administrative and regulatory oversight in order to most effectively leverage the issues. The following section provides an in-depth review of existing U.S. institutional and legal strategies for abating/mitigating the effect of urbanization and industrialization on freshwater ecosystems. This overview section on institutional and legal strategies concludes with a summary of key international institutional and legal strategies for use by developed and developing countries around the world.

U.S. institutions and legal authorities

Utilizing the Clean Water Act and other federal laws

Federal oversight of water quality began with the 1972 Federal Water Pollution Control Act (FWPCA) when the EPA was charged with defining water quality standards and funding large proportions of local infrastructural improvement projects to help meet these standards. The Clean Water Act (CWA) of 1977 amended the responsibilities of the EPA to include permitting of all point source discharges. In 1987, Congress approved revisions to the CWA that brought more focus to the control of nonpoint source discharges. Funding for sewage and wastewater treatment plant construction projects were phased out and a state revolving fund was developed to support a broader base of projects including infrastructure improvements, implementation of Best Management Practices (BMPs), purchase of sensitive lands, wetland restoration and brownfield clean-up. CWA sections relevant to reducing threats associated with urbanization and industrialization include:

- **Section 402** deals with point sources of pollution through the National Pollutant Discharge Elimination System (NPDES) of permitting, and requires that all point source discharges have an approved permit.
- **Section 319** is the nonpoint source program, which is non-regulatory. It requires states to develop a nonpoint source pollution management plan. Once approved by the EPA, 319 grants are issued to provide funding to help implement plans.
- **Section 401** requires state certification of federal projects resulting in discharge into a state's waterbody,

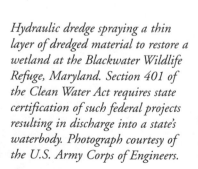

Hydraulic dredge spraying a thin layer of dredged material to restore a wetland at the Blackwater Wildlife Refuge, Maryland. Section 401 of the Clean Water Act requires state certification of such federal projects resulting in discharge into a state's waterbody. Photograph courtesy of the U.S. Army Corps of Engineers.

such as U.S. Army Corps of Engineers (Corps) projects or EPA approved NPDES permits. Certification must indicate that discharge will not threaten declared water quality standards for that receiving water.

- **Section 404** deals with the filling of waterbodies with dredged or fill material. Pertaining most often to wetlands, but applicable to all surface waters, this section is administered jointly by the EPA and the Corps. The Corps is responsible for permit issuance. In order of decreasing desirability, avoidance of filling is optimal, followed by minimizing the affected area, and finally compensating for any losses. This final option is also referred to as the "no net loss" federal policy assertion heard frequently: if an acre of wetland is destroyed, an acre must be created or restored elsewhere.

- **Section 304** requires the EPA to develop national quality standards for industrial wastewater discharges.

- **Clean Water Act Amendments,** particularly Section 303(d), require the maintenance of minimal water quality levels in all streams throughout the U.S. through the establishment of Total Maximum Daily Loads (TMDLs).

The CWA provides a framework for influencing policy and development to reduce or minimize urban impacts to freshwater in the United States. Many how-to guides have been written on ways to direct or halt detrimental activities and to implement or encourage beneficial activities in the context of the CWA. Some of these approaches and a list of resources can be found at the end of this section.

Other federal legislation having direct influence over freshwater quality includes the Resource Conservation and Recovery Act (1976); the Federal Insecticides, Fungicides and Rodenticides Act (1947); the Toxic Substances Control Act (1976); and the Pollution Prevention Act (1990).

While EPA is the regulatory agency, the United States Geological Survey (USGS) has no regulatory mandate and therefore serves as a national, natural science and technology research agency. USGS can provide conservation practitioners with data, tools and strategies useful to those interested in urban water quality issues. The USGS Water Resources Division

provides data and technical information to assist in determining problems and devising appropriate strategies for freshwater conservation in urban areas. Hydrologic data, biochemical data, GIS data layers and local publications and case studies are also available to assist in the assessment and monitoring of the watershed of interest. Two particularly relevant programs are the USGS Science in Your Watershed program (at http://www.usgs.gov/wsc) and the National Water Quality Assessment (NAWQA) program. NAWQA (http://water. usgs.gov/nawqa) is a data collection and synthesis initiative that began in 1991 aimed at acquiring long-term standardized data on the hydrology, chemistry, habitat of aquatic ecosystems, and land use of 50 major watersheds and aquifers throughout the United States to inform decision-making and policy development.

Engaging state governments in clean-up activities

Much of the administration and day-to-day activities that occur from CWA mandates have been turned over to state governments. State level initiatives are developed to meet or exceed federal mandates on water issues and/or to preserve/restore something valuable to the state and its people. Section 303(d) of the CWA Amendments requires each state to develop a prioritized list of impaired waters with and identified problem pollutant(s) every four years. This list can be found at www.epa.gov/owow/tmdl. The state is then required to develop a clean up plan for each impaired waterbody. The goal of these clean-up plans is to meet or improve upon that stream's established TMDL's. According to the EPA, a TMDL is defined as the amount of pollutant (e.g., phosphorus, sediment), or property of a pollutant (e.g., biological oxygen demand), from point, nonpoint, and natural background sources that may be discharged to a water quality-limited receiving water. Any pollutant loading above the TMDL results in a violation of applicable water quality standards.

A powerful way to protect freshwater from urban pollution is to participate in the process of TMDL development. TMDL development is a public process, so a well-informed advocate can ensure that TMDLs are set to adequately protect the waterbody of interest Clean Water Network has published a handbook entitled *The Ripple Effect* that provides detailed information on how to participate in the development of watershed cleanup plans. This guide can be found on line at: www.cwn.org/docs/publications/ripple/ along with a very helpful toolkit for the development and evaluation of TMDL's. The first step in becoming part of the cleanup plan process is to gather information (Frey 2001). For example, find out what pollutants are causing problems in your favorite waterbody, when it is scheduled for clean up, and ask to be on the agency's mailing list for your waterbody. Basic questions to ask about any cleanup plan include:

- Does the cleanup plan set daily pollution limits?
- Does the cleanup plan account for all sources of the pollutant?
- Does the cleanup plan include a margin of safety?
- Does the plan take seasonal variations, such as river flow and temperature, into account?
- Is there a plan to implement the pollution reductions?
- Is it reasonable to think that the cleanup plan's actions will actually be implemented? That they will result in cleaner water?
- Is there a monitoring plan?
- Are there milestones for water quality improvements?

The National Pollution Discharge Elimination System regulates point source discharges in urban areas, primarily from wastewater treatment facilities, stormwater drains and industrial discharges. Specific information on permits issued in your area is available in the Envirofacts data warehouse at www.epa.org/enviro/index_java.html. Identifying the major polluters and knowing the compliance rate of those facilities can help prioritize action either in the form of facilitation of pollution reductions or accountability of consistently negligent dischargers.

Worthy of note is the recent shift in financial burden to individual states of federal mandates on water quality issues with direct ties to urban developments such as wastewater treatment, municipal waste and sewage sludge disposal. The establishment or expansion of funding mechanisms such as fees, environmental taxes, bond issues and revolving loan funds can provide states with funds necessary to protect water quality (Fiorino 1995).

Other valuable information on the internet about using the CWA to abate the effects of urbanization and industrialization on freshwater ecosystems includes:

- *Saving our Watersheds: A Field Guide to Watershed Restoration Using TMDLs.* http://www.nwf.org/watersheds/fieldguide/index.html
- EPA's TMDL website. http://www.epa.gov/owow/tmdl
- American Rivers: *Using the Clean Water Act/The Clean Water Toolkit.* http://americanrivers.org/cleanwatertoolkit/default.htm
- The River Network looks at the Clean Water Act on a state-by-state basis at http://www.rivernetwork.org/cleanwater/cwa_search.asp

Participating in local planning processes

The management of land uses and development lies primarily with local governments. Therefore, influencing planning, ordinance development, outreach, and restoration at the local level provide a unique opportunity to protect freshwater resources from impacts of urbanization in a proactive manner.

Incorporating concepts of smart growth, or sustainable development, such as conservation subdivisions, greenspace preservation, and low-impact development into county and city level development plans can lessen the impacts of development on natural ecosystems, including freshwater ecosystems. The EPA identifies the following universal characteristics of smart growth (USEPA 2002b):

- Development is economically viable and preserves open space, natural resources, and habitats for indigenous species.
- Development projects that enhance the economy, the community, and the environment receive expedited approval.
- Existing infrastructure is maintained and enhanced but expanded when appropriate to serve current and new residents.
- There is a beneficial collaboration among the community, the nonprofit sector, and the public and private sectors.
- Compact development is focused on existing or planned transportation facilities.
- Development is limited in ecologically significant areas.

Many different approaches exist for achieving the goals of smart growth. One well-defined approach to accomplishing smart growth is Low Impact Development.

Low Impact Development (LID) is a design strategy developed to incorporate broad planning strategies and individual site planning methods into a unified approach aimed at maintaining the natural hydrologic regime of a developing watershed. In Prince George's County, Maryland's Department of Environmental Resources has been refining this approach and implementing its principals within the county. The goals of LID are comprehensive, covering the entire planning process from master planning to community buy-in and involvement, and can be summarized as follows (MD Department of Environmental Resources 1999):

- Provide an improved technology for environmental protection of receiving waters.
- Provide economic incentives that encourage environmentally sensitive development.
- Develop the full potential of environmentally sensitive site planning and design.
- Encourage public education and participation in environmental protection.
- Help build communities based on environmental stewardship.
- Reduce construction and maintenance costs of the stormwater infrastructure.
- Introduce new concepts, technologies, and objectives for stormwater management such as micro-management and multifunctional landscape features (bioretention areas, swales, and conservation areas); mimic or replicate hydrologic functions; and maintain the ecological/biological integrity of receiving streams.
- Encourage flexibility in regulations that allows innovative engineering and site planning to promote smart growth principles.
- Encourage debate on the economic, environmental, and technical viability and applicability of current stormwater practices and alternative approaches.

The Low Impact Development design strategies manual produced by Prince George's County Department of Environmental Resources describes this approach and gives specific implementation guidelines. It can be found on-line at http://www.go princegeorgescounty.com/Government/AgencyIndex/ DER/PPD/LID/LiDNatl.pdf.

Individual developments can also incorporate strategic planning and protective construction methods can dramatically reduce the influence of development on the five key ecological factors necessary to maintain a healthy aquatic ecosystem. This is particularly important for developments adjacent to or within freshwater ecosystems. Important considerations in such circumstances include minimum lot area and frontage; structure setbacks; clearing limitations; timber harvesting limitations; erosion and sedimentation control; sewage disposal; and provisions for nonconforming uses. Wisconsin also has a well-developed shoreland zoning program available through the Wisconsin Department of Natural Resources Shoreland Management Program at http://www.dnr. state.wi.us/org/water/wm/dsfm/shore/title.htm.

Conservation subdivisions are gaining popularity among urban planners. These subdivisions are designed to reduce lot sizes and impervious surface cover while increasing greenspace, or areas remaining in a natural land cover type. Greenspace has the potential to benefit freshwater ecosystems, landowners and the larger community. Designed properly, greenspace should protect sensitive features such as wetlands or riparian vegetation, provide wildlife habitat and serve as a source of recreation opportunity and added aesthetics to homeowners. In the U.S., a greenway, or a linear park, that increases and connects greenspace was established in Athens, Georgia. A portion of this greenway protects over 450 acres of floodplain and marshland along the Oconee River. Property values adjacent to, or near to, this greenspace are substantially higher than property values on similar homes not located near this park, benefiting individual home owners. Higher property taxes on these higher value homes also generate a significant tax revenue that benefits the community as a whole (Nelson et al. 2002).

Further information on land use planning can be found at:

- The Low Impact Development Center at http:// www.lowimpactdevelopment.org
- The University of Georgia's Institute of Ecology Office of Public Service and Outreach offers publications

Box 4-18. Etowah River Watershed, Georgia

The Etowah River is a major tributary of the Coosa River System, which drains metropolitan Atlanta. Sprawl from Atlanta's rapidly growing metropolis has earned six of the counties within the Etowah basin the title of the fastest-growing counties in America (U.S. Bureau of the Census 2001). Development pressures are enormous.

The Etowah River is also home to 91 native fish, of which 14 have been extirpated, three are federally protected, two are endemic and five have state-level protection (Burkhead *et al.* 1997). This biodiversity has been challenged by a long agricultural history, the development of the Lake Allatoona reservoir, and a variety of pressures extending from urbanization. Many of the tributaries of the Etowah River drainage network no longer meet their designated uses and sedimentation and nutrient enrichment from urban runoff

Etowah River, Georgia. Photograph by Candace Stoughton/TNC.

threaten the viability of Lake Allatoona as a drinking water source and for recreation, a $90 million per year industry. Many of the tributaries within the mid- and lower reaches of the Etowah River drainage network face these same threats no longer supporting designated uses. Growing concern among citizens, local government officials, and scientists provided the impetus to organize, form partnerships, and work toward the protection of the Etowah River basin.

In 1996, the Upper Etowah River Alliance (UERA) was formed representing the five counties occupying the Etowah River basin above Lake Allatoona. UERA's mission is "to provide regional leadership and education for maintaining the natural beauty and quality of the Upper Etowah River Watershed, which meets the needs of property owners, a prosperous economy and the environment." In order to best accomplish this mission, UERA hosted public meetings throughout the watershed and solicited public input regarding watershed protection priorities and strategies. Subsequently, UERA applied for and received a Clean Water Act Section 319 grant to develop twenty nonpoint source BMPs and demonstration sites throughout the watershed including streambank restoration, retrofiting of failing septic tanks, native plant xeriscaping and porous pavement installations.

Since UERA needed technical, scientific and practical information to implement, monitor, and evaluate the effectiveness of these BMPs, a unique, powerful, and mutually beneficial partnership emerged between UERA and the University of Georgia. The University developed a course involving students from many disciplines including ecology, environmental engineering, forestry, environmental design, and law. Each semester students team up and choose a project to fulfill an information need identified by UERA. Project products have since provided UERA and the people of the Upper Etowah with information on fundraising, restoration, ordinance development and much

Urban sprawl encroaches on Lake Allatoona. Photograph by Candace Stoughton/TNC. Flight courtesy of South Wings.

more. Many projects have already been used to implement conservation activities including the adoption of a conservation subdivision ordinance, the development of state legislation to make development rights transferable, and the creation of a regional greenspace plan.

For more information visit the University of Georgia Institute of Ecology Office of Public Service and Outreach at http://outreach.ecology.uga.edu/etowah.html. Reports from the University of Georgia Etowah Practicum course are available at http://outreach.ecology.uga.edu/etowah/main.html. While projects are catered to the specific needs and conditions in the Etowah River basin, much of the information is broadly applicable. Information about the HCP can be accessed at www.etowahhcp.org and details specific to the UERA can be attained at http://www.etowahriver.org.

on and sample ordinances for conservation subdivisions, conservation easements, transferable development rights and greenway planning. http://outreach.ecology.uga.edu/publications.html
- Planners Web at http://www.plannersweb.com, especially the Sprawl Guide at www.plannersweb.com/sprawl. See "solutions" page and "resources" page for technical reports, current news articles, case studies and links to other valuable resources.
- Smart Growth On-line at http://www.smartgrowth.org houses a wealth of on-line reports on smart growth as it pertains to the urban environment.

Establishing or supporting a local watershed organization is often a useful device for addressing issues that cross geo-political boundaries. For example, often several counties will contain land area draining into a single lake or river network. Collaboration among these governments is essential to the protection of a waterbody. Establishing and supporting a crossboundary watershed coalition is a great way to achieve this collaboration. The watershed coalition can provide technical advice on development and water quality issues within a watershed and coordinate the efforts of individual governments optimizing the benefits of watershed protection.

International institutions and legal authorities

Several international governing policies or directives exist and may help decrease the threat of urbanization to freshwater ecosystems.

Agenda 21, adopted by 178 governments in 1992 at the United Nations Conference on Environment and Development (Rio de Janerio (Brazil)), is a comprehensive plan for global, national, and local action toward achieving sustainable development. Chapter 18 of the agenda articulates the objectives of global development and management of freshwater resources. Major goals include the dramatic increase in access to safe drinking water and basic sanitation. Of particular relevance to freshwater protection in urban environments is language promoting sustainable human settlements, sustaining biological diversity, the safe use of toxic chemicals and managing hazardous wastes. Possibly the most tangible aspect of Agenda 21 was the development and implementation of a Local Agenda 21 for all communities. Each plan would include the full participation of the community, assess current conditions, set targets for specific goals, and establish monitoring and reporting programs. As part of Agenda 21, local authorities are to develop a Local Agenda 21 for their communities. For more information visit http://www.un.

Volunteers help clean up the Conasauga River in Georgia. Photograph by George Ivey/TNC.

org/esa/sustdev/tech_coop/water/water.htm. Visit the Global Development Research Center's web site on Local Agenda 21 (http://www.gdrc.org/uem/la21/la21.html) for excellent documentation of existing Local Agenda 21s and how-to guides for creating local Agenda 21 programs.

Probably the single largest threat to freshwater ecosystems in urban areas of the developing world is wastewater. Wastewater, from municipal, commercial or industrial sources requires deliberate management to ensure the protection of freshwater resources. In developing nations management plans may not exist yet or may have been developed but are not practiced. The World Bank recommends a river basin or national-scale approach to wastewater management involving the following aspects (World Bank Group 1998):

- Establish a lead organization and involve stakeholders
- Identify broad goals
- Define specific, measurable objectives
- Formulate and assess possible strategies
- Select the preferred strategy, and then implement and monitor it

The following organizations produce publications and provide support for urban freshwater conservation in developing countries:

- The Global Development Research Center, www.grdc.org
- The World Wildlife Fund, www.panda.org
- The World Bank Group, www.worldbank.org
- The United Nations Development Program, www.undp.org
- The United Nations Educational Scientific and Cultural Organization, www.unesco.org

COMMUNITY-BASED STRATEGIES

Community members acting in a concerted effort to protect water resources is a necessary component of any pollution control strategy. Individual and business buy-in help halt pollution at its source, thereby eliminating the need for elaborate clean-up efforts once

pollutants have been released into a watershed. Also, a unified voice within the community will influence local, state, and federal policy crucial to the protection of freshwater resources.

Education and outreach campaigns help provide community members with an awareness of the effect of their individual actions and decisions on the place where they live. Such campaigns should help the community members understand their connection to the watershed in which they live, and how to properly live within it (Schueler 2000). News and radio ads on topics such as lawn care and disposal of municipal wastes, etc. (e.g., http://comnet.org/local/orgs/hrwc/ie/ietk.htm), watershed labeling to help citizens understand the interconnectedness of the natural and built environments, and road signs identifying watershed boundaries all encourage people to recognize their position in the landscape and promote a sense of belonging. Another tactic is to label stormwater drains with phrases such as "No dumping. This drain empties into the Hudson River." Hosting workshops, participating in local fairs and providing programs to schools, educate all sectors of the community. Encouraging volunteer participation in river or lake clean-ups or water monitoring activities helps get work done and educates community members.

An educated community can turn into an active community. Interested persons can form an advocacy group, or open a chapter of an already established group. Local citizen groups can conduct water quality monitoring, participate in stewardship activities, represent a concerned public during relevant decision making, serve as a watchdog group, and can lead further educational campaigns. In the United States, funding sources for such groups may come from government sources such as EPA's 319 Clean Water Action grants or from private sources, many of which are listed on the River Network's website at http://www.rivernetwork.org/library/libfundir.cfm. Sustaining funds often come from membership fees/donations. Citizen groups also often rely heavily on volunteers and partnerships. A local printing company may donate photocopies and envelopes. Partnerships with universities can provide expert support and/or lab services such as water quality or soil testing.

FORESTRY

Virgin timber in Costa Rica. Photograph by Jeffrey Brown.

Introduction

Approximately 3.9 billion hectares of forest occur globally, with 95% considered natural forest and five percent plantation forest (FAO 2000). Much of this forest occurs in tropical latitudes (47%). Of global forested land, 51% lies within 10 km of major transportation infrastructures and therefore is easily accessible for harvest. In addition to wood and paper products, forests provide humans with areas for hunting and recreation as well as a wide range of other ecosystem services including carbon sequestration, habitat for wildlife, and watershed protection.

Today, timber harvest in many tropical regions is occurring at high and largely unsustainable rates, ranging from 1m³ per hectare (Bolivia and Zambia) to 34m³ per hectare (Brazil). In the industrialized world, in 1996, more than 475 million m³ of timber were har-

vested in the U.S. alone, with over 350 million m³ from private lands. In the U.S., most of the private land harvest occurs in the East and most of the public land harvest occurs in the West (harvests from public lands have been decreasing since the mid-1980s). Timber harvest methods include selective felling, accounting for approximately 62% of all harvests, and clear cutting, accounting for approximately 38% of all harvests (USDA Forest Service 2000). Across the globe, most harvesting occurs in existing natural forests, or those forests comprised mostly of indigenous species not planted by humans (FAO 1998). Plantation forestry or tree farming (forests planted or seeded with non-native species, or occasionally indigenous species that are generally even-aged and regularly spaced (FAO 1998)) is increasingly common, particularly in China, India, the Russian Federation, and the United States (FAO 2000). The most common plantation grown trees are *Pinus,*

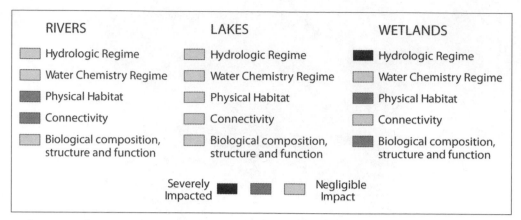

FIGURE 4-21. Summary of Impacts of Forestry on Freshwater Ecosystems

Eucalyptus, and *Acacia.* Plantation forestry produces about 35% of global roundwood supply though occupying only 5% of total harvestable lands.

The Effects of Forestry on Freshwater Ecosystems

Forestry harms freshwater ecosystems by contributing erosion and sedimentation as well as fertilizers and pesticides to freshwater ecosystems and by altering the runoff to and recharging associated with these ecosystems. Forestry also harms aquatic habitat directly by contributing to a loss of woody debris, increasing water temperatures, and siltation of substrate. However, many variables contribute to the magnitude of these threats including harvest rates and methods, stand improvement and vegetation management, and the location of these practices within a watershed (FAO 2000). Forestry also often requires the construction and maintenance of roads and other infrastructure such as stream crossings, skidding trails and log landings. The establishment of this infrastructure is often the most detrimental forestry-related activity to freshwater ecosystems (Megahan 1980; Clapham *et al.* 1998).

THE HYDROLOGIC REGIME

Logging alters the hydrologic regimes of freshwater ecosystems associated with forests by reducing transpiration and infiltration rates across harvested areas. These effects are particularly extreme in wetlands. Roads and tracks further alter hydrology by compact-

ing soils, contributing to the formation of erosion gullies, and facilitating more rapid delivery of rainwater to freshwater ecosystems due to a greater amount of overland flow and reduced amount of infiltration and subsurface flow. Even when roads are well maintained in an attempt to reduce the effect on freshwater ecosystems, these roads are often left unmaintained once harvest activities terminate and problems may go unnoticed for years (Tetra Tech Inc. 2001). The removal of litter and understory vegetation exposing soil surfaces will also increase overland flow and erosion.

Collectively, these attributes alter streamflow and flood characteristics. For example, following the clear cutting of a small catchment, streamflow was 28% greater than expected without harvest and stormwater volume delivered to streams was greater (peak flows increased and flood flow recession time increased) (Swank *et al.* 2001). The reduced infiltration rates associated with logging roads and exposed soils can lessen groundwater recharge. The size of the harvested area, the type of tree harvested, and the location of the harvest all play a role in determining the severity of hydrologic alteration. For example, two streams in the northeast U.S. experienced increased total stream flow, direct runoff, and groundwater recharge after some thinning and clear cutting within the watershed. However, where harvest took place in the uplands and only pines were removed, altered hydrology persisted for only one year. Where harvest occurred in the riparian zone, coupled with herbiciding of understory vegetation and where hardwoods were removed, alterations lasted up to six years after harvest activity (Bent 2001).

A logging road crosses a dry river bed. During heavy rains damaged tributaries like this one carry gravel, silt, and debris into Walbran Creek on Vancouver Island, British Columbia, Canada. Photograph by Richard Boyce.

PHYSICAL HABITAT CONDITIONS

The main avenues by which forestry practices can affect freshwater habitat conditions are through erosion and sedimentation and the reduction of terrestrial debris such as branches and tree falls. Forestry practices are responsible for approximately six percent of all sediment pollution in U.S. streams and rivers (Firehock 1991). Erosion sources include roads, skidding of logs, and intense site preparations. Sheet and gully erosion is common and mass failure of roads and slopes can occur in steep areas. Harvest activities can increase erosion rates from less than 0.1 tons per acre per year to approximately 0.25 (e.g., road construction) to five tons per acre per year (e.g., roller chopping) (Stednick 2000). Whether or not mobile soil reaches a waterbody depends on the areal extent of the disturbance and the proximity to receiving water.

Although erosion associated with forestry practices is relatively short-lived, effects of associated sediment on freshwater ecosystems are longer in duration. A long term study of sediment yields and export in the Southern Appalachian mountains of North Carolina found sediment yields persisted at a measured location downstream of forest harvest at levels nearly 50% above pre-harvest levels for 15 years after the cessation of forestry activities (Swank *et al.* 2001). Locally sedimentation events can be extreme when forestry

activities are poorly managed. The South Fork Salmon River watershed in Idaho was logged intensively from the 1940s through the 1960s, increasing annual sediment yields from about 23,200 metric tons to 73,000 metric tons. Excess soil buried the beds of rivers and streams throughout the watershed causing channel bed aggradations, loss of substrate diversity and the filling of pool habitats. Consequently, salmon reproduction reached an all-time low (Megahan *et al.* 1992).

Riparian forests are unique zones responsible for processes critical to the maintenance of freshwater ecosystem integrity. In open forestry, riparian forests may be cleared entirely or changed functionally by selective harvest. Managers of plantation forests may clear native vegetation adjacent to waterbodies to plant a monoculture of even-aged trees with commercial value. The maturing monoculture and the eventual harvest of these trees will compromise riparian function. Disturbance of riparian forests mobilizes sediment directly adjacent to receiving waters and removes the buffer between upland erosion and the waterbody. Removal of riparian vegetation also eliminates the valuable contribution of woody debris to freshwater ecosystems, which provides habitat and cover for invertebrates and fishes (Gregory *et al.* 1991), influences the morphology of channels and the hydrologic and sediment regimes (Gurnell 1995), and mediates water

Helicopter spraying herbicide over a clearcut. Photograph by Robyn Hertz/BLM.

temperature fluctuations, all attributes integral to the habitat requirements of native species (Agee 1988).

THE WATER CHEMISTRY REGIME

Pollutants from forestry practices (e.g., fertilizers, herbicides, insecticides, and wood preservatives), as well as nutrients mobilized or released due to forest disturbance, affect water quality in adjacent and nearby freshwater ecosystems. Although forestry practices contribute fewer contaminants than agriculture and urban land uses, forestry practices contribute nitrogen, potassium, calcium and magnesium, and phosphorus to freshwater ecosystems (Stednick 2000). The amount of a contaminant that reaches the receiving water depends on the severity of the disturbance, its proximity to water, the presence and condition of a riparian zone, and physical factors specific to the region.

Fertilizer application related to forestry also significantly contributes contaminants to freshwater ecosystems. Broadcast-applied fertilizers, if applied in excess or at a time of year when nutrient uptake is slow, may contaminate surface waters. Reports on the severity of nutrient impairment associated with fertilizing of forestry lands vary widely. Studies of rock phosphate applications to upland forests in the United Kingdom found elevated phosphorus levels in lentic waters for

up to five years, along with increased algal growth, though effects were not severe enough to alter trophic status (Swift 1990). Small to moderate increases in nutrient concentrations have been shown in the United States following fertilizer activity and concentrations may not return to pre-harvest condition for up to six to eight weeks (Stednick 2000).

Pesticides are also used in forestry (e.g., to prevent damage to tree crop, suppress understory plant growth that may impede seedling establishment, and prevent pest infestations of harvested timber), though not significantly (while forest lands make up 16% of the land area in the United States, only about one percent of total pesticide applications occurs on these lands (Pimentel and Levitan 1986)). Applications in plantation forests make up the majority of pesticide use in forestry and this use is increasing (Dubois *et al.* 1999). Most application occurs by aerial broadcast. Field studies of herbicide applications showed low stream residues with low persistence times except when directly applied to small headwater streams (Neary and Michael 1996).

CONNECTIVITY

Forestry can impair connectivity within freshwater ecosystems. The removal of trees, as well as the planting of fast growing monocultures on plantation forestry, can alter evapotranspiration rates, changing soil moisture levels and water tables. The soil compaction that occurs during harvest reduces infiltration rates and increases runoff rates, further altering vertical connectivity (Ferguson 1996). Increased runoff may produce flood flows that reach their peak more rapidly and occur more frequently. On the other hand, channel entrenchment can occur as sediment delivery increases due to forestry activities, which ultimately results in reduced flood frequencies (Dunne, 1978). Both alter the lateral connection between a river and its floodplain. Road crossings, common in forestry lands, result in a longitudinal disconnect as these dams, bridges, and culverts are often barriers to fish movement and debris flows (Roni 2002).

BIOLOGICAL COMPOSITION AND INTERACTIONS

Forestry practices result in habitat quality declines for freshwater ecosystems, even if for a short time (Naiman et al. 1998). Even the most benign forest harvest methods will lead to some alteration of freshwater ecosystem function, shifting the trophic structure of an aquatic community from heterotrophic to autotrophic (Garman and Moring 1991; France et al. 1996). For example, streams draining recently clearcut native forests experienced a shift in their vertical structure (Trayler and Davis 1998), as well as changes in abundance, biomass and functional group composition of benthic invertebrates (Stone and Wallace 1998).

The effects of forestry practices are most pronounced in plantation forestry. Mature plantation forests differ ecologically from mature natural forests. These differences may lead to shifts in the biology of aquatic systems within, or adjacent to, these forests even when active harvest is not occurring. Following harvest of a plantation forest, and during the regeneration period, aquatic systems are exposed to changing conditions that can affect community structure. Plantation forestry also reduces the diversity of litter inputs to freshwater systems and has been linked to depressed abundances and diver-

sity of fungi (Laitung et al. 2002) and invertebrates (Ormerod et al. 1993).

Sediment from accelerated erosion associated with many logging activities can clog and bury the substratum, resulting in the dramatic decline of aquatic invertebrate richness and abundance (Trayler 1998), buried fish eggs and increased juvenile and adult fish mortality (Henley 2000), and well as depressed salamander populations (Conner 1988).

Strategies for Mitigating/Abating the Effect of Forestry on Freshwater Ecosystems

A range of technical strategies or Best Management Practices (BMPs) exist to reduce the effect of forestry practices on freshwater ecosystems. Legal and institutional strategies may be more appropriate for refining areas where forestry takes place to protect sensitive habitat and important ecological processes.

TECHNICAL STRATEGIES

More disruptive forestry activities like clear cutting and road construction contribute significant levels of runoff, sediment, and other pollutants to freshwater ecosystems. The these practices can be changed or abated through application of the BMPs described in the three categories listed below: improving the method of harvest, improving riparian management, and reducing the impacts of road construction and maintenance. For maximum effectiveness, industry personnel, agencies and organizations, and other vested stakeholders should work together to identify BMPs and implement them at the appropriate scale (e.g., both at individual locations and across entire watersheds) (Bisson et al. 1992).

Improving the method of harvest

Both timber harvest methods (clearcut and selective) have their benefits and drawbacks. Ultimately, the management of either method determines the level of threat to nearby freshwater ecosystems. Both require the use of BMPs for effective mitigation.

After harvest, felled trees must be removed from the forest for future processing. Two techniques exist for removing trees: skidding and yarding. **Skidding**

Yarders harvest trees on a steep slope near on Vancourver Island, British Columbia, Canada. Only a few trees are left along the ridgeline. Photograph by Richard Boyce.

involves dragging or carrying logs along the ground to landing areas. Skidding can be accomplished by machinery or animals but requires trails which can result in compacted soils that are susceptible to erosion. Landings are areas where logs are staged for treatment and loading onto trucks for transport to a mill. *Yarding* involves lifting logs off the ground by cable, helicopters, balloons and cranes and transporting them to landing areas. Yarding is less damaging to freshwaters but tends to be more expensive and may damage valuable timber (Smith *et al.* 1997). Both landings and skidding trails result in severe soil compaction along trails and at landing areas. BMPs related to reducing these effects include revegetation of trails after harvest (Virginia Department of Forestry 2001), selecting and using logging equipment to minimize impacts on local waterbodies (Smith *et al.* 1997), and creating landings in areas with minimal slope (e.g., 2–5%) and on well-drained soils with proper drainage structures installed.

Additionally, proper care should be taken to reduce freshwater contamination from equipment maintenance and storage of substances associated with logging activities (Virginia Department of Forestry 2001). Harvesting activities should be scheduled at locations and times to best avoid damage to lakes, rivers and wetlands (e.g., avoid harvesting near streams and in wetlands and minimize harvesting activities during or prior to major storm events).

After harvest, BMPs should be implemented to promote vegetation regrowth and the maintenance of a high proportion of the preexisting plant and animal diversity in the forest. Rapid replanting immediately following harvest, and maintenance of wind breaks and seed sources, are important to the rapid stabilization of forest function protective of aquatic ecosystems.

BMPs related to improving harvest methods described in the EPA's National Management Measures to Control Nonpoint Source Pollution from Forestry (Tetra Tech Inc. 2001) include:

- Based on information obtained from site visits, make any alterations to the harvesting plan that are necessary or prudent to protect soils from erosion and surface waters from sedimentation or other forms of pollution.
- Fell trees away from water courses whenever possible, keeping logging debris from the channel, except where debris placement is specifically prescribed for fish or wildlife habitat.
- Immediately remove any tree accidentally felled in a waterway.
- Remove slash from the water body and place it above the normal high water line or flood to prevent downstream transport.
- Leave sufficient slash throughout the harvest site and distribute it to provide good ground cover and minimize erosion after the timber harvest.

A clearcut in Oregon. Photograph by Steve Hillebrand/USFWS.

Improving riparian management

The appropriate management of riparian areas, often termed Riparian Management Zones (RMZ) or Streamside Management Areas (SMA), can also help mitigate of impacts of timber harvest activities. Adequate management of riparian areas themselves is central to the ability of these areas to mitigate the effects on freshwater ecosystems of forestry practices in the landscape. A management plan should be in place prior to the commencement of logging activities that indicates the amount and type of harvest, timing of operations, and methods for reforestation. The plan should indicate how to maintain a diversity of uneven-aged species as well as adequate soil quality to sustain infiltration, denitrification, and water holding capacity. Essentially, the plan should take into consideration resource values within the riparian area for heightened protection: economic, social, cultural, and environmental.

Variables that can be altered to meet different management objectives are the width of the riparian zone and the type of harvest restriction designated within this zone. Most experts recommend that such areas be a minimum of 50 to 100 feet wide (Phillips *et al.* 2000). Two approaches exist for determining appropriate widths for riparian areas: (1) fixed width or standard width determined by slope or water body type and (2) variable width determined by site specific conditions including factors such as vegetation characteristics, geomorphology, animal and plant species present, and the sensitivity of land to disturbance (Phillips *et al.* 2000).

Best Management Practices related to improving management within riparian areas described in the EPA's *National Management Measures to Control Nonpoint Source Pollution from Forestry* (Tetra Tech Inc. 2001) include:

- Minimize disturbances that would expose the mineral soil of the SMA forest floor. Do not operate skidders or other heavy machinery in the SMA.
- Locate all landings, portable sawmills, and roads outside the SMA.
- Restrict mechanical site preparation in the SMA, and encourage natural revegetation, seeding, and hand planting
- Limit pesticide and fertilizer usage in the SMA. Establish buffers for pesticide application for all flowing streams.
- Directionally fell trees away from streams to prevent logging slash and organic debris from entering the waterbody. Remove slash and debris unless consultation with a fisheries biologist indicates that it should be left in the stream for large woody debris.
- Apply harvesting restrictions in the SMA to maintain its integrity.

Reducing the impacts of road construction and maintenance

Best Management Practices related to mitigating the effect of road construction and maintenance attempt to minimize sediment delivery by altering the location, density, design, drainage, construction, and maintenance of these roads. BMPs for forest roads are numerous and often highly technical. For simplicity, road BMPs will be discussed in brief under three main headings: road construction, road maintenance, and stream crossings.

Road construction

Road design and construction are site-specific and dictated by factors such as soils, topography, and method of harvest. Most erosion occurs during, and immediately following, the construction of roads making the implementation of BMPs during these activities imperative to the successful protection of freshwater resources from forestry. Roads are best located on naturally low grade features and should follow natural contours (Montana DNRC 2002). Road design should effectively remove water from the road without increased sediment export (Grace 2002). Length and width of road and amount of fill material should be minimized. Stabilizing road sideslopes can greatly reduce erosion (Swift Jr. 1984, Grace 2000).

Best Management Practices related to mitigating the effects of road surface construction described in the EPA's *National Management Measures To Control Nonpoint Source Pollution From Forestry* (Tetra Tech Inc. 2001) include:

- Follow the design developed during preharvest planning to minimize erosion by properly timing and limiting ground disturbance operations.
- During road construction, operate equipment to minimize unintentional movement of excavated material downslope.
- Properly dispose of organic debris generated during road construction
- Prevent slash from entering streams and promptly remove slash that accidentally enters streams to prevent problems related to slash accumulation
- Compact the road base at the proper moisture content, surfacing, and grading to give the designed road surface drainage shaping.
- When soil moisture is high, promptly suspend earthwork operations and weatherproof the partially completed work.
- If the use of borrow or gravel pits is needed, locate rock quarries, gravel pits, and borrow pits outside of streamside management areas and above the 50-year flood level of any water. Avoid excavating below the water table.

Best Management Practices related to mitigating the effects of road surface drainage described in the EPA's *National Management Measures To Control Nonpoint Source Pollution From Forestry* (Tetra Tech Inc. 2001) include:

- Install surface drainage controls at intervals that remove storm water from the roadbed before the flow gains enough volume and velocity to erode the surface. Route discharge onto forest floor so that water disperses and infiltrates.
- Install turnouts, wing ditches, and dips to disperse runoff and reduce the amount of road surface drainage that flows directly into watercourses.
- Install appropriate sediment control structures to trap suspended sediment transported by runoff and prevent its discharge into aquatic environments.

Best Management Practices related to stabilizing road slopes described in the EPA's *National Management Measures To Control Nonpoint Source Pollution From Forestry* (Tetra Tech Inc. 2001) include:

- Visit locations where roads are to be constructed on steep slopes or cut into hillsides to verify that these are the most favorable locations for the roads.
- Use straw bales, straw mulch, grass seeding, hydromulch, and other erosion control and revegetation techniques to stabilize slopes and minimize erosion.
- Compact the fill to minimize erosion and ensure road stability.
- Revegetate or stabilize disturbed areas.

Road maintenance

Proper road management and maintenance can reduce erosion and pollutant runoff. Freshwater ecosystems will benefit from periodic scrutiny of road integrity, evaluation and maintenance of installed BMPs, and the management of use, timing of use, and dust production on roads (Palone and Todd 1997). Following the cessation of harvest activity, roads should be closed if they will no longer be needed, but drainage features should continue to function until roadways revegetate, or until the following harvest season.

Best Management Practices related to mitigating the effects of road maintenance described in the EPA's *National Management Measures To Control Nonpoint Source Pollution From Forestry* (Tetra Tech Inc. 2001) include:

- Blade and reshape the road to conserve existing surface material; to retain original, crowned, self-draining cross section; and to prevent or remove berms (except those designed for slope protection) and other irregularities that retard normal surface runoff.
- Maintain road surfaces by mowing, patching, or resurfacing as necessary.
- Clear road inlet and outlet ditches, catch basins, culverts, and road-crossing structures of obstructions as necessary.
- Remove any debris that enters surface waters from a winter road or skid trails located over surface waters before a thaw.
- Build erosion barriers on any skid trails that are steep enough to erode.
- Abate dust problems during summer dry periods.

BMPs have also been developed for wet conditions, winter weather, road closure, and decommissioning.

Stream crossings

Most of the BMPs related to stream crossings are also applicable to wetland areas. First and foremost, the number of stream crossings should be minimized. Where stream crossings are necessary, emphasis should be on the location and design of these crossings, as these road segments are usually regarded as having the greatest potential to impact water quality (Grace 2002).

Best Management Practices related to mitigating the effects and maintenance of stream crossings described in the EPA's *National Management Measures To Control Nonpoint Source Pollution From Forestry* (Tetra Tech Inc. 2001) include:

- Based on information obtained from site visits, make any alterations to the harvest plan that are necessary or prudent to protect surface waters from sedimentation or other forms of pollution and to ensure the adequacy of fish passage.
- Construct stream crossings to minimize erosion and sedimentation. Keep machinery out of water. Avoid construction during rain, high flow events, or migratory fish spawning periods. Attempt to construct crossing at right angle to stream and where stream is narrow. Maintain grade over the entire length of crossing.

Stream crossing restoration, before (left) and after (right), in Quartz Creek Watershed, Kootenai National Forest, Montana. Photographs courtesy of the USDA Forest Service.

- Install a stream crossing that is appropriate to the situation and conditions. Categories of crossings include bridges, fords, and culverts each being appropriate to different circumstances.
- When temporary stream crossings are no longer needed, and as soon as possible upon completion of operations, remove culverts and log crossings to maintain adequate streamflow. Restore channels to pre-project size and shape by removing fill materials used in temporary crossing.
- During and after logging activities, ensure that all culverts are open and functional.

BMPs related to improving fish passage at stream crossings include:

- On streams with spawning areas, avoid construction during egg incubation periods.
- Design and construct stream crossings for fish passage according to site-specific information on stream characteristics and the fish populations in the stream where the passage is to be installed. In order of preference, the following types of structures are recommended for fish passage: bridges, bottomless culverts or log culverts, embedded metal culverts, nonembedded culverts, then baffled culverts.

Other forestry activities may also require careful planning and the use of BMPs to protect rivers, streams, wetlands, and lakes. Site preparation, forest replanting/regeneration, fire management, and disease control need to be considered when determining how forest land will be managed to protect freshwater ecosystems. For explicit, state-specific forestry BMP information relevant to the protection of water quality visit Water Quality and BMPs for Loggers at www.usabmp.net.

INSTITUTIONAL AND LEGAL STRATEGIES

Institutional and legal strategies are often the most effective means to influence land use practices including those related to improving forestry practices or reducing the effect of these practices on freshwater ecosystems. This section is divided into U.S. and international institutional and legal strategies.

U.S. institutions and legal authorities

Utilizing federal forestry protection and environmental protection legislation

Two major federal acts govern forestry operations and activities for the protection of freshwater ecosystems in the United States: the Clean Water Act and the Coastal Zone Act Neither of these acts address forestry explicitly; rather they restrict polluting practices and promote mitigation and abatement of pollution. Section 208 of the Clean Water Act (CWA) mandates state-level management plans to protect against water pollution and Section 319 applies to forestry operations through its nonpoint source control language. Section 404 of the CWA restricts the dredging and filling of water bodies, although silviculture operations are often exempt from these restrictions. Section 6217 of the Coastal Zone Act Reauthorization Amendments (CZARA) of 1990 requires the use of management measures to prevent nonpoint source pollution from reaching coastal waters. The amendments require coastal states, including the Great Lakes, to submit Coastal Nonpoint Pollution Control Programs to the Environmental Protection Agency and the National Oceanic and Atmospheric Administration. As a result, EPA has developed literature on management measures appropriate for forestry activities. Explicit in the act is the necessity of public participation in all aspects of designed state programs.

Both the CWA and the CZARA include programs through which funding may be obtained to mitigate the effect of forestry practices on freshwater ecosystems. For information on funding sources refer to:

- A state and local government guide to environmental program funding alternatives, available at www.epa.gov/owow/nps/MMGI/funding.html
- A catalog of federal funding sources for watershed protection, available at www.epa.gov/owow/watershed/wacademy/fund.html
- Clean water state revolving loan web site at www.epa.gov/OWM/finan.html

The National Forest Management Act (NFMA) and the National Environmental Policy Act (NEPA) also significantly affect forestry practices. In 1976, NFMA recognized the need to protect and improve water resources on national forest lands and worked to accomplish this through the requirement of Land and Resource Management Plans (LRMPs) that identify water resources and report management activities necessary to protect these resources. LRMPs are revised periodically and are open to public review and comment. The NFMA has been used to protect freshwater ecosystems from logging activities on many occasions through its diversity provisions. For example, the conservation of the Cow Knob salamander in George Washington National Forest was accomplished by revising the LRMP to exclude logging activities from prime Cow Knob salamander habitat (Zaber 1998). For more information about how the NFNA can be used to save species, please see *Southern Lessons: Saving species through the National Forest Management Act,* Defenders of Wildlife (Zaber 1998), www.defenders.org/pubs/sfor01.htm. NEPA requires all federal agencies including the U.S. Department of Agriculture Forest Service to produce Environmental Impact Statements (EISs) for activities affecting public lands and that these statements be reviewed by the EPA. All EISs are open to public review and are posted at www.epa.gov/compliance/nepa/current/index.html.

Engaging state and local governments in improving forestry practices

The EPA is responsible for the oversight of state-level management of forestry operations. However, individual states develop their own management approaches and adequate protections for freshwater ecosystems may be integrated into these approaches. Many states have state forest practice acts or nonpoint source management programs providing a framework for natural resource conservation specific to forestry activities. These usually rely heavily on BMPs. States generally take one of two approaches to the development of management guidelines. The state agency responsible for the oversight of forestry activities may produce guidelines and then release these guidelines for public review. Alternatively, the state agency may opt to involve stakeholders in the development process, then usually the guidelines are released for a public review period. It is the later process, though more complicated and often a greater time investment, from which management practices most likely will be adopted

rapidly and with less resistance because stakeholder opinion was incorporated into the guidelines themselves (Phillips *et al.* 2000). Guidelines may be voluntary, or regulated, or a combination of the two. Most guidelines require the implementation of specific management practices. One state that offers more flexibility is North Carolina. North Carolina developed standards for forest lands, but how those standards are met is up to the landowner or logger. North Carolina also tightened compliance with the state sedimentation pollution legislation (Chapter 179, Senate bill 379) from which forest activities had previously been exempt Language was modified to only allow exemption if BMPs were used at a site and when standards for water quality protection were met (North Carolina Divison of Forest Resources 1989).

Several states require pre-harvest plans. If they are not required in a state, effort should be put toward establishing legislation mandating their preparation and approval. These plans are site-specific and usually developed by the land manager. Plans should identify areas to be harvested and areas needing special protection (such as wetlands or steep slopes). The plan should also contain information on the timing of harvest activity, the layout, design, construction and maintenance of roads and other infrastructure (skidding trails, landings, stream crossings, etc.), and methods for site preparation, harvest and forest regeneration. Forest management plans are open for public review. Public meetings required by law provide a good forum for holding managers accountable for freshwater ecosystem protection.

Any regulatory agenda must recognize and consider the different types of forest landowners—non-industrial private, industrial private, and public. Non-industrial private forest landowners hold the majority of forested land (Smith 1994). These landowners have highly variable values and priorities ranging from those who live on the land and harvest occasionally to supplement income to those who conduct more industrial-like forestry practices that provide the main source of income for that landowner. Landowners may or may not have a strong conservation ethic. Generally, private property rights are central to this type of landowner and infringing upon these rights requires careful consideration. Industrial private landowners, such as Weyerhaeuser and Georgia Pacific, own property for commercial reasons and manage these lands for continual economic returns. However, the advent and increased exposure of sustainable forestry has resulted in the addition of several other landowner values including protection of the environment and ensuring the perpetuation of forested lands into the future (Palone and Todd 1997). Industrial private landowners generally conduct relatively intensive silviculture throughout large land holdings (Smith 1994). These landowners rely heavily on lobbying to influence public policy. Public forest landowners (forestry agencies) face the challenge of managing lands for multiple purposes. Those harvesting on public lands face scrutiny from the general public. On most public lands, timber production is low on the management agenda. However, where timber production is a primary management objective, silvicultural practices are often intensive (Smith 1994).

Information and education programs are a critical element in any campaign to increase the adoption of non-polluting management practices. Programs can include workshops, logger and landowner training, reporting requirements, site visits, and the development of informational brochures. These programs can be carried out by state forest or natural resource agencies, university extension services, or even local governments. For more information about state forestry laws please visit the Defenders of Wildlife website www.defenders.org/states/publications/stforestrylaws.html. Please also refer to www.epa.gov/agriculture/forestry.html for an extensive list of links to federal and state forestry agencies and university departments and extension offices.

International institutions and legal authorities

Several international agreements address forest resource issues. Water resource protection is inherent in the sustainable management of global forest resources under such agreements. Two useful documents emerged from the 1992 United Nations Conference on Environment and Development (UNCED). The first is a set of guiding principles entitled "Non-Legally Binding Authoritative Statement of Principles for a Global Consensus on the Management, Conservation, and Sustainable Development of All Types of Forests." As evident in the title,

these principles are voluntary and lack enforceability, yet they are a step toward consensus building among nations necessary to the achievement of sustainable forest management. These principles promote increased international cooperation, support and technology transfer and non-discriminatory trade, with a reduction of tariff barriers allowing better market access and prices, which will allow for conservation of forest resources within impoverished countries (Fletcher 1995). The second agreement produced from the UNCED meetings is Agenda 21, an action plan for sustainable development introduced in the urbanization subsection of this module. Chapter 11 of Agenda 21 addresses global forest issues. Again, this plan articulates voluntary actions that nations should take to achieve sustainable forest development in the coming century. Actions fall into four program areas: (1) sustaining the multiple roles and functions of forests, (2) protecting, conserving and sustainably managing forests, (3) promoting efficient utilization and assessment, and (4) planning, assessment, and periodical evaluations. Developing a local Agenda 21 will work toward protecting freshwater resources from the threats of forestry activities.

Timber certification is another avenue used internationally and domestically to encourage forestry practices that protect the natural environment, including freshwater ecosystems. Certification may also promote socially responsible and economically viable forest management. Certification is attained by performance standards and assessments are set by a certifying organization. The Forest Stewardship Council (FSC) has been providing international certification since 1993. The Sustainable Forestry Initiative (SFI) is a U.S.-based program developed by the forestry industry. The most expansive certification program is the Pan European Forest Certification (PEFC) system in Europe. Standards necessary to qualify for certification vary widely, but, with some research into options, concerned citizens can pressure forestry operations that are known polluters to become certified. A motivation for large-scale operations to become certified is to avoid criticism and environmental controversy (Fletcher et al. 2002). This, coupled with the economic benefits of certification such as price premiums in specialized markets and access to a broader market, may be enough to

Lumber certified by the Forest Stewardship Council. Photograph courtesy of the Forest Stewardship Council.

influence a landowner or timber harvest corporation to implement management programs necessary to become certified.

For more information visit the websites of existing certification programs:

- Forest Stewardship Council: www.fscus.org
- Sustainable Forestry Institution: www.afandpa.org
- Pan European Forest Certification: www.pefc.org
- International Organization for Standardization: www.iso.org
- Canadian Standards Association: www.csa-inter national.org/certification/forestry/
- Smartwood: www.smartwood.org
- Forest Certification Watch: http://certification watch.org
- Global Institute of Sustainable Forestry: http:// research.yale.edu/gisf/index.html
- International Institute for Environment and Develop: Forestry and Landuse http://www.iied.org/ forestry/index.html
- IUCN Forest Conservation Programme: http://www. iucn.org/themes/fcp/home.html

Sustainable Forestry and Certification Watch also provides information on the available programs (www.certificationwatch.org).

COMMUNITY-BASED STRATEGIES

Local authorities and citizens can take a number of actions to ensure that forestry practices are compatible with the maintenance of freshwater ecosystem health. First, local authorities can require the use of certified wood for use in all public works projects. Barcelona, Spain, uses only FSC certified wood for their public works. Second, local authorities and citizens can encourage or require that local forestry be managed to meet sound certification standards. Finally, work toward raising awareness within your community about the importance of responsible forest management (WWF 2001). For more detailed information on steps local authorities can take to promote responsible forest management read the World Wildlife Fund for Nature report titled *Local Authorities Can Make a Difference!*, available online at www.panda. org/downloads/europe/LA_brochure.pdf.

At the community level, activism is a helpful tool in the prevention of freshwater ecosystem degradation due to poor forestry activities. Many watchdog and advocacy groups have been founded for this purpose. Most are regionally-based, allowing them to best address local issues. Partnering with existing groups or developing a group where needed may increase the capacity for conservationist and concerned citizens to advance freshwater protection agendas. Also, these groups can often provide sound information on the status of forestry corporations and landowners, their practices, compliance with environmental regulations, participation in voluntary programs, etc. Having the benefit of experience, these organizations may also be able to advise others on how to approach a landowner or corporation about an issue of concern. Some of the more prominent or active organizations engaged in forest advocacy include:

- The Dogwood Alliance: www.dogwood alliance.org
- National Forest Protection Alliance: www.forestadvocate.org
- Heartwood: www.heartwood.org
- Oregon Natural Resource Council: www.onrc.org

For a more complete list of organizations engaged in forest protection, conservation, and restoration, please visit the website of Defend the Forests (www.defendtheforests.org).

MINING

Introduction

Mining extracts resources to supply energy (oil, gas, and coal) and the raw materials necessary for manufacturing and commerce (metals, gravel, and sand). Mining is a global industry that occurs at small and large scales conducted by entities ranging from large multi-national corporations to independent artisans. Although mining activities occupy a relatively small proportion of land area, the localized effects of these activities on freshwater ecosystems can be severe. Mining activities can both occur in or adjacent to freshwater ecosystems (e.g., gold mining, sand and gravel mining, etc.), require water for mining processes and extraction methods, and necessitate changing the hydrologic regime or physical habitat conditions of freshwater ecosystems. Water used in mining, or passing through mining sites, also often becomes contaminated with materials used in or byproducts associated with mining activities including acids, sediments and heavy metals (Kelly 1988).

The mineral mining process includes five stages, as described by Ripley *et al.* (1979): exploration, development, extraction, beneficiation (concentration of desired material), and processing. Methods of extraction vary widely based on the material and the location of that material in the landscape, but can generally be categorized as surface mining (e.g., instream gravel mining, strip mining, mountaintop mining) or underground mining (e.g., drift mining, deep mining). Mining sites generally include all or several of the following features: infrastructure such as roads, offices, fueling stations; heap leach piles (for the leaching of low grade ore); stockpiles; tailings impoundments or ponds; and waste heaps for overburden (non-target) material (National Research Council 1999). The processes used to extract desired materials generally fall into four categories: drilling, blasting, mucking (or loading), and transporting.

The major types of mined materials include oil and gas, coal, and hardrock minerals (e.g., gold). Each of these material types require different extraction methods as discussed below:

OIL AND GAS

Fossil fuels currently comprise the vast majority of global energy sources, with oil being the primary source and the demands for natural gas continuing to grow. Globally, oil production is greatest in the Middle East and growing in importance in Russia and the Caspian Region (OECD/IEA 2002). Natural gas reserves are more widely dispersed with significant reserves throughout North America, the former Soviet Union, Asia, and Oceania (ENI 2003). Oil and gas are mined from deep wells drilled into the earth's surface. On-site pits or closed circuit systems are used to contain extracted non-target materials and waste. Prospecting may lead to the creation of unproductive wells that require plugging in a manner that is protective of groundwater quality. If productive, wells are

A mine in northern Mexico. Photograph by Adriel Heisey.

cased and oil/gas is removed. Gas generally flows unaided. Flow of oil may be encouraged with the use of acid to dissolve impediments or the rock may be fractured using a special fluid. An oil well may flow unaided or may require a lift system to extract desired materials. A second and third effort to extract remaining oil in a reservoir may require the injection of various fluids. Separation of oil from non-target materials occurs and is stored on-site until distributed (Gauthier-Warinner 2000).

COAL

Coal extraction for energy production has occurred for centuries. Major coal producing countries include the U.S., Germany, the former Soviet Union, and China (Kelly 1988). Other countries and regions anticipated to be large coal producers include South Africa, Australia, India, Indonesia, and Latin America (OECD/IEA 2002). Coal is third only to oil and gas in importance of extractive industries, producing approximately 4.5 billion tons annually valued at $175 billion (Crowson 1992). When coal strips are near the surface and horizontally oriented, surface

mining is employed. Overburden is blasted and removed from the mining site to reach coal strip. Approximately 30% of hard coal mining occurs in surface mines (Buchanan and Brenkley 1994). The remainder of coal mining activity occurs as underground operations, with reserves often far below the earth's surface. To extract coal from such reserves, a series of tunnels and pillars are created. Commonly, water from underlying aquifers must continually be pumped out of these tunnels.

HARDROCK MINING

Hardrock mining is used to extract nearly all minerals (except coal) and metals. Gold, silver, copper, zinc, lead, and nickel are the most commonly mined metals. In the U.S., gold, copper and iron ore are the top three metals produced (Macdonald 2002). According to the EPA's toxic release inventory, hardrock mining released more toxic waste than any other monitored industry in 2000 (USEPA 2002). Each industry has unique mining methods, although many of the threats these industries pose to freshwater ecosystems are similar. For example, gold is found in alluvial sediments;

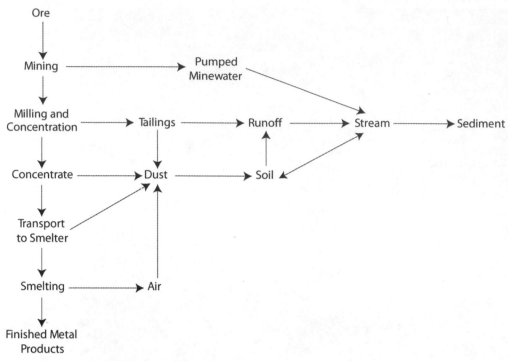

FIGURE 4-22. Mining Activities and Transport of Pollutants to the Aquatic Environment
Source: Adapted from Kelly 1998.

therefore, the majority of mining occurs in or near riverbeds (USGS 2003). Gold in bed sediments is generally extracted using placer mining methods, or those that use gravity and water to separate minerals from alluvium. Gold may also be harvested from surface or underground mines. Most gold mining methods employ the use of mercury to amalgamate gold particles and cyanide for heap leaching. Concentrations of these substances are highly toxic to freshwater ecosystems. The top three countries for gold production are South Africa, the United States, and Australia, in order of importance (USGS 2003). The gold mining industry encompasses a large informal sector, especially in developing countries such as Brazil (Cleary and Thorton 1994), Ghana, and Ecuador (IIED 2002b), making monitoring and enforcement of sound practices difficult.

SAND AND GRAVEL

Sand and gravel resources are abundant and well-dispersed globally. Although sand and gravel earn minimal price per unit weight, extraction quantities are significant worldwide (IIED 2002a) and supply local construction and industrial markets. The U.S. is by far the world's leading producer and consumer of sand and gravel (USGS 2003). The primary sources of sand and gravel are river floodplains and channels. Given the location of these reserves, the volume of materials removed, and the dispersion of mining activities globally, extracting these materials may affect the greatest expanses of freshwater ecosystems compared to other mined materials.

The Effects of Mining on Freshwater Ecosystems

The effects of mining on freshwater ecosystems vary with scale, intensity, proximity to water, geologic setting and mining operation. Effects may be localized, such as aquifer depletion, or far-reaching, such as sediment mobilization. Effects also vary widely in their longevity. While turbidity caused by mining may be short lived, metals and chemicals introduced into freshwater ecosystems by mining activities may persist in an aquatic environment for years, decades, or

*Limestone mining
operations, North Lake
Huron, Michigan.
Photograph by Harold
E. Malde*

longer. Please find below an examination of the effects of activities associated with the four major mining industries on the key ecological factors of freshwater ecosystems.

THE HYDROLOGIC REGIME

Mining activities often require water to extract resources and raw materials or require reforming freshwater ecosystems themselves to allow for the mining activities. Extraction of either groundwater or surface water for mining activities and even the mining activities themselves alter the hydrologic regime of freshwater ecosystems in a myriad of ways.

Mining that occurs in freshwater ecosystems (e.g., sand and gravel mining, etc.) alters channel morphology on a localized scale. Deeper and wider channel sections created from mining activities tend to lower the river stage and associated water table. The balance of exchange between groundwater and surface water in these altered channels shifts, resulting in some river reaches with diminished aquifer recharge and other reaches with diminished surface water recharge (Mas-Pla *et al.* 1999).

Pit lakes and artificial lakes created for water storage often remain after cessation of mining activities and can significantly alter the hydrologic balance

within a watershed by intercepting underlying aquifers and preventing groundwater movement to the aquifer downslope of the pit (National Research Council 1999). In the Niederlausitz coal mining region of Germany, pit lakes have the potential to hold four billion cubic meters of water that would otherwise be part of the hydrologic regime (Werner *et al.* 2001).

Mining that requires groundwater pumping to either remove water from areas to allow for mining activities (e.g., to allow for underground coal mining or to release coalbed methane) or for mining processes themselves can remove so much water that they create a cone of depression in the underlying aquifer and significantly alter the exchange between groundwater and surface waters. The excavation of coal seams can create new subsurface flow paths further altering hydrology (Bonta *et al.* 1992). These changes can effect the surface and subsurface hydrology far outside the actual mining site and even extend into adjacent watersheds (Bonta *et al.* 1992, Zipper *et al.* 1997).

Water that is excavated from either surface or groundwater to allow for mining activities or for mining processes can also be discharged directly into local streams, rivers and lakes. The timing and amount of discharge also alters the hydrologic regime in the recipient freshwater ecosystem.

The clear water of 12 Mile Creek, Alaska, receives a heavy sediment load from Birch Creek, which has active placer mining operations upstream. Photograph courtesy of the USGS.

Finally, changes to natural soil stratigraphy, through various mining and mine reclamation processes, also alter the hydrologic characteristics of soils, thereby influencing the flow of water to surface waters (Guebert and Gardner 2001) and groundwater (Liu *et al.* 1997).

PHYSICAL HABITAT CONDITIONS

The most extreme examples of mining impacts to the physical habitat of freshwater ecosystems are those where the water body is used for some portion of the mining process, e.g., gold mining, instream gravel and sand mining, and the mountaintop mining of coal. Additionally, habitat alterations may result from excess sedimentation, lowered base levels, and increased temperatures.

The placer method of goal mining uses water and gravity to separate gold particles from alluvial sediment. Methods to collect sediments vary with their location. Dredging is used to collect submerged sediments. Hydraulic dismount methods employ the use of water jets to blast away river terraces. All non-target material is washed into waterways resulting in tremendously high turbidity and shoaling (Kligerman *et al.* 2001). The downstream deposition of sediment

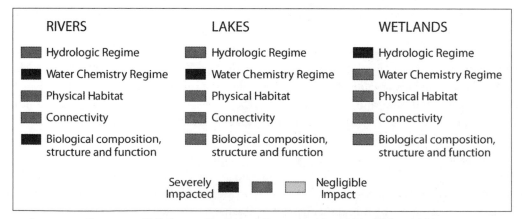

FIGURE 4-23. Summary of Impacts of Mining on Freshwater Ecosystems (can be highly variable)

Normally a steep, gravel-bed, braided river, this system in the Philippines filled with fine tailings after a containment leak from a large open cut copper mining operation. Photograph by Dr. Geoff Pickup.

disturbed by placer mining can cover spawning habitat, and change channel bed and bank morphology (National Research Council 1999, Wanty *et al.* 1999). The placer mining methods employed may also have a dramatic effect on the extent of habitat alteration and on water quality degradation from turbidity. Very little disturbance was measured in an Alaska stream where suction dredging was used. Elevated turbidity was short-lived and well within regulated standards. Where heavy equipment is used to remove sediment from river beds, to be replaced after separation activities take place, reclaimed beds are unstable, resulting in persistent turbidity and bank erosion and altered bed morphology (Wanty *et al.* 1999). Mining activities concluded long ago may continue to affect freshwater ecosystems for many years. For example, in an area of intense hydraulic gold mining in Georgia, floodplain sedimentation rates increased dramatically during the time period of active mining. Currently, the occurrence of overbank floods is low, therefore erosive flows transport sediments downstream rather than depositing them in the floodplain. This causes severe sedimentation problems in the reservoir downstream of historic mining activities where mobilized sediments are deposited (Leigh 1994).

The implications of in-channel gravel and sand mining are similar to those of gold placer mining. Removal of bed materials changes channel morphology and the available bedload, suspending more sediment in the water column and altering flow patterns (Rivier and Sequier 1985). These alterations combine to change habitat characteristics in both upstream and downstream directions (Kondolf 1994). Gravel bed streams have been shown to respond to these alterations by increasing channel width, the surface area of pools and the distance between riffle habitats (Brown *et al.* 1998). Pools may fill with mobilized sediment, creating a more homogeneous environment lacking typical habitat diversity. Upstream from mining pits, lateral and vertical erosion, or headcutting, can occur affecting flow characteristics, temperature, bank stability, available cover and siltation (Meador and Layher 1998). Wider channels created by gravel mining result in decreased flood frequency, eliminating floodplain habitat availability (Brown *et al.* 1998).

Mountaintop coal mining is a highly controversial method of coal extraction. This is due, in part, to its effects on aquatic habitat. Mountain tops are cleared of forest, then blasted and bulldozed in order to reach coal seams under the surface. Overburden material is dumped into adjacent valleys to create what are termed valley fills. To date, nearly 1,450 km of streams have been buried under the overburden from mountaintop removal coal mining in Central Appalachia, and over half of this occurred in West Virginia (USFWS 1998). Moreover, this amount may be a considerable underestimate (Meyer and Wallace 2001). While research relating explicitly to mountain-

Mountaintop mining operation near Kayford Mountain, West Virginia. Photograph by Vivian Stockman. Flight courtesy of SouthWings.

top mining is scarce, the loss of headwater streams has been well documented. Such loss results in increased flood frequency and severity, erosion, sedimentation and the loss valuable habitat, spawning grounds and thermal refugia (Meyer and Wallace 2001).

THE WATER CHEMISTRY REGIME

Mining can dramatically increase the delivery of various elements to receiving waters. Chemical loads may originate from mining processes as target material is concentrated and extracted from non-target materials, or from heaps of waste materials left exposed to weathering processes that break down, transform and mobilize elements. Delivery may be isolated and temporary, as is usually the case with products created during the beneficiation process. Chemicals leached from waste material left onsite after decommission of a mine site may have extremely long term effects, as is the case with acid mine drainage. The more common pollutants reaching aquatic systems from hard rock mining include iron, manganese, aluminum, zinc, cadmium, lead, and other metals (Younger 2000) along with sulfate, acid drainage, nitrate and suspended solids (National Research Council 1999). Cyanide and mercury, used in beneficiation processes, often reach

freshwater ecosystems. Finally, petroleum-based compounds frequently contaminate waters near oil and natural gas mining operations.

Acid mine drainage is considered the most serious and persistent effect of mining activities on adjacent land and nearby waters (IIED 2002a). Any extraction of minerals containing sulfide has the potential to be a source of acid mine drainage, although some types of deposits are more likely to produce acid mine drainage than others (Kelly 1988). The mobilization and oxidation of sulfide containing minerals create pollutants harmful to freshwater ecosystems. Three aspects of acid mine drainage can alter the chemical regime of a waterbody: acidic pH, iron precipitate, and heavy metals (Kelly 1988). Acid drainage will vary in its level of acidity and concentration of metals and can permeate soils or run off from soil surfaces to contaminate groundwater and surface water sources. Tailings, overburden, open pit and underground workings can all produce acid mine drainage. Once the process of acid drainage production begins it is difficult to halt (National Research Council 1999) and may continue to produce pollutants for centuries (Warhurst 1994b). Acid mine drainage is a common pollutant from coal, metal, and sand and gravel mines.

Heavy metal pollution is another major implication

of mining activity in a watershed. Materials laden with metallic compounds are removed from a relatively stable location embedded within the earth and placed in storage or waste heaps on the earth's surface, vulnerable to chemical breakdown processes and mobilization. For example, coal often occurs in association with several other metals including arsenic, cadmium, cobalt, copper, lead, and zinc (Monterroso and Macias 1998). At a mining site in New Zealand, elevated levels of arsenic, copper, and zinc were found in the adjacent wetland complex (Black and Craw 2001). Heavy metals can reach freshwater ecosystems adhered to sediment particles or suspended in runoff. The highest levels of the metals found in the New Zealand study occurred in the winter when rainfall is high (Black and Craw 2001). In lotic waters, metals tend to remain in suspension or settle out into bed sediments. Resuspension of metals in bed sediments commonly occurs as hydrologic fluctuations change the velocity and discharge of these waterways. In suspension, metals can be transported great distances (Kelly 1988). The fate of metals is different in lentic waters. In these slow-moving waters, metals settle out of suspension quickly and accumulate in bottom sediments. Vertical mixing and the disturbance of bottom sediments by fish, humans, or boat activity can resuspend metals but is far less common than in lotic waters. Metals and metalloids may cycle through a system but they will not degrade to more innocuous substances, making metal contamination a longterm concern (National Research Council 1999).

Chemicals released during the beneficiation process also alter the chemical regime of freshwater ecosystems. Gold mining operations, especially small-scale or artisanal operations, provide one of the most severe examples. Discharge from gold mining activities often contains dangerously high levels of metals, metalloids, and cyanide (Tarras-Wahlberg et al. 2000). The use of mercury to amalgamate gold particles has been found in sediments and in plant and animal tissues in aquatic ecosystems throughout the world. Several processes employed by many hard rock mining industries use cyanide, and its use is increasing, because it allows for economically viable extraction of increasingly lower grade ores (Wireman 2000). For gold mining, cyanide applied to piled ore induces the gold to leach out of the ore. Cyanide is acutely toxic,

yet in its free form, will break down quickly into benign substances. Therefore, it is usually only found within a few kilometers of mining operations. However, cyanide can combine to form metal cyanide complexes much more difficult to break down and can be detected at distances up to 50 km from a mining site (Tarras-Wahlberg et al. 2000).

Oil mining poses the greatest risk to groundwater, although surface waters are vulnerable to contamination from oil mining as well. Contaminants associated with mining operations include hydrocarbons, heavy metals, chlorides, and sediment. Drilled wells can be a source of oil contamination in aquifers if a well is operated without casing or if the integrity of the casing fails. Water is commonly inserted into injection wells to force oil toward the producing well. This water may be laden with salts and chemicals used in processing methods, potentially contaminating aquifers. Leaks or breaks in storage tanks and piping can discharge oil directly into surface waters, or onto land where oil can reach surface waters via overland flows, or percolate through soils to groundwater (Gauthier-Warinner 2000).

Several other phenomena associated with mining also alter water chemistry regimes. Salt water intrusion into aquifers has been shown to increase near coastal areas due to the alteration in water exchange between a channel and groundwater source caused by instream mining (Mas-Pla et al. 1999). Pit lakes remaining after the completion of mining activities often have very poor water quality since they are often contaminated with metals, chemicals, and salts. Their waters may contaminate natural waterbodies if water is exchanged via flooding, or infiltration to groundwater, and can be harmful to colonizing organisms, migratory birds and terrestrial wildlife (National Research Council 1999).

CONNECTIVITY

Mining activity may cause permanent or short-lived disconnects within aquatic ecosystems. Metal and contaminant toxicities have reached levels high enough to result in avoidance behaviors in fishes (Delonay et al. 1995; Woodward et al. 1997). Valley-filling activities, which bury headwater streams, disconnect an entire watershed from valuable headwater sources. Organisms that rely on headwater environments

Valley filling can bury headwater streams, such as this one in West Virginia, disconnecting rivers from their headwater sources. Photograph by Vivian Stockman. Flight courtesy of SouthWings.

for migration, spawning and thermal refuge are disconnected from environments ideal for certain elements of their life cycles. Headwaters are also the location of extensive detrital accumulations and nutrient processing for export to downstream communities. Loss of the connectivity between headwaters and the rest of a river network can result in alterations to nutrient availability and retention (Meyer and Wallace 2001). Oil spills can create a barrier to the movement of organisms between habitats for long periods of time. Channel incision, a common geomorphic response to in-channel mining creates disconnects between running waters and their floodplain environment (Leigh 1994). Finally vertical connectivity can be compromised as the exchanges and linkages between groundwaters and surface waters are altered during and after mining activities (Choubey 1991; National Research Council 1999).

BIOLOGICAL COMPOSITION AND INTERACTIONS

The main pathways by which mining affects freshwater biodiversity are via contaminant delivery and physical habitat manipulation. Contamination can be lethal or sub-lethal. Examples of sub-lethal contamination include changes in behavior, physiology, and/or reproductive capacity of individuals. For both contamination and habitat alterations, entire species may find an impacted area uninhabitable while other, more tolerant species, may fill space left by the exodus of sensitive species. For example, a shift from sensitive to tolerant invertebrate taxa was quantified downstream of coal mining activity in Spain. Richness decreased with increasing conductivity, sulfates, metal concentrations, and silt accumulation (Garcia-Criado *et al.* 2002). Substitutions or deletions of species caused changes in community structure and species interactions.

Most metals are toxic to aquatic organisms even at low concentrations. The cases of mercury and crude oil contamination serve as representative examples of the many substances from mining activities that have the potential to harm aquatic biota. Mercury from gold mining can occur at toxic levels and is persistent in aquatic environments, causing impairment in invertebrates (e.g., Clements *et al.* 1988) and fishes. Mercury is a known neurotoxin which readily accumulates and concentrates in the tissues of organisms (Leady and Gottgens 2001). Once stored in tissue it can be passed to offspring, often producing young with anorexia, lethargy, muscle ataxia, visual impairment and other central nervous system disorders (Hilson 2002). Mercury can affect mammals, birds, and humans that feed on contaminated aquatic organisms. Oil spills in freshwater ecosystems result in shifts in microbial communities from those dominated by heterotrophic species to a community dominated by hydrocarbon utilizing species (Obire and Okudo 1997, Il'inskii *et al.* 1998). Oil contamination has also been connected to impairment of amphibians (Mahaney 1994), benthic invertebrates (Bhattacharyya *et al.* 2003), fishes and mammals (USEPA 2003).

Turbidity and sedimentation problems associated with in-channel mining and runoff from land-based mining can reduce the amount of light penetrating the waters surface and lead to a decline in primary producers, especially algae. This decrease in food availability can cascade through an aquatic food web (Henley *et al.* 2000). Silt-intolerant species are lost from locations downstream of in-channel mining and changes to pool-riffle habitat structure further alter fish and invertebrate communities (Brown *et al.* 1998). The loss of headwater streams to valley fill from mountaintop coal mining translates to a loss of unique habitats and thermal refugia, directly impacting the biota. Further,

shifts in nutrient sources and processing and sediment dynamics of the entire watershed can occur, which may have indirect effects on individuals, species and communities (Meyer and Wallace 2001).

Strategies for Mitigating/Abating the Effect of Mining on Freshwater Ecosystems

Strategies for mitigating or abating the effect of mining on freshwater ecosystems include improving mining practices during mining and at the time of mine closure as well as influencing the laws and policies that place restrictions on mining activities and reduce environmental harm. The factors necessary to consider in planning for a mining operation that minimizes alterations to freshwater ecosystems include site location, dust control, solid waste and liquid effluents management and disposal, disaster avoidance, site closure, mitigation, remediation, and restoration (Barbour 1994).

TECHNICAL STRATEGIES

Technical strategies can be categorized into those to pursue during active mining and those to pursue at mine closure.

A plant to treat acid water drained from Iron Mountain Mine in California, which once mined gold, copper, and zinc. Photograph courtesy of NOAA Restoration Center & Damage Assessment and Restoration Program.

Strategies to pursue during active mining

Proper planning, management, treatment, and disposal of mining waste (overburden, waste rock, tailings, and heap leach spent ore) and chemical use during active mining help protect nearby freshwaters from mine-related contamination. Preventing mass failure and erosion of mine waste (e.g., overburden and mine waste) helps minimize contamination of nearby freshwaters. Tailings and heap leach spent ore are generally laden with chemicals used in the beneficiation process and can easily result in contamination of nearby freshwaters if not adequately managed:

- Tailings usually occur as a slurry and are contained in retention/settling ponds. After settling, water is discharged and requires proper treatment to ensure quality of discharge. Settled material requires disposal and should consider future leaching potential and dust production potential, which can blow contaminates great distances.
- Heap leach spent ore is placed on a lining and is then treated with chemicals. Leachate should be collected from channels constructed around heaps, processed to extract desired material, and reused to continue leaching process. Technical strategies should work toward creating a closed system where contaminated solutions are recycled internally and no external exchange occurs (IIED 2002a).

Technical strategies for the mitigation of in-channel mining are of limited usefulness since the harm to freshwater ecosystems is caused almost entirely by the extraction and subsequent loss of bed materials themselves, not how the bed materials are extracted (Brown *et al.* 1998). Potential control measures include bank stabilization, re-vegetation, buffer strips, and devices to control headcutting and filtering and/or recycling of wash water prior to discharge (Meador and Layher 1998). Because of the minimal potential to mitigate impacts of in-channel mining, prohibition is often the best strategy (Kondolf and Lyons 1992). In fact, many countries prohibit in-channel mining including the United Kingdom, Germany, France, the Netherlands, and Switzerland (Kondolf 1997).

Strategies to pursue at mine closure

The manner in which a mine is closed, or decommissioned, plays a large part in determining the pollution potential of a mining site. Closures may include removing and disposing of chemicals; removing structures, roadways and ditches; plugging shafts; treating waste and capping tailings; backfilling pits; and active water management (Wireman 2000). Two remediation tasks common to most mining closures and necessary to prevent freshwater degradation are chemical management and decontamination of water following the cessation of dewatering activities.

Preventing the onset of the processes that create acid mine drainage, and halting and/or containing the drainage once it has begun are among the most important measures associated with mine operation and closure. Management of acid mine drainage (AMD) falls into one of two categories: controlled placement of overburden materials and water management. Systems designed to treat AMD after its creation include: adding neutralizing agent to the AMD; procedures for ensuring iron oxidation; and settling ponds for removing iron, manganese, and other co-precipitates.

Contaminated water that fills mines and mined areas after closure should be treated through hydrological interventions, active treatments, and passive treatments to prevent contamination of receiving waters (aquifers and natural surface waters). Hydrologic interventions attempt to prevent the infiltration of water into mining areas and the flow from mining areas into nearby rivers and aquifers. Active treatment methods generally rely on conventional wastewater treatment units to accomplish three steps: (1) oxidation, (2) dosing with alkali, and (3) accelerated sedimentation. This treatment method is usually adequate for improving water quality to a level acceptable for discharge but requires constant monetary and energy inputs. Passive treatments rely on natural energy sources and ecological processes such as can be created in constructed wetlands. In Britain, treatment methods have combined active treatment for the first several years with a shift to a passive system allowing for economically feasible yet long-term treatment of contaminated mine water (Younger 2000).

Conversion of mined land to other uses is another strategy for decreasing the spread of contaminants to freshwaters. For example, converting mined lands to native forest or grassland is the least sediment producing of all alternatives and improves the ecological connection of the land to associated rivers, lakes, and wetlands.

INSTITUTIONAL AND LEGAL STRATEGIES

Government regulations may restrict mining operations to protect freshwater ecosystems. However, as described below, legislation pertaining to mining is often minimal or minimally enforced. In some instances, legal reform may be necessary to change existing practice.

U.S. institutions and legal authorities

Utilizing existing federal and state laws

In the United States, the Forest Service, the Bureau of Land Management, and several other agencies within the Department of the Interior administer mining on public lands. However, federal mining laws only minimally protect freshwaters from mining activities. The General Mining Law of 1872 still governs public land mining today with little revision to accommodate the

modern context. Coal mining is the only mining sector under specific national level regulation. The Office of Surface Mining Reclamation and Enforcement (OSM) administers and enforces the Surface Mining and Control Reclamation Act of 1977. This agency generally delegates regulatory program development to individual states and requires the preparation of an operation and reclamation plan for all coal operations (Wireman 2000). For more information about the OSM, please visit http://www.osmre.gov/osm.htm. Activities within waterways, such as sand and gravel mining, are regulated by the U.S. Army Corps of Engineers.

Regulation of mining on private lands generally falls under the jurisdiction of the EPA and state governments. Regulation of other mining sectors not described within the previous paragraph also generally falls to state governments. However, state governments often face enforcement challenges due to insufficient operating budgets, a scarcity of staff, and pressure to ignore violations and resultant environmental impacts (Hilliard 1994). A list of links to most state mining agencies can be found in the U.S. Department of Labor website at www.msha.gov/SITEINF1.

Mining activities must also operate within standards set by the Clean Water Act (CWA), the Coastal Zone Act (CZA) and the Safe Drinking Water Act

A strip mine in Montana. Photograph courtesy of USFWS.

(SDWA). These acts require discharge permits and set water quality standards that polluters must meet. SWDA provisions can help protect aquifers with good drinking water supply potential from injection fluids commonly used in oil and natural gas mining (Gauthier-Warinner 2000). The Comprehensive Environmental Response, Compensation and Liability Act (CERCLA or Superfund) provides provisions necessary to facilitate the clean up of highly polluted abandoned mine sites by the EPA, or requires the clean up be done by the responsible parties.

Numerous policies and regulations in the U.S. may be used to mitigate the effects of a mining operation on freshwater ecosystems. Information about chemical releases from mining facilities (required under the Toxic Release Inventory administered by the EPA) is publicly available through www.epa.gov/tri (required by the Emergency Planning and Communities Right-to-Know Act of 1986) and can be used to identify sources of water quality problems in a watershed. Through NEPA, all new mining activities requiring a permit from a federal government agency or occurring on public lands must assess the potential environmental impacts of these operations and identify ways to mitigate these impacts and public comment must be solicited and assessed within this assessment. The resulting draft Environmental Impact Statement (EIS) must also include a public comment period prior to acceptance of the EIS and permit issuance. Participation by scientists and community members in this process can force an aquatic conservation agenda that might otherwise remain inadequately addressed. For more information on EIS and a list of those under current review visit http://www.epa.gov/compliance/nepa.

Influencing reform of federal and state mining laws

Promoting more stringent mining regulations is another mechanism to protect freshwater ecosystems. Many advocate reform of the 1872 General Mining Law since this law remains much as it did 125 years ago and allows mining of minerals on public lands with little liability and no environmental provisions (Mining Policy Center 2003). Writing to government

officials, teaming up with advocacy groups that are working toward this end, or getting press coverage on this issue will contribute to the achievement of reform. Ensuring that proposed environmental provisions are adequately protective of freshwater ecosystems is also necessary for effective reform. Visit the Mineral Policy Center (www.mineralpolicy.org) for details on the current status of reform initiatives and ideas on how to get involved.

Another reform strategy involves promoting state laws and policies with adequate provisions for protecting freshwaters from mining activities. In Montana, citizens approved a law prohibiting the establishment of any new mining operations that employ the use of cyanide. Wisconsin issued a moratorium on new sulfide ore mining permits until the applicant demonstrates proposed techniques for producing no AMD at mine closure (Environmental Law Institute 2000). As of 2002, 50 mines had been evaluated, none of which were able to meet this prerequisite (IIED 2002a).

International institutions and legal authorities

Most public policy, both existing and proposed, is retrospective in that it regulates the pollution problem rather than being proactive and attempting to reduce pollution before it is produced. Proactive policy approaches emphasize pollution prevention through the facilitation of technological improvements and improved managerial capacity and capitalize on the theory that enabling economic efficiency through policy will result in improved environmental management because it further increases the operation's efficiency. Energy and chemical inputs can be reduced, waste production minimized, and recovery maximized when capacity allows for innovation (Warhurst 1994a). Examples of such proactive policies include incentives, credits, loans, privatization, research and development, and environmental management systems (Warhurst 1994a; Environmental Law Institute 2000). The Environmental Law Institute (ELI) proposes a proactive framework for pollution and mining that emphasizes pollution prevention over pollution control (Environmental Law Institute 2000). In assessing the potential for countries in the Americas to achieve such a framework, ELI identified several weaknesses. Most countries need specific goals, measures, and technical guidance as well as more legal tools and policies that facilitate and ensure closure planning, financial assurance, privatization, public participation, economic incentives, and liability (Environmental Law Institute 2000).

While several international agreements are relevant to the mining industry, none directly address freshwater conservation. The Biological Diversity Convention of 1992 protects biodiversity from human activities including mining and the Basel Convention of the Trade in Hazardous Wastes of 1989 prohibits transboundary movement of hazardous wastes including metals. Agenda 21 promotes sustainable development across all land-use types and is discussed in more detail elsewhere in this document (see forestry and urbanization components of this subsection for more information). A Compendium of Links to International Mining Law is available within the U.S. Department of Labor's Mine Safety and Health Administration website at http://www.msha.gov/minelink/compend/intermng.htm which also provides links to information on mining policy for individual countries. See also http://www.iipm-mpri.org for information about mining and mining reform in Latin America and the Caribbean. Documents relevant to mining and sustainable development are available through http://www.natural-resources.org/minerals/CD/sustdev.htm and http://www.iied.org/mmsd/global_act/research.html.

COMMUNITY-BASED STRATEGIES

Effective community-based strategies for abating the effects of mining on freshwater ecosystems center on organizing, advocacy and accountability. Partnering with existing watchdog organizations or forming one in your community can help bring polluters into the public forum and subject to scrutiny. Relationships between a community and a mining operation need not be adversarial. Communicating acceptable conduct may be enough to influence the practices of a mining operation as companies generally want to remain in good standing with the local community. Occasionally, conflict between a community's desire for environmental protection and a mining company's mode of operation will escalate and in these cases, communities may elect to bring a lawsuit against a polluter.

In the United States, state and federal programs exist to help communities clean up abandoned mine sites that may still be contributing to the impairment of freshwater ecosystems. For example, the Appalachian Clean Stream Initiative's mission is "to facilitate and coordinate citizen groups, university researchers, the coal industry, corporations, the environmental community, and local, state, and federal government agencies that are involved in cleaning up streams polluted by acid drainage" and draws upon federal and private funds to accomplish this task. For more information visit http://www.osmre.gov/acsihome.htm. Also, the Clean Water Act has state revolving funds that provide low interest loans to those interested in nonpoint source pollution mitigation projects such as replanting and soil stabilization, dispersion of contaminated runoff, and the control or collection of sediments associated with mining sites.

RECREATION

Introduction

Humans use rivers, lakes, and wetlands for many recreational purposes including fishing, boating, and swimming. Enjoying freshwater ecosystems for recreational pursuits provides people with a break from everyday life and provides a broader economic base to regions with recreational assets. For example, recreational fishing brings over 30 million people to freshwater ecosystems each year and is a $36 billion industry in the United States (U.S. Department of the Interior *et al.* 2002). However, sometimes freshwater ecosystems can be overutilized for recreational purposes, creating harmful effects for the underlying ecosystem as well as making the location less desirable for continued recreation.

Fishing on the Russian River in Alaska. Photograph courtesy USFWS.

The Effects of Recreation on Freshwater Ecosystems

As a whole, recreation poses a modest threat to freshwater ecosystems when compared to more ubiquitous and intensive uses of land and water such as those associated with agriculture and with dams and diversions. However, the type and severity of these effects varies with site conditions such as ecosystem type, climate, and geographic setting, as well as with the characteristics of recreational activity itself (e.g., the type of recreation, and the intensity and frequency of use) (Sun and Walsh 1998). For example:

- Recreational fishing may harm native fisheries and stocking practices can significantly alter underlying freshwater ecosystems.
- Motorized water vehicle use (e.g., jet boats, fishing boats with outboard motors, speed boats, etc.) and associated infrastructure contributes to heightened noise levels, pollution, trash, and habitat degradation, thereby harming freshwater ecosystems, particularly in areas with a high density of these vehicles. In the U.S., private citizens own over 17 million motorized water vehicles (NMMA 2002).
- Recreation effects expand considerably if the harm to freshwater ecosystems caused by facilities and infrastructures (e.g., buildings, docks, flood control levees, etc.) developed in support of recreational activities and located in or adjacent to freshwater ecosystems are also taken into consideration.

The following sections summarize the specific effects of fishing, motorized vehicle operation, and recreation-related development on the five key ecological factors defining freshwater ecosystems. For more information about the effects of second home development on freshwater ecosystems, please review the text associated with urbanization included within this subchapter.

HYDROLOGIC REGIME

Recreational activities seldom directly alter the hydrologic regime of freshwater ecosystems. However, a few notable exceptions exist. Rivers which contain impoundments (e.g., reservoirs behind dams) may be managed for recreational purposes, although these purposes are usually secondary to the primary purpose of the structure (e.g., hydropower production, flood control, and water supply). Please see the Water Use and Management subchapter for more information about the effects of dams and reservoirs on the hydrologic regime of freshwater ecosystems.

Development of lake or riverfront property often includes infrastructure for flood control. The installation of facilities and infrastructure (e.g., levees, dikes, flood walls, canals, etc.) to protect shoreline developments and facilitate recreation can also alter natural hydrologic processes. Collectively, they may work to decrease floods, minimize water level fluctuations, homogenize flow patterns and lead to the loss or impairment of riparian wetlands and floodplains. Demands for water use during peak visitation months of recreational areas can place heavy demands on waterbodies reducing the quantity of water in available in an ecosystem (UNEP 2001).

Soil compaction from heavy foot traffic, bicycles, and off-road vehicles within and adjacent to freshwater ecosystems can significantly decrease the infiltration capacity of soils and increase the imperviousness of these areas, effectively increasing runoff. Campgrounds, parking lots, boat launches, homes and resorts add impervious surface further increasing runoff. These changes may alter the timing and magnitude of water entering freshwater ecosystems from precipitation.

PHYSICAL HABITAT CONDITIONS

Recreation alters the physical habitat conditions of freshwater ecosystems by physically changing the morphology of or removing substrate from freshwater ecosystems. Physically changing the morphology of freshwater ecosystem shifts the type and quality of habitat available to aquatic organisms, wading birds, and other wildlife. For example, increasing the slope of the nearshore environment in lakes to improve swimming and boating conditions and arming shorelines with walls or retention devices reduces access to shore and floodplain habitats, nutrient exchange, flood flow refugia, and spawning in some fish. Recreation infrastructure development (beaches, marinas, homes, etc.) and invasive plant species removal practices can further reduce valuable habitat for aquatic organisms through the reduction of macrophyte growth (Bryan and Scarnecchia 1992). Turbidity caused by motorboats can mobilize sediment, which can then settle on and even smother aquatic habitats (National Research Council Committee on Restoration and Aquatic Ecosystems 1992). Trampling and activity in swimming areas

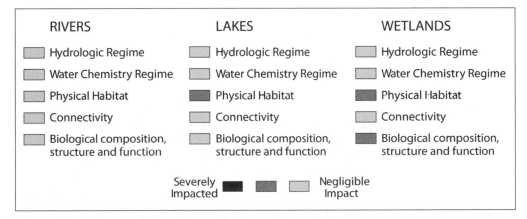

FIGURE 4-24. Summary of Impacts of Recreation on Freshwater Ecosystems

Channel modifications to the South Fork Zumbro River, Minnesota, to protect a golf course. Photograph courtesy USACE.

degrade habitat and severely restrict the use of these areas to only the most hardy organisms. Land-based recreational activities further threaten aquatic habitat by contributing erosion from construction activities as well as foot and vehicle traffic and by contributing to warmer water temperatures through from riparian clearing for development (Hammitt and Cole 1998). This clearing also reduces sources of coarse woody debris (Christensen *et al.* 1996).

THE WATER CHEMISTRY REGIME

Motorized boating and marinas pollute freshwater ecosystems with oil and gas, hydrocarbon byproducts, sewage and pet waste, trash, toxic metals and other chemicals, solvents, antifreeze, detergents, sediments and nutrients (USEPA 2003). Recreational boating is the main source of MTBE (methyl tertbutyl ether)— a gasoline additive and suspected carcinogen with high water solubility, high mobility, and low biodegradability—in aquatic ecosystems (Reuter *et al.* 1988). MTBE concentrations were greatest during peak boating season and in boat docking areas most likely as a result of gas spillage during engine startup (An *et al.* 2002). Homes, commercial developments, golf courses, parks and other development spurred by

the growth of recreational activity in and around a river or lake can contribute further contaminants. Finally, contaminants also extend from management activities designed to promote recreational activities (e.g., application of herbicides, dredging, etc.).

CONNECTIVITY

Dams and canals are commonly associated with water-related recreational activities. Please refer to the text about dams within the Water Use and Management subchapter for a thorough examination of the effect of dams on connectivity within freshwater ecosystems.

BIOLOGICAL COMPOSITION AND INTERACTIONS

Recreation activities alter the biological composition within freshwater ecosystems through the practice of fish stocking, the transport of invasive alien species, the overharvesting of desirable species, and the loss of sensitive species. Please refer to the subchapter dedicated to overharvesting and fisheries management and invasive alien species for more information about this topic.

Strategies for Mitigating/Abating the Effect of Recreation on Freshwater Ecosystems

As with other threats, the effects of recreation on freshwater ecosystems can be reduced or eliminated by implementing specific appropriate technical, legal and institutional, and/or community-based strategies.

TECHNICAL STRATEGIES

Technical strategies for reducing the effect of recreation and associated development on freshwater ecosystems generally include Best Management Practices to reduce erosion, minimize pollutants, and diminish harm to specific habitats:

- Reduce land and shoreline erosion
  - Avoid converting vegetated shorelines to beaches. Installed beaches should have a very gradual slope (e.g., one foot of vertical drop for every ten feet of horizontal distance). Locate beaches in areas with minimal wave action and away from springs or flowing water. Add sand with largest acceptable grain size such as pea-gravel.
  - Include no-wake zones to prevent wave action from eroding shoreline.
  - Construct docks to allow water to flow beneath.
  - Avoid constructing paths to waterfront that cut directly down slope.
- Minimize the release of pollutants
  - Prohibit the use soap or shampoo in the water.
  - Avoid spilling gas, oil, paint, etc. while maintaining boats. Require fueling on trailer before launching when possible.
  - Require proper storage and disposal of wastewater, trash and fish waste created while boating.
  - Use untreated wood, plastic, or metal to construct docks.

For more information about reducing pollutants associated with marinas, please see:
- Shipshape Shores and Waters: A handbook for Marina Operators and Recreational Boaters, EPA report EPA-841-B-03-001 (available on-line at http://www.epa.gov/owow/nps/marinashd-bk2003.pdf).
- National Clean Boating Campaign website: www.cleanboating.org.
- Diminish harm to specific habitats
  - Remove plants only where they seriously interfere with recreational use.
  - Avoid damaging or draining wetland areas. Build boardwalks over, or create paths around, wetlands.

Boaters on the Cumberland River near Nashville, Tennessee. Photograph courtesy of the USACE.

- Retain or plant native trees along shoreline.

The University of Minnesota Cooperative Extension Service lists other BMPs as well as a series of fact sheets (University of Minnesota Extension Service 2002) available on-line at http://www.extension.umn.edu/distribution/naturalresources/DD6946.html.

INSTITUTIONAL AND LEGAL STRATEGIES

Local ordinances as well as state and federal legislation and incentive programs also are useful to reduce recreation or mitigate the effects of existing recreation on freshwater ecosystems.

U.S. institutions and legal authorities

The federal agencies most heavily involved with the management of freshwater recreation activities are the FWS and the EPA. For over 120 years, FWS has been responsible for managing fishery resources. FWS runs the National Fish Hatchery System, which rears and releases both native and non-native game fishes into waters throughout the United States, as explained in detail within the Overharvesting and Fisheries Management subchapter. EPA regulates recreation to improve water quality and aquatic life within freshwater ecosystems. However, most of the decisions about the recreational use of freshwaters lie with state agencies. Please refer to the overharvesting and Fisheries Management subchapter of this guide for information about strategies related to stocking decisions.

Controlling how, and how often, a particular recreational activity occurs can help minimize effects of recreation on freshwater ecosystems. For example, restricting and even prohibiting motorized boating helps to limit the harm caused by this activity, create a more peaceful setting for shoreland owners, and enhance other recreational experiences such as swimming, paddling, and fishing. Controlling motorboat density is another option. In some circumstances, even non-motor craft can cause significant harm to a system. For example, canoe and kayak passage density on a river reach in Belgium reached 15 vessels per minute, and boat dragging and grounding changed aquatic and riparian habitat. To protect the freshwater

ecosystem, including spawning activities, vegetation growth, and nesting sites for wading birds, authorities of the Walloon Region limited the hours of authorized canoe and kayak use and set minimum flow standards below which they prohibit canoe and kayak use (Gerard and De Bast 2000). Damage from recreational use can be minimized through the use of designated areas for specific activities: defining a swimming area, managing development associated with recreation, etc.

COMMUNITY-BASED STRATEGIES

River and watershed groups as well as lake associations allow community members an opportunity to form a united voice advocating for and facilitating the maintenance or achievement of the community's goals for a given waterbody. These groups have effectively influenced local and state government decisions, educated users and landowners about the value of these ecosystems, and worked together with government agencies and others to monitor conditions within and the effect of changed activities on these ecosystems. They have also acted as watchdog organizations and promoted the enforcement of local ordinances.

The following list of steps, adapted from the Minnesota Lakes Association, provides a sequential process for forming community-based organizations dedicated to rivers, lakes, and watersheds:

1. List reasons for forming a river, lake, or watershed association. Ask other local river, lake, or watershed associations for advice or support.
2. Hold a public meeting. Invite everyone—individuals, groups, or business owners—who might have an interest in the particular river, lake, or watershed.
3. Reserve a convenient location at a time and date that doesn't conflict with other events.
4. Choose a leader and recording secretary for the meeting. Discuss the river, lake, or watershed in general and then focus on specific issues common to all participants.
5. Invite participation on a four- or five-person steering committee to establish the river, lake, or watershed association. The steering committee will select a name, write articles of incorporation, file for non-profit status, draft bylaws and a mis-

sion statement, and develop a slate of candidates for the river, lake, or watershed association's board of directors.

6. Once the steering committee has finished, set the first official meeting of the river, lake, or watershed association to vote on the by-laws, elect a board of directors, vote on dues, and develop committees to support future action.

7. Schedule an annual meeting and perhaps other social events throughout the year.

Drawing upon the appreciation recreationists have

for aquatic environments can be a conservationist's most powerful tool in working toward the protection of freshwater ecosystems. Outreach activities can educate users on how their actions may impact the rivers and lakes from which they derive a great deal of pleasure. The National Clean Boating Campaign at www.cleanboating.org provides an extensive list of links to best management practices for boaters and marina operators as well as links to reports on the ecological effects associated with boating.

—*Authored by Rebecca Esselman and David Allan*

Overharvesting and Fisheries Management

Introduction

Freshwater biota is a source of food and income for many cultures. Although catches from freshwater ecosystems account for only approximately 12% (8.2 million metric tons) of total human fish consumption (FAO 1999a), freshwater fish are a major source of protein and micronutrients for a large percentage of the world's population especially in land-locked countries. The population of Cambodia, for example, gets roughly 60 percent of its total animal protein from the fishery resources of Tonle Sap, a large freshwater lake (MRC 1977). In Malawi, the freshwater catch provides about 70–75% of the animal protein for both urban and rural low-income families (FAO 1996). While the principal use of harvested freshwater biota is as a food source, subsidiary uses include trade (e.g., specimens, pelts, animal parts), medicinal products, ornamental products, fertilizer, and biological control of insects and weeds, and, increasingly, recreation. Recreational fisheries are also important components of local or regional economies and are increasingly promoted in developing nations as a major income-generating activity. The extent of recreational fishing is poorly documented, but estimates suggest that the annual global harvest exceeds two millions tons (FAO 1999).

Unfortunately, inland native fishery records indicate that harvest rates in capture fisheries[18] exceed sustainable levels (FAO 1999b). Overharvesting has contributed to 29% of freshwater fish extinctions globally (Harrison and Stiassny 1999). When combined with other stresses, overexploitation and mismanagement of aquatic biota contributes to the collapse of a region's freshwater biodiversity. Obviously, the collapse of native fisheries also significantly affects human populations dependent on this food source.

Offsetting this decline in native fisheries is the tremendous expansion of hatcheries and aquaculture over the past few decades. Unfortunately, hatcheries and aquaculture cause ecological harm as well by releasing fish that compete with native populations for habitat and food. These fish also carry disease, parasites, and predation into freshwater ecosystems. For example, in the Pacific Northwest of North America, hatchery-raised salmon have brought many of the remaining native stocks to the brink of extinction. The same can be said for salmon and freshwater trout species in the northeastern United States. Furthermore, the rapid rise in aquaculture production in recent decades hides the decline of natural fisheries and the role played by aquaculture itself in degrading inland and coastal systems through habitat conversion, pollution, introduction of foreign diseases to native stocks, hybridization and weakening of native stocks, and the accidental release of IAS.

While finfish currently represent the major group of freshwater fauna exploited for human use, other animal groups may be locally or regionally significant. Mollusk shells are used in the production of pearls, and several species of mammals are harvested for meat, hides, and medicinal purposes. Table 4-6 lists these animal groups and their primary uses.

With few exceptions, aquatic and riparian plants are not heavily exploited in the wild state. Plants are collected for use as: food (e.g., wild rice–*Zizania palustris L*; Spirulina alga; edible aroid–*Araceae*; taro–*Colocasia* and *Cyrtosperma chamissonis*); ornamentals (e.g., laceplant–*Aponogeton* spp.; pitcher plants–*Sarracenia rubra* ssp. *jonesii*); building materials (e.g., reeds for thatch); and medicines. Globally, aquatic plants make a relatively minor contribution to human nutrition and resource needs, but they may be locally important in less developed regions of the world especially during periods of food shortage (WCMC 1998).

---

[18] Capture fisheries refer to exploitation of naturally occurring sources of freshwater fishes in contrast to harvesting of fish stock through aquaculture.

TABLE 4-6. Animal Groups Exploited in Inland Waters

Group	Use
Crustaceans (crayfishes, shrimps)	Food
Mollusks (mussels, clams)	Food, pearls
Frogs (mainly Ranidae)	Food
Crocodilians	Food, leather, ranch stock
Chelonians (turtles, especially softshells [Trionychidae])	Food, medicinal products (esp. East Asia)
Waterfowl (ducks, geese, and others)	Food, sport hunting
Fur-bearing mammals (beavers Castor, otters [subfamily Lutrinae] and muskrats [Ondatra zibethicus, Neofiber alleni]	Skins
Sirenians (manatees [Trichechidae])	Food

Source: WCMC 1998.

The Effect of Overharvesting and Fisheries Management on Freshwater Ecosystems

Determining the effect of overharvesting or fisheries management practices usually begins with an adequate assessment of the current fish stock followed by an assessment of the effect of overharvesting or fisheries management practices. Accurate assessment of harvest is difficult to establish because data on inland fisheries landings are poor, especially in developing nations. Illegal, unreported, and unregulated (IUU)[19] harvesting contributes to this information vacuum. IUU harvesting practices in small-scale fisheries include use of dynamite and other explosives and poisons to kill fish.

Despite these difficulties in assessing harvests and fisheries management, estimates suggest a five-fold increase in total freshwater harvests globally over the past 50 years (Coull 1993). Human population growth, hence greater demand, and improvements in harvesting techniques and equipment have fueled larger harvests. However, increased harvests has seriously affected biodiversity and is responsible, in part, for depleted populations of many taxa and species extinctions. Overharvesting[20] is a major contributor to this decline, particularly in Central and South America, Africa, and Asia. While generally less of a critical factor in Europe and North America today, past practices and overharvesting set the stage for the endangerment of many species. For example, overharvesting of salmon in the Pacific Northwest, lake trout in the Great Lakes, salmon in the Northeast, and mussels in the Midwest U.S. led to precipitous declines and extirpation of local populations. Intensive hunting of beaver and river otter in North America in the 18th and 19th century for pelts and a variety of wetland and riparian birds (e.g., herons, egrets, and bitterns) for women's apparel was responsible for the near elimination of these taxa from most of their natural habitat Overharvesting over the past several decades, perhaps in combination with other factors, contributed to the global decline in amphibian and reptilian populations (Houlahan et al. 2000).

In some regions of the world the decline of native freshwater biodiversity from overharvesting has reached alarming proportions. Current harvest of turtles in China and other countries of Southeast Asia for domestic and international markets threaten virtually all

---

[19] IUU includes: (1) illegal operations that are in contravention of laws governing harvesting; (2) unreported and misreported activities and yields; and (3) unregulated activities are inconsistent with conservation and management objectives.

[20] Overharvesting includes exploitation of animals and plants for commercial or subsistence purposes at levels that exceed the natural ability of the species to maintain its population levels, thereby endangering its survival.

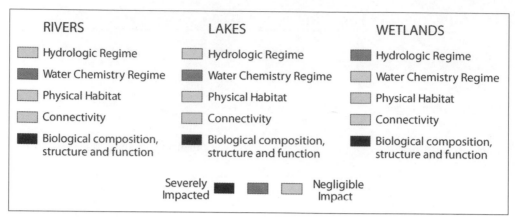

FIGURE 4-25. Summary of Impacts of Overharvesting and Fisheries Management on Freshwater Ecosystems

endemic species (TRAFFIC 2000). High demand for frog legs in some regions of the world as human food has been linked to a marked decline in native frogs in Europe, India, and Bangladesh (Blaustein and Wake 1990). In France alone, annual consumption is 3,000 to 4,000 tons, and each ton consists of about 20,000 frogs (Blaustein and Wake 1995). Recreational, subsistence, and illegal hunting has also depleted local crocodile populations throughout tropical regions, especially in Asia. Many crocodilian species throughout Asia are now seriously endangered or threatened and require immediate protection. Overharvesting and capture of juvenile fish in the once species-rich Lake Victoria (eastern Africa) have resulted in rapidly depleting stocks. Fish catches have been falling since 1993 in land-locked Malawi and Uganda, as have the landings of the commercially important Nile perch (*Lates niloticus*) for all countries bordering the lake (ECES 2003). Ten nations (including six in Asia) accounted for almost two-thirds of the global freshwater capture total in 1996. China's production alone amounted to 1.7 million tons, or 23% of global harvest. Other top producers, in descending order include: India, Bangladesh, Indonesia, Tanzania, Russian Federation, Thailand, Uganda, the Philippines, and Brazil.

In addition to the ecological consequences of overharvesting native populations, fish stocking practices also harm freshwater ecosystems. Fish stocking supports a large and growing recreational fishing community. Estimates suggest that 50 million recreational anglers spend $24 billion annually. In the U.S., this industry provides 1.3 million jobs. However, stocking practices alter the balance of freshwater ecosystems and introduce species, genes, and disease to these ecosystems. These costs must be adequately considered in any stocking decision.

The remainder of this section provides examples of species endangerment as a result of overharvesting and describes how overharvesting and poor fisheries management practices harm freshwater ecosystems. Because the specific effects vary considerably depending on the ecosystem in question, the management of species populations and degree of overharvesting of a particular species, the relationship of species within each ecosystem, and the degree and modality of overharvesting or management practice, this section will not include an analysis of the specific effects of overharvesting and fisheries management on the key ecological factors.

EXAMPLES OF SPECIES ENDANGERMENT CAUSED BY OVERHARVESTING AND FISHERIES MISMANAGEMENT

Expanding product demand continues to drive overharvesting and management of freshwater biota. The following section highlights examples of overharvesting of and management problems related to specific freshwater animals and plants including mammals, herpetofauna, fish, mollusks, and wetland plants. This summary illustrates current or historical root causes and barriers to management and conservation efforts.

TABLE 4-7. Reported World Freshwater Fisheries Production (values expressed in million tons)

	1990	1992	1994	1995	1996	1997	1998	1999[21]
Inland Capture[22]	6.6	6.3	6.7	7.2	7.4	7.5	8.0	8.2
Inland Aquaculture	8.2	9.4	12.1	14.1	16.0	17.6	18.7	19.8
Inland Total	14.8	15.7	18.8	21.4	23.4	25.1	26.7	28.0
Inland + Marine (World) Total	99.0	101.7	112.3	116.1	120.3	122.4	117.2	125.2
Total Inland % of World Total	14.9	15.4	16.7	18.4	19.5	20.5	22.8	22.4
Capture % of Total Inland	44.6	40.1	35.6	33.6	31.6	29.9	30.0	29.3
Capture % if Total World	6.7	6.2	6.0	6.2	6.2	6.1	6.8	6.5

Source: FAO 1999.

[21] Preliminary estimates.

[22] Inland capture fisheries include freshwater and diadromous fish caught in inland waters, freshwater mollusks and crustaceans.

Mammals

Dolphin:

Endemic to China's Yangtzee River, the baiji dolphin (*Lipotes vexillifer*) is threatened with extinction. Once plentiful and hunted for meat as well as killed by fishermen since they were deemed competitors for fish, the population declined to 6,000 in the late 1950s and to less than 200 today (Ames 1991, Mufson 1997). Since 1975 it has been protected under Chinese law. This dolphin is probably the most threatened of all cetaceans and is classified endangered under CITES. Hunting, accidental catching, and electrocution by fishermen, collision with motorboats, and development of dams and floodgates on the river where they live all contributed to this decline. Dams and flood gates that blocked fish and dolphin migration also induced food stress and limited opportunities for propagation. While a nature reserve has been established for the dolphin, the area is too small for these wide-ranging mammals. Their low population, scattered and isolated over 1,900 km of the river, compromises their ability to establish and maintain social bonds. Additionally, continued expansion of flow regulation projects (e.g., Three Gorges Dam) will further fragment and change their habitat (Nowak 1997a).

Manatee:

Manatee (*Trichechus* spp.) were once widespread in rivers and along coasts in the southeastern U.S. (e.g.,

Florida), the Caribbean, and the Amazonian region. This species was hunted extensively in the 18th and 19th centuries for their meat and hides to manufacture heavy-duty leather. Coastal development has also contributed to their decline. Commercial hunting of the Amazonian species (*Trichechus inunguis*) continued at a heavy rate for almost 200 years beginning in the late 18th century. Annual harvest rates were 4,000–10,000 in Brazil alone from 1935 though the early 1960s (Nowak 1997b). In response to the rapidly falling population, Brazil gave legal protection to the manatee in 1973. However, subsistence hunting and local commercial killing has continued throughout the manatee range. In Colombia, manatee meat regularly sells at local markets for prices lower than beef, and manatee bones are used for engraving and home remedies in the Dominican Republic and Mexico. In Puerto Rico, some coastal communities still consume manatee meat during holiday celebrations even though laws protect the manatee (CSN 2002). Today approximately 2,000 of the West Indian species (*Trichechus manatus*) survive in the United States.

Beavers:

Heavy hunting pressure for pelts in the 18th and 19th centuries significantly reduced beaver (*Castor* spp.) populations in Europe and North America. By the start of the 20th century these wetland dwelling animals were eliminated from much of their natural

Baiji or Chinese river dolphin. Photograph courtesy of the Institute of Hydrobiology, the Chinese Academy of Sciences.

Manatee and nursing baby. Photograph by Gaylen Rathburn/USFWS.

range except in remote areas. Fortunately, recovery efforts for this species have shown tremendous success. Beaver populations have recovered to pre-settlement levels in many boreal forests of Canada and have reached carrying capacity for available habitat in much of the U.S. due to the effects of law, reintroduction[23] efforts, and management programs. For example, in response to eliminating native beaver populations, Sweden reintroduced 80 beavers between 1922 and 1939. Seventy years later, the population was estimated at 100,000 individuals and still increasing and expanding its range (Bridgham 1995, Göran 1995).

---

[23] Reintroduction is the intentional movement of an organism into part of its native range from which it has disappeared or become extirpated in historic times as a result of human activities or natural catastrophe. Its use as a conservation tool is increasingly important.

Beaver. Photograph courtesy of U.S. Fish and Wildlife Service.

Giant river otter. Photograph © Frank Hajek, Frankfurt Zoological Society Giant Otter Project.

Otters:

The giant river otter (*Pteronura brasiliensis*), largest of the 13 otter species, is endemic to the rainforests and rivers of South America but heavily hunted for it's fur. Between 1950 and 1970, Peru exported more than 20,000 pelts and Brazil exported more than 40,000 during the 1960s (Grzelewski 2002, WWF 2003, WWF-LC 2003). The actual number of animals killed was probably much higher. Although the otter received protection through listing under CITES beginning in 1973, Venezuela did not ban hunting until 1979. Despite protection status, the population has not yet rebounded and still faces hunting pressure from poachers and fishermen. Additional stressors include inadequate food sources as a result of overfishing and pollution, habitat loss, and disease. The current population of river otters is estimated at 1,000 to 5,000 individuals.

Mountains of shells pile up on the shore of the Mississippi River from the harvest of mussels to supply the button industry. Photograph © Musser Public Library/Oscar Grossheim Collection.

Mussels

In addition to their economic importance, freshwater mussels perform important water quality functions. Mussels are filter feeders and can pump up to 40 liters of water per hour through their bodies in their quest for oxygen and food. Mussels are also important as environmental monitors of rivers, streams, ponds, and lakes because they are: (1) sensitive to environmental conditions; (2) slow growing and long-lived (from a decade to over a century); (3) near the bottom of the foodchain; and (4) dependent on hosts (fish) for reproduction. Their reproductive success depends on water conditions (e.g., temperature, nutrients, oxygen level) and the presence of fish hosts. If hosts are not present, their reproductive cycle cannot be completed. Most mussel species have only one host fish species.[24]

The United States has the greatest diversity of freshwater mussels in the world, and supports nearly 300 of the 1,000 species occurring globally. Despite their importance and widespread occurrence, 72% of all species in the U.S. are endangered, threatened, or of special concern (Williams and Neves 2003). While deteriorating environmental conditions (e.g., sedimentation, pollution, regulation of river flow) and

invasive species (e.g., zebra mussel) are major stress factors, exhaustive overharvesting in the past has also contributed to mussel decline.

Extensive harvesting of mussels began in the middle of the 19th century in the U.S. Mussels were first harvested as a source of freshwater pearls, then for buttons, and finally for the cultured pearl industry. Harvesting pressures in combination with deteriorating environmental conditions extirpated local beds in many regions in the eastern half of the country especially in the Mississippi, Ohio, and Tennessee river basins. A minimum of 50 species (20 of which are now considered endangered, threatened or of special concern) were exploited by the end of the (pearl) button industry era. Exports of shells (to Japan for the cultured pearl industry) exceeded 22,000 tons in 1968. At the height of button industry (1916), almost six billion buttons were produced (Anthony and Downing 2001). Exports in the early 1990s leveled off to about 4,500 tons (Baker 1993). While some states and localities in the U.S. have implemented management and harvesting restrictions (e.g., limits on size and species, harvesting season, means of capture, licensing fees), no federal regulations exist for mussels

---

[24] For example, trout (*Salmo* spp.) are hosts of eastern pearlshell mussel (*Margaritifera margaritifera*). The alewife floater (*Anodonta implicate*) depends on only three species of anadromous fish: American shad (*Alosa sapidissima*), alewives (*Alosa pseudoharengus*), and blue-backed herring (*Alosa aestivalis*). The more tolerant carp (*Cyprinus* spp.) and white suckers (*Catostomus commersoni*) are hosts to the eastern floater mussel (*Pyganodon cataracta*).

unless species are on the federal list of endangered or threatened species (Williams and Neves 2003).

Turtles

Globally, approximately 290 freshwater turtle and tortoise species exist, with the largest numbers of species in Asia (>90), South America (>60), and North America (>55). While some species occur in more than one region, most do not. For example, all Australian and Papua New Guinean and most Asian species are endemic. The greatest overlap occurs between the two Americas (CI 2002). This high degree of endemism is one of the challenges for conservation efforts. Extensive harvesting and deteriorating environmental conditions contribute to imperilment of these species. Consequences of reduction in population size are serious for turtles but may not be immediately recognizable. Their life history characteristics (e.g., long life, high adult survivorship, low recruitment, multiple habit types) make it difficult for populations to recover from chronic stress, such as overharvesting or habitat degradation. Consequently, native populations of turtles are poor candidates for sustainable harvesting programs.

Recent increased demand for turtle species, especially in Asia, have brought many species in the wild to the brink of extinction. All of the Asian species are commercially harvested; 75% of these species are now either threatened or endangered and 18 are critically endangered. One species, the Yunnan box turtle (*Cuora yunnanensis*) is already considered extinct (CRF 2000). Collection for trade is the most significant current threat for most Asian turtle species (Van Dijk *et al.* 2000). Other hunting pressures include use for food; for medicine, tonics, and elixirs; and for release in religious (Buddhist) ceremonies. In 1996 Hong Kong alone imported more than 3,500 tons for direct consumption. This represents more than three million turtles. By 1998, the amount was 12,000 tons.

The United States exports more than seven million turtles every year as pets or food products and imports more than 30,000, the majority caught in the wild (Orenstein 2001). Of the 55 species in the U.S., 25 species (45%) are in need of conservation action, and 21 species (38%) receive or are candidates for protection under the Endangered Species Act (ENN 1999). Since 1993, approximately 10,000 soft-shell turtles were exported from the U.S. and in some years the number exported exceeded 30,000

Turtles for sale at Guangzhou market, China. Photograph courtesy of Andreas Budischek, Vienna, Austria, ISV—Internationale Schildkroeten Vereinigung/Tortoise Trust

American eel. Illustration by Duane Raver/USFWS.

(CTTC 2002). Recent annual catches of the freshwater turtle family Chelydridae (snapping turtle) include over 40 tons in Minnesota and 50 tons in southern Ontario (Canada); one wholesaler in Louisiana purchased more than 17 tons of alligator snapping turtle (representing over 1200 individuals) over a two-year period in the mid-1980s (Burke *et al.* 2000).

Scientists have shown that annual harvesting of only 10% of the adult population of a common species (such as snapping turtles) would result in a 50% decline in adults within 15 years. Further complicating this situation is the effect of turtle egg harvesting of both common and protected species. Loss of turtle eggs is a serious impediment to stabilizing population declines that result from harvesting adults and juveniles. Given these facts, clearly the current freshwater turtle harvest rates are unsustainable and have already caused dramatic population declines. For additional information about global turtle harvesting and its consequences, please consider *Survivors in Armor* by R. Orenstein.

Fish

Eels:

The American eel (*Anguilla rostrata*) is a slow growing and late maturing catadromous freshwater fish that spawns in the ocean. Its habitats include open oceans, coasts and estuaries, rivers and streams, lakes, and ponds. Its geographic range includes southern Greenland, eastern coast of North America, the St. Lawrence River and Lake Ontario, the Mississippi drainage basin, Central America, and northern South America. American eels spawn only in the Sargasso Sea (east of the Bahamas).

American eels are harvested for food at different life stages including elvers (young), juveniles (yellow eels), and adults (silver eels). In the 1970s and 1980s, commercial harvest rates in the U.S. were approximately 2,000 tons per year. In 1981, commercial catch[25] was more than 318 tons in both Maryland and Virginia (NOAA 2003). This increased catch has caused a marked decline in eel populations. For example, the number of juvenile eels migrating to Lake Ontario fell

---

[25] Catch is the total fish captured from an area over some period of time, including fish that are caught but released or discarded instead of being landed; it can be recorded by weight or number. In contrast, harvest is the total number or weight of fish caught and kept from an area over a period of time. Landings are the number or weight of fish unloaded at a dock by commercial fishermen or brought to shore by recreational fishermen. Landings are reported at the points at which fish are brought to shore.

from 935,000 in 1985 to approximately 8,000 in 1993 and to levels approaching zero in 2001. Declines have also been documented in New York and Virginia, as well as in New Brunswick and Prince Edward Island in Canada (SeaWeb 2003). In addition to high harvesting rates, other threats contributing to this decline include habitat loss, pollution, loss of juveniles passing through hydropower turbines, disease from introduced parasites, and oceanographic changes. Limited information exists about full extent and geographic distribution of the decline, impacts associated with human activity, and life history and ecology of the species. Additionally, this species has received very limited management attention and little effort in long term monitoring of population trends and understanding potential threats to its survival (SeaWeb 2003).

Sturgeon:

Twenty-seven species of sturgeon and the related paddlefish (*Polyodon* spp.) exist worldwide. Sturgeon are generally large (some species may exceed 4.5 meters in length and one ton in weight), long-lived (some species live for more than 100 years) (NRDC 2001), and all are anadromous. Recent increased demand for caviar, especially from the highly prized beluga sturgeon (*Huso huso*) in the Caspian Sea, has resulted in intensive fishing pressures. Legal and illegal harvests and other stressors have caused the population of this species to decline by more than 90% in the past two decades. However, many species of sturgeon are threatened with local extirpation or extinction as a result of overharvesting as well as other factors including pollution, habitat loss, and altered hydrology.

In the recent past, the Caspian Sea provided 95% of total world caviar production. Official harvest fell from a peak of about 30,000 tons in the late 1970s to less than one-tenth that figure in the late 1990s. Estimated illegal catch in the four former Soviet Republics is 10 to 12 times higher than the legal take. A recent status report of the beluga sturgeon showed: (1) 85% of the entire beluga population consists of immature fish (average age of 8.4 years), suggesting a population severely depleted and nearly incapable of supporting itself by natural recruitment; (2) a 40% decline in mature sturgeon in only 7 years and the absence of mature specimens in many parts of the range; and (3) dramatic decline in numbers of beluga sturgeon even in areas that historically had large populations. The United States imports 80% of the total legal beluga caviar harvest, and the prices may exceed the global average market value (CITIES 2002).

In order to protect populations from extinction, The 2001 "Paris Agreement" reduced total allowable harvest for the year 2002 by 10% for five sturgeon species to a Caspian-wide quota of 142 tons (CITIES 2002). However, many resource managers still consider this allowable harvest unsustainable and have

Beluga sturgeon. Photograph by Alexander Masur.

proposed total, temporary bans. The Fish and Wildlife Service has recently proposed listing the beluga sturgeon as an endangered species under the Endangered Species Act, which would prohibit all importation of beluga caviar into the United States (Caviar Emptor 2002). The United States currently imports 80% of all legally harvested beluga caviar.

Salmon:

Once plentiful in their range, salmon (*Oncorhynchus* spp.) have been overharvested and their full recovery made impossible by loss of suitable habitat. Pacific Northwest salmon have disappeared from about 40% of their historical breeding ranges in Washington, Oregon, Idaho, and California (NRC 1995), and about half of the approximately 400 original Pacific coast stocks[26] of salmon and steelhead have been eliminated through overharvesting and other factors. Of the remaining stocks, almost 80% are at high or moderate risk of extinction (Nehlsen *et al.* 1991). Precipitous declines of Pacific salmon species began around the turn of the century, with most salmon harvests peaking before this time (Chinook salmon in 1883, sockeye in 1898, and steelhead trout in 1892) (NPPC 1986). By the late 1990s, Pacific salmon abundance was 10–15% of what it had been in the 1800s. This decline resulted in economic loss and job displacement for communities throughout the region. However, salmon still contribute significantly to the regional economy. As recently as 1988, sport and commercial salmon fishing generated more than $1.25 billion for the regional economy (NCSE 1999) and $196 million in 1996 for Washington State alone.

Like the Pacific salmon, the Atlantic salmon is also a prized commercial and sport fish with important cultural significance. It spends most of its life in the North Atlantic Ocean from the Arctic Circle to Portugal in the eastern Atlantic and from Iceland and southern Greenland south to the Connecticut River in the U.S in the western Atlantic. It generally returns to its natal stream for spawning one to three times during its life.[27] Its population has been declining for the past two decades and is now at its lowest point in history, falling by five-fold for some stocks. Between 1994 and 1999 the number of adult fish available to return to North American rivers dropped from approximately 200,000 to 80,000 (ASF 2002). In 1999, only 1,452 adults returned to U.S. rivers. Like the Pacific salmon, the factors responsible for this decline include overfishing, habitat destruction, loss of access to spawning grounds by dams and other obstructions, pollution, and possibly changes in sea temperature.

In 1999, 26 distinct population segments of Pacific salmon were listed under the U.S. Endangered Species Act (NCSE 1999). Atlantic salmon joined this list in 2000 (NOAA 2000). Both government and commercial interests are actively working to prevent further salmon species extinction. These efforts include: (1) reducing sea-based harvests; (2) improvement of habitat including access to spawning grounds; (3) hatchery rearing and release of native populations; (4) expanding development of mariculture[28] to prevent exhaustion of native population; and (5) voluntarily retiring of commercial licenses. A good source for additional material on the history and status of the Pacific salmon industry is *Salmon Without Rivers* by J. Lichatowich.

Trout cod:

Trout cod (*Maccullochella macquariensis*) is an aggressive top predator that feeds primarily on aquatic insects, crustaceans, and small fish. Originally found throughout Murray-Darling river system (New South Wales and Victoria, Australia), only two breeding populations remain in the wild (portions of the Murray River and a translocated population in Seven Creeks). Severe declines in population have been attributed to overharvesting, habitat fragmentation

---

[26] Stock refers to a subunit or population of a species that possess genetic differences that are adaptive to the environment conditions. Stocks have unique characteristics for which the adaptive significance is not obvious. The 'stock' concept (developed in 1940 by W. Rich) is important in fisheries management especially conservation aspects.

[27] A major distinction between the Pacific and Atlantic salmon is the ability of the Atlantic salmon to spawn and return to its natal stream more than once during its lifetime; the Pacific salmon spawn only once.

[28] Mariculture is saltwater fish farming.

A Puget Sound, Washington, salmon catch ca. 1900. Photograph courtesy of the Museum of History and Industry, Seattle.

and degradation (especially desnagging and siltation), and hydrologic alteration. Despite its endangered status, harvesting pressure continues, perhaps due in part to its similar appearance to the Murray cod (*Maccullochella peelii peelii*). Recovery plans include restocking selected rivers in the historical range and habitat improvements including sand removal, establishment of pool-riffle runs, provision of additional cover, and replacement of snags in the river (Brown *et al.* 1998, NFAI 2001).

Wetland plants

Collection by plant hobbyists and for commercial resale, as well as the indirect consequences of these activities (e.g., drainage, change of hydrologic regime, pollution) and natural stressors (e.g., disease, weather-related conditions), contribute to declining populations and local extirpations of some wetland plant species. Some examples of plants that have been threatened, in part as a result of overharvesting and are currently listed or are candidates for listing include: the mountain sweet pitcher plant (*Sarracenia rubra* ssp. *jonesii*), the green pitcher plant (*Sarracenia oreophila*), swamp pink (*Helonias bullata*), and the

Wenatchee Mountains checker-mallow (*Sidalcea oregana* var. *calva*). Conservation and management plans implemented by federal and state agencies as a consequence of federal or state endangered or threatened listings help protect these species by removing stress factors (e.g., improving altered hydrology, removing invasive species, monitoring against harvesting, etc.).

THE ECOLOGICAL HARM CAUSED BY OVERHARVESTING

Large-scale freshwater harvests select out target species, ages, and sizes. As overharvesting reduces the population, a threshold point is reached at which the probability of extinction increases significantly. Chance events such as climatic stress (e.g., drought), random variation in sex ratios, disease, or additional human disturbance make species recovery improbable (Soulé and Simberloff 1986). Heavily exploited areas often show a decline in age or size at maturity, and cumulative effect tends to be a gradual shift in genetic makeup. Harvests of reproducing populations (e.g., spawning salmon) result in loss of genetic variability and put future stocks at risk to natural and human-induced stressors (Harvey 2001).

TABLE 4-8. Examples of Economically or Ecologically Important Fish in the U.S. Whose Stocks Have Been Depleted by Overharvesting and Are Now Listed as Endangered.

Name	Location	Principal Causes	Notes
Atlantic salmon (*Salmo salar*)	North Atlantic Ocean and freshwater tributaries from southeastern Canada and northeastern U.S. and from Russia's White Sea to Portugal	Pollution, commercial driftnet fishing, and dams	
Beluga sturgeon (*Huso huso*)	Caspian Sea, Russia	Habitat loss, pollution, dams, overfishing, poaching	
Bonytail (*Gila elegans*)	Colorado River basin, U.S.	Poisoned as "trash" fish; habitat loss, dams, and flow regulation	Originally one of most abundant fish in basin
Coastal cutthroat trout (*Oncorhynchus clarki clarki*)	Washington and Oregon, U.S.	Habitat loss, hatcheries, overfishing	
Colorado pikeminnow (*Ptychocheilus lucius*)	Colorado River basin, U.S.	Poisoned as "trash" fish; habitat loss, dams and flow regulation, invasive non-native species	Historically abundant in range & important human food source
Humpback chub (*Gila cypha*)	Colorado River basin, U.S.	Poisoned as "trash" fish; habitat loss, dams and flow regulation, invasive non-native species	Slow and steady recovery
Lahontan cutthroat trout (*Oncorhynchus clarki henshawi*)	Truckee and Walker rivers in Nevada and California, U.S.	Water diversions, pollution, overfishing, invasive non-native species	
Lost River sucker (*Deltistes luxatus*)	Klamath Basin (Oregon/California), U.S.	Dams, water diversions, overharvesting; pollution, habitat loss, sedimentation	
Pacific salmon (*Oncorhynchus* spp.)	Northeastern Pacific ocean, northwestern U.S. and western Canada rivers	Historical overharvesting, dams, sedimentation, hatchery fish production, habitat loss	
Pallid sturgeon (*Scaphirhynchus albus*)	Missouri, lower Yellowstone, Mississippi, and Atchafalaya rivers, U.S.	Channelization, levees, impoundments, pollution, harvesting	
Razorback sucker (*Xyrauchen texanus*)	Colorado River basin, U.S.	Poisoned as "trash" fish; habitat loss, dams and flow regulation, invasive non-native species, pollution, pollution by hormone-disrupting chemicals	
Shortnose sturgeon (*Acipenser brevirostrum*)	Estuarine and river habitats, east coast U.S.	By-catch, water intake entrapment, pollution, overharvesting, dam and bridge construction, habitat alteration, dredging	

Overharvesting and fisheries mismanagement may result in the decline or elimination of keystone species. The presence or absence of a keystone species controls trophic structure (foodweb interactions) of an ecosystem and important biogeochemical and biogeophysical interactions. Since species are linked through trophic interactions such as predator-prey and host-parasite, loss of a species may result in a domino effect on the biotic composition and function of the community. Impacts of species loss can be felt on multiple spatial scales, from the stream reach to watershed and waterbasin. These impacts are most frequently manifested by disruption to food chains and habitat changes. For some species, this domino effect may be partially offset by foodweb redundancy.[29]

Species differ in the rates and pathways by which they process resources, in their effects on the physical environment, and in their interactions with other species. Thus, changes in species composition likely alter ecosystem processes through changes in the functional traits of biota. This can alter ecosystem processes, such as nitrogen uptake by vegetation, which in turn modifies community processes, such as competition and herbivory, feeding back to further changes in community composition. Species-induced changes in ecosystem processes can also alter regional processes, such as methane emissions from beaver ponds, nutrient transfers, and water purification, extending the impacts beyond the original zone of species change (Chapin *et al.* 1997). For example:

- Beavers are ecosystem engineers that alter hydrology, aeration, and carbon inputs to soil. Through the construction of dams and modification of stream channels beavers increase areal extent, depth, and longevity of flooding in wetlands. These changes influence production of greenhouse gases such as methane and carbon dioxide.
- Through their suspension feeding, mussels influence phytoplankton ecology, nutrient cycling, and water quality; filtration rates of bivalves are estimated at 10–100% of the water column per day.

Additionally, mollusks contribute a significant portion of freshwater macrobenthic biomass and their parasitic larvae impact fish mortality (Strayer *et al.* 1999, Anthony and Downing 2001).

- Anadromous fish are important transport vectors of nutrients and energy between oceans and rivers. Although most salmon stocks spend most of their lives in the ocean, they eventually return to rivers and streams to spawn and die. Carcasses of spent salmon are an important food source for aquatic invertebrates and other creatures that directly consume salmon tissue, as well as for the species that consume these species. Additionally, evidence suggests that riparian vegetation also benefits directly from carcass-derived nutrient input and indirectly by increased seed dispersal from animals attracted to the area by the carcasses and other opportunistic feeding.

Strategies for Mitigating/Abating the Effect of Overharvesting on Freshwater Ecosystems

Across the globe, resource managers, policy makers, businesses, and consumers generally recognize that maintenance of a biological resource for sustainable yields requires strategies that prevent overexploitation (Coates 2001). Strategies include both technical improvements (e.g., equipment, monitoring harvests and status of wild stock, improved hatchery operations) and conservation-driven legal restrictions (e.g., establishment of limits and timing of harvests, mechanisms for enforcement, etc.) as well as local community efforts.

TECHNICAL STRATEGIES

Technical strategies for reducing the harm caused by overharvesting and inappropriate management practices include either improving harvesting methods and practices used or improving fisheries management itself. These two types of approaches are discussed below.

---

[29] Foodweb redundancy is the number of links in the foodweb that perform the same "function." Complex foodwebs frequently have greater redundancy.

Improving harvesting methods and practices

The methods and practices used to raise and collect wild and non-wild stock (aquaculture and hatcheries) may themselves contribute to overharvesting. Technical strategies related to improving methods and practices related to these different types of stock include:

Wild stock:

Some netting methods used in commercial harvesting result in the capture of non-target fish. In both developed and developing nations netting can result in large bycatch.[30] This problem is more serious in ocean harvests of freshwater migratory fish such as salmon and eels and in large lake systems (e.g., Lake Victoria and Lake Tanganyika in Africa and the Great Lakes in North America) than in rivers. Estimated freshwater bycatch is nearly 25% of the overall catch (FAO 1999b).

Changes to harvesting gear and techniques can significantly reduce landings of non-target species. Selective harvest can be employed in both the commercial and recreational industry and can aid in monitoring stock populations. Fishwheels[31] and fishtraps, once commonly used in salmon fishing in the Pacific Northwest, are devices that permit live capture of target species while allowing non-target species to continue their migration and spawning. Live capture eliminates the use of nets and hooks (sources of high mortality) and permits the release of egg bearing females. It also provides an opportunity for tagging and release for monitoring (health of the stock) and can be used when traditional net fishing is closed. Where netting is practiced, use of appropriate gear is paramount to prevent capture of undersized fish and non-target fauna, such as otters and turtles. For fisheries using hooks, modifying types and sizes of lures and bait is effective in reducing non-target species, and elimination of lead weights can reduce incidence of wetland waterfowl mortality resulting from lead poisoning.

Aquaculture:

Four primary markets exist for aquaculture[32] production: (1) human and animal food; (2) restocking for native fish; (3) ornamental fish; and (4) and sport fisheries. The largest single market is for human consumption. Globally, the primary fish produced for human consumption include the carp (*Hypophthalmichthys molitrix, Gypfinns carpio,* other species), channel catfish (*Ictalurus punctatus*), Tilapia spp., eels (*Anguilla* spp.), milkfish (*Chanos chanos*), rainbow trout (*Oncorhynchus mykiss*), and salmon (*Salmo salar*). Although aquaculture production may relieve harvesting pressure from wild stock, it presents a suite of environmental challenges that threaten ecosystem function, biodiversity, and the health of aquatic fauna and flora. These challenges include resource depletion, water quality deterioration, hybridization with wild stock, predation, and disease. Ecologically sound fish farms should: (1) not be based partly on or open to surrounding ecosystems; (2) avoid crowded conditions; (3) utilize agricultural and other organic and processed waste for food and not fishmeal; and (4) follow the precautionary approach involving nonindigenous stocks, alien species and genetically modified organisms.

Hatcheries:

Although data on global hatchery output are not systematically collected, estimates suggest that hatcheries produce 180 million juveniles per day, 99% of which

---

[30] Bycatch applies to fish, birds, turtles, and mammals that are captured by a fishing operation but that are not kept and sold as a commercial product because they have little or no commercial value, are the wrong sex, or otherwise do not meet regulatory requirements.

[31] Fishwheels work on the principle of using submerged mechanical buckets to capture fish during their upstream migration and moving them into a live holding pen. The holding pen is located in the water where the flowing current delivers oxygen to the fish. Fish are then removed by knotless mesh dipnets and returned to the stream if they are not target specimens or "landed" if they meet specifications.

[32] Aquaculture is farming fish and other aquatic organisms. Land-based systems may be integrated with agriculture by stocking fish in rice fields and ponds (especially in developing nations). Water-based systems involve stocking fish directly in enclosures or attaching them to substrates in water bodies such as rivers, lakes, reservoirs, or bays.

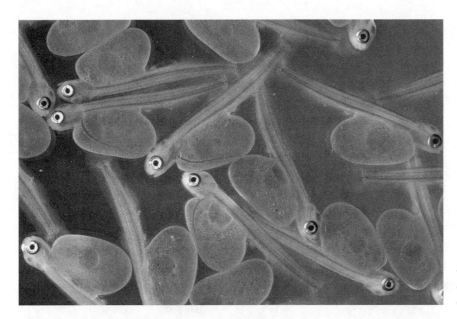

*Newly-hatched salmon alevins.
Photograph courtesy of the Fish
and Wildlife Service.*

are finfish and most destined for release to the wild. The estimated releases of hatchery-raised juvenile salmon in North America alone is five billion fish (Harvey 2001). Hatcheries were developed to (1) compensate for overharvesting; (2) compensate for habitat deterioration and/or loss; (3) buffer against natural variation; (4) provide additional stock for harvest; and (5) conserve threatened stocks and species. However, their operation may harm wild stocks. Threats of hatchery reared and released fish include: (1) capture of wild specimens in a mixed (hatchery and wild) stock; (2) spread of disease and parasites; (3) genetic hybridization of wild stock through cross-breeding thereby risking fitness of wild stocks; (4) competition for food and other resources and negative social interaction; (4) reduced fitness of hatchery raised fish; and (6) use as a substitute for habitat protection and harvest regulation and avoiding substantive improvements to environmental and management needs (Lichatowich 2003, NWFSC 2003).

Developing better management plans

Conservation of freshwater biodiversity requires ecologically sound and sustainable resource management schemes. The basic outline for these schemes includes development and implementation of national and regional guidance and management plans for harvesting. Additionally, strong governance of laws and policies that regulate harvesting are critical to effective management. However, many management plans of commercial and recreational harvests are less than effective due to uncertainty in stock abundance, commodity price, cost of harvests, political constraints, and budgets, as well as inadequate information about biological characteristics of target species (Hilborn 1994). To address these concerns, a management framework should be specific to the target species, environmental considerations, and social/ecomomic interests of the region. Management plans should include all of the relevant elements presented below:

- Establish annual harvest levels on the basis of scientific recommendations that incorporate the precautionary principle.
- Include multi-annual and ecosystem-oriented management strategies that encompass all species harvested; these must be considered when harvest levels are established.
- Utilize equipment and techniques that focus on species conservation (e.g., selective fishing gear, installation of exit windows on nets, measures to reduce juveniles and nontarget species discards).
- Replace traditional area-wide fisheries designation by a spatial and temporal division into areas of harvest and protection and enforcement of these delineations; identification is based on research and follows scientific recommendations.

Aquaculture in the Tam Giang lagoon, Vietnam. Photograph by Paul Insua Cao.

- Prohibit or reduce of harvest (commercial and/or recreational) where justified by endangered status of species.
- Include adequate monitoring and inspections of harvesting activities.
- Consider advocacy such as:
  - Promote the reduction of commercial fisheries where overcapacity exists with respect to available resources and sustainable harvest guidelines.
  - Limit or eliminate subsidies to commercial harvesting enterprises since these have historically resulted in increased harvesting effort and pressure on the resources.
  - Facilitate buyouts of harvesting licenses to encourage early retirement from the industry. As part of the equation to minimize overharvesting, buyouts will foster a higher catch ratio for the remaining harvesters thereby ensuring a more financially secure environment for the employment sector.

Freshwater biota is often considered common property or free and is therefore vulnerable to exploitation. The effectiveness of efforts to curb over-harvesting varies geographically and is often a function of local and regional economics and culture. Incentives, pricing mechanisms, as well as political, market, and institutional stability all contribute to the effectiveness of management programs (Klaphake *et al.* 2001).

LEGAL AND INSTITUTIONAL STRATEGIES

Policies at all levels of governance are necessary to better manage harvesting practices. Fortunately, as described below, local, national, and international institutions and legal instruments promote the adoption of sound freshwater biota management policies and plans.

U.S. institutions and legal authorities

State laws and public agencies govern the management of most freshwater species in the United States. These agencies (state departments of fish and game or wildlife) are responsible for stocking non-native fish to streams to serve recreational interests as well as introducing native fish to new stream segments. Improving conditions for freshwater biodiversity should begin with influencing the policies and practices of state agencies.

Federal laws and public agencies also govern the management of freshwater species in the United States, particularly those species listed as threatened or endangered under the Endangered Species Act (ESA) or regarding overharvesting or to protect critical breeding and feeding grounds within streams designated wild and scenic under the Wild and Scenic Rivers Act (WSRS). The federal agencies most heavily involved with fisheries management in the U.S. include the Fish and Wildlife Service (FWS) and the Environmental Protection Agency (EPA). The FWS has managed fishery resources for over 120 years. It runs the National Fish Hatchery System, which rears and releases both native and non-native game fish into waters throughout the United States. The EPA regulates recreational fishing practices as they affect water quality and aquatic life within freshwater ecosystems.

If influencing public agencies to adopt recreational fishing practices supportive of freshwater biodiversity, the American Fisheries Society (AFS) recommends improved management practices and regulations that (AFS 2003):

1. Include fishery goals that are: realistic and attainable and have measurable objectives; compatible with broader, ecological management objectives; and easily understood by anglers.
2. Involve the angling public in all phases of planning, development, and implementation of special regulations therefore minimizing conflict.
3. Include assessment measures which recognize fiscal and temporal constraints as well as include peer-reviewed evaluation techniques which anticipate and minimize possible short-comings.
4. Recognize that unforeseen problems (i.e. concentrated fishing pressure, increased hooking and handling mortality, etc.) arise regularly during implementation and evaluation of special regulations.
5. Communicate evaluation results to the public and the professional community.

International institutions and legal authorities

Growing recognition of threats to biodiversity has resulted in modifying existing as well as developing new declarations, conventions, and international organizations within and outside the United Nations framework. While many of these instruments are not specific to harvesting freshwater biota, they do address issues of sustainability (hence protection from overharvesting and protection of endangered species). Examples include the Ramsar Convention (on Wetlands), the United Nations Framework on Climate Change, and the Convention on International Watercourses.

The following international laws and treaties are particularly important regarding overharvesting:

- **United Nations Convention on the Law of the Sea (LOS):** Living Resources Provisions (Buck 1994) contain relevant provisions regarding anadromous and catadromous fish stocks:
  - *Anadromous stocks* (e.g., salmon, sturgeon, and striped bass): the LOS Convention assigns primary interest in and responsibility for anadromous fish stocks to the country in whose rivers the stocks originate. Enforcement of regulations concerning anadromous fish stocks beyond the EEZ[33] will be done through negotiated agreement
  - *Catadromous stocks* (e.g., American eels): the LOS Convention gives the coastal country where these species spend most of their lives the responsibility for managing them, and prohibits harvesting them on the high seas. International cooperation is required where these species migrate through several EEZs.

- **Convention on Biological Diversity (CBD):** The three goals of the CBD are to promote the conservation of biodiversity, the sustainable use of its components, and the fair and equitable sharing of benefits arising out of the utilization of genetic resources. Among other obligations, the CBD requires participating nations to: (1) conserve biological diversity within their jurisdiction and cooperate in preserving biological diversity in areas outside areas of national jurisdiction; (2) develop and implement strategies, plans, or programs for the conservation and sustainable use of biological diversity; (3) monitor elements of biological diversity; and (4) support research, training, and general

---

[33] EEZ refers to the Exclusive Economic Zone in which coastal states have effective management jurisdiction for its development and economic growth. Maximum distance from shore that a maritime nation can claim for its EEZ is about 370 km.

education to foster an awareness of the importance of biodiversity (CIESIN 2003).

• **CITES (Convention on International Trade in Endangered Species of Wild Fauna and Flora):** The aim of this international agreement is to ensure that international trade in wild animals and plants does not threaten their survival. It provides varying degrees of protection to more than 30,000 species of animals and plants globally. Species covered by CITES include three groups: those threatened with extinction, species not necessarily threatened with extinction but in which trade must be controlled in order to avoid utilization that would threaten their survival, and species that are protected in at least one country which has asked other CITES Parties for assistance in controlling the trade (CITES 2003). Although legally binding for those nations who have signed the agreement, it does not take the place of national laws. It provides a framework for the signatory nations to adopt their own domestic legislation to ensure that CITES is implemented at the national level.

In addition to these multilateral instruments there are many bilateral agreements that establish and implement harvesting management plans. For example, the United States actively participates in a cooperative bilateral salmon agreement with Canada as well as broader regional agreements for both Atlantic and Pacific stocks.

Numerous international organizations provide policy and action support for conservation and sustainable management of biological resources by providing integrated information on their status, trends, distribution and use. They work with Secretariats of major international conventions and other key agencies (e.g., Food and Agricultural Organization, International Institute for Environment and Development) to facilitate information transfer and coordination of policies across participating nations. Examples of these organizations and agencies include: World Conservation and Monitoring Center (WCMC), World Conservation Union (IUCN), United Nations Environmental Program (UNEP), and the World Wildlife Fund (WCMC 2000).

COMMUNITY-BASED STRATEGIES

People living within a river or lake basin that rely on subsistence fishing are a part of the ecosystem. Many spend most of their life observing the system and utilizing the benefits it provides (such as fish) on a daily basis. Their knowledge includes both ecological aspects of importance for the capture of fish as well as utility aspects, such as human fish consumption, processing and marketing. Local knowledge also covers long time horizons, often reaching beyond lifetimes of individual people. Therefore, the success of any strategy to abate overharvesting threats needs to incorporate local knowledge and community support. For example, in the Mekong River, the systematic compiling of local knowledge throughout the basin provided information at various scales, which is now considered of crucial value for the basin planning process under the advisement of the Mekong River Commission (Bao *et. al.* 2000; Valbo-Jørgensen and Poulsen, 2000). Furthermore, the process of bringing local knowledge to the forefront has the added benefit of bringing local communities and government agencies together to work toward a common goal. Working together often increases stakeholder motivation and participation in fisheries management, including monitoring and data collection.

—Authored by Ronald Bjorkland and Catherine Pringle

Invasive Alien Species

Introduction

Invasive alien species are a leading cause of species endangerment and extinction in freshwater ecosystems (Claudi & Leach 1999, Harrison and Stiassny 1999). Sometimes called introduced non-native species or invasive species, the most commonly used term for these species is invasive alien species (IAS) defined as "an *alien species* (a species, subspecies, or lower taxon, introduced outside its natural past or present distribution and includes any part, (e.g., gametes, seeds, eggs, or propagules) of such species that might survive and subsequently reproduce), whose introduction and/or spread threaten biodiversity."[34] Although any introduced species will have some influence on the host ecosystem, most influences are benign and their impacts are undetectable. Only a few rise to the level of IAS, but these few reap substantial damage.

Although information about IAS is generally incomplete, IAS are thought to cause or contribute to more than 70% of native North American freshwater species extinctions during the twentieth century (Williams *et al.* 1989). A survey of 31 fish introduction studies in Europe, North America, Australia, and New Zealand found that introduced alien fish species reduced or eliminated native fish populations in 77% of the cases. IAS contributed to 76 of the 167 freshwater species listed at some degree of risk in Mexico (Contreras-Balderas *et al.* 2002). Invasive alien fish species are the leading cause of decline for 22 species of native fish now classified as endangered, vulnerable or rare in Australia (Wager and Jackson 1993). Information on IAS introductions is available through FAO's Database on Introductions of Aquatic Species (DIAS) (search for DIAS at www.fao.org) and through FishBase, another on-line database developed by FAO and World Fish Center in collaboration with others (www.fishbase.org) (Figure 4-26).

Invasive alien species spread both intentionally and unintentionally. Intentional introductions include stocking of IAS by fisheries management agencies to serve recreational interests, planting of IAS for erosion control within riparian areas, and utilization of natural freshwater ecosystems (e.g., lakes) to breed IAS for commercial sale (aquaculture). Unintentional introductions include the escape of IAS from aquaculture facilities (including artificial and natural freshwater ecosystems), and IAS introductions carried by ships and other transportation vectors, and other factors.

Intentional introductions due to aquaculture and stocking account for the greatest number of IAS entering freshwater ecosystems. The concern regarding these introductions is that about one-third of these species have documented adverse ecological effects. The top five IAS introductions from aquaculture and stocking are: common carp (*Cyprinus carpio*), Mozambique tilapia (*Oreochromis mossambicus*), rainbow trout (*Oncorhynchus mykiss*), largemouth bass (*Micropterus salmoides*), and brown trout (*Salmo trutta*). Table 4-9 summarizes various intentional and unintentional pathways of entry for IAS into freshwater ecosystems.

Often, the threat posed by introducing a species, even one recognized as an IAS, is not fully understood, leading to resource management decisions with devastating ecological consequences. For example, some of the most dramatic trade-offs between economic benefits and ecological costs involve introductions of common carp (*Cyprinus carpio*), the most widely introduced species into freshwater ecosystems. In 1996, 1.99 million tons of common carp were produced through aquaculture (FAO 1999a). Although a tremendous food source, native species have suffered in lakes and rivers where this species has been introduced. By feeding at the bottom of lakes and rivers, common carp increase siltation and turbidity, decreasing water

---

[34] The definition for invasive alien species was developed at the CBD's Sixth Conference of the Parties (Decision VI/23).

TABLE 4-9. Pathways of Entry of IAS into Freshwater Ecosystems. (Ciruna *et al.* 2004)

Pathway of Entry	Means of Introduction: I = Intentional, U = Unintentional
Aquaria (Private)	1. (I/U) Aquaria plants and animals escape/released into the environment 2. (U) Pathogens, parasites, algae associated with aquaria plants/pets escape into the environment 3. Introduction (I) of fish for ornamental purposes into private garden ponds
Aquaria (Public)	1. (I/U) Display organisms escape/released into the environment 2. (I/U) Organisms transported with display species escape/released into the environment
Bait	1. (I/U) Live bait and/or its live packaging (e.g., aquatic plants) released/escaped into the environment 2. (U) Organisms associated with live bait/packaging released into the environment
Biological Supply	1. (I/U) Organisms intended for scientific study released into the environment 2. (I/U) Organisms used for classroom study escape/released into the environment 3. (I/U) Organisms associated with study specimens escape/released into the environment
Shipping Vessels (land, water, and air transport)	1. (U) Organisms released when ships discharge ballast water 2. (U) Organisms attached to interior or exterior structures and equipment (i.e., fouling organisms) released into the environment 3. (U) Organisms contaminating cargo (e.g., wood casks, water containers) released into the environment
Cargo	1. (I) Organisms released into the environment 2. (U) Organisms contaminating cargo (e.g., wood products) released into the environment
Dry Docks/Jetties	1. (U) Organisms attached to structures that have been relocated 2. (U) Organisms released when ballast water is discharged
Floating Debris	1. (U) Organisms moving on garbage (e.g., bottles, buoys, nets, packaging) that have been relocated
Fisheries & Game (Recreational)	1. (I/U) Release of organisms for sporting purposes, including organisms intended to serve as their forage (e.g., tadpoles for bass). Also included are associated organisms (e.g., pathogens) that are unintentionally released 2. (U) Escape of fisheries stocks, game species (e.g., bullfrogs), and their associated organisms during transport, transplantation and/or holding for growth. 3. (U) Introduction of organisms associated with relocated fishing gear (e.g., lines, nets, floats) 4. (I/U) Introduction of aquatic plants and associated material to enhance habitat fisheries/game stocks 5. (U) Release of organisms (esp. pathogens and parasites) form waste produced by processing of fish/game 6. (U) Release of organisms (esp. pathogens and parasites) along with introduced fish
Food (aquaculture & agriculture)	1. (U) Escape of animals and their associated organisms from holding facilities/transport containers 2. (I/U) Release of organisms by private citizens for propagation and harvest. Includes associated organisms 3. (I) Government sanctioned release of organisms for propagation and harvest 4. (I/U) Organisms associated with food packaging and released into the environment when packaging is discarded.
Horticulture & Flora Culture	1. (I/U) Introduction of plants and associated organisms into gardens, waterways, and riparian areas 2. (U) Introduction of organisms associated with water and soil storage/transport media.
Pest Control	1. (I/U) Release of organisms as biological control agents. Includes their associated organisms.

Pathway of Entry	Means of Introduction: I = Intentional, U = Unintentional
Restoration	1. (I/U) Introduction of organisms (esp. plants and fish) and their associated organisms for habitat restoration/conservation purposes. 2. (U) Release of organisms associated with re-introduced or established native species.
Water Diversion Projects	1. (I/U) Movement of organisms into new aquatic systems as a result of projects designed to redirect the flow of water (e.g., inter-basin water transfer, canals, dams, and diversions)
Recreation	1. (U) Introduction of organisms associated with relocated recreational gear (e.g., SCUBA tanks, rafts, inner tubes, ATVs, hiking boots, etc.) 2. (I/U) Movement of organisms along transportation corridors—roads, trails, etc.
Natural Dispersal & Hitchhiking	1. (I/U) Dispersal of organisms under their own influence or aided by other organisms (e.g., birds moving snails from one wetland system into another)
Military and Development Actions	1. (U) Introduction of organisms associated with transport of military and development aid.
Drinking Water Shipments	1. (U) Introduction of organisms associated with bottled water.
Smuggling	1. (I) Illegal transport of organisms

clarity and harming native species (Fuller *et al.* 1999). They have been associated with the disappearance of native fishes in Argentina, Venezuela, Mexico, Kenya, India, and elsewhere (Welcomme 1988).

The primary source of unintentional IAS introductions is people. For example, human migration has long served as a source of species introductions because people tend to bring plants and animals with them and unwittingly contribute IAS as well as diseases and other pathogens to their new locales. People also tend to live near freshwaters, making these ecosystems extremely vulnerable to IAS invasion. Indeed, remote areas with less human disturbance receive fewer IAS than areas that are in the middle of trade routes or that host immense human settlement and activity (Drake *et al.* 1989). A wide range of factors contribute to IAS establishment success in new ecosystems. For example, freshwater ecosystems with degraded water quantity and quality caused by dams, interbasin water transfers, effluent release etc., are more vulnerable to IAS invasion (Heinz Center 2003). Additionally, in comparison to their terrestrial counterparts, freshwater ecosystems are more vulnerable to IAS invasion due to differences in their species distribution patterns. Freshwater biodiversity is often highly localized with discrete areas (e.g., small lakes, stream portions, or even single springs) harboring unique, locally evolved forms of life. Because of the

nature of this habitat, freshwater species cannot readily migrate outside their drainage basins to avoid IAS invasion. Biological invasions are more prominent drivers of biodiversity change in freshwater systems than in terrestrial systems (Sala *et al.* 2000).

IAS issues will likely increase in importance as our population grows. Human population growth will likely demand more fish and this demand will likely cause the aquaculture industry to expand further, thereby increasing pathways for IAS invasions. Aquaculture production has doubled in the past decade and now supplies one-third of the world's fish and seafood (Naylor *et al.* 2000). Equally true, as wealth grows in different regions globally, demand for alien plants and animals is likely to increase resulting in more IAS introductions through the horticulture, the pet trade, tourism, and recreational activities.

The Effects of IAS on Freshwater Ecosystems

IAS directly reduce native species abundance through predation, hybridization, parasitism, or competition. IAS also affect the five key ecological factors of freshwater ecosystems: the hydrologic regime, the water chemistry regime, connectivity, physical habitat conditions, and biological composition and interactions. However, these effects vary significantly based on the

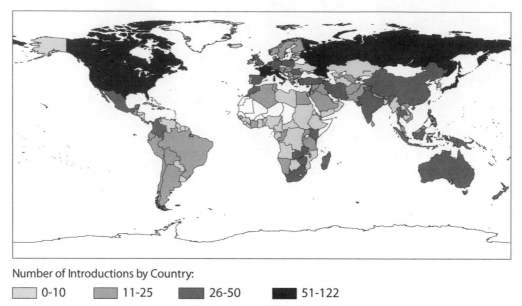

Number of Introductions by Country:

| 0-10 | 11-25 | 26-50 | 51-122 |

FIGURE 4-26. Number of Freshwater Species Introductions by Country (DIAS).

Data Source: DIAS-Database on Introduction of Aquatic Species, Food and Agriculture Organization of the United Nations, http://www.fao.org/figis/servlet/static?dom=root&xml=Introsp/introsp_s.xml.

invading species, the extent of the invasion, and the vulnerability of the ecosystem being invaded. Because of the range of possible effects of IAS, this chapter summarizes these effects broadly, includes a few illustrative examples of the harm caused by IAS, and explains how to assess the threat of invasive alien species—a critical step before appropriate strategies can be pursued to address IAS eradication or abatement.

SUMMARY OF THE EFFECTS OF IAS ON FRESHWATER ECOSYSTEMS

Table 4-10 summarizes the effects of IAS on freshwater ecosystems. Loss and degradation of biodiversity due to IAS can occur at all biological levels: genes, populations, species, community, and habitat/ecosystem levels. Effects of individual IAS introductions vary in terms of the period of time between introduction and spread, severity of impact, interaction with other threats, and ability to cascade throughout an entire ecosystem (Levin e 2000; McNeely *et al.* 2001; Wilcove *et al.* 1998). The following examples provide a detailed look at some of the more typical effects of IAS:

1) **Native species may be harmed by interactions between successfully established IAS and native**
species during reproduction. Erosion of the native gene pools can occur directly through hybridization resulting in sterile offspring and an associated decrease in population size, and introgression, or gene swapping of native species by more productive IAS, or indirectly through competition resulting in a reduced population from which to draw genetic material. The most explicit example of the consequences of these types of interactions is hybridization followed by the erosion of the gene pool of native species, such as hybridization between invasive alien trout species (rainbow trout (*Oncorhynchus mykiss*)) and native trout populations (cutthroat trout (*Salmo clarki*)) (Campton 1987), and between mallard ducks (*Anas platyrhynchos*) released in the wild for hunting in Florida and the native Florida mottled duck (*Anas fulvigula fulvigula*), whose existence is now threatened by hybridization (Ryhmer and Simberloff 1996).

2) **Native species may be replaced by stronger and more robust introduced IAS.** Introductions of the quilted melania (*Thiara granifera*) and the red rimmed melania (*Melanoides tuberculata*), freshwater snails native to subtropical and tropical areas of northern and eastern Africa and southern

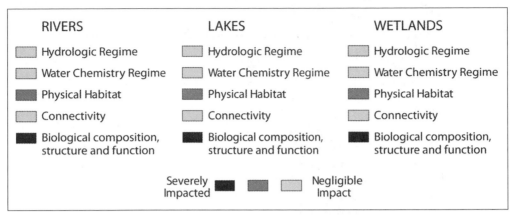

FIGURE 4-27. Summary of Impacts of Invasive Alien Species on Freshwater Ecosystems

Asia, into North America has led to decline or disappearance of several native snail populations (Contreras-Arquieta and Contreras-Balderas, 1999). Thiarids not only out compete native species, but are resistant to predation thereby reducing food availability to molluscivore fishes.

3) **Native species may be harmed by parasites and diseases carried by and destructive behavior of IAS.** In addition to out-competing native snails, quilted and red rimmed melania are also vectors for several dangerous invasive alien parasites such as *Clonorchis sinesis* (Chinese liver fluke), *Paragonimus westermani* (oriental lung fluke), *Philophtalmus* spp. (eye fluke of birds, which occasionally infects mammals), and *Centrocestus formosanus,* a trematode which infective stages that penetrate the gills of fish in high numbers causing severe damage and even death. *C. formosanus* has caused serious infections in cultured fish in Florida and Mexico and in wild fish stocks in Texas affecting several threatened or endangered fishes such as the fountain darter (*Etheostoma fonticola*), Devils River minnow (*Dionda diaboli*), Rio Grande darter (*Etheostoma grahami*), Proserpine shiner (*Cyprinella proserpina*), Comanche Springs pupfish (*Cyprinodon elegans*) and Pecos gambusia (*Gambusia nobilis*) (Mitchell *et al.* 2000). Introductions of the Louisiana crayfish (*Procambarus clarkii* or *P. Clarkii*), native to the south central part of the United States and northeastern Mexico to other areas have infected fish in these ecosystems with a crayfish plague (caused by

Aphanomyces astaci). *P. clarkii* is also physically destructive creating burrowing holes through earthen dams and causing damage in levees, or water control structures, and contributes to public or veterinary health problems because *P. clarkii* is an intermediate host for several parasitic helminthes of vertebrates. In ecosystems with *P. clarkii* introductions, dramatic changes occurred in invertebrate assemblages, benthic algae and macrophyte biomass and productivity was affected, which in turn led to decreased fish populations.

4) **Native species may be harmed by the cascading or ecosystem-wide effects of IAS introductions.** In Lake Erie, native green algae declined precipitously due to the colonization of zebra mussels (*Dreissena polymorpha*) and quagga mussels (*Dreissena bugnesis*). Since the native green algae is the primary producer in the system, its decline contributed to the mass extinction of native Unionidae clams (Schloesser and Nalepa 1994). Zebra and quagga mussels intercept organic detritus that normally supports chironomids, mayflies, and amphipods. These species are food for fish including bass and yellow perch, so invasive mussel colonization has also contributed to a decline in these species. In the Mississippi River basin, researchers predict that zebra mussel invasions will reduce native mussel species by as much as 50% within this decade. This river basin contains more native species of freshwater mussels than any other river system in the world. The loss of its native

TABLE 4-10. Ecological Impacts of IAS to Freshwater Ecosystems. (Modified from Ciruna *et al.* 2004)

Ecological Factors	Impacts
Change in Physical Habitat	Loss of native habitat
	Creation of non-native habitat and ecological niches
	Loss of native habitat heteogeneity/complexity
	Alteration of riparian habitat
	Alteration of soil structure/composition
	Alteration of microclimate(s)
	Alteration of bed/bank stability and structure
	Alteration of instream habitat/channel morphology
	Alteration of organic matter
	Alteration of stream shading/light availability
	Alteration of water temperature regime
	Alteration of nutrient regime
	Alteration of sediment regime
	Alteration of light levels
Change in Hydrologic Regime	Alteration of surface water flow regime
	Alteration of surface water run-off regime
	Alteration of groundwater regime
	Alteration of soil moisture regime
	Alteration of evapotranspiration regime
Change in Water Chemistry Regime	Alteration of dissolved oxygen concentration(s)
	Alteration of dissolved mineral concentrations
	Alteration of dissolved organic matter
	Alteration of turbidity
	Alteration of pH
Change in Connectivity	Alteration of latitudinal connectivity (e.g., river–floodplain connectivity)
	Alteration of longitudinal connectivity (e.g., upstream–downstream connectivity), vertical connectivity (e.g., river–groundwater connection through the hyporheic zone)
Biological Community Impacts	Loss of native species
	Alteration of native trophic structure and intractions
	Alteration of native community composition
	Loss of native species richness and diversity
	Alteration of native food web structure
	Alteration of native community structure
	Alteration of native community function
	Alteration of native biomass
	Alteration of native primary and secondary productivity
	Alteration of native keystone species' dominance
Species Population Impacts	Loss of or decrease in native species populations through predation
	Loss of or decrease in native species populations through competition for food, shelter, habitat, and other important resources
	Loss of or decrease in native species populations through pathogens/parasites carried by invasive alien species
	Dispersal/relocation of native species populations through over-crowding and aggressive behavior
	Decrease in reproduction rate and fecundity of native species populations
	Decrease in fecundity of native species populations
	Decrease in growth rates of native species populations
	Alteration of meta-population dynamics of native species populations
	Alteration of behavior in native species populations
Genetic Impacts	Loss of genetic variability through hybridization
	Loss of genetic variability through introgression/gene-swapping (i.e., erosion of the native species population's gene pool)

*The Comanche Springs pupfish (*Cyprinodon elegans*), an endangered species native to Texas, has been adversely affected by invasive alien parasites.*

mussels could result in the extinction of up to 140 species. Because native mussels play an important role in nutrient cycling and sediment mixing, their loss could diminish the viability of the Mississippi River ecosystem.

Bermuda grass (*Cynodon dactylon*), an IAS introduced into the southeastern U.S. for livestock forage and lawns, has completely changed many streams in the southeast by forming a carpet on stream bottoms. This carpet increases the resistance of substrates to disturbance during floods and eliminates the scoured habitat preferred by native fish and invertebrates (i.e., spawning areas). It also creates habitat for the fathead minnow and other invasive alien fish that compete with natives and facilitates establishment of watercress, aquatic buttercups and other plant IAS. The result is a short-circuit of the natural succession because it creates an invasion complex or invasional meltdown (Simberloff 1999) in which one invading species facilitates additional invaders (Ricciardi 2001).

Common carp (*Cyprinus carpio*), introduced into the Murray-Darling River System in Australia, have reached such high densities (e.g., biomass of 3,144 kg) (Gehrke *et al.* 1995) that they may contribute to bank erosion as well as increased turbidity and elevated nutrient concen-

trations. These alterations to physical and chemical conditions have ecological consequences, such as increased phytoplankton density in response to elevated nutrient levels, and reduced aquatic macrophyte growth (a consequence of disturbance of the substrates that support submerged aquatic vegetation, especially delicate species). Reduced plant biomass and cover may affect important habitat conditions for invertebrates and fish, and also fish food resources (Arthington 1991; Koehn *et al.* 2000). The massive biomass shifts that occur in rivers infested with carp represent major redirection of energy flow through the ecosystem.

Not all IAS impacts are equally detectable and in some cases it may not be clear what symptoms to look for (Allendorf 1991, Gaffney and Allen 1992). For example, a large volume of literature exists on changes in species composition resulting from predation. However, predation is much easier to detect than genetic effects or allelopathy and may be a secondary effect of IAS. Distinguishing between impacts caused by IAS and those caused by other threats is also often difficult. An example is the introduction of Nile perch (*Lates niloticus*) in Lake Victoria. Initially the decline of the haplochromine cichlid populations was attributed almost completely to predation of Nile perch. Later, it was discovered that increased eutrophication

*Common carp (*Cyprinus carpio*). Illustration by Duane Raver, U.S. Fish and Wildlife Service.*

through pollution and over-exploitation may have also played a role (Pitcher and Hart 1995).

ASSESSING THE THREAT OF IAS ON FRESHWATER ECOSYSTEMS

An IAS threats assessment helps rank the relative significance of any individual IAS and helps prioritize what to do once an IAS has invaded or is deemed to represent an imminent threat of invading a particular area of interest. A threats assessment is also a vital precursor to setting realistic conservation goals and developing effective and scale-appropriate threat abatement strategies.

The following four categories prove useful in ranking the relative importance of the threat posed by an IAS. Wittenberg and Crock (2001) use a version of these categories to assign a numeric score to each IAS for a particular area of interest. They recommend assigning high scores for IAS that meet more than one criteria in any category:

What is the current and potential extent of the IAS?

The greater the geographical range, abundance or density, and variety of habitats that the species invades, the greater its potential for damage. Under this category, priorities are assigned to species in order to: prevent the establishment of new IAS; eliminate small, rapidly growing infestations; prevent large infestations from expanding; and reduce or eliminate large infestations. Assigning priorities in the following sequence may prove useful here:

- Species not yet on the site but which are present and rapidly establishing nearby.
- Species present on the site as new populations or outliers of larger infestations, especially if they are expanding rapidly.
- Species present on the site in large infestations that continue to expand.
- Species present on the site in large infestations, which are not expanding.

Reality is also a critical factor here. For example, practitioners should also identify certain species or infestations that cannot be controlled with available resources.

What is the current and potential effect of the IAS?

IAS causing the greatest degree of harm to native species populations, communities, and ecosystems may constitute the most severe problems, especially if they affect conservation targets, rare or keystone species, communities, or ecosystem processes. In general, IAS that have strong effects on ecosystem processes or parameters will likely have strong effects on community composition and structure and native species populations. Priorities under this category should be aligned with the management goals for the particular conservation area. The following sequence for assigning priorities in this category may prove useful:

- IAS that alter ecosystem processes, such as sedimentation, nutrient cycling, hydrologic regime, or other relative ecosystem processes. These species change the rules of the game, often altering conditions so radically that few native plants and animals can survive.

- IAS that kill, parasitize, hybridize, or out-compete natives and dominate otherwise undisturbed native communities.
- IAS that:
  - prevent or depress recruitment or regeneration of native species; or
  - reduce or eliminate resources, such as food, cover, spawning sites, used by native species; or
  - promote populations of IAS by providing them with resources otherwise unavailable in the area; or
  - significantly increase seed distribution of invasive alien plants or enhance invasive alien plants in some other way.
- IAS that overtake and exclude native species following natural disturbances such as floods, droughts, or hurricanes, thereby altering natural succession or impeding restoration of natural communities. Note that species of this type should be assigned higher priority in areas subject to repeated disturbances.

What is the value of the area that the IAS is currently or may potentially infest?

IAS with a high potential for further spread have the potential to cause greater damage, especially if they are deemed likely to spread to distant but currently uninfested portions of the areas of interest. The questions in this category address the likelihood that the IAS under evaluation will spread to new areas within the region or increase in abundance in areas already occupied, and how quickly it could do so if not controlled. The following sequence for assigning priorities in this category may prove useful:

- Infestations that occur in areas associated with or adjacent to areas containing conservation targets.
- Infestations that occur in less highly valued areas. For example, areas already badly infested with other invasive alien species may be given low priority.

How difficult is it to control the IAS?

IAS that are more difficult to control or prevent from spreading have the potential to cause greater damage. The following sequence for assigning priorities in this category may help evaluate the ease of control, accessibility of invaded sites, and the likelihood that known control measures will cause collateral damage to native species:

- IAS likely to be controlled or eradicated with available technology and resources and which desirable native species will replace with little further input.
- IAS likely to be controlled but will not be replaced by desirable natives without an active restoration program requiring substantial resources.
- IAS difficult to control with available technology and resources and/or whose control will likely result in substantial damage to other, desirable species and/or enhance other IAS.
- IAS unlikely to be controlled with available technology and resources.
- Finally, IAS whose populations are decreasing or those that colonize only disturbed areas and do not move into (relatively) undisturbed habitats or affect recovery from the disturbance can be assigned the lowest priorities.

IAS often take a long time to establish themselves in a new ecosystem before the population spreads explosively. Figure 4-28 represents an IAS invasion. A species might have several populations at different phases of infestation within a large area. This figure illustrates the advantages of prevention and early detection strategies. Some species reach a threshold abundance above which they become irreversibly established (i.e., impossible to eradicate completely) within just a few years, whereas other species may require many decades or even centuries to reach this threshold. Species for which there are no successful control methods may cross this threshold with smaller patches or fewer individuals than those that respond well to management actions.

As illustrated in Figure 4-27, once an IAS takes off and is successfully reproducing, it will be almost impossible to eradicate. As a rule, the later the response react to an invasion, the more time, money, and effort will be spent attempting to control the invasion with a diminishing hope of ever truly eradicating the species from a site. In order to prevent repeated invasions, it may be necessary to eliminate one or more pathways of entry. If this is not done, control efforts will be undone by later re-invasions. For IAS that are not yet at a site, eliminating potential

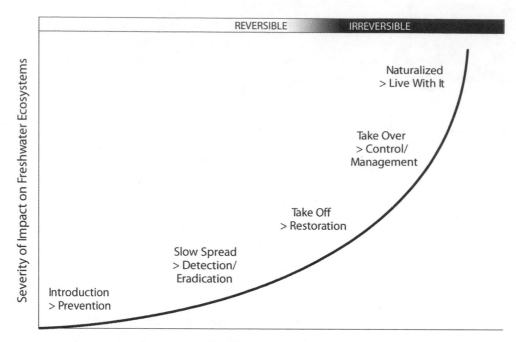

FIGURE 4-28. Lifecycle of an Invasive Alien Species Infestation with Associated Threat Abatement Strategies by Infestation Phase
Source: Modified from The Invasive Species Initiative Charter, The Nature Conservancy, 2002.

pathways of entry is the most effective and efficient threat abatement strategy.

Although guidelines for assessing the effect of invasive alien animals are limited, a number of useful resources exist for addressing invasive alien plants. For more information about such approaches, the following resources are recommended:

- Randall *et al.* (2003) have recently developed a specific threat assessment for invasive plants. It can be found at: http://tncweeds.ucdavis.edu/
- Handbook for Ranking Exotic Plants for Management and Control (Hiebert, R.D. and Stubbendieck, J. (1993) Denver, CO)
- Australia's National Weeds Strategy: http://www.weeds.org.au/nws.htm

Strategies for Mitigating/Abating the Effect of Invasive Alien Freshwater Species on Freshwater Ecosystems

Strategies for abating or mitigating the effect of IAS on freshwater ecosystems fall into one of four categories:

- Prevention
- Early detection and eradication
- Control
- Mitigation

Early detection and eradication, control, and mitigation are often considered collectively as management-based approaches. Figure 4-28 summarizes when to employ strategies in each category with regards to the various stages of an IAS infestation.

These categories are equally relevant when considering technical, legal and institutional, or community-based approaches to threat abatement associated with IAS.

TECHNICAL STRATEGIES

Prevention

"An ounce of prevention is worth a pound of cure" summarizes the most enduring strategy for abating threats from IAS. Once an introduced species has become established, particularly if it has become invasive, it becomes extremely difficult to eradicate. Most

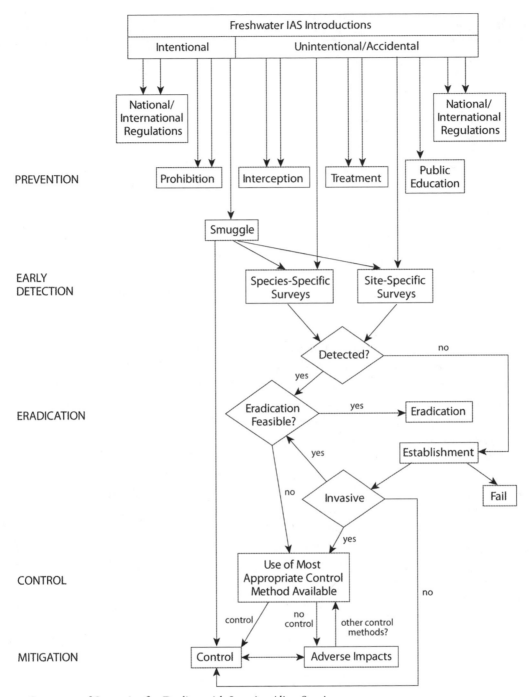

FIGURE 4-29. Summary of Strategies for Dealing with Invasive Alien Species
Source: Modified from Wittenberg and Crock, 2001.

attempts to eradicate such species fail, and even failed attempts are often expensive. Once eradication has failed, society is faced with damage and management costs in perpetuity (Wittenberg and Crock 2001).

Human activities are the primary means for the tremendous increase of species moving from one part of the world to another, especially through trade, travel, tourism, and transport. The great increase in the importation of IAS for economic or aesthetic reasons often leads to more species invading native ecosystems, with disastrous results. IAS can enter a site through either intentional or accidental introductions.

Intentional introductions are the result of a deliberate action to relocate an organism. The predominant pathways for intentional introductions of freshwater IAS include:

- Horticultural trade (e.g., tamarisk, purple loosestrife, water chestnut, and Russian olive);
- Intentional fisheries releases to expand recreation fisheries (e.g., European brown trout);
- Bait bucket transfer of invasive alien forage fishes and crayfish combined with recent advance in technology enabling anglers to transport their live bait over greater distances;
- Pets released into the wild acquired from the aquarium trade (e.g., red-eared slider, carp, and bullfrog); and
- Escape from aquaculture pens (e.g., tilapia, Atlantic salmon).

Historically, few if any of the intentionally introduced plant and animal species were tested to determine their effect on native species and ecosystems.

Accidental introductions occur when species hitch a ride on humans, trade goods, or vehicles. The most critical pathways for freshwater IAS accidental introductions are listed here:

- **Ballast water of ships**
  Ballast water from just a single ship can contain hundreds of species. On average one tanker releases about 240 million organisms into the surrounding water on each voyage. Probably the most infamous introduction via ballast water is that of the zebra mussel into the Great Lakes in North America (Wittenberg and Crock 2001). At present, mid-ocean ballast water exchange remains the primary treatment option recommended for international ship traffic (Figure 4-29). In most parts of the world ballast water exchange occurs on a voluntary basis, but some countries are considering the possibility of a mandatory approach. Ballast water exchange at sea can prove difficult and do not necessarily result in the removal of all biota. Other options for treatment include filter systems at water intakes, irradiation using ultraviolet light, drinking water treatment methods, heat treatment with waste heat of the engines, and dumping ballast water into land-based plants used for sewage treatment. The cost of purging ballast water at sea or of

chemical or ultraviolet light treatment is not negligible, but it pales in comparison to the economic and ecosystem cost of such introductions.

- **Ballast water tank sediment**
  Although ballast water favors pelagic (open-water) species, the sediment carried by ballast water tanks favors ground-dwelling species. Ballast water can be exchanged during the voyage, but the sediment is not easily flushed out.

- **Hull fouling and hitchhiking**
  The greatest IAS risks are associated with boats or ships and machinery kept in ports or at docks for some time and then transferred to a new destination. Recreational boaters within the U.S., even kayakers and rafters, often unintentionally transfer species from one water body to another. Plant species may be wrapped around a boat's propeller, zebra mussels may be attached to the bottom of the boat, and fish bait carrying invasive species may cling to various surfaces. Please refer to the Stop Aquatic Hitchhikers web site (www.ProtectYour Waters.net) for strategies for dealing with hull fouling and hitchhiking.

Quite often after the initial introduction and colonization of an IAS, these species continue to expand their range and colonize new ecosystems. Some species undergo an explosive expansion of their range after barriers are removed or new pathways are opened by human activity even if the initial introduction happened a long time ago. Knowledge of these natural barriers is basic to containment programs.

Structures which link otherwise unconnected freshwater ecosystems are an important pathway for spreading freshwater compatible IAS into new watersheds. For example, the completion of the Welland Canal between Lake Ontario and Lake Erie, enabled the sea lamprey (*Petromyzon marinus*), to spread to other lakes and river systems. The opening of the Suez Canal initiated an influx of hundreds of Red Sea species into the Mediterranean Sea.

For more comprehensive information on pathways, please refer to the following resources:

- Gregory M. Ruiz and James T. Carlton, Editors, 2001. *Pathways of Invasion: Strategies for Management across Space and Time*. Island Press, Washington,

BOX 4-19. Release of Invasive Alien Fish by Aquarium Hobbyists

Each year, over 2000 species, representing nearly 150 million invasive alien freshwater and marine fishes, are imported into the U.S. for use in the aquarium trade. Unfortunately, some of these invasive alien fishes are released into the wild each year. Hobbyists may not be able to take their fish with them when they move, or they simply may lose interest in maintaining an aquarium. Fish may also be released if they outgrow the aquarium or if they appear to be in poor health.

*Midas cichlid (*Cichlasoma citrinellum*). Photograph courtesy of the Florida Fish and Wildlife Conservation Commission.*

Currently, approximately 185 different species of invasive alien fishes have been caught in open waters of the U.S., and 75 of these are known to have established breeding populations. Over half of these introductions are due to the release or escape of aquarium fishes. Because many of these fish are native to tropical regions of the world, their thermal requirements usually prevent them from surviving in temperate areas. In the U.S., therefore, most introduced fishes have become established in Florida, Texas, and the Southwest. Examples include a number of cichlids, such as the oscar, Jack Dempsey, jewelfish, convict cichlid, Midas cichlid, and spotted tilapia; and livebearers, such as swordtails, platies, and mollies, and armored catfishes. The goldfish, a native of China, is one of the few examples of a temperate aquarium species that now is established throughout the U.S..

Alternative means for disposing of unwanted pet fish that should be followed instead of release into freshwater ecosystems include:

- Return it to a local pet shop for resale or trade.
- Give it to another hobbyist, an aquarium in a professional office, a museum, a public aquarium, or zoological park.
- Donate it to a public institution, such as a school, nursing home, hospital, or prison.
- If these options are not available, rather than release fish into the wild, they should be euthanized. One option for tropical fish is exposure to very cold temperatures which act as a natural (and fatal) anesthetic.

Edited from the U.S. Department of the Interior Geological Survey Non-indigenous Aquatic Species website "Problems with the Release of Exotic Fish" at http://nas.er.usgs.gov/fishes/dont_rel.html.

DC. This is the symposium volume arising out of the November 1999 GISP conference on pathways.
- Washington Sea Grant Program, *Pathways of Aquatic Introduction: American Fisheries Society Position on Introductions of Aquatic Species.*
- ORTEP Association, The Netherlands, *Pathways of Introduction and the Ecological and Economic Impacts of Invasive Species.*

Exclusion methods based on pathways rather than on individual species provide the most efficient way to concentrate IAS prevention efforts at national ports of entry. Strategies related to prevention include:

- *Intercepting IAS through inspections and imposition of fines*

Accidental introductions are best addressed before export or upon arrival of imported goods. Inspection programs often catch numerous unintentional and intentional IAS introductions. Fees and confiscation associated with shipments containing banned species can help motivate compliance with such regulations. Obviously, implementation of this strategy requires not only relevant regulations but also adequate staffing at ports of entry. Also, requiring recreational boaters to use boat

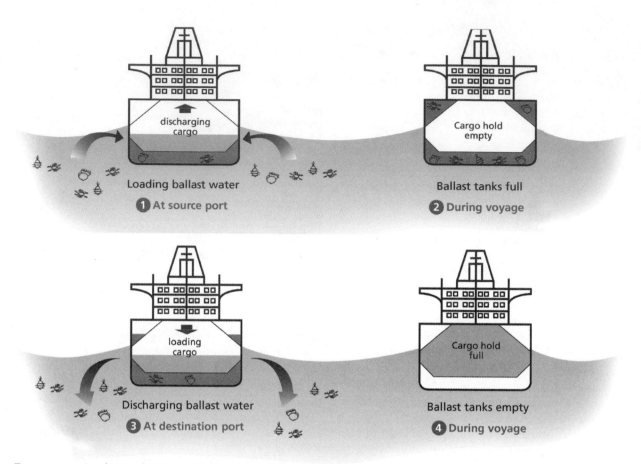

FIGURE 4-30. Loading and Release of Ballast Water from a Tanker.

Source: Figure courtesy of GloBallast, International Martime Organization, http://www.globallast.imo.org.

washing stations enroute to or from infested water bodies may help decrease the spread of hitchhiking IAS from one place to another.

- *Eliminating IAS through treating cont animated materials*

  If goods and their packaging material or holding containers are suspected to be contaminated with IAS, treatment can help eliminate this threat. Treatment may involve biocide applications (e.g. fumigation, pesticide application), water immersion, heat and cold treatment, pressure, or irradiation. As with the last strategy, implementation of this strategy also requires relevant regulations and adequate staffing at ports of entry.

- *Restricting IAS entry by prohibiting commodities suspected of contamination*

  Trade prohibitions related to particular high-risk products, source regions, or routes may prove nec-

essary in certain situations. Under the World Trade Organization—Sanitary and Phytosanitary Agreement (WTO SPS Agreement) member countries have the right to take sanitary and phytosanitary measures to the extent necessary to protect human, animal, and plant life or health provided these measures are based on scientific principles and are not maintained without sufficient scientific evidence (Wittenberg and Crock 2001).

- *Using education to reduce IAS introductions*

  Education is a key component of successful prevention and management methods for IAS. The public can be a considerable advocate in reducing IAS introductions through voluntary actions and in supporting preventative measures. The public as well as the companies concerned should perceive preventative measures as necessary aspects of travel and trade to care for the future commercial and natural environment. Education should focus on raising awareness of the reasons for the restrictions and regulatory actions, as well as explaining the environmental and economic risks associated with IAS invasions.

The following resources provide additional information on preventative strategies for freshwater IAS:

- 100th Meridian Initiative—A Strategic Approach to Prevent the Western Spread of Zebra Mussels and Other Aquatic Nuisance Species, U.S. Fish and Wildlife Service for the Western Regional Panel 100th Meridian Initiative. Cooperative effort between state, provincial, and federal agencies to prevent the westward spread of zebra mussels and other aquatic nuisance species in North America
- A Model Comprehensive State Management Plan for the Prevention and Control of Nonindigenous Aquatic Nuisance Species, Great Lakes Commission, January 1996
- Ballast Water Management, U.S. Coast Guard
- Exotic Policy: An International Joint Commission White Paper on Policies for the Prevention of the Invasion of the Great Lakes by Exotic Organisms, Eric Reeves, July 1999
- FICMNEW Pulling Together: National Goal 1—Effective Prevention, Part of FICMNEW's national strategy for invasive plant management
- Guide to Noxious Weed Prevention Practices (Word document), U.S. Department of Agriculture, Forest Service, Version 1, July 5, 2001
- How to Prevent the Spread of Noxious Weeds, Bureau of Land Management, Environmental Education
- IUCN Guidelines for the Prevention of Biodiversity Loss Caused by Alien Invasive Species, Prepared by the Species Survival Commission, Invasive Species Specialist Group. Approved February 2000.
- IPlants: Invasive Plants and the Nursery Industry—How should we prevent exotic plants from becoming invasive pests?, Meredith Hall, Undergraduate Senior Thesis in Environmental Studies, Brown University, Spring 2000
- Invasive Alien Species—How to Address One of the Greatest Threats to Biodiversity: A Toolkit of Best Prevention and Management Practices, CAB International on behalf of the Global Invasive Species Program, 2001
- Legislation, Regulation and Policy for the Prevention and Control of Nonindigenous Aquatic Nuisance Species: Model Guidance for Great lakes Jurisdictions, Approved by the Great Lakes Panel on Aquatic Nuisance Species, Prepared by: Great Lakes Commission
- Plan for the Prevention and Control of Nonindigenous Aquatic Nuisance Species in the Colorado River Basin, Draft plan for consideration by the Colorado River Fish and Wildlife Council, December 1998

Management

Once IAS have become established at a particular location, management-based approaches become most appropriate. Management-based approaches include early detection and eradication, control, and mitigation. Eradication is the most desirable, but often the most difficult approach. When eradication has failed and an IAS has become established at a particular site, control is the next best management option. Control strategies can be divided into containment, i.e., keeping species within a defined area, and control in a stricter sense, i.e., suppressing population levels of an IAS to below an acceptable threshold. If these three management approaches cannot be employed, or are not effective, the last option is mitigating the impact of the IAS on native organisms and ecosystems—i.e., find the best way in which to live with the IAS.

Early detection and eradication

Early detection of an IAS before it has had the opportunity to take hold within an ecosystem is crucial for successful eradication. A system of regular surveys to find newly established species is one of the best approaches for early detection. Those responsible for implementing the surveys need training in how to administer such tools, but may find a good source of information in groups using or familiar with the natural environment (e.g., ecotour operators, fishers, and the concerned public). Such surveys may focus on either searching for specific species across a conservation area or searching a particular conservation area or locations within a conservation area for IAS.

Frequency and timing of surveys are important. The potential range of newly arrived invaders needs to be considered along with the climate of the region. Some invaders may be difficult to detect in one season and easier in others. The design of any survey should take into consideration and make special notation of these factors. Records taken on data collection efforts should indicate the species found, their location, sampling date, and the action taken. In the case of most groups of IAS, voucher specimens should be collected and preserved. When local knowledge is not adequate to make an authoritative identification, material should be sent for specialist identification. Local and regional museums are a good starting point for advice on identification of invasives, but there are also specialized international services available. BioNET International is a global network for capacity building in taxonomy, and contact with your local network may help identify regional expertise (http://www.bionet-intl.org). The Expert Centre for Taxonomic Identification (ETI) maintains an internet database of taxonomists (http://www.eti.uva.nl/database/WTD.html). The Global Taxonomy Initiative recently started under the Convention on Biological Diversity will also be a valuable resource in this area in future.

Eradication can be a successful and cost-effective solution in response to early detected IAS. However, a careful analysis of the costs and likelihood of success must be made and adequate resources mobilized before implementation of any eradication effort. Successful eradication programs in the past have been based on mechanical control, e.g., hand-pulling of weeds or handpicking of snails; chemical control, e.g., using toxic baits against vertebrates; habitat management, e.g., restoration of an instream flow regime; and fishing out invasive fishes. For more information about these and other control methods, please see the information below beneath Control. Most eradication programs need to employ several different methods. Eradication should only be pursued with adequate funding and stakeholder commitment. The more rapid the response to a new invasion, the more likely it is that eradication will succeed.

For a detailed review of early detection and eradication methods please refer to: Global Invasive Species Programme's *The Invasive Alien Species-A Toolkit of Best Prevention and Management Practices.* 2001 http://www.cabi-bioscience.ch/wwwgisp/gtcsum.htm.

Control

Containment of IAS is a special form of control. The aim of containment is to restrict the spread of an IAS and to contain the population within a defined area. The population(s) of the IAS is then suppressed using a variety of methods along the border of the defined area of containment, individuals and colonies spreading beyond this are eradicated, and introductions into areas outside the defined containment area are prevented. The distinction between containment and eradication is not always clear-cut. Containment programs need clearly defined goals: barriers beyond which the IAS should not spread, habitats that are not to be colonized and invaded, etc. In order to establish these parameters, practitioners need a clear understanding of why the containment is being done in the first place (e.g., to protect particular areas or habitats from invasion, to allow time to mobilize other control or eradication measures, etc). An important component of a containment program is the ability to rapidly detect new infestations of the IAS both spreading from the margins of its distribution or in completely new areas, so that control measures can be implemented in as timely a manner as possible. These new infestations will initially be at very low densities so early detection will be challenging.

The chances for successful containment of IAS are relatively good for species living in freshwater habitats. For example, many river drainages are connected by artificial canals that enable IAS to spread between river systems. However, canals are rather small corridors IAS introductions through these pathways can be stopped by creating barriers, restricting traffic, and other measures.

Traditional control methods for IAS involve reducing the density and abundance of the species to below an acceptable threshold. The harm caused by the IAS under this threshold is considered acceptable with regard to damage to freshwater biodiversity. It is not always clear what this level should be set at in order to

Mechanical harvesting of hydrilla from Wakulla Springs, Florida. Photograph by J. Schardt/Florida DEP.

achieve the management objective but a good starting point is to examine how the IAS affects the natural range of variability of key ecological factors for the target freshwater species and ecosystems.

Suppression of the IAS population below the identified acceptable threshold can tip the competitive balance in favor of native species. The weakened state of the IAS allows native species to regain ground and even further decrease the abundance of the IAS. In rare cases this might even lead to extinction of the IAS (especially combined with habitat restoration efforts to support native species and put intact natural systems back in place), but this is clearly not the principle goal of control efforts.

Methods exist for controlling IAS include mechanical control, chemical control, biological control, and habitat management. Available literature and expertise should always be consulted to determine the most effective method for the particular species in question.

(1) Mechanical Control. Mechanical control involves directly removing individuals of the IAS either by hand tools or machinery. Winches and mechanical harvesters may be necessary for larger plants. In many cases mechanical control methods can control or even eradicate in small-scale infestations of IAS. The downside of the method is the fact that it is labor intensive. Most manual work is expensive and

has to be repeated for several years to remove all individuals.

The effectiveness of mechanical control methods will vary depending on the species. For example, plant parts of some species, left in contact with soil, may survive and grow, (e.g., Japanese knotweed (*Fallopia japonica*), an IAS in Europe and North America, will regenerate from rhizome fragments of less than 1 gram). If there is no information available about the plant's response to uprooting, some simple tests should be carried out to discover the effectiveness of various treatment options and options for the residues, e.g., composting or burning, etc.

Fishing can be considered a mechanical or manual control as well. Fishing IAS can be effective in keeping populations down to an acceptable level and can be a money source for other management activities in the area. This is a rare case where control does not involve costs, but earns money. It does, however, give rise to the concern that the invasive alien fish may become a valuable commodity that should be preserved in order to continue to generate this income and also increases the risk of providing the incentive for some individuals to spread the invasive alien fishes to new areas. Furthermore, there are many instances where recreational fishing will not reduce the target population sufficiently.

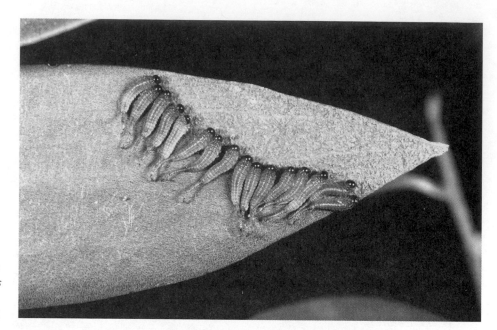

An example of biological control—day-old sawfly larvae devour a leaf of the invasive alien plant species melaleuca. Photograph by Jason Stanley/USDA ARS.

(2) Chemical Control. Chemical control involves the application of chemical herbicides and pesticides to IAS. Chemical control is often very effective as a short-term solution, and relatively inexpensive when com-pared to labor costs associated with mechanical control. Major drawbacks of chemical control are that repeated applications increase the cost associated with approach as well as its effect on native species. It may also provide a selective pressure enabling an IAS to develop resistance to these chemicals.

Herbicides, such as glyphosate and 2,4-D, have been used extensively around the world as a quick and effective means of controlling weeds in freshwater environments. However, since they are nonselective and more difficult to apply directly to the invasive alien plant in water, they are more likely to cause harm to native species. The fish poison rotenone is sometimes used to control fish IAS in ponds and other small water bodies. This method is efficient for the eradication of species, but its non-selective character means that effects will extend to other species and communities as well.

(3) Biological Control. Biological control involves the intentional use of populations of upper trophic level organisms (natural predators) to suppress IAS populations. When it is successful, biological control is highly cost effective and permanent.

Classical biological control typically involves the introduction of natural enemies from the original range of the IAS into new areas where the alien species is invasive. Since IAS are usually introduced into new environments without their natural enemies, they often grow and/or reproduce more vigorously in the ecosystem of introduction. Natural enemies for introduction are selected on the basis of their host specificity to minimize or eliminate any risk of effects on native species. The aim of introducing the particular IAS enemy is not the eradication of IAS, but to reduce its competitiveness with native species, hence reducing its density and its impact on the environment. Classical biological control against water weeds has been particularly promising and has produced several success stories. Conservation managers are coming to realize that classical biological control, if used following modern protocols such as the International Plant Protection Convention's *Code of Conduct for the Import and Release of Exotic Biological Control Agents*, provides a promising approach to solve many IAS problems.

However, others argue that this type of biological control is too risky since it leads to the introduction of another potentially problematic species. These critics often argue for the inclusion of non-self-sustaining methods. Non-self-sustaining methods include:

- Mass release of sterile males to reduce the number of offspring in the next generation;
- Inducing host resistance (plants) against IAS; and
- Inundative biological control using pathogens, parasitoids, or predators that will not reproduce and survive effectively in the ecosystem. Large-scale or mass releases of natural enemies are made to react quickly to control an IAS population.

(4) Habitat Management—Changing Abiotic Factors. Most invasions of IAS are caused or favored by human disturbance of freshwater ecosystems. In some cases, freshwater IAS control results from improving the health of the underlying ecosystem by restoring water quality, addressing eutrophication and pollution problems, or even restoring the natural flow regime of the ecosystem. Please refer to the other subchapters within this chapter for strategies that can be used to abate the threat of human land and water use and management.

Mitigation

If eradication, containment, and control are not options or have failed in managing an IAS, the last resort is to find a way to live with this species and mitigate impacts on freshwater biodiversity. Mitigation as used in this context differs from containment and control in that the activity undertaken does not directly affect the IAS in question but rather focuses on alleviating the affect of the IAS on native species and their ecosystem. At its simplest and perhaps most extreme form it could mean the translocation of a viable population of the endangered species to an ecosystem where the IAS of concern does not occur or, in the case of a rehabilitated system, no longer occurs.

LEGAL AND INSTITUTIONAL STRATEGIES

Effective prevention and management requires not only national legal frameworks but also often concerted bilateral, regional, or global action based on common objectives and jointly agreed international standards. Currently, more than 50 global and multilateral "soft" law instruments (agreements, codes of conduct, and technical guidance documents) exist that deal with IAS. They cover terrestrial, marine, freshwater, wetlands, and coastal ecosystems, as well as processes and pathways that generate introductions. IUCN (2000) provides a summary of these international instruments and is a useful resource for more

---

Box 4-20. A Success Story: Sea Lamprey Control in the Great Lakes

The Great Lakes are a valuable resource shared by Canada and the United States. Over 40 million people depend on the Great Lakes to provide food, drinking water, and recreation. The fishery alone generates up to $4 billion for the region annually, offering recreational angling opportunities and providing 75,000 jobs. The health of the Great Lakes fishery is under constant threat from habitat loss, pollution, and IAS, including sea lampreys.

Sea lampreys are primitive migratory fish native to the Atlantic Ocean. In the Great Lakes they have no commercial value and fish do not normally feed on them. Lacking jaws, their round mouths form a sucking disc filled with sharp, horn-shaped teeth that surround a rasping tongue. They attach to fish with their suction mouth and teeth and use their tongue to rasp through a fish's scales and skin so they can feed on its blood and body fluids. A single sea lamprey will destroy up to 40 lb. (18 kg.) of fish during its adult lifetime. Sea lampreys are so destructive that, under some conditions, only 1 out of 7 fish attacked will survive. This contributed significantly to the collapse of the Great Lakes lake trout fishery: annual harvests in Lake Huron and Lake Superior declined from 15 million pounds to 300,000 pounds by the 1960s.

Sea lampreys entered the Great Lakes from the Atlantic Ocean through shipping canals and were first observed in Lake Ontario in the 1830's. Niagara Falls acted as a natural barrier preventing sea lamprey movement to Lakes Erie, Huron, Michigan, and Superior. However, when the Welland Canal was deepened in 1919, sea lampreys gained access to the rest of the Great Lakes. By 1938, they had invaded all of the Great Lakes. In

(continues)

Box 4-20. *Continued*

1955, the governments of the United States and Canada created the Great Lakes Fishery Commission to control sea lampreys, coordinate research and improve the fishery. The control program uses several techniques to attack sea lampreys during different stages of its life cycle. Adult sea lampreys swim upstream to spawn and then die. Fertilized eggs hatch into small larvae which burrow into stream bottoms and feed on debris and algae for an average 3 to 6 years before they transform into a parasitic adult. The adults migrate into the Great Lakes where they spend 12 to 20 months feeding on fish. The complete life cycle, from egg to adult, takes an average of 5 to 8 years to complete.

Sea lamprey mouth. Photograph courtesy of the Great Lakes Sea Grant Network Exotic Species Graphics Library.

Sea lamprey control in the Great Lakes has been tremendously successful. Ongoing control efforts have resulted in a 90% reduction of sea lamprey populations in most areas, creating a healthy environment for fish survival and spawning. Although it is impossible to completely rid the Great Lakes of sea lampreys, through continued cooperation and support, their populations can be managed at levels that lessen the impact to the Great Lakes aquatic communities. Currently the control program includes four strategies:

- *Lampricide:* 3-trifluoromethyl-4-nitrophenol (TFM) kills sea lamprey larvae in streams with a limited effect on other freshwater species. TFM treatment at regular intervals occurs across about 175 Great Lakes streams. Despite the success of TFM, it is a costly control method and the Great Lakes Fishery Commission prefers to reduce its use.

- *Barriers:* Barriers now block the upstream migration of spawning sea lampreys but allow other fish to pass with minimal disruption. Newer designs include velocity barriers that take advantage of the lampreys' poor swimming ability, electrical barriers that repel sea lampreys during the spawning run without risk to other fish or animals, and adjustable-crest barriers which can be inflated during the spawning run and then deflated to allow other fish to pass during the rest of the year.

- *The Sterile-Male-Release-Technique:* Each year male sea lampreys are collected and sterilized. When they are released back into streams the sterile males compete with normal males for spawning females. Spawning sea lampreys and sterile males die after the spawning run. Assessment has indicated that fewer sea lamprey eggs hatch in streams where this technique is used.

Sea lampreys attached to a lake trout. Photograph courtesy of the U.S. Fish and Wildlife Service.

- *Trapping:* Sea lamprey traps operate at various locations throughout the Great Lakes, often in association with barriers. Traps are designed to catch lampreys as they travel upstream to spawn.

For more information about sea lampreys and available learning resources, please visit the Great Lakes Fishery Commission's website at www.glfc.org.

detailed information on legal issues relating to IAS. International legal instruments are often, though not always, fairly general in character. National legislation and regulations are necessary to operationalize these instruments within individual countries.

Nations that have legislation relevant to abating and mitigating IAS threats have developed these policies across numerous government sectors and over a long time period. As a result, national policies are often fragmented, contain inconsistencies in terminology, and may be difficult to enforce. Where possible, national frameworks should be established, streamlined or strengthened to:

- harmonize objectives and scope,
- standardize terminology,
- implement measures to prevent unwanted introductions,
- support mechanisms for early warning systems,
- provide management measures, including the restoration of native biodiversity, and
- promote compliance and accountability (Wittenberg and Crock 2001).

U.S. institutions and legal authorities

The following summary of relevant U.S. federal policy regarding, and agencies with significant roles for dealing with, IAS is modified from Corn *et al.* 1999, *Harmful Alien Species: Issues for Congress.* Please visit http://laws.fws.gov/lawsdigest/indx.html for information on relevant state level agencies and policies. U.S. federal law concerning freshwater IAS is highly fragmented. No laws focus on the broad problems of IAS, their interception, prevention, and control across a variety of industries and habitats. Some laws, though not directly addressed at IAS control or prevention, have effects that may limit such introductions. Below is a brief overview of existing laws, presented in chronological order of enactment, which affect IAS introduction, prevention, and control. All of the laws presented below can also be found at: http://laws.fws.gov/lawsdigest/indx.html

Lacey Act

Originally enacted in 1900, the Lacey Act, as amended in 1998, makes it illegal to import, export, sell, receive, acquire, or purchase fish, wildlife, or plants taken, possessed, transported, or sold in violation of U.S. or tribal law. In addition, the Lacey Act makes it unlawful to engage in interstate or foreign commerce involving any fish, wildlife, or plant material taken, possessed, transported, or sold in violation of state or foreign law. Specific provisions authorize the federal government to prescribe requirements and issue permits for importing of wild animals and birds under humane and healthful conditions. This law may be useful in regulating some instances of IAS introduction, if only indirectly.

The Animal Damage Control Act

The Animal Damage Control Act, originally enacted in 1931, is the primary statute under which the Animal and Plant Health Inspection Service (APHIS) operates its Wildlife Services (WS) program. The Animal Damage Control Act gives APHIS the authority to control wildlife damage on federal, state, or private land and address damage problems caused by IAS such as nutria, blackbirds, European starlings, and monk parakeets. In 1991, Congress amended the Animal Damage Control Act specifically to add the brown tree snake to the list of animals that the WS program monitors and controls.

National Environmental Policy Act (NEPA)

NEPA requires that federal government agencies consider the environmental effects of their actions. The primary mechanism to achieve this end is the preparation of environmental impact statements (EISs) for major federal actions affecting the environment. Agencies are expected not only to prepare EISs, but also to comment on the EISs prepared by other agencies. This law could apply to introductions of IAS if a federal action might affect the risk of introducing of IAS and thereby have a significant impact on the environment.

If NEPA is triggered, the opportunity for significant analysis of the proposed action through an EIS is great. The analysis may result in modification or abandonment of some actions or alternatives due to a consideration of the effects of the action(s) on IAS introductions and the effect of the IAS introduction on the environment.

Endangered Species Act (ESA)

The ESA offers strong protection for species that are rare or at risk of extinction. These protections may create a vehicle for IAS regulation. ESA could prevent a federal agency from introducing an IAS that could harm endangered or threatened species. Such an introduction would trigger consultation with the U.S. Fish and Wildlife Service (FWS) or National Marine Fisheries Service (NMFS) to determine whether the introduction (or action leading to introduction) would tend to jeopardize the continued existence of the rare or at risk species. ESA could also require the issuance of an incidental take permit if the actions of another entity or even a private citizen in relation to an IAS introduction could result in the death of a listed species. For example, in the Pacific Northwest, the threat to resident salmon species protected under ESA is a major argument being used against the introduction or expansion of Atlantic salmon aquaculture.

Nonindigenous Aquatic Nuisance Prevention and Control Act of 1990 (NANPCA)

NANPCA established a federal program to prevent the introduction of and to control the spread of aquatic IAS and the brown tree snake. The USFWS, the Coast Guard, the EPA, the U.S. Army Corps of Engineers, and the National Oceanic and Atmospheric Administration share responsibilities for implementation, acting cooperatively as members of an Aquatic Nuisance Species Task Force (ANSTF) to develop a program for protection, monitoring, control, and research. The ANSTF conducts studies and reports to Congress: (1) to identify areas where ballast water exchange does not pose an environmental threat; (2) to assess whether aquatic IAS threaten the ecological characteristics and economic uses of U.S. waters other than the Great Lakes; (3) to determine the need for controls on vessels entering U.S. waters other than the Great Lakes; and (4) to identify and evaluate approaches for reducing the risk of negative impacts associated with intentional introduction of aquatic IAS. For more information on the ANSTF and for links to aquatic IAS state management plans, please refer to: http://anstaskforce.gov/.

Under NANPCA, state governors are authorized to submit: (1) comprehensive aquatic IAS management plans to the ANSTF for approval which identify areas or activities for which technical and financial assistance is needed; and (2) public facility management plans to the Assistant Secretary of the Army (Civil Works) for approval identifying public facilities for which technical and financial assistance is needed. Grants are authorized to states for implementing approved management plans, with a maximum federal share of 75% of the cost of each comprehensive management plan and 50% of each public facility management plan.

The NANPCA directs the Coast Guard to issue regulations to prevent the introduction and spread of aquatic IAS into the Great Lakes through the ballast water of vessels, setting civil and criminal penalties for violation of these regulations. It also encourages the Secretary of Transportation, through the International Maritime Organization, to negotiate with foreign countries on the prevention and control of the unintentional introduction of aquatic IAS. In addition, NANPCA directs the U.S. Army Corps of Engineers to: (1) develop a program of research and technology for the environmentally sound control of zebra mussels in and around public facilities; and (2) make available information on the control methods.

Alien Species Prevention and Enforcement Act (ASPEA)

ASPEA (39 U.S.C. 3015; 106 Stat. 1774) makes it illegal to ship certain plants and animals through the mail, including those implied through a number of the laws indicated above. However, ASPEA appears to do very little to prevent the introduction of invasive alien species especially if the sender is unaware of the inclusion of the items to be shipped under the prohibitions of the above laws.

Executive Order 13112

Executive Order 13112 on Invasive Species, signed by President Clinton on February 3, 1999, seeks to prevent the introduction of IAS and provide for their control and minimize their impacts through better coordination of federal agency efforts under a National Invasive Species Management Plan to be developed by an interagency Invasive Species Council. This law directs all federal agencies to address IAS concerns as well as refrain from actions likely to increase invasive alien species problems. The Invasive Species Council, supported by an advisory committee, is also to develop recommendations for international cooperation, promote a network to document and monitor IAS impacts, and encourage development of an information-sharing system on IAS.

Agency Responsibilities

The various U.S. agencies have responsibilities regarding IAS. In some cases (e.g., APHIS), IAS account for a substantial portion of the agency's workload; in others (e.g., Coast Guard), IAS are a minor part of the agency's responsibilities:

Agencies and programs within the U.S. Department of Agriculture (USDA)

- **Agricultural Research Service (ARS).** ARS provides scientific and technical support for other USDA agencies. Such support has focused on detection technology for ports of entry, systematics for rapid identification of IAS, and pesticide application technology. ARS conducts research on biologically based pest management programs at more than 40 locations, involving more than 200 researchers and expending more than $100 million annually. In addition, ARS helps monitor specific IAS (e.g., ground, aerial, and satellite monitoring of leafy spurge and other weed species).

- **Animal and Plant Health Inspection Service (APHIS).** Through an agriculture quarantine inspection program conducted at 178 U.S. ports of entry, APHIS conducts pre-clearance activities, permit decisions, treatment efforts, detection surveys, and eradication efforts to prevent the introduction of specific IAS that would threaten U.S. agricultural production and natural ecosystems. Only APHIS has emergency authority to deal with an incipient alien species invasion. Domestically, APHIS cooperates with federal and state agencies as well as non-governmental organizations to detect, contain, and eradicate IAS before they become established.

- **Natural Resources Conservation Service (NRCS).** NRCS administers the Environmental Quality Incentive Program (EQIP), the Wildlife Habitat Improvement Program (WHIP), and Wetlands Reserve Program (WRP), which distribute monies to priority projects at the state level. IAS is one of the fundable topic areas. NRCS also provides natural resource conservation information provider to private landowners, including IAS information. In addition to providing plant guides for restoring native plant communities, the NRCS plants website (http://plants.usda.gov) provides access to state noxious weed lists, invasive plant lists, and links to key sources of weed species biology and management information.

- **Cooperative State Research, Education, and Extension Service (CSREES).** Although CSREES's National Research Initiative Competitive Grants Program does not currently identify specific topics with a research focus on IAS, several programs support research relevant to improving understanding of IAS. In addition, other CSREES initiatives fund research on best management practices for cost effective, environmentally safe control of IAS using biological, chemical, cultural, and mechanical practices as well as IAS management to maximize effective and cost effective pest control and exclusion.

- **Economic Research Service (ERS).** ERS has developed decision-making tools for comparing the consequences of invasive alien plant invasions with possible control costs. ERS considers both direct and indirect human costs of ecosystem disruptions as well as the costs and potential adverse consequences of alternative control methods.

- **Committee on Environment and Natural Resources Research (CENR).** CENR, a program of the National Science and Technology Council (NSTC), was established to advise and assist the NSTC in increasing the effectiveness and productivity of federal research and development efforts in the area of the environment and natural resources. CENR addresses science policy as well as research and development that cut across agency boundaries and provides a formal mechanism for interagency coordination relevant to domestic and international environmental and natural resources issues. CENR has identified IAS as a priority focus for integrated ecosystem research. CENR members

A plant pathologist from the USDA Agricultural Research Service researches treatments to stem the growth of invasive Eurasian watermilfoil. Photograph by Brian Prechtel/USDA ARS.

include representatives from the White House, NOAA, Smithsonian Institution, EPA, DOE, NASA, NSF, USDA, OMB, DOI, DHHS, DOT, DHUD, DOD, DOS, FEMA, Tennessee Valley Authority, Office of the Coordinator for Meteorology, Central Intelligence Agency, and Council on Environmental Quality.

- **Farm Service Agency (FSA).** In managing the Conservation Reserve Program, FSA requires all participants to control invasive alien plants, insects, and other undesirable species on enrolled lands.
- **Forest Service.** The Forest Service administers a number of cooperative programs that assist partnerships and encourage forest stewardship for non-industrial

forest landowners, including control of IAS The Forest Service conducts several research programs focused on IAS, including ecological studies to support restoration of sites after the control/eradication of invasive alien plants, such as kudzu in the southern United States; and yellow starthistle, spotted knapweed, and leafy spurge in Idaho. In addition, the Forest Service seeks to control and mitigate the impacts from invasive alien insects, such as the Asian longhorned beetle, gypsy moth, hemlock woolly adelgid, and browntail moth. The agency conducts disease research, such as to control butternut canker and to select trees genetically resistant to Dutch elm disease, pitch canker, and white pine blister rust.

- **Federal Interagency Committee for Management of Noxious and Exotic Weeds (FICMNEW)** is a committee composed of various agency representatives from the Departments of Agriculture, the Interior, Transportation, Defense, and Energy. FICMNEW fosters cooperative work on integrated ecological approaches to management of invasive alien plants on federal lands and provides technical assistance on private lands.

Agencies and programs within the U.S. Department of Commerce

- **National Oceanic and Atmospheric Administration (NOAA).** NOAA funds research in several program areas, including outreach to prevent and control invasions in marine environments, Chesapeake Bay ballast water management, and an economic evaluation of the costs of IAS. Under the National Invasive Species Act, NOAA funds research on such topics as identifying pathways of introduction, developing cost effective prevention methods, developing effective controls that minimize ecological damage, and identifying dispersal mechanisms of established IAS that might lead to safeguards and protocols to prevent or slow the spread of related IAS. NOAA's Great Lakes Environmental Research Lab has spent millions of dollars on research on IAS impacts in the Great Lakes, focusing on zebra mussels. In addition, NOAA laboratories conduct research on introduced oyster diseases and shrimp viruses. NOAA also funds graduate student fellowships related to aquatic IAS research.
- **National Sea Grant College Program.** NOAA has a major role in research regarding aquatic IAS under the Nonindigenous Aquatic Nuisance Presentation and Control Act. NOAA's Sea Grant program manages a competitive research grant program for all aspects of aquatic IAS issues, including for the development of ballast water management technology. This program funds research, education, and outreach to address threats from IAS, with specific research supported on the biology and life history of IAS; ecosystem effects of IAS, including socioeconomic analysis of costs and benefits; control and mitigation options; prevention of new introductions;

and reduction in the spread of established populations of IAS. Funding for this program, which includes out-reach, has averaged about $2.8 million per year.

Agencies and programs within the U.S. Department of Defense (DOD)

- **The Department of Defense (DOD)** has a number of programs for reducing the threat from IAS. These include the Navy's ballast water management policy; efforts to control brown tree snakes chemically in cooperation and partnership with the Armed Forces Pest Management Board and the National Wildlife Research Center; and through maintenance of a noxious and nuisance plant management information system. A DOD Invasive Species Management Program seeks to prevent the entry of IAS into the United States, to control IAS present on DOD installations, and to restore DOD lands using native plants.
- **Army Corps of Engineers (the Corps).** The Army Corps of Engineers supports an aquatic plant control research effort within an Aquatic Plant Management Program as well as a zebra mussel research effort within Zebra Mussel Operations Management. The Corps also supports broader DOD initiatives described above. The Corps had a number of control programs, including the Aquatic Plant Control Program, Zebra Mussel Program, and the Removal of Aquatic Growth Program. The Corps has a number of research programs focused on IAS. The Aquatic Plant Control Research Program (APCRP) has provided effective, economical and environmentally compatible technologies for identifying, assessing, and managing aquatic plant problems for over 30 years. The Zebra Mussel Program is the only federally authorized research program for zebra mussel control. It is also authorized to implement a 50% federal/50% local cost arrangement with state and local governments for managing aquatic invasive alien plants in waterways not under the control of the Corps or other federal agencies. In addition, the Corps is conducting a Chicago Channel Dispersal Barrier Study to determine effective measures to limit the dispersal of aquatic IAS.

Agencies and programs within the U.S. Department of the Interior

- **Bureau of Land Management (BLM).** BLM focuses its IAS efforts primarily on controlling invasive alien plants. BLM's Partners Against Weeds is an action plan to prevent and control the spread of noxious weeds on public lands. In addition, BLM has instituted a Communication and Environmental Education Plan to help prevent and control the spread of noxious weeds on public lands. BLM has adopted specific policies to address weed infestation, and BLM's Director has identified invasive weeds as a top priority for the agency. APHIS regulates IAS on BLM land under a Memorandum of Understanding between APHIS and BLM. BLM requires that plant IAS be used on its grazing lands only in situations where native species are not available in sufficient quantities or are incapable of maintaining or achieving properly functioning conditions and biological health.

- **Bureau of Reclamation (BOR).** The Bureau of Reclamation is responsible for programs that control IAS that infest water systems, including reservoirs, rivers, distribution canals, etc. Species such as zebra mussels, Chinese mitten crabs, hydrilla, and water hyacinth obstruct water flow, reduce recreational access, and can cause structural damage. BOR manages invasive alien species through its integrated pest management program through various reclamation-enabling statutes and directives.

- **Fish and Wildlife Service (FWS).** FWS efforts related to IAS focus on preventing the introductions and spread of IAS and, where feasible and warranted, to control those species that have become established. The Endangered Species Act authorizes FWS involvement if a proposed introduction of an IAS or other activity seems likely to harm a species protected under the ESA.

  FWS regulations concerning seized or forfeited organisms prohibit the release of any IAS into the wild. Such species may be returned to suitable habitat in (1) the country of export (if known) after consultation with and at the expense of the country of export, or (2) a country within the historic range of the species which is party to the Convention on International Trade in Endangered Species of Wild Fauna and Flora after consultation with and at the expense of such country.

  The Wild Bird Conservation Act: FWS regulates the management and importation of invasive alien birds, including any egg or offspring thereof, excluding domestic poultry, dead sport-hunted birds, dead museum specimens, dead scientific specimens, products manufactured from such birds, or birds in 10 taxonomic families specified in this law.

  FWS has multiple programs to address management and control of IAS. The FWS works with ANSTF and leads efforts to develop and implement cooperative plans to manage and control infestations of aquatic IAS across the country. The National Wildlife Refuge System has invasive species teams that review strategies and recommend potential pilot projects involving IAS. In addition, IAS issues are included within comprehensive conservation plans for refuge units. The FWS also has several habitat restoration programs that restore habitat degraded by IAS as part of their overall habitat restoration activities.

- **Geological Survey (USGS).** The Biological Resources Division of USGS focuses on researching factors influencing the invasion by alien species and the effects of IAS on ecosystem processes, native species, and landscape dynamics, especially on Department of the Interior lands. The program deals with the following elements: identification and reporting of new invasions and assessment of environmental risks; monitoring methods; determination of the effects of IAS and the susceptibility of habitats to invasions; control approaches and methods; and development of regional and national IAS information systems. Through the National Biological Information Infrastructure, USGS facilitates documentation, dissemination, and integration of IAS information. USGS currently focuses on a small number of highly invasive alien species in the Great Lakes and eastern waterways and wetlands, riparian ecosystems, and Hawaii as well as invasive alien plants on western rangelands. USGS also manages the national Nonindigenous Aquatic Nuisance Species Database as well as several regional databases (e.g., Hawaii, Colorado plateau, and northern prairie).

- **National Park Service (NPS).** NPS manages more than 83 million acres, and approximately 200 parks have identified IAS as an important resource management threat. NPS management policies prohibit the introduction of IAS to a few situations and require the use of an integrated pest management approach to remove or control invasive alien species on NPS units. As part of its regulation of fishing in park units, NPS prohibits the use of most bait fish (live or dead), except in specially designated waters in order to reduce the likelihood of the introduction or spread of IAS. Waters which may be so designated are limited to those where IAS are already established, where scientific data indicate that the introduction of additional numbers or types of IAS would not hurt populations of native species, and where park management plans do not call for elimination of IAS. The NPS has special regulations to minimize the potential for spreading zebra mussels and other aquatic IAS at the St. Croix National Scenic Riverway.

Agencies and programs within the U.S. Department of State

The Department of State engages in negotiations, international treaty activities, and regional and bilateral efforts related to IAS, such as participating in bilateral efforts with China to address the invasion of the Asian longhorned beetle, working with South Pacific countries to raise awareness of the need to control the spread of the brown tree snake, and negotiating with the International Maritime Organization to develop a treaty to address the introduction of IAS through ballast water. Efforts of the Department of State focus on safeguarding biodiversity values and reducing ecological impacts, reducing economic impacts, managing trade and other economic consequences of actions taken to control IAS, and reconciling the need to identify and restrict pathways of entry for IAS with the necessity of maintaining human commerce.

Agencies and programs within the U.S. Department of Transportation

Under the Nonindigenous Aquatic Nuisance Prevention and Control Act the Coast Guard is responsible for developing and implementing a ballast water management program to minimize the likelihood that IAS can be transported to the United States in the ballast water of long-distance ocean vessels, as described previously.

Agencies and programs of the U.S. Environmental Protection Agency (EPA)

EPA regulates IAS by establishing criteria for the issuance of permits to operate aquaculture projects. EPA requires that the applicant demonstrate to the satisfaction of the EPA Director that if the species to be cultivated in the aquaculture project is not native to the immediate geographical area, there will be minimal adverse effects on the native flora and fauna to the area, and the total commercial value of the introduced species is equal to or greater than that of the displaced or affected native flora and fauna.

EPA has authority under three statutes that can be used to control and manage IAS. The Clean Water Act permits EPA to treat IAS as point source and nonpoint source pollutants. Accordingly, the EPA could set discharge limits for point sources such as ballast water from ships.

EPA reviews all Environmental Impact Statements under NEPA. This review, conducted in EPA's regional offices, now includes an explicit consideration of the proposed action with regard to IAS.

EPA conducts research on the risks associated with IAS and monitors the extent of IAS spread by ecosystem type as part of EPA's research and development authority. EPA has a number of research and monitoring programs that can be modified to contribute to the overall assessment of IAS. Two examples are the Environmental Monitoring and Assessment Program (EMAP) and Regional Vulnerability (ReVA).

For more information about U.S. federal and state policies and agencies with responsibilities regarding IAS, please refer to:

- *National Management Plan: Meeting the Invasive Species Challenge,* National Invasive Species Council, January 18, 2001, http://invasivespecies.gov/council/nmp.shtml
- U.S. Congress, Office of Technology Assessment. 1993. Harmful Non-indigenous Species in the United States. OTAF-565. U.S. Government

Printing Office. Washington, DC. 391 pp. http://www.wws.princeton.edu/~ota/disk1/1993/9325_.html

- *The Paradox of United States Alien Species Law,* IUCN Country Report, Marc Miller, 11/8/1999
- List of Laws and Regulations (Federal and State): http://www.invasivespecies.gov/laws/main.shtml
- Various State Laws in each state: http://laws.fws.gov/lawsdigest/indx.html
- *Harmful Alien Species: Issues for Congress,* M. Lynne Corn, Eugene H. Buck, Jean Rawson, and Eric Fischer, Resources, Science and Industry Division, April 8, 1999
- *Noxious Weed Control Policy and Classification System,* Oregon Department of Agriculture, Noxious Weed Control Program, 2001
- NR-22. *Improved Cooperative Management of Invasive Species,* National Governors' Association
- *APHIS Weed Policy 2000–2002,* U.S. Department of Agriculture, Animal & Plant Health Inspection Service, Plant Protection and Quarantine
- *Draft Action Plan for the Noxious Weeds Program* (January 2002), Comments Open Until March 29, 2002
- U.S. Department of Agriculture, Animal and Plant Health Inspection Service, Plant Protection and Quarantine
- *Pacific Northwest Region Noxious Weed Policy & Strategic Plan,* U.S. Department of Agriculture, Forest Service, August 1999
- *Partners Against Weeds, An Action Plan for the Bureau of Land Management,* U.S. Department of Interior, Bureau of Land Management
- *Preserving Our Natural Heritage—A Strategic Plan for Managing Invasive Alien Plants on National Park Systems Land*
- *A Binational Canadian–U.S. Ballast Water Research Strategy,* Policy Position of the Great Lakes Panel on Aquatic Nuisance Species, February 1998
- *Analysis of Laws & Policies Concerning Exotic Invasions of the Great Lakes,* Office of Great Lakes, Michigan Department of Environmental Quality, March 15, 1999
- *Ballast Water Management Policy Statement,* Adopted by the Great Lakes Panel on Aquatic Nuisance Species, March 2001
- *Exotics and Public Policy in the Great Lakes,* The Results of a Workshop at the Biennial Great Lakes Water Quality Forum in Milwaukee, Wisconsin, September 23 and 26, 1999
- *Exotic Policy: An International Joint Commission White Paper on Policies for the Prevention of the Invasion of the Great Lakes by Exotic Organisms,* Eric Reeves, July 1999
- *Guidance for Information and Education Efforts for the Prevention and Control of Aquatic Nuisance Species in the Great Lakes,* Policy Position of the Great Lakes Panel on Aquatic Nuisance Species, June 1997
- *Report to Congress—Findings Conclusions, and Recommendations of the Intentional Introductions Policy Review,* Aquatic Nuisance Species (ANS) Task Force, March 1994
- *Research Guidance for the Prevention and Control of Nonindigenous Aquatic Nuisance Species in the Great Lakes,* Policy Position of the Great Lakes Panel on Aquatic Nuisance Species, December 1996
- *Draft Action Plan—National Early Warning and Rapid Response System For Invasive Plants in the United States* (March 15, 2002) (Word document)
- Federal Interagency Committee for the Management of Noxious and Exotic Weeds (FICMNEW)
- *FICMNEW's Pulling Together: National Goal 2—Effective Control,* Part of FICMNEW's national strategy for invasive plant management.

International institutions and legal authorities

Non-governmental organizations have been the prominent force in focusing international attention on the threats associated with IAS introductions. Between 1982 and 1988, the Scientific Committee on Problems of the Environment (SCOPE) engaged scientists and experts in an effort to document the nature of the IAS threat. The results of this effort appeared in a number of books including a synthesis entitled *Biological Invasions—A Global Perspective* (1989). This synthesis clearly established that IAS could harm ecosystem functioning and that they effect virtually all ecosystems due to the massive breakdown of global biogeographic barriers to migration. In 1996, the International Union for the Conservation of Nature (IUCN) developed and released the document Draft *IUCN Guidelines for the*

Prevention of Biodiversity Loss due to Biological Invasion. It focuses on recommendations for reducing the risks of biodiversity loss caused by IAS, as envisioned under article 8(h) of the Convention on Biological Diversity.

Based on recommendations from SCOPE and IUCN, the Global Invasive Species Programme (GISP) was established in 1997 with the mission of conserving biodiversity and sustaining human livelihoods by minimizing the spread and impact of IAS. GISP aims to achieve this mission by providing a global vision and by catalyzing efforts to implement this vision at all scales. GISP created the GISP Partnership Network comprised of scientific and technical experts on IAS issues from around the world. GISP stakeholders include governments, intergovernmental organizations, non-governmental organizations, academic institutions, and the private sector. Although GISP partners can be found throughout the world, its services are primarily intended to benefit developing countries and the institutions that support sustainable development.

As countries become more aware of the implications of IAS, they tend to look inward, and focus on protecting themselves. The GISP partnership-based initiatives encourage countries to recognize that they cannot solve this problem by working exclusively within their own borders. By their very definition, IAS are an international problem. GISP helps bring together governments and other institutions to share experience and cooperate in efforts to address national and regional problems.

GISP works in a similar manner with international organizations to prevent the isolated, sector-focused approaches to the IAS issue that can lead to duplicative efforts and ineffective policies. For example, the GISP Partnership Network enables governments, environmental groups, and trade industries to work together and engage in positive, constructive dialogue. Examples of services provided by the GISP Partnership Network include:

- Raising awareness of the IAS threat and potential solutions through relevant organizations and frameworks at national and international levels;
- Creating linkages among governments, between governments and the private sector, and across disciplines;
- Networking databases and providing a gateway for information on IAS issues and expertise;
- Designing and co-hosting workshops on strategic planning, priority setting, and the development of new and better tools to address the IAS threat;
- Summarizing scientific and technical information in order to make it readily available to policy makers, scientists, educators, and other audiences; and

Volunteers pull knapweed along the Salmon River, Idaho. Photograph by Jerry Asher/BLM.

TABLE 4-11. Summary of Major International and Continental Agreements with Provisions Pertaining to Invasive Alien Species

---

UN Convention on Biological Diversity (CBD) (1992), www.biodiv.org
Article 8 (h). Parties to "prevent the introduction of, control or eradicate those invasive alien species which threaten ecosystems, habitats, or species."

Cartegena Protocol on Biosafety to the CBD (Montreal 2000), www.biodiv.org
Protocol's objective is to contribute to ensuring adequate level of protection in the safe transfer, handling and use of living modified organisms resulting form modern biotechnology that may have adverse effects on the conservation and sustainable use of biological diversity.

United Nations Convention on the Law of the Sea (Montego Bay 1982), www.un.org/Depts/los/losconv1.html
Article 196. States to take all measures necessary to prevent, reduce and control the intentional or accidental introduction of species, alien or new, to a particular part of the marine environment, which may cause significant and harmful changes.

Convention on Wetlands of International Importance, especially as Waterfowl Habitat (Ramsar 1971), www.ramsar.org
COP 7 — Resolution VII.14 on Invasive Species and Wetlands

Convention on Migratory Species of Wild Animals (Bonn 1979), www.wcmc.org.uk/cms/
Range State Parties of Endangered Migratory Species (Annex 1) to prevent, reduce or control factors that are endangering or likely to further endanger the species, including invasive alien species. (Article III (4) (c)). Agreements for Annex II Migratory Species to provide for strict control of the introduction of, or control of already introduced invasive alien species detrimental to the migratory species (Article V (5) (e)).

Convention on the Law of Non-navigational Uses of International Watercourses (New York 1997), www.un.org
Watercourse States take all necessary measures to prevent the introduction of species, alien or new, into an international watercourse. (Article 22).

International Plant Protection Convention (Rome 1951, as amended 1997) www.fao.org/legal/treaties
Creates an international regime to prevent spread and introduction of pests of plants and plant products through the use of sanitary and phytosanitary measures by parties to this convention. Parties establish national plant protection organizations and agree to cooperate on information exchange and on the development of International Standards for Phytosanitary Measures.

World Trade Organisation (WTO) Agreement on the Application of Sanitary and Phytosanitary Measures (Marakesh 1995), www.wto.org/english/tratop_e/sps_e/sps_e.htm
A supplementary agreement to the WTO Agreement. Applicable to all sanitary and phytosanitary measures directly or indirectly affecting international trade.

International Health Regulations (Geneva 1982), www.who.int/emc/IHR/int_regs.html
To ensure maximum security against the international spread of diseases with a minimum of interference with world traffic. Regulations strengthen the use of epidemiological principles as applied internationally, to detect, reduce, or eliminate the sources from which infection spreads, to improve sanitation in and around ports and airports, to prevent the dissemination of vectors and to encourage epidemiological activities on the national level.

North American Free Trade Agreement (1982), www.sice.oas.org/tradee.asp#NAFTA
Each Party may adopt, maintain, or apply any sanitary or phytosanitary measure necessary for the protection of human, animal, plant life or health in its territory. (Article 712(1)). Each Party shall adapt any of its sanitary or phytosanitary measures relating to the introduction, establishment, or spread of an animal or plant pest or disease taking into account conditions relating to transportation and handling, between those areas. (Article 716).

North American Agreement on Environmental Cooperation (1993) www.cec.org
The Council of the Commission on Environmental Cooperation may develop recommendations regarding invasive alien species which may be harmful. (Article 10 (2) (h)).

IUCN Guidelines for the Prevention of Biodiversity Loss Caused by Alien Invasive Species (2000), www.iucn.org/themes/ssc/pubs/policy/invasivesEng.htm
Guidelines designed to increase awareness and understanding of the impact of invasive alien species. Provides guidance for the prevention of introduction, re-introduction, and control an eradication of invasive alien species.

Guidelines for the Control and Management of Ships' Ballast Water to Minimize the Transfer of Harmful Aquatic Organisms and Pathogens (International Maritime Organisation 1997), www.imo.org
Provides guidance and strategies to minimize the risk of unwanted organisms and pathogens from ballast water and sediment discharge. (Resolution A.868 (29)).

Code of Conduct for Responsible Fisheries (FAO 1995), www.fao.org/fi/agreem/codecond/ficonde.asp
Encourages legal and administrative framework to facilitate responsible aquaculture. Including pre-introduction discussion with neighboring nations when alien stocks are to be introduced into transboundary aquatic ecosystems. Harmful effects of alien and genetically altered stocks to be minimized especially where significant potential exists for spread into other nations beyond the country of origin. Adverse genetic and disease effects to wild stock from genetic improvement and alien species to be minimized

Code of Conduct for the import and release of exotic biological control agents (FAO 1995), www.fao.org
Aims to facilitate the safe import, export, and release of such agents by introducing procedures of an internationally acceptable level for all public and private entities involved, particularly where national legislation to regulate their use does not exist or is inadequate. Outlines specific responsibilities for authorities of an exporting country, which should ensure that relevant regulations of the importing country are followed in exports of biological control agents.

Preventing the Introduction of Invasive Alien Species (International Civil Aviation Organisation 1998), www.icao.int/icao/end/res/a32_9.htm
Resolution A-32-9. Urges all signatory nations to use their civil aviation authorities to assist in reducing the risk of introducing, through civil air transportation, potentially invasive species to areas outside their natural range. Requests the ICAO Council to work with other United Nations organizations to identify approaches that the ICAO might take in assisting to reduce the risk of introducing potential invasive species.

- Supporting partners in the design of projects and programs to minimize the spread and impact of IAS.

Table 4-11 provides a summary of these major international agreements with their relevant provisions for invasive alien species excerpted from the Global Strategy on Invasive Alien Species (2001).

In addition to these international laws, policies, and guidelines, a number of useful documents have been developed by international non-governmental organizations which contain recommendations for addressing invasive alien species globally:

- Invasive Alien Species—How to Address One of the Greatest Threats to Biodiversity: A Toolkit of Best Prevention and Management Practices, CAB International on behalf of the Global Invasive Species Program, 2001
- IUCN Policy Recommendations Papers for the Sixth Meeting of the Conference of the Parties to the Convention on Biological Diversity (COP6), April 7–19, 2002, The Hague, Netherlands
- Alien Species That Threaten Ecosystems, Habitats or Species: Recommendations, April 2002 (Word document)
- IUCN Guidelines for the Prevention of Biodiversity Loss caused by Alien Invasive Species (Word document)

COMMUNITY-BASED STRATEGIES

Public awareness combined with volunteer efforts is critically important for abating localized IAS threats. In freshwater ecosystems across the world, volunteers are the front line of defense against IAS as well as helping to prevent their spread. Volunteers greatly increase the number of eyes looking out for invaders, and since most volunteers live or recreate on the water body they monitor, they visit it often and know it well enough to spot anything unusual. Volunteer involvement also means increased public awareness about IAS, which means more people taking precautions to prevent the spread of these troublesome invaders. Volunteer monitoring should definitely be considered for nearly any IAS abatement effort.

—Authored by Kristine Ciruna

REFERENCES

Water Use and Management

DAMS

American Rivers. 2002a. Lessons learned from the Fort Edward Dam Removal. http://www.americanrivers. org/tableofcontents/lessonslearned.htm [23 Oct. 2002].

————. 2002b. Who is FERC? What is relicensing? http://www.americanrivers.org/hydropowertoolkit/ meetferc.htm [23 Oct. 2002].

————. 2002c. Toolkit—Hydropower Dam Reform. 14 Steps of the Relicensing Process. http://www. amrivers.org/damremovaltoolkit/damremovalcosts.htm [23 Oct. 2002].

————. 2002d. Removal of the Edwards Dam in Maine. http://www.amrivers.org/tableofcontents/ sskennebec.htm [27 Jan. 2003].

Amoros, C. 2001. Connectivity and biocomplexity in riverine floodplains. Presentation at 1st International Symposium on Landscape Dynamics of Riverine Corridors, Ascona, Switzerland, March 25–30, 2001. http://www.riverine-landscapes.ch/amoros.htm [28 Jan. 2003].

Arthington, A.H.. 1998. Comparative Evaluation of Environmental flow Assessment Techniques: Review of Holistic Methodologies. Land and Water Resources Research and Development Corporation Occasional Paper 26/98.

Bednarek, A.T. 2001. Undamming rivers: A review of the ecological impacts of dam removal. Environmental Management 27(6): 803–814.

Ben-David, M., T.A. Hanley, and D.M. Schell. 1998. Fertilization of terrestrial vegetation by spawning pacific salmon: the role of flooding and predator activity. Oikos 83:47–55.

Bissell, R.E. 2001. A participatory approach to strategic planning. Dams and development: A new framework for decision-making. Environment 43(7): 37–40.

Bolling, D.M. and River Network. (1994). How to Save a River: A Handbook for Citizen Action. Island Press, Washington, DC. 266 pp.

(BRec) U.S. Bureau of Reclamation. 1980. Safety Evaluation of Existing Dams. Government Printing Office, Washington, DC.

————. 2002. Managing Water in the American West. http://www.usbr.gov/main/what/who.html [17 Oct. 2002].

Brizga, S.O., A. Arthington, S.J. Choy, M.J. Kennard, S. Mackay, and B. Pusey. 2002 Benchmarking, a new 'top-down' methodology for assessing environmental flows in Australian rivers. Environmental Flows 2002: 4th Ecohydraulics Symposium, Cape Town, South Africa, 3–8 Mar 2002. (World Meeting Number 000 5997).

Chao, B.E. 1991. Man, water and a global sea level. EOS, Transactions of the American Geophysical Union 72: 492.

————. 1995. Anthropogenic impact on global geodynamics due to reservoir water impoundment. Geophysical Research Letters 22: 3529–3532.

(CFRTAC) Clark Fork River Technical Assistance Committee. 2003. Site History. About the Milltown Reservoir Site. http://www.clarkforkoptions.org/SiteHistory.asp [29 Jan. 2003].

Chesapeake Bay Program. 2002. Passage Restoration website. http://www.chesapeakebay.net/fishpass.htm [13 Oct. 2002].

Collier, M., R.H. Webb, and J.C. Schmiudt. 1996. Dams and Rivers. A Primer on the Downstream Effects of Dams. U.S. Geological Survey Circular 1126. U.S. Geological Survey, Denver, CO. 94 pp.

Collier, M., R.H. Webb, and E.D. Andrews. 1997. Experimental flooding in the Grand Canyon. Scientific American 276:82–89.

Counihan, T.D., A.T. Miller, M.G. Mesa, and M.J. Parsley. 1998. The effects of dissolved gas supersaturation on white sturgeon larvae. Transactions of the American Fisheries Society 127(2): 316–322.

Curry, R.A., J. Gehrels, D.L. Noakes, and R. Swainson. 1994. Effects of river fluctuations on groundwater discharge through brook trout, Salvelinus fontinalis, spawning and incubation habitats. Hydrobiologia 277: 121–134.

Décamps, H. 1984. Biology of regulated rivers in France. *In*, Lillehammer, A. and S.J. Saltveit (ed). Regulated Rivers. Oslo University Press, Oslo, Norway.

Décamps, H., M. Fortune, F. Gazelle, and G. Pautou. 1988. Historical influence of man on the riparian dynamics of a fluvial landscape. Landscape Ecology 1: 163–173.

Delaney, R.L. and M.R. Craig. 1997. Longitudinal Changes in Mississippi River Floodplain Structure. USGS Project Status Reports 97–02. http://www.umesc.usgs.gov/reports_publications/psrs/psr_1997_02.html [28 Jan. 2003].

(DSE) Deutsche Stiftung fur internationale Entwicklung. 1998. Partnership for Transboundary Water Management—an Area of Action for Policy Dialogue. Annual Report 1998. http://www.dse.de/aktuell/jb98ef.htm [20 Oct. 2002].

Dister, E., D. Goemer, P. Obrdlik, P. Petermann, and E. Schneider. 1990. Water management and ecological perspectives of the Upper Rhine's floodplains. Regulated Rivers 5: 1–15

Dooley, J.H., and K.M. Paulson. 2003. Engineered Large Woody Debris, for Aquatic, riparian and Upland Habitats. http://www.elwdsystems.com/pdf/dooley_paulson.pdf [30 Jan 2003].

Dudgeon, D. 2000. Large-scale hydrological changes in tropical Asia: Prospects for riverine biodiversity. BioScience 50(9) 793–806.

Echeverria, J.D., P. Barrow, and R. Roos-Collins. 1989. Rivers at Risk: The Concerned Citizen's Guide to Hydropower. Island Press, Washington, DC. 217 pp.

Eltson, R., J. Colt, P. Frelier, M. Mayberr, and W. Maslen. 1997. Differential diagnosis of gas emboli in the gills of steelhead and other salmonid fish. Journal of Aquatic Animal Health 9(4): 258–264.

Endangered Species Coalition. 2001. Testimony of David S. Wilcove, Senior Ecologist, Before the Fisheries, Wildlife and Water Subcommittee of the Senate Environment and Public Works Committee, May 9, 2001. http://www.stopextinction.org/News/News.cfm?ID=74&c=13 [24 Oct. 2002].

(FERC) Federal Energy Regulatory Commission. 2002a. FERC Homepage. http://www.ferc.fed.us/About/about.htm [13 Sept 2002].

———. 2002b. Hydropower. http://www.ferc.gov/hydro/docs/waterpwr.htm [15 Oct. 2002].

Flavin, C., H. French, G. Gardner, S. Dunn, R. Engleman, B. Halweil, L. Mastny, A.P. McGinn, D. Nierenberg, M. Renner, and L. Starke. 2002. State of the World 2002. The Worldwatch Institute, Washington, DC. 265 pp.

Flecker, A.S. 1997. Habitat modification by tropical fish: environmental heterogeneity and the variability of interaction strength. Journal of the North American Benthological Society 16:286–295.

Freeman, M.C., C.M. Pringle, E.A. Greathouse, and B.J. Freeman. *In press.* Ecosystem-level consequences of migratory faunal depletion caused by dams. Transactions of American Fisheries Society.

Freeman, R. 2002. Harnessing the restoration potential of artificial floods. Conservation in Practice 3(2): 34–38.

Friends of the River Narmada. 2002. Sardar Sarovar Project. http://www.narmada.org/index.html [19 Oct. 2002].

Galay, V.J. 1983. Causes of river bed degradation. Water Resources Research 19: 1057–1090.

Glase, J.D. 1994 Evaluation of Artificially Constructed Side Channels as Habitat for Salmonids in the Trinity River, Northern California, 1991–1993. Progress Report. USFWS Trinity River Restoration Program. Weaverville, CA. 55 pp. Text website http://www.krisweb.com/biblio/regional/klamath_trinity/glaseside.pdf [14 Oct. 2002].

Glasser, S.P. 2000. Hydromodifications-dams, diversions, return flows and other alterations of natural water flows, In G.F. Dissmeyer (ed.). Drinking Water from Forests and Grasslands. A Synthesis of the Scientific Literature. U.S. Depart of Agriculture, Forest Service, Southern Research Station, Ashville, NC. General Technical Report SRS-39. 246 pp.

Gleick, P. H. 2000. The World's Water. 2000–2001. The Biennial Report on Freshwater Resources. Island Press, Washington, DC. 313 pp.

Golz, E. 1994. Bed degradation: nature causes, countermeasures. Water Science and Technology 29: 325–333

Gosse, J.P. 1963. Le milieu aquatique et l'écologie des poisson dans la région de Yangambi'. Ann. Mus. R. Afr. Cent. Zoo 116:113–270.

Haeuber, R.A. and W.K. Michener. 1998. Policy implications of recent natural and managed floods. BioScience 48(9): 765–772.

Hall, C.A.S. 1972. Migration and metabolism in a temperate stream ecosystem. Ecology 53:585–604.

Haynes, H.B.N. 1983. Groundwater and stream ecology. Hydrobiologia 100:93–99.

Hart, D.D, T.E. Johnson, K.L. Bushaw-Newton, R.J. Horwitz, A.T. Bednarek, D.F. Charles, D.A. Kreeger, and D.J. Velinsky. 2002. Dam Removal: challenges and opportunities for ecological research and river restoration. BioScience 52(8): 669–681.

Hart, D.D. and N.L. Poff. 2002. A special section on dam removal and river restoration. BioScience 52(8): 653–655.

Heinz Center. 2002. Dam Removal: Science and Decision Making. Washington, DC. 221 pp.

Horn, A.J. and C.R. Goldman. 1994. Limnology, 2nd edition. McGraw-Hill, Inc. New York, NY. 576 pp.

Hulse, D., S. Gregory, and J. Baker (eds.). 2002. Willamette River Basin Planning Atlas. Trajectories of Environmental and Ecological Change. Oregon State University Press, Corvallis, OR. 178 pp.

(HRC) Hydropower Reform Coalition. 1997. Relicensing Tool Kit: Guidelines for effective participation in the FERC relicensing process. 37 pp.

(HRC) Hydropower Reform Coalition. 2000. Hydropower Reform Toolkit and Hydropower Reform Information Kit. http://www.amrivers.org/hydropowertoolkit/default.htm [15 Sept. 2002].

Hutchins, D. A. M. and K. W. Bruland. 1998. Iron-limited diatom growth and Si:N uptake rations in a coastal upwelling. Nature 393: 561–64.

(IRN) International Rivers Network. 2002a. Fish passage impasse at Fort Halifax Dam. River Revival Bulletin 40, Sept. 5, 2002. http://www.irn.org/revival/decom/index.asp?id=bulletins/rrb40.html [12 Oct. 2002].

———. 2002b. Dam Removal: The International Experience. http://www.irn.org/revival/decom/brochure/rrpt3.html [12 Sept. 2002].

———. 2002c. Latvia-Dam removed to restore salmon and spawning areas. River Revival Bulletin 41, Oct 3, 2002. http://www.irn.org/revival/decom/index.asp?id=bulletins/rrb41.html [25 Oct. 2002].

———. 2002d. Reviving the World's Rivers: Technical Challenges. Decommissioning Methods. http://www.irn.org/revival/decom/brochure/rrpt5.html [23 October 2002].

Ittekkot, V., C. Humborg, and P. Schafer. 2000. Hydrological alterations and marine biogeochemistry: a silicate issue? BioScience 50: 776–792.

(IUCN) The World Conservation Union. 2002. Environmental flows and international watercourses. Environmental Law Programme Newsletter 1: 4–7.

Jobin, W. R. (1998). Sustainable management for dams and waters. Lewis Publishers, Boca Raton, FL. 265 pp.

Johnson, S.E., and B.E. Graber. 2002. Enlisting the social sciences in decisions about dam removal. BioScience 52(8): 731–738.

Junk, W.J. 1999. The flood pulse concept of large rivers: Learning from the tropics. River Ecosystem Concepts 115 (3): 261–280. Archiv fur Hydrobiologie. Supplementband

Junk, W.J., P.B. Bayley, and R.E. Sparks. 1989. The flood pulse concept in river-floodplain system. Proceedings of the International Large River Symposium, pp. 110–127, Canadian. Special Publication of Fisheries and Aquatic Sciences 106.

Justic, D., N. N. Rabelais., and R. E. Turner. 1995. Stoichiometric nutrient balance and origin of coastal eutrophication. Marine Pollution Bulletin 30: 41–46.

Keller, E. A., and G. M. Kondolf. 1990. Groundwater and fluvial processes: selected observations. Groundwater geomorphology: The role of subsurface water in earth-surface processes and landforms. Special Paper—Geological Society of America 252: 319–340.

Kennebec Coalition. 1999. A River Reborn. Benefits for People and Wildlife of the Kennebec River following the Removal of Edwards Dam. http://www.tu.org/newstand/library_pdfs/edwards-web.pdf [20 Aug. 2002].

Kerr, G.R., and H. Reheis 2002. Apalachicola-Chattahoochee-Flint River Basin Compact Alabama-Coosa-Tallapoosa River Basin Compact http://www.dnr.state.ga.us/dnr/environ/outreach_files/intwatplan_files/actlette.pdf [24 Jan. 2003].

Kowalewski, M., G.E.A. Serrano, K.W. Flessa, and G.A. Goodfriend. 2000. Dead delta's former productivity: two trillion shells at the mouth of the Colorado River. Geology 28:1059–1062.

Lemly, A.D., S.E. Finger, and M.K. Nelson. 1993. Annual Review: sources and impacts of irrigation drainwater contaminants in arid wetlands. Environmental Toxicology and Chemistry 12:2265–2279.

Leopold, L. 1990. Closing Remarks, In Colorado River Ecology and Dame Management. National Academy Press, Washington, DC. 276 pp.

Lovett, R. 1999. As salmon stage disappearing act, dams may too. Science 284: 574–575.

Lutz, D.S. 1995. Gas supersaturation and gas bubble trauma in fish downstream from a Midwestern reservoir. Transactions of the American Fisheries Society 124(3): 423–436.

Maclin, E., and M. Bowman (eds.). 2002. The ecology of dam removal. A summary of benefits and impacts. American Rivers, Washington, DC. 15 pp. http://www.amrivers.org/damremovaltoolkit/ecologyofdam removal.htm [12 Sept. 2002].

Maclin, E., and M. Sicchio. 1999. Dam Removal success Stories: Restoring Rivers Through Selective Removal of Dams that Don't Make Sense. Friends of the Earth, American Rivers, and Trout Unlimited. 176 pp.

March, J.G., J.P. Benstead, C.M. Pringle, and F. N. Scatena. 2003. Damming tropical island streams: problems, solutions and alternatives. BioScience 53(11): 1069–1078.

McCully, P. 2001. Silenced Rivers. The Ecology and Politics of Large Dams. Zed Books, London, United Kingdom. 359 pp.

McDonald, G., R. Mclaughlin and S. McKinley. 2001. Fish Passage: Concepts, Application and Evaluation-Great Lakes Tributary Streams. A summary report for the Great Lakes Fishery Commission Sponsored Workshop, Feb 2–3, 2001. 24 pp.

(MHB) Mississippi Headwaters Board. 2002. Homepage. http://www.mhbriverwatch.dst.mn.us/about_mhb/index.htm [21 Oct. 2002].

Miller, G.T. 2001. Living in the Environment Wadsworth Biological Series. Belmont, CA.

Molles, M.C., Jr., C.S. Crawford, L.M. Ellis, H.M. Valett, and C.N. Dahm. 1998. Managed flooding for riparian ecosystem restoration. BioScience 48(9): 749–756.

(MRC) Mekong River Commission. Homepage. http://www.mrcmekong.org/ [20 Oct. 2002].

Nilsson, C., and K. Berggren 2000. 2000. Alterations of riparian ecosystems caused by river regulation. BioScience 50(9): 783–792.

(NRC) National Research Council. 1983. Safety of Existing Dams: Evaluation and Improvement National Academy Press, Washington, DC.

———. 1985. Safety of Dams: Flood and Earthquake Criteria. National Academy Press, Washington, DC.

———. 1998. New Directions in Water Resource Planning for the U.S. Army Corps of Engineers. National Academy Press, Washington, DC.

———. 1999. U.S. Committee on Watershed Management. New Strategies for America's Watersheds. National Academy Press, Washington, DC. 311 pp.

(NWSRS) National Wild and Scenic Rivers System. Homepage http://www.nps.gov/rivers/ [18 Oct. 2002].

Odeh, M. (ed.). 1999. Innovations in Fish Passage Technology. American Fisheries Society, Bethesda, MD. 224 pp.

———. 2000. Advances in Fish Passage Technology: Engineering Design and Biological Evaluation. American Fisheries Society, Bethesda, MD. 170 pp.

(ORBC) Ohio River Basin Commission. 2002. Introduction. http://www.orbcinterstate.org/introduction.htm [17 Oct. 2002].

Otto, B. 2000. Paying for Dam Removal: a guide to selected funding sources. American Rivers, Washington, DC. 110 pp. http://www.amrivers.org/docs/PDR-color.pdf [21 Oct. 2002].

Pielou, E.C. 1998. Fresh Water. University of Chicago Press, Chicago, IL. 275 pp.

Philips, J.D. 2001. Sedimentation in bottomland hardwoods downstream of an east Texas dam. Environmental Geology 40(7): 860–868.

Poff, N.L., and D.D. Hart. 2002. How dams vary and why it matters of the emerging science of dam removal. BioScience 52(8): 659–668.

Postel, S., and Richter, B.D. 2003. Rivers for Life: Managing Water for People and Nature. Island Press, Washington, DC. 240pp.

Postel, S.L., J.I. Morrison, and P.H. Gleick. 1998. Allocating freshwater to aquatic ecosystems: the case of the Colorado River Delta. International Water 23: 119–123.

Prakash, A. 2002. Farakka barrage causes concern, both upstream and downstream. http://www.cyberbangladesh.org/concern.txt [12 Sept. 2002].

Pringle, C. M. 2004. Cumulative and interacting effects of altered hydrology and contaminant transport: Ecological patterns in wildlife of global concern. *In:* Holland, M. E. Blood and L. Schaffer (eds.) Achieving Sustainable Systems: A Web of Connections. Island Press, Washington, DC..

Pringle, C.M. 2001a. Hydrologic connectivity and the management of biological reserves: A global perspective. Ecological Applications 11:981–998.

———. 2001b. Hydrologic connectivity: A call for greater emphasis in wilderness management. International Journal of Wilderness 7(3):21–26.

———. 2000. Riverine Connectivity: Conservation and management implications for remnant natural areas in complex landscapes. Plenary Talk, Verhandlungen Internationals Verein. Limnol. 27:1149–1164.

Pringle, C. M., and F. J. Triska. 2000. Emergent biological patterns and surface-subsurface interactions at landscape scales, Chapter 7, pp. 167–193. *In:* J. B. Jones and P. J. Mulholland (eds.) Stream and groundwaters. Academic Press.

Pringle, C.M., M. Freeman, and B. Freeman. 2000. Regional effects of hydrologic alterations on riverine macrobiota in the New World: Tropical-temperate comparisons. BioScience 50: 807–823.

River Alliance of Wisconsin. 2000. Dam removal down under: River Alliance shares Wisconsin Experience with Australia. Sept. 28, 2000 News Release. http://www.wisconsinrivers.org/NR0928.html [21 Oct. 2002].

River Alliance of Wisconsin and Trout Unlimited. 2000. Dam Removal: A Citizen's Guide to Restoring Rivers.

Richter, B.D., J.V. Baumgartner, J. Powell, and D.P. Braun. 1996. A method for assessing hydrologic alteration within ecosystems. Conservation Biology 10(4): 1163–1174.

Roberts, T.R. 1993. Commentary. Just another dammed river? Negative impacts of Pak Mun Dam on fish of the Mekong Basin. Natural History Bulletin of Siam Society. 41: 105–133.

Rosenberg, D.M., P. McCully, and C.M. Pringle. 2000. Global scale environmental effects of hydrological alterations: introduction. BioScience 50(9):746–751.

(RWESA) Rivers Watch East and Southeast Asia. 2002. Progress Report of Thai Baan Research. Findings of Community-Based Research on the Impacts of Opening Pak Mun Dam Gates in Thailand. http://www.rwesa.org/pakmun2nd.html [25 Oct. 2002].

Ryan, B.A., E.M. Dawley and R.A. Nelson. 2000. Modeling the effects of supersaturated dissolved gas on resident aquatic biota in the main-stem Snake and Columbia Rivers. North American Journal of Fisheries Management 20(1): 192–204.

Schramm, H.L., Jr., M.A. Eggleton, and R.M. Mayo. 2000. Habitat conservation and creation: invoking the flood-pulse concept to enhance fisheries in the lower Mississippi River. Polish Archives of Hydrobiology 47 (1): 45–62.

Sinha, M., M.K. Mukhopadhyay, P. Mitra, M.M. Bagghi, and H.C. Karamkar. 1996. Impact of Farakka Barrage on the hydrology and fishery of the Hooghly estuary. Estuaries 19(3): 710–722.

Speece, R.E. 1994. Lateral thinking solves stratification problems. Water Quality International 3: 12–15.

Strayer, D.L., D.C. Hunter, L.C. Smith, and C.K. Borg. 1994. Distribution, abundance, and the roles of freshwater clams (Bivalvisa, Unionidae) in the freshwater tidal Hudson River. Freshwater Biology 31:239–248.

Tanzeema, S., and I.M. Faisal. 2001. Sharing the Ganges: a critical analysis of the water sharing treaties. Water Policy 3(1): 18–28.

Tharme, R.E., and J.M. King. 1998. Development of the Building Block Methodology for Instream Flow Assessments and Supporting Research on the Effects of Different Magnitude Flows on Riverine Ecosystems. Water Research Commission Report No. 576/1/98, Cape Town, South Africa.

The Aspen Institute. 2002. Dam Removal. A New Option for a New Century. 81 pp. http://www.aspeninst.org/eee/pdfs/damremovaloption.pdf [28 Jan. 2003].

(TNC) The Nature Conservancy. 2002. Flow Restoration Database. 36 pp.

(TNRCM) The Natural Resources Council of Maine. 2003. Benefits and Impacts of Removal of the Edwards Dam. According to FERC's Final Environmental Impact Statement. http://www.maineenvironment.org/news/waterpress/benefits.htm [28 Jan. 2003].

Tockner. K, F. Alard, and J.V. Ward. 2000. An extension of the floodplain concept. Hydrological Processes 14(16-17): 2861–2883.

Tracy, R. 2000. Existing Information Analysis. Flow and Sediment Regime. Lewis River Hydroelectric Projects. USDA Forest Service, Gifford Pinchot National Forest. http://www.fs.fed.us/gpnf/forest-administration/ferc/lewis/documents/20020718-01-eia-instream-sediment.pdf [28 Jan. 2003].

Trout Unlimited. 2002. Small Dams Campaign. http://www.tu.org/small_dams/ [10 Sept. 2002].

Turner, R.E., N. Qureshi, N.N. Rabelais, Q. Dortch, D. Justic, R.F. Shaw, and J. Cope. 1998. Fluctuating silicate: nitrate ratios and coastal plankton food webs. Proc. Natl. Acad. Sci., USA 95: 13048–51.

(USACE) United States Army Corps of Engineers. 2002a. Improving Salmon Passage. Final. Lower Snake River Juvenile Salmon Migratory Feasibility Environmental Report. 55 pp. http://www.nww.usace.army.mil/lsr/final_fseis/study_kit/summary.pdf [13 Sept. 2002].

———. 2002b. National Inventory of Dams. http://crunch.tec.army.mil/nid/webpages/nid.cfm [11 Oct. 2002].

———. 2002c. Homepage. http://www.hq.usace.army.mil/history/brief3.htm [10 Sept. 2002].

(USEPA) U.S. Environmental Protection Agency. 1999. The national survey of mercury concentrations in fish: Data base summary 1990–95. http://www.epa.gov/ost/fish/mercurydata.html [24 Oct. 2002].

———. 2002. Section 404 of the Clean Water Act: An Overview. http://www.epa.gov/owow/wetlands/facts/fact10.html [16 Oct. 2002].

(USFWS) U.S. Fish and Wildlife Service. 2002. General Statistics for Endangered Species. (Data current as of 10/25/2002). http://ecos.fws.gov/servlet/TessStatReport [25 Oct. 2002].

Van Ginkel, C.E., B.C. Hohls, and E. Vermaak. 2001. A Ceratium hirundinella (O.F. Mueller) bloom in Hartbeespoort Dam, South Africa. Water south Africa 27(2): 269–276.

Vincke, P. P., and I. Thiaw. 1995. Contribution de la Coopération internationale de la Belgique à la conservation de la diversité biologique. Parks 5(2). http://bch-cbd.naturalsciences.be/belgium/contribution/cooperation/ann2.htm [25 Oct. 2002].

Wallin, P. and R.R. Haberman. 1992. People Protecting Rivers: A collection of Lessons from Successful Grassroots Activists. River Network, Portland, OR. 72 pp.

Ward, J.V. 1982. Ecological aspects of stream regulation: responses in downstream lotic reaches. Wat. Poll. Mgnt. Reviews (New Delhi) 2:1–26.

———. 1985. Thermal characteristics of running water. Hydrobiologia 125:31–46.

———. 1986. Altitudinal zonation in a Rocky Mountain stream. Arch. Hydrobiol. Suppl. (Monogr. Beiträge) 74:133–199.

————. 1988. Riverine-wetland interaction. *In*, Sharitz, R.R. and J.W. Gibbons. (eds.). Freshwater wetlands and wildlife. U.S. Dep. Energy, Oak Ridge, TN.

Ward, J.V. and J.A. Stanford. 1989. Riverine ecosystems: the influence of man on catchment dynamics and fish ecology. *In:* Dodge, D.P. (ed.). Proceedings of the International Large River Symposium. Can. Spec. Publ. Fish Aquat. Sci. 106.

Waters, T.F. 1995. Sediments in Streams. Sources, Biological Effects and Control. Monograph 7. American Fisheries Society, Bethesda, MD. 251 pp.

(WCD) World Commission on Dams. (2000). Dams and Development: A New Framework for Decision-making. The Report of the World Commission on Dams. Earthscan, London, United Kingdom. 404 pp.

Webster, I.T., B.S. Sherman, M. Bormans, and G. Jones. 2000. Management strategies for cyanobacterial blooms in an impounded lowland river. Regulated Rivers: Research and Management 16(5): 513–525.

Welcomme, R.L. 1979. Fisheries Ecology of Floodplain Rivers. Longman, London. 317 pp.

Wetzel, R.G. 1983. Limnology. W.B. Saunders, Philadelphia, PA. 743 pp.

Williams, P. 2000. Restoring living rivers. http://www.igc.org/igc/en/hl/10004204076/hl9.html [10 Sept. 2002].

Willson, M.F., S.M. Gende, and B.H. Marston. 1998. Fish and the forest. BioScience 48:455–462.

Wilson, S.F., R.P. Bio, and V. Craig. 2001. Footprint Impacts of Hydroelectric Development on Coarse Woody Debris: An Assessment of Vancouver Island Watershed. Report prepared for BC Hydro-Bridge Coastal Fish and Wildlife Restoration Program. 23 pp.

World Bank. 2002. Fish Passages. http://www.worldbank.org/html/fpd/em/hydro/fp.stm [13 Oct. 2002].

SURFACE WATER DIVERSIONS

Acharya, G. 1997. Incentive measures for the conservation of biodiversity in inland water systems. Paper presented at 8th Session of the Global Biodiversity Forum, Montreal, Canada.

American Rivers. 2002. Texas' Guadalupe River is one of America's most endangered rivers. The future of the river hinges on protecting instream flows. http://www.amrivers.org/mostendangered/guadalupe2002.htm [04 Nov 2002]

————. 2003. Little Tennessee River Basin. River restoration case study: Hydropower Reform. http://www.amrivers.org/hydropowertoolkit/littletennesseecasestudy.htm [24 Jan. 2003].

Arthington, A.H., and R.L. Welcomme. 1995. The Condition of Large River Systems of the World, *In*, Armantrout, N.B. (ed.). Conditions of the World's Aquatic Habitats. Proceedings of the First World Fisheries Congress, Theme 1. Oxford and IBH Publishing Co., Pvt. Ltd., New Delhi, India. 411 pp.

BBC News. 2002. Dead Sea in danger. http://news.bbc.co.uk/2/hi/middle_east/392442.stm [16 Nov 2002].

Benstead, J.P., J.G. March, C.M. Pringle, and F.B. Scatena. 1999. Effects of a low-head dam and water abstraction on migratory tropical stream biota. Ecological Applications 9: 656–668.

(BLM) Bureau of Land Management (in press 2002). Draft environmental Impact Statement: Walker Lake, Nevada.

Busch, D.E., and S.D. Smith. 1995. Mechanisms associated with decline of woody species in riparian ecosystems of the southwestern U.S. Ecological Monographs 65(3): 347–370.

Cahill, T.A., E.A. Gearhart, T.E. Gill, D.A. Gillette, and J.S. Reid. 1996. Saltating particles, playa crusts and dust aerosols at Owens(dry) Lake, California. Earth Surface Processes and Landforms 21: 621–637.

Cascadia Times. 2002. Water in the West. The Struggle for Water in the Desert. http://www.waterinthewest.org/riverbasins/riogrande/riogrande.htm [10 Nov. 2002]

Castle, A. 1999. Water Rights Law—Prior Appropriation. http://profs.lp.findlaw.com/water/water_1.html [07 Nov. 2002].

(CDG) China Development Gateway. 2002. Project Introduction. Wanjiazhai Water Control Project http://www.chinagate.com.cn/english/1405.htm [06 Jan 2003].

(CEC) Commission for Environmental Cooperation. 2001. North American Boundary and Transboundary Inland Water Management Report. Éditions Yvon Blais, Montréal, Canada. 218 pp. http://www.cec.org/files/pdf/LAWPOLICY/NAELP7e.pdf [16 Dec. 2002].

(CGLG) Council of Great Lakes Governors. 2002. Great Lakes Water Management Governance. http://www.cglg.org/projects/water/ [18 Sept. 2002]

Chang, G. 2002. The problem with water, Part II. The Jamestown Foundation China Brief 2 (20), October 10, 2002. http://china.jamestown.org/index.htm [06 Jan 2003].

Clyma, W., and M.S. Shafique. 2001. Basin-wide water management concepts for the new millennium. Presented at the 94th annual meeting of the American Society of Agricultural Engineers, Sacramento, CA, 30 July–August, 2001

(CNS) China News Service. 2002. World-level trans-valley water transfer of Yellow River is successful in Shanxi. http://www.enviroinfo.org.cn/Water_Conservation/Water_Transfer_Allocation/e102117_en.htm [06 Jan 2003].

(COA) City of Albuquerque. 2002a. Angostura Diversion–Dual Canal Conveyance. http://www.cabq.gov/water resources/angosturadiversion.html. [21 Jan. 2003].

———. 2000b. San Juan-Chama Diversion Project http://www.cabq.gov/waterresources/sjc.html [21 Jan. 2003].

Coates, D. 2001. Biodiversity and fisheries management opportunities in the Mekong River Basin. Presented at the Blue Millennium: Managing Global Fisheries for Biodiversity thematic workshop. Victoria, British Columbia, Canada. 40 pp. http://www.unep.org/bpsp/Fisheries/Fisheries Case Studies/COATES.pdf [09 Dec. 2002].

Covalla, E., C. Pandarinath, J. Williams, and A. Wingo. 2001. Managing Agricultural Water Impacts. http://ambient.2y.net/wingo/projects/water/e497/e497/e497.html [25 Sept. 2002]

(CVIOG) Carl Vinson Institute of Government. 2001. Georgia Joint Comprehensive State Water Plan Study. http://www.cviog.uga.edu/water/news/01-12.pdf [13 Dec. 2002].

Davies, B.R., and J. Day. 1998. Vanishing Waters. University of Cape Town Press, Cape Town, South Africa. 487 pp.

Davies, B.R., M. Thoms, and M. Meador. 1992. An assessment of the ecological impacts of interbasin transfers, and their threats to river basin integrity and conservation. Aquatic Conservation 2(4): 325–349.

Day. J.C., and F. Quinn. 1992. Water Diversion and Export: Learning from Canadian Experience. Canadian Association of Geographers Public Issues Committee, No. 1. 215 pp.

(DEFRA) Department for Environment, Food and Rural Affairs. 2002. The Ramsar Convention. English and European Wildlife Issues. http://www.defra.gov.uk/wildlife-countryside/ewd/ewd10.htm [14 Nov. 2002].

de Moor, A.P. 2001. Perverse Incentives. Subsidies and Sustainable Development: Key Issues and Reform Strategies. Earth Council, San Jose, Costa Rica. http://www.ecouncil.ac.cr/rio/focus/report/english/subsidies/chap5.htm [25 Sept 2002].

de Moor, A.P., and Calamai, P. 1997. Subsidizing Unsustainable Development. Undermining the Earth with Public Funds. Earth Council, San Jose, Costa Rica. 77 pp.

(ENN) Environmental News Network. 2002. Lebanon taps river at the center of Israel row. Reuters, October 17, 2002. http://www.enn.com/news/wire-stories/2002/10/10172002/reu_48733.asp [30 Oct. 2002].

(ENS) Environmental News Service. 2001. The disappearance of Dojran Lake. October 16, 2001. http://ens-news.com/ens/oct2001/2001/-10-16-03.asp [31 Oct. 2002]. N. Dokovska.

Environment Canada. 2002. Water—How we share it. http://www.ec.gc.ca/water/en/info/pubs/primer/e_prim07.htm [16 Sept. 2002].

Florida Wildlife Federation. 2002. Resolution for the Protection of the Apalachicola-Chattahoochee-Flint and Alabama-Coosa-Tallapoosa River Basins. http://www.flawildlife.org/pubs/fwn-6-00/apalch.htm [13 Dec. 2002].

Gibbins, C.N., M.J. Jeffries, and C. Soulsby. 2000. Impacts of an interbasin water transfer: distribution and abundance of Micronecta poweri (Insecta: Corixidae) in the River Wear, north-east England. Aquatic Conservation: Marine and Freshwater Ecosystems 10(2): 103–115.

Gillilan, D.M., and T.C. Brown. 1997. Instream Flow Protection. Seeking a Balance in western Water Use. Island Press, Washington, DC. 417 pp.

Glasser, S.F. 2000. Hydromodifications—Dams, Diversions, Return Flows, and Other Alterations of Natural Water Flows: In Dissmeyer, G.E. (ed.). Drinking Water from Forests and Grasslands. USDA Forest Service, Southern Research Station, Ashville, NC. 246 pp.

Gleick, P.H. 2000. The changing water paradigm. A look at twenty-first century water resource development. Water International 25(1): 127–138.

Golladay, S.W., and C.L. Hax. 1995. Effects of an engineered flow disturbance on meiofauna in a north Texas prairie stream. Journal of the North American Benthological Society 14(3): 404–413.

Heimlich, R.E., K.D. Wiebe, R. Classen, D. Gadsby, and R.M. House. 1998. Wetlands and Agriculture: private interests and public benefits. Agricultural Economics Report 765. 104 pp. http://www.ers.usda.gov/publications/aer765/aer765f.pdf [08 Nov. 2002].

Hertelin, L. 1999. Lake Winnepeg Regulation. Churchill-Nelson River Diversion Project in the Crees of Northern Manitoba. A working paper of the World Commission on Dams. http://www.damsreport.org/docs/kbase/contrib/soc205.pdf [21 Jan. 2003].

(IUCN) World Conservation Union. 2002. 'Environmental flows' and international watercourses. Newsletter 1: 4–7.

Jehl, D. 2002. In race to tap the Euphrates, the upper hand is upstream. New York Times, August 25, 2002.

Kentula, M.E. 1999. Restoration, Creation, and Recovery of Wetlands. Wetland Restoration and Creation. National Water Summary on Wetland Resources. U.S. Geological Survey Water Supply Paper 2425. http://water.usgs.gov/nwsum/WSP2425/restoration.html [25 Jan. 2003].

Kilgour, D.M., and A. Dinar. 1995. Are stable agreements for sharing international river waters now possible? The World Bank (Agriculture and Natural Resources Department, Agricultural Policies Division).

Kingsford, R.T. 2000. Ecological impacts of dams, water diversions and river management on floodplain wetlands in Australia. Australian Journal of Ecology 25: 109–127.

Kingsford, R.T., and R.F. Thomas. 2001. Changing Water Regime and Wetland Habitat on the Lower Murrumbidgee Floodplain of the Murrumbidgee River in Arid Australia. Report to Environment Australia. http://www.npws.nsw.gov.au/wildlife/lower_murrumbidgee/lower_murrumbidgee_section1.pdf [22 Jan. 2003].

Living Lakes. 2003. Lake Characteristic. Mono Lake. Homepage. http://www.livinglakes.org/mono/ [22 Jan. 2003].

Loch, J.S., A.J. Derksen, M.E. Hora, and R.B. Oetting. 1979. Potential effects of exotic fish species on Manitoba: an impact assessment of the Garrison Diversion Unit. Technical Report of Fisheries and Marine Services (Canada). No. 838. 43 pp.

MacDonnell, L.J. 1999. From Reclamation to Sustainability. Water, Agriculture, and the Environment in the American West University Press of Colorado, Niwot, CO. 385 pp.

MacDonnell, L.J., and S.F. Bates (eds.). 1993. Natural Resources Policy and Law. Island Press, Washington, DC. 241 pp.

Manitoba Hydro. 2003. Churchill River Diversion. http://www.hydro.mb.ca/issues/churchill_river_diversion.shtml [22 Jan. 2003].

March, J.G., J.P. Benstead, C.M. Pringle, and F. N. Scatena. 1998. Migratory drift of larval amphidromous shrimps in two tropical streams, Puerto Rico. Freshwater Biology 40:1–14.

———. 2003. Damming tropical island streams: problems, solutions and alternatives. BioScience 53(11):1069–1078.

Marking, L.L., T.D. Bills, J.J. Rach, and S.J. Grabowski. 1983. Chemical control of fish and fish eggs in the Garrison Diversion Unit, North Dakota. North American Journal of Fisheries Management 3(4): 410–418.

McIvor, C.C., J.A. Ley, and R.D. Bjork. 1994. Changes in Freshwater Inflows From the Everglades to Florida Bay Including Effects on Biota and Biotic Processes: a Review: In, Davis, S.M., J.C. Ogden, and W.A. Park, (eds.) Everglades: The Ecosystem and its Restoration. St. Lucie Press, Boca Raton, FL. 826 pp.

Mitsch, W.J. and J.G. Gosselink. 1993. Wetlands. 2nd edition. VanNostrand Reinhold, New York, NY. 722 pp.

Nabhan, G.P., and A.R. Holdsworth. 1998. Water Diversion and Impoundment. State of the Sonoran Desert Biome: Uniqueness, Biodiversity, Threats and the Adequacy of Protection in the Sonoran Bioregion. http://alic.arid.arizona.edu/sonoran/documents/nabhan/db_h2odiversion.html [22 Jan. 2003].

(NRC) National Research Council. 1992. Restoration of Aquatic Ecosystems. Science, Technology, and Public Policy. National Academy Press, Washington, DC. 552 pp.

(NRCS) Natural Resources Conservation Service. 2002. Farmbill 2002. Conservation Provisions Overview. http://www.nrcs.usda.gov/programs/farmbill/2002/pdf/ConsProv.pdf [Nov. 10, 2002].

(NRDC) Natural Resources Defense Council. 2002. Water Subsidies. Clean Water & Oceans: Water Conservation & Restoration: In Brief: FAQs http://www.nrdc.org/water/conservation/qsubs.asp [Sept. 24, 2002].

(NRLC) Natural Resources Law Center. 1997. Restoring the Waters. University of Colorado School of Law, Boulder, CO. 64 pp.

(NSWEPA) New South Wales Environmental Protection Agency. 2002. Backgrounder. Water. http://www.epa.nsw.gov.au/soe/soe2000/bw/ 15 Nov. 2002]

Ono, Y. 1996. Citizen's work to protect Chitose River. World Rivers Review 11(5). http://www.irn.org/pubs/wrr/9612/chitose.html [15 Nov. 2002].

(OTA) Office of Technology Assistance. 1983. Technologies Affecting Surface Water Storage and Delivery. In, Water-Related Technologies for Sustainable Agriculture in U.S. Arid/Semiarid Lands. OTA-F-212, Washington, DC.

(PCFFA) Pacific Coast Federation of Fisherman's Association. 2001. News Release. Court Ruling Against Klamath Irrigators Gives Lower River Salmon Fishermen a Chance for Survival. http://www.pcffa.org/pr01-1nw.htm [22 Jan. 2003].

Peberdy, K. 1998. The making of a wetland. Wildfowl and Wetlands 124:16–19.

People's Daily. 2001. South-North Water Diversion Project to Benefit 300 Million Chinese. Dec. 26, 2001.

Postel, S. 1997. Last Oasis. Facing Water Scarcity. W.W. Norton and Co., New York, NY. 239 pp.

Pringle, C.M. 1997. Exploring how disturbance is transmitted upstream: going against the flow. Journal of the American Benthological Society. 16:425–438.

———. 2000. Threats to U.S. public lands from cumulative hydrologic alterations outside their boundaries. Ecological Applications 10(4):971–989.

Pringle, C.M., F.N. Scatena, P. Paaby-Hansen, and M. Núñez-Ferrera. 2000. River conservation in Latin American and the Caribbean. In (Boone, P.J., B.R. Davies and G.E. Petts, eds.) Global Perspectives on river conservation: Science, Policy and Practice. John Wiley and Sons, Ltd., New York, NY.

Rivernet. 2002. The Spanish National Hydrological Plan. Save The Delta Of The Ebro. The Spanish National Hydrological Plan (SNHP) and the Social Opposition to the Transference of Water from the River Ebro to Other River Basins. http://www.rivernet.org/Iberian/deltaebro/savethedelta.htm [13 Dec. 2002].

Shane, E.B. 2001. Water rights and Gila River III: the Winters doctrine goes underground. Water Law Review 4(2):397–417.

Snaddon, C.D., and B.R. Davies. 1998. A preliminary assessment of the effects of a small South African inter-basin water transfer on discharge and invertebrate community structure. Regulated Rivers: Research and Management 14(54): 421–441.

Snaddon, C.D., B.R. Davies, and M. Wishart. 2000. A Global Overview of Interbasin Water Transfer Schemes, with an Appraisal of their Ecological, Socio-Economic and Socio-Political Implications, and Recommendations for Their Management. Foundation for Water Research, Bucks, United Kingdom.

Söderqvist, T. 2002. Constructed wetlands as nitrogen sinks in southern Sweden: an empirical analysis of cost determinants. Ecological Engineering 19(2):161–173.

(TCWN) Tennessee Clean Water Network. 2002. Homepage. http://www.tcwn.org/Library/WetLands/Endangered_Rivers.htm [22 Jan. 2003].

Terpstra, P.M.J. 1999. Options for closed water systems: sustainable water management. Water Science and Technology 39(5): 65–72.

Texas Observer. 2002. The Rights of a River. Environmentalists Stake a Radical Claim to the Water in the Guadalupe. June 21, 2002. http://www.texasobserver.org/showArticle.asp? ArticleID=759 [04 Nov 2002]. J. Bernstein

The League of Women Voters. 2002. Where We Stand. Protecting Our Natural Resources. Water. http://www.lwv.org/where/protecting/watcr_pg2.html [12 Dec. 2002].

Tiner, R. 1998. In search of Swampland. A Wetland Sourcebook and Field Guide. Rutgers University Press, New Brunswick, NJ. 264 pp.

(UNDESA) United Nations Department of Economic and Social Affairs. 2002. Jordan and Israel Announce Project to Save Dead Sea. http://www.johannesburgsummit.org/html/whats_new/feature_story33.htm [15 Nov. 2002].

(UNESCO) United Nations Educational, Scientific and Cultural Organization. 1999. Inter Basin Water Transfer. http://www.worldwatercouncil.org/Vision/Documents/IWBTReport.PDF [09 Dec. 2002].

(USACE) United States Army Corps of Engineers. 2003. The U.S. Army Corps of Engineers Regulatory Program Overview. http://www.usace.army.mil/inet/functions/cw/cecwo/reg/oceover.htm [22 Jan. 2003].

(USEPA) United States Environmental Protection Agency. 2003a. Wetlands. Clean Water Act, Section 404. http://www.epa.gov/owow/wetlands/regs/sec404.html [22 Jan. 2003].

———. 2003b. Wetlands. Section 10 of the Rivers and Harbors Appropriation Act of 1899. http://www.epa.gov/owow/wetlands/regs/sect10.html [22 Jan. 2003].

(USFWS) United States Fish and Wildlife Service. 2002a. Upper Colorado River Endangered Fish Recovery Program. http://mountain-prairie.fws.gov/coloradoriver/Index.htm [15 Sept. 2002].

———. 2002b. Stillwater National Wildlife Refuge Complex. Draft Environmental Impact Statement for the Comprehensive Plan and Boundary Revision. Summary. Portland, OR. 51 pp.

US Water News. 2003. Work begins on huge China water-diversion project. January 2003. http://www.uswater-news.com/archives/arcglobal/3worbeg01.html [06 Jan 2003].

Vidthayanon, C., and M. Kottelat. 1995. First record of Abbottina rivularis (Cyprinidae: Gobioninae) from the Mekong basin. Japan Journal of Icthyology 41: 463–465.

WaterWatch. 2002. Water Law Basics. http://www.waterwatch.org/waterlaw.html [08 Nov. 2002].

World Bank. 1997. World Bank provides U.S. $400 million loan for China water project. News Release No. 97/1375/EAP. http://www.worldbank.org/html/extdr/extme/1375.htm [06 Jan 2003].

(WWBWC) Walla Walla Basin Water Council. 2002. http://www.wwbwc.org/Main_Pages/Projects/Flows/Flows.htm [Sept 25, 2002].

(WWF) World Wildlife Fund. 2001. The EU Dimension of the Spanish National Hydrological Plan. http://archive.panda.org/europe/freshwater/regional/spain-nhp-eu.html [13 Dec. 2002].

(WWI) WorldWatch Institute. 2002. Irrigation issues: efficiency of irrigation systems. http://www.orst.edu/instruction/bi301/irrigati.htm [17 Sept. 2002].

Yardas, D. 1996. Lahontan Valley Wetlands, Nevada. In, Restoring the Wetlands, Natural Resources Law Center, University of Colorado School of Law, Denver, CO., p 14–16.

Yu, X. 1983. Possible Effects of the Proposed Eastern Transfer Route on the Fish Stock of the Principal Water Bodies along the Course, In, Biswas, A.K., Z. Dakang, J.E. Nickum, and L. Changming (eds.). 1983. Long-distance Water Transfer: A Chinese Case Study and International Experiences. Tycooly International Publishing Limited, Dublin, Ireland. 417 pp.

Altered Bed and Bank Structure

(ARMCANZ) Agriculture and Resource Management Council of Australia and New Zealand. 2000. Floodplain Management in Australia: Best Practice Principles and Guidelines. http://www.dpiwe.tas.gov.au/inter.nsf/Web Pages/RPIO-4YQ6V4?open [02 Dec. 2002].

Arner, D.H., H.R. Robinette, J.E. Fraiser, and M.H. Gray. 1975. Report on the effects of channelization modification on the Luxapalila River. *In*, Symposium on Stream Channel modification, Harrisonburg, VA, pp 77–96.

————. 1976. Effects of channelization of the Luxapalila River on fish, aquatic invertebrates, water quality, and fur bearers. Report No. FWS/OBS-76/08. Office of Biological Services, Fish and Wildlife Service, U.S. Department of the Interior, Washington, DC.

Bree, T., and C. Cunnane. 1980. The effect of arterial drainage on flood magnitude, In Project 5.1 of the International Hydrological Programme. Casebook of methods of computation of quantitative changes in the hydrological regimen of river basins due to human activities. UNESCO.

Brookes, A. 1988. Channelized Rivers. Perspectives for Environmental Management. John Wiley and Sons, Chichester, England. 326 pp.

————. 1996. River Restoration Experience in Northern Europe. *In*, Brookes, A. and F.D. Shields (eds.), River Channel Restoration. Guiding Principles for Sustainable Projects. John Wiley and Sons, Chichester, England. 433 pp.

Brookes, A., and F.G. Shields, Jr. 1996. Perspectives in River Channel Restoration, *In*, Brookes, A., and F.D. Shields (eds.), River Channel Restoration. Guiding Principles for Sustainable Projects. John Wiley and Sons, Chichester, England. 433 pp.

Brown, C.M., G.T. Decker, R.W. Pierce, and T.M. Brandt. 2002. Applying Natural Channel Design Philosophy to the Restoration of Inland Native Fish Habitat. http://mountain-prairie.fws.gov/pfw/r6pfw2h16.htm [02 Dec. 2002].

Canterbury, J.H. 1972. Channelization—the farmer's friend. Soil Conservation 38: 23–24.

Close P., and J. Lieschke. 2002. Rehabilitating Elwood Canal and Elster Creek, Victoria: An Assessment of Impacts on Native Freshwater Fish. http://home.vicnet.net.au/~earthcare/cnlfront.htm [16 Jan. 2003].

Cooper, W.E., and L.B. Crowder. 1979. Patterns of predation in simple and complex environments in Predator-Prey Systems in Fisheries Management, pp. 257–267.

Florsheim, J. and J.F. Mount 2000. Intentional levee breaches as a restoration tool. http://watershed.ucdavis.edu/crg/product.asp?var=%2206%22 [Jan 15, 2003].

Funk, J.L., and J.W. Robinson. 1974. Changes in the channel in the lower Missouri River and effects on fish and wildlife. Aquatic Series II, Missouri Department of Conservation, Jefferson City, MO.

Griffin, C.B. 1999. Watershed councils: an emerging form of public participation in natural resource management. Journal of the American Water Resources Association 35(3): 505–518.

Grimes, D.J. 1975. Release of sediment-bound coliforms by dredging. Applied Microbiology 29:109–111.

Hawaii. 2002. Chapter 6: Hydromodifications—Channelization, Channel Modification, Dams, Stream and Shoreline Erosion. Part III-Management Measures for Hydromodification. http://www.hawaii.gov/dbedt/czm/III-Hydromodifications.pdf [26 Nov. 2002].

(IUCN) The World Conservation Union. Towards the sustainable management of Sahelian floodplains.

Koebel, J.W. 1995. An historical perspective on the Kissimmee River restoration project. Restoration Ecology 3(3): 149–159.

Kondolf, M. 2002. Geomorphology in river restoration. http://www.laep.ced.berkeley.edu/people/kondolf/restoration/restoration.html [29 Nov. 2002].

Lockwood, L.J., and S.L. Pimm. 1999. When does restoration succeed? *In*, Weiher, E. and P.A. Keddy (eds.),

Ecological Assembly Rules: Perspectives, Advances, Retreats. Cambridge University Press, Cambridge, United Kingdom.

Lopinot, A.C. 1972. Channelized streams and ditches in Illinois. Illinois Department of Conservation, Division of Fisheries. Special Fisheries Report #35. 59 pp.

Mason, C.F. 1995. River Management and Mammal Populations, *In*, Harper, D.M., and A.J.C. Ferguson (eds.), The Ecological Basis for River Management. John Wiley and Sons, Chichester, England. 614 pp.

(MCCIS) Marquette County Community Information System. 2003. Great Lakes Water Levels. http://www.mqtinfo.org/planningeduc0026.asp [14 Jan 2003].

(MCWA) Mokelumne-Cosumnes Watershed Alliance. 2002. Lower Cosumnes and Mokelumne Rivers. Feasibility Study. http://mcwatershed.org/cosumnes/cosumnes.html [15 Jan. 2003].

Mitchell, M.S. 2003. By Lakes' Restless Edge. Erosion Control. http://www.forester.net/ecm_0205_lakes.html [08 Jan 2003].

Mullen, M.W., and B.E. Allison. 1999. Stakeholder involvement and social capital: keys to watershed management success in Alabama. Journal of the American Water Resources Association 35(3): 655–662.

Newson, M. 1992. Land, Water and Development. River Basin Systems and their Sustainable Management. Routledge, London, United Kingdom. 351 pp.

(NIPC) Northeastern Illinois Planning Commission. 2002. A Guidebook for Local Government Officials. www.nipc.cog.il.us/protect_nature_docs/Stream,%20Lake,%20and%20Wetland%20Protection.DOC [04 Dec. 2002].

(NRC) National Research Council. 1992. Restoration of Aquatic Ecosystems. National Research Council, Washington, DC. 552 pp.

(NRCS) Natural Resources Conservation Service. 2002. Homepage. http://www.nrcs.usda.gov [03 Dec. 2002].

Sammell, E.A., J.A. Baker, and R.A. Brackley. 1966. Water resources of the Ipswich River Basin, Massachusetts. Water supply Paper 1826, Geological survey, U.S. Department of the Interior, Washington, DC.

Shankman, D., and S.A. Samson. 1991. Channelization effects on Obion river Flooding, Western Tennessee. Water Resources Bulletin 21(2): 247–254.

Shields Jr., F.G. 1996. Hydraulic and Hydrologic Stability, *In*, Brookes, A., and F.D. Shields (eds.), River Channel Restoration. Guiding Principles for Sustainable Projects. John Wiley and Sons, Chichester, England. 433 pp.

Simpson, P.W., J.R. Newman, M.A. Keirn, R.M. Matter, and P.A. Guthrie. 1982. Manual of Stream Alteration Impacts on fish and Wildlife. Report No. FWS/oBS-82-24. Office of Biological Services, Fish and Wildlife Service, U.S. Department of the Interior. 155 pp.

UC Davis News. 2000. Using Levee Breaches to Restore Habitat, Control Floods. (Nov. 9th, 2000). http://www.news.ucdavis.edu/news_releases/11.00/news_levee_breaches.html [15 Jan. 2003].

(USACE) United States Army Corps of Engineers. 2002a. The Atchafalaya Basin Project http://www.mvn.usace.army.mil/pao/bro/AtchafalayaBasinProject.pdf [29 Nov. 2002].

———. 2002b. Napa River Flood Protection Project. http://www.spk.usace.army.mil/civ/napa/history.html [03 Dec. 2002].

(USEPA) United States Environmental Protection Agency. 2002a. Hydromodification. http://www.epa.gov/reg3wapd/nps/pdf/de_hydromodification.pdf [29 Nov. 2002].

———. 2002b. Mississippi River Basin Challenges. A Background to Channelization/Navigation on the Mississippi River. http://www.epa.gov/msbasin/navigation.htm [29 Nov. 2002].

Ward, J.V., K. Tockner, U. Uehlinger, and F. Malard. 2001. Understanding natural patterns and processes in river corridors as the basis for effective river restoration. Regulated rivers Research and Management 17:311–323.

Wyzga, B. 1993. River response to channel regulation: case study of the Raba River, Carpathians, Poland. Earth surface Processes and Landforms 18(6): 541–556.

GROUNDWATER OVEREXPLOITATION

Alghariani, A.A. 1999. Environmental impact assessment and remediation of groundwater mining in northern Libya. Presentation at Water Management in Arid Zones Workshop, The United Nations University, Médenine, Tunisia, Oct. 18–22, 1999. http://www.unu.edu/land/Tunisia_booklet.doc [15 Nov. 2002].

Alley, W.M., T.E. Reilly, and O.L. Franke. 1999. Sustainability of Ground-Water Resources. U.S. Geological Survey Circular 1186. Denver, CO. 80 pp.

American Rivers. 1999a. Sprawl Called Worst Threat Facing Nation's Rivers Today. http://www.american rivers.org/pressrelease/pressmersanpedro1999.htm [20 Nov. 2002].

———. 1999b. Threat: Sprawl, Groundwater Pumping. Upper San Pedro River. http://www.americanrivers.org/mostendangered/uppersanpedro1999.htm [23 Nov. 2002].

(AWR) Arizona Water Resources. 2000. Recharge Project to Protect San Pedro Flow. News Briefs 8(5). http://ag.arizona.edu/AZWATER/awr/mar00/news.htm [23 Nov. 2002].

Ayelel, T. and S.A. Al Shadily. 2000. Some of the engineering geological and hydrogeological problems and conditions of Ethiopia and Yemen. Acra Geologica Universitatis Comenianae 55:51–62.

(BLM) Bureau of Land Management. 2002. San Pedro Riparian National Conservation Area. http://azwww.az.blm.gov/tfo/spnca/spnca-info.html [22 Nov. 2002].

Blue Planet Foundation. (2002). Homepage: http://www.blueplanetfoundation.com/ [22 Nov. 2002].

Briggs, M. 1996. Riparian Ecosystem Recovery in Arid Lands. Strategies and References. University of Arizona Press, Tucson, AZ. 159 pp.

Brooks, D. 2000. Water: Local-level Management. http://www.idrc.ca/books/996/05part3.htm [17 Jan. 2003].

CalFed. 1998. CalFed and Groundwater http://www.grac.org/spring98/calfed.htm [20 Nov. 2002].

Davies, B., and J. Day. 1998. Vanishing WatersUniversity of Cape town Press, Cape Town, South Africa. 487 pp.

(DOI) Department of Interior. 2000. Federal Funding Will Help Protect San Pedro River Flows, San Pedro Riparian National Conservation Area. http://www.doi.gov/news/archives/000307.html [23 Nov. 2002].

Ezcurra, E., and M. Maziri-Hiriat. 1996. Are Megacities viable? —A cautionary tale from Mexico City. Environment 38: 26–31.

(FEMP) Federal Energy Management Program. 2003. Federal Water Conservation Projects. 2000 Federal Water Management Award Winners. http://www.eren.doe.gov/femp/techassist/waterconserve_projects.html [18 Jan. 2003].

Fetter, C. W. 1994. Applied Hydrogeology. 3rd edition. Macmillan, New York, NY.

Freeze, R.A., and J.A. Cherry. 1979. Groundwater. Prentice-Hall, Inc. Englewood Cliffs, NJ. 604 pp.

Gale, J., D. Line, D. Osmond, S. Coffey, J. Spooner, J. Arnold, T. Hoban, and R. Wimberley. 1993. Evaluation of the experimental Rural Clean Water Program. United States Environmental Protection Agency, EPA-841-R-93-005 http://h2osparc.wq.ncsu.edu/info/rcwp/index.html [21 Nov. 2002].

(GEM) Groundwater Education in Michigan. 2002. Michigan Drinking Water. http://www.gem.msu.edu/gw/mi_water.html [22 Nov. 2002].

(GF) Groundwater Foundation. 2002a. Groundwater Basics. http://www.groundwater.org/GWBasics/what isgw.htm [13 Nov. 2002].

———. 2002b. Using Technology to Conduct a Contaminant Source Survey: a Primer for Small Communities. Groundwater Foundation, Lincoln, NE. http://www.groundwater.org/ProgEvent/ACTTprimer10-02.pdf [22 Nov. 2002]

Gleick, P.H. (ed.). 1993. Water in Crisis. A Guide to the World's Fresh Water Resources. Oxford University Press, New York, NY. 473 pp.

Gleick, P.H. 2000. The World's Water 2000–2001. The Biennial Report on Freshwater Resources. Island Press, Washington, DC. 315 pp.

Haasz, D. 1999. Enhancing the prospects for water demand management in California. Pacific Institute Report, Spring 1999: 6–8. http://www.pacinst.org/pi report/spring99n1.pdf

Hunt, S. 1990. Quest for water. IDRC Reports 18 (4): 8–9. http://idrinfo.idrc.ca/Archive/ReportsINTRA/pdfs/v18n4e/108920.pdf [24 Nov. 2002].

Irrigation Journal. 1994. Irrigation survey. Jan–Feb.

Lopez, A., and C. Morales. 2002. Integrated Management of River Basins in the Mediterranean region: Sustainable Water for Nature and Food. 42 pp. http://www.riob.org/ag2002/docs/iucn01.PDF. [17 Jan 2003].

Johnson, G., D. Cosgrove, and M. Lovell. 1998. Eastern Snake River Plain—Estimates of Surface & Groundwater Interaction. http://imnh.isu.edu/digitalatlas/hydr/snakervr/esgwi.htm [20 Nov. 2002].

Kidd, J. 2002. Groundwater. A North American Resource. A Discussion Paper. http://www.cec.org/files/pdf/LAWPOLICY/water_disucssion-e1.pdf [17 Jan. 2003].

Lierong, L. 2002. Groundwater resources exploitation in China. http://www.lanl.gov/chinawater/documents/lilierong.pdf [18 Nov. 2002].

Massachusetts. 1999. Sample Impervious Surface Zoning Bylaw. (Based on a bylaw developed by the Town of Mashpee). http://www.state.ma.us/dep/brp/dws/files/IMPSURZB.doc [20 Nov. 2002].

Morgan, A.V. 2002. Mexico city: A Megacity with Big Problems. http://www.science.uwaterloo.ca/earth/waton/mexico.html [25 Nov. 2002].

Morris, E.E., and W.V. Bush. 1996. Extent and Source of Saltwater Intrusion into the Alluvial Aquifer near Brinkley, Arkansas, 1984. U.S. Geological Survey Water-Resources Investigations Report 85–4322. 123 pp.

National Land and Water Resources Audit 2001. Australian Natural Resources Atlas. Water resources-allocation and uses-Australia. http://audit.ea.gov.au/anra/water/water_frame.cfm?region_code=AUS [18 Nov. 2002].

(NRC) National Research Council. 1992. Water Transfers in the West. Efficiency, Equity, and the Environment. National Academy Press, Washington, DC. 300 pp.

———. 2000. Investigationg Groundwater Systems on Regional and National Scales. National Academy Press, Washington, DC. 143 pp.

Planet Ark. 2000. Factbox—The how, where and cost of salinity. http://www.planetark.org/dailynewsstory.cfm?newsid=8868 [15 Nov. 2002].

Poland. J.F., B.E. Lofgren, R.L. Ireland, and R.G. Pugh. 1975. Land Subsidence in the San Joaquin Valley, California, as of 1972. U.S. Geological Survey Professional Paper 437-H. Reston, VA.

Postel, S. 1999. Pillar of Sand. Can the Irrigation Miracle Last? W.W. Norton, New York, NY. 313 pp.

———. 2001. Growing more food with less water. Scientific American 284 (2): 46.

Postel, S., J.I. Morrison, and P.H. Gleick. 1998. Allocating freshwater to aquatic ecosystems: the case of the Colorado River delta. International Water Resources Association 23:119–125.

Potworowski, A. 1990. A taste of salt. IDRC Reports 18 (4): 10. http://idrinfo.idrc.ca/Archive/ReportsINTRA/pdfs/v18n4e/108921.pdf [24 Nov. 2002].

Reisner, M. 1993. Cadillac Desert: The American West and Its Disappearing Water. Penguine, New York, NY.

(SADC) Southern African Development Community. 2002. Water use in SADC countries. http://www.sadcwscu.org.ls/programme/groundwater/prog_groundprog_stats_sheet2.htm [18 Nov. 2002].

Saliba, B.C., and D.B. Bush. 1987. Water Markets in Theory and Practice. Market Transfers, Water Values, and Public Policy. Westview Press, Boulder, CO. 273 pp.

Sampat, P. 2000. Deep Trouble. The Hidden Threat of Groundwater Pollution. Worldwatch Paper 154. Worldwatch Institute, Washington, DC. 55 pp.

Seiler, K.P. and W. Lindner. 1995. Near-surface and deep groundwaters. Journal of Hydrology 165(1–4): 33–44.

Shane, E.B. 2001. Water rights and the Gila River III: the Winters Doctrine goes underground. Water Law Review 4(2): 397–417.

Shiklomanov, I.A. 1997. Comprehensive Assessment of the Freshwater Resources of the World: Assessment of

Water Resources and Water Availability in the World. World Meterological Organization and Stockholm Environment Institute. Stockholm, Sweden.

Smart Growth America. 2002. Paving Our Way to Water Shortages: How Sprawl Aggravates the Effects of Drought. Executive Summary. http://www.smartgrowthamerica.org/waterexecsum.html [20 Nov. 2002].

Stromberg, J.C. 1992. Riparian mesquite forests: a review of their ecology, threats, and recovery potential. Journal of the Arizona-Nevada Academy of Science 26: 97–100.

(TNC) The Nature Conservancy. 2000. San Pedro River. http://www.lastgreatplaces.org/SanPedro/conserve_efforts.html [18 Jan. 2003].

———. 2002. Another link for the world-class San Pedro River. The Nature Conservancy of Arizona acquires farm to restore river and wildlife habitat. http://nature.org/wherewework/northamerica/states/arizona/press/press754.html [18 Jan. 2003].

(TSHA) Texas State Historical Association. 2002. The Handbook of Texas. Toothless Blindcat. http://www.tsha.utexas.edu/handbook/online/articles/view/TT/tft1.html [18 Jan. 2003].

(UN) United Nations. 1989. Charter on Ground-Water Management (as adopted by the Economic Commission for Europe at its forty-fourth session by decision E (44)). http://www.internationalwaterlaw.org/RegionalDocs/Groundwater_Charter.htm - GROUNDWATER STRATEGIES [17 Jan. 2003].

(USEPA) U.S. Environmental Protection Agency. 1999. Safe Drinking Water Act, Section 1429. Ground Water Report to Congress. Office of Water, Washington, DC. 56 pp.

———. 2001. A Guidebook of Financial Tools, Section 6: Tools for Lowering Costs, United States Environmental Protection Agency, Environmental Finance Program. http://www.epa.gov/efinpage/guidbk98/gbk6.htm [21 Nov. 2001].

(USGS) United States Geological Survey. 1999a. Ground Water. http://capp.water.usgs.gov/GIP/gw_gip/index.html [14 Nov. 2002].

———. 1999b. Land Subsidence in the United States. U.S. Geological Survey Circular 1182. Reston, VA.

———. 2002. Concepts for National Assessment of Water Availability and Use. U.S. Geological Survey Circular 1223. Reston, VA. http://pubs.water.usgs.gov/circ1223/ [22 Nov. 2002].

Winter, T.C., J.W. Harvey, O.L. Franke, and W.M. Alley. 1998. Ground Water and Surface Water: A Single Resource. U.S. Geological Survey Circular 1139. Reston, VA.

(WRI) World Resources Institute. 2002. Water: the Challenge for Mexico City. http://www.wri.org/wri/wr-96-97/ee_b1.html [25 Nov. 2002].

World Water Forum. 2000. Presentation at the 2nd World Water Forum. http://www.worldwaterforum.net/Dossiers/docs/Russia_session.pdf [18 Nov. 2002]

Yahyaoui, H., and M. Ouessar. 1999. Withdrawal impacts on piezometric and chemical characteristics of groundwater in the arid regions of Tunisia: case of Zeuss-Koutine water table. Presentation at Water Management in Arid Zones workshop, The United Nations University, Médenine, Tunisia, Oct. 18–22, 1999. http://www.unu.edu/land/Tunisia_booklet.doc [15 Nov. 2002].

Land Use

AGRICULTURE

Administration Floodplain Management Task Force. 1994. Science of floodplain management into the 21st century. Washington, DC: 144.

Al-Ahamadi, M.E., G. Jones and J. Dottridge. 1994. Agricultural production or conservation of groundwater? A case study of the wajid aquifer, Saudi Arabia. Groundwater—drought, pollution and management. C. Reeve, and J. Watts. Rotterdam, A. A. Balkema.

Albrecht, V., and M. Wenzel. 1996. A view from the private sector. Mitigation banking: Theory and practice. L. L. Marsh, D.R. Porter, and D.A. Salvesen. Washington, DC., Island Press.

Allan, J.D. 1995. Stream ecology. Structure and function of running waters. London, Chapman & Hall.

Allan, J.D. and A.S. Flecker. 1993. "Biodiversity conservation in running waters." BioScience 43(1): 32–44.

ANS (1995). Wetlands are more than mere swamps. Philadelphia, PA, The Academy of Natural Sciences.

Bellows, B. 2002. Protecting water quality on organic farms. Fayetteville, AK, Appropriate Technology Transfer for Rural Areas.

Brinson, M.M., and A.I. Malvarez. 2002. "Temperate freshwater wetlands: Types, status, and threats." Environmental Conservation 29(2): 115–133.

Carey, A.E. 1991. Agriculture, agricultural chemicals, and water quality. Agriculture and the environment: The 1991 yearbook of agriculture. D.T. Smith. Washington, DC, United States Department of Agriculture, US Government Printing Office.

Carpenter, S.R., N.F. Caraco, D.L. Correll, R.W. Howarth, A.N. Sharpley, and V.H. Smith. 1998. "Nonpoint pollution of surface waters with phosphorus and nitrogen." Ecological Applications 8(3): 559–568.

Clapham, W.B. J., L. Granat, M.M. Holland, H.M. Keller, L. Lijklema, S. Lofgren, W. Rast, S.O. Ryding, J.A. Thorton, and L. Vermes. 1998. In, Human activities in the drainage basin as sources of nonpoint pollutants. Assessment and control of nonpoing source pollution of aquatic ecosystems. J.A. Thorton, W. Rast, C.C. Holland, G. Jolankai, and S.O. Ryding (eds.). Paris, The Parthenon Publishing Group. 23: 113–216.

Colborn, T., and K. Thayer. 2000. "Aquatic ecosystems: Harbingers of endocrine disruption." Ecological Applications 10(4): 949–957.

Cross, F.B., and R.E. Moss. 1987. Historic changes in fish communities and aquatic habitats in plains streams of Kansas. In, Community and evolutionary ecology of north American stream fishes. W.J. Matthews, and D.C. Heins (eds.). Norman, OK, University of Oklahoma Press: 155–165.

Cuffney, T.F., M.R. Meador, S.D. Porter, and M. E. Gurtz. 2000. "Responses of physical, chemical, and biological indicators of water quality to a gradient of agricultural land use in the Yakima river basin, Washington." Environmental Monitoring and Assessment 64(1): 259–270.

de Haan, C., H. Steinfeld, and H. Blackburn. 1997. Livestock & the environment: Finding a balance. Brussels, European Commission Directorate-General for Development, Development Policy, Sustainable Development, and Natural Resources.

Decamps, H., M. Fortune, F. Gazelle, and G. Pautou. 1988. "Historical influence of man on the riparian dynamics of a fluvial landscape." Landscape Ecology 1(3): 163–173.

Detenbeck, N.E., S.M. Galatowitsch, J. Atkinson, and H. Ball. 1999. "Evaluating perturbations and developing restoration strategies for inland wetlands in the great lakes basin." Wetlands 19(4): 789–820.

Diamond, J.M., D.W. Bressler, and V.B. Serveiss. 2002. "Assessing relationships between human land uses and the decline of native mussels, fish, and macroinvertebrates in the clinch and powell river watershed, USA." Environmental Toxicology and Chemistry 21(6): 1147–1155.

Doering, O.C., F. Diaz-Hermelo, C. Howard, R. Heimlich, F. Hitzhusen, R. Kazmierczack, J. Lee, L. Libby, W. Milton, T. Prato, and M. O. Ribaudo. 1999. Evaluation of the economic costs and benefits of methods for reducing nutrient loads to the Gulf of Mexico. Washington, D.C., National Atmospheric and Oceanic Administration: 137.

Epstein, L., S. Bassein, F.G. Zalom, and L.R. Wilhoit. 2001. "Changes in pest management practice in almond orchards during the rainy season in California, USA." Agriculture, Ecosystems & Environment 83(1–2): 111–120.

Eswaran, H. 1991. Sustainable agriculture in developing countries: Challenges and the U.S. Role. Agriculture and the environment: The 1991 yearbook of agriculture. D.T. Smith. Washington, DC, U.S. Department of Agriculture.

FAO. 1988. A soil conservation strategy for Africa. Rome, Food and Agriculture Organization: 14.

———. 2000. Statistical databases, Food and Agriculture Organization of the United Nations. 2003.

Foster, D.R. 1992. "Land-use history (1730–1990) and vegetation dynamics in central New England, USA." Journal of Ecology 80: 753–772.

Gleick, P.H. (ed.). 1993. Water in crisis a guide to the world's fresh water resources. New York, Oxford University Press.

Goldman-Carter, J., and G. McCallie (1996). An environmentalist's perspective—time for a reality check. *In*, Mitigation banking: Theory and practice. L.L. Marsh, D.R. Porter, and D.A. Salvesen (eds.). Washington, DC, Island Press.

Greenhalgh, S., and A. Sauer. 2003. Awakening the dead zone: An investment for agriculture, water quality, and climate change. Washington, DC., World Resources Institute: 24.

Gregory, S.V., F.J. Swanson, W.A. McKee, and K.W. Cummins. 1991. "An ecosystem perspective of riparian zones: Focus on links between land and water." BioScience 41(8): 540–551.

Hancock, P.J. 2002. "Human impacts on the stream-groundwater exchange zone." Environmental Management 29(6): 763–781.

Harding, J.S., E.F. Benfield, P.V. Bolstad, G.S. Helfman, and E.B.D. Jones, III. 1998. "Stream biodiversity: The ghost of land use past." Proceedings of the National Academy of Sciences 95: 14843–14847.

Harris, J.M. 1990. World agriculture and the environment. New York, NY, Garland Publishing, Inc.

Jeffery, R.C.V., and P.M. Chooye 1991. "The peoples role in wetlands management—the Zambian initiative." Landscape and Urban Planning 20(1–3): 73–79.

Karr, J.R., and I.J. Schlosser. 1978. "Water resources and the land-water interface." Science 201(21): 229–234.

Kolpin, D.W., E.T. Furlong, M.T. Meyer, E.M. Thurman, S.D. Zaugg, L.B. Barber, and H.T. Buxton. 2002. "Pharmaceuticals, hormones, and other organic wastewater contaminants in us streams, 1999–2000: A national reconnaissance." Environmental Science & Technology 36(6): 1202–1211.

Lammert, M., and J.D. Allan. 1999. "Environmental auditing. Assessing biotic integrity of streams: Effects of scale in measuring the influence of land use/cover and habitat structure on fish and macroinvertebrates." Environmental Management 23(2): 257–270.

Lawton, L.A. and G.A. Codd. 1993. "Cyanobacterial (blue-green algae) toxins and their significance in U.K. and European waters." Journal of the Institute of Water and Environmental Management.

Lemly, A.D., R.T. Kingsford, and J.R. Thompson. 2000. "Irrigated agriculture and wildlife conservation: Conflict on a global scale." Environmental Management 25(5): 485–512.

Lenat, D.R. and J.K. Crawford. 1994. "Effects of land-use on water-quality and aquatic biota of 3 north-Carolina piedmont streams." Hydrobiologia 294(3): 185–199.

Line, D.E., W.A. Harman, G.D. Jennings, E.J. Thompson, and D.L. Osmond. 2000. "Nonpoint-source pollutant load reductions associated with livestock exclusion." Journal of Environmental Quality 29: 1882–1890.

Lowrance, R., L.S. Altier, J.D. Newbold, R.R. Schnabel, P.M. Groffman, J.M. Denver, D.L. Correll, J.W. Gilliam, J.L. Robinson, R.B. Brinsfield, K.W. Staver, W. Lucas, and A.H. Todd. 1997. "Water quality functions of riparian forest buffers in Chesapeake bay watersheds." Environmental Management 21(5): 687–712.

McPherson, B.F., and R. Halley. 1997. The south Florida environment: A region under stress. Denver, CO, USGS.

Minnesota Pollution Control Agency. 2000. "Oxygen-poor 'dead zone' links gulf of Mexico with Minnesota waters." Minnesota Environment (November 2000).

Mississippi River/Gulf of Mexico Watershed Nutrient Task Force. 2001. Action plan for reducing, mitigating, and controlling hypoxia in the northern gulf of Mexico. Washington, DC, U.S. Environmental Protection Agency: 36.

Molnar, J.J., A. Bitto, and G. Brant. 2001. Paths and barriers perceived by small and limited resource farmers. Auburn, AL, Auburn University.

Molnar, J.J., T. Hoban, J.D. Parrish, and M. Futreal. 1997. Industrialization of agriculture: Trends, spatial patterns, and implications for field-level application by the NRCS. Washington, DC, Natural Resources Conservation Service, Social Sciences Institute.

Myers, D.N., K.D. Metzker, and S. Davis. 2000. Status and trends in suspended-sediment discharge, soil erosion and conservation tillage in the Maumee river basin—Ohio, Michigan and Indiana. Washington, DC, United State Geological Survey: 45.

Naiman, R.J., J.J. Magnuson, D.M. McKnight, and J. A. Stanford, Eds. 1995. The freshwater imperative; a research agenda. Washington, DC, Island Press.

National Research Council. 1995. Wetlands: Characteristics and boundaries. Washington, DC, National Academy Press.

National Research Council. 2001. Compensating for wetland losses under the clean water act. Washington, DC, National Academies Press.

National Research Council Committee on Long-Range Soil and Water Conservation. 1993. Soil and water quality: An agenda for agriculture. Washington, DC, National Academy Press.

National Research Council Committee on Restoration and Aquatic Ecosystems. 1992. Restoration of aquatic ecosystems. Washington, DC, National Academy Press.

National Research Council Committee on Sustainable Agriculture and the Environment in the Humid Tropics. 1993. Sustainable agriculture and the environment in the humid tropics. Washington DC, National Academy Press.

North Plains Ground Water District (unknown). Ogallala aquifer, North Plains Ground Water District. 2003.

NRCS. 1997. Water quality and agriculture; status, conditions and trends. Washington, DC, Natural Resources Conservation Service.

Oakley, P. 1991. "The concept of participation in development." Landscape and Urban Planning 20 (1–3): 115–122.

Palmer, T. 1994. Lifelines: The case for river conservation. Washington DC, Island Press.

Postel, S.L. 1993. Water and agriculture. In, Water in crisis: a guide to the world's fresh water resources. P.H. Gleick. New York, Oxford University Press: 56–66.

Prasad, R. 1994. Groundwater utilization and management in the state of Karnataka in India. In, Groundwater-drought, pollution and management. C. Reeve and J. Watts (eds.). Rotterdam, A.A. Balkema.

Pyrovetsi, M., and G. Daoutopoulos. 1999. "Farmers' needs for nature conservation education in Greece." Journal of Environmental Management 56(2): 147–157.

Quinn, J.M., R.B. Williamson, R.K. Smith, and M.L. Vickers. 1992. "Effects of riparian grazing and channelization on streams in Southland, New Zealand. 2. Benthic invertebrates." New Zealand Journal of Marine and Freshwater Research 26(2): 259–273.

Richards, C., and G. Host. 1994. "Examining land-use influences on stream habitats and macroinvertebrates—a GIS approach." Water Resources Bulletin 30(4): 729–738.

Rickerl, D.H., L.L. Janssen, and R. Woodland. 2000. "Buffered wetlands in agricultural landscapes in the prairie pothole region: Environmental, agronomic, and economic evaluations." Journal of Soil and Water Conservation 55(2): 220–225.

Roth, N.E., D.J. Allan, and D.L. Erickson. 1996. "Landscape influences on stream biotic integrity assessed at multiple spatial scales." Landscape Ecology 11(3): 141–156.

Sierra Club. 2002. Changes to wetlands permitting rules threaten our streams and wetlands. The Sierra Club. 2003.

Smith, D.T. (ed.). 1991. Agriculture and the environment: The 1991 yearbook of agriculture. Washington, DC, United States Department of Agriculture, US Government Printing Office.

Solley, W.B., R.R. Pierce, and H.A. Perlman. 1995. Estimated use of water in the United States in 1995. Washington DC, US Geological Survey.

Stanners, D., and P. Bourdeau, Eds. 1995. Europe's environment, the dobris assessment. Copenhagen, European Environment Agency.

Steinfeld, H., C. de Haan, and H. Blackburn. 1997. Livestock—environment interactions: Issues and options. Brussels, European Commission Directorate-General for Development, Development Policy, Sustainable Development, and Natural Resources.

Stonehouse, D.P. 1999. "Economic evaluation of on-farm conservation practices in the great lakes region of north America." Environmetrics 10(4): 505–520.

Thompson, J.R., and G. Polet. 2000. "Hydrology and land use in a sahelian floodplain wetland." Wetlands 20(4): 639–659.

Thompson, T.D.E. 1996. Interactive elements of catchment ecosystems: Agriculture. Multiple land use and catchment management, Scotland, The Macaulay Land Use Research Institute.

Thorton, J.A., W. Rast, C.C. Holland, G. Jolankai, and S. O. Ryding, Eds. 1999. Assessment and control of non-poing source pollution of aquatic ecosystems. Man and the biosphere. Paris, The Parthenon Publishing Group.

Turner, M. G. 1990. "Landscape changes in nine rural counties in Georgia." Photogrammetric Engineering and Remote Sensing 56(3): 379–386.

UCIPM. 1999. Water quality and ipm annual report, University of California Statewide Integrated Pest Management Program. 2003.

Uri, N.D. 1999. Agriculture and the environment. Commack, NY, Nova Science Publishers, Inc.

U.S. Bureau of the Census. 1990. Statistical abstract of the United States, 1990: The national data book. Washington DC, U.S. Department of Commerce: 991.

USDA and USEPA. 1999. Unified national strategy for animal feeding operations. Washington, DC, U.S. Department of Agriculture and U.S. Environmental Protection Agency.

USEPA. 2000. The quality of our nation's waters. A summary of the national water quality inventory: 1998 report to congress, USEPA Office of Water: 20.

USEPA. 2002. EPA and agriculture working together to improve America's waters, US Environmental Protection Agency.

USEPA. 2003. Protecting and restoring America's wetlands: Agency actions to improve mitigation and further the goal of "no net loss" of wetlands, U.S. Environmental Protection Agency.

USGS. A systematic approach to understanding nutrients and pesticides, National Water Quality Assessment.

USGS. 2001. Selected findings and current perspectives on urban and agricultural water quality by the national water-quality assessment program, US Geological Survey.

Warrington, P. 2000. Best management practices to protect water quality from nonpoint source pollution, British Columbia Lake Stewardship Society.

Waskom, R.M. 1994. Best management practices for Colorado agriculture: An overview, Colorado State University Cooperative Extension and Colorado Department of Agriculture.

Welcomme, R.L. 1979. Fisheries ecology of floodplain rivers. London, UK, Longman.

Williams, J.D., M.L. Warren, K.S. Cummings, J.L. Harris, and R.J. Neves. 1993. "Conservation status of freshwater mussels of the united-states and Canada." Fisheries 18(9): 6–22.

Wilson, G.A. 1996. "Farmer environmental attitudes and esa participation." Geoforum 27(2): 115–131.

WRI. 2000. People and ecosystems: The fraying web of life. Washington, DC, World Resources Institute, United Nations Development Programme, the World Bank and United Nations Environment Programme.

Zhang, W.L., Z.X. Tian, N. Zhang, and X.Q. Li. 1996. Nitrate pollution of groundwater in northern China. Agriculture, Ecosystems and Environment 59: 223–31,

Zedler, J.B. 1997. Restoring the nation's wetlands; why, where and how? Principles of conservation biology. G. K. Meffe and C. R. Carroll. Sunderland, MA, Sinauer Associates, Inc.

Urbanization

Aldous, P.J., and J. Turrell. 1994. Atrazine concentrations in chalk aquifers and the implications for future water treatment. In, Groundwater: Drought, pollution and management. C. Reeve, and C.D. Watts (eds.). Rotterdam, UK, A.A. Balkema.

Allan, J.D. 1995. Stream ecology. Structure and function of running waters. London, Chapman & Hall.

American Planning Association. 1996. Growing smart legislative guidebook. Chicago, IL, APA Planners Press.

Arnold, C.L., and J.C, Gibbons. 1996. "Impervious surface coverage: The emergence of a key environmental indicator." Journal of the American Planning Association 62(2): 243–258.

Bamford, H.A., F.C. Ko, and J.E. Baker. 2002. "Seasonal and annual air-water exchange of polychlorinated biphenyls across Baltimore harbor and the northern Chesapeake bay." Environmental Science & Technology 36(20): 4245–4252.

Beacham, T.D., and C.B. Murray. 1990. "Temperature, egg size, and development of embryos and alevins of five species of pacific salmon: A comparative analysis." Transactions of the American Fisheries Society 119: 927–945.

Bjork, S. 1994. Restoration of lakes through sediment removal- lake trummen, Sweden. In, Restoration of lake ecosystems: A holistic approach. M Eiseltova (eds.). Gloucester, UK, International Waterfowl and Wetlands Research Bureau.

Boon, P.J., B.R. Davies, and G.E. Petts, Eds. 2000. Global perspectives on river conservation: Science. Policy and practice. Chichester, John Wiley & Sons, Ltd.

Bourgine, F., J.I. Chapman, and H. Kerai. 1994. Removal of organic compounds from a groundwater in an urban area near London. In, Groundwater: Drought, pollution and management C. Reeve and C.D. Watts (eds.). Rotterdam, UK, A. A. Balkema.

Brinson, M.M., and A.I. Malvarez. 2002. "Temperate freshwater wetlands: Types, status, and threats." Environmental Conservation 29(2): 115–133.

Burkhead, N.M., S.J. Walsh, B.J. Freeman, and J.D. Williams. 1997. Status and restoration of the etowah river, an imperiled southern appalachian ecosystem. In, Aquatic fauna in peril: The southeastern perspective. G.W. Benz, and D.E. Collins (eds.). Decatur, GA, Southeastern Aquatic Research Institute, Lenz Design and Communications.

Carpenter, S.R., N.F. Caraco, D.L. Correll, R.W. Howarth, A.N. Sharpley, and V.H. Smith. 1998. "Nonpoint pollution of surface waters with phosphorus and nitrogen." Ecological Applications 8(3): 559–568.

Chafik, A., M. Cheggour, D. Cossa and S.B.M. Sifeddine. 2001. "Quality of Moroccan Atlantic coastal waters: Water monitoring and mussel watching." Aquatic Living Resources 14(4): 239–249.

Clapham, W.B.J., L. Granat, M.M. Holland, H.M. Keller, L. Lijklema, S. Lofgren, W. Rast, S.O. Ryding, J.A. Thorton, and L. Vermes. 1998a. Human activities in the drainage basin as sources of nonpoint pollutants. In, Assessment and control of nonpoing source pollution of aquatic ecosystems: A practical approach. J.A. Thorton, W. Rast, C.C. Holland, G. Jolankai, and S.O. Ryding (eds.). Paris, UNESCO and The Parthenon Publishing Group.

Clapham, W.B.J., A.J. Davenport, M.M. Holland, W. Rast, S.O. Ryding, and J.A. Thorton. 1998b. Available nonpoint source pollution control measures. In, Assessment and control of nonpoint source pollution of aquatic systems: A practical approach. J.A. Thorton, W. Rast, M.M. Holland, G. Jolankai, and S.O. Ryding (eds.). Paris, UNESCO and The Parthenon Publishing Group.

Colborn, T., and C. Clement, Eds. 1992. Chemically-induced alterations in sexual and functional development: The wildlife/human connection. Princeton, New Jersey, Princeton Scientific.

Colborn, T., and K. Thayer. 2000. "Aquatic ecosystems: Harbingers of endocrine disruption." Ecological Applications 10(4): 949–957.

Cooke, R.A., E.B. Welch, S.A. Peterson, and P.R. Newroth, Eds. 1993. Restoration and management of lakes and reservoirs. Boca Raton, FL, Lewis Publishers.

Couch, C., and P. Hamilton. 2002. Effects of urbanization of stream ecosystems, U.S. Geological Survey. 2002.

CWP. 2000. Nutrient movement from the lawn to the stream. In, The practice of watershed protection. T.R. Schueler and H.K. Holland (eds.). Ellicott City, MD, The Center for Watershed Protection.

CWP. 2003a. Managing non-stormwater discharges. http://www.cwp.org/non-stormwater_discharges.html.

CWP. 2003b. Stormwater management practices. http://www.cwp.org/stormwater_practices.html.

Dennehy, K.F., D.W. Litke, C.M. Tate, S.L. Qi, P.B. McMahon, B.W. Bruce, R.A. Kimbrough, and J.S. Heiny 1998. Water quality in the south platte river basin, Colorado, Nebraska, and Wyoming, 1992–95: U.S. Geological survey circular 1167, U.S. Geological Survey.

Department of Environmental Resources. 1999. Low-impact development: An integrated design approach. Maryland, Prince Georges's County, Maryland Department of Environmental Resources: 150.

Diamond, J.M., D.W. Bressler, and V.B. Serveiss. 2002. "Assessing relationships between human land uses and the decline of native mussels, fish, and macroinvertebrates in the clinch and powell river watershed, USA." Environmental Toxicology and Chemistry 21(6): 1147–1155.

Dudgeon, D., S. Choowaew, and S-C Ho. 2000. River conservation in south-east Asia. *In*, Global perspectives on river conservation: Science, policy and practice. P.J. Boon, B.R. Davies, and G.E. Petts (eds.). Chichester, John Wiley & Sons, Ltd.

Duke, L.D. 2000. Practical pollution prevention emphasized for industrial stormwater. *In*, The practice of watershed protection. T.R. Schueler, and H.K. Holland (eds.). Ellicott City, MD, The Center for Watershed Protection.

Dunne, T., and L.B. Leopold. 1978. Water in environmental planning. New York, W.H. Freeman & Co.

Ehrenfeld, J.G. 2000. "Evaluating wetlands within an urban context." Ecological Engineering 15(3–4): 253–265.

Fiorino, D.J. 1995. Making environmental policy. Berkeley, CA, University of California Press.

Forman, R.T.T., and L.E. Alexander. 1998. "Roads and their major ecological effects." Annual Review of Ecology and Systematics 29: 207–231.

Foster, D.R., G. Motzkin, and B. Slater. 1998. "Land-use history as long-term broad-scale disturbance: Regional forest dynamics in central New England." Ecosystems 1: 96–119.

Foster, I.D.L., and S.M. Charlesworth. 1996. "Heavy metals in the hydrologic cycle: Trends and explanations." Hydrological Processes 10(2): 227–261.

France, R., H. Culbert, and R. Peters. 1996. "Decreased carbon and nutrient input to boreal lakes from particulate organic matter following riparian clear cutting." Environmental Management 20(4): 579–583.

Frey, M. 2001. The ripple effect: How to make waves in the turbulent world of watershed cleanup plans. Washington, DC, Clean Water Network.

Gafny, S., M. Goren, and A. Gasith. 2000. "Habitat condition and fish assemblage structure in a coastal Mediterranean stream (yarqon, Israel) receiving domestic effluent." Hydrobiologia 422: 319–330.

Gleick, P.H. (ed.). 1993. Water in crisis a guide to the world's fresh water resources. New York, Oxford University Press.

Gopal, B. 2000. River conservation in the Indian sub-continent. *In*, Global perspectives on river conservation: Science, policy and practice. P.J. Boon, B.R. Davies, and G.E. Petts (eds.). Chichester, John Wiley & Sons, Ltd.

Gregory, K.J., R.J. Davis, and P.W. Downs. 1992. "Identification of river channel change due to urbanization." Applied Geography 12: 299–318.

Gregory, S.V., F.J. Swanson, W.A. Mckee, and K.W. Cummins. 1991. "An ecosystem perspective of riparian zones: Focus on links between land and water." BioScience 41(8): 540–551.

Guy, H.P. 1965. Residential construction and sedimentation at Kensington, Maryland. Proceedings of the federal interagency sedimentation conference 1963.

Hanisch, C. 1998. Environmental Science & Technology 32: 176a–179a.

Harper, D., and T. Brown, Eds. 1998. The sustainable management of tropical catchments. Chichester, John Wiley & Sons Ltd.

Holland, C.C., J.E. Honea, S.E. Gwin, and M.E. Kentula. 1995. "Wetland degradation and loss in the rapidly urbanizing area of Portland, Oregon." Wetlands 15(4): 336–345.

Horne, A.J., and C.R. Goldman. 1994. Limnology. New York, McGraw-Hill, Inc.

Horowitz, A.J., M. Meybeck, Z. Idlafkih, and E. Biger. 1999. "Variations in trace element geochemistry in the Seine river basin based on floodplain deposits and bed sediments." Hydrological Processes 13: 1329–1340.

Jagals, P. 1997. "Stormwater runoff from typical developed and developing south African urban developments: Definitely not for swimming." Water Science and Technology 35(11–12): 133–140.

Jeppesen, E., M. Sondergaard, M. Sondergaard, and K. Christofferson, Eds. 1998. The structuring role of submerged macrophytes in lakes. New York, Springer-Verlag.

Klein, R.D. 1990. Protecting the aquatic environment from the effects of golf courses. Maryland Line, MD, Community and Environmental Defense Association: 54.

Kollar, K.L., and P. Macauley. 1980. "Water requirements for industrial development." Journal of the American Water Works Association 72(1): 2–9.

Landis, M.S., A.F. Vette, and G.J. Keeler. 2002. "Atmospheric mercury in the lake Michigan basin: Influence of the Chicago Gary urban area." Environmental Science & Technology 36(21): 4508–4517.

Lawton, L.A., and G.A. Codd. 1993. "Cyanobacterial (blue-green algae) toxins and their significance in U.K. and European waters." Journal of the Institute of Water and Environmental Management.

Lenat, D.R., and J.K. Crawford. 1994. "Effects of land-use on water-quality and aquatic biota of 3 north-Carolina piedmont streams." Hydrobiologia 294(3): 185–199.

Lindqvist, O., and H. Rodhe. 1985. Tellus 37B: 136–159.

Ludwig, J.P., J.P. Giesy, C.L. Summer, W. Bowerman, R. Aulerich, S. Bursian, H.J. Auman, P.D. Jones, L.L. Williams, D.E. Tillitt, and M. Gilbertson. 1993. "A comparison of water-quality criteria for the great lakes based on human and wildlife health." Journal of Great Lakes Research 19(4): 789–807.

Mainstone, C.P., and W. Parr. 2002. "Phosphorus in rivers—ecology and management." Science of the Total Environment 282: 25–47.

Mcpherson, B.F., and R. Halley. 1997. The south Florida environment: A region under stress. Denver, CO, USGS.

Mielke, H. W., C.R. Gonzales, M.K. Smith, and P.W. Mielke. 2000. "Quantities and associations of lead, zinc, cadmium, manganese, chromium, nickel, vanadium, and copper in fresh Mississippi delta alluvium and new Orleans alluvial soils." The Science of the Total Environment 246: 249–259.

Moore, K.M., and S.V. Gregory. 1988. "Summer habitat utilization and ecology of cutthroat trout fry (salmo clarki) in cascade mountain streams." Canadian Journal of Fisheries and Aquatic Sciences 45: 1921–1930.

Moraes, R., P. Gerhard, L. Andersson, J. Sturve, S. Rauch, and S. Molander. 2003. "Establishing causality between exposure to metals and effects on fish." Human and Ecological Risk Assessment 9(1): 149–169.

Naiman, R.J., and M.G. Turner. 2000. "A future perspective on north America's freshwater ecosystems." Ecological Applications 10(4): 958–970.

National Research Council Committee on Restoration and Aquatic Ecosystems. 1992. Restoration of aquatic ecosystems. Washington, DC, National Academy Press.

Nelson, N., J. Dorfman, and L. Fowler. 2002. The potential for community forests to be self-financing: An hedonic analysis of the enhancement value of Georgia's trees. Athens, GA, Office of Public Service and Outreach, University of Georgia's College of Environment and Design: 24.

Odell, K.M. 1994. "Water-quality in the shingle creek basin, Florida, before and after wastewater diversion." Journal of Environmental Quality 23(3): 563–571.

Offenberg, J.H., and J.E. Baker. 2000. "PCBS and PAHS in southern lake Michigan in 1994 and 1995: Urban atmospheric influences and long-term declines." Journal of Great Lakes Research 26(2): 196–208.

Pedersen, E.R., and M.A. Perkins. 1986. "The use of benthic invertebrate data for evaluating impacts of urban runoff." Hydrobiologia 139: 13–22.

Pereira, H.C. 1973. Land use and water resources in temperate and tropical climates. Cambridge, Cambridge University Press.

Peterson, A., R. Reznick, S. Hedin, M. Hendges, and D. Dunlap. 1998. Guidebook of best management practices for Michigan watersheds. Lansing, MI, Michigan Department of Environmental Quality: 59.

Pluhowski, E.J. 1970. Urbanization and its effect on the temperature of streams in Long Island, New York. Washington DC, United States Geological Survey.

Poff, N.L., D.J. Allan, M.B. Bain, J.R. Karr, K.L. Prestegaard, B.D. Richter, R.E. Sparks, and J.C. Stromberg. 1997. "The natural flow regime: A paradigm for conservation and restoration of riverine ecosystems." BioScience 47: 769–784.

Rast, W. 1998. Introduction. *In*, Assessment and control of nonpoint source pollution of aquatic ecosystems: A practical approach. J.A. Thorton, W. Rast, M.M. Holland, G. Jolankai and S.O. Ryding (eds.). Paris, UNESCO and the Parthenon Publishing Group.

Rhodes, B.L., and R.A. Cahill. 1999. "Geomorphological assessment of sediment contamination in an urban stream system." Applied Geochemistry 14(459–83).

Richards, C., R.J. Haro, L.B. Johnson, and G.E. Host. 1997. "Catchment and reach-scale properties as indicators of macroinvertebrate species traits." Freshwater Biology 37: 219–230.

Riley, A.L. 1998. Restoring streams in cities: A guide for planners, policymakers, and citizens. Washington, DC, Island Press.

Rolland, R.M. 2000. "A review of chemically-induced alterations in thyroid and vitamin a status from field studies of wildlife and fish." Journal of Wildlife Diseases 36(4): 615–635.

Ryding, S.O., and J.A. Thorton. 1998. Types of aquatic pollutants, impacts on water quality and determination of critical levels. *In*, Assessment and control of nonpoing source pollution of aquatic ecosystems: A practical approach. J.A. Thorton, W. Rast, C.C. Holland, G. Jolankai, and S.O. Ryding (eds.). Paris, UNESCO and The Parthenon Publishing Group.

Schueler, T.R. 1987. Controlling urban runoff: A practical manual for planning and designing urban bmp's. Washington, DC, Metropolitan Washington Council of Governments.

Schueler, T.R. 2000. On watershed education. *In*, The practice of watershed protection. T.R. Schueler, and H.K. Holland (eds.). Ellicott City, MD, The Center for Watershed Protection.

Schueler, T.R., and H.K. Holland, Eds. 2000. The practice of watershed protection. Ellicott City, MD, Center for Watershed Protection.

Seabrook, C. 1997. EPA slams metro streams. The Atlanta Journal/The Atlanta Constitution. Atlanta, GA.

Soares, C. 1999. Environmental technology and economics: Sustainable development in industry. Boston, Butterworth Heinemann.

Solley, W.B., R.R. Pierce, and H.A. Perlman. 1995. Estimated use of water in the united states in 1995. Washington DC, U.S. Geological Survey.

Sparks, B.L., and D.L. Strayer. 1998. "Effects of low dissolved oxygen on juvenile elliptic complanata (bivalvia: Unionidae)." Journal of the North American Benthological Society 17(1): 129–134.

Srinivas, H. 2003. An integrated urban water strategy. www.gdrc.org/uem/water/urban-water.html.

Stranko, S., and W. Rodney. 2001. Habitat quality and biological integrity assessment of freshwater streams in the saint mary's river watershed, Maryland Department of Natural Resources: 27.

The Heinz Center. 2002. The state of the nation's ecosystems: Measuring the lands, waters, and living resources of the united states. Cambridge, The Heinz Center: 270.

Thorton, J.A., W. Rast, C.C. Holland, G. Jolankai, and S.O. Ryding, Eds. 1999. Assessment and control of nonpoing source pollution of aquatic ecosystems. Man and the biosphere. Paris, The Parthenon Publishing Group.

United Nations Commission on Sustainable Development. 1997. Comprehensive assessment of the freshwater resources of the world: Report of the secretary-general to the fifth session of the commission on sustainable development. New York, United Nations.

UNPD. 2002. World urbanization prospects: The 2001 revision. New York, United Nations Population Division.

U.S. Bureau of the Census. 2001. 100 fastest growing counties. 2002. http://eire.census.gov/popest/data/counties/tables/CO-EST2001-11.php.

USEPA. 1992. Storm water management for construction activities; developing pollution prevention plans and best management practices. Washington DC, U.S. Environmental Protection Agency, Office of Water: 290.

———. 1993. Guidance specifying management measures for sources of nonpoint pollution in coastal waters. Washington, DC, USEPA, Office of Water.

———. 1997. Urbanization and streams: Studies of hydrologic impacts. Washington, DC, USEPA Office of Water: 18.

———. 1999a. Introduction to the national pretreatment program. Washington, DC, USEPA, Office of Wastewater Management.

———. 1999b. Preliminary data summary of urban stormwater best management practices. Washington DC, USEPA.

———. 2000a. National conference on urban water resource management and protection. Chicago, IL, USEPA.

———. 2000b. The quality of our nation's waters. A summary of the national water quality inventory: 1998 report to congress, USEPA Office of Water: 20.

———. 2002a. Section 319 success stories volume iii: The successful implementation of the clean water act's section 319 nonpoint source pollution program. Washington, DC, United States Environmental Protection Agency, Office of Water.

———. 2002b. Sustainable communities: Putting wetlands to work in your watershed. Washington DC, USEPA: 4.

USGS. 1999. Status and trends of the nation's biological resources. Washington, DC, United States Geological Survey.

———. 2002. A systematic approach to understanding nutrients and pesticides. http://water.usgs.gov/nawqa.

Wang, L.Z., J. Lyons, P. Kanehl, R. Bannerman and E. Emmons (2000). "Watershed urbanization and changes in fish communities in southeastern Wisconsin streams." Journal of the American Water Resources Association 36(5): 1173–1189.

Wilber, W.G. and J.V. Hunter. 1979. "The impact of urbanization of the distribution of heavy metals in bottom sediments of the saddle river." Water Resources Bulletin 15: 790–800.

Wohl, E.E. (ed.). 2000. Inland flood hazards: Human, riparian, and aquatic communities. Cambridge, Cambridge University Press.

World Bank Group. 1998. Pollution prevention and abatement handbook, 1998: Toward cleaner production. Washington, DC, The World Bank.

World Resources Institute, United Nations Environment Programme, United Nations Development Programme and The World Bank. 1996. World Resources 1996–97. A guide to the global environment: The urban environment. Washington DC, World Resources Institute: 400.

FORESTRY

Agee, J.K. 1988. Successional dynamics in forest riparian zones. *In*, Streamside management: Riparian wildlife and forestry interactions. K.J. Raedeke (eds.). Seattle, WA, Institute of Forest Resources, University of Washington.

Askew, G.R., and T.M. Williams. 1984. "Sediment concentrations from intensively prepared wetland sites." Southern Journal of Applied Forestry 8: 152–157.

Batzer, D.P., C.R. Jackson, and M. Mosner. 2000. "Influences of riparian logging on plants and invertebrates in small, depressional wetlands of Georgia, USA." Hydrobiologia 441(1–3): 123–132.

Bent, G.C. 2001. "Effects of forest-management activities on runoff components and groundwater recharge to quabbin reservoir, central Massachusetts." Forest Ecology and Management 143(1–3): 115–129.

Bisson, P.A., T.P. Quinn, G.H. Reeves, and S.H. Gregory. 1992. Best management practices, cumulative effects, and long-term trends in fish abundance in pacific northwest river systems. *In*, Watershed management: Balancing sustainablility and environmental change. R.J. Naiman (eds.). New York, NY, Springer-Verlag.

Clapham, W.B.J., Granat, L., M.M. Holland, H.M. Keller, L. Lijklema, S. Lofgren, W. Rast, S.O. Ryding, J.A. Thorton, and L. Vermes. 1998. Human activities in the drainage basin as sources of nonpoint pollutants. *In*, Assessment and control of nonpoing source pollution of aquatic ecosystems: A practical approach. J.A. Thorton, W. Rast, C.C. Holland, G. Jolankai, and S.O. Ryding (eds.). Paris, UNESCO and The Parthenon Publishing Group.

Cubbage, F.W. 1991. "Public regulation of private forestry; pro-active policy responses." Journal of Forestry 89(12): 31–35.

Defenders of Wildlife. 2000. State forestry laws. Albuquerque, NM, Defenders of Wildlife: 58.

Dubois, M.R., K. Mcnabb, and T.J. Straka. 1999. "Costs and cost trends for forestry practices in the south." Forest Landowner 58: 3–8.

FAO. 1998. Forest resource assessment 2000: Terms and definitions. Rome, Food and Agriculture Organization.
———. 2000. Global forest resources assessment 2000. Rome, Food and Agriculture Organization.

Fenn, ME., M.A. Poth, and A.J.D. 1984. "Nitrogen excess in north American ecosystems: Predisposing factors, ecosystem responses, and management strategies." Ecological Applications 8: 706–733.

Firehock, K. 1991. Virginia's erosion and sediment control law: A citizen's action guide. Arlington, VA, Izaak Walton League of America.

Flaspohler, D.J., C.J.F. Huckins, B.R. Bub, and P.J. Van Dusen. 2002. "Temporal patterns in aquatic and avian communities following selective logging in the upper great lakes region." Forest Science 48(2): 339–349.

Fletcher, R., M. Rickenbach, and E. Hansen. 2002. Forest certification in north America. Corvallis, OR, Oregon State University Extension Service.

Fletcher, S. 1995. International forest agreements: Current status. Washington, DC, Environment and Natural Resources Policy Division, Congressional Research Service.

France, R., H. Culbert, and R. Peters. 1996. "Decreased carbon and nutrient input to boreal lakes from particulate organic matter following riparian clear cutting." Environmental Management 20(4): 579–583.

Garman, G.C., and J.R. Moring. 1991. "Initial effects of deforestation on physical characteristics of a boreal river." Hydrobiologia 209(1): 29–37.

Garman, G.C., and J.R. Moring. 1993. "Diet and annual production of 2 boreal river fishes following clear-cut logging." Environmental Biology of Fishes 36(3): 301–311.

Grace, J.M. 2000. "Forest road sideslopes and soil conservation techniques." Journal of Soil and Water Conservation 55(1): 96–101.

Grace, J.M. 2002. Overview of best management practices related to forest roads: The southern states. American Society of Agricultural Engineers Annual International Meeting, Chicago, IL.

Green, W.D., W.B. Stuart, and J.V. Perumpral. 1983. Skidder and tire size effects on soil compaction. St. Joseph, MI, American Society of Agriculture and Engineering: 16.

Gregory, S.V., F.J. Swanson, W.A. Mckee, and K.W. Cummins. 1991. "An ecosystem perspective of riparian zones: Focus on links between land and water." BioScience 41(8): 540–551.

Irland, L.C., and J.F. Connors. 1994. "State nonpoint source programs affecting forestry: The 12 northeastern states." Northern Journal of Applied Forestry 11(1): 5–11.

Laitung, B., J.L. Pretty, E. Chauvet, and M. Dobson. 2002. "Response of aquatic hypomycete communities to enhanced stream retention in areas impacted by commercial forestry." Freshwater Biology 47(2): 313–323.

Lockaby, B.G., R.G. Clawson, K. Flynn, R.B. Rummer, J.S. Meadows, J.S. Stokes, and J.A. Stanturf. 1997. "Influence of harvesting on biogeochemical exchange in sheetflow and soil processes in a eutrophic floodplain forest." Forest Ecology and Management 90: 187–194.

Malmer, A., and H. Grip. 1994. "Converting tropical rain-forest to forest plantation in sabah, malaysia. 2. Effects on nutrient dynamics and net losses in streamwater." Hydrological Processes 8(3): 195–209.

May, C.L. 2002. "Debris flows through different forest age classes in the central Oregon coast range." Journal of the American Water Resources Association 38(4): 1097–1113.

Megahan, W.F. 1980. Nonpoint source pollution from forestry activities in the western united states: Results of recent research and research needs. U.S. Forestry and Water Quality: What course in the 80's? Proceedings of the Water Pollution Control Federation Seminar., Richmond, VA.

Megahan, W.G., J.P. Potyondy, and K.A. Seyedbagheri. 1992. Best management practices and cumulative effects from sedimentation in the south fork salmon river: An Idaho case study. *In*, Watershed management: Balancing sustainability and environmental change. R.J. Naiman (eds.). New York, NY, Springer-Verlag.

Montana DNRC. 2002. Best management practices (BMPS) for forestry in Montana. Missoula, MT, Montana Department of Natural Resources and Conservation.

Naiman, R.J., K.L. Fetherston, S.J. Mckay, and J. Chen. 1998. Riparian forests. *In*, River ecology and management: Lessions from the pacific coastal ecoregion. R.J. Naiman, and R.E. Bilby (eds.). New York, NY, Springer-Verlag.

Neary, D.G., and J.L. Michael. 1996. "Herbicides—protecting long-term sustainability and water quality in forest ecosystems." New Zealand Journal of Forestry Science 26(1/2): 241–264.

Nisbet, T.R. 2001. "The role of forest management in controlling diffuse pollution in U.K. forestry." Forest Ecology and Management 143(1–3): 215–226.

North Carolina Divison of Forest Resources. 1989. Forest practices guidelines related to water quality, NC Division of Forest Resources, Department of Environment, Health, and Natural Resources: 10.

Ormerod, S.J., S.D. Rundle, E.C. Lloyd, and A.A. Douglas. 1993. "The influence of riparian management on the habitat structure and macroinvertebrate communities of upland streams draining plantation forests." Journal of Applied Ecology 30(1): 13–24.

Palone, R.S., and A.H. Todd (eds.). 1997. Chesapeake bay riparian handbook: A guide for establishing and maintaining riparian forest buffers. Radnor, PA, USDA Forest Service.

Phillips, M.J., L.W. Swift, and C.R. Blinn. 2000. Best management practices for riparian areas. *In*, Riparian management in forests of the continental eastern united states. E.S. Verry, J.W. Hornbeck, and C.A. Dolloff (eds.). Boca Raton, FL, Lewis Publishers.

Pimentel, D., and L. Levitan. 1986. "Pesticides: Amounts applied and amounts reaching pests." BioScience 36(2): 86–91.

Reid, L.M. 1998. Cumulative watershed effects and watershed analysis. *In*, River ecology and management: Lessons from the pacific coastal ecoregion. R.J. Naiman, and R.E. Bilby (eds.). New York, Springer-Verlag.

Smith, D.M. 1994. The forests of the united states. *In*, Regional silviculture of the united states. J.W. Barrett (eds.). New York, NY, John Wiley & Sons, Inc.

Smith, D.M., B.C. Larson, M.J. Kelty, and P.M.S. Ashton. 1997. The practice of silviculture: Applied forest ecology. New York, NY, John Wiley & Sons, Inc.

Stednick, J.D. 2000. Timber management. *In*, Drinking water from forests and grasslands: A synthesis of the scientific literature. General technical report SRS-39. G.E. Dissmeyer (eds.). Washington, DC, U.S. Department of Agriculture, Forest Service.

Stone, M.K., and J.B. Wallace. 1998. "Long-term recovery of a mountain stream from clear-cut logging: The effects of forest succession on benthic invertebrate community structure." Freshwater Biology 39(1): 151–169.

Sun, G., S.G. McNulty, J.P. Shepard, D.M. Amatya, H. Riekerk, N.B. Comerford, W. Skaggs, and L. Swift, Jr. 2001. "Effects of timber management on the hydrology of wetland forests in the southern united states." Forest Ecology and Management 143(1–3): 227–236.

Sun, G., H. Riekerk, and N.B. Comerford. 1998. "Modeling the hydrologic impacts of forest harvest on flatwoods." Journal of American Water Resource Association 34: 843–854.

Swank, W.T., J.M. Vose, and K.J. Elliott. 2001. "Long-term hydrologic and water quality responses following commercial clearcutting of mixed hardwoods on a southern appalachian catchment." Forest Ecology and Management 143(1–3): 163–178.

Swift, D.W. 1990. Nutrient enrichment of Scottish lochs and reservoirs with particular reference to the impact of forest fertilization. Medmenham, UK, Water Research Center.

Swift, Jr., L.W. 1984. "Soil losses from roadbeds and cut and fill slopes in the southern appalachian mountains." Southern Journal of Applied Forestry 8(4): 209–215.

Tennessee Department of Agriculture Division of Forestry. 2003. Silviculture options.

Tetra Tech Inc. 2001. National management measures to control nonpoint source pollution from forestry (draft). Fairfax, VA, US Environmental Protection Agency, Office of Water.

Trayler, K.M., and J.A. Davis. 1998. "Forestry impacts and the vertical distribution of stream invertebrates in south-western Australia." Freshwater Biology 40(2): 331–342.

USDA Forest Service. 2000. U.S. Forest facts and historical trends. Washington, DC, U.S. Department of Agriculture Forest Service.

USEPA. 2003. Managing nonpoint source pollution from forestry. http://www.epa.gov/owow/nps/facts/point8.htm.

Virginia Department of Forestry. 2001. Forestry bmp guide for Virginia, Virginia Department of Forestry: 33.

WWF. 2001. Local authorities can make a difference; the role of local authorities in promoting responsible forest management. Brussels, Belgium, World Wildlife Fund for Nature: 20.

Zaber, D.J. 1998. Southern lessons: Saving species through the national forest management act, Defenders of Wildlife.

MINING

Barbour, A.K. 1994. Mining non-ferrous metals. In, Mining and its environmental impact. M.W. Hester, and R.M. Harrison (eds.). Cambridge, Royal Society of Chemistry.

Bhattacharyya, S., P.L. Klerks, and J.A. Nyman. 2003. "Toxicity to freshwater organisms from oils and oil spill chemical treatments in laboratory microcosms." Environmental Pollution 122(2): 205–215.

Black, A., and D. Craw. 2001. "Arsenic, copper and zinc occurrence at the wangaloa coal mine, southeast otago, new Zealand." International Journal of Coal Geology 45(2–3): 181–193.

Bonta, J.V., C.R. Amerman, W.A. Dick, G.F. Hall, T.J. Harlukowicz, A.C. Razem, and N.E. Smeck. 1992. "Impact of surface coal-mining on 3 Ohio watersheds—physical conditions and groundwater hydrology." Water Resources Bulletin 28(3): 577–596.

Brown, A.V., M.M. Lyttle, and K.B. Brown. 1998. "Impacts of gravel mining on gravel bed streams." Transactions of the American Fisheries Society 127(6): 979–994.

Buchanan, D.J., and D. Brenkley. 1994. Green coal mining. In, Mining and its environmental impact. R.E. Hester, and R.M. Harrison (eds.). Cambridge, Royal Society of Chemistry.

Choubey, V.D. 1991. "Hydrogeological and environmental-impact of coal-mining, Jharia coalfield, India." Environmental Geology and Water Sciences 17(3): 185–194.

Cleary, D., and I. Thorton. 1994. The environmental impact of gold mining in the Brazilian Amazon. In, Mining and its environmental impact. R.E. Hester, and R.M. Harrison (eds.). Cambridge, Royal Society of Chemistry.

Clements, W.H., D.S. Cherry, and J. Cairns Jr. 1988. "The impact of heavy metals on macroinvertebrate communities: A comparison of observational and experimental results." Canadian Journal of Fisheries and Aquatic Science 45: 2017–2025.

Crowson, P.C.F. 1992. "An international perspective on the U.K. coal industry." Min. Technology July/August: 215–221.

Delonay, A.J., E.E. Little, J. Lipton, D. Woodward, and J. Hansen. 1995. Avoidance response as evidence of injury: The use of behavioral testing in support of natural resource damage assessments. In, Environmental toxicology and risk assessment. T.W. LaPoint, F.T. Price, and E.E. Little (eds.). Philadelphia, American Society for Testing and Materials.

Environmental Law Institute. 2000. Pollution prevention and mining: A proposed framework for the Americas. Washington, DC, Environmental Law Institute.

Garcia-Criado, F., M. Fernandez-Alaez, and C. Fernandez-Alaez. 2002. "Relationship between benthic assemblage structure and coal mining in the Boeza river basin (Spain)." Archiv Fur Hydrobiologie 154(4): 665–689.

Gauthier-Warinner, R.J. 2000. Oil and gas development. *In*, Drinking water from forests and grasslands: A synthesis of the scientific literature. General technical report SRS-39. G.E. Dissmeyer (eds.). Washington, DC, U.S. Department of Agriculture, Forest Service.

Guebert, M.D., and T.W. Gardner. 2001. "Macropore flow on a reclaimed surface mine: Infiltration and hillslope hydrology." Geomorphology 39 (3–4): 151–169.

Henley, W.F., M.A. Patterson, R.J. Neves, and A.D. Lemly. 2000. "Effects of sedimentation and turbidity on lotic food webs: A concise review for natural resource managers." Reviews in Fisheries Science 8(2): 125–139.

Hilliard, T.J. 1994. States' right, miners' wrongs: Case studies of water contamination from hardrock mining, and the failure of states to prevent it. Washington, DC, Mineral Policy Center, American Fisheries Society, American Rivers and Trout Unlimited: 25.

Hilson, G. 2002. "The environmental impact of small-scale gold mining in Ghana: Identifying problems and possible solutions." Geographical Journal 168: 57–72.

IIED. 2002a. Breaking new ground: The report of the mining, minerals, and sustainable development project. London, International Institute for Environment and Development and the World Business Council for Sustainable Development.

IIED. 2002b. Global report on artisanal and small-scale mining. London, International Institute for Environment and Development and the World Business Council for Sustainable Development.

Il'inskii, V.V., O.V. Porshneva, T.I. Komarova, and T.V. Koronelli. 1998. "The effect of petroleum hydrocarbons on the hydrocarbon-oxidizing bacteriocenosis in the southeast part of the Mozhaiskoe water storage basin." Microbiology 67(2): 220–225.

Kelly, M. 1988. Mining and the freshwater environment. London, Elsevier Applied Science.

Kligerman, D.C., E.L. La Rovere, and M.A. Costa. 2001. "Management challenges on small-scale gold mining activities in Brazil." Environmental Research 87(3): 181–198.

Kondolf, G.M. 1994. "Geomorphic and environmental-effects of instream gravel mining." Landscape and Urban Planning 28(2–3): 225–243.

Kondolf, G.M. 1997. "Hungry water: Effects of dams and gravel mining on river channels." Environmental Management 21: 533–551.

Kondolf, G.M., and J. Lyons. 1992. Impacts of in-stream sand and gravel mining on stream habitat and fish communities including a survey on the Big Rib river, marathon county, Wisconsin. Madison, WI, Wisconsin Department of Natural Resources.

Leady, B.S., and J.F. Gottgens. 2001. "Mercury accumulation in sediment cores and along food chains in two regions of the Brazilian pantanal." Wetlands Ecology and Management 9(4): 349–361.

Leigh, D.S. 1994. "Mercury contamination and floodplain sedimentation from former gold mines in north Georgia." Water Resources Bulletin 40(4): 739–748.

Liu, J., D. Elsworth, and R.J. Matetic. 1997. "Evaluation of the post-mining groundwater regime following longwall mining." Hydrological Processes 11(15): 1945–1961.

Macdonald, A. 2002. Industry in transition: A profile of the north American mining sector. Winnipeg, International Institute for Sustainable Development.

Mahaney, P.A. 1994. "Effects of fresh-water petroleum contamination on amphibian hatching and metamorphosis." Environmental Toxicology and Chemistry 13(2): 259–265.

Mas-Pla, J., R. Montaner, and J. Sola. 1999. "Groundwater resources and quality variations caused by gravel mining in coastal streams." Journal of Hydrology 216(3–4): 197–213.

Meador, M.R., and A.O. Layher. 1998. "Instream sand and gravel mining: Environmental issues and regulatory process in the united states." Fisheries 23(11): 6–13.

Meyer, J.L., and J.B. Wallace. 2001. Lost linkages and lotic ecology: Rediscovering small streams. *In*, Ecology: Achievement and challenge. N.J. Huntly, and S. Levin (eds.), M.C. Press.

Mining Policy Center. 2003. The last American dinosaur: The 1872 mining law. Washington, DC, Mineral Policy Center: 6.

Monterroso, C. and F. Macias. 1998. "Drainage waters affected by pyrite oxidation in a coal mine in Galicia (NW Spain): Composition and mineral stability." Science of the Total Environment 216: 121–132.

National Research Council. 1999. Hardrock mining on federal lands. Washington, DC, National Academy Press.

NMA. 2003. U.S. Coal production by state, 1993–2002. 2003. http://www.nma.org/pdf/c_production.pdf.

Obire, O., and I.V. Okudo. 1997. "Effect of crude oil pollution on a freshwater stream in Nigeria." Discovery and Innovation 9(1–2): 25–32.

OECD/IEA. 2002. World energy outlook: 2002. Paris, Organisation for Economic Cooperation and Development, International Energy Agency.

OSM. 2003. Acid mine drainage. http://www.osmre.gov/amdint.htm.

Ripley, E.A., R.E. Redmann and J. Maxwell. 1979. Environmental impact of mining in Canada. Kingston, Ontario, Centre for Resources Studies, Queens University.

Rivier, B., and J. Sequier. 1985. Physical and biological effects of gravel extraction in river beds. *In*, Habitat modification of freshwater fisheries. J.S. Alabaster (ed.). London, Butterworth.

Tarras-Wahlberg, N.H., A. Flachier, G. Fredriksson, S. Lane, N. Lundberg, and O. Sangfors. 2000. "Environmental impact of small-scale and artisanal gold mining in southern Ecuador—implications for the setting of environmental standards and for the management of small-scale mining operations." Ambio 29(8): 484–491.

USEPA. 2002. 2000 toxics release inventory public data release report. Washington, DC, United States Environmental Protection Agency: 16.

USFWS. 1998. Permitted stream losses due to valley filling in Kentucky, Pennsylvania, Virginia, and West Virginia: A partial inventory. State College, PA, United States Fish and Wildlife Service.

USGS. 2003. Mineral commodity summaries 2003. Washington, DC, United States Geological Survey: 202.

Wanty, R.B., B. Wang, J. Vohden, P.H. Briggs, and A.L. Meier (1999). Regional baseline geochemistry and environmental effects of gold placer mining operations on the fortymile river, eastern Alaska. Washington, DC, United State Geological Survey.

Warhurst, A. 1994a. Environmental best-practice in metals production. *In*, Mining and its environmental impact. R.E. Hester, and R.M. Harrison (eds.). Cambridge, The Royal Society of Chemistry.

———. 1994b. Environmental degradation from mining and mineral processing in developing countries: Corporate responses and national policies. Paris, Organisation for economic cooperation and development: 89.

Werner, F., F. Bilek, and L. Luckner. 2001. "Impact of regional groundwater flow on the water quality of an old post-mining lake." Ecological Engineering 17(2–3): 133–142.

Wireman, M. 2000. Hardrock mining. *In*, Drinking water from forests and grasslands: A synthesis of the scientific literature. General technical report SRS-39. G.E. Dissmeyer (eds.). Washington, DC, U.S. Department of Agriculture, Forest Service.

Woodward, D.F., J.N. Goldstein, A.M. Farag, and W.G. Brumbaugh. 1997. "Cutthroat trout avoidance of metals and conditions characteristic of a mining waste site: Coeur d'alene river, Idaho." Transactions of the American Fisheries Society 126(4): 699–706.

Younger, P.L. 2000. "Holistic remedial strategies for short- and long-term water pollution from abandoned mines." Transactions of the Institution of Mining and Metallurgy Section a-Mining Technology 109: A210–A218.

Zipper, C., W. Balfour, R. Roth, and J. Randolph. 1997. "Domestic water supply impacts by underground coal mining in Virginia, USA." Environmental Geology 29(1/2): 84–93.

RECREATION

Adams, S., C.A. Frissell, and B.E. Rieman. 2001. "Geography of invasion in mountain streams: Consequences of headwater lake fish introductions." Ecosystems 4(4): 296–307.

AFS. 2003. AFS policy statement #28: Special fishing regulations for managing freshwater sport fisheries (abbreviated). http://www.fisheries.org/Public_Affairs/Policy_Statements/ps_28a.shtml.

An, Y.J., D.H. Kampbell, and G.W. Sewell. 2002. "Water quality at five marinas in lake texoma as related to methyl tert-butyl ether (MTBE)." Environmental Pollution 118(3): 331–336.

Aznar, J.C., A. Dervieux, and P. Grillas. 2003. "Association between aquatic vegetation and landscape indicators of human pressure." Wetlands 23(1): 149–160.

Bryan, M.D., and D.L. Scarnecchia. 1992. "Species richness, composition, and abundance of fish larvae and juveniles inhabiting natural and developed shorelines of a glacial Iowa lake." Environmental Biology of Fishes 35(4): 329–341.

Christensen, D.L., B.R. Herwig, D.E. Schindler, and S.R. Carpenter. 1996. "Impacts of lakeshore residential development on coarse woody debris in north temperate lakes." Ecological Applications 6(4): 1143–1149.

Edington, J.M., and M.A. Edington. 1986. Ecology, recreation and tourism. Cambridge, Cambridge University Press.

FAPEL. 2003. All you need to know about the boating restriction regulations. http://www.fapel.org/english/anmoto15.htm.

Ferry, M.C., and A.S. Deller. 1996. "Review of factors affecting the distribution and abundance of waterfowl in shallow-water habitats of Chesapeake bay." Estuaries 19(2A): 272–278.

Garber, S.D., and J. Burger. 1995. "A 20-yr study documenting the relationship between turtle decline and human recreation." Ecological Applications 5(4): 1151–1162.

Gerard, P., and B. De Bast. 2000. "Restriction of the circulation of small pleasure boats on the rivers of Wallonia, Belgium." Fisheries Management and Ecology 7(1–2): 139–143.

Hammitt, W.E., and D.N. Cole. 1998. Wildland recreation: Ecology and management. New York, John Wiley & Sons, Inc.

Mackie, G.L. 1991. "Biology of exotic zebra mussel, *dreissena polymorpha*, in relation to native bivalves and its potential impact in lake St. Clair." Hydrobiologia 219: 251–268.

Maxted, J.R., R.A. Eskin, S.B. Weisberg, and F.W. Kutz. 1997. "The ecological condition of dead-end canals of the Delaware and Maryland coastal bays." Estuaries 20(2): 319–327.

MDEP. 1994. Mandatory shoreland zoning act. 2003. http://www.maine.gov/dep/blwq/docstand/ip-shore.htm.

Minnesota Lakes Association. 2001. Organizing a lake association. http://www.shorelandmanagement.org/quick/ol.html.

National Research Council Committee on Restoration and Aquatic Ecosystems. 1992. Restoration of aquatic ecosystems. Washington, DC, National Academy Press.

NMMA. 2002. Boating at a glance 2002: Facts and figures. Chicago, IL, National Marine Manufacturing Association.

Parker, B.R., D.W. Schindler, D.B. Donald, and R.S. Anderson. 2001. "The effects of stocking and removal of a nonnative salmonid on the plankton of an alpine lake." Ecosystems 4(4): 334–345.

Pilliod, D.S., and C.R. Peterson. 2001. "Local and landscape effects of introduced trout on amphibians in historically fishless watersheds." Ecosystems 4(4): 322–333.

Poff, N.L., D.J. Allan, M.B. Bain, J.R. Karr, K.L. Prestegaard, B.D. Richter, R.E. Sparks, and J.C. Stromberg.

1997. "The natural flow regime: A paradigm for conservation and restoration of riverine ecosystems." BioScience 47: 769–784.

Reuter, J.E., B.C. Allen, R.C. Richards, J.F. Pankow, C.R. Goldman, R.L. Scholl, and J.S. Seyfried. 1988. "Concentration, sources, and fate of the gasoline oxygenate methyl tert-butyl ether (MTBE) in a multiple-use lake." Environmental Science & Technology 32: 3666–3672.

Schindler, D.E., R.A. Knapp, and P.R. Leavitt. 2001. "Alteration of nutrient cycles and algal production resulting from fish introductions into mountain lakes." Ecosystems 4(4): 308–321.

Schnaiberg, J., J. Riera, M.G. Turner, and P.R. Voss. 2002. "Explaining human settlement patterns in a recreational lake district: Vilas county, Wisconsin, USA." Environmental Management 30(1): 24–34.

Sun, D. and D. Walsh. 1998. "Review of studies on environmental impacts of recreation and tourism in Australia." Journal of Environmental Management 53(4): 323–338.

U.S. Department of the Interior, U.S. Fish and Wildlife Service, Department of Commerce and U.S. Census Bureau. 2002. 2001 national survey of fishing, hunting, and wildlife-associated recreation. Washington, DC, U.S. Fish and Wildlife Service: 170.

UNEP. 2001. Tourism's three main impact areas. http://www.uneptie.org/pc/tourism/sust-tourism/env-3main.htm#natres.

University of Minnesota Extension Service. 2002. Protecting our waters: Shoreland best management practices. http://www.extension.umn.edu/distribution/naturalresources/DD6946.html.

USEPA. 2003. Shipshape shores and waters. Washington, DC, United States Environmental Protection Agency Office of Wetlands, Oceans and Watersheds: 17.

Overharvesting

(AFS) Atlantic Salmon Federation. 2002. The Atlantic salmon. http://www.asf.ca/Overall/atlsalm.html [22 Feb. 2003].

Ames, M.H. 1991. Saving some cetaceans may require captive breeding. Work on bottlenose dolphin may be applies to the Baiji. BioScience 41(11): 746–749.

Anthony, J.L., and J.A. Downing. 2000. Exploitation trajectory of a declining fauna: a century of freshwater mussel fisheries in North America. Canadian Journal of Fisheries and Aquatic Sciences 58(10): 2071–2090.

Baker, P.M. 1993. Resource management: a shell exporter's perspective, in Cummings, K.S., A.C. Buchanan, and L.M. Koch (eds.). Conservation and Management of Freshwater Mussels. Proceedings of a symposium. Illinois Natural History Survey, Champaign, IL.

Bao, T. Q., K. Bouakhamvongsa, S. Chan, T. Phommavong, A.F. Poulsen, P. Rukawoma, U. Suntornratana, D.V. Tien, T.T. Tuan, N.T. Tung, J. Valbo-Jørgensen, S. Viravong, and N. Yoorong 2001. Local Knowledge in the Study of River Fish Biology: Experiences from the Mekong. Mekong development Series No. 1, 22 pp, Mekong River Commission, Phnom Penh, ISSN: 1680–4023

Barzyk, J.E. 1999. Turtles in crisis: the Asian food markets. http://www.tortoisetrust.org/articles/asia.html [20 Feb. 2003].

Blaustein, A.R., and D.B. Wake. 1990. Declining amphibian populations: a global phenomenon. TREE 5(7): 203–204.

———. 1995. The puzzle of declining amphibian populations. Scientific American 272(4): 52–57.

Bridgham, S.D., C.A. Johnston, J. Pastor, and K. Updegraff. 1995. Potential feedbacks of northern wetlands on climate change. BioScience 45(4): 262–275.

Brown, A., S. Nicol, and J. Koehn. 1998. Trout Cod (Maccullochella Macquariensis) Recovery Plan. National Heritage Trust, Tasmania, Australia. http://neptune3.galib.uga.edu/cgi-bin/homepage.cgi?style=&_id=80c012cf-1058040154-408&_cc=1 [21 Feb. 2003].

Buck, E.H. 1994. CRS Report for Congress 95-4 ENR. United Nations Convention on the Law of the Sea:

Living Resources Provisions. http://www.ncseonline.org/NLE/CRSreports/Marine/mar-9.cfm?&CFID= 6894420&CFTOKEN=95483054 [25 Feb. 2003].

Burke, V.J. J.E. Lovich, and J.W. Gibbons. Conservation of Freshwater Turtles, *In*, Klemens, M.W. (ed). Turtle Conservation. Smithsonian Institution Press, Washington, DC. Pp 156–179.

Caviar Emptor. 2002. Support builds for protection of beluga sturgeon. http://www.caviaremptor.org/ press_122802.html [21 Feb. 2003].

Chapin, F.S. III, B.H. Walker, R.J. Hobbs, D.U. Hooper, J.H. Lawton, O.E. Sala, and D. Tilman. 1997. Biotic control over the functioning of ecosystems. 277 (5325): 500–504.

(CI) Conservation International. 2002. A proposed Plan for the Conservation of the World's Tortoises and Freshwater Turtles. I. Executive Summary. http://www.zooreach.org/News/India/plan.PDF [20 Feb. 2003].

(CIESIN) Center for International Earth Science Information Network. 2003. Environmental Treaties and Resource Indicators (ENTRI)-UNEP Summary File. Convention On Biological Diversity. http://sedac. ciesin.org/pidb/register/reg-170.rrr.html [25 Feb. 2003].

(CITES) Convention on International Trade in Endangered Species of Wild Fauna and Flora. 2002. Caspian Sea states to resume caviar trade. Press Release. http://www.cites.org/eng/news/press/020306_caviar_ resumption.shtml [21 Feb. 2003].

———. 2003. Homepage http://www.cites.org/ [25 Feb. 2003].

Coates, D. 2001. Biodiversity and Fisheries Management Options in the Mekong River Basin. A Blue Millennium report, a project of the United Nations Environmental Program. 38 pp.

Coull, J.R. 1993. World Fisheries Resources. Routledge, New York, NY. 267 pp.

(CRF) Chelonian Research Foundation. 2000. Scientists Say Half of Asia's Turtles Endangered. TRAFFIC Press Release. Turtle and Tortoise Newsletter, 2000, 3:13–14. http://www.chelonian.org/ttn/archives/ttn3/pp13-14.shtml [20 Feb 2003].

(CSN) Caribbean Stranding Network. 2002. Survival of Marine Animals in Danger of Extinction. http://rcv.caribe.net/english/supervivencia.htm [03 Feb. 2003].

(CTTC) California Turtle and Tortoise Club. 2002. United States Submissions for Consideration at CITES COP1. http://www.tortoise.org/conservation/citescop12.html [20 Feb. 2003].

Drammeh, Q.K.L. 2000. Illegal, unreported and unregulated fishing in small-scale marine and inland capture fisheries. Paper prepared for the Expert Consultation on Illegal, Unreported and Unregulated Fishing, Organized by the Government of Australia in Cooperation with FAO, Sydney, Australia, 15–19 May 2000. http://www.fao.org/DOCREP/005/Y3274E/y3274e09.htm - fn109 [12 Feb. 2003].

Dudgeon, D. 1992. Endangered ecosystems: a review of the conservation status of tropical Asian rivers. Hydrobiologia 248: 167–191.

———. 2002. An inventory of riverine biodiversity in monsoonal Asia: present status and conservation challenges. Water Science and Technology 45(11): 11–19.

(ECES) Earth Crash Earth Spirit. 2003. Documenting the Collapse of a Dying Planet. Ecosystem Destruction: Overfishing, Bycatch, and Destructive Fishing Practices. http://eces.org/ec/ecosystems/lakevictoria.shtml-021301 [01 Feb. 2003].

(ENN) Environmental News Network. 1999. Half of world's turtles face extinction, scientists say. http:// www.cnn.com/NATURE/9908/27/fresh.turtle.enn/ [20 Feb. 2003].

(FAO) Food and Agriculture Organization (of the United Nations). 1999. The State of World Fisheries and Aquaculture 1998. Rome, Italy. 112 pp.

Gende, S.M., R.T. Edwards, M.F. Willson, and M.S. Wipfli. 2002. Pacific Salmon in Aquatic and Terrestrial Ecosystems. BioScience 52(10): 917–929.

(GOA) Government of Alberta. 2002. Bull Trout. http://www3.gov.ab.ca/srd/fw/threatsp/bt_stat.html [21 Feb. 2003].

Göran, H. 1995. Reintroduction of beaver in Sweden—an early success. http://info.metla.fi/iufro95abs/d1pap147.htm [03 Feb. 2003].

Grzelewski, D. 2002. Otterly Fascinating. Smithsonian Magazine (Nov. 2002).

Haro, A., W. Richkus, K. Whalen, A. Hoar, W. Dieter Bush, S. Lary, T. Brush, and D. Dixon. 2000. Population decline of the American eel: implications for research and management Fisheries. 25(9): 7–16.

Harvey, B. 2001. Biodiversity and Fisheries. Chapter 1: Synthesis Report. A Primer for Planners. A Blue Millennium report, a project of the United Nations Environmental Program. 64 pp.

Helfield J.M., and R.J. Naiman. 2001. Effects of salmon-derived nitrogen on riparian forest growth and implications for stream productivity. Ecology 82(9): 2403–2415.

Hilborn, R. 1994. Uncertainty, risk, and the precautionary principle, *In*, Pikitch, E.K., D.D. Huppert, and M.P. Sissenwine (eds.). Global Trends: Fisheries Management, Vol. 20, American Fisheries Society Symposium. Pp. 100–106.

Houlahan, J.E., C.S. Findlay, B.R. Schmidt, A.H. Meyer, and S.L. Kuzmin. 2000. Quantitative evidence for global amphibian population declines. Nature 404: 752–755.

Klaphake, A., W. Scheumann, and D. R. Schliep. 2001. Biodiversity and International Water Policy. International Agreements and Experiences Related to the Protection of Freshwater Ecosystems. Study on behalf of the Federal Ministry of Environment, Bonn, Germany. 36 pp.

Lichatowich, J. 2003. Salmon Hatcheries: Past, Present and Future. Report for Oregon Business Council. http://www.orbusinesscouncil.org/docs/hatcheries.pdf [24 Feb. 2003].

Mufson, S. 1997. Fabled dolphins face extinction in Yangtze. Washington Post. http://www.washingtonpost.com/wp-srv/inatl/longterm/china/stories/dam120997.htm [06 Feb. 2003].

(NCSE) National Council for Science and the Environment. 1999. CRS Report for Congress. 98–666: Pacific Salmon and Anadromous Trout: Management Under the Endangered Species Act. http://www.ncseonline.org/nle/crsreports/biodiversity/biodv-22.cfm?&CFID=4529292&CFTOKEN=40523692 [22 Feb. 2003].

Nehlsen, W., J.E. Williams, and J.A. Lichatowich. 1991. Pacific salmon at the crossroads: stocks at risk from California, Oregon, Idaho, and Washington. Fisheries 16(2): 4–21.

(NFAI) Native Fish Australia Incorporated. 2001. Trout Cod. http://www.nativefish.asn.au/troutcod.html [21 Feb. 2003].

(NOAA) National Oceanic and Atmospheric Administration. 2002. Atlantic Salmon. An Endangered Population. Atlantic salmon in eight Maine rivers were declared "endangered" on November 13, 2000. http://www.nero.nmfs.gov/atsalmon/ [22 Feb. 2003].

———. 2003. Species Information, American eel Anguilla rostrata. http://noaa.chesapeakebay.net/spc/eel.htm. [19 Feb. 2003].

(NPPC) Northwest Power Planning Council. 1986. Compilation of Information on Salmon and Steelhead Losses in the Columbia River Basin. Portland, OR.

Nowak, R. M. 1997a. Baiji, or Whitefin Dolphin. Mammals of the World. On-line 5.1. The Johns Hopkins University Press. http://www.press.jhu.edu/books/walkers_mammals_of_the_world/cetacea/cetacea.lipotidae.lipotes.html [06 Feb. 2003].

———. 1997b. Mammals of the World. Online 5.1. The Johns Hopkins University Press. http://www.press.jhu.edu/books/walker/sirenia/sirenia.trichechidae.trichechus.html [03 Feb. 2003].

(NRC) National Research Council. 1995. New Management Approach Needed to Restore Pacific Salmon Populations. Released Nov. 8, 1995. http://web.outsideonline.com/news/ozone/salmon.html [22 Feb. 2003].

(NRDC) Natural Resources Defense Council. 2001. Caviar Emptor. http://www.nrdc.org/wildlife/fish/caviar.asp [21 Feb. 2003].

(NWFSC) Northwest Fisheries Science Center. 2003. Salmon Hatchery Q&As. http://www.nwfsc.noaa.gov/Q&A/ - risks [24 Feb. 2003].

Orenstein, R. Survivors in Armor. 2001. Turtles, Tortoises and Terrapins. Key Porter Books, Toronto. 308 pp.

Revenga, C., J. Brunner, N. Henninger, K. Kassem, and R. Payne. 2000. Pilot Analysis of Global Ecosystems: Freshwater Systems. World Resources Institute, Washington, DC. 100 pp.

Sea Web. 2003. American Eel Decline http://www.seaweb.org/background/book/american_eels.html [19 Feb. 2003].

Soulé, M.E., and D. Simberloff. 1986. What do genetics and ecology tell us about the design of nature-reserves. Biological Conservation 35(1): 19–40.

Strayer, D.L., N.F. Caraco, J.J. Cole, S. Findlay, and M.L. Pace. 1999. Transformation of freshwater ecosystems by bivalves. BioScience 49(1): 19–27.

TRAFFIC. 2000. Half of Asia's freshwater turtles endangered. http://www.traffic.org/news/turtles.html [10 Feb. 2003].

(USFWS) U.S. Fish and Wildlife Service. 1999. A Chronology of Bull Trout Events http://www.r1.fws.gov/news/bulltrout/bullchron_fnl.htm [21 Feb. 2003].

Valbo-Jørgensen, J., and A.F. Poulsen. 2000. Using Local Knowledge as a Research Tool in the Study of River Fish Biology: Experiences from the Mekong. In, Environment, Development and Sustainability, Volume 2 (Nos. 3–4): 253–276.

Van Dijk, P.P, B.L. Stuart, and G.J. Rhodin (eds.). 2000. Asian Turtle Trade. Proceedings of a Workshop on Conservation and Trade of Freshwater Turtles and Tortoises in Asia. Chelonian Research Monographs no. 2: 13–14.

(WCMC) World Conservation Monitoring Centre. 1998. Freshwater Biodiversity: a preliminary global assessment. http://www.unep-wcmc.org/ [11 Feb. 2003].

(WCMC) World Conservation Monitoring Centre. 2000. Biodiversity Assessment Programme Strategic Development Plan 1996–2000. http://www.grida.no/enrin/biodiv/biodiv/pubs/wcmc2.htm [11 Mar 2003].

Williams, J.D., and R.J. Neves. 2003. Freshwater mussels: a neglected and declining aquatic resource. http://biology.usgs.gov/s+t/noframe/f076.htm - 15629 [19 Feb. 2003].

Williams, J.E., J.E. Johnson, D.A. Hendrickson, S. Contreras-Balderas, J. D. Williams, M. Navarro-Mendoza, D.E. McAllister, and J.E. Deacon. 1989. Fishes of North America endangered, threatened, or of special concern. 1989. Fisheries 14(6): 2–20.

Wipfli, M.S., J.P. Hudson, D.T. Chaloner, and J.P. Caouette. 1999. Influence of salmon spawner densities on stream productivity in southeast Alaska. Canadian Journal of Fisheries and Aquatic Sciences 56(9): 1600–1611.

(WWF) World Wildlife Fund. 2003. Giant river otters. http://www.wwfguianas.org/feat_spec_giant_otter.htm [04 Feb. 2003]

(WWF-LC) World Wildlife Fund–Latin America and Caribbean. 2003. Trouble in paradise: threats to an endangered species' new refuge. http://www.panda.org/about_wwf/where_we_work/latin_america_and_caribbean/where/peru/JTHF_profile6.cfm [04 Feb. 2003].

Invasive Alien Species

Alexander, G.R. 1977. Consumption of small trout by large predatory brown trout in the Norht Branch of the Au Sable River, Michigan, Michigan Department of Natural Resources, Fisheries Research Report no. 1855:1–26.

Allendorf, F.W. 1991. Ecological and genetic effects of fish introductions: synthesis and recommendations. Can. J. Fish. Aquat. Sci. 48 (Suppl. 1): 178–181.

Anonymous. 1997a. National policy on introductions and transfers of aquatic organisms.

Anonymous 1997b. Recommended actions to address marine Non-Indigenous Species (NIS) issues in Washington.

Aquatic Nuisance Species Task Force. 2003. web site: http://www.anstaskforce.gov/

Arthington, A.H. 1991. The ecological and genetic impacts of introduced freshwater fishes in Australia. Canadian Journal of Fisheries and Aquatic Sciences 48 (Suppl. 1): 33–44.

Ashton, P.J., and D.S. Mitchell. 1989. Aquatic plants: patterns and modes of invasion, attributes of invading species and assessment of control programs. In, Biological Invasions: A Global Perspective. SCOPE 37, (eds. Drake, J.A., H.A. Mooney, F. diCastri, R.H. Groves, F.J. Kruger, M. Rejmanek, and M. Williamson). J. Wiley and Sons, New York, pp. 111–154.

Bills, T.D., D.A. Johnson, and J.H. Selgeby. 1992. Effects of a lampricide treatment on ruffe and other nontarget fish in the Brule River, Brule, Wisconsin, Phase 2. Special report, National Fisheries Research Center, La Crosse, WI.

Bradford, D.F., F. Tabatabai, and D.M. Graber. 1993. Isolation of remaining populations of the native frog, Rana muscosa, by introduced fishes in Sequoia and Kings Canyon National Parks. Conservation Biology 7:882–888.

Bright, C. 1998. Bio-invasions, in Worldwatch Reader 1998, (eds. Brown and Ayers). Worldwatch Institute, Washington, DC, pp. 115–133.

Bright, C. 1998. Life Out of Bounds. Bioinvasion in a Borderless World. The Worldwatch Alert Series. W.W. Norton and Co., New York. 287 p.

Busiahn, T. R. 1993. Can the ruffe be contained before it becomes YOUR problem? Fisheries, Vol. 18, No.8:22–23.

Campton, D.E. 1987. Natural hybridization and introgression in fishes: methods of detection and genetic interpretation. Pages 161–192 in N. Ryman and F. Utter, editors. *Population genetics and fishery management*. University of Washington Press, Seattle, WA.

Carl, G.C., W.A. Clemens, and C.C. Lindsey. 1959. The fresh-water fishes of British Columbia. British Columbia Provincial Museum Handbook No. 5.

Carl, G.C., and C.J. Guiget. 1972. Alien Animals in British Columbia. British Columbia Povincial Museum Handbook No. 14.

Carlton, James. T. 2000. Global change and biological invasions in the oceans In, Mooney, H., and R. Hobbs (eds.). Invasives in a changing world. Island Press, Washington, DC.

Chew, R.L. 1972. The failure of largemouth bass, Micropterus salmoides floridanus (LeSueur), to spawn in eutrophic, overcrowded environments. Proceedings of the Annual Conference of the Southeastern Association of Game and Fish Commissioners 26:306–319.

Ciruna, K.A., L.A. Meyerson, and A. Gutierrez. 2004. The ecological and socio-economic impacts of invasive alien species in inland water ecosystems. Report to the Conservation on Biological Diversity on behalf of the Global Invasive Species Programme, Washington, DC pp. 34.

Chevassus, B. 1979. Hybridization in salmonids: results and perspectives. Aquaculture 17:113–128.

Claudi, R., and J.H. Leach (eds.). 1999. Nonindigenous Freshwater Organisms: Vectors, Biology, and Impacts. Lewis Publ., 464 pp.

Clemens, W.A., D.S. Rawson, and J. McHugh. 1939. A biological survey of Okanagan Lake, British Columbia. Fish. Res. Bd. Can., Bull. 56, pp1–70.

Conner, J.V., R.P. Gallagher, and M.F. Chatry. 1980. Larval evidence for natural reproduction of the grass carp (Ctenopharyngodon idelola) in the lower Mississippi River. Proceedings of the Fourth Annual Larval Fish Conference, Biological Services Program, National Power Plant Team, Ann Arbor, Michigan, FWS/OBS-80/43:1–19.

Contreras-Arquieta, A. and S. Contreras-Balderas. 1999. Description, biology and ecological impact of the screw snail Thiara tuberculata (Müller, 1774) (Gasteropoda:Thiaridae) in Mexico. In, Non-indigenous freshwater organisms: vectors, biology and impacts (Claudi, R. and J.H. Leach eds.). Lewis Publishers, Boca Raton, USA. pp 151–160.

Contreras-Balderas, S., P. Almada-Villela, M.L. Lozano-Vilano, and M.E. García-Ramírez. 2002. Freshwater fish at risk or extinct in México. Rev. Fish Biol. Fish., 12:241–251.

Courtenay W.R. Jr. 1978. Biological impacts of introduced species and management policy in Florida. *In*, Man, R. (ed.). Exotic Species in Mariculture. The MIT Press, Cambridge, Massachusetts, and, London, England.

Courtenay, W.R. Jr. and J.N. Taylor. 1986. Strategies for reducing risks from introductions of aquatic organisms: a philosophical perspective. Fisheries 11(2):30–33.

Crossman, E.J. 1991. Introduced freshwater fishes: a review of the North American perspective with emphasis on Canada. Can. J. Fish. Aquat. Sci. 48 (Suppl. 1):46–57.

Drake, J.A. et al. 1989. Biological Invasions: A Global Perspective. Wiley, Chichester, UK. Vol 37.

Drost, C.A., and G. M. Fellers. 1996. Collapse of a regional frog fauna in the Yosemite area of the California Sierra Nevada, USA. Conservation Biology 10:414–425.

Dudley, T. 2003. Exotic Species in Aquatic Ecosystems. Pacific Research Institute, Oakland, California.

Ernst, C.H., J.E. Lovich, and R.W. Barbour. 1994. Turtles of the United States and Canada. Smithsonian Institution Press, Washington, DC. 578 pp.

FAO. 2002. The State of World Fisheries and Aquaculture. Rome, Food and Agriculture Organization.

Farmer, J. 1996. Park Service preys on lake trout. High Country News, Vol. 28, No. 15.

Ferguson, M. 1989. The impact of introduced species on native species with emphasis on genetics. Can. Soc. Zoo. Bull. 20:6–7.

Ferguson, M. 1990. The genetic impact of introduced fishes on native species. Can. J. Zool. 68:1053–1057.

Flecker, A.S., and C.R. Townsend. Community-wide consequences of trout introduction in New Zealand Streams, *In*, F.B. Samson and F.L. Knopf (eds.). 1996. Ecosystem Management Selected Readings. Springer, New York, NY. p 203–215.

Forester, T.S., and J.M. Lawrence. 1978. Effects of grass carp and carp on populations of bluegill and largemouth bass in ponds. Transactions of the American Fisheries Society 107(1):172–175.

Fuller, P.L., L.G. Nico, and J.D. Williams. 1999. Nonindigenous Fishes Introduced into Inland Waters of the United States. Special Publication 27. American Fisheries Society, Bethesda, MD. 613 pp.

Gaffney, P. and S.K. Allen. 1992. Genetic aspects of introduction and transfer of mollusks. Journal of Shellfish Research 11:535–538.

Gehrke, P.C., P. Brown, C.B. Schiller, D.B. Moffatt, and A.M. Bruce. 1995. River regulation and fish communities in the Murray Darling River system, Australia. Regulated Rivers: Research and Management 11: 363–375.

Gumbart, D. 2002. The Nature Conservancy of Connecticut's Director of Ecological Management, personal communication.

Heinz Center. 2003. The State of the Nation's Ecosystems: Measuring the Lands, Waters, and Living Resources of the United States. Cambridge University Press, Washington, DC. 270 pp.

Hiebert, R.D., and J. Stubbendieck. 1993. Handbook for Ranking Exotic Plants for Management and Control. National Park Research Report NPS/NRMWRO/NRR-93/08.

Hill, K., 1979. Wildlife inspector. Fla. Wildl. 33(2):17–22.

Hocutt, C.H. 1984. Toward the development of an environmental ethic for exotic fishes. p. 374-385. *In*, W.R. Courtenay, Jr. and J.R. Stauffer, Jr. (eds.). Distribution, biology and management of exotic fishes. Johns Hopkins University Press, Baltimore, MD.

Hoshovsky, M.C., and L. Anderson. 2000. Egeria densa Planchon. *In*, Bossard, C.C., J.M. Randall, and M.C. Hoshovsky (eds.). Invasive Plants of California's Wildlands. University of California Press, Berkeley.

Johnson, L.E. and D.K. Padilla. 1996. Geographic spread of exotic species: ecological lessons and opportunities from the invasion of the zebra mussel Dressena polymorpha. Biological Conservation 78: 23–33.

Koehn, J., A. Brumley, and P.C. Gehrke. 2000. Managing the Impacts of Carp. Bureau of Resource Sciences, Canberra. 247 pp.

Kohler, C.C. 1986. Strategies for reducing risks from introductions of aquatic organisms. Fisheries, 11(2):2–3

Kohler, C.C. and W.R. Courtenay, Jr. 1986a. Regulating introduced aquatic species: a review of past initiatives. Fisheries, Vol. 11, No.2: 34–38.

Kohler, C.C., and W.R. Courtenay, Jr. 1986b. American Fisheries Society position on introductions of aquatic species. Fisheries 11(2):39–42.

Kolar, C., and D. Lodge. 2000. Freshwater nonindigenous species: interactions with other global changes. In, Mooney, H., and R. Hobbs (eds.). Invasives in a changing world. Island Press, Washington, DC.

Larkin, P.A. 1956. Interspecific competition and population control in freshwater fish.

Larkin, P.A. 1979. Predator-prey relations in fishes; An overview of the theory, 13–22. In, H. Clepper (ed.). Predator-prey systems in fisheries management Sport Fishing Institute, Washington, DC.

Leach, J.H., and C.A. Lewis. 1991. Fish introductions in Canada: provincial views and regulations. Can. J. Fish. Aquat. Sci., Vol. 48 (Suppl. 1):156–161.

Levine, J.M. 2000. Species diversity and biological invasions: relating local process to community pattern. Science 288: 852–854.

Litvak, M.K., and N.E. Mandrak. 1993. Ecology of freshwater bait-fish use in Canada and the United States. Fisheries, 18(12):6–13.

Loope, L. L., P. G. Sanchez, P. W. Tarr, W. L. Loope, and R. L. Anderson. 1988. Biological invasions of arid land nature reserves. Biological Conservation 44:95–118.

Lovich, J.E. 1997. Wildlife as weeds. pp. 46-51. J. Lovich, J. Randall, and M. Kelly (eds.). Proceedings California Exotic Pest Plant Council Symposium '96.

Ludwig, H.R. Jr. 1995. Bait bucket transfer potential between the Mississippi and the Hudson Bay watersheds. Master's thesis, North Dakota State University, Fargo.

Ludwig, H.R., Jr., and J.A. Leitch. 1996. Interbasin transfer of aquatic biota via anglers' bait buckets. Fisheries, 21(7):14–161.

Luiselli, L., M. Capula, D. Capizzi, E. Filippi, V.T. Jesus, and C. Anibaldi. 1997. Problems for conservation of pond turtles (Emys orbicularis) in central Italy: is the introduced red-eared turtle (Trachemys scripta) a serious threat. Chelonian Conservation and Biology 2:417–419.

MacDonald, D.W., L.L. Loope, M.B. Usher, and O. Hamann. 1989. Wildlife conservation and the invasion of nature reserves by introduced species: a global perspective, In, Drake, J.A., H.A. Mooney, F. diCastri, R.H. Groves, F.J. Kruger, M. Rejmanek, and M. Williamson(eds.). Biological Invasions: A Global Perspective. SCOPE 37, J. Wiley and Sons, New York pp. 215–255.

Mack, Richard N. 2000. Assessing the extent, status, and dynamism of plant invasions: current and emerging approaches. In, Mooney, Harold, and Richard Hobbs (eds.) Invasives in a changing world. Island Press, Washington, DC.

Mandrak, N.E. 1989. Potential invasion of the Great Lakes by fish species associated with climatic warming. Great Lakes Res. 15:306–316.

Manning, E. 1995. Bleak future for cutthroat. High Country news Vol. 27, No.8.

Marsden, J.E. 1993. Responding to aquatic pest species: control or management? Fisheries 18: 4–5.

McCoid, M.J. 1995. Alien reptiles and amphibians. Pages 433–437 In, Laroe, E.T., G.S. Farris, C.E. Puckett, P.D. Doran, and M.J. Mac, (eds.). Our living resources: a report to the nation on the distribution, abundance, and health of U.S. plants, animals, and ecosystems. U.S. Department of the Interior, National Biological Service, Washington, DC. 530 p.

McKeown, S. 1978. Hawaiian reptiles and amphibians. Oriental Publishing Company Honolulu. 80 p.

McKnight, B.N. 1993. Biological Pollutions. The Control and Impact of Invasive Exotic Species. Indiana Academy of Science, Indianapolis. 261 p.

McNeely, J.A. et al. (eds.). 2001. Global Strategy on Invasive Alien Species. IUCN, Gland, Switzerland.

Meisner, J.D., J.S. Rosenfeld, and H.A. Reiger. 1988. The role of groundwater in the impact of climatic warming on stream salmonines. Fisheries 13(3):2–8.

Meronek, T.G., F.A. Copes, and D.W. Coble. 1995. A summary of bait regulations in north central United States. Fisheries 20(11):16–23.

Miller, R.R., J.D. Williams, and J.E. Williams. 1989. Extinctions of North American fishes during the past century. Fisheries (Bethesda) 14(6):22–38.

Mills, E.L., J.H. Leach, J.T. Carlton, and C.L. Secor. 1994. Exotic species and the integrity of the Great Lakes. Lessons from the Past BioScience 44(10): 666–676.

Minckley, W.L., and J.E. Deacon. 1968. Southwestern fishes and the enigma of "endangered species." Science 159(3822):1424–1432.

Ministry of Environment Lands and Parks Website. http://www.env.gov.bc.ca/fsh/.

Mitchell, A.J., M.J. Salmon, D.G. Huffman, A.E. Goodwin, and T.M. Brandt. 2000. Prevalence and Pathogenicity of a Heterophyid Trematode Infecting the Gills of an Endangered Fish, the Fountain Darter, in Two Central Texas Spring-Fed Rivers. Journal of Aquatic Animal Health. Vol. 12, No. 4, pp. 283–289.

Montana State University Extension (MSU). 1997. Extension Bulletin: Mapping Noxious Weeds in Montana. Bozeman, MT.

Mooney, H.A., and R.V. Hobbs. 2000. Invasive Species in a Changing World. Island Press, Washington, DC. 457 pp.

Moyle, P.B., and R. Nichols. 1974. Decline of the native fish fauna of the Sierra Nevada foothills, Central California, American Midland Naturalist 92:72–83.

Moyle, P.B. 1976. Fish introductions in California: History and impact on native fishes. Biological Conservation 9:101–118.

Moyle, P.J., H.W. Li, and B.A. Barton. 1986. The Frankenstein effect: impact of introduced fishes on native fishes in North America, In, Stroud, R.H. (ed.). Fish Culture in Fisheries Management, American Fisheries Society, Bethesda, MD.

National Geographic Society. 1998. Alien Invasion. America's Battle with Alien Animals and Plants. National Geographic Society, Washington, DC.

Nalepon, T.F., and D.W. Schloesser (eds.). 1993. Zebra Mussels. Biology, Impacts, and Control. Lewis Publishers, Boca Raton. 810 p.

Naylor, R., R.J. Goldberg, J.H. Primavera, N. Kautsky, M.C.M. Beveridge, J. Clay, C. Folke, J. Lubchenco, H. Mooney, and M. Troell. 2000. Effect of aquaculture on world fish supplies. *Nature* 405: 1017–1024.

Nico, L.G., and P.L. Fuller. 1999. Spatial and Temporal patterns of nonindigenous fish introductions in the United States. Fisheries 24(1): 16–26.

Pitcher, T.J., and P.J.B. Hart (eds.). 1995. The Impact of Species Changes in African Lakes. Chapman and Hall, London. 601 p.

Parsons, P.A. 1982. Adaptive strategies of colonizing animal species. Geological Review 57:117–148.

Pratt, C.M., W.H. Blust, and J.H. Selgeby. 1992. Ruffe, Gymnocephalus cernuus: newly introduced in North America. Can. J. Fish. Aquat. Sci 49;1616–1618.

Randonski, G.C., N.S. Prosser, R.G. Martin, and R.H. Stroud. 1984. Exotic fishes and sport fishing, p. 313–319. In, W.R. Courtenay, Jr and J.R. Stauffer, Jr [ed] Distribution, biology and management of exotic fishes. Johns Hopkins University Press, Baltimore, MD.

Raguso, J. 1993. Bait well choices. Trailer Boats 22(6):28–29.

Rice, J. 1995. Rare native fish found in Utah, then poisoned by mistake. High Country News Vol. 27. No. 22.

Rhymer, J.M., and D. Simberloff. 1996. Extinction by hybridization and introgression. Annu. Rev. Ecol. Syst. 27: 83–109.

Ricciardi, A. 2001. Facilitative interactions among aquatic invaders: is an "invasional meltdown" occurring in the Great Lakes? Can. J. Fish. Aquat. Sci. 58: 2513–2525

Richardson, M.J., and F.G. Whoriskey. 1992. Factors influencing the production of turbidity by goldfish. (Carrasius auratus). Can. J. Zool. 70(8):1585–1589.

Ring, R. 1995. The West's fisheries spin out of control. High Country News, Vol. 27, No. 17.

Rosen, P.C. and C.R. Schwalbe. 1995. Bullfrogs: introduced predators in southwestern wetlands. Pages 452-454 *In*, Laroe, E. T., G. S. Farris, C. E. Puckett, P. D. Doran, and M. J. Mac (eds.). Our living resources: a report to the nation on the distribution, abundance, and health of U.S. plants, animals, and ecosystems. U.S. Department of the Interior, National Biological Service, Washington, DC. 530 p.

Ruesink, J.L., I.M. Parker, M.J. Groom, and P.M.. Kareifva. 1995. Reducing the risks of Non-indigenous Species introductions. BioScience 45: 465–477.

Sala, O.E., F.S. Chapin III, J.J. Armesto, R. Berlow, J. Bloomfield, R. Dirzo, E. Huber-Sanwald, L.F. Huenneke, R.B. Jackson, A. Kinzig, R. Leemans, D. Lodge, H.A. Mooney, M. Oesterheld, N.L. Poff, M.T. Sykes, B.H. Walker, M. Walker, and D.H. Wall. 2000. Global biodiversity scenarios for the year 2100. Science 287: 1770–1774.

Schloesser, D.W., and Nalepa, T.F. 1994. Dramatic decline of unionid bivalves in offshore waters of western Lake Erie after infestation by the zebra mussel Dreissena polymorpha. Canadian Journal of Fisheries and Aquatic Sciences 51, 2234–42

Scott, W.B., and E.J. Crossman. 1973. Freshwater fishes of Canada. Bulletin 184. Fisheries Research Board of Canada. Ottawa.

Shafland, P.L. 1979. Alien fish introductions with special reference to Florida. Fisheries (Bethesda) 4(3):18–24.

Shafland, P.L., and W.M. Lewis. 1984. Terminology associated with introduced organisms. Fisheries 9(4):17–18.

Shafland, P.L. 1986. A review of Florida's efforts to regulate, assess and manage exotic fishes. Fisheries 10(2):20–25

Sharpe, F.P. 1962. Some observations of the feeding habits of brown trout. Progressive Fish-Culturist 24(2):60–64.

Simberloff, C. 1981. Community effects of introduced species, 53–81. *In*, M.H. Nitecki (ed.). Biotic crises in ecological and evolutionary time. Academic Press, Inc., New York.

Simberloff, D., B. Von Holle. 1999. Positive interactions of nonindigenous species: invasion meltdown? *Biological Invasions* 1(1): 21–32.

Smith, S.L. 1976. Behavioural suppression of spawning in largemouth bass by interspecific competition for space within spawning areas. Transactions of the American Fisheries Society 105(6):682–685.

Stroud, R.H. 1969. Conference on exotic fishes and related problems. Sport Fishing Institute Bulletin 203:4–9.

Swingle, H.S. 1957. A repressive factor controlling reproduction in fishes. Proceedings of the Pacific Science Congress 8(1953):865–871.

Taylor, J.N., W.R. Courtenay Jr., and J.A. McCann. 1984. Known impacts of exotic fishes in the continental United States. *In*, W.R. Courtenay, Jr., and J.R. Stauffer, Jr. (ed.). Distribution, biology and management of exotic fishes. Johns Hopkins University Press, Baltimore, MD.

The Nature Conservancy. 2001. Abating the Threat to Biodiversity from Invasive Alien Species: A Business Plan for Engaging the Core Strengths of The Nature Conservancy.

The Nature Conservancy 2000. The Five-S Framework for Site Conservation: A practitioner's handbook for site conservation planning and measuring conservation success.

Tu, Mandy. 2002. Early Detection and Cooperation Prevents the Establishment and Spread of a Severe Invasive Plant Pest into the Connecticut River: A Success Story. The Nature Conservancy's Wildland Invasive Species Team. http://tncweeds.ucdavis.edu/success/ct001/ct001.rtf.

Turner, B.E. (ed.). 1988. Codes of practice and manual of procedures for consideration of introductions and transfers of marine and freshwater organisms. ICES Co-operative Research Report No. 159. 44pp.

United States Geological Survey Press Release. 1994. Earth Stewards Conservation Education Program launched. Fish and Wildlife Service. National Biological Information Infrastructure. National Biological Survey http://biology.usgs.gov/pr/newsrelease/1994/5-24.html.

Wager, R., and P. Jackson. 1993. The action plan for Australian freshwater species. Australian Nature Conservation Agency (ANCA), Endangered Species Program, Project No. 147. Canberra, Australia: ANCA.

Wallen, I.E. 1951. The direct effect of turbidity on fishes. Bulletin of the Oklahoma Agricultural and Mechanical College, Biological Series no. 2, 48(2):1–27.

Wattendorf, B. 1997. Butterfly peacock bass. High Country News, Vol.29, No.12.

Welcomme, R.L. 1988. International Introductions of Inland Aquatic Species. FAO Fisheries Tech. Pap. No. 294. Food and Agriculture Organization of the United Nations, Rome, Italy.

Welcomme, R.L. 1986. International measures for the control of introductions of aquatic organisms. Fisheries, 11(2):4–9.

Wilcove S., D. Rothstein, J. Dubow, A. Phillips, and E. Losos. 1998. Quantifying threats to imperiled species in the United States. BioScience. p 607–615.

Williams, J.E., J.E., Johnson, D.A. Hendrickson, S. Contreras-Balderas, J.D. Williams, M. Navarro-Mendoza, D.E. McAllister, and J.E. Deacon. 1989. Fishes of North America Endangered, Threatened, or of Special Concern. *Fisheries* 14: 2–20.

Wittenberg, R., M.J.W. Crock, (eds.). (2001) Invasive alien species: a toolkit of best prevention and management practices. Wallingford, Oxon, UK; CABI Publishing, 228 pp. Pbk. ISBN 0851995691.

Van Driesche, J., and R. Van Driesche. 2000. Nature Out of Place. Biological Invasions in the Global Age. Island Press, Washington, DC. 363 p.

Vermont Invasive Exotic Plant Fact Sheet 1998. Brazilian elodea, Egeria densa Planch. The Nature Conservancy of Vermont, Vermont Department of Environmental Conservation, and the Vermont Department of Fish and Wildlife. Available at http://www.anr.state.vt.us/dec/waterq/ans/objects/befs.pdf.

Chapter 5

Measuring Freshwater Biodiversity Conservation Success

David Braun

OVERVIEW AND LEARNING OBJECTIVES

This chapter explores how to design and implement a credible and cost-effective freshwater monitoring program guided by an appropriate team of experts and support staff. Specifically, this chapter describes the importance of, and methods for, identifying monitoring program purposes, priorities, and indicators; crucial components of a monitoring program such as determining when and where to monitor, what methods to use, and who should actually do the monitoring; and useful approaches for analyzing the data collected and using this information to increase conservation effectiveness through adaptive management. This chapter builds directly on Chapters 3 and 4, which focus on setting freshwater conservation priorities within and across conservation areas and on identifying and abating threats to conservation targets at these scales. Figure 5-1 explains the context of this informa-

DESIGNING A FRESHWATER MONITORING PROGRAM:
PURPOSES, PRIORITIES, AND INDICATORS

tion in relation to the
entire guide.

Designing a freshwater monitoring program can seem a daunting task. Almost an infinite number of characteristics of freshwater ecosystems exists to monitor, including characteristics of all five key ecological factors —the hydrologic regime, the water chemistry regime, physical habitat conditions, connectivity, and biological composition and interactions. Without careful planning, limited resources can be lost to data collection of questionable usefulness. The solution to this problem is to determine: (1) the exact intended purposes of the monitoring program; (2) the priority of each of these purposes; and (3) what indicators to monitor in order to satisfy programmatic purposes and priorities. As suggested elsewhere in this guide, a conceptual ecological model is a very useful device for determining targets and indicators and understanding threats. It is also useful for determining how to measure success.

Purposes of a Freshwater Monitoring Program

Monitoring for freshwater conservation needs to address three types of questions: (i) the status of the focal targets and the effects of conservation actions on them, (ii) the status of threats to these targets and the effects of conservation actions on this status, and (iii) gaps in scientific knowledge about the targets and the system overall. Consider:

- As described in Chapter 3, planning for each conservation area should identify a suite of focal conservation targets, the key ecological factors shaping the integrity of each target, and conservation goals for each target based on these key factors. These key factors, along with their indicators and information on their acceptable ranges of variation, frame a list of questions about each target, including, *"What is the status or trend for [factor X] and does it meet specified conservation goals?"* For example, needed information may include whether a particular fish

species is present in acceptable numbers or if nitrate levels remain below some critical threshold.

- As described in Chapter 4, planning for each conservation area should identify the critical threats to each focal target and specific strategies to abate them. Taken together, the assessments of threats and strategies for the targets frame a second list of questions, including, *"What is the status or trend for [threat Y] and are the conservation strategies having the desired effect(s) on this threat?"* For example, it may be important to determine whether a dam operator is keeping the daily variation in releases within some desired pattern and whether ecosystem health (as quantified by available habitat, particular fish populations, and macroinvertebrate populations) is responding positively to these changes. Another example might be whether the implementation of alternative farming practices has reduced sediment runoff.

- Finally, reducing gaps in scientific knowledge helps improve conservation effectiveness. These gaps may relate to the targets, the key factors affecting target integrity, acceptable ranges of variation within these key factors, the ways that particular threats affect the targets, the relative importance of different sources of these threats, or the ways that different conservation actions can improve target status. For example, in order to set sound conservation goals, more information about the natural composition of the fish community in a stream may be needed, including how temperature variation affects biotic composition, and the extent of reduction in flood magnitudes that a river system can tolerate and still sustain its biodiversity.

Priorities in a Freshwater Monitoring Program

The resources available to carry out a monitoring program will rarely be optimal. The following criteria can help focus monitoring efforts and direct limited funds appropriately. These criteria should also help determine whether to begin the monitoring now or later and how much investment is needed for the effort.

Global processes, including geology and climate, interact to produce...

The Watershed Context of Freshwater Ecosystems

- Location
- Waterhed vegetation cover
- Watershed elevation, gradient, and drainage patterns

which establishes the natural patterns of variation in...

The Five Key Ecological Factors of Freshwater Ecosystems

- Hydrology
- Physical habitat structure
- Water chemistry
- Connectivity
- Biological composition and interactions

which in turn can be altered by...

Human Activities

- Land use and management
- Water use and management
- Invasive alien species
- Overharvesting and fisheries management

because of the adverse effects these activities can have on...

Geophysical Conditions	Aquatic Biological Conditions
- Watershed vegetation cover - Soil erosion rates - Surface and groundwater hydrology - Soil and water chemistry - Channel/shoreline morphology	- Taxonomic and genetic composition - Individual health - Biological processes - Ecological processes - Evolutionary processes

which must be prevented or abated by...

Conservation Strategies

- Restoration and land/water protection
- Specific land use policies and practices
- Specific sustainable water management policies and practices
- Invasive alien species management policies and practices
- Fisheries management and harvesting policies and practices
- Etc.

and we improve our success through...

Monitoring and Adaptive Management

FIGURE 5.1.

Although all are important, the first two are critical considerations:

- **Degree of Alternation.** The greater the suspected degree of departure of a key ecological factor from its acceptable range of variation, the higher the priority of monitoring that factor. In addition, the greater the likelihood that some emerging threat(s) will push one or more key ecological factors outside their acceptable ranges of variation, the higher the priority for monitoring that factor.

- **Urgency of Threat.** Threats always vary in their urgency, depending on their severity and scope, whether they are already active or only anticipated to take place, and, if only anticipated, how likely they are to take place. The more immediate a threat—the greater its severity and scope and the greater its likelihood of affecting the target—the higher the priority for monitoring that threat. In addition, the more immediate a threat, the higher the priority for monitoring the effectiveness of any conservation actions aimed at that threat. The urgency of a threat will also influence the kinds of indicators selected for monitoring that threat, as discussed below.

- **Ecological Uncertainty.** Knowledge about conservation targets is often incomplete (e.g., what are its key ecological processes, interactions among factors, relationships between biotic and abiotic processes, etc.). Although this uncertainty may have little bearing on conservation plans, more often both the uncertainty and the risk are high. The higher the uncertainty about an ecological relationship, and the higher the risk associated with making incorrect assumptions about this relationship, the higher the priority of collecting data to reduce this uncertainty. One of the most common causes of ecological uncertainty is the absence of historic or recent data regarding key ecological factors or regarding the conservation target itself (population dynamics, distribution, etc.). Without such data, demonstrating change will be elusive. Establishing such baseline data for a target may therefore be a high priority for reducing ecological uncertainty.

- **Conservation Uncertainty.** Uncertainties will always exist about whether specific conservation actions are working at all or about whether conservation actions are having as much effect as hoped. Such uncertainty can be particularly unwelcome, the more altered a key factor, the higher the severity of the stresses affecting it, or the more alarming the trend in its status. But even if the need for conservation action is not dire, few can afford to waste resources on actions that don't work well. The greater the uncertainty about the effectiveness of particular conservation actions, both ongoing and planned, the higher the priority of collecting data to reduce this uncertainty. The absence of historic or recent baseline data for a target is one of the most common causes of conservation uncertainty. Without baseline data, it will be impossible to demonstrate that a change has taken place following implementation of any conservation strategy. Establishing baseline data for a target may therefore be a high priority for reducing conservation uncertainty as well.

Sound adaptive management will always demand reliable monitoring data. However, monitoring need not always address every single key factor. In relatively less-threatened landscapes, integrative indicators may be used that provide information on several factors at the same time, as explained by Appendix B.

Choosing Indicators in a Freshwater Monitoring Program

Once the purposes and priorities for a monitoring program are established, the next step is determining the indicators to monitor. This section explains the reasons for using indicators and criteria to consider in selecting indicators

WHAT ARE INDICATORS?

Indicators are ecological characteristics that can be directly measured. Some aspects of freshwater ecosystems appear easy to measure, given the right equipment, for example water temperature, nutrient levels, river discharge, lake levels, etc. Other aspects of freshwater ecosystems appear to pose greater challenges, for example the integrity of floodplain vegetation or river-bottom fish communities. Where direct measure-

Water level monitor. Photograph by Jane M. Rohling/USFWS.

ments are available, they prove very useful. However, direct measurements are not always available.

In situations where direct measurements are either not available or not useful, indicators may be used. For instance, scientists rarely measure river or stream discharge directly since doing so is technically difficult and expensive if not impossible.[1] Instead, scientists estimate river or stream discharge by measuring the stage (height) of the water and the shape of the channel. Measuring the chemical characteristics of water, such as the concentration of some agricultural chemical, is even more difficult by direct measurements. Chemicals in freshwater ecosystems may be dissolved in the water, may attach themselves to particles of clay or organic matter, or may bind with other chemicals; they may break down into other chemicals through natural reactions in the water; they may be consumed or absorbed by living organisms, by which they may be modified into other chemical forms or simply retained as part of living and dead biomass; and they may become incorporated into the mineral, organic, and living matter in the sediments of the water body just as easily. Freshwater ecologists and toxicologists therefore have developed indicators

for many types of chemicals, usually based on measurements of their presence in only a few components of the ecosystem (e.g., in the water and absorbed into sediments).

DESIRABLE CHARACTERISTICS OF FRESHWATER INDICATORS

Indicators must produce credible evidence with which to answer specific monitoring questions, analogous to the evidence that a prosecuting attorney might use in court or a doctor might use in diagnosing an illness. The most desirable characteristics of indicators, whether for freshwater monitoring or any other kind of conservation-related monitoring, include:

- **Scientific Relevance.** The indicator must provide a scientifically sound and unambiguous assessment of the key ecological factor, stress, or source of stress that it is intended to measure. An unambiguous indicator is one that, for all practical purposes, responds exclusively to that which it is intended to measure. For example, the population density of a

---

[1] This would require forcing the entire flow through a strcture that directly measures the volume of water passing through.

particular riverine fish could be selected as an indicator of the connectivity between the river and its floodplain. The rationale for this selection might derive from scientific evidence that this fish reproduces successfully only when it has access to floodplain wetlands during floods. If the relationship were well established by previous research, and if no other ecological variables also affected the fish population, then this indicator would be based on sound reasoning. On the other hand, if the fish population depends not only on floodplain inundation but on the availability of a critical prey species or on the susceptibility of the fish to an exotic parasite, then this indicator would not be based on good science and would likely work poorly for assessing the status of connectivity in the system.

- **Sensitivity.** The indicator must be sensitive to change in the key ecological factor, stress, or source

it is intended to measure, along its entire range of variation, and be able to register incremental changes along that entire range as well, particularly changes that correspond to critical ecological thresholds. For example, an area occupied by a certain bottom-land tree species—as measured from aerial photographs—could be used as an indicator of the integrity of the river-floodplain connection. The rationale for this might be that the species is known to colonize floodplain soils only through flooding. However, this species might in fact be long-lived and, once mature, insensitive to changes in the pattern of inundation. In fact, the species may colonize new patches on the floodplain only following certain kinds of flood disturbances that occur only once every several decades even under natural conditions. As a result, the area covered by the species might change little for many decades,

Sampling aquatic invertebrates. Photograph by Charles Morris/USACE.

even if recruitment has ceased due to the construction of an upstream dam. The measurements from the aerial photographs would therefore not be sufficiently sensitive to the ecological factor of interest to justify its use as an indicator.

- **Timeliness.** The indicator must respond promptly to any change in the key ecological factor, stress, or source it is intended to measure. For example, it may take a few years for a stream's macroinvertebrate assemblage to change in response to a new pollutant, or for the pollutant to accumulate to unhealthy levels in the tissues of the stream's fishes. Direct measurement of the pollutant in water samples, on the other hand, should allow detection of the change right away. Indicators that respond rapidly (or immediately) to a change in a target or factor are termed "leading" indicators; those that respond more slowly are termed "lagging" indicators. In the aforementioned example, the concentration of the pollutant in actual water samples would be a leading indicator, while measurements of macro-invertebrate assemblage composition or fish tissue accumulations would serve as lagging indicators. However, leading indicators may not always be the best choice. For example, the direct measurement of a pollutant in water samples may require the collection of large numbers of samples, particularly during high-flow events, at large numbers of locations, as well as require costly laboratory procedures to detect the small amounts present in each sample. The proposed lagging indicators alternatively will provide information on the effects of the pollutant integrated or averaged over a longer period of time. Although lagged, this information may be more reliable, less expensive, and still sufficiently timely to allow corrective actions.
- **Measurability.** The indicator must be consistently measurable by some practical, repeatable method that produces results with good accuracy and precision. For example, it may someday be possible to monitor fish species and their population sizes in a river using arrays of underwater acoustic (sonar) sensors combined with three-dimensional image recording and pattern-recognition software. However, this technology is not yet practical for everyday application (it remains highly experimental as well as quite costly). More conventional fish monitoring methods, involving nets and electrical shocking techniques, have their own limitations and biases. However, these limitations and biases are well-known and understood, the techniques are highly reliable, and the results are highly repeatable. In other words, they may not be ideal, but they get the job done. In addition, other stakeholders will give greater credibility to data collected with widely recognized, standard methods. For example, the U.S. Environmental Protection Agency, U.S. Geological Survey, American Society of Civil Engineers, and, working together, American Public Health Association and American Water Works Association, all maintain catalogs of scientifically approved standard methods for monitoring hydrology and water chemistry in the U.S. (see resource lists, below).

- **Community Relevance.** Key ecological factors, stresses, and sources of stress need to be measurable in ways that other stake-holders also find useful and, preferably, easy to understand. Successful freshwater conservation depends on support—or at least tolerance—from the community living in the watershed and from other stakeholders in the use of its water resources. Indicators often play a crucial role in informing not only the science of the conservation effort, but the larger community as well. Indicators that the public and/or other stakeholders do not understand may impede conservation efforts. Alternatively, other stake-holders —including governmental agencies—may already be using indicators of their own for managing freshwater resources. If these indicators are useful, use them—the communication value will be important.
- **Cost-effectiveness.** The costs of freshwater monitoring include the costs of equipment and supplies, field staff time, transportation (including transporting samples to an off-site laboratory), data management, and, when necessary, contracts with laboratories and with experts to analyze or interpret data. With all the pressures on conservation resources, it is vital that every indicator selected provide the maximum amount of information for the effort and expense. The general rule is, the greater the level of detail, accuracy, and precision desired in an indicator, the greater its cost. When

considering costs, include both the cost of getting started and the costs of keeping the program going. Automated equipment, for example, may require a significant outlay at the start, but provide significant savings in staff time and laboratory expenses in the long run, as well as generating a much more detailed monitoring record than possible with simpler methods.

For almost any aspect of a freshwater ecosystem, a wide range of indicators exists. Please refer to Appendix B for an overview of options for indicators related to the five key factors in freshwater ecological integrity. Appendix B also provides information about integrative indicators.

DESIGNING A FRESHWATER MONITORING PROGRAM: CRUCIAL COMPONENTS OF A MONITORING PROGRAM

Important Considerations in Designing a Monitoring Program

Decisions about monitoring purposes, priorities, and indicators provide the foundation for addressing six critical considerations for monitoring programs: (1) whether to measure any covariates along with other field measurements; (2) when to collect field measurements and samples, how often to repeat the fieldwork, and for how long; (3) where to collect these field measurements and samples; (4) what methods to use for collecting these field measurements and samples and for handling and analyzing the samples brought in from field; (5) how to ensure quality control for monitoring data; and (6) who is going to do the work. These six considerations clearly depend closely on each other.

DECIDING WHETHER TO MONITOR COVARIATES

Interpreting some indicators may be difficult without also having data on covariates to assess. Covariates are environmental variables that strongly influence the status of some other variable but that may be controlled by different environmental conditions. For example, the temperature of the surface water in a lake depends on the influences of runoff from its watershed, but also depends on the time of day, the time of year, and the air temperature at the time of measurement. Time of day, time of year, and air temperature are thus covariates for lake surface water temperature. If a monitoring program fails to collect data on such covariates, it runs the risk of

being unable to properly interpret its core monitoring data. Thus, to continue the same example, if surface water temperature measurements are collected at a lake for a few years but no record is kept of the time of day, time of year, and air temperature at the same time, the data collected will likely not prove useful for any conservation purpose. If the data are highly variable, it will be impossible to determine if surface water temperatures have actually become more variable, or if the measurements were simply taken randomly in either the early morning or the late afternoon without any consistency. Similarly, if the average surface water temperature rises, it will be impossible to determine if the weather has been warmer, or if human activities in the water-shed are causing the change.

Common examples of covariates in freshwater ecosystem monitoring include the following:

- Storm runoff carries many pollutants, including eroded soils, into freshwater systems. The more intense the runoff, the higher the total amount, or the load, of each pollutant carried in the runoff. The load, of each pollutant carried in the runoff. The load of a pollutant in a river or stream depends on two variables: the concentration of the pollutant in the water (i.e., the amount present in a given unit of volume, such as milligrams of nitrate per liter of water) and the amount of water flowing in the stream (expressed as volume per unit of time). Evaluating the degree of runoff pollution and the effectiveness of conservation strategies to reduce the runoff requires examining not only the concentrations of pollutants but also their loads.

Stream discharge is thus a covariate for monitoring runoff pollution.

- The rain and snow falling anywhere in the world contains a dilute soup of chemicals, that derive from nature and as a side effect of many human activities. For example, rainfall along the ocean coasts usually contains measurable levels of ocean salt, since the water in the clouds derives in part from droplets of spray blown off the ocean surface. Similarly, rain and snow over many parts of the U.S. contain significant levels of nitrate and sulfate, and have a significantly lowered pH, as a result of air pollution from power plants, industry, motor vehicles, and agricultural activities. Monitoring the concentration of crucial chemical variables in precipitation will help to distinguish the effects of land-based strategies to reduce runoff pollution from the effects of variation in atmospheric deposition. Rain and snow concentrations of several chemical variables therefore may be covariates for monitoring some kinds of pollution.

Covariates should be monitored on the same sampling schedule as the indicators with which they are associated (see below). Usually, but not always, covariates should also be monitored at the same sampling locations as the variables with which they are associated, as well (see also below).

DEVELOPING A MONITORING SCHEDULE

Answering the question of when to monitor each freshwater indicator and associated covariates is greatly simplified by considering the following components:

- Initiation—when to start;
- Timing—whether to monitor randomly, regularly (e.g., always at the same time of day) or only at times determined by external trigger conditions;
- Frequency—how often to monitor within and across the years;
- Duration—for how many years; and
- Consistency—whether to maintain the same methods

over time, or alternate high- and low-intensity methods.

Responses to each of these components should rest first on conservation need, and secondly on capacity.

Deciding when to initiate monitoring is largely a matter of priorities (see above). The choices of timing, frequency, duration, and consistency for monitoring each indicator (and associated covariates) will depend foremost on what is known or expected of the range of variability of the indicator or covariate. That is, deciding when to monitor is primarily a matter of deciding how to sample that range of variability over time in order to obtain information with the accuracy and precision needed. Conservation practitioners working with freshwater targets generally should consider the following criteria:

- Measurements expected to exhibit significant or unpredictable variation from day to day or week to week may require more frequent monitoring. For example, capturing the full pattern of variation of stream flow often requires measuring stream flow daily or even hourly using automatic instruments.
- Indicators of cumulative or average conditions may require only seasonal or annual measurement. For example, the composition of the benthic invertebrate community in a stream may need to be monitored only once a year, although always at the same time of year.
- Indicators that vary in response to specific events may require monitoring that is synchronized with these particular kinds of events. For example, water chemistry in a lake may vary in response to storm runoff, the spreading of fertilizer in surrounding fields, or specific dam operations upstream. Catching information on the effects of these events will require monitoring the water at the same time as the events take place, including a short period before and after as well.
- Experiments to evaluate the effectiveness of specific conservation actions will require monitoring before, during, and after those actions, to ensure scientifically reliable results.
- Determining statistical trends in field experiments affected by large numbers of uncontrollable factors (e.g., the weather, stakeholder actions, population

growth) also may require monitoring both more often within each year and over a greater number of years to produce reliable results.

- Determining statistical trends in attributes that may change only slowly (or with a delay) in response to threats or conservation actions will also require monitoring over a greater number of years to produce reliable results.
- Adaptive management in systems where any one of several stakeholders can affect ecological conditions, where there is any uncertainty about target integrity or the effects of conservation action, or where conservation management is evolving as more is learned about the system (and that covers almost any conservation area), will require both:
  - baseline monitoring: comprehensive monitoring of conditions before initiating conservation efforts against which to compare future conditions; and
  - ongoing monitoring: monitoring that continues so long as conservation efforts or attention persist.

The biggest stumbling block to devising appropriate sampling schedules is often knowing or developing expectations for the range of variability in each indicator or covariate. Knowing or having models of what external factors drive the variability will help. Measurements that are readily affected by the weather or unpredictable human behavior exhibit the greatest variability. Data from previous monitoring in a particular conservation area or in neighboring watersheds will also provide crucial information on variability, as will the experiences of other conservation projects pursuing similar strategies in similar landscapes.

As noted above, decisions about sampling schedules will also depend on programmatic capacity. Regardless of whether a program has the capacity to do the monitoring itself or must carry out the monitoring in partnership with others, the amount of monitoring that can take place will depend on the resources available. The more often monitoring occurs, and the more locations to monitor, the more costly the monitoring will be. Fortunately, some of these costs can be controlled by taking advantage of economies of scale, such as purchasing automatic monitoring equipment that reduces field time and/or the need for field staff or obtaining discounts on

laboratory services. Volunteers can also assist, with appropriate training and supervision. Inevitably, though, compromises will be necessary.

DETERMINING WHERE TO MONITOR

Most conservation questions—whether concerning target integrity, threats, or knowledge gaps—pertain to different geographic zones or sets of localities within the overall conservation area. Answering these questions requires focusing monitoring precisely within these zones. The selection of locations for monitoring within these zones, in turn, requires a careful consideration of both the scientific needs at hand, and the physical opportunities available.

Considerations in selecting sampling locations include:

- One or more targets may associate with specific macrohabitats or geomorphic settings; monitoring the status or trends in the integrity of such targets will require sampling those specific settings.
- Assessing the cumulative impacts of human activities, including conservation actions, on conditions within a conservation zone will require monitoring those conditions toward the lower (downstream or downgradient) end of that zone.
- Different human activities, including conservation actions, may affect conditions within different sub-watersheds within a conservation zone. Assessing the cumulative impacts of these different activities may require monitoring those conditions toward the lower (downstream, downgradient) end of each sub-watershed.
- Assessing the impacts of human activities, including conservation actions, that occur within only a limited portion of a conservation zone may require monitoring those conditions both above (upstream, up-gradient) and below (down-stream, down-gradient) those impacts.
- Assessing the impacts of particular conservation strategies may require monitoring conditions associated both with the area of implementation of each such strategy and with one or more comparable areas within which the strategy has not been implemented. The area of implementation of a field-based strategy is called a treatment area, while an

area excluded from this implementation is called a control area.[2]

- Assessing the status and trends in target integrity and threats often will benefit from monitoring at reference as well as conservation sites. Reference sites are nearby locations (e.g., stream reaches, lakes, or wetlands) selected for their relative absence of human impacts on biological diversity, but which otherwise share most environmental conditions in common with a particular conservation area or specific zones within it. Comparing target conditions within a conservation area (or specific zones within it) to conditions at a reference site will help to determine how well conservation targets are doing, and will help explain the effects of any covariates acting on indicators.[3]

The selection of sampling locations also hinges on crucial logistical and institutional criteria:

- Avoid sampling locations that:
  - require unusually large amounts of time or costs to reach, particularly if the kind of information expected does not warrant this time or expense or can be obtained elsewhere with less effort;
  - are affected by highly localized or unique environmental conditions that are not representative of the area of interest, such as a narrow and steep bedrock gorge in an otherwise wide and gently sloping valley, or the foot of a dam or bridge;
  - entail unacceptable safety hazards, such as dangerous routes of access;
  - are susceptible to environmental hazards or to vandalism, that may make it undesirable to leave equipment or sampling markers in place; or
  - are prohibited because of access restrictions.

- Consider utilizing locations that are (or have been) monitored by other parties, or allow a monitoring program in partnership with others. In such cases, their institutional history and agenda may dictate the use of particular sampling locations to accommodate the monitoring design.

- Save costs by taking advantage of economies of scale and using volunteers, as noted above. However, the costs of monitoring increase more or less directly with the total number of sampling locations used. Therefore, one of the statistical methods for "optimizing" the number of sampling locations and the number of visits (sampling schedule) per location may be appropriate (U.S. Department of Agriculture 1997).

Covariates generally require sampling at the same locations as the variables or indicators with which they are associated, precisely because their purpose is to help explain the variability of those variables or indicators. However, sometimes this will not be the case. For example, weather information may help interpret stream discharge. Although the logical location for monitoring stream discharge would be at or near the bottom of a watershed, a weather station at this location would not necessarily provide entire representative data on meteorological conditions across the watershed. Instead, spatially representative weather monitoring stations across the watershed would yield more useful weather data.

CHOOSING WHAT METHODS TO USE

Most methods for field measurement, field sampling, sample handling, and laboratory analysis are well

---

[2] The most effective use of treatment and control areas in freshwater monitoring involves the use of a paired-watershed design. Watersheds (usually small sub-watersheds) within which a specific treatment (strategy) is applied are paired with others (the control sites) in which the treatment is not applied. The control and treatment sites must otherwise differ in as few environmentally significant respects as possible, including land use. However, using a paired-watershed design may not be possible in all areas. An alternative is then to use an upstream/downstream design, in which conditions are monitored both above and below the area in which a treatment is applied. A monitoring location immediately upstream from the treatment area serves as the control site, while monitoring immediately downstream provides information on the cumulative condition of both the control and treatment areas combined. The greatest benefit from the use of treatment and control sites—whether using a paired-watershed or an upstream-downstream design—comes from monitoring both before and after implementation of the treatments. The resulting monitoring design is often identified by its acronym, BACT (for Before-After Control-Treatment), sometimes also shown as BACI (Before-After Control-Impact). For further information on paired-watershed, upstream-downstream, and BACT sampling designs, see USDA 1997; USEPA 1997.

[3] The selection and use of reference sites takes some care. However, it is central to the use of many indicators (USEPA 1997).

Scientists discuss possible monitoring locations. Photograph by Brian Richter/TNC.

established and documented in widely available reference works, such as those listed at the end of this chapter. Here, we offer only general criteria for selecting the right methods to use in a particular conservation area. In general, the more urgent the priority for the monitoring, the greater the level of detail, precision, and reliability in data needed.

- Methods that produce more accurate and precise results, or that can detect very low concentrations of chemicals, usually cost more. However, sometimes these methods are what must be used in order to reduce critical uncertainties.
- Methods that save labor in the field generally cost more at the start, for buying or leasing the equipment, but reduce the cost per sample in the long run. In particular, automated and electronically aided methods usually initially cost more than manual methods, but quickly pay for themselves in higher densities of data and lower costs per measurement.
- Automated and electronically aided field methods are more prone to equipment malfunction and more sensitive to mishandling than are manual methods, but all require comparable levels of field operator training and practice.
- All field methods are susceptible to human error, resulting in problems with data quality that

demand comparable quality control procedures (see below).
- Laboratory measurements on field samples are generally more accurate than field-based measurements, but also entail greater costs in sample handling and logistics, payments to contractors, and potential additional problems with data quality control (see below).

Other factors to consider in selecting methods for each indicator include:

- Partners, particularly governmental agencies, usually follow specific standard methods. They will use them in their own monitoring, so using those same methods will ensure consistency and comparability. In some cases, such partners may require that all collaborators follow their standard methods.
- Consider using methods comparable to those used previously at the project site or in neighboring watersheds by partners, community-based groups, or other stake-holders.
- Water chemistry analyses must distinguish between the concentration of substances that are dissolved in the water (and therefore more biologically available) and the concentrations of these same substances that are present only in particulate form or adsorbed to other particulate matter. Analyzing

samples for dissolved substances alone requires filtering the samples, often at the time the samples are collected in the field. Filtering requires additional equipment and operator training.

- The concentrations of many chemicals and the distributions of many aquatic species can vary over space within a sampling location, in response to variation in water flow and mixing (both vertically and horizontally within the water body), or variation in microhabitat conditions. For example, on any given day, many aquatic species will differ in their occurrences among banks, bars, pools, riffles, runs, bed zones with different substrates, and around woody debris. Proper monitoring at an individual sampling location therefore generally demands methods for collecting a representative sample for the entire location.

MANAGING DATA QUALITY

Unreliable data is the undoing of any monitoring program. Reliability refers to the accuracy, precision, representativeness, comparability, and completeness of collected data. A conservation program burdened with unreliable data may fall into incorrect interpretations of monitoring data, or be unable to arrive at any interpretation at all. Every monitoring program therefore must establish and strictly enforce a set of quality assurance procedures, to protect the reliability of the data. The higher the priority for the monitoring, the more rigorous the quality assurance program needs to be

Quality assurance procedures address problems that arise for several reasons, any of which can arise in any monitoring program:

- Field samples can become contaminated during collection, because of failures to keep the sampling equipment and containers in proper condition;
- Field samples can deteriorate or become contaminated during handling through failures to follow proper procedures for handling and storage;
- Field samples and measurements can be taken incorrectly due to failures to follow standard procedures, failures to maintain equipment, or simply equipment malfunction;
- Field measurements and even sample labels can be recorded incorrectly by distracted field staff; and
- All measurement methods are subject to statistical error from the myriad other factors that affect sample condition and equipment operations.

There are two types of quality assurance procedures. Quality assessment (QA) procedures involve the use of specialized samples and tests to assess the quality of your monitoring data. Quality control (QC) procedures

Scientists review water temperature data. Photograph by Lynda Richardson.

are ones used to ensure that monitoring samples are collected and measurements taken consistently in the first place, and with minimal error. Together, these procedures are often identified by the acronym, QA/QC. As indicated earlier, different kinds of monitoring questions will require different levels of QA/QC to ensure an appropriate level of monitoring reliability.

Quality control procedures typically include documenting and following:

- Standard procedures for collecting samples and taking measurements in the field;
- Standard procedures for sample handling, custody, and transport;
- Standard good laboratory practices;
- Standard procedures for maintaining and calibrating equipment;
- Standard procedures for maintaining field and laboratory records; and
- Standard procedures for supervision and training.

Quality assessment procedures are often most carefully developed for working with water chemistry samples. Such procedures typically include some combination of the following (U.S. Department of Agriculture 1997):

- Collecting and analyzing blank and known (also termed spiked) samples. A blank sample consists only of chemically purified (distilled, de-ionized) water. A known or spiked sample is one in which a known amount of some substance has been introduced, for later measurement. Usually there is one blank or spike included in every twenty samples analyzed;
- Collecting and analyzing duplicate samples. A duplicate sample should be included for every twenty samples analyzed;
- Submitting duplicate samples to other laboratories (e.g., once a year);
- Having a partner simultaneously collect and analyze duplicate samples or collect duplicate field measurements;
- Regularly auditing the occurrence of recording errors; and
- Regularly comparing measurement results to an expected range of values, to look for unexpectedly high or low values that result from measurement errors.

IDENTIFYING WHO WILL DO THE MONITORING

Although clearly important, engaging in adequate monitoring to measure conservation success may seem both overly expensive and excessively time consuming. However, other entities and individuals may also be engaged within a particular project area and may be interested in sharing the burden of monitoring. Knowing the current status and past history of monitoring in a particular watershed is important for two reasons. First, this knowledge helps practitioners avoid duplicative efforts; if all parties can share their monitoring data, including their QA/QC data and information on methods, everyone benefits. Second, this knowledge help synchronize the use of particular methods and indicators; building on any knowledge base already developed and using methods compatible with these information gathering efforts will help ease communication challenges and allow for the generation of comparable data. In fact, it may be possible to build a consortium of parties interested in monitoring in a project area, coordinating activities and sharing results.

Among the many kinds of partners in a monitoring effort, organized volunteers often prove highly valuable. Local community groups and schools often have a strong interest in the freshwaters and aquatic life around them. Organizations and considerable published information exist to assist such local groups in developing the skills they need to produce useful and highly credible monitoring data.

Putting It All Together

Carrying out all of the steps above for planning a monitoring program will result in long, linked lists of questions, priorities, partners, indicators, covariates, sampling locations and schedules, monitoring methods, and QA/QC procedures. These lists require refinement and pruning to bring monitoring plans down to a manageable level capable of implementation. The pruning should start with a search for opportunities to simplify the plan, by reducing the number of monitoring locations, simplifying the sampling schedule, and adopting a smaller number of standardized indicators and methods.

Assembling a complete monitoring plan requires identifying those conservation questions that demand the most immediate monitoring, or at least an immediate cycle of baseline monitoring, and what monitoring activities they entail. This effort will also, as a corollary, identify those conservation questions for which the monitoring might be delayed, or started at a reduced level of intensity, should available resources prove more limited. The planning effort should also identify the costs of all monitoring activities, information about who can carry out specific parts of the monitoring, and the funding and other resources available for these specific parts of the monitoring.

Monitoring plans are usually assembled in steps, beginning with a tabulation of the highest priority monitoring efforts, their costs, and who will do the work. The team can then successively add additional components to the plan based on conservation priority until the plan reaches the limits of what is possible with the resources available. The results of this incremental approach may define only a worst-case plan, that includes only a minimal set of monitoring tasks, including only those that absolutely must take place or at least must begin right away. On the other hand, the results may define a best-case plan that fully supports everything needed. Between these two extremes will fall many variants, differing in when different monitoring efforts begin and at what level of intensity. If all the resources and potential partnerships available can not support even the worst-case scenario, a serious problem exists. In all likelihood, however, the most feasible plan will fall somewhere between the two extremes.

A great deal will be learned once work begins, which will likely cause readjustment of monitoring activities. Equipment or contractors won't work out, locations will be harder to reach than expected, and the system may not behave in expected ways. Indeed, making sense of the data will often prove to be one of the next biggest hurdles to overcome.

Each indicator and method selected, and each set of QA/QC procedures, will generate data that demand their own careful analysis. Generally, the procedures for simply summarizing as well as analyzing the data will be described in the reference works for that indicator, method, or QA/QC procedure. In addition, there are numerous published works available, and listed below, which present simple ways for tabulating and making basic sense of freshwater monitoring data. These need not involve elaborate statistical procedures, although those may also be appropriate under some circumstances. As with the design of the monitoring program itself, there is no substitute for having the right experts available from the start.

One very important last recommendation: keep good monitoring records. Keep them in a form that is safe and suitable for analysis. Paper records can burn, fall into the river, or get lost All data should be transferred to a computer database as soon as possible (and keep a backup, too). Some kinds of monitoring also generate enormous quantities of data. For example, an automatic device that measures water stage, temperature, pH, salinity, turbidity, and dissolved oxygen once every 15 minutes, along with the date and time of the measurement (such devices are readily available) will generate 768 items of data every day, or more than 280,000 observations each year. Adequately anticipate computer needs for storing this amount of information.

KEY TO CONSERVATION SUCCESS—MONITORING WITHIN AN ADAPTIVE MANAGEMENT FRAMEWORK

Conservation projects face many challenges. One of the most perplexing challenges is the reality that practitioners must move forward with conservation efforts despite enormous uncertainties. Uncertainties will be encountered over:

• the ecology of targets, how they function, what environmental conditions and processes are crucial to their integrity, and how they vary naturally over time and space;

• how, and to what extent, different human activities may alter these targets, their crucial driving processes, and their natural variation;

• the potential effectiveness of different conservation

strategies to prevent or abate these impacts, and the magnitude and geographic scope of implementation necessary for their success;

- the availability of financial resources for the implementation of these different strategies, and the willingness of partners to support or pursue them;
- the potential economic and social consequences of alternative conservation strategies; and
- the willingness of different stakeholders—many of whom may not support conservation, even if they do not oppose it—to cooperate with conservation efforts across a landscape.

Conservation efforts should not be delayed indefinitely while uncertainties are resolved, for two crucial reasons: (1) the answers may not be forthcoming; and (2) the pace of present changes to the land, water, and freshwater life, and/or the extent of past changes, pose urgent threats to freshwater biodiversity. In the best of scenarios, conservation action should proceed while practitioners explicitly acknowledge the uncertainties they face and look for ways to solve them while moving forward. This should be done in a manner that both engages and respects the values of all stakeholders and helps everyone use best available science to inform management decisions. This way is called adaptive management.

Adaptive management is both a philosophy and a specific body of methods. As a philosophy, its central tenet is that conservation programs must be designed so that they learn as much as possible, as rapidly and accurately as possible, and can adapt promptly to what is learned. In practice, this means:

- **Translate uncertainties into hypotheses.** When faced with scientific uncertainties, decisions must still be made and conservation activities should proceed. However, in proceeding with conservation activities, information should be collected to help address these uncertainties. If these uncertainties are framed as hypotheses, they will more likely be resolved through careful scientific inquiry.
- **Engage stakeholders in identifying and testing hypotheses.** Every stakeholder will have different knowledge and uncertainties about the landscape and its freshwater systems. Engaging all stakeholders in identifying these differences in knowledge, and ways to test and resolve them helps gain stakehold-

er support for specific conservation actions or eliminate opposition to such actions. This process transforms uncertainties from a potential source of conflict to a reason for collaboration.

- **Use new knowledge gained to inform and improve conservation.** Monitoring will generate information that changes understanding about a conservation target—for example, concerning it's distribution and life stages, the key ecological factors upon which it depends, and threats to it's existence or continued persistence. In turn, strategies can be refined and improved for abating threats and enhancing conditions for conservation targets. Components of any conservation planning effort should be considered in an iterative fashion so that they may be continuously improved. Adaptive management makes such iterative reconsideration possible.
- **Treat the entire conservation effort as an experiment.** Resolving uncertainties one by one can become a source of institutional friction, consume much effort, and delay significant conservation action. Moving forward with conservation action requires that the stakeholders become comfortable with the idea that the entire conservation effort is an experiment where conservation actions themselves play crucial roles. For example, as noted above, the entire conservation effort will face uncertainties about the ecology of each target, its vulnerability to human alteration, and the effectiveness and potential human consequences of alternative strategies to prevent or undo such alteration. The more that is collectively known about these aspects by sharing monitoring results, the greater chance for building organizational, institutional, and individual ownership for conservation progress and success.

Adaptive management improves the probability of conservation effectiveness. Measuring conservation success gives the necessary information to fuel the adaptive management engine. Improving conservation success requires that adaptive management be an integral part of any conservation effort.

REFERENCES

	General monitoring design	Selecting indicators	Standard methods & equipment	Monitoring partnerships	Interpreting monitoring data
Adopt-a-Stream Foundation. 1996. Streamkeeper's Field Guide: Watershed Inventory and Stream Monitoring Methods. pp. 300.	•	•	•	•	•
American Water Works Association and American Public Health Association. 1998. *Standard Methods for the Examination of Water and Wastewater,* 20th Edition. ISBN 0-87553-235-7.			•		•
Bunte, K., and S.R. Abt. 2001. Sampling Surface and Subsurface Particle-Size Distributions in Wadable Gravel- and Cobble-Bed Streams for Analyses in Sediment Transport, Hydraulics, and Streambed Monitoring. U.S. Department of Agriculture, Forest Service, Rocky Mountain Research Station, General Technical Report RMRS-GTR-74. Fort Collins, CO. Online: http://www.fs.fed.us/rm/pubs/rmrs_gtr74.html.			•		•
Cairns, J., Jr., P.V. McCormick, and B.R. Niederlehner. 1993. A Proposed Framework for Developing Indicators of Ecosystem Health. *Hydrobiologia* 263: 1–44.		•			
Dolloff, C.A., D.G. Hankin, and G.H. Reeves. 1993. Basinwide Estimation of Habitat and Fish Populations in Streams. U.S. Forest Service. 36 pp. Online: http://www.srs.fs.usda.gov/pubs/gtr/gtr_se083.pdf.	•	•	•		•
Downes, B.J., et al., 2002. *Monitoring Ecological Impacts: Concepts and Practice in Flowing Waters.* Cambridge University Press, New York.	•	•	•		•
Federal Interagency Stream Restoration Working Group. 1998. *Stream Corridor Restoration: Principles, Processes, and Practices.* U.S. Government Printing Office Item No. 0120-A; SuDocs No. A 57.6/2:EN3/PT.653. ISBN-0-934213-59-3. Online: http://www.nrcs.usda.gov/technical/stream_restoration.	•	•	•		•
Gordon, N.D., T.A. McMahon, and B.L. Finlayson. 1992. *Stream Hydrology: An Introduction for Ecologists.* John Wiley & Sons, New York.			•		•
Grant, G.E., J.E. Duval, G.J. Koerper, and J.L. Fogg. 1992. *XSPRO: A Channel Cross-Section Analyzer.* Technical Note 387, Bureau of Land Management, Denver, CO.			•		
Harrelson, C.C., C.L. Rawlins, and J.P. Potyondy. 1994. *Stream Channel Reference Sites: An Illustrated Guide to Field Technique.* U.S. Department of Agriculture, Forest Service, Rocky Mountain Forest and Range Experiment Station, General Technical Report RM-245. Fort Collins, CO.					

	General monitoring design	Selecting indicators	Standard methods & equipment	Monitoring partnerships	Interpreting monitoring data
Hauer, F.R., and G.A. Lamberti, editors. 1996. *Methods in Stream Ecology.* Academic Press, New York.		•	•		•
Hem, J.D. 1985. *Study and Interpretation of the Chemical Characteristics of Natural Water.* 3rd Edition. U.S. Geological Survey, Water-Supply Report 2254. Reston, VA.					•
Karr, J.R., and E.W. Chu. 1999. *Restoring Life in Running Waters.* Island Press, Washington, DC.	•	•	•		•
Karr, J.R., K.D. Fausch, P.L. Angermeier, P.R. Yant, and I.J. Schlosser. 1986. *Assessing Biological Integrity in Running Waters: A Method and Its Rationale.* Special Publication Number 5. Illinois Natural History Survey, Champaign, Illinois, USA.	•	•			•
Margoluis, R., and N. Salafsky. 2001. *Is Our Project Succeeding? A Guide to Threat Reduction Assessment for Conservation.* Washington, DC: Biodiversity Support Program. Online: http://www.bsponline.org (a version of this work was also published in *Conservation Biology* 13 (4): 830–841).	•	•			•
Mason, C.F. 1991. *Biology of Freshwater Pollution.* 2nd Edition. Longman Scientific and Technical Books/John Wiley & Sons, New York.			•		•
National Environmental Methods Index. A comprehensive listing and guidance site for environmental monitoring methods. Online: http://www.nemi.gov.	•	•	•	•	•
Clarkson, B.R., B.K. Sorrell, P.N. Reeves, P.D. Champion, T.R. Partridge, and B.D. Clarkson. 2002. Handbook for Monitoring Wetland Condition. Coordinated Monitoring of New Zealand Wetlands. A Ministry of the Environment Sustainable Management Fund Project 74 pp. Online: http://www.wetlandtrust.org.nz/documents/Handbook.pdf.	•	•	•	•	•
Oak Ridge National Laboratory, Environmental Sciences Division, Biological Indicators Program. Guidance on freshwater biological indicator selection. Online: http://www.esd.ornl.gov/programs/bioindicators/.		•			
New Guidelines for management planning for Ramsar sites and other wetlands (Resolution VIII.xx) Online: http://www.ramsar.org/key_res_viii_index_e.htm.	•		•		
Guidelines for establishing and strengthening local communities' and indigenous people's participation in the management of wetlands (Resolution VII.8) Online: http://www.ramsar.org/key_guide_indigenous.htm.				•	

	General monitoring design	Selecting indicators	Standard methods & equipment	Monitoring partnerships	Interpreting monitoring data
Richter, B.D., J.V. Baumgartner, D.P. Braun, and J. Powell. 1998. A spatial assessment of hydrologic alteration within a river network. *Regulated Rivers* 14:329–340.					•
Richter, B.D., J.V. Baumgartner, J. Powell, and D.P. Braun. 1996. A method for assessing hydrologic alteration within ecosystems. *Conservation Biology* 10:1163–1174.		•		•	•
Rosgen, D. 1996. *Applied River Morphology.* Wildland Hydrology, Inc., Pagosa Springs, CO.			•		•
Saterson, K., R. Margoluis, and N. Salafsky. 1999. *Measuring Conservation Impact: An Interdisciplinary Approach to Project Monitoring and Evaluation.* Biodiversity Support Program, Washington, DC. Online: http://www.bsponline.org.	•	•			•
The Nature Conservancy. 1996. *Hydrologic Monitoring Manual.* Version 4.1. Available from the Freshwater Initiative.			•		
U.S. Department of Agriculture, Natural Resources Conservation Service, National Water and Climate Center, Water Quality Assessment and Monitoring Program: Tools for estimating water quality sample sizes, converting measurement units, analyzing lake nutrient data, etc. Online: http://www.wcc.nrcs.usda.gov/wqam/wqam-tools.html.			•		•
U.S. Department of Agriculture, Natural Resources Conservation Service, National Water and Climate Center, Water Quality Assessment and Monitoring Program: Guidance on Sampling Equipment. Online: http://www.wcc.nrcs.usda.gov/wqam/wqam-sampling.html.			•		
U.S. Department of Agriculture. 1997. *National Handbook of Water Quality Monitoring Part 1.* Natural Resources Conservation Service, Publication 450-Part 600. National Water and Climate Center, Portland, OR. http://www.wcc.nrcs.usda.gov/wqam/wqam-docs.html.			•		•
U.S. Department of Agriculture. 1998. Stream Visual Assessment Protocol. Natural Resources Conservation Service, NWCC-TN-99-1. National Water and Climate Center, Portland, OR. http://www.wcc.nrcs.usda.gov/water/quality/frame/wqam/Guidance_Documents/guidance_documents.html.		•	•		
U.S. Department of Agriculture. 1999. *A Procedure to Estimate the Response of Aquatic Systems to Changes in Phosphorus and Nitrogen Inputs.* Natural Resources Conservation Service, National Water and Climate Center, Portland, OR. http://www.wcc.nrcs.usda.gov/wqam/wqam-docs.html.					•

	General monitoring design	Selecting indicators	Standard methods & equipment	Monitoring partnerships	Interpreting monitoring data
U.S. Department of Agriculture. 2002. *National Handbook of Water Quality Monitoring, Part 2, Analysis of Water Quality Monitoring Data.* Natural Resources Conservation Service, Publication 450-Part 615. National Water and Climate Center, Portland, OR. http://www.wcc.nrcs.usda.gov/wqam/wqam-docs.html.			•		•
U.S. Department of the Interior, Bureau of Land Management, Riparian Recovery Initiative, guidance on riparian monitoring and assessment, including visual assessment protocols and use of aerial photography. Online: http://www.blm.gov/riparian/tech.htm.	•	•	•		•
U.S. Environmental Protection Agency. 2003. *Volunteer Estuary Monitoring: A Methods Manual, Second Edition,* Office of Water, Office of Wetlands, Oceans and Watersheds, National Estuary Program, Washington, DC. http://www.epa.gov/owow/estuaries/monitor.	•				
U.S. Environmental Protection Agency, Office of Water, Office of Wetlands, Oceans and Watersheds, Guidance on Monitoring and Assessing Water Quality (includes lakes, streams and rivers, estuaries and coastal marine waters). Online: http://www.epa.gov/owow/monitoring/bioassess.html	•	•	•		•
U.S. Environmental Protection Agency. 1991. Voluntary Lake Monitoring. EPA 440-4-91-002, Office of Water, Washington, DC. Online: http://www.epa.gov/volunteer/lake.			•	•	
U.S. Environmental Protection Agency. 1997. *Monitoring Consortiums: A Cost-Effective Means To Enhancing Watershed Data Collection And Analysis.* EPA 841-R-97-006), May 1997, Office of Water, Office of Wetlands, Oceans and Watersheds, Assessment and Watershed Protection Division, Watershed Academy, Information Transfer Series, No. 3, Washington, DC. Online: http://www.epa.gov/owow/watershed/wacademy/its03/mon_cons.pdf.				•	
U.S. Environmental Protection Agency. 1997. *Monitoring Guidance for Determining the Effectiveness of Nonpoint Source Controls.* EPA 841-B-96-004, November, 1997, Office of Water, Office of Wetlands, Oceans and Watersheds, Washington, DC.	•				•
U.S. Environmental Protection Agency. 1997. *Volunteer Stream Monitoring: A Methods Manual.* EPA 841-B-97-003, November 1997, Office of Water, Washington, DC. Online: http://www.epa.gov/volunteer/stream/stream.pdf.			•	•	
U.S. Environmental Protection Agency. 1999. *Rapid Bioassessment Protocols for Use in Streams and Wadeable Rivers: Periphyton, Benthic Macroinvertebrates, and Fish,* 2nd Edition. EPA 841-B-99-002, July 1999, Office of Water, Washington, DC. Online: http://www.epa.gov/owowwtr1/monitoring/rbp/index.html.	•	•	•		•

	General monitoring design	Selecting indicators	Standard methods & equipment	Monitoring partnerships	Interpreting monitoring data
U.S. Environmental Protection Agency. 2001. Indicators for Monitoring Biological Integrity of Inland, Freshwater Wetlands: A Survey of North American Technical Literature (1990–2000). EPA 843-R-01-001, October, 2001, Office of Water, Wetlands Division, Washington, DC. Online: http://www.epa.gov/owow/wetlands/bawwg/monindicators.pdf.		•			
U.S. Environmental Protection Agency. 2001. *Volunteer Wetland Monitoring: An Introduction and Resource Guide.* EPA 843-B-00-001, December 2001, Office of Water, Office of Wetlands, Oceans and Watersheds, Washington, DC. Online: http://www.epa.gov/owow/wetlands/monitor/volmonitor.pdf.			•	•	
U.S. Geological Survey. 1993. *National Water Summary 1990–91* compiled by R.W. Paulson, E.B. Chase, J.S. Williams, and D.W. Moody, U.S. Geological Survey Water-Supply Paper 2400, Reston, VA.					•
U.S. Geological Survey: National Water-Quality Assessment (NAWQA) Method, Sampling, and Analytical Protocols. Online: http://water.usgs.gov/nawqa/protocols/doc_list.html.			•		
U.S. Geological Survey: Techniques of Water-Resources Investigations Reports. Online: http://water.usgs.gov/pubs/twri.			•		
Vives, P. Tomas. 1996. Monitoring Mediterranean Wetlands: A Methodological Guide. Wetlands International and Instituto da Conservacao da Natureza. 140 pp. Online: http://www.wetlands.org/pubs&/wetland_pub.html.	•	•	•	•	•

Ecological Characteristics of Freshwater Ecosystem Type

Kristine Ciruna and Allison Aldous

This appendix provides an overview of the three principle types of freshwater ecosystems: lakes and ponds, rivers and streams, and wetlands. Specifically, this appendix examines how lakes and ponds, rivers and streams, and wetlands are formed and how variations in their key ecological factors—hydrologic regime, water chemistry regime, physical habitat conditions, connectivity, and biological composition and interactions—make these ecosystems unique from one another. Gaining a deeper understanding of these freshwater ecosystem types and how they function will help inform assessments of ecosystem health and integrity, the relevance of particular threats to these ecosystems, and the design of effective monitoring programs for measuring conservation success.

LAKES AND PONDS

Lakes are inland depressions containing standing water. They vary in size from small lakes of less than a hectare, to large bodies of open water covering thousands of square kilometers such as the Great Lakes bordering the U.S. and Canada. The difference between a lake and a pond is in the depth and not the size. In a pond, sunlight reaches all the way to the bottom, whereas in a lake the light does not reach the bottom. It is possible, therefore, for a pond to be larger in surface area than a lake. The lack of light at the bottom of lakes limits and usually eliminates plant growth, which, in turn, affects the distribution of plant-eating organisms. Although ponds and lakes are different, given the relative simplicity of ponds and the need to provide more explanation about lakes, the remainder of this section focuses exclusively on lakes.

Formation of Lakes

The formation of a lake begins with a depression or basin within a relatively flat geologic feature with higher ground all around. A lake is formed when this depression collects water. Water can enter a lake in four ways: from groundwater (seepage lake); inflow from a stream; overland flow from the surrounding watershed; and/or precipitation falling directly on its surface. Seepage lakes, because they are supported mostly by groundwater discharge, tend to have smaller watersheds and therefore tend to have better water quality due to fewer contaminants entering from surface runoff. Please refer to Table A-1 for a complete review of lake types and formational processes. Water can leave a lake in three ways: seepage outward into the groundwater system; outflow through a stream; or evapotranspiration (the combined effects of direct evaporation and transpiration by aquatic and shoreline plants).

Key Ecological Factors of Lakes

The ecological integrity of a lake ecosystem depends on the status and interrelationships among its key ecological factors—physical habitat conditions, hydrologic regime, water chemistry regime, connectivity and biological composition and interactions. Each suite of key ecological factors for a lake ecosystem uniquely contributes to the lake's ecological integrity. Physical habitat conditions and water chem-

TABLE A-I. Seepage and Drainage Lakes

Depressions or basins which provide the foundation for lakes to form are themselves formed through a variety of different processes and phenomena. These result in different lake types, as described below.

Lake Type	Formation
Tectonic Lakes	Tectonic lakes from faulting and warping of the Earth's crust (e.g., African Rift Lakes; Lake Baikal, USSR)
Volcanic Caldera Lake	Volcanic caldera lakes form in the caldera or depression left after the collapse of a volcanic peak (post eruption or discharge) (e.g., Crater Lake , Oregon, U.S.A.)
Maars	Maars form by volcanic explosions below the Earth's surface, which produce low crater rims at the surface of the volcano. These low crater rims are built on fragments of rock with little or no volcanic material. If these embryonic volcanoes do not evolve further, they often fill with water and become small deep lakes (e.g., lakes in the Eiffel district of Germany)
Meteor Impact Lake	The crater caused by a meteorite crashing into the Earth may also form a basin within which a lake may form. Meteor impacts are the rarest cause of lake formation. Only five crater lakes are known to exist; Kaalijarv on the Island of Osel (Saaremaa) in the Baltic, Laguna Negra Campo del Ciele in the Gran Chaco of Argentina, Lake Bosumtwi in Ghana, Lonar Lake in western India, and Ungava Lake in Ungava, Quebec, Canada.
Landslide Lakes	Landslide of large quantities of consolidated material into the floor of a stream valley may form a dam behind which a lake may form (e.g., Warner mountain range of NE California, U.S.A. is characterized by this type of lake basin.)
Solution Lakes	Solution lakes form by water percolating through the solution of soluble rock, usually limestone/karst. A large number of solution lakes occur in the calcareous parts of the Alps.
River Plunge-Pool Lakes	River plunge-pool lakes form through the corrosive power of a waterfall which excavates a basin below the fall. If the river is diverted, the rock basin left at the base of the fall may contain a plunge-pool lake (e.g., Falls Lake and Castle Lake lie at the bottom of dry escarpments that were formerly large waterfalls at the head of the Lower Coulee, Washington, U.S.A.)
River Levee Lakes	Where a river reaches its endpoint—which may be an ocean, a large lake or desert wetland—the sediment of the river is abruptly deposited due to the sudden decrease in current velocity. Similarly, when a river overflows its banks and spreads across its floodplain, the water slows and quickly drops its load of sediment. Both cases result in the formation of raised ridges of deposited sediment, called "natural levees," that can trap water behind them and thereby form lakes (e.g., Lake Pontchartrain on the Mississippi Delta; Lake Tineo on the Orinoco River floodplain).
Oxbow Lakes	Oxbow lakes form as a river meanders across its floodplain creating loops of the channel that later become cut off or isolated from the river by silting. Numerous examples also occur along the Darling and Murray rivers in Australia where oxbow lakes are terms billabongs.
Floodplain Lakes	Floodplain lakes form from hollow in the floodplain of a river which are filled by the river when it overflows its banks during times of flooding. Common along the Amazon River's floodplain.
Ice-Dammed Lakes	On glaciated mountains, a stream may be dammed by the edge of a glacier and form an isolated lake. This damming of a stream occurs when the glacier of a main valley extends far enough down to dam a tributary stream, or alternatively, when a lateral glacier dams the main stream. These dams are usually not permanent, since they are constantly melting (e.g., Lake Missoula, Montana)

Lake Type	Formation
Ice-Scour Lakes	Ice-scour lakes may form in glacial basins created when pre-existing fractures and shatter belts on hard bedrock are excavated by glaciers as they advance and retreat (e.g., prominent European examples of ice-scour basins are found in Finland; in the U.S. and Canada, the Great Lakes are ice-scour lakes)
Glacial Cirque Lakes	The heads of glaciated valleys are often molded by glacial ice action into amphitheater-like basins, termed cirques. True cirques are generally small and shallow, although a few deep cirques have been found. Cirque lakes occur in practically every glaciated mountain range. Numerous examples of cirque lakes are found in the Cordilleran chains of North America.
Glacial Glint Lakes	In glaciated regions, ice may accumulate in valleys with small outlets, eventually creating large rock basins within which glint lakes may form as the glacial ice melts. A number of examples of glacial glint lakes occur in Scotland such as Loch Rannoch, Loch Ericht, Loch Ossian, and Loch Treig, which radiate from the ice cauldron that occupied Rannoch Moor.
Glacial Kettle Lakes	Glacial kettle lakes form by the deposition of blocks of ice washed out with glacial drift material from glaciers as they retreat. As these blocks of ice melt, they leave distinctly steep-sided basins that, when filled with water, form kettle lakes. Numerous freshwater ponds on the Midwestern plains, termed prairie potholes, are examples of kettle lakes on the central plains of North America.
Thermokarst Lakes	In regions of perennially frozen ground, lakes may form by local thawing. Such lakes are analogous to kettle lakes, with one exceptional feature: the position of a kettle lake is determined by the presence of a discrete mass of buried ice, whereas the position of a local thaw lake is determined by extraneous events causing local melting. Examples of thermokarst lakes are found in the interior of eastern Alaska. The permafrost in this region is unstable; once soil in this area thaws, it will not reform a perennially frozen layer. Once formation of a thermokarst lake begins, the embryonic lake progressively increases in area.

istry regime are the main drivers determining the biological interactions and resultant biodiversity for a lake. This is in contrast to river ecosystems where the hydrologic regime is the master variable that drives all other environmental processes such as physical habitat and water chemistry.

PHYSICAL HABITAT CONDITIONS

The morphology or shape of a lake basin has important effects on nearly all of the key ecological factors of a lake. Subsequent modifying events of water and sediment movements within the basin from drainage and seepage further act to modify a lake's morphology. These changes occur over a very long time period as compared to that of a river's channel.

Lakes can have extreme changes in relief in terms of lake depth. Different types of habitat and thus different communities occur at different depths as illustrated by bathymetric maps.

The most commonly used parameters to describe a lake's morphology are: lake surface area, volume, maximum depth, shoreline complexity and maximum length or fetch. These lake morphology characteristics determine the likelihood of thermal stratification and the resultant community types within a lake. The maximum length or fetch of a lake determines the direction of maximum wind interaction with the surface water of a lake. This is important because wind and wave action contribute a large proportion of dissolved oxygen content in the water. Shoreline complexity is the ratio of the length of the shoreline to the circumference of a circle of area equal to that of the lake. Shoreline complexity is of considerable interest because it reflects the potential for greater development of littoral zone communities in proportion to the volume of the lake.

Lakes are three-dimensional systems comparable in structural complexity to that of forest ecosystems. Both have changes in light and temperature from top to bottom which structure the organization of biodiversity. A typical lake contains three broad zones with unique biological communities: the littoral zone, pelagic zone, and benthic zone.

- The *littoral zone* is a transitional zone between terrestrial and freshwater communities. It is the shallow edge or near-shore area of the lake, where sunlight fully penetrates to the bottom and enables emergent and submergent aquatic plants (macrophytes) to grow.
- The *pelagic zone* is the area of open water. It is further subdivided into the euphotic and profundal zones. The *euphotic zone* extends from the surface down to the depth to which light ceases to penetrate or at which light levels become too low for photosynthesizers to exist. Phytoplankton (suspended algae) exists within this zone. The *profundal zone* occurs below the euphotic zone. It is the deeper open water area into which light does not penetrate.
- Lastly, the *benthic zone* consists of the lake bottom and contains accumulated sediments and detritus (dead, decaying organic matter).

HYDROLOGIC REGIME

The morphology of the lake basin, its connection to rivers and groundwater, the lake's stratification structure, and exposure to wind are all important factors that determine a lake's hydrologic regime. Water movements influence not only the distribution of nutrients, but also the distribution of microorganisms and plankton and hence the location of lake community types.

Two terms commonly used to describe lake hydrology are water budgets and water levels. Water budgets describe the amount of water flowing through, or into and out of, a freshwater ecosystems at any given point in time. Water levels and fluctuations in these levels also help describe lake ecosystem hydrologic function. Lake water level fluctuations include:

- *Short-term Fluctuations:* Temporary water level extremes can occur through phenomena such as storm surges and seiches caused by winds or atmospheric pressure changes, and tend to occur locally. They usually occur over a short time span since the water levels return to normal within a few hours or days. The effect of this type of fluctuation on littoral and coastal wetland communities is minimal.
- *Seasonal Fluctuations:* Lake levels are affected seasonally by evaporation, precipitation, watershed runoff and groundwater flow. Water levels have a fairly regular seasonal cycle, with minimum levels in the dry season, and maximum levels in the wet season.
- *Long-Term Fluctuations:* Long-term fluctuations in water levels do not occur cyclically, since there are no regular patterns or predictable changes. The range in these fluctuations can be extreme. Long term fluctuations are due to climatic variations which occur over several years. Precipitation, evaporation, and temperature are the dominant factors which control lake water levels. Changes in these elements caused by climatic variations affect the supply of water to lakes.

WATER CHEMISTRY REGIME

Water chemistry plays a crucial role in shaping the biological composition and dynamics of lake ecosystems —perhaps far more than it does in shaping river ecosystems. This crucial role arises because of both the longer residence time of water flow through a lake than a river and the way that water chemistry in lakes varies with depth, which in turn depends closely on the unique way that water temperature shapes the circulation of lake water. Three crucial aspects of water chemistry for lakes are water temperature, dissolved gases, nutrients, minerals, and turbidity.

Water temperature

Water temperature is extremely important for all freshwater ecosystems, including lakes, for three key reasons:

- Most freshwater organisms are cold-blooded. They are not able to regulate their own body temperature or metabolism and therefore need to rely on external temperature for their metabolic processes;

- All freshwater organisms have specific temperature ranges for which they can exist. Temperature therefore plays a key role in defining community structure. Cooler or warmer temperatures outside their range will lead to death; and
- Temperature influences other aspects of water chemistry, including dissolved oxygen, which all freshwater organisms need to survive. The concentration of dissolved oxygen has an *inverse* relationship with water temperature; the warmer the water, the less dissolved oxygen it can hold.

The dynamics of thermal stratification and mixing make water temperature an even greater factor for lake ecosystems. Lake water is seldom the same temperature from top to bottom. The least dense water forms the topmost layer, with successively denser layers at increasing depths. Provided none of the water is colder than 4°C, this simply means that the warmest water is at the top, and the coolest at the bottom. This is because at a temperature above 4°C the warmer the water the lower its density. Below 4°C the behavior of water changes radically. Instead of becoming more dense as it cools, it becomes less dense. No other liquid behaves in this way. This is why lakes and ponds freeze from the surface downward.

Many lakes, particularly in areas with greater daily or seasonal temperature variability, will stratify based on temperature. Water of different temperatures will form distinct layers within the lake where the temperature of the water will change sharply within a few centimeters. Therefore, a stratified lake is more accurately thought of as layered rather than smooth temperature gradient from top to bottom.

The process of thermal stratification and mixing in lakes is driven by the way that water changes density as it changes temperature. This process occurs in any climate where air temperature varies daily and with the seasons, and is especially pronounced in high latitudes and at high elevations. Typically in summer, when air temperatures are consistently warm, most lakes form a warm layer near the surface, that floats on top of the colder, deeper water. This warm layer is called the *epilimnion* and is well mixed by wave action. The bottom of the epilimnetic layer is where the mixing stops and the metalimnion layer begins. The *metalimnion* layer contains placid water, in which the temperature falls quickly as you go deeper forming a thermocline. Anyone who has gone swimming in a lake with a thermocline knows the shock of the cold water that you meet, when you dive deep enough to cross this boundary. The deepest water layer is the *hypolimnion*. It is the layer of cool/cold water at the bottom of the lake. Lakes shallower than ten meters generally do not develop a stable thermocline; their wave action can stir the water to such a depth that the boundary never forms for very long; at the other extreme, deep lakes almost always develop a thermocline. In general, the deeper the lake and the more sheltered it is from the wind, the more readily it stratifies and the longer the stratification lasts.

As the season progresses, night-time temperatures begin to fall, and water that warms and floats during the day increasingly cools and sinks at night. This destroys the thermocline, allowing deeper water to mix with shallow water; this is called turnover. During winter, when the water temperature falls below 4°C, in turn, the lake will stratify again. The formation of ice in fact reduces the effect of wind on mixing in the lake waters, making it still easier for the winter strati-

---

Box A-1. Why Ice Floats

The warmer the water, the faster its molecules are moving, the more space occupied by these molecules, and the less dense or lighter the water. As water cools toward 4°C, the molecules, move less quickly and take up less individual space, allowing the water to become more dense. Below 4°C, the slow-moving molecules begin to arrange themselves into a solid crystal; but the arrangement of electrons and protons in the water molecules forces them to line up in a way that takes up more space than when they were still moving freely. As the water changes from liquid to solid, it becomes less dense. This is why ice floats!

fication to develop and persist. Then, in the spring, the warming of air temperatures first eliminates any ice, then eliminates the presence of any water cooler than 4°C. The alternating of warmer days and cooler nights also promotes turnover, which prevents the formation of a thermocline until air temperatures are consistently high both night and day, at which point the spring turnover cycle ends and summer stratification resumes.

Dissolved gases, nutrients, and minerals

The second most ecologically important component of lake water chemistry are dissolved gases and minerals, particularly dissolved oxygen, pH, specific conductivity and the concentrations of nutrients (compounds containing nitrogen and phosphorus). Other compounds may also exert a strong influence in particular lakes, including dissolved minerals such as calcium, magnesium, silica, sulfur, and iron.

Dissolved Oxygen

Oxygen is a crucial requirement of all life in water. The concentration of oxygen in water in turn depends on three factors: (1) the temperature of the water; (2) the ability of aquatic plants and algae to generate oxygen as a byproduct of photosynthesis; and (3) the rate at which aquatic organisms respire and consume the oxygen that is available.

The dissolved oxygen concentration in the epilimnion remains high throughout the summer because of photosynthesis and absorption from the air. However, conditions in the hypolimnion vary with biological productivity. In nutrient-rich lakes, hypolimnetic dissolved oxygen declines during the summer because it is cut-off from all sources of oxygen, while organisms continue to respire and consume oxygen. The bottom layer of the lake and even the entire hypolimnion may eventually become anoxictotally devoid of oxygen. Decaying organic matter, which can be exacerbated by high plant and algae production, also consumes oxygen, potentially further depleting oxygen in nutrient-rich lakes. In nutrient-poor lakes, low phytoplankton biomass allows deeper light penetration and less decomposition. Phyto-

plankton are able to exist relatively deeper in the water column and less oxygen is consumed by decomposition. The dissolved oxygen concentration may even increase with depth below the thermocline in such cases as cold water can hold more dissolved oxygen than warm water. In extremely deep, unproductive lakes, dissolved oxygen may persist at high concentrations near 100% saturation throughout the water column year-round. These differences between nutrient rich and nutrient poor lakes tend to disappear during fall and spring turnover.

pH

pH is a standard measure of the hydrogen ion concentration of the water and is represented using a logarithmic scale. The concentration of hydrogen ions in water determines whether the water is acidic or basic. A pH of seven is neutral. This is the pH of water when you remove all dissolved gases, minerals, and organic compounds. Highly acidic water—water with a pH well below seven—can break down and dissolve a wide range of mineral and organic matter, and in the extreme is toxic. At the other end of the spectrum, water with a very low concentration of hydrogen ions and therefore a high pH is called basic water. Highly basic water can also break down and dissolve both mineral and organic matter, and can be highly corrosive.

The pH in most lakes has a natural range of variation that hovers between six and nine depending on the surface runoff and underlying geology of the watershed and the lake's zone of groundwater contribution. Rainfall is not only water. Water in the atmosphere absorbs a wide range of gases that actually make it highly acidic. Carbon dioxide (CO_2), a common gas in the air, dissolves easily in water and releases large amounts of hydrogen ions as it dissolves. Other gases that atmostpheric water typically absorbs include sulfur and nitrogen oxides, released as pollutants from our factories and automobiles. Once dissolved in water, these gases that form sulfuric and nitric acids, the compounds responsible for acid rain. When rain water and snow-melt percolate into the soil, they pick up additional acid-forming compounds from the organic matter in the soil and absorb additional CO_2 released by soil microbes.

Fortunately, geology and photosynthetic aquatic organisms play a large role in neutralizing the water coming into most lakes. The minerals that dissolve from most geologic formations, especially from limestone and other forms of carbonate rock, have the ability to bind with and reduce the concentration of hydrogen ions in the water, thereby maintaining a relatively stable pH in the range of seven to eight. The ability to hold down the acidity of water is called the buffering capacity or acid neutralizing capacity of a lake's water chemistry, and it depends on the concentration of acid-neutralizing compounds such as dissolved carbonate minerals. Aquatic photosynthetic organisms also help by absorbing CO_2 from the water. Lakes in granite regions, in contrast, tend to be more acidic because granite does not provide any buffering capacity to runoff. At the other extreme, lakes in some rare cases may contain high concentrations of minerals that remove almost all hydrogen ions from the water. Such alkali lakes typically form in locations where hot pressurized water rises to the surface from deep in the Earth's crust (e.g., hot springs), or where groundwater seeps out onto a desert valley floor where it evaporates, leaving a concentrated, salty, alkaline soup. Only rare and highly specialized organisms can survive in alkaline springs and lakes.

Aquatic species tolerate various ranges of pH. For most aquatic organisms, a pH below four or above ten is toxic, although there are exceptions. Very few aquatic organisms tolerate pH values below five or above nine for a short duration of time. Pulses of runoff and snow-melt, for example, typically have low pH values. On the other hand, as noted earlier, groundwater discharges typically contain higher concentrations of dissolved minerals, that may temporarily or continuously hold the pH above eight. Organisms that live in such environments must be able to tolerate these spikes in pH.

The pH of lake water determines more than simply whether the water is toxic to some species and not to others. It also determines whether the various organic and mineral chemicals entering a lake will remain dissolved in the water in a form that plants and microbes can use. In particular, it affects what nutrients can dissolve. For example, phosphate minerals play a vital role in the nutrient dynamics of lake (and

river) ecosystem. Phosphate minerals dissolve very poorly in waters with elevated pH levels, but much better in waters with lowered levels. We noted above that, during thermal stratification, the hypolimnion in some lakes can become completely anoxic. The process by which the hypolimnion becomes anoxic also produces CO, which in turn lowers the pH of the hypolimnion; these conditions favor the dissolving of phosphate minerals. During spring and fall turnover, the dissolved phosphate then becomes mixed throughout the water of the lake, providing a vital pulse of nutrients.

Nitrogen and Phosphorus

The nutrients nitrogen (N) and phosphorus (P) play key roles in lake ecosystem dynamics. Nitrogen and phosphorus, along with carbon (C), oxygen (O), and hydrogen (H) are the basic chemical building blocks of all life. C, O, and H are available to all aquatic organisms from dissolved gases (O, CO_2) and from water itself. Every cell in every freshwater (and terrestrial) species requires some minimal amount of nitrogen to function. Although nitrogen is the most abundant gas in air, it dissolves very poorly in water. Nitrogen becomes soluble only when converted into a different chemical form, which often requires the presence of extreme heat. Lightning, for example, can convert nitrogen gas into nitrogen oxides, that can then dissolve in rainwater and become available to life on Earth. A few specialized bacteria have also mastered the complex chemistry required to convert nitrogen gas into usable forms; as they grow and die, they release this soluble nitrogen into runoff and groundwater. Together, atmospheric events and the activities of nitrogen fixing bacteria are the primary ways that nitrogen is delivered to terrestrial and aquatic ecosystems. Plants and algae take up the dissolved nitrogen and, when they are eaten, deliver this precious commodity to other organisms on up the food chain. Nitrogen is constantly in flux, being captured at one end of the cycle and released back to the atmosphere at the other.

All organisms also need some minimal amount of phosphorus in every cell for their most essential functions of metabolism and reproduction. Phosphorus does not occur as a gas; it only occurs in mineral form and is not common or evenly distributed. Although phosphorus can dissolve in water, the conditions that it requires are highly selective: phosphorus is delivered to freshwater organisms through runoff or groundwater discharges and through turnover in a stratified lake that releases dissolved phosphorus from the hypolimnion. Plants and algae absorb this nutrient as quickly as they can, making it available to their own cells and, eventually, to the rest of the food chain.

The concentrations of nitrogen and phosphorus in lake water determine or limit how much total biomass the lake can support. Unfortunately, humans have developed vast technologies for creating soluble forms of nitrogen and phosphorus for use in everything from fertilizers to laundry detergents. The quantities of soluble nitrogen and phosphorus released by human activities sometimes can overwhelm lake ecosystems, utterly changing their food webs and productivity in ways that completely alter their biodiversity.

Other Dissolved Minerals

Several other dissolved minerals play ecologically important roles in shaping the chemistry of lakes. Diatoms, a common form of aquatic microorganism, build a framework of silica within and around their cells. Dissolved Silica (sand) therefore is a limiting mineral for diatom population growth. Other ecologically important dissolved minerals include calcium (Ca) and magnesium (Mg), iron (Fe), and sulfur (S).

Lakes with high concentration of Ca and Mg are called *hardwater lakes* while those with low concentration of these ions are called *softwater lakes.* Concentrations of other ions, especially bicarbonate, are highly correlated with the concentration of the hardness ions, especially calcium. The concentrations of these ions influence the lake's ability to maintain nutrients in solution, to keep potentially toxic metals from dissolving, and to assimilate pollutants.

Iron and sulfur are also vital to all aquatic and terrestrial life, but both require special circumstances to become dissolved in water and available to supply the primary producers. Iron dissolves almost exclusively in water that is both anoxic and acidic; it therefore becomes dissolved in lake water in only two ways— from discharges of acidic groundwater and from

chemical reactions in benthic sediments during thermal stratification when the hypolimnion takes on these special chemical properties. Subsequent turnover then makes the iron available to the entire lake ecosystem, although the mineral rapidly loses its solubility once turnover begins. Sulfur enters the water through the dissolving of a variety of geologic materials. Sulfur exists in two forms in lake water (sulfate and hydrogen sulfide), both of which are soluble and provide nutrition to different spectra of organisms.

In addition to the importance of the specific minerals discussed above, the total of all dissolved minerals in lake water also matters to the ecosystem. This is referred to as the total dissolved solids (TDS) or salinity of a particular waterbody. Both TDS and the relative amounts or ratios of different ions influence what species can best survive in the lake in addition to affecting many important chemical reactions that occur in the water. Under the right circumstances, lakes can develop a *chemocline,* which has a similar shape to a thermocline. Chemoclines occur when the layer of water at the bottom is dense because of dissolved chemicals entering from groundwater seeps up through the lake floor, as well as from accumulated products of decomposing detritus that have become so concentrated that they affect water density. The chemocline separates relatively pure water above from water with dissolved chemicals below.

Turbidity

Primary productivity in lakes by aquatic plants and algae requires the right mixture of nutrients, temperature, and sunlight. Season, shading from surrounding terrestrial vegetation and landforms, and cloudiness in the atmosphere all affect how much light reaches the surface of a lake. Once sunlight reaches the surface of a lake, however, the most important variable determining how useful it will be is the clarity of the water. The greater the clarity, the more deeply the light can penetrate, supporting photosynthesis to the greatest possible depth. The converse of water clarity is turbidity, the ability of water to attenuate or block the passage of light. The more turbid a lake's water, the less light penetration.

Three factors determine the turbidity of lake

water: plankton, suspended non-living matter, and dissolved minerals. Plankton are suspended algae (phytoplankton) and small animals (zooplankton) in the water column. Plankton thrive where sunlight and nutrients come together. However, the more plankton that thrive in the water, the more their presence contributes to turbidity, thereby reducing light penetration.

Suspended non-living matter consists of particles of plant litter, silt, and clay. Silt and clay may wash into lakes during storm runoff from the surrounding watershed or arise from the lake bottom by storms, wave action, and seasonal overturn. Because of their size and shape, such mineral particles may remain suspended for days or weeks, before they finally settle back out. Particles of plant litter similarly get washed in and stirred up, but they disappear through a combination of settling out and being consumed by microbes and larger organisms in the water.

Dissolved chemicals affect turbidity by changing the spectrum of colors of light that get absorbed as the light penetrates the water. Lakes with high concentrations of dissolved minerals appear blue, because the water absorbs red colors more rapidly with depth. Because different algae respond best to different light spectra, dissolved mineral content also affects algae diversity and distribution. Other lakes may have high concentrations of dissolved organic matter, often because their watersheds contain high densities of swamps and other permanent wetlands. The dark brown color of their waters absorbs blue light more readily than it does red, again affecting conditions for algae.

Turbidity in lake water affects more than the depth to which different algae species can live and the depth to which light can penetrate to support photosynthesis. It also affects the ability of aquatic animals to navigate underwater. Many fishes, reptiles, diving birds, and even crustaceans depend on their sight in the water to locate their plant food or prey; aquatic prey animals, in turn, often depend on sight to help them avoid predators. The turbidity of water and the color(s) of light that penetrate it strongly determine the suitability of available habitat for these species.

Lakes all have natural patterns of variation in their turbidity, driven by the changes of season and thermal stratification, patterns of runoff, sediment disturbance, and so forth. The animals and plants that live in or feed in lakes therefore have evolved ways to tolerate or take advantage of this variation. Changing a lake's turbidity regime by altering its primary productivity or sediment inputs will change the biological dynamics and therefore the fish assemblages and community structure found to exist within the lake.

CONNECTIVITY

The physical location of a lake within its larger landscape determines its connection to water sources which in turn play a major role in defining the lake's abiotic characteristics and resultant community types. Lakes positioned within a river drainage that have both an inflow and an outflow are driven by the hydrologic regime and water chemistry regime of the river. Lakes positioned at the headwaters of a river drainage with only an outflow to a river are driven hydrologically by groundwater flow and precipitation events. Lakes with no surface water connection to a river drainage are termed seepage lakes and again are driven hydrologically by groundwater flow and precipitation events.

The littoral zone is an ecotone between freshwater and terrestrial systems. It is an extremely productive zone that sustains an incredible wealth of biodiversity. The littoral zone is home to a highly productive nearshore lake community that supports spawning, rearing, refuge and feeding habitat for a diverse array of fish, bird and macroinvertebrate species.

Species composition in lakes is driven by their historic formation and temporal connectivity. Relict lakes are those that were once part of a large waterbody presumably sharing a common species pool that has since receded to form a number of smaller lakes. These lakes tend to share similar species assemblages and community types. Solus lakes are those that formed in isolation which were never a part of a larger water system or species pool. Solus lakes tend to be species poor with relatively distinct species assemblages. Relict and solus lake types are similar to landbridge and oceanic islands respectively in terms of their historical formation, extinction and colonization potential, and community structure (Ciruna 1999).

BIOLOGICAL COMPOSITION AND INTERACTIONS

Biological composition and interactions for lakes are summarized in the following two sections on lake productivity and biodiversity.

Productivity

The concentrations of the nutrients nitrogen (N) and phosphorous (P) determine the productivity of a lake. Productivity starts with the process of photosynthesis, where the energy from sunlight is combined with the essential nutrients (nitrogen, phosphorus, carbon, oxygen, and hydrogen) to create new living matter. As we also noted earlier, plants and algae are the primary producers in all ecosystems, both aquatic and terrestrial. The concentrations of nitrogen and phosphorus entering a lake determine the trophic or nutrition or growth status of a lake. Lakes are defined as being oligotrophic, mesotrophic or eutrophic depending on their productivity. *Oligotrophic lakes* are naturally poor in nutrients. These lakes generally have watersheds with infertile soils that release relatively little nitrogen and phosphorus leading to poorly productive lakes. Many seepage lakes are oligotrophic because of their generally small watershed areas and therefore smaller contributions of surface runoff into the lake. Oligotrophic lakes generally have clear, cold water; a sandy or gravel bottom; with little plankton or plant life. *Mesotrophic lakes* are intermediate in status between oligotrophic and eutrophic lakes. *Eutrophic (well-nourished) lakes* are nutrient-rich lakes. They typically have large contributing watersheds with rich organic soils or agricultural soils enriched with artificial fertilizers that yield higher nutrients. These lakes generally have a mucky bottom; cloudy, turbid, warm water; and rich plankton and plant life. Changes in land use practices, especially agricultural application of fertilizers, can increase the productivity of a lake from oligotrophic to eutrophic.

The species that comprise the natural communities of a lake have evolved with their lake's productivity regime. Eutrophic, mesotrophic and oligotrophic lakes therefore have a very different community compositions based on differences in their productivity regime and its intimate relationship to the community's trophic structure. Changing the productivity regime of a lake to a range outside its natural range of variation such as through application of fertilizers or acid deposition, will dramatically alter the lake's ecological integrity.

Not all biomass in lakes (or in rivers, as we discuss below) arises from primary productivity in the water itself. The vegetation covering the watershed of every lake, and especially the vegetation immediately surrounding the lake, provides a source of plant matter washed and blown into the lake. Microorganisms and macro-invertebrates then attack and break down this plant litter, and are in turn eaten by other organisms, thus adding to the total amount of living matter supported by the ecosystem. In oligotrophic lakes, terrestrial plant litter is the most important source of matter supporting the entire food web. In naturally eutrophic lakes, terrestrial plant litter contributes only a small fraction to the ecosystem's productivity. The aquatic organisms that feed on and break down terrestrial plant litter may be quite different from those that feed on living aquatic plants and algae. The magnitude and relative importance of plant litter to a lake ecosystem's productivity thus can have a significant impact on its overall biodiversity.

Biodiversity

Each of the three main zones within a lake has a unique set of habitat characteristics, which in turn gives rise to a distinct community type. The *littoral zone* provides habitat for the greatest number of lake-dwelling and lake-using species. The food web in littoral zone communities rests on a large biomass of primary producers, primarily aquatic plants. These aquatic plants provide a food source and substrate for algae and invertebrates and provide habitat refuge for fish, especially young of the year and other organisms that are very different from the open water environment. This zone is also generally the warmest zone of the lake, which further stimulates primary productivity and the diversity of species within this zone. The productivity of the littoral zone also attracts terrestrial and avian species who feed on this richness, including browsers such as ungulates (tapir, moose) and ducks, and predators such as raccoons, otters, and herons.

As stated above, the *euphotic zone* is the portion of the pelagic or open water zone of a lake where photosynthesis can occur and hence where open-water primary producers (phytoplankton or suspended algae) live. Phytoplankton grow suspended in open water by taking up nutrients from the water and energy from sunlight. If their populations are dense, the water will become noticeably green or brown and will have low transparency. The euphotic zone holds the greatest biomass of primary producers in the lake—in essence, it drives the trophic structure of the entire lake ecosystem, providing most of the food that supports the rest of the biota in a lake as well as most of the dissolved oxygen in the lake. Zooplankton (small animals that swim about in open water), are the primary consumers that feed on the phytoplankton, and are in turn consumed by planktivores such as small fish, which are in turn consumed by larger piscivorous fish. Some predatory birds, such as eagles and osprey, also consume fish directly from the pelagic zone.

Lastly, the *benthic zone* at the bottom of the lake can be abundant with animals including macroinvertebrates and microinvertebrates such as crustaceans and insect larvae, mollusks, and burrowing worms. The upper layer of sediments may be mixed by the activity of the benthic organisms that live there, often to a depth of 2–5 centimeters in rich organic sediments. The productivity of this zone largely depends on the organic content of the sediment, the amount of physical structure, and in some cases the rate of fish predation. Sandy substrates are constantly shifting and therefore do not provide stable habitat for most species. They also provide relatively little organic matter (food) and poor refuge from fish. Sandy substrates therefore harbor the least diversity among all examples of benthic environments. Rocky bottoms offer a high diversity of habitats and provide hiding places from predators, substrate for invertebrates, and pockets of organic food. Flat mucky bottoms provide abundant food for benthic organisms but are less protected and offer a lower structural diversity of habitats. Most importantly, the benthic zone is where the decomposers live. All dead matter within a lake sinks to the bottom where bacteria, fungi, and decomposers breakdown organic matter to be recycled as nutrients.

The physical characteristics of the water column largely determine a lake's biological characteristics. Important physical characteristics include temperature, light transparency, and wave action, as well as the total abundance of inorganic nutrients, which is largely a watershed characteristic. Putting all of the littoral, pelagic, and benthic zone communities together provides a picture of a lake's trophic pyramid —the movement of energy and nutrients through the lake ecosystem through biological interactions. For example, consider the primary producers. Since they need light (as well as nutrients) they are generally found within the littoral and euphotic zones. Primary producers are consumed by primary consumers, the herbivores such as zooplankton. Secondary consumers such as planktivores are small fish that eat zooplankton and invertebrates. Planktivores are less restricted in where they can live and grow in a lake. Larger carnivorous fish at the top of the trophic pyramid are the least restricted in where they can live and grow in a lake. These individual trophic levels may be idealized as a food chain; in fact many organisms are omnivorous and are not necessarily restricted to a distinct level. Consumers in particular often shift levels throughout their life cycle. For example, a larval fish may initially eat fine particulate material that includes algae, bacteria and detritus. As it matures, it may switch and graze on larger zoo-plankton and ultimately end up feeding on forage fish or even young game fish (top predators) when it reaches maturity. Decomposers also offer an interesting example. They include bacteria, fungi, and other micro-organisms. They are found in all zones of a lake and feed on the remains of all freshwater organisms. Through their activities they break down or help decay organic matter, returning it to an inorganic state. Some of the decayed material is subsequently recycled as nutrients such as phosphorus and nitrogen, which then become readily available for new plant growth. Carbon is released largely as carbon dioxide that acts to lower the pH of bottom waters. In anoxic zones, some carbon can be released as methane gas. In the benthic zone where they are the dominant life form, oxidation of organic matter by the decomposers (respiration) in the benthic zone is responsible for the depletion of dissolved oxygen over the course of the summer, potentially leading to anoxic conditions.

RIVERS

Flowing-water ecosystems—rivers and streams—are distinguished by water moving along distinct channels within a watershed, creating diverse but often challenging habitat for a unique array of organisms. Factors such as the amount of water, the source of the water, the gradient through which it flows, the substrate over which it flows, how the flow naturally changes over time, and the location of the ecosystem within a watershed all combine to further determine the type of river ecosystem and the organisms living in it and dependent on it. Nearly all stream and river ecosystems are directly connected longitudinally to other streams and rivers (and to lakes, and wetlands as well), and eventually to estuarine and marine ecosystems. This connectivity serves a critical role in movement of energy, material, and biota. Riparian ecosystems serve as lateral connections for streams and rivers to terrestrial ecosystems, providing key habitat (e.g., floodplains as fish nurseries), material inputs (e.g., woody debris for structure and nutrients), and ecological processes (e.g., temperature control from shading) to these ecosystems. Rivers and streams often interact strongly with their adjacent floodplain or riparian corridors, so that it sometimes makes sense to treat the river and floodplain together as a single ecosystem. This is particularly true in large river valleys where seasonal flooding covers vast areas of the adjacent lowlands for months at a time. A panoply of terrestrial species also use rivers and streams and their adjacent riparian areas as habitat and for foraging.

Streams and rivers vary dramatically in their size, from the smallest headwaters high in a mountain range to the largest rivers such as the Amazon, Mississippi, Congo, Danube, Mekong, or Nile. The terms stream and river are general terms for relatively small and large flowing waters, respectively, and have no precise meanings beyond this. Flowing waters form drainage networks across a watershed: small streams high in a watershed join to form larger streams, that join to form rivers, which will eventually drain out to the sea. During this journey, changes occur in the physical, chemical, hydrologic, and biological aspects of flowing waters.

Formation of River Systems

Nearly all rivers start in hilly or mountainous areas except for rivers that begin underground such as in limestone caverns and rivers that begin as meltwater from the ends of glaciers. The life of most rivers begins as an indeterminate point in a slight depression in the ground where groundwater happens to ooze out as a gentle seep. This depression also collects runoff flowing down rills on the surface of the surrounding slope. Eventually seepage in the bottom of the depression augmented by the water entering the rills from the surrounding slopes adds up to enough water to erode a self-sustaining permanent channel. What makes a true stream distinct from water draining over irregular ground is the self-sustaining character of its channel. The first trickles of water erode an incipient channel, which then guides later flows. The later flows progressively widen and deepen the channel until it becomes a valley with the water confined to the bottom of it.

This description may give the impression that headwater stream channels are continuously digging and widening their channels. They are in fact doing just that but very slowly. Once established after a major geologic disturbance, they quickly reach a condition where they change very little from one year to the next. The shape of the channel reaches a kind of balance or equilibrium with the amount of water available to shape it and with the character of the geologic raw material. However, gradually they erode the entire landscape downward; that is one of the principal reasons why, over millions of years, even the tallest mountains are worn down.

The faster the water moves in a channel, the more material it is able to lift up and suspend or carry along with it. The slower the water moves, the more likely materials will fall out of suspension. The net result of all this is that streams and rivers act like giant conveyor belts, picking up materials when they are moving fast and dropping much of that material when they later slow down. Understanding this property helps explain how river systems form, how they change, and the effects of human activities on their function.

Key Ecological Factors of Rivers and Streams

The ecological integrity of all stream and river ecosystems depend on the status and interrelationships among their key ecological factors. Each suite of key ecological factors for a river ecosystem contributes uniquely to that river's ecological integrity. The hydrologic regime is by far the master variable onto which all other key ecological factors depend for their formation and existence within river ecosystems.

PHYSICAL HABITAT CONDITIONS

River ecosystems provide a great diversity of habitats. Within each segment of the overall system the characteristics of habitat vary as well. Both the large-scale characteristics and finescale details of a river ecosystem depend on the terrain, vegetation, and climate of its watershed; whether the slope (gradient) of the channel is steep or gentle; whether the channel flows over solid rock or loose material; and both the quantity and composition of the sediments and large woody debris that it carries. In addition, river ecosystems are dynamic at both the large and fine spatial scales, largely through the processes of erosion, deposition, and channel migration. Successful conservation of river ecosystems requires adequate consideration of both the large-scale and fine-scale features of habitat, their natural variation over time, and the factors that shape or impair them.

Large-scale variation in river habitat

Stream order and river zone are two terms used to classify differences in stream and river habitat:

Stream Order

Stream order is a term used to classify the different types of streams and rivers within a drainage network based on stream/tributary relationships. Under Strahler's well-known classification, the uppermost channels in a drainage network (i.e., headwater channels with no upstream tributaries) are designated as first-order streams down to their first confluence. A second-order stream is formed below the confluence of two first-order channels. Third-order streams are created when two second-order channels join, and so on. However, the intersection of a channel with another channel of lower order does not raise the order of the stream below the intersection (e.g., a fourth-order stream intersecting with a second-order stream is still a fourth-order stream below the intersection). Within a watershed, stream order correlates well with other descriptive features of the watershed, such as its drainage area or the cumulative length of river channel. When matched with information on river zone (see below), stream order also provides information on channel gradient, shape, bed material, and rate of channel migration, all of which strongly shape the biodiversity of individual stream sections.

River Zone

River ecosystems generally have three zones: a headwater zone, a mid-reach or transfer zone, and a lower mainstem zone. Channel erosion, conveyance of the eroded material (transfer), and deposition occur in all zones, but their patterns of interaction differ from each zone to the next in ways that create significant differences in habitat. The zone concept focuses on the most dominant processes within each zone.

The ***headwaters zone*** is generally characterized by narrow stream valleys with a steep gradient. This steep gradient enables the stream to move coarse and sometimes large debris such as boulders and large cobbles. In this zone erosion is greater than deposition. The continuous erosion within the channel is balanced by the continuous erosion of geologic materials into the channel from the surrounding land area. This is a zone of degradation. The headwater zone transitions into an ***intermediate mid-reach or transfer zone*** with wider streams that have lower gradients. In this zone the river begins to meander and interact with relatively narrow floodplains. In the mid-reach or transfer zone, the river transitions from carrying gravels and finer substrates to depositing the larger loads carried from the headwaters. Further downstream is the ***lower mainstem zone.*** This zone is characterized as having a wide and deep channel with a low gradient and therefore low velocity and strong floodplain interaction. All of the river's load will settle out in this zone. The river builds up new land by depositing some of the material it is carrying. This process is called ***aggradation.*** At the delta or river mouth the river deposits the last of its load. This is a zone of deposition. These zones and their associated processes thereby transform a river and its related drainage network to a conveyor belt of energy, materials, nutrients, and organisms.

Fine-scale variation in river habitat

Within the different zones of a river system, habitat varies from one **reach** to the next. A reach is a length of a river or stream and its associated valley with a distinctive mixture of geologic conditions, channel gradient, and watershed vegetation. The diversity of habitat conditions among reaches in a river ecosystem contributes significantly to the system's overall biodiversity because each type of reach typically harbors a distinctive freshwater community.

The geologic conditions of a reach (and its position within the watershed) determine both the channel gradient and the types of substrate materials that make up the channel bank and bed. Substrate material also strongly influences how much material the flow can suspend during high-flow events. Together, these factors strongly influence the types of habitat present in the reach, and habitat types, in turn, affect diversity of species. For example, a steep reach flowing through a zone of gravel and boulders will provide a great diversity of crevices and sheltered locations in the stream bank and bed, but few areas of soft bottom sediments. A relatively low gradient reach flowing over exposed bedrock will have relatively few sheltered places and even fewer areas of soft bottom sediments. A reach flowing through a low-gradient floodplain will have relatively few solidly protected locations but an abundance of soft bottom sediments.

The geologic conditions of each reach also influences the manner and extent to which groundwater affects stream conditions. Specifically, the geologic conditions of a reach and its relative position within the watershed together determine whether and how readily groundwater can discharge into the channel or, conversely, whether and how readily stream water can soak downward from the channel into the groundwater system. A reach in which more groundwater enters the channel than leaves it is called a gaining reach; one in which more water leaves than enters is called a losing reach. Gaining reaches occur when the elevation

of groundwater in the watershed immediately adjacent to the channel is higher than the water in the channel itself and when the geologic materials surrounding the channel are conductive enough that the groundwater can actually flow into the channel. Losing reaches occur when the elevation of the groundwater system immediately surrounding the channel is lower than the elevation of the water in the channel itself and when the geologic materials surrounding the channel are conductive enough that the groundwater can actually seep downward out of the channel. A reach may be either losing or gaining over time, because the elevation of water in the channel and in the groundwater system both can vary over time in response to seasonal precipitation regimes and other watershed-scale dynamics. During the dry season, groundwater contributes the only water source in many streams. River flow contributed by groundwater is called **baseflow**. Baseflow is a fairly constant and dependable supply of river water unless the aquifer or river surface flow regime is severely altered. The pattern of interaction of the channel water with the groundwater system influences such ecologically critical conditions as the stability, temperature, and chemistry of baseflow.

Taken together, the influences of geology, gradient, and adjacent vegetation therefore also shape three other ecologically important features of habitat in each reach: the riparian zone; pool, riffle, and bar structure; and hyporheic zone dynamics.

The Riparian Zone

No discussion of habitat in individual stream or river reaches can be complete without touching on the relationship of the stream or river to its adjacent **riparian zone.** At times of low flow, the river remains in its channel. At times of high flow such as large storm events, the river overflows its banks and inundates the surrounding land. The resulting riparian zone is the zone onto which the stream or river water spreads when it rises out of its channel, whether during flows that barely exceed the bank-full discharge or during extreme floods that occur once only every 500 years or more. Along reaches where channel migration has carved an actual floodplain, the floodplain and riparian zone will be the same. Along reaches without a distinct floodplain, the riparian zone will consist of whatever landforms lie in the path of the spreading flood waters. In either case, the amount of land inundated depends on the size of the storm event and the topography of the riparian zone itself. High flood flows also help prevent the colonization of riparian areas by non-specialized terrestrial species.

Flood waters slow down when they rise out of their banks and spread across the riparian zone. This hydrologic effect has several significant ecological effects. First, the over flow water infiltrates the surrounding floodplain and works its way downward to become a part of the groundwater system. The more water that flows into the surrounding floodplain, the more energy absorbed by the riparian zone. Further, as the water slows down by spreading into the floodplain, it drops much of its load of suspended sediment, creating new soils and habitat. While inundated, the riparian zone provides more slowly flowing waters, in which many river fauna can find refuge from the turbulent flood flows of the main channel as well as habitat for feeding, spawning, and rearing. Finally, as the flood event subsides and the river level drops, water, sediment, nutrients, and aquatic biota transfer back into the river channel.

The riparian zone of a reach serves a number of important functions for the river ecosystem depending on the zone of the river in which it occurs. In the headwater zone, the riparian zone provides almost complete shading of the stream channel and therefore serves to cool the temperature of the water. It also supplies leaf litter nutrients to the river. For all zones of the river, the riparian zone provides bank stability, and acts as a barrier to surface runoff of sediments and chemicals. It also provides critical habitat for a wide range of animals that function within both terrestrial and freshwater ecosystems such as birds that feed on emergent adult aquatic insects and fishes and for most amphibian and reptile species that use both ecosystems for critical life history stages.

Floodplains are narrow or nonexistent in a river's headwaters. Therefore, flood-dependent and flood-tolerant plant communities tend to be limited in distribution in this river zone. These communities may occur in the headwaters zone only immediately alongside the channel or in wet areas near the stream's source. On the other hand, woody vegetation bordering streams in the headwater zone often create a canopy that leaves little open sky visible from the channel. The vegetation surrounding streams in most headwater zones also provide a regular supply of plant litter to the stream, along with sediment. Some of this litter gets flushed downstream into the transfer and lower mainstem zones, where they support important ecological processes. For example, logs and woody debris from headwater forests in Pacific Northwest region of the U.S. and Canada support food chains and instream habitat structure from the mountains all the way out to the sea (Maser and Sedell 1994).

Reaches in the transfer zone of a river system typically have wider riparian zones than found in the headwaters, along with true floodplains. Plant communities associated with these riparian areas often vary due to differences in elevation, soil type, flooding frequency, and soil moisture. Localized differences in erosion and deposition of sediment add complexity and diversity to the types of plant communities that become established.

The true floodplains found in reaches of both the transfer and lower mainstem zones of river systems often make them attractive for agricultural or residential development. Such development is often accompanied by the construction of barriers, such as artificial levees, to prevent the river from flooding its floodplain, and by the removal of the native vegetation and disturbance to the floodplain soils. Such development tends to significantly alter stream processes involving flooding, erosion/deposition, import or export of organic matter and sediment, stream corridor habitat diversity, and water quality characteristics.

The riparian zones of reaches in the lower mainstem zone typically harbor distinct plant communities adapted to increased sediment deposition, broader floodplains, and greater water volume. Large floodplain wetlands and strongly flood-dependent plant communities dominate the riparian zone, particularly on deep, rich alluvial soils of floodplains. These plant communities, such as bottomland hardwood forests, are generally highly productive and biologically diverse. The slower flow in the channel also allows marsh vegetation, rooted floating or free-floating plants, and submerged aquatic plant beds to thrive.

Box A-2. Scouring and Deposition at a Bend in a River

If you are given a choice to build your dream house along a river, would you choose to build it along ther inside or outside bend of a river? The answer is the inside! You will continuously gain property as sdediment from the outside bend is deposited on its bank. The outside bend will continue to be scoured so your house would mostly likely fall into a river at some point. However, the ultimate answer would be not to build along the river's flood-plain as your house will inevitably be flooded.

Pools, Riffles, and Bars

Pools and riffles provide a great variety of ecological habitat for aquatic plants and animals. Pools form in places where physical obstacles cause the flow in the channel to swing sideways or downward, eroding a deep pool. The most common type of pool is found at bends in the river. The river's flow hits the outer bank and scours out the bank and bed of the channel, and deposits the sediment downstream on the inside bend. Pools can also be found in backwaters, below falls, or behind log dams.

Riffles, in turn, are relatively straight and shallow stretches of channel, which cause the flow of water to ripple vertically all the way to the water surface. The constant agitation of the water surface allows more air bubbles to become entrapped in the water, resulting in more oxygen dissolving into the water. Riffles form downstream of pools and also along sections of the channel where the bed materials are relatively coarse or are otherwise relatively resistant to erosion.

Pools and riffles differ in more than simply depth. In pools, deeper (and perhaps cooler) water may not mix with surface water; in riffles, all water is thoroughly mixed. Large woody debris and other plant litter can collect in pools but not in riffles, creating extra places of shelter in the former but not the latter. On the other hand, pools tend to collect fine sediments because their waters move so much more slowly, resulting in bottom sediments with little diversity of habitat; riffles are places where the current continuously clears out the fine particles, maintaining more openings in the substrate material. The highest quality pools are those with deep, slow-moving water and overhanging banks. They contain the greatest biomass of fish. Young fish prefer riffles because that is where

their bite-sized food is found in greatest supply—insects and other invertebrates. Filter-feeding fauna, such as mussels, also prefer riffles for their stability and ready supply of food. Riffles and their underlying substrate also provide more places for all smaller fauna to take refuge. In addition, gravel-bottomed riffles are chief spawning sites for many fish as they provide a fresh supply of dissolved oxygen and experience little accumulation of fine sediment that might smother eggs. On the other hand, riffles are apt to dry up during periods of low flow, while pools serve as refuges for aquatic life during these periods.

Bars are bands or ridges of sediment deposited in the channel by a stream or river immediately following flood flows and high flow pulses. Reaches immediately downstream of bends and obstructions tend to be areas of greatest bar formation since they tend to experience more dramatic velocity decreases and decreased velocity results in material deposition. When the stream or river returns to low flow conditions, these depositional areas become exposed bars of sand and gravel, which provide seeding beds and crucial habitat for a wide range of species such as insects and amphibians.

The Hyporheic Zone

The water visible in the channel is almost always directly linked to groundwater. The gravel, sand, and fractured bedrock lining the sides and bottom of the channel contain lots of empty space in the form of micro- and macroscopic pores, interstices, and fissures. This space will always fill up with water so that the water table immediately adjacent to the channel lies at roughly the same elevation as the water in the channel itself. Water and organisms can move readily between pore spaces adjacent to the channel and the water in the channel itself.

The transition is not abrupt—it takes place in what is known as the *hyporheic zone*. Normally, the hyporheic zone is either the same width as, or only a little wider than, the channel itself, but occasionally it extends as far as two or three km beyond the banks on either side so that the hidden hyporheic river is far wider than the visible river. The hyporheic zone may also not be continuous, but occur in only localized patches distributed like beads on a string along the length of a reach. Hyporheic water differs in various ways from the adjacent river water. It seldom flows at more than a few centimeters per hour; it contains less oxygen and more carbon dioxide than the water of the river proper; its temperature moderates against anticipated seasonal variation; and it contains more dissolved minerals. Hyporheic water also differs from the true groundwater below it. Compared to the surrounding groundwater, hyporheic water flows faster, contains more oxygen and less carbon dioxide, its temperature is more variable, and it contains more dissolved organic matter.

The hyporheic zone provides home to a diverse array of micro-organisms and macro-invertebrates found nowhere else. However, many animals live there for only part of their lives. Stoneflies, for example, live there only as naiads, their immature form before they transform into a winged adult. Other animals move up into the open channel and down into hyporheic water at will. The hyporheic zone provides a dry season refuge for them if the channel dries up or a wet season refuge for them if the flow is damagingly strong when the river is raging. The width, chemistry, temperature regime, and rate of flow of water in the hyporheic zone vary from one reach to the next, and consequently so does the composition of the natural community for which it provides habitat. This variation arises from the unique combination of watershed and channel geology and hydrology found in each reach, that together shape hyporheic zone dynamics.

HYDROLOGIC REGIME

The most notable feature of streams and rivers, of course, is the flow of water. Stream flow consists of both baseflow and runoff from the surrounding watershed. Baseflow consists of water that flows into the stream from groundwater; it sustains stream flow during periods of little or no precipitation.

The hydrologic regime is different for every river and stream, and is shaped by the interaction of climate, geology, topography, and watershed vegetation. The hydrologic regime will also vary as a result of differences in these factors over space, and as a result of differences in the size of the relevant watershed or sub-watershed. For every river or stream, however, the hydrologic regime can be characterized by five ecologically-relevant attributes:

- **Magnitude** - the amount of water passing a fixed point in the river at a specific point in time;
- **Frequency** - how often a particular condition, such as a large flood, has occurred;
- **Duration** - the length of time that a specific flow condition lasts, such as the duration of extremely low flow conditions;
- **Timing** - the time of year at which particular flow events occur, such as the day and month of floods or low flow conditions;
- **Rate of change** - how quickly the flow changes, as flows rise or fall from day-to-day.

These terms prove useful when describing a river's annual and inter-annual pattern of low flows, flood flows, and high flow pulses.

The natural flow paradigm springs from an understanding that freshwater and riparian organisms depend upon, or can tolerate, a range of flow conditions specific to each species. For example, certain fish species will move into floodplain areas during flood events to spawn, feed, or escape predation from other species occupying the main channel. If flooding occurs at the right time of the year, and lasts for the right amount of time, these fish populations will benefit from the flood event. On the other hand, other species may be adversely affected by the same flood. For example, benthic (bottom-dwelling) macroinvertebrates may be scoured from the streambed or riparian trees may become stressed or die from prolonged flooding and associated oxygen deprivation. Also important is the rate at which flow levels change. If the river level rises too fast, it can trap animals such as amphibians and reptiles on the floodplain. Conversely, young plants such as cottonwoods taking root on the floodplain can die from moisture stress if their growing root systems cannot keep up with the dropping water table linked to falling river levels.

Natural low flow conditions can be equally important. Prolonged natural droughts might help certain plants such as baldcypress trees become established on the floodplain, before river levels again rise up around their growing trunks. In the river channel, low flows will concentrate fish and other aquatic organisms, benefiting predators such as larger fish or wading birds. If low flows are too severe, or last for too long due to human influences, large numbers of individuals may perish and jeopardize the local populations of certain species. Thus, where the conservation of all freshwater species is important, rather than trying to prescribe a flow regime that benefits some species all of the time, a better approach is to restore or sustain a natural flow regime for a particular river. The species that are found in each river have endured many trials of adverse flow conditions, exploited many occasions of favorable flow, and have managed to persist in their native rivers over long periods of time. Until very recently in evolutionary time, the variation in river flows has been dictated largely by natural climatic and environmental conditions. These natural river flows have influenced the development of behavioral (e.g., floodplain spawning), physiological (e.g., tolerance for oxygen deprivation), and morphological (e.g., body shape) traits in riverine species. Thus, perpetuation of the natural flow regime is the best approach for conserving the full richness of a river's biological diversity.

Flow regimes exert a strong influence on other ecosystem conditions as well. Water chemistry, temperature, nutrient cycling, oxygen availability, and the geomorphic processes that shape river channels and floodplains are tightly coupled to streamflow variation. Natural flow regimes are therefore intimately linked to many different aspects of a river's ecological integrity.

WATER CHEMISTRY REGIME

Water chemistry can change dramatically from reach to reach depending on the location of the reach within the larger drainage network, its lateral and vertical connectivity, and its underlying geologic and climatic conditions. The role of pH, calcium, magnesium, iron, sulfur, nitrogen and phosphorus, and turbidity in structuring freshwater communities is presented in detail in the previous lake water chemistry section. Please review the previous section for more information about these aspects of the water chemistry regime. Instead, this section will focus on the roles of temperature and dissolved oxygen in structuring aquatic biodiversity.

Water temperature

Water temperature has diverse effects on the biodiversity of river ecosystems. The aquatic communities of rivers and streams are often defined by their relative temperatures, e.g., cold water versus warm water communities. A river may (and often does) change from a cold water system in the headwaters or mid-reach area to a warm water system in the lower mainstem area. Temperature affects the rate at which eggs develop and juveniles grow as well as the productivity of the river community. Seasonal changes in temperature often act as a cue to synchronize a species' life cycle to seasonal changes in the environment for efficient use of resources.

The temperature of flowing waters in rivers and streams usually varies reach by reach as well as seasonally, depending on climate, elevation, riparian vegetation and the relative contribution of groundwater inputs. Large river reaches tend to harbor warm-water communities as bank shading has a negligible cooling effect. Large rivers also have less variable temperatures than small streams because of their greater volume of water. Most large river reaches also tend to be located near the terminus of the river drainage network, typically at low elevations that have warmer air temperatures than higher elevations.

Daily temperature fluctuations are common in small streams due to daily air temperature variation and the effect of solar radiation. Small streams tend to contain cool-water communities if they have sufficient riparian shading and/or are located at higher elevations. Small streams may also contain cool to cold water communities if they have substantial groundwater contribution. Lastly, glaciers also play a significant role in driving river water temperature. There is generally an attenuation in river temperature from cold to warm water conditions the farther the river reach is from the glacial source.

Dissolved oxygen

Dissolved oxygen in flowing river systems is usually always near saturation and therefore is usually not a limiting factor for the selection of habitat by river biota. However, increasing water temperature and/or decreasing flow can decrease the concentration of dissolved oxygen in a river reach and thus alter its community composition. Droughts can therefore be particularly stressful events. Other factors that influence lowered dissolved oxygen levels include reaches or areas of the river with high decomposition rates (e.g., stagnant backwaters), high contributions of oxygen-poor groundwater, or high contributions of oxygen-poor lake or reservoir water.

CONNECTIVITY

The connection between a river and its associated freshwater features (groundwater, floodplain, upstream areas, etc.) is essential for the survival of many species. Connectivity exists horizontally, or longitudinally, vertically, and laterally, as described below.

- **Upstream–downstream connectivity.** Nearly all stream and river ecosystems are directly connected longitudinally to other streams and rivers (and ponds and lakes as well), and eventually to estuarine and marine ecosystems. This connectivity serves a critical role in the movement of energy, material, and biota throughout the entire system.
- **Surface–groundwater connectivity.** As discussed earlier, the hyporheic zone is the zone in which the exchange of water, dissolved materials and organisms between surface water and groundwater takes place. This zone plays an important role to stream biota by providing a dry-season refuge for stream macroinvertebrates if the channel dries up or a wet-season refuge for them if the flow is damagingly strong when the river is raging. The width, chemistry, temperature regime, and rate of flow of water in the hyporheic zone vary from one reach to the next, and consequently so does the composition of the natural community for which it provides habitat.
- **Stream–riparian zone connectivity.** Riparian ecosystems serve as lateral connections for streams and rivers to the terrestrial world, providing key habitat (e.g., floodplains as fish nurseries), material inputs (e.g., woody debris for structure and nutrients), and ecological processes (e.g., temperature control from shading) to these ecosystems. Riparian systems also serve as key habitats for terrestrial species through their provision of water, forage, shelter, and migratory corridors.

The changing sequence of plant communities along streams from headwaters to mouth is an important source of biodiversity and resiliency to change. Although many, or perhaps most, of a stream corridor's plant communities might be fragmented, a continuous corridor of native plant communities is desirable. Restoring vegetative connectivity in even a portion of a stream will usually improve conditions and increase its beneficial functions.

BIOLOGICAL COMPOSITION AND INTERACTIONS

Physical, chemical, hydrologic and other factors influence biological composition and interactions in river ecosystems and within different reaches along the same river. The differences in species found in different types of reaches also result in differences in community structure and inter-species interactions among reach types. More importantly, community dynamics in each reach strongly influence, and are influenced by, community dynamics in neighboring reaches, in both the up- and down-stream direction. This relational inter-dependence is described more fully by an explanation of river ecosystem food webs and the river continuum concept.

A river ecosystem actually has two food chains that converge to form its larger food web. Every ecosystem must have some process by which the basic ingredients of life—carbon, oxygen, hydrogen, nitrogen, phosphorus, and other elements—are assembled and incorporated into living matter. A great deal of such primary production takes place in river ecosystems. However, river ecosystems also benefit from primary production that takes place on the adjacent land. Each of these pathways builds biomass for rivers and streams.

Primary production occurring directly in streams and rivers is called autochthonous production. The primary producers are algae, diatoms and aquatic plants. Most of this instream primary production occurs from algae and diatoms along reaches where ample sunlight reaches the water surface and where limiting nutrients are in ample supply. The more area of water along a reach that meets these conditions, the higher the level of productivity. Diatoms consist mostly of lipids and sugars that are easily digested and nutritious to animals. Algae, on the other hand, are made up of mostly cellulose and some sugar. They are not as nutritious or digestible as diatoms. Therefore primary consumers (herbivores) prefer to eat diatoms over algae. Examples of such primary consumers are snails scraping diatoms (and some algae) off rocks in the stream.

Primary production washed into a stream from the adjacent land is called allochthonous production. The main ingredient of allochthonous production is plant litter and dissolved organic molecules produced by the decomposition of plant matter in the adjacent soils. Allochthonous production is usually the dominant source of production in a river's headwater streams, where the adjacent vegetation provides plentiful organic litter and also provides enough shade to limit autochthonous production.

Allochthonous production supports a food chain that differs from that supported by autochthonous production. Bacteria and fungi breakdown the solid litter. In turn, other aquatic animals seek out this growing bounty of microbes as their own food.

The unifier of these two distinct food chains are secondary consumers or predators. Predators feed off all consumers regardless of feeding guild hence connecting the two food chains together. Also helping with this process are depositional collectors that breakdown dead organic matter off the river bottom, recycling the nutrients back to the primary producers. As you move downstream in a river system, more and more of the nutrients come from the recycling of dead freshwater biota rather than through fresh inputs of nutrients from the adjacent watershed.

Together all of these relationships form the river continuum concept (Vannote *et al.* 1989). The concept captures the changes in biological communities from a rivers' headwaters to its mouth in relation to habitat and food web dynamics. The concept only applies to perennial streams, and may be more accurate in temperate than in tropical climates. In general, however, it is useful to think of river systems as supporting a complex gradient of biological conditions from headwaters to its mouth.

WETLANDS

Wetlands are an ecotone or transitional zone between terrestrial and freshwater ecosystems. They support both freshwater and terrestrial species. Wetlands are areas where water covers the soil, or is present either at or near the surface of the soil for varying periods of time during the year, including the growing season. The prolonged presence of water creates conditions that favor the growth of specially adapted plants and promote the development of characteristic wetland soils. Wetlands occur on every continent except Antarctica. Fifty-six percent of the world's wetlands are in tropical and subtropical regions. The remaining are primarily boreal peatland in arctic and sub-arctic regions.

Wetlands are among the most productive ecosystems in the world, comparable to rain forests and coral reefs. They are also one of the most highly threatened ecosystems in the world—they are drained or reclaimed and converted to other land uses such as forestry, agriculture, and residential uses or modified to serve water needs by groundwater extraction as well as through the placement of dams and diversions. Today, only half of the world's wetlands remain.

Wetlands perform many important services within a watershed:

- They filter out pollutants, excess nutrients and sediments from water that passes through them;
- They hold back floods in the wet season and release water in times of drought; and

- They provide critical habitat for numerous species of waterfowl, wading and shore birds that breed in wetlands or use them as stopover sites during migration, and provide critical habitat for amphibian species that are rapidly declining world-wide.

Formation of Wetlands

Wetlands form in landscapes where water can be captured and persist and so promote the development of hydric soils and obligate wetland plant and animal communities. Geologic conditions favorable for wetland development include areas that have fine textured surficial soils or peat with low hydraulic conductivity and sufficient thickness to store water. The presence of impermeable bedrock near the land surface may favor the development of wetland areas. The three topographic positions that favor wetland formation are depressions, breaks in slope, and permafrost areas.

- *Depressions* are the most common setting for freshwater wetlands because water tends to pool and be held in topographic lows. Some examples include kettle holes, bogs, prairie potholes, and large flooded forest wetlands such as in the Amazon Basin. Geologically, depressions may be formed by movement of glaciers and water; action of wind, waves, and tides; and/or by processes associated with tectonics, subsidence, or collapse. Water sources to freshwater depressional wetlands include surface flow (either in rivers or via overland flow), groundwater discharge, and precipitation. Water out-puts include surface water outflow, groundwater recharge, and evapotranspiration.
- *Breaks in slope* are a less common setting for wetland formation. These wetlands occur where groundwater moves through aquifers and discharges at geologic discontinuities. Examples include sloping fens, seeps, and riparian and lacustrine wetlands along rivers and lakes where groundwater discharges upslope of the river or lake margin. The major source of water is groundwater, although this source can be supplemented by surface flow and precipitation. Water leaves these wetlands by surface flow and evapotranspiration.
- *Permafrost* wetlands are found in very flat landscapes at high latitudes such as the arctic, where deeper soils are frozen year-round. Precipitation is held in saturated surface soils because the deeper soils are permanently frozen and act as a barrier to groundwater passage. The surface soils thaw for the brief but intense arctic summer. Many permafrost wetlands have a characteristic polygon patterning formed by freeze-thaw cycles. Precipitation and surface flow are the only sources of water, and water is lost by evapotranspiration and surface outflow.

Wetlands found at any of these three topographic positions may differ substantially, depending on their hydrogeologic setting (HGS). HGS is a three-dimensional description of the position of the wetland in the watershed, and plays a leading role in determining essential characteristics of a wetland. HGS includes:

a) Surficial and bedrock geologic deposits over which water travels, including thickness and permeability of the soils, land surface slope, surface topography, and composition and hydraulic properties of the underlying geologic materials;

b) Position of the wetland in the landscape (i.e., Top or bottom of the watershed? Adjacent to another water body? Does the landscape have much or little topographic relief?); and

c) Climate.

These three components coupled with the hydrologic regime (which itself is a function of the HGS) explain much about water chemistry, hydroperiod, and soil biogeochemistry, which in turn will dictate the plant and animal biodiversity supported by that environment. An understanding of the HGS will help simplify the identification of key ecological factors and threats to wetland viability. Below are some descriptive examples of the HGS of different wetland types.

- *Rich fens* in temperate, glaciated regions of the northern U.S. and southern Canada, the Netherlands, and England are small depressional wetlands fed by groundwater discharge and precipitation. Rich fens often are found in gently rolling landscapes, either at the top or bottom of typically small watersheds. Shallow groundwater travels over permeable limestone deposits of variable thickness before discharging into the fen, which contribute calcium and other base cations that raise the pH to seven or eight. Rich fens develop in moist climates, where precipitation exceeds evapotranspiration. If these fens are not impacted by agricultural runoff or elevated atmospheric deposition, nutrient inputs such as nitrogen and phosphorus are very low. The soils are high in organic matter, because the constantly elevated water table inhibits organic matter decomposition. These nutrient-poor, alkaline ecosystems harbor a wide diversity of native plants and animals.

- *Flooded tropical forest wetlands* in the upper Amazon Basin of Peru, Colombia, Venezuela, and Brazil form in large flat landscapes where the water table rises and falls by several meters with the annual flood pulse. Surface water and precipitation/evapotranspiration are the only hydrologic sources and outlets. The origin of the surface water flow is the Andean mountains to the west, and so the flood pulse is reliant on snowmelt that travels off these forested slopes. Water travels down river channels and overtops the banks to flood the adjacent forest. Precipitation is seasonal with heavy rains in the wet seasons and lighter rains during the dry season. Wetland soils are mostly clays, which are eroded and deposited along the major rivers. Waters are turbid from the heavy sediment load and highly discolored from incomplete decomposition of organic plant matter. The native plant and animal communities have evolved with the annual hydrologic fluctuations, which result in periods of high water with little bare ground, and periods of low water with exposed soils.

- *Boreal bogs* form in central and northern Canada, Alaska, northern Europe, and Russia. The groundwater hydraulic head (i.e., groundwater pressure) underlying the surface peat usually supports a high water table, particularly during drought, but that groundwater rarely is discharged at the surface. Therefore, bogs are fed primarily by precipitation. Because the precipitation feeding these wetlands is usually dilute in dissolved substances, they tend to be poorly buffered, acidic, and nutrient-poor. The climate where bogs are found is cool and humid, which slows organic matter decomposition and favors peat accumulation. Species diversity in boreal bogs tends to be low, perhaps because few species

are specifically adapted to these harsh environmental conditions.

- *Vernal pools* are depressions that fill with water temporarily, usually during times of high water table levels or spring runoff. The isolation of these unique features from other water bodies, the presence of associated predatory species (e.g., fish species), and the cycle of wet and dry periods has fostered the evolution of species of plants and animals that are uniquely adapted to these features. For example, the vernal pools located in the northeastern U.S. are home to fairy shrimp, mole salamanders, and wood frogs that exist only in association with vernal pools. Therefore, vernal pools are defined both by their hydrologic regime, by their lack of connectivity to other freshwater ecosystems, and by their specialized biological composition and interactions.

Key Ecological Factors for Wetlands

The ecological integrity of all wetland ecosystems depends on the status and interrelationships among its key ecological factors. Each key ecological factor contributes uniquely to the wetland's ecological integrity. These factors often are best summarized in the form of a conceptual ecological model.

HYDROLOGIC REGIME

The formation, persistence, size, soil type, biogeochemical properties, and vegetative composition of a wetland are controlled by its hydrologic regime. For example:

- the hydrologic regime controls nutrient transport into and out of wetlands;
- the flooding regime determines redoximorphic properties of the soil (i.e., whether it is oxic or anoxic), which control the chemical transformations of nutrients and metals;
- concentrations of different solutes such as salts and nutrients are dependent upon the relative contributions of different water sources;
- the timing and duration of surface water flooding control sediment transport;
- many plant species have evolved to germinate under

certain water levels, so the hydroperiod controls which seedlings can germinate from the seed bank;

- water level fluctuations often control plant and animal species composition due to specific tolerance ranges of those species to flooding; and
- extended periods of flooding result in soil anoxia, which impedes organic matter decomposition and leads to the formation of peat.

Small changes in wetland hydrology can significantly affect the chemical and physical properties of a wetland. For example, a lowered water table can promote oxidizing conditions, leading to increased organic matter oxidation, soil loss, and land subsidence. This changes the wetland's ability to store water. It also concentrates nutrients that are not oxidized along with the carbon. Changes in the hydroperiod have severe impacts on wetland plant and animal communities. Invasive alien species often invade wetlands when there is a shift in hydrology and a subsequent loss of native species with narrower tolerance ranges to water level.

The hydrologic regime of a wetland is best described using detailed knowledge of the wetland's water budget and its hydroperiod. The water budget is a quantitative description of the contributions of all water sources and outflows. Sources include precipitation (P), groundwater discharge $(GW)_i$, surface water inflow $(SW)_i$, and tides $(T)_i$. Outflows include evapotranspiration (ET), groundwater recharge (GW), surface water outflow (SW), and tides $(T)_t$. The difference between the annual sources and outflows is the water storage:

$$[P + GW + SW + T] - [ET + GW + SW + T] = storage$$

The hydroperiod is a description of annual fluctuations in the water table, and illustrates the timing and duration of flooding. It is displayed quantitatively by graphing time (usually months) on the x-axis and water table elevation on the y-axis. For example, the hydrograph of a tropical floodplain wetland in Brazil rises from December through March during the rainy season and when the pulse of snowmelt from the Andes reaches the lower elevations. Water levels are high in April and May, start to fall in June, and are low from July through November. In contrast, a temperate rich fen would have a relatively flat hydroperiod because the water table in this groundwater-supported ecosystem does not fluctuate much over the course of the year. However, irregular fluctuations will arise in response to precipitation events.

PHYSICAL HABITAT CONDITIONS

The most important physical habitat conditions for wetlands are soil composition and structure, particularly relating to "hydric" soils. Hydric soils provide a reactive surface for a specialized suite of microbially-mediated biogeochemical reactions. They are the medium in which many of the wetland chemical transformations occur and the primary storage area of plant nutrients.

Hydric soils are produced under anoxic conditions. When wetlands are flooded with little turbulence, a gradient of dissolved oxygen develops. The upper water column generally remains oxidized because of its proximity to air. However, oxygen diffusion from the air through the water column and into the soil is slow, and plants and microbes that respire in the soil often deplete dissolved oxygen in soil pore spaces more rapidly than it is replenished. Anoxic conditions develop in the soil, and soil microbes begin to reduce other available compounds for energy production (nitrogen, manganese, iron, sulfur, organic molecules, in that order). The redox potential is a measure of anoxia.

There are two types of hydric soils: organic soils (also known as peats or histosols) and mineral soils. *Peat* develops when plant decomposition is slowed by low oxygen availability and low temperatures, and the resulting partially decomposed organic matter accumulates in the upper soil horizon. Soils are classified as peats if they have greater than about 30% organic matter. *Hydric mineral soils* have lower organic matter content. They are distinguished from upland mineral soils by their geochemical properties. In hydric mineral soils, metals such as iron and manganese are reduced and become more soluble, so they are leached from the soil profile. Hydric mineral soils are identified by color because the metals give non-hydric soils their bright red, yellow, brown, and orange colors. Hydric soils therefore have muted light grey colors.

Peat and mineral soils differ physically in many

important ways. Organic soils can hold more water than mineral soils. They tend to have lower pH because of the organic acids produced by decomposing organic matter, and because they lack the buffering cations frequently found in mineral soils. Peat bulk density is lower than mineral soils. Hydraulic conductivity is high in hydric mineral soils, but variable in peats, depending on compaction. Nutrient availability generally is higher in mineral soils than peat because nutrients often are tied up in the organic matter and not available for plant or microbial uptake.

With the exception of peat harvesting for horticulture, wetland soils are not directly affected by anthropogenic threats. However, they can be altered indirectly. For example, a change in wetland hydroperiod from dam construction or flow regulation may alter rates of organic matter accumulation.

WATER CHEMISTRY REGIME

Wetland water chemistry is a result of hydrology, geologic setting, type of soils and vegetation, and human activity within or near the wetland. Wetlands dominated by surface water inflow reflect the chemistry of the associated watershed. Wetlands that receive surface water or groundwater inflow, have limited outflow, and lose water primarily to evapotranspiration have a high concentration of chemicals and may contain brackish or saline water. Examples of such wetlands are the saline playas, wetlands associated with the Great Salt Lake in Utah, and the permanent and semi-permanent prairie potholes in the mid-west of Canada and the U.S. In contrast, wetlands such as bogs that receive water primarily from precipitation and lose water by surface water outflow or groundwater recharge tend to have lower concentrations of chemicals. Wetlands influenced strongly by groundwater discharge such as fens have water chemistries that reflect the geologic substrate over which groundwater passes. In most cases, wetlands receive water from more than one source, so the resultant water chemistry is a composite chemistry of the various sources.

Seasonal patterns of nutrient uptake and release are characteristics of many wetlands. In temperate climates, nutrient retention is greatest in the growing season primarily because of higher plant productivity

as well as microbial activity in the water column and sediments. Much of this is released at the end of the growing season when plants are senescing and decomposing.

Nitrogen and phosphorus

Dissolved nutrients such as nitrogen and phosphorus are important determinants of wetland properties. Some wetlands such as boreal fens and bogs have low availability of nitrogen and phosphorus, and plant production is usually limited by nutrient availability. These plant communities have evolved nutrient-use efficiency mechanisms such as carnivory, nutrient translocation from senescing tissues to growing ones, and mycorrhizal symbioses. Nutrient-poor wetlands tend to be net sinks for nutrients. This is particularly true for peatlands, where nitrogen and phosphorus are bound to partially decomposed organic matter. Other wetlands such as floodplains and tidal wetlands receive a regular pulse of nutrient-laden water and those plants tend to have fewer nutrient-use efficiency mechanisms.

Phosphorus is transported to and from wetlands bound to mineral or organic soil particles. It does not have a gaseous phase, and does not undergo biogeochemical redox reactions, although it can be adsorbed or released by other compounds when they undergo redox reactions. Phosphorus can be bound in many different forms, with different degrees of availability to plants and microbes.

Nitrogen can be transported into wetlands as nitrate in groundwater or surface water, as organic nitrogen bound to organic compounds, or it can be fixed from the atmosphere by nitrogen-fixing organisms such as Alder and some cyanobacteria. Nitrogen undergoes a variety of microbially-mediated redox reactions, including nitrate reduction to ammonium under anoxic conditions, and denitrification of nitrate. In the anoxic conditions of many wetland soils, most nitrogen is found as reduced ammonium.

But too much of a good thing can be bad. Anthropogenic nutrient loading to wetlands is a serious problem around the globe. Nitrogen and phosphorus from municipal wastewater, excess fertilizer in agricultural runoff, and atmospheric deposition are wreaking havoc on aquatic systems. Elevated nutrient availability often favors exotic and weedy species, reduces species diversity by removing nutrient limitation constraints, and feeds cyanobacterial blooms that shade and choke out native plants and animals.

Conductivity and pH

Both pH and conductivity are good diagnostic tools for understanding wetland properties, such as water sources, without doing an entire water budget. They can be measured quickly and inexpensively with a probe.

The pH is an inverse measure of the concentration of protons. Acidic wetlands (e.g., pH of four to six) tend to have low rates of plant production, slow decomposition, organic soils, and low inputs of buffering cations such as calcium from limestone. Alkaline wetlands (e.g., pH of six to eight) tend to have mineral soils, higher plant production and decomposition, and a source of cations.

Conductivity is a measure of the capacity of water to conduct an electric current, which is directly proportional to the concentration of cations and anions in solution. Wetlands with low conductivity surface water (<100 S/cm) tend to be dominated by precipitation such as bogs and poor fens. If the conductivity is slightly higher (e.g., 100–200 S/cm), there may be a groundwater source that passes over rocks and soil with little leaching capacity, such as granite. Wetlands with significant groundwater inputs in landscapes with highly leachable geologic strata may have surface water conductivities as high as 800 S/cm. Floodplain wetlands with a large source of sediment-laden water have very high conductivities (1000–10,000 S/cm). Saline waters may have conductivities as high as 5000 S/cm.

Dissolved oxygen

As discussed above in the section on soils, the concentration of dissolved oxygen in wetland surface water and porewater dictates the relative rares of many physical and biotic processes.

Other chemical variables

A variety of water chemistry constituents may be specific to individual wetland types. For example, salinity is important for wetlands in closed basins such as the Great Salt Lake, where all water losses are from evapotranspiration which concentrates salts. Calcium is an important water constituent for wetlands formed on limestone bedrock, such as karst marshes along the Yucatan coast of Mexico, and rich fens in temperate regions. Turbidity is an important parameter for many floodplain wetlands.

CONNECTIVITY

Wetlands are connected to the rest of the watershed by hydrology. Both surface water and groundwater usually travel over and through other ecosystems before reaching wetlands. For wetlands to function with high integrity, those hydrologic connections must remain intact.

For example, floodplain wetlands are connected to rivers, and they receive water from overbank flow at times of high water volume. These wetlands store water at peak flow and retard the movement of floodwater in the river. In another example, prairie potholes are fed by shallow, local groundwater flow. If groundwater is pumped and used for irrigation, the connection between wetland and water supply is cut off, and the wetland probably will degrade.

Connectivity of wetlands to the rest of the landscape is important for many plant and animal species. For example, salamanders breed in wetlands but migrate to upland areas as adults. If the wetland for breeding is isolated from the upland by an impassable feature such as a road, the habitat is no longer viable for that population.

BIOLOGICAL COMPOSITION AND INTERACTIONS

Hydrology is the driving influence on the occurrence and abundance of plant and animal species in wetlands. Wetland plants exhibit distinct morphological, physiological, and reproductive adaptations that enable them to tolerate specific hydroperiods and hydric soils that sometimes go anoxic. As hydrologic conditions vary from periodic or seasonal saturation to permanent inundation, the vegetation will also vary from a transitional grouping of species that can tolerate wet soils, to species specifically adapted to long periods of inundation. Wetland plants that live only in wetlands and cannot tolerate dry soils are termed obligate wetlands species. Those that can tolerate flooded conditions, but also survive in uplands, are termed facultative wetland species. Many invasive alien plant species are facultative.

Wetland plants and animals need oxygen or a similar source of energy for respiration. Many have evolved clever mechanisms to cope with soil anoxia. Some plants "pump" oxygen into the rooting zone through specialized cells called aerenchyma or specialized organs such as pneumatophores. Amphibians can absorb oxygen through their skin. Some tropical wetland fish can gulp air and absorb oxygen from their gut lining.

The combination of shallow water, high levels of inorganic nutrients, and high rates of primary productivity in wetlands is ideal for the development of organisms that are the primary consumers within the food web such as many species of insects, mollusks, and crustaceans. Some animals consume the aboveground live vegetation (herbivore-carnivore food web); others utilize the dead plant leaves and stems (detritivores), which break down in the water to form small, nutrient-enriched particles of organic material called detritus.

Some organisms need wetlands for part of their life cycle. Many species of fish will use wetlands for nursery grounds and migrate to open water at maturity. Some amphibians have an aquatic as well as a terrestrial life stage (e.g., frogs and salamanders). Many waterfowl species nest in emergent vegetation and rear their young in highly productive shallow wetland waters.

REFERENCES

Ciruna, K.A. 1999. The implications of lake history for conservation biology. Ph.D. dissertation. Department of Zoology, University of Toronto, Toronto, Ontario.

Hutchinson, G.E. 1957. A Treatise on Limnology. Volume 1. Geography, Physics and Chemistry. John Wiley and Sons, Inc., New York.

Maser, C., and J. Sedell. 1994. From the forest to the sea: the ecology of wood in streams, rivers, estuaries, and oceans. St. Lucie Press, Delray Beach, FL.

Appendix B

Indicators of Freshwater Ecological Integrity
David Braun

Chapters 2 and 3 introduced the five categories of key factors in freshwater ecological integrity—the hydrologic regime, the water chemistry regime, physical habitat conditions, connectivity, and biological composition and interactions. As explained in Chapters 3 and 4, threats to freshwater ecological integrity involve alterations to these key factors. This appendix introduces and summarizes information about indicators recognized and commonly used in freshwater conservation for each of the five categories of key ecological factors. This appendix lists both specific indicators for individual key ecological factors as well as integrative indicators. Chapter 5 provides more information about the use of these indicators for measuring conservation success and engaging in adaptive management.

INDICATORS OF THE FIVE KEY FACTORS

The Hydrologic Regime

Hydrologists rely on a wide range of indicators of hydrologic variation in rivers and streams. These indicators include simple measures, such as the average discharge for each month of the year, and more complex measures, such as the return frequency (average number of years between recurrences) for high and low flows of particular magnitudes. All of these indicators derive from a variety of measurement types that estimate discharge.

Discharge, defined as the total volume of water moving through a channel per unit of time, cannot be directly measured without confining the entire flow into a pipe or other structure. In natural channels, the water moves at different rates depending on location in the channel, horizontally, vertically, and in the vicinity of any irregularities in channel shape, such as bends, boulders, bars, and woody debris. As a result, measuring discharge directly, in theory, would require measuring the rate and direction of movement of the water continuously at every point in the channel cross-section. The more practical alternative is to collect such measurements at only a sample of locations across the channel cross-section and use the results to estimate total discharge. The more complex the channel form, however, the less reliable such measurements become.

Discharge can also be estimated for a watershed even without direct discharge measurements, through the use of regional curves. A regional curve is an equation that describes the relationship between the size and shape of a watershed and the way it responds to weather conditions, calculated for a group of highly similar watersheds in a limited area with consistent geology and climate. A regional curve is developed and calibrated using those watersheds in the area for which the necessary data are available. The resulting curve equation can then be applied to other watersheds within the same area, for which actual flow data are limited or missing.

Alternatively and most commonly, discharge can be estimated in rivers and streams by measuring the stage or elevation of the water in the channel.

TABLE B-1. Indicators of the Five Key Factors

Variable	Indicator
River/Stream Discharge	Velocity/Cross-section estimates
	Stage-based estimates using a rating curve
	Stage-based estimates using weirs or flumes
	Stage-based estimates using predictive equations
	Estimates on regional curves
River/Stream Elevation	Stage-based estimates
Lake Level	Stage-based estimate
Groundwater Elevation	Well-based estimation of potentiometric surface
Groundwater Flow	Tracer-based estimates
	Estimates based on predictive equations

Typically, stage and discharge follow a consistent relationship to each other in any straight channel section. This relationship typically can be described by a simple logarithmic equation. However, this relationship is not perfect. Changes in water temperature and sediment load, bed and bank vegetation, channel erosion and deposition, and the movement of large objects all cause the relationship to change from moment to moment in natural channels. As a result, a graph of stage versus discharge can be somewhat messy in its details even when the overall pattern is stable. Using stage as an indicator of discharge therefore requires collecting repeated measurements of both flow and stage over a range of flow conditions, from low to high discharge. These data allow the construction of a rating curve for a monitoring location, which shows the average relationship between the two variables. By periodically updating this curve with new data, the effects of changes in channel morphology and flow patterns can also be tracked. Of course, developing a rating curve requires collecting at least some measurements of discharge, in order to calculate the curve; this method therefore runs into the same problems noted above.

Two alternatives also exist for estimating discharge from measurements of stage:

- For small channels, use a weir or flume to measure flow. These are structures through or over which the water must flow, built with a fixed geometry. The geometry generates a highly consistent relationship between stage and discharge. Of course, installing such a structure requires artificially altering the channel itself, thereby potentially disturbing habitat conditions, and is practicable only for small channels.

- Use a theoretical rating curve for a channel section based on standardized measurements of channel gradient, shape, and roughness or the ease with which water can move over the channel bed and banks without resistance. These measurements, collected following widely accepted procedures, get entered into an equation or computer model based on a suite of equations to arrive at the estimated rating curve.

Sometimes, of course, the critical concern for a river or stream may be stage or water level alone. And for lakes and wetlands, stage will almost always be the most important surface water variable. Measuring surface water elevation in lakes and wetlands is technically no different than in running waters, with the same limitation: whatever location selected for the monitoring will only provide data from a single sample point in the system.

Groundwater hydrologic variation is more difficult to measure than surface water variation because it occurs out of sight. Measuring the depth of water in wells provides information on the elevation of the groundwater surface in an unconfined aquifer, or on

TABLE B-2. Indicators of Water Chemistry

Variable	Indicator
General water properties	Estimates based on in-situ data at multiple locations/depths
	Estimates based on samples from multiple locations/depths
	Estimates from composited samples
Water column constituents	Estimates based on in-situ data at multiple locations/depths
	Estimates based on samples from multiple locations/depths
	Estimates from composited samples
Sediment constituents	Pore-water composition
	Sediment solid-matter composition
Organism constituents	Whole-organism composition
	Organ/organelle composition
Physiological response	Response-specific enzyme concentrations in organisms

the water pressure in a confined aquifer, depending on the type of aquifer tapped by each well. These measurements constitute samples of the groundwater elevation or pressure, from which the overall distribution of elevation or pressure values may be extrapolated, so long as the elevation of the ground surface is also known for each well. A map of the well water levels for an individual aquifer will resemble the kind of contour map that one might construct for ground surface elevation; such a groundwater map is called a map of the potentiometric surface for an aquifer. The rate of groundwater flow between any two well locations may be estimated by using non-toxic tracer chemicals and determining how long it takes for water to move from one location to the other; or by applying equations based on properties of the geologic materials present and the slope of the potentiometric surface.

Finally, hydrologic indicators may also include measurements of the extent of inundation of floodplains or wetlands. These indicators may be selected and monitored using direct field measurements at select sampling locations or using aerial or satellite imagery.

The Water Chemistry Regime

Indicators of water chemistry derive from measurements of general properties of the water and the concentrations of specific constituents. General properties of freshwater bodies include temperature, pH, water color, salinity, and clarity/turbidity. The chemical constituents of freshwater bodies can include dissolved gases (e.g., oxygen), nutrients (e.g., molecules containing nitrogen, phosphorus, carbon, etc.) dissolved in the water and incorporated into particulate matter, dissolved and particulate metals, organic matter from natural and human sources, and other substances. Measuring such properties and constituents poses special problems. The properties and composition of freshwaters always vary from one location and depth to the next within the water body and always vary over time—not just from one year or season to the next, but sometimes from moment to moment as well. Further, as noted earlier, chemicals in freshwater ecosystems may occur in a variety of forms and in a variety of components of the ecosystem. They also change their forms and locations within the system over time—they may be absorbed, deposited, consumed, transformed, flushed away by water movement, and even converted into gases that escape into the air. In turn, monitoring can produce measurements for only a few components of the ecosystem (e.g., water and sediments), from only a limited number of locations, at any given time. The resulting data therefore serve only as indicators of water chemistry conditions across the system as a whole.

A sample of water removed from a stream or lake for study immediately begins to change temperature and exchange gases once exposed to the air. These changes in turn lead to changes in pH and the condition of many chemical constituents. Therefore, what is measured on the shore or in a boat is only an approximation for what conditions were like in situ. Because water chemistry in a sample begins to change the moment it is collected into a container, samples collected for examination on the shore or in a boat should be measured as soon as possible after collection and samples collected for shipment to a lab or for other later measurement always need to be stabilized by being placed on ice and sometimes treated with additional chemicals for preservation.

Samples collected for examination on the shore, in the boat, or in a laboratory can be examined individually, or mixed together (with specific quantities of each portion noted for future duplication) into a composite sample. The mixing of composite samples helps deal with the fact that, noted above and in Chapter 5, the concentrations of many aquatic chemicals can vary over time in response to changes in surface water flow and other highly changeable conditions. For example, the first surge of runoff from a storm often carries the greatest concentrations of natural plant matter and many pollutants. Proper monitoring of storm runoff therefore generally demands methods that sample this short-term variation, usually by collecting several sub-samples over the course of the storm event and combining them into a single composite sample for analysis. There are two ways to create a composite water sample from a river or stream. Flow-weighted composite samples combine the sub-samples in direct relation to the intensity of stream discharge at the time each sub-sample was taken. Creating this kind of composite samples therefore requires monitoring stream discharge as well. Time-weighted composite samples combine the sub-samples according to the time interval between the sub-samples (e.g., see USDA 1997, listed in the references for Chapter 5). In lakes and deeper rivers, depth-weighted composite samples may prove useful. The creation of a composite sample allows investigators to examine average conditions across the water body either at a single time or across the duration of some hydrologic event, without having to analyze individually every single sub-sample.

The components of the freshwater ecosystem most often used for measuring chemistry include the water itself, the sediments in the water body, and plant and animal tissues:

- Water samples are generally called water column samples, to denote that they are taken from some specific vertical position in the water. Water column samples can be examined either to determine the separate quantities of dissolved and suspended (particulate) matter present or to determine the total concentration of any particular constituent.

- Sediments collected from the bottom of a stream, river, lake, or pond provide important chemical information because they incorporate particulate matter from the water column, contain pore water that may have a composition different from that in the water column, and can absorb chemicals onto the mineral and organic matter present.

- Aquatic plants incorporate chemicals from the water column and bottom sediments into their cells through direct absorption; aquatic animals incorporate such chemicals though their foods and by absorption through their body walls. In turn, these chemicals in aquatic animals can simply become part of their biomass, or can become isolated in discrete organs or organelles. Toxic metals, for example, often become concentrated in the livers of vertebrates; organo-chlorine pollutants in fatty tissues. Analyzing animal tissues for evidence of some chemicals therefore must take into account what tissues need to be examined.

- Many organisms also produce chemicals, such as particular types of enzymes, in response to exposure to irritating or poisonous chemicals. Measurements of the levels of these enzymes particularly in aquatic animals can be used as indicators of the exposure of the organism to the triggering substance.

- Finally, some scientists have suggested using the presence/absence or relative densities of particular aquatic invertebrate taxa as indicators of the effects of particular contaminants.

Physical Habitat Conditions

Indicators of physical habitat conditions derive from measurements taken at a number of spatial scales. As discussed in Chapters 2 and 3, and Appendix A, rivers,

TABLE B-3. Indicators of Physical Habitat

Variable	Indicator
Channel/Shoreline Survey	Location and form detectable in remote imagery
	Location and description at/along survey transects
Channel/Shoreline Profile	Profile details along transects
	Geomorphic profile type along transects
Microhabitat Distribution	Microhabitat occurences along transects
	Woody debris occurences along transects
Vegetative Structure	Species composition
Particle Size	Statistics from samples along transects

wetlands and lakes are geomorphically dynamic at several spatial scales. These scales range from the individual particles of mineral and organic matter that make up the substrate; to larger features created by boulders, woody debris and vegetation; to the overall configuration of the shores, banks, and bottom; to overall size and form. Individual measurements at these different scales provide information on the magnitudes of specific variables, such as mean bed particle size, channel entrenchment, sediment accumulation, or the density of large woody debris per unit of river or shoreline distance, or can be used to categorize channel and shoreline form and stability. Repeated measurements provide the information for assessing the rates of change in these same measurements or the rates of specific processes, such as the rate of channel migration or shoreline recession.

At coarse spatial scales, measurements taken from aerial and satellite imagery often provide less expensive but equally reliable information on the size (extent), location, and overall shape of wetlands and open waters than would on-the-ground surveying. Such imagery may also be available over a long span of years, as well, providing a useful means for examining patterns and rates of change over time. Such imagery does not provide bathymetric data, of course; these require direct surveying either by mechanical or echolocation (e.g., sonar) methods. At finer scales, measurements taken along survey transects—along-shore, up/down-channel, cross-channel, and across the shore and wetland profile—can be used to record topographic and sediment size data and details of channel, wetland and shore form, including occurrences of large woody debris and other habitat-forming structures. At still finer scales, artificial objects can be placed into the bed or across the channel or shore profile, to help detect sediment erosion and deposition (e.g., scour chains) or the types of sediments transported (e.g., sediment traps, core samples). Many of these finer-scale methods involve collecting samples or sample measurements at only select locations along each transect, which itself only provides a sample of the larger system. A number of excellent visual assessment protocols also exist for rapidly collecting information along channels, wetlands and shorelines on habitat form, quality, and stability. These protocols emphasize visual criteria and checklists over more detailed measurement. Please use the list of additional resources included at the end of Chapter 5 for more information about these protocols.

Connectivity

Chapter 2 and Appendix A describe the three types of connectivity that influence ecosystem dynamics in river ecosystems: surface-groundwater connectivity, upstream-downstream connectivity, and river-riparian area connectivity. Lakes and wetlands have similar types of connectivity. The last two types of connectivity clearly lend themselves to examination using maps, geographic databases (e.g., databases of dam locations and their characteristics), and remote imagery. However, indicators developed from such sources may not be completely reliable, for four reasons.

- First, not all potential structures that can be tabulated in this manner necessarily present barriers to the movement of water and biota. For example, some low-height dams may present no more of a barrier to fish migrations than a natural beaver dam or log jam. The effects of the structure as a barrier may need to be verified through an examination of the actual behavior of potentially affected biota; and structures (or other impediments, see below) may pose barriers to the movement of some biota but not others.

- Second, not all structural barriers may be detectable in remote imagery or recorded in geographic databases. For example, farmers on floodplains may construct levees to reduce flooding of their fields, and/or dredge out drainage channels so that the streams do not overtop their banks so often. Such efforts may not be detectable from existing maps or imagery and may require intensive surveys to inventory.

- Third, not all breaks in the connectivity of surface waters will be caused by structural barriers such as dams. Water diversions and alterations to the groundwater system (see below) can cause stream or river waters to dry up along a reach, preventing the movement of aquatic biota; and chemical and thermal discharges can make some reaches so unsuitable that many aquatic biota will not attempt or survive passage. Mapping these other types of barriers may require using other geographic data or conducting separate surveys.

- Finally, artificial structures may not change the pattern of connectivity along a river. Specifically, dams built at locations where naturally impassible waterfalls once existed may not make the river less passable—or may make the river less passable only for biota traveling in the downstream direction.

Surface to groundwater connectivity does not lend itself as readily to examination using geographic information systems and remote imagery. Except where groundwater depletion causes surface water entirely to disappear, remote imagery and conventional geographic databases will not necessarily provide information on either the location or magnitude of water movement between surface waters and the groundwater system. Where precise groundwater elevation data (i.e., potentiometric data) are available to compare with equally precise surface water elevation data,

investigators can develop estimates for the average or seasonal relationships between the two systems; changes in baseflow can also provide information on changes in connectivity. In the absence of, or in conjunction with such data, indicators may be developed based on transects of wells and surface staff gauges. Field crews can also carry out a synoptic survey of stream baseflow, measuring baseflow simultaneously at multiple stations along a stream reach to determine where and at what rate groundwater is entering or being recharged from the stream channel. Alternatively, in areas where stream flow has become fragmented into isolated wet and dry reaches, indicators may be developed for flow fragmentation by repeatedly surveying the size and distribution of surface water remnants.

Biological Composition and Interactions

The published literature on biological indicators for freshwater ecosystems is vast, largely because such indicators are so useful for assessing the integrity of these systems. Bioassessment indicators are in fact becoming common components of governmental water monitoring programs in many countries. Several useful summaries of this field are available (e.g., Karr and Chu, 1999) and many are provided at the end of Chapter 5.

The freshwater targets for a conservation area may be individual species (or particular populations or genetic stocks of individual species), assemblages of species, ecological communities, or ecological systems. The indicators needed for each of these scales of biological complexity will differ. However, the status of some individual species (or assemblages of species) may be useful indicators of the integrity of a community or ecological system. Biological indicators may also be grouped together into indicators of biological pattern (e.g., composition and spatial structure) and biological process (e.g., population or successional dynamics) although some overlap exists between these two categories of indicators.

Table B-4 summarizes the kinds of biological indicators that can be used in freshwater ecosystems. The principles underlying this table are quite simple, despite the apparent complexity of the resulting choices. At the level of individual species, the status of the

TABLE B-4. Indicators of Connectivity

Variable	Indicator
Up/Downstream Connectivity	GIS- and remote imagery-based tabulations of barriers
	Field survey-based tabulations of barriers
	Biologically-confirmed tabulations of barriers
Water-Floodzone Connectivity	GIS- and remote imagery-based tabulations of barriers
	Field survey-based tabulations of barriers
	Biologically-confirmed tabulations of barriers
Surface-Groundwater Connectivity	GIS- and imgery-based measures of disconnection
	Estimates from surface vs. groundwater elevation data
	Estimates from synoptic and other field survey data

target may be tracked by looking at: (a) abundance, whether the species occupies the entire range across which it is expected to occur, and how fragmented the distribution of individual populations may be within that range; (b) detailed demographic variables such as age, size and gender ratios; (c) genetic markers that give evidence of population in- versus out-breeding, isolation, and hybridization; and (d) indicators of the health of the individual organisms. For example, annual census surveys and data on spatial occurrence might be used to track the overall abundance and distribution of a species of fish; the size and age distribution of males and females might be used to track recruitment and patterns of mortality; eroded fins, lesions, tumors, malformed external organs, and evidence of parasites might be used to track patterns of health; accumulation of metals or pesticides in specific organ tissues might be used to track levels of exposure to harmful chemicals; and genetic markers in individuals found in different localities might provide evidence concerning genetic isolation or hybridization.

Individual species may also serve as indicators of the condition of an overall assemblage, community, or ecological system, so long as they meet all the criteria for useful indicators discussed above. Typically, indicator species will include those that are especially characteristic of, play a keystone role in, or are especially sensitive to alteration to key driving processes in some particular community or ecosystem. For example, the status of a wide-ranging, highly mobile aquatic species such as a sturgeon or river dolphin may provide a good indicator of overall connectivity and water quality in a large river ecosystem; the status of an annual plant species that colonizes freshly exposed mud banks may provide a good indicator of the integrity of the hydrologic and sediment delivery regimes; and so forth.

Indicators that incorporate information from many species at once will be useful for monitoring biological response at the scale of species assemblages, communities, and ecosystems. The simplest of these will combine species into major taxa, functional groups, or groups typical of different seral (successional) stages in response to characteristic disturbance processes. Data on the abundance and proportions of these groups, and perhaps their spatial distributions, can then be tabulated together to create an index of the integrity of interactions among species overall. For example, some fish species in a river basin may readily tolerate murky water and muddy, silt-covered river bottoms, while others may require clear water for capturing prey, avoiding predators, seeking mates, and finding nesting locations. An indicator based on the relative proportions of turbidity-tolerant versus intolerant fish species might then provide useful information on a critical aspect of the aquatic habitat. Some of the best-known freshwater biological indicators rest on this general concept: different taxa of aquatic insect larvae have been found to be sensitive to variation in hydrology and pollutant concentrations; different taxa of algae and diatoms (those that live in the water column and those that live on solid surfaces) are sensitive to variation in nutrient pollution, as are different taxa of insect larvae, mollusks, and both fish and

TABLE B-5. Biological Indicators in Freshwater Ecosystems

Elements	Variable	Indicator
Species	*Pattern*	
	Genetic composition	Genetic markers
	Demographics	Age/size/gender structure
	Abundance	Number(s)/size(s) of population(s)
	Range	Spatial distribution; fragmentation
	Process	
	Genetic isolation, mutation, and hybridization	Genetic markers
	Aggregation/dispersion; migration	Spatial distribution; movement
	Recruitment, mortality	Number/size/structure of population(s)
	Health	Disease, deformities, body size & growth rates, bioaccumulation of contaminents
Assemblages	*Pattern*	
	Taxonomic composition	Taxonomic richness
	Demographics	Taxonomic abundance, dominance
	Range	Spatial distribution; fragmentation
	Process	
	Competition and exclusion	Taxonomic richness, dominance; spatial dominance
Community	*Pattern*	
	Taxonomic composition	Abundance of keystone, charactersitic, sensitive species
	Functional composition	Abundance of keystone, charactersitic, sensitive functional groups, guilds, seral stages
	Range	Spatial distribution of co-occurences of characteristic taxa
	Spatial structure	Spatial (horizontal, vertical) distribution of characteristic functional groups, guilds, seral stages
	Process	
	Succession	Spatial (horizontal, vertical) distribution of characteristic functional groups, guilds, seral stages
	Predation	Predator dominance (by numbers, biomass); prey demographics
	Herbivory	Herbivore dominance (by number, biomass)
	Productivity	Biomass; chlorophyll-a production
	Trophic dynamics	Abundance of keystone, charactersitic, funcational groups; number of trophic links
Ecosystem	*Pattern*	
	Taxonomic composition	Abundance of keystone, characteristic, sensitive species
	Functional composition	Abundance of keystone, characteristic, sensitive communities, seral stages
	Range	Spatial distribution of co-occurences of characteristic communities
	Spatial structure	Spatial (horizontal, vertical) distribution of characteristic communities, seral stages
	Process	
	Succession	Spatial (horizontal, vertical) distribution of characteristic communities, seral stages
	Predation	Predator dominance (by numbers, biomass); prey demographics
	Herbivory	Hebrivore dominance (by numbers, biomass)
	Productivity	Biomass; chlorophyll-a production
	Trophic dynamics	Abundance of keystone, charactersitic communities; number of trophic links

amphibians that feed on these microorganisms. Further, the more geographically widespread the taxa used in such indicators, the more widely these indicators can be applied. For these reasons, indicators based on freshwater algae, diatoms, and benthic macroinvertebrates are among the most common bioassessment indicators in use today.

All indicators of biological pattern and process rely on samples collected at limited numbers of places and at specific times. Biological conditions vary naturally in aquatic and floodplain settings, from one location and geomorphic setting to the next, as well as over time—moment to moment as well as season to season and year to year. For example, the composition of benthic macroinvertebrates samples from riffle or bar settings will almost always differ naturally from those collected from deep pools; a census of fishes or annual plants on the floodplain in October will potentially give different results than one carried out in March; and so forth. As a result, analyses of aquatic biological data will only produce meaningful results when they involve comparisons among samples collected with the same methods, from the same kinds of locations, at the same times of the year. Additionally, samples collected during or immediately after a storm may also produce different results than those collected following several calm days. All standard methods for monitoring freshwater biological conditions include procedures for ensuring sample reliability and comparability.

INTEGRATIVE INDICATORS

Biological indicators may be extended one step further to construct integrative indicators. These are indicators that provide information on a large number of ecological variables at once, thereby providing a kind of summary of conditions in a community or ecological system. There are two general kinds of integrative indicators: (1) Broad-spectrum indicators and (2) Multi-metric indicators.

Broad-spectrum indicators are simple biological indicators for use with species, assemblage, community, and ecosystem targets, but with one special design criterion: The indicator must be sensitive not to just one or two driving processes but to large numbers at once. The variation in such broad-spectrum indicators therefore provides an indication of how well all of the included processes are operating overall—whether their collective variation is within some overall range of variation. For example, some freshwater mussel species in North America may provide useful integrative information because they are simultaneously sensitive to stream hydrology and geomorphic dynamics, turbidity and sedimentation, temperature, pH, the presence of toxic chemicals, the spectrum of microorganisms available as food in the water column (which itself depends on nutrient loads and other variables), the availability of fish species that can serve as hosts for the mussels' parasitic larvae (glochidia), and the density of predators-itself limited by the availability of riparian habitat. Extremely common species of mussels may not be sensitive enough to all these variables to show much variation; and extremely rare species of mussels will not be widespread enough to be useful. But species of intermediate sensitivity and range may provide consistent integrative information on the overall integrity of a riverine system.

Measurements of the status of a riparian forest community similarly may collectively serve as a useful integrative or broad-spectrum indicator. Riparian forest vegetation in any single location will vary in composition in response to variation in both surface and groundwater hydrology, sedimentation, nutrient and other chemical concentrations, and connectivity with upstream sources of propagules. In addition, a healthy riparian ecosystem will provide habitat for a wide range of fauna, including aquatic vertebrates that use flooded bottomland for feeding and spawning habitat or that depend on nutrients and coarse plant matter flushed into the river from the riparian community during floods. Some measure of the overall status of the riparian forest community—as indicated by data concerning the integrity of both biotic pattern and process—therefore may provide a useful integrative indicator of the overall integrity of a river system's hydrology, geomorphic variation, chemistry, connectivity, and stream-floodplain interactions. Visual assessment protocols exist for using information on riparian forest community condition in precisely this manner (see resource list at end of Chapter 5). However, caution should be used in determining which aspects of these communities to monitor. For example, it may be useful to consider variation in age classes and recruitment of new trees, not simply the presence of mature trees of different taxa, given the fact that some riparian tree species are very long lived (e.g., cottonwoods).

Multi-metric indicators combine information on a large number of ecological variables at once into an overall index of the integrity of a freshwater community or ecological system; each included variable is considered a metric. The concept underlying multi-metric indexes is that no single aspect of a freshwater community or ecosystem will be sensitive to alterations in all key driving processes nor sensitive at the same speeds. For example, one species of aquatic insect may be highly sensitive to the arrival of an agricultural pesticide, but then disappear from the stream once the concentration of the pesticide passes some minimal threshold. At the same time, some other species of insect may tolerate a moderate concentration of this same pesticide, but then gradually decline in abundance as the concentration rises. Measurements of the presence and densities of these two species, combined into a composite index, would therefore provide information on biological response to the pesticide over a wider range of conditions than either could alone. By combining a number of such metrics, investigators can create far more sophisticated indexes than illustrated in this example, that vary according to how many key factors have been altered, and the degree to which they have been altered, system-wide. The measurements for each metric typically are ranked along a scale, for example from one to five, indicating a scale for highly altered to unaltered conditions. The rank values for the individual metrics are then summed (some may be weighted, as well), to produce an overall index value or score.

Scientists and water quality agencies in the midwestern U.S., for example, have developed a type of multi-metric index called the Fish Index of Biological Integrity, or Fish IBI. The following are the most common metrics used in Fish IBI in the mid-western U.S. (modified from Karr and Chu, 1999):

- Number of native fish species
- Number of riffle-benthic insectivores
- Number of water column insectivores
- Number of pool-benthic insectivores
- Number of intolerant species
- Relative abundance of individuals of tolerant species
- Relative abundance of omnivores
- Relative abundance of specialized insectivores
- Relative abundance of top carnivores
- Relative abundance of diseased individuals

Visual assessment protocols for stream habitat condition (see above) have also been used to construct multi-metric indicators of stream habitat integrity. Sources of additional information on such overall habitat quality indicators are also listed at the end of Chapter 5.

Integrative indicators have one important limitation. They cannot be used to determine whether a change in the status of the overall indicator has resulted from any single cause since they combine multiple sources of information or metrics that are sensitive to a wide range of stresses to the community or ecosystem. Assessing the causal relationships among the key factors in a freshwater ecosystem, or between these key factors and human impacts, requires a more detailed assessment using individual metrics or indicators of the kinds described previously.

Contributors

Allison Aldous has held positions with The Nature Conservancy's Worldwide Office and Oregon program providing expertise and oversight related to wetland conservation efforts, research, and monitoring. Allison has a Ph.D. in Natural Resources from Cornell University, a M.S. in Plant Sciences, and a B.S. in Biochemistry from McGill University.

David Allan is a Professor of Conservation Biology and Ecosystem Management at the School of Natural Resources and Environment at the University of Michigan. He has served on numerous scientific advisory boards and committees, works with watershed councils and environmental organizations, and publishes extensively. David has a Ph.D. in Ecology from the University of Michigan and a B.S. in Zoology from the University of British Columbia.

Ronald Bjorkland is a conservation ecologist specializing in freshwater systems. Ron has worked as a consultant and with NGOs and government agencies facilitating the interface between science and policy decision-making both in and outside of the United States. Ron has Ph.D. from the University of Georgia researching water quality trends and land use patterns in the southeastern United States.

David Braun has held numerous freshwater-related positions with and served on a wide variety of science related advisory groups for The Nature Conservancy since 1993, helping guide programs and projects toward strategic actions and opportunities. David holds an M.S. in Hydrology from the University of Arizona as well as a Ph.D. from the University of Michigan and an A.B. from Harvard in Anthropology.

Mark Bryer directs The Nature Conservancy's Chesapeake Bay Initiative and previously worked as an aquatic ecologist for the Conservancy's Freshwater Initiative with significant international exposure. Mark holds an M.F.S. in Ecology and Hydrology from Yale University and a B.S. in Water Resource Engineering from Lehigh University.

Kristine Ciruna is Coordinator of Conservation Programs for The Nature Conservancy of Canada focusing on the development and implementation of a freshwater biodiversity conservation program for the province. She has over ten years of international experience in freshwater conservation and received her Ph.D. in Aquatic Ecology from the University of Toronto.

Jonathan Higgins is Senior Ecologist for The Nature Conservancy's Global Conservation Approach Team and has worked in ecology and conservation planning professionally and academically for more than 20 years. Jonathan has a Ph.D. and an M.S. in Ecology and Evolutionary Biology from the University of Illinois at Chicago and a B.A. from Grinnell College.

Rebecca Esselman contributes to multi-scale conservation planning and management, the development of learning tools, and research related to freshwater ecosystems for The Nature Conservancy and others. She holds an M.S. in Conservation Ecology and Sustainable Development from the University of Georgia and a B.S. in Botany from Michigan State University.

Mary Khoury is Aquatic Ecologist for the Great Lakes Program of The Nature Conservancy and previously contributed to freshwater ecoregional priority setting for the Conservancy. Mary has an M.S. in Resource Ecology and Management from the University of Michigan's School of Natural Resources and Environment and a B.A. in History and Studies in the Environment from Yale University.

Catherine M. Pringle is a Professor of Ecology at the Institute of Ecology at the University of Georgia. She has numerous scientific appointments and publications of national and international significance and a Post Doctoral in Botany from the University of California at Berkeley, a Ph.D. in Aquatic Ecology, an M.A. in Natural Resources, and a B.A. in Botany from the University of Michigan at Ann Arbor.

Nicole S. Rousmaniere was a graphic artist and publications manager for The Nature Conservancy's Sustainable Waters Program, Freshwater Initiative, and Conservation Science Division. Nicole is currently pursuing a Master's degree in environmental management focused on urban ecology and environmental design at the School of Forestry and Environmental Studies at Yale University.

Nicole Silk is Director of Partnership Development for The Nature Conservancy's Sustainable Waters Program and previously directed the Conservancy's Freshwater Learning Center. Nicole has twenty years of experience in conservation and holds a J.D. in Law from the University of California at Davis and a B.A. in Economics and Ecology from the University of California at Santa Cruz.

Index